EVERYMAN'S LIBRARY

EVERYMAN,
I WILL GO WITH THEE,
AND BE THY GUIDE,
IN THY MOST NEED
TO GO BY THY SIDE

ILLUSTRATIONS

ALEXANDER VON HUMBOLDT

SELECTED WRITINGS

EDITED AND INTRODUCED
BY ANDREA WULF

EVERYMAN'S LIBRARY
Alfred A. Knopf New York London Toronto

THIS IS A BORZOI BOOK
PUBLISHED BY ALFRED A. KNOPF

First included in Everyman's Library, 2018

Alexander Humboldt: *Personal Narrative of a Journey to the Equinoctial Regions
of the New Continent*
Abridgement, translation and notes copyright © Jason Wilson, 1995
All rights reserved. The translator has asserted his moral rights
Reprinted with the kind permission of Penguin Books, London

Extracts from:

Alexander von Humboldt and Aimé Bonpland: *Essay on the
Geography of Plants*
Translated by Sylvie Romanowski, edited by Stephen T. Jackson
Copyright © 2009 by The University of Chicago

Reprinted by kind permission of The University of Chicago Press,
Chicago and London

Owing to limitations of space, page 793 constitutes an extension of the
copyright page.

Selection and editorial material copyright © 2018 by
Everyman's Library
Introduction copyright © 2018 by Andrea Wulf

Map (pp. 4–5) by Nigel Andrews, originally published in the Penguin
Classics edition of *Personal Narrative*, 1995

All rights reserved. Published in the United States by Alfred A. Knopf, a
division of Penguin Random House LLC, New York, and in Canada by
Penguin Random House Canada Limited, Toronto. Distributed by
Penguin Random House LLC, New York. Published in the United
Kingdom by Everyman's Library, 50 Albemarle Street, London W1S 4DB
and distributed by Penguin Random House UK, 20 Vauxhall Bridge Road,
London SW1V 2SA.

www.randomhouse/everymans
www.everymanslibrary.co.uk

ISBN 978-1-101-90807-5 (US)
978-1-84159-387-6 (UK)

A CIP catalogue reference for this book is available from the
British Library

Book design by Barbara de Wilde and Carol Devine Carson

Typography by Peter B. Willberg

Typeset in the UK by Input Data Services Ltd, Isle Abbotts, Somerset

Printed and bound in Germany by GGP Media GmbH, Pössneck

CONTENTS

v

ALEXANDER von HUMBOLDT

SELECTED WRITINGS

EDITED AND INTRODUCED
BY ANDREA WULF

EVERYMAN'S LIBRARY
Alfred A. Knopf New York London Toronto
387

THIS IS A BORZOI BOOK
PUBLISHED BY ALFRED A. KNOPF

First included in Everyman's Library, 2018

Alexander Humboldt: *Personal Narrative of a Journey to the Equinoctial Regions
of the New Continent*
Abridgement, translation and notes copyright © Jason Wilson, 1995
All rights reserved. The translator has asserted his moral rights
Reprinted with the kind permission of Penguin Books, London

Extracts from:

Alexander von Humboldt and Aimé Bonpland: *Essay on the
Geography of Plants*
Translated by Sylvie Romanowski, edited by Stephen T. Jackson
Copyright © 2009 by The University of Chicago

Reprinted by kind permission of The University of Chicago Press,
Chicago and London

Owing to limitations of space, page 793 constitutes an extension of the
copyright page.

Selection and editorial material copyright © 2018 by
Everyman's Library
Introduction copyright © 2018 by Andrea Wulf

Map (pp. 4–5) by Nigel Andrews, originally published in the Penguin
Classics edition of *Personal Narrative*, 1995

www.randomhouse/everymans
www.everymanslibrary.co.uk

ISBN 978-1-101-90807-5 (US)
978-1-84159-387-6 (UK)

A CIP catalogue reference for this book is available from the
British Library

Book design by Barbara de Wilde and Carol Devine Carson

Typography by Peter B. Willberg

Typeset in the UK by Input Data Services Ltd, Isle Abbotts, Somerset

Printed and bound in Germany by GGP Media GmbH, Pössneck

C O N T E N T S

ILLUSTRATIONS

INTRODUCTION

On 14 September 1869, the centennial of the birth of German scientist Alexander von Humboldt was celebrated across the world. Thousands of people came together in Europe, Africa, Australia and in the Americas. There were parties in Buenos Aires and Mexico City, as well as in Melbourne and Adelaide. In Moscow Humboldt was hailed as the 'Shakespeare of sciences' and in Alexandria in Egypt fireworks illuminated the sky. In Berlin 80,000 people trudged through torrential rain to celebrate the most famous resident of their city. Some of the greatest festivities were organized in the United States – from San Francisco to Philadelphia, from Chicago to Charleston. In New York 25,000 people marched along Manhattan's cobbled streets which were lined with flags and colourful bunting. The crowds assembled in Central Park to unveil a Humboldt bust which still stands today opposite the Natural History Museum at the Naturalists' Gate on Central Park West and 77th Street. Humboldt's fame, the *Daily News* in London reported, was 'in some sort bound up with the universe itself'.

Almost forgotten today – at least in the English-speaking world – Humboldt was described by his contemporaries as the most famous man in the world after Napoleon. His name still lingers everywhere from the Humboldt Current, which runs along the west coast of South America, to the Humboldt penguin and a fierce six-foot giant squid. There are towns, rivers, and mountains across the globe that carry his name. There is the Mare Humboldtianum on the moon, the Humboldt Glacier in Greenland and mountain ranges in New Zealand, South Africa and China. Even the state of Nevada was almost called Humboldt when its name was debated in the 1860s. More places, plants and animals are named after Humboldt than anyone else.

Ralph Waldo Emerson called him 'one of those wonders of the world' and Thomas Jefferson described him as 'one of the greatest ornaments of the age'. Johann Wolfgang von Goethe, Germany's greatest poet, declared that spending a few days

vii

with Humboldt was like 'having lived several years', and Charles Darwin believed that the German explorer was 'one of the greatest men the world has ever produced'. Humboldt inspired scientists, poets, artists, politicians and revolutionaries. Simón Bolívar, the man who liberated the Spanish colonies, admired him, and the American painter Frederic Edwin Church followed Humboldt's footsteps through South America. Walt Whitman wrote his celebrated poetry collection *Leaves of Grass* with a copy of one of Humboldt's books on his desk and the Romantic poet Robert Southey said that he was 'among travellers what Wordsworth is among poets'.

*

So, who was this man? Alexander von Humboldt was a visionary scientist and explorer who changed the way we understand nature. Born in 1769 into a wealthy Prussian aristocratic family, he was daringly adventurous and his five-year voyage of exploration to Latin America (1799–1804) shaped his life and made him legendary across the world. He and his older brother Wilhelm were brought up on the family estate at Tegel, just outside Berlin. It was an unhappy childhood, Alexander von Humboldt later said. Their beloved father died when they were young and their emotionally cold mother never showed much affection – but she did provide the best education then available in Prussia. The boys were tutored by several Enlightenment thinkers who instilled in them a love of truth, liberty and knowledge. But Alexander escaped the classroom whenever he could to ramble through the countryside, collecting and sketching plants, animals and rocks. When he returned with his pockets full of insects and plants his family nicknamed him 'the little apothecary'. He dreamed of adventures in faraway countries and felt stifled at 'Castle Boredom', as he called Tegel, but Marie Elisabeth von Humboldt made it clear that she expected her sons to become civil servants in the Prussian administration.

In 1791, after completing his studies in economy, mathematics, languages and finance, Alexander von Humboldt enrolled at the prestigious mining academy in Freiberg, a small town near Dresden. It was a compromise that would prepare him for a career in the Prussian Ministry of Mines – to appease his mother – but it allowed him to indulge his interest in science and geology. He was curious and restless – impelled by a 'perpetual drive', he wrote, as if chased by '10,000 pigs' – but deeply unhappy. He travelled across Europe, climbed the Alps, experimented with so-called 'animal electricity', investigated mines, examined plants and spent many weeks in Jena with Goethe. The time with Goethe, Humboldt later recalled, 'affected me powerfully' – it changed him from being a scientist who based his research on purely empirical and rational methods to one who believed that imagination and emotional responses were as important, and equipped him with 'new organs' through which to see and understand the natural world.

In 1796, Marie Elisabeth von Humboldt died but neither Alexander, nor his brother Wilhelm went to her funeral. Four weeks later, Alexander was talking about his 'great voyage'. He was rich, independent, and couldn't wait to travel the world. It took a while to organize the expedition but in June 1799 Humboldt and his travel companion the French botanist, Aimé Bonpland, left Europe with the permission of the Spanish king to explore the Spanish colonies in South America. For five years they travelled through what is today Venezuela, Cuba, Colombia, Ecuador, Peru and Mexico – with a brief stopover in the United States to meet Thomas Jefferson on their return to Europe.

During those five years Humboldt paddled deep into the rainforest where few white men had ever gone and climbed the highest volcanoes in the Andes. He risked his life many times – when he experimented with electric eels in the great plains of Venezuela or when he clung to narrow ledges inside craters to collect sulfuric air samples. He drank the deadly curare poison at the Orinoco, swam next to crocodiles and boas, and was almost killed by a jaguar. He scoured the archives in Mexico City and Havana, climbed majestic Chimborazo which was then believed to be the highest mountain in the world, and measured the cold ocean current which would later carry his name. He collected indigenous languages, sketched Inca ruins, copied Aztec manuscripts and discovered the Brazil nut. He (and Bonpland) collected 60,000 plant specimens, and Humboldt drew the most accurate maps of South America ever made, filled 4,000 diary pages, produced hundreds of sketches and drawings, and conducted tens of thousands of astronomical, geological and meteorological observations. Charles Darwin called him the 'greatest scientific traveller who ever lived'.

As Humboldt travelled across South America, he began to see nature in a completely new way – and he saw connections everywhere. His mind, his brother Wilhelm believed, was made 'to connect ideas, to detect chains of things'. In the jungle he observed jaguars chasing capybaras, and at sea he recorded how flying fish escaped the dolphins' sharp teeth, only to be caught mid-air by albatrosses – later noting how plants and animals 'limit each other's numbers' (an idea which Charles Darwin underlined in his copy of Humboldt's book). Humboldt talked about nature as a global force where everything was connected from the smallest insect to the tallest tree. 'In this great chain of causes and effects,' he said, 'no single fact can be considered in isolation.' Instead of understanding flora and fauna in taxonomic units as other scientists did, he saw nature as a living organism pulsating with life, and pre-dated James Lovelock's Gaia Theory by more than a century. 'Nature is a living whole', Humboldt said, 'not a dead aggregate.'

Humboldt knew that travelling provided the knowledge that was needed to understand the world. Scientists had to look at flora, fauna, rock strata and climate globally, he insisted. Failure to do so would make them like those geologists who constructed the entire world 'according to the shape of the nearest hills surrounding them'. As Humboldt explored the world, he collected the data and impressions that made him realize that humankind was destroying the environment. Humboldt noted how mining exploited the land and the indigenous people; how huge swathes of forests had been destroyed to make way for plantations; how irrigation desiccated the soil and how ruthless pearl fishing had depleted the oyster stocks at the Venezuelan coast. Humboldt already predicted harmful human-induced climate change in 1800 – because he compared and connected what he saw. He warned of the devastating consequences of monoculture, deforestation and irrigation. He was a prescient environmentalist who talked of 'mankind's mischief ... which disturbs nature's order'. His diary entry in November 1801 revealed that he worried about a future in which humankind might expand into space. If that happened, he wrote, we would take our lethal mix of vice and greed which already had left earth 'barren' and 'ravaged', and spread it across other planets.

After his expedition Humboldt moved to Paris where he lived for more than twenty years. He became the centre of scientific enquiry – he experimented, gave lectures, rushed to scientific meetings and published many of his books. He was so famous that cab drivers didn't need an address, just the information 'chez Monsieur de Humboldt', to know where to take visitors. But in 1827 he reluctantly moved to Berlin, a city he hated. Having spent his fortune on his expedition as well as on hundreds of lavish engravings and maps that illustrated his many publications, Humboldt was desperately short of money. The Prussian king, Friedrich Wilhelm III, had paid him an annual stipend for more than two decades and insisted on his return. The king had run out of patience and wrote to Humboldt that 'you must already have completed the publication of the works, which you believed could only be accomplished satisfactorily in Paris'. Humboldt, by now 'poor as a church mouse', as he admitted, didn't have much of a choice.

He still managed to have some fun, though. Two years later, in 1829, he went on another expedition – this time to Russia, with all expenses paid by the Russian tsar. At the age of sixty, Humboldt travelled 10,000 miles in six months – crossing the border into China and Mongolia as well as racing through anthrax-infested steppes in Siberia. He was as restless as he had been as a young man. For the remaining thirty years of his life, Humboldt was based in Berlin and employed as the king's chamberlain. It was the beginning of what Humboldt called his 'swinging of a pendulum' – a life in which he chased the king's movements from one castle to the next summer residence and back to Berlin, always on the road and always loaded with manuscripts and boxes full of notes. The only time he had for himself and to write his books was between midnight and three o'clock in the morning.

By the end of his life, he received some 3,000 letters a year and welcomed a never-ending stream of visitors. He had become the greatest attraction of Berlin and for young scientists it was a rite of passage to meet the great Humboldt. He was so famous that his portrait was placed in the Great Exhibition in London and his birthday was celebrated as far away as Hong Kong. Everybody knew Humboldt. As one American journalist claimed: 'Ask any schoolboy who Humboldt is, and the answer will be given.'

Humboldt died on 6 May 1859, just a few months before his ninetieth birthday. As the news of his death travelled across the world, people everywhere mourned 'the great, good and venerated Humboldt', as the United States ambassador to Prussia said. Eulogies were given from Berlin to Mexico City. He had been, the Prussian king had once said, simply 'the greatest man since the Deluge'.

*

Since I published my book *The Invention of Nature* in 2015, my readers have asked me often which of Humboldt's books I would recommend. There is no quick answer to this question. Humboldt was such a prolific writer that not even he himself knew exactly what was published when and in which language. It doesn't help that some of his books were published in different formats and editions, or as part of a series, but then also separately as single volumes. The chance to bring some of his writing together in one volume has been a wonderful experience. It has been a privilege to make this selection – though I have to admit that it hasn't been easy. There is so much that couldn't be included here but I tried to choose sections and passages that illustrate the breadth of Humboldt's interests, while at the same time focusing on the books which he wrote for the general reader rather than scientific colleagues.

Prose was for Humboldt as important as the content. When he wrote his book *Views of Nature*, for example, he insisted that his publisher did not change a single syllable because otherwise the 'melody' of the sentences would be destroyed. For Humboldt, nature was a painting drawn on a canvas of empirical observation, but infused with emotions, imagination and poetic descriptions. He wrote of leaves that unfolded to 'greet the rising sun like the morning song of the birds' and of monkeys that filled the jungle with 'melancholy howling'. In the mists at the rapids of the Orinoco, rainbows danced in a game of hide-and-seek – 'optical magic', he called it. 'What speaks to the soul', Humboldt wrote, 'escapes our measurements.'

This new nature writing was so seductive, Goethe told Humboldt, 'that I plunged with you into the wildest regions'. Henry David Thoreau devoured Humboldt's books and found an answer to his dilemma on how to be a poet *and* a naturalist. *Walden* would have been a very different book without Humboldt. John Muir, father of the national parks in the United States, read Humboldt's books with a pencil in hand – underlining and writing as he went along, inspired by Humboldt's revolutionary ideas about the role of forests in the ecosystem. The French writer François-René de Chateaubriand thought Humboldt's writing was so extraordinary that 'you believe you are surfing the waves with him, losing yourself with him in the depths of the woods', and Jules Verne mined Humboldt's descriptions of South America for his *Voyages Extraordinaires* series. Even Captain Nemo in his famous *Twenty Thousand Leagues Under the Sea* owned the complete works of Humboldt.

*

Personal Narrative of Travels to the Equinoctial Regions of the New Continent

Originally published in seven volumes, *Personal Narrative* is part travel account, part scientific treatise, following Humboldt and Bonpland's expedition through Latin America chronologically from their departure in June 1799. Humboldt never completed *Personal Narrative*. The last volume ends with their arrival at the Río Magdalena in today's Colombia on 20 April 1801 – not even halfway through the expedition. First published in French (1814–31), it was almost immediately translated into English by Helen Maria Williams, a poet and writer who lived in Paris and who worked closely with Humboldt.

It was a book that changed Charles Darwin's life. 'My admiration of his famous personal narrative (part of which I almost know by heart),' Darwin later wrote, 'determined me to travel in distant countries, and led me to volunteer as naturalist in her Majesty's ship Beagle.' British Romantic poets William Wordsworth, Robert Southey and Samuel Taylor Coleridge read it too. Southey was so impressed that he visited Humboldt in Paris, declaring that Humboldt united his vast knowledge with 'a painters eye and a poets feeling'. Wordsworth copied a passage from *Personal Narrative* in which Humboldt described the myths of the 'great waters' at the Orinoco almost verbatim in his sonnets on the River Duddon. *Personal Narrative* was a huge success at the time.

The edition here is a much abridged version that focuses mainly on the journey aspect of the book rather than on the scientific observations. It's a 1995 translation from the original French edition.

Essay on the Geography of Plants

Published in 1807 in French and German, this was the first volume that Humboldt published after his expedition to Latin America. It was sold with a large three-foot-by-two-foot hand-coloured fold-out, his so-called '*Naturgemälde*' – an engraving that illustrates Humboldt's ability to make connections. It also shows that he was one of the founders of what we call infographics today.

The *Naturgemälde* (depicted on pages 354–355 in this volume) shows Chimborazo, a mountain that was elemental for Humboldt's vision of nature, in cross-section. Written onto the mountain are the names of the plants according to the altitude where Humboldt had found them. To the left and right of the mountain are columns with comparative data about gravity, temperature, chemical composition of the air and the boiling point of water amongst other things – also all arranged according to altitude. The *Naturgemälde* is packed with complex scientific data but easily understandable because Humboldt presented them visually. He used this new graphic approach so that he could appeal to his readers' imagination, he told a friend, because 'the world likes to *see*'.

The *Essay on the Geography of Plants* is almost like one long caption of the *Naturgemälde*. The introduction which is reproduced here, explains Humboldt's new ideas about plant distribution and nature as a web of life. Instead of classification, Humboldt revealed relationships between plants, climate and geography. He explained the idea of vegetation zones – 'long bands' as he called them – that were slung across the globe. In *Essay on the Geography of Plants*, Humboldt painted a picture of global patterns but also looked at history, economy and geology.

Views of Nature

Of all of the books that Humboldt published, *Views of Nature* was his favourite. It was a new literary genre in which he combined evocative writing and rich landscape descriptions with scientific observation in a blueprint for much of nature writing today. Humboldt took his readers into rainforests teeming with life, up snowy mountains, above stupendous waterfalls and across enormous deserts. Published first as *Ansichten der Natur* in Germany in 1808, it was eventually available in eleven languages. An extended edition in 1849 was the first to be published in English (in two competing translations under two titles, *Aspects of Nature* and *Views of Nature*) and became a bestseller at the time.

These translations have not aged well because the elegance and liveliness of the original prose was gagged and tamed into stodgy Victorian fare. In 2014, Chicago University Press published a new translation which makes for much better reading. Released of its Victorian corset, Humboldt's words are once again singing off the page. Sanitized expressions from the 1849 edition such as a 'glowing surface' are finally allowed to become Humboldt's 'glowing womb of the earth'; or a convoluted phrase such as 'carbonized turvy covering' is translated into the much more palatable 'charred grass'.

I've selected some of the chapters which illustrate Humboldt's interconnected thinking such as 'Steppes and Deserts' in which he compares similar zones across the globe – northern European heaths, the Llanos in Venezuela, the Pampas in Argentina, the Prairies in the Midwest, African deserts and steppes in Asia and Russia. Or the beautiful 'Nocturnal Wildlife of the Primeval Forest' in which he conjures up the teaming life of the rainforest and describes nature as a living organism where 'everything announces a world of active, organic powers'.

For reasons of space and readability, I've decided to leave out Humboldt's scientific annotations which he placed at the end of each chapter and which in some cases are longer than the actual text. For those interested in Humboldt's detailed scientific thinking, these endnotes are also worth reading. Some are little essays, others are fragments of thoughts that point towards future discoveries, including evolutionary ideas long before Darwin published his *Origin of Species*.

Views of the Cordilleras and Monuments of the Indigenous Peoples of the Americas

This was Humboldt's most lavish and opulent publication – two volumes which contained sixty-nine engravings depicting landscapes, art, buildings and manuscripts related to his expedition. First published in Paris as *Vues des Cordillères et monumens des peuples indigènes de l'Amérique* in seven instalments between 1810 and 1813, an English translation became available in 1814. The English edition was a less monumental two-volume octavo edition which included all the text but only twenty engravings.

The French large folio edition is so big that one can hardly lift the volumes. The engravings (twenty-three are in colour) range from volcanoes such as Chimborazo and Cotopaxi to Inca ruins in Peru, the famous Mexican Sun Stone which is today in the National Museum of Anthropology in Mexico

City and Aztec manuscripts. Each illustration is accompanied by an explanatory text that varies in length from a few sentences to dozens of pages. I've selected a few images with their explanatory text that illustrate the wide-ranging subjects of this publication, from the Quindío (or Quindiu) Pass – a trail at almost 12,000 feet that was known to be the most dangerous and difficult in all the Andes – to the Inca palace of Cañar (now called Ingapirca) in today's Ecuador.

Views of the Cordilleras shows that Humboldt wasn't just fascinated by nature. He was interested in everything – he recorded the languages of the indigenous people, he copied Aztec manuscripts and he sketched Inca monuments. Unlike most Europeans, he did not regard these people as barbaric savages. When he arrived back home in 1804, Humboldt didn't only bring with him a new concept of nature but he also showed Europeans that the ancient civilizations of Latin America were sophisticated cultures with rich languages, architecture and art.

The edition used here is not the nineteenth-century English translation but a new translation published by Chicago University Press in 2012 based on the original French text.

Political Essay on the Island of Cuba

First published in French in 1826 as part of the *Personal Narrative*, Humboldt's book *Political Essay on the Island of Cuba* is not exactly a thrilling read. It's a dense and data-based book in which he brought together his observations on geography, plants, conflicts of race, Spanish exploits, and the environmental consequences of colonialism. He provided information about revenues and military defence, about roads and ports, about demographics as well as economic data on trade and agriculture. But *Political Essay on the Island of Cuba* is an important publication because it also includes Humboldt's outspoken criticism of slavery. Though the Spanish king, Carlos IV, had granted him the rare permission to explore the Spanish Latin American territories, Humboldt did not hold back in his condemnation of colonial rule

I've selected only the short section from the book related to slavery which Humboldt called 'the greatest evil ever to have afflicted humanity'. During his expedition Humboldt went twice to Cuba where he remarked how 'every drop of sugarcane juice cost blood and groans'. As much as he admired the United States for their concepts of liberty and equality, Humboldt never stopped criticizing their failure to abolish slavery. In 1856 an English translation of *Political Essay on the Island of Cuba* was published in the United States by a pro-southern, pro-slavery journalist – an unauthorized edition that left out Humboldt's criticism of slavery. Unsurprisingly, Humboldt was furious. In response he issued a press release that was published in newspapers across the United States, denouncing the edition and declaring that the deleted sections were the most important in the book.

Cosmos. Sketch of a Physical Description of the Universe

In 1845 and much delayed, Humboldt published the first volume of *Cosmos* – the book that would make him famous across the world. It was an instant bestseller. First published in German, it was soon translated into many other languages. 'Were the republic of letters to alter its constitution,' one reviewer of *Cosmos* wrote, 'and choose a sovereign, the intellectual sceptre would be offered to Alexander von Humboldt.' In the history of publishing, the book's popularity was 'epoch making', Humboldt's German publisher announced. He had never seen so many orders.

Cosmos was unlike any previous book about nature. Humboldt took his readers on a journey from outer space to earth, from botany to poetry and landscape painting, from microscopic organism to northern lights. He wrote of the migration of the human race, comets and geomagnetism. At a time when other scientists crawled into their ever-narrowing disciplines Humboldt wrote a book that did exactly the opposite. In *Cosmos*, Humboldt spoke of a 'wonderful web of organic life'.

Over the next twenty-four years, until his death in 1859, Humboldt published five volumes. The first volume was a journey through the external world – from nebulae and stars to volcanoes, plants and humans. The second volume was a voyage of the mind through human history from ancient Greeks to modern times. The last three volumes were more specialized scientific publications that didn't appeal so much to the general readership – which is the reason why I've only included selections from the first two volumes.

From the first volume I've chosen what I think is the most important part of *Cosmos*: the long introduction of almost one hundred pages. This is the nineteenth-century English version which suffers from some heavy-handed Victorian translation but it's still an amazing piece of writing. In this introduction Humboldt spelled out his vision – of a world that pulsated with life. Everything was part of this 'never-ending activity of the animated forces' (my translation), Humboldt wrote. Nature was a 'living whole' where organisms were bound together in a 'net-like intricate fabric' (my translation). More than any other of his books, the introduction of *Cosmos* brings together Humboldt's ideas and new concepts. Here he explains everything – from his belief in connections and comparisons to his insistence that scientific knowledge adds to the magical beauty of nature (rather than diminishing it). 'Descriptions of nature,' he wrote, 'may be sharply defined and scientifically correct, without being deprived thereby of the vivifying breath of imagination.'

In the second volume Humboldt wrote about human history from ancient civilizations to modern times. No scientific publication had ever attempted anything similar. He wrote about poetry, art and gardens, as well as about feelings and emotions. I've selected his 'survey' of nature descriptions in literature in which Humboldt gallops from ancient Greece to contemporary explorers, from Persian poetry to Dante and Shakespeare, as well as his chapter on landscape painting. In *Cosmos* Humboldt brought everything together, writing of the 'deeply-seated bond which unites natural knowledge with poetry and with artistic feeling'. He believed that descriptions of nature by poets and artists were as truthful as the latest scientific discoveries.

*

For me Humboldt is the link between the arts and the sciences; between the Enlightenment and the poetry of the Romantics. He connects Newton's *Opticks*, which explained that rainbows were created by light refracting through raindrops, to poets such as John Keats, who declared that Newton 'had destroyed all the Poetry of the rainbow, by reducing it to a prism'.

Humboldt remains important for so many reasons. He gave us the concept of nature as a web of life and as a global force; he's the forgotten father of environmentalism; he united the arts and the sciences; and he saw the earth as an interconnected whole. In short, he was 'the wonderful Humboldt,' as Ralph Waldo Emerson wrote in his journal, who 'with his extended centre & expanded wings, marches like an army, gathering all things as he goes'.

Andrea Wulf

ANDREA WULF's books include *The Brother Gardeners: Botany, Empire and the Birth of an Obsession* and *The Invention of Nature*, her biography of Alexander von Humboldt, which won the Royal Society Science Book Award in 2016 and the Costa Award for Biography in 2015.

SELECT BIBLIOGRAPHY

SIGRID ACHENBACH, *Kunst um Humboldt: Reisestudien aus Mittel- und Süd-amerika von Rugendas, Bellermann und Hildebrandt im Berliner Kupferstich-kabinett*, SMB Kupferstichkabinett and Staatliche Museen zu Berlin, Berlin and Munich, 2009.

DOUGLAS BOTTING, *Humboldt and the Cosmos*, Sphere Books, London, 1973.

KARL BRUHNS (ed.), *Life of Alexander von Humboldt*, Longmans, Green and Co., London, 1873.

REX CLARK and OLIVER LUBRICH (eds), *Transatlantic Echoes: Alexander von Humboldt in World Literature*, Berghahn Books, New York and Oxford, 2012.

REX CLARK and OLIVER LUBRICH (eds), *Cosmos and Colonialism: Alexander von Humboldt in Cultural Criticism*, Berghahn Books, New York and Oxford, 2012.

ANDREW CUNNINGHAM and NICHOLAS JARDINE (eds), *Romanticism and the Sciences*, Cambridge University Press, Cambridge, 1990.

MANFRED GEIER, *Die Brüder Humboldt: Eine Biographie*, Rowohlt Taschenbuch Verlag, Hamburg, 2010.

GERARD HELFERICH, *Humboldt's Cosmos*, Gotham Books, New York, 2005.

FRANK HOLL, *Alexander von Humboldt: Mein Vielbewegtes Leben*, Die Andere Bibliothek, Berlin, 2017.

OLIVER LUBRICH (ed.), *Alexander von Humboldt: Das Graphische Gesamtwerk*, Lambert Schneider, Darmstadt, 2014.

AARON SACHS, *The Humboldt Current: Nineteenth-Century Exploration and the Roots of American Environmentalism*, Viking, New York, 2006.

ANDREA WULF, *The Invention of Nature: Alexander von Humboldt's New World*, Knopf, New York, 2015; *The Invention of Nature: The Adventures of Alexander von Humboldt, The Lost Hero of Science*, John Murray, London, 2015.

SELECTION OF HUMBOLDT'S PUBLISHED DIARIES AND LETTERS

MARGOT FAAK (ed.), *Alexander von Humboldt: Reise durch Venezuela. Auswahl aus den Amerikanischen Reisetagebüchern*, Akademie Verlag, Berlin, 2000.

ALEXANDER VON HUMBOLDT

MARGOT FAAK (ed.), *Alexander von Humboldt: Reise auf dem Río Magdalena, durch die Anden und Mexico,* Akademie Verlag, Berlin, 2003.

MARGOT FAAK (ed.), *Alexander von Humboldt: Lateinamerika am Vorabend der Unabhängigkeitsrevolution. Eine Anthologie von Impressionen und Urteilen aus seinen Reisetagebüchern,* Akademie Verlag, Berlin, 1982.

NICOLAS HOSSARD (ed.) *Alexander von Humboldt et Aimé Bonpland. Correspondance 1805–1858,* L'Harmattan, Paris, 2004.

ILSE JAHN and FRITZ G. LANGE (eds), *Die Jugendbriefe Alexander von Humboldts 1787–1799,* Akademie Verlag, Berlin, 1973.

ULRIKE MOHEIT (ed.) *Alexander von Humboldt: Briefe aus Amerika 1799–1804,* Akademie Verlag, Berlin, 1993.

C H R O N O L O G Y

———

DATE	AUTHOR'S LIFE	LITERARY CONTEXT
1768		
1769	Born 14 September in Berlin, Prussia.	Smollett: *The History and Adventures of an Atom.*
1770		
1772		*Göttinger Hainbund* literary group founded, part of the *Sturm und Drang* movement.
1773		Wheatley: *Poems on various subjects.*
1774		Goethe: *The Sorrows of Young Werther.*
1776		Paine: *Common Sense.* Klinger: *Sturm und Drang.*
1777–87	Humboldt and his brother Wilhelm are educated at their home, Castle Tegel, by private tutors.	
1779	His father Alexander Georg von Humboldt dies.	Lessing: *Nathan the Wise.* Schiller: *The Robbers.*
1780		Lessing: *The Education of Mankind.*
1781		Kant: *Critique of Pure Reason.*
1782		Wieland: *The Golden Mirror.* Laclos: *Les Liaisons dangereuses.*
1783		Kant: *Prolegomena to any future Metaphysics.*
1784		Herder: *Outlines of a Philosophy of the History of Man.* Schiller: *Love and Intrigue.*
1785		
1786		Schiller: *Philosophical Letters.*
1787	Studies government administration and political economy for six months at the	

First voyage of Captain James Cook on HMS *Endeavour* (to 1771).

Birth of Hegel. Birth of Beethoven.
Cook's second Pacific voyage (to 1775). Friedrich II of Prussia (Frederick the Great) makes huge territorial gains in First Partition of Poland.

The Sons of Liberty destroy a shipment of tea sent by the East India Company to Boston Harbor in protest against the Tea Act (1773); this becomes known as the Boston Tea Party.

American Declaration of Independence. Cook's third voyage.

Cook dies after the attempted kidnap of Kalani'ōpu'u, ruling chief of Hawaii. Birth of geographer Carl Ritter.
Death of Maria Theresa of Austria, ruler of the Habsburg Empire; succeeded by her son Joseph II (Holy Roman Emperor since 1765).
Joseph II begins a series of far-reaching judicial and administrative reforms. Dohm's publication of *On the Civic Improvement of the Jews* in Prussia provokes a storm of criticism.

The Treaty of Paris is signed, ending the American Revolutionary War; Britain formally acknowledges American independence. The Treaties of Versailles are signed, ending conflict between Britain, France and Spain.

Friedrich II organizes the German League of Princes, opposing any redistribution of territory within the German Empire.
Friedrich II of Prussia dies; succeeded by his nephew Friedrich Wilhelm II. A devotee of the arts, he does not share his uncle's military and political gifts. Nevertheless Prussia continues to achieve considerable expansion. Sierra Leone colonized by freed slaves arriving from England.
Mozart: *Don Giovanni.*

DATE	AUTHOR'S LIFE	LITERARY CONTEXT
1787 *cont.*	University of Frankfurt an der Oder, having been intended by his mother for a political career.	
1788	Matriculates at the University of Göttingen. Studies science, mathematics and languages.	Wächter: *Legends of the Past.* Kant: *Critique of Practical Reason.* Hutton: *Theory of the Earth.*
1789	Develops his interest in natural history and botany after meeting Georg Forster.	Blake: *Songs of Innocence.* Equiano: *The Interesting Narrative of the Life of Olaudah Equiano.*
1790	Publishes his first book, *Mineralogische Beobachtungen über einige Basalte am Rhein,* and travels with Forster in Europe, where he meets scientists and explorers such as Joseph Banks and Captain William Bligh. Studies finance and economics at academy of trade in Hamburg.	Burke: *Reflections on the Revolution in France.*
1791	Enrols at Freiburg School of Mines.	Paine: *Rights of Man.*
1792	After graduation he is appointed to a role as inspector in Bayreuth and the Fichtel Mountains for the Department of Mines.	Wollstonecraft: *A Vindication of the Rights of Woman.*
1793	Publishes *Florae Fribergensis specimen,* a compendium of his botanical research around the mines of Freiburg.	
1794	His brother Wilhelm von Humboldt moves to Jena where Alexander is subsequently introduced to Schiller and Goethe.	
1795	Tours Italy and Switzerland studying geology and botany. Publishes a philosophical allegory in Schiller's periodical *Die Horen.*	Goethe: *Wilhelm Meister's Years of Apprenticeship* (to 1796); *Roman Elegies.* Schiller: *On the Aesthetic Education of Man.*
1796	His mother Marie Elisabeth dies. Neither Humboldt nor his brother attends her funeral.	Fichte: *Foundations of Natural Right.*

French Revolution sends shockwaves through Europe. Meeting of States General; Third Estate adopts title of National Assembly. The storming of the Bastille on 14 July. Abolition of feudal privileges; secularization of church lands. In Berlin the monumental Brandenburg Gate is built. Death of Emperor Joseph II, succeeded by Leopold II. Civil Constitution of the Clergy in France. Mozart: *Così fan tutte.*

Attempting to flee France, Louis XVI is captured at Varennes. The Declaration of Pillnitz is issued by Prussia and Austria (Holy Roman Empire) in support of Louis XVI against the French Revolution. Slave rebellion in Haiti against French colonial rule.
Abolition of the monarchy in France; trial of Louis XVI (Dec). France declares war on Austria, the beginning of the French Revolutionary, later Napoleonic Wars (to 1815).

Execution of Louis XVI (Jan) and of Marie Antoinette (Oct). France declares war on Britain and Spain. Charlotte Corday assassinates Jean-Paul Marat in his bath. Reign of Terror begins under Robespierre. Second Partition of Poland.
Thermidorian Reaction: Robespierre and Saint-Just are arrested and executed. *Allgemeines Preussisches Landrecht* – a new and more liberal law code instituted in Prussia.

The Peace of Basel is signed between France and Prussia. The Alliance of St Petersburg is formed between Britain, Russia and Austria against France. Third Partition of Poland eliminates independent Polish state. Rule of Directory in France.

French victories in Italy. Napoleon Bonaparte occupies Venice.

DATE	AUTHOR'S LIFE	LITERARY CONTEXT
1797	Publishes the results of his research on muscular irritability and 'animal electricity', in which he experimented on his own body.	Schelling: *Ideas towards a Philosophy of Nature.*
1798	Moves to Paris where he meets the French botanist Aimé Bonpland.	Wordsworth and Coleridge: *The Lyrical Ballads.* Schlegel brothers edit *Das Athenäum,* manifesto of German Romanticism (to 1800).
1799	Travels to Madrid where he receives permission from the Spanish king Carlos IV to travel to the Spanish colonies in South America. Humboldt and Bonpland leave Spain in June to sail to South America, arriving in Cumaná 41 days later.	Schlegel: *Lucinde.* Schiller: *Wallenstein.*
1800	Travels to Caracas, Lake Valencia and then crosses the Llanos to reach the Orinoco. For 75 gruelling days Humboldt and Bonpland paddle along the Orinoco and the surrounding river networks, travelling 1,400 miles.	Mme de Staël: *De la littérature.* Schiller: *Mary Stuart.*
1801	After three months in Cuba, Humboldt and Bonpland return to South America in March. They travel from Cartagena to Bogotá and then across the high Andes to Quito.	Schiller: *The Maid of Orleans.*
1802	During his six-month stay in Quito, Humboldt climbs every reachable volcano, including Chimborazo which was then believed to be the highest mountain in the world. He arrives in Lima in October, having travelled almost 1,000 miles across the Andes.	Chateaubriand: *Génie du Christianisme.*
1803	Lands in Acapulco, Mexico in March and travels to Mexico City where he spends almost a year. He works in the archives,	Birth of Ralph Waldo Emerson.

CHRONOLOGY

DATE	AUTHOR'S LIFE	LITERARY CONTEXT
1803 *cont.*	visits silver mines and studies Aztec culture and hieroglyphs.	
1804	Journeys from Mexico City to Veracruz, before sailing again to Cuba. In April, Humboldt sails from Havana for the United States in order to meet Thomas Jefferson. A heavy storm causes passengers and crew to fear for their lives. On reaching Philadelphia, Humboldt travels to Washington, DC, to meet with Jefferson, establishing a lifelong friendship and correspondence. Humboldt returns to Europe in August, settling in Paris, where he meets the future leader of Venezuelan independence, Simón Bolívar.	Schiller: *William Tell*. Death of Kant.
1805	Travels to Italy, visits Rome and Naples, and climbs Mount Vesuvius. Humboldt becomes a full member of the Academy of Sciences in Berlin. In November, he returns to Berlin for the first time in nine years, and receives a Cabinet order entitling him to a pension of 2,500 thalers annually, 500 thalers of which are from the funds of the Academy.	Death of Schiller.
1806	Begins an intense series of magnetic observations in Berlin.	
1807	Publishes *Essay on the Geography of Plants* which is accompanied by his stunning *Naturgemälde*, a picture of nature as an interconnected whole.	Hegel: *The Phenomenology of Spirit*. Mme de Staël: *Corinne*.

CHRONOLOGY

Napoleon crowns himself Emperor of the French. Napoleon plans invasion of Britain. Spain declares war on Britain. The Lewis and Clark Expedition sets out from Camp Dubois, Illinois, beginning a journey to the Pacific Coast of America. Dessalines, leader of the successful slave revolt, takes power in an independent Haiti.

Napoleon crowns himself King of Italy, where the *Code Napoléon* is extended. War of the Third Coalition (Britain, Russia and Austria) opens with Ulm campaign. Napoleon occupies Vienna (Nov). Battle of Austerlitz (Dec): Napoleon defeats Austrian and Russian armies. Admiral Lord Nelson obtains a decisive victory at the Battle of Trafalgar (21 October), but dies shortly afterwards from a gunshot wound sustained during the battle.

Treaty of Paris between France and Prussia (Feb). Scharnhorst advocates the formation of a national militia in Prussia (April). Friedrich Wilhelm III fails to join with Britain, Austria and Russia, in the hope of annexing Hanover (dynastically allied to Britain), but by September is provoked into war against Napoleon. Prussia suffers overwhelming defeats at Jena and Auerstädt (Oct). Emperor Francis II abdicates the Holy Roman Empire and becomes Emperor Francis I of Austria; end of Holy Roman Empire. Joseph Bonaparte becomes King of Naples and Sicily; Louis Bonaparte becomes King of Holland.
Treaty of Tilsit: Prussia obliged to cede all her possessions west of the Elbe, all gains from the Second and Third Partitions of Poland, and required to pay an exorbitant contribution to Napoleon's finances as well as accept French occupation of much of her territories. Faced with the collapse of the state, Friedrich Wilhelm III accepts moderate reformist measures. Emancipation of serfs begun. Scharnhorst's army reforms. British Parliament passes Act to abolish the Slave Trade in British colonies.

DATE	AUTHOR'S LIFE	LITERARY CONTEXT
1808	Publishes *Views of Nature*, his favourite book. Moves back to Paris where he quickly establishes himself as the centre of scientifc enquiry. He lectures, writes, and performs hygrometric experiments with Joseph Louis Gay-Lussac.	Goethe: *Faust* (I). Fichte: *Addresses to the German Nation*.
1809	Meets the French mathematician François Arago.	Goethe: *Elective Affinities*. Chateaubriand: *Les Mémoires d'outre-tombe* (to 1841). Birth of Poe, Gogol and Tennyson.
1810	Publishes *Views of the Cordilleras* (to 1813). Humboldt's brother Wilhelm founds the first university in Berlin, which today carries the name of the brothers.	Goethe: *Theory of Colours*.
1811	Publishes first volume of *Political Essay on the Kingdom of New Spain*.	
1812		Byron publishes first two cantos of *Childe Harold's Pilgrimage*. Grimm brothers: *Children's and Household Tales*.
1813		Austen: *Pride and Prejudice*. Mme de Staël: *De l'Allemagne*.
1814	Humboldt uses his influence to protect the Natural History Museum and Botanical Garden in Paris from the occupying allied forces. Later visits his brother in London and tries to convince the British to give him permission to travel to India. Publishes the first volume of *Personal Narrative* (to 1826).	Wordsworth: *The Excursion*. Scott: *Waverley*. Austen: *Mansfield Park*.
1815	Humboldt is attacked by the German press for living in Paris and being unpatriotic. Elected Fellow of the Royal Society, London.	Austen: *Emma*.

CHRONOLOGY

Prussia's reforming minister, Karl Stein, dismissed at Napoleon's request. Formation at Königsberg of the Moral and Scientific Union (*Tugendbund*), influential movement embodying German idealism and patriotic fervour. French invasion of Spain; abdication of Ferdinand VII .

In South America, colonists in Quito take power from Spanish administration. Birth of Charles Darwin. Educational reforms in Prussia. Austria re-enters war and is defeated at Battle of Wagram.

Napoleon divorces Joséphine and marries Archduchess Marie Louise of Austria. Joseph Bonaparte King of Spain. The Hidalgo revolt triggers the Mexican War of Independence against the Spanish colonial government (to 1821). Colonists in Buenos Aires seize power. The Supreme Junta of Caracas is established after a coup.

Venezuelan independence from Spain proclaimed. Reform of economic policy in Prussia; restrictive power of guilds abolished.

Jews in Prussia are granted equality of civil rights. Prussia and Austria are in an enforced alliance with Napoleon, and have to support French attack on Russia. Following Napoleon's retreat from Moscow, Prussia disengages herself from the French alliance. Devastating earthquake in Caracas; Spanish regain control.

Treaty of Kalisz: Prussia (later with Austria) allies with Russia against France. War of Liberation begins. Napoleon suffers his first major defeat at Battle of Leipzig. Wellington crosses the Pyrenees into France. Simón Bolívar proclaims 'War to the Death'; retakes Caracas. Civil war in Venezuela.

Allied invasion of France and fall of Paris; Napoleon abdicates and is exiled to Elba. Congress of Vienna (to 1815). Restoration of monarchy in France (Louis XVIII).

Napoleon escapes from Elba and retakes Paris during the 'Hundred Days'; defeated by the British and Prussian armies at the Battle of Waterloo. Napoleon exiled on St Helena. Treaty of Paris: France reduced to 1790 borders, large war indemnity imposed. Prussia loses most of the eastern territory gained in the partitions of Poland, but makes gains on her western frontier at the expense of other German states (reduced from 300 to 39).

DATE	AUTHOR'S LIFE	LITERARY CONTEXT
1815 *cont.*		
1816	Bonpland returns to South America.	Keats: 'On First Looking into Chapman's Homer'. Marcet: *Conversations on Political Economy*. Constant: *Adolphe*.
1817	Creates the first isothermal chart. Travels again to London to get permission to enter British-ruled India but is once again refused.	Coleridge: *Biographia Literaria*.
1818	Travels yet again to London but the East India Company continues to block his plans.	Mary Shelley: *Frankenstein*.
1819		Schopenhauer: *The World as Will and Idea*. Byron: *Don Juan* (to 1824).
1820		Hegel: *Philosophy of Right*. Percy Bysshe Shelley: *Prometheus Unbound*. Keats: *Hyperion*; *Lamia*.
1821	Prepares abortive expedition to India. British intransigence is probably caused by his outspoken criticism of Spanish colonial rule in South America.	Kleist: *Prinz Friedrich von Homburg*.
1822	Humboldt is made a Foreign Honorary Member of the American Academy of Arts and Sciences and travels through Italy.	Pushkin: *The Prisoner of the Caucasus*. De Quincey: *Confessions of an English Opium Eater*. Death of Shelley.

CHRONOLOGY

Friedrich Wilhelm III joins conservative Holy Roman Alliance with Austria and Russia; his government under Chancellor Hardenberg continues to promote liberal reforms. Birth of Otto von Bismarck. Restored to his throne, Ferdinand VII dispatches Spanish army to South America.

First meeting at Frankfurt of German Confederation set up to replace the Holy Roman Empire. René Laennec invents the stethoscope.

Rossini: *The Barber of Seville.*

Altenstein's educational reforms. Prussian universities become centres of radicalism, demanding centralized, national German power.

Congress of Aix-la-Chapelle; end of allied occupation of France. Birth of Karl Marx. Prussia suffering from bad harvests and floods; laws introduced to free internal trade. Chile declares independence.

The Peterloo Massacre in Manchester, England, results in around fifteen deaths after cavalry charge into a crowd of some 60,000 people demanding parliamentary reform. The repressive Six Acts are passed as a result.

The liberal reform movement grows strongest in southern Germany; Metternich (Austrian Chancellor) persuades German Confederation to accept repressive Carlsbad Decrees. Bolívar's march across the Andes and defeat of the Spanish at Battle of Boyacá. Bolívar becomes the first President of Gran Colombia (comprising modern Ecuador, Colombia, Panama and Venezuela).

The discovery of Antarctica by Fabian Gottlieb von Bellinghausen and Mikhail Lazarev. Liberia is founded by the American Colonization Society to enable the migration of free-born or manumitted African Americans to West Africa. The shift to the right in Berlin is echoed throughout Germany, and by 1820 the reform movement is effectively halted. Revolutions in Spain, Portugal, and the Two Sicilies. Assassination of the Duc de Berry (heir presumptive to the French throne); repressive measures taken by government.

Death of Napoleon. Fall of Richelieu ministry in France. Ultra-royalists take over government (to 1827); impose stringent censorship laws. The Greek War of Independence (to 1830). Peruvian independence declared. Weber: *Der Freischütz.*

Pedro I of Brazil declares Brazilian independence and founds the Empire of Brazil. Nicéphore Niépce creates the first photographic image using heliography. Schubert writes his *Unfinished Symphony.*

DATE	AUTHOR'S LIFE	LITERARY CONTEXT
1823	Geologist Charles Lyell visits him in Paris. Humboldt visits Berlin for the first time since 1808.	Pushkin: *Eugene Onegin* (to 1831).
1824		Death of Byron in Greece.
1825		
1826	*Political Essay on the Island of Cuba* published. Visits Goethe in Weimar.	Eichendorff: *Memoirs of a Good-for-Nothing.* J. F. Cooper: *The Last of the Mohicans.*
1827	Desperately short of money, Humboldt is forced to accede to the demands of Friedrich Wilhelm III that he settle in Berlin. Leaves Paris, travelling via London where he meets Isambard Kingdom Brunel. Humboldt and Brunel descend in a diving bell to the bottom of the Thames to inspect the leaks in the new Thames tunnel. Humboldt arrives in Berlin on 12 May. Takes up duties as chamberlain at the Prussian royal court. Begins long lecture series which later forms the basis for his book *Cosmos*. Guadalupe Victoria, first President of the newly independent Mexico, grants him honorary Mexican citizenship.	Audubon: *The Birds of America* (to 1838).
1828	Hosts conference in Berlin which attracts around 500 scientists from across Europe.	Hazlitt: *Life of Napoleon* (to 1830).
1829	On the invitation of Russian minister of finance Count Georg von Cancrin, Humboldt leads a six-month-long expedition, funded by the Russian government. Accompanied by	Irving: *Chronicle of the Conquest of Granada.*

CHRONOLOGY

Monroe Doctrine extends US protection to newly independent South American republics. French invasion of Spain; Ferdinand VII restored. Mary Anning discovers the first complete plesiosaurus at Lyme Regis, Dorset.

Death of Louis XVIII and succession of Charles X in France. Berlin Polytechnic opens. Beethoven completes his Ninth Symphony, including the setting of Schiller's *Ode to Joy*. Antonio José de Sucre inflicts major defeat on the Spanish at the Battle of Ayacucho (Peru).
The Republic of Bolivia is created, named after Simón Bolívar. Naturalist William John Burchell begins his Brazilian expedition. Accession of reactionary Tsar Nicholas I in Russia; Liberal Decembrist uprising suppressed. Law against sacrilege in France.
Treaty of Akkerman between Russia and Turkey. Russia declares war on Persia (to 1828). Mendelssohn's Overture to *A Midsummer Night's Dream*; Schubert: *Death and the Maiden* quartet; Weber's *Oberon*.

Villèle's Ultra-royalist government defeated in French general election; Villèle resigns (1828); Martignac forms moderate ministry. British, French and Russian ships destroy Turkish fleet at Battle of Navarino during Greek War of Independence. Joseph Fourier first proposes the existence of the greenhouse effect. Death of Beethoven. Bellini: *Il Pirata*.

Bolívar declares war on Peru, later declaring himself dictator of Gran Colombia. Argentina and Brazil recognize the independence of Uruguay. Russo-Turkish War (to 1829).
Polignac's Ultra-royalist ministry. First excavations at the sanctuary at Olympia are made by a team lead by French architect Abel Blouet. Rossini: *William Tell*.

DATE	AUTHOR'S LIFE	LITERARY CONTEXT
1829 *cont.*	Gustav Rose, a mineralogist, and the botanist Christian Gottfried Ehrenberg, the party covers a distance of almost 10,000 miles all the way to the Mongolian and Chinese border. Makes important speech on geomagnetism to Imperial Academy in St Petersburg, influential in triggering an international collaboration to collect more data, known as the 'Magnetic Crusade'.	
1830	First of several diplomatic missions to Paris where he is sent by Friedrich Wilhelm III to acknowledge King Louis Philippe's accession. From now on Humboldt travels regularly to Paris from Berlin to continue his scientific work.	Stendhal: *Le Rouge et le Noir*.
1831	Visits Goethe in Weimar for the last time.	Balzac: *La Peau de chagrin*.
1832		Death of Goethe. Clausewitz: *On War*.
1833		
1834	Starts work on *Cosmos*.	
1835	Wilhem von Humboldt dies.	Tocqueville: *De la démocratie en Amérique* (vol. I: vol. II, 1840).
1837		Martineau: *Society in America*.
1839	Darwin sends Humboldt a copy of *The Voyage of the Beagle*.	Darwin: *The Voyage of the Beagle*. Poe: *The Fall of the House of Usher*. Townsend: *The Narrative of a Journey across the Rocky Mountains to the Columbia River. and a Visit to the Sandwich Islands*.

CHRONOLOGY

July Revolution in France; Louis Philippe comes to power. Liberal constitutions granted in Brunswick, Saxony, Hanover and Hesse-Kassel. Belgians revolt against King of Holland. Charles Lyell publishes *Principles of Geology* (to 1833), 'being an attempt to explain the former changes of the earth's surface, by reference to causes now in action'. The Indian Removal Act is passed, marking a systemic effort by the United States government to remove Native American tribes from their land. The Royal Geographical Society is formed in London. London Protocol recognizes Greece as an independent state. Death of Simón Bolívar. Disintegration of Gran Colombia. Berlioz: *Symphonie Fantastique.*

Voyage of HMS *Beagle* (with the young Charles Darwin aboard), dispatched to carry out a hydrographic survey of the southern coast of South America. Polish rebellion suppressed.

Militant German students attempt to seize Frankfurt, dissolve the Diet, and proclaim a German republic; mass meeting of southern German radicals expresses approval of national unification, republican government and popular sovereignty; Metternich rallies German princes to crush the liberal, nationalist movement. Bill for Parliamentary Reform passes in Britain. Slavery abolished throughout the British Empire.

Charles Darwin arrives at the Galapagos Islands. British authorities make English the medium of higher education in India, leading to its becoming the official language of public business. Bellini: *I Puritani.*

Accession of Queen Victoria in Britain.

The Treaty of London is signed by Belgium, the Netherlands, Britain, Austria, Russia, France and the German Confederation, recognizing Belgian independence from the Netherlands.

DATE	AUTHOR'S LIFE	LITERARY CONTEXT
1840	Humboldt's court duties become more onerous under the new king Friedrich Wilhelm IV.	Lermontov: *A Hero of Our Time*.
1842	Visits London where he meets Charles Darwin.	
1843	Completes three-volume *Asie Centrale* on his Russian expedition, dedicated to Tsar Nicholas.	Dickens: *Martin Chuzzlewit* (to 1844).
1844		Dumas: *Les Trois Mousquetaires*; *Le Comte de Monte Cristo*. Heine: *Germany: A Winter's Tale*.
1845	Meets the British botanist Joseph Dalton Hooker in Paris. Publishes first volume of *Cosmos*.	Douglass: *Narrative of the Life of Frederick Douglass, an American Slave*.
1846		Balzac: *Cousin Bette*.
1847	The second volume of *Cosmos* is published, and is so popular that, according to the publisher, people fight 'regular battles' over possession of a copy.	C. Brontë: *Jane Eyre*. E. Brontë: *Wuthering Heights*. A. Brontë: *Agnes Grey*. Thackeray: *Vanity Fair* (to 1848).
1848	Humboldt marches at the head of the funeral procession for the fallen revolutionaries in Berlin.	Marx and Engels: *The Communist Manifesto*. Mill: *Principles of Political Economy*. A. Dumas *fils*: *La Dame aux Camélias*.
1849	Disappointment at failure of the 1848 revolutions. Publishes an extended edition of *Views of Nature* which becomes an international bestseller.	C. Brontë: *Shirley*. Death of Edgar Allen Poe.
1850		Wordsworth: *The Prelude*.
1851		Melville: *Moby-Dick*.
1852		Stowe: *Uncle Tom's Cabin*.
1854		Grimm brothers: *The German Dictionary* begins publication. Thoreau: *Walden*.
1855		Trollope: *The Warden*. Whitman: *Leaves of Grass*.

CHRONOLOGY

HISTORICAL EVENTS

The Treaty of Waitangi is signed by the Maori and the British, declaring British sovereignty and resulting in the founding of New Zealand as a colony of the British Empire. Friedrich Wilhelm IV becomes King of Prussia after the death of his father, Friedrich Wilhelm III.
Ada Lovelace writes the first computer algorithm in her *Notes* on her translation of an article by Luigi Menabrea.

Bad harvests and potato blight affect most of western Europe (to 1846).
New Zealand Wars (to 1872).

The Mexican–American War over the annexation of Texas begins (to 1848).
Verdi: *Macbeth*.

Short-lived revolutions in Berlin, throughout Germany, and elsewhere in Europe – notably Paris, Vienna, Prague, Venice, Milan, Rome, Naples. Abdication of Louis Philippe; Second Republic in France. Inspired by the expeditions of Humboldt and Darwin, Alfred Russel Wallace and Henry Walter Bates set off to explore the Amazon, with the intention of charting the Río Negro, collecting specimens and making notes on the people, flora and fauna they encounter.
Frankfurt National Assembly (1848–9) offers German imperial crown to Friedrich Wilhelm IV, who rejects it. Californian Gold Rush sees widespread violence against Native American tribes leading to catastrophic decline in population.

The Fugitive Slave Act is passed in the United States, requiring that all fugitive slaves must be returned to their masters, even if captured in free states.
Louis Napoleon's coup d'état; Empire proclaimed in 1852. George Perkins Marsh's expedition to Egypt and Palestine.
David Livingstone crosses southern Africa from west to east, discovering the Victoria Falls en route (to 1856).

The removal of Stamp Duty from British newspapers causes proliferation of new publications.

DATE	AUTHOR'S LIFE	LITERARY CONTEXT
1856	Publishes a complaint that the US edition of *Political Essay on the Island of Cuba* had left out his criticism of slavery.	Barrett Browning: *Aurora Leigh*.
1857	Suffers minor stroke in February.	Baudelaire: *Les Fleurs du mal*. Flaubert: *Madame Bovary*.
1858	Aimé Bonpland dies in South America.	Gray: *Gray's Anatomy*.
1859	Dies in Berlin on 6 May and is given a grand funeral through the streets of Berlin before being interred at the family resting-place in Castle Tegel on 10 May.	Darwin: *The Origin of Species*. Dickens: *A Tale of Two Cities*. Eliot: *Adam Bede*.
1862	The fifth volume of *Cosmos* is published posthumously, based on Humboldt's notes.	Hugo: *Les Misérables*.

CHRONOLOGY

Peace of Paris ends Crimean War (began 1853). William Walker usurps the presidency of the Republic of Nicaragua with the intent of reinstating slavery, but is defeated by a coalition of Central American armies in 1857.

France and Britain declare war on China (second Opium War, to 1860). The University of Calcutta and the University of Bombay are established in British-ruled India. The Indian Mutiny begins, a major uprising against the rule of the British East India Company.

The first transatlantic telegraph cable is laid, reaching from Ireland to Newfoundland. John Hanning Speke discovers the source of the Nile.

Death of Carl Ritter. Ground is broken for the Suez Canal. The largest slave auction in US history is held in Savannah, Georgia; 436 men, women, children, and infants are sold over two days. The Brazil–Venezuela border is agreed, following the water divide between the Amazon and the Orinoco basins. Joseph Prestwich and John Evans report the results of their research into the gravel-pits of the Somme valley, establishing human history back to the Paleolithic era. Frederic Edwin Church's painting *The Heart of the Andes*, inspired by Humboldt, is exhibited in New York.

EDITORIAL NOTE

Discrepancies in editorial style inevitably occur in a volume drawn from both British and American sources, and including translations from different periods. Readers will appreciate that this is a selection, and we decided not to impose on it a rigorously consistent house style, especially as this would have involved making changes to scholarly editions.

ALEXANDER VON HUMBOLDT:
SELECTED WRITINGS

PERSONAL NARRATIVE OF TRAVELS TO THE EQUINOCTIAL REGIONS OF THE NEW CONTINENT

1814–29

Abridged and translated by Jason Wilson

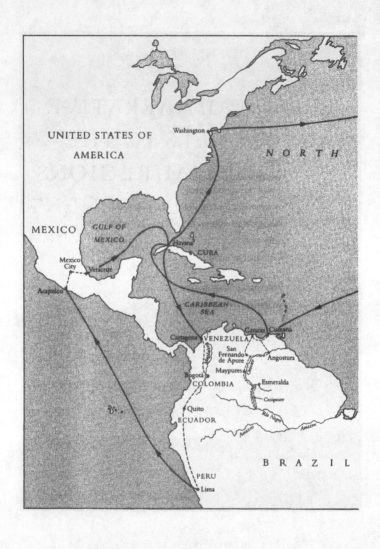

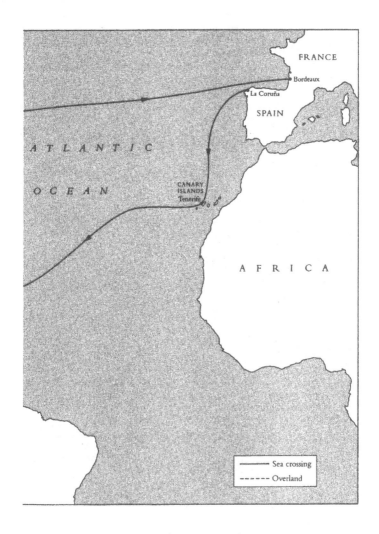

HUMBOLDT'S ROUTE, 1799–1804

CONTENTS

INTRODUCTION*

TWELVE YEARS HAVE elapsed since I left Europe to explore the interior of the New Continent. From my earliest days I was excited by studying nature, and was sensitive to the wild beauty of a landscape bristling with mountains and covered in forests. I found that travelling out there compensated for a hard and often agitated life. But pleasure was not the only fruit of my decision to contribute to the progress of the physical sciences. For a long time I had prepared myself for the observations that were the main object of my journey to the torrid zone. I was equipped with instruments that were easy and convenient to use, made by the ablest artists, and I enjoyed the protection of a government that, far from blocking my way, constantly honoured me with its confidence. I was supported by a brave and learned friend whose keenness and equanimity never let me down, despite the exhaustion and dangers we faced.

Under such favourable circumstances, and crossing regions long unknown to most European nations, including Spain itself, Bonpland and I collected a considerable number of materials, which when published may throw light on the history of nations, and on our knowledge about nature. Our research developed in so many unpredictable directions that we could not include everything in the form of a travel journal, and have therefore placed our observations in a series of separate works.

Two main aims guided my travels, published as the *Relation historique*.[1] I wanted to make known the countries I visited, and to collect those facts that helped elucidate the new science vaguely named the Natural History of the World, Theory of the Earth or Physical Geography. Of these two aims, the

* Editorial Notes to this section can be found on pp. 325–45

second seemed the more important. I was passionately keen on botany and certain aspects of zoology, and flattered myself that our researches might add some new species to those already known. However, rather than discovering new, isolated facts I preferred linking already known ones together. The discovery of a new genus seemed to me far less interesting than an observation on the geographical relations of plants, or the migration of social plants, and the heights that different plants reach on the peaks of the cordilleras.

The natural sciences are connected by the same ties that link all natural phenomena together. The classification of species, which we should consider as fundamental to botany, and whose study has been facilitated by introducing natural methods, is to plant geography what descriptive mineralogy is to the rocks that form the outer crust of the earth. To understand the laws observed in the rocks, and to determine the age of successive formations and identify them from the most distant regions, a geologist should know the simple fossils that make up the mass of mountains. The same goes for the natural history that deals with how plants are related to each other, and with the soil and air. The advancement of plant geography depends greatly on descriptive botany; it would hinder the advancement of the sciences to postulate general ideas by neglecting particular facts.

Such considerations have guided my researches, and were always present in my mind as I prepared for the journey. When I began to read the many travel books, which form such an interesting branch of modern literature, I regretted that previous learned travellers seldom possessed a wide enough knowledge to avail themselves of what they saw. It seemed to me that what had been obtained had not kept up with the immense progress of several sciences in the late eighteenth century, especially geology, the history and modifications of the atmosphere, and the physiology of plants and animals. Despite new and accurate instruments I was disappointed, and most scientists would agree with me, that while the number of precise instruments multiplied we were still ignorant of the height of so many mountains and plains; of the periodical oscillations of the aerial oceans; the limit of perpetual snow under the polar caps and on the borders of the torrid zones; the variable intensity of magnetic forces; and many equally important phenomena.

Maritime expeditions and voyages round the world have rightly conferred fame on naturalists and astronomers appointed by their governments, but while these distinguished men have given precise notions of the coasts of countries, of the natural history of the ocean and islands, their expeditions have advanced neither geology nor general physics as travels into the interior of a continent should have. Interest in the natural sciences has trailed behind geography and nautical astronomy. During long sea-voyages, a traveller hardly ever sees land; and when land is after a long wait it is often stripped of its most beautiful products. Sometimes, beyond a sterile coast, a ridge of high mountains covered in forests is glimpsed, but its distance only frustrates the traveller.

Land journeys are made very tiresome by having to transport instruments and collections, but these difficulties are compensated by real advantages. It is not by sailing along a coast that the direction, geology and climate of a chain of mountains can be discovered. The wider a continent is the greater the range of its soil and the richness of its animal and vegetable products, and the further the central chain of mountains lies from the ocean coast the greater the variety of stony strata that can be seen, which reveal the history of the earth. Just as every individual can be seen as particular, so can we recognize individuality in the arrangement of brute matter in rocks, in the distribution and relationships of plants and animals. The great problem of the physical description of the planet is how to determine the laws that relate the phenomena of life with inanimate nature.

In trying to explain the motives that led me to travel into the interior of a continent I can only outline what my ideas were at an age when we do not have a fair estimate of our faculties. What I had planned in my youth has not been completely carried out. I did not travel as far as I had intended when I sailed for South America; nor did it give me the number of results I expected. The Madrid Court had given me permission in 1799 to sail on the Acapulco galleon and visit the Philippine Islands after crossing its New World colonies. I had hoped to return to Europe across Asia, the Persian Gulf and Baghdad. With respect to the works that Bonpland and I have published, we hope that their imperfections, obvious to both of us, will not be attributed to a lack of keenness, nor to publishing too quickly. A determined will and an active perseverance are not always sufficient to overcome every obstacle.

Having outlined the general aim, I will now briefly glance at the collections and observations we made. The maritime war during our stay in America made communications with Europe very uncertain and, in order for us to avoid losses, forced us to make three different collections. The first we sent to Spain and France, the second to the United States and England, and the third, the most considerable, remained constantly with us. Towards the end of our journey this last collection formed forty-two boxes containing a herbal of 6,000 equinoctial plants, seeds, shells and insects, and geological specimens from Chimborazo, New Granada and the banks of the Amazon, never seen in Europe before. After our journey up the Orinoco, we left a part of this collection in Cuba in order to pick it up on our return from Peru and Mexico. The rest followed us for five years along the Andes chain, across New Spain, from the Pacific shores to the West Indian seas. The carrying of these objects, and the minute care they required, created unbelievable difficulties, quite unknown in the wildest parts of Europe. Our progress was often held up by having to drag after us for five and six months at a time from twelve to twenty loaded mules, change these mules every eight to ten days, and oversee the Indians employed on these caravans. Often, to add new geological specimens to our collections, we had to throw away others collected long before. Such sacrifices were no less painful than what we lost through accidents. We learned too late that the warm humidity and the frequent falls of our mules prevented us from preserving our hastily prepared animal skins and the fish and reptiles in alcohol. I note these banal details to show that we had no means of bringing back many of the objects of zoological and comparative anatomical interest whose descriptions and drawings we have published. Despite these obstacles, and the expenses entailed, I was pleased that I had decided before leaving to send duplicates of all we had collected to Europe. It is worth repeating that in seas infested with pirates a traveller can only be sure of what he takes with him. Only a few duplicates that we sent from America were saved, most fell into the hands of people ignorant of the sciences. When a ship is held in a foreign port, boxes containing dried plants or stones are merely forgotten, and not sent on as indicated to scientific men. Our geological collections taken in the Pacific had a happier fate. We are indebted for their safety to the generous work of Sir Joseph Banks, President of the Royal Society of London, who, in the middle of Europe's political turmoils, has struggled ceaselessly to consolidate the ties that unite scientific men of all nations.

The same reasons that slowed our communications also delayed the publication of our work, which has to be accompanied by a number of engravings and maps. If such difficulties are met when governments are paying, how much worse they are when paid by private individuals. It would have been impossible to overcome these difficulties if the enthusiasm of the editors had not been matched by public reaction. More than two thirds of our work has now been published. The maps of the Orinoco, the Casiquiare and the Magdalena rivers, based on my astronomical observations, together with several hundred plants, have been engraved and are ready to appear. I shall not leave Europe on my Asian journey before I have finished publishing my travels to the New World.

In our publications Bonpland and I have considered every phenomenon under different aspects, and classed our observations according to the relations they each have with one another. To convey an idea of the method followed, I will outline what we used in order to describe the volcanoes of Antisana and Pichincha, as well as Jorullo, which on the night of the 20th of September 1759 rose 1,578 feet up from the plains of Mexico. We fixed the position of these remarkable mountains in longitude and latitude by astronomical observations. We took the heights of different parts with a barometer, and determined the dip of the needle and magnetic forces. We collected plants that grew on the slopes of these volcanoes, and specimens of different rocks. We found out the exact height above sea-level at which we made each collection. We noted down the humidity, the temperature, the electricity and the transparency of the air on the brinks of Pichincha and Jorullo; we drew the topographical plans and geological profiles of these volcanoes by measuring vertical bases and altitude angles. In order to judge the correctness of our calculations we have preserved all the details of our field notes.

We could have included all these details in a work devoted solely to volcanoes in Peru and New Spain. Had I written the physical description of a single province I could have incorporated separate chapters on geography, mineralogy and botany, but how could I break the narrative of our travels, or an essay on customs and the great phenomena of general physics, by tiresomely enumerating the produce of the land, or describing new species and making dry astronomical observations? Had I decided to write a book that included in the same chapter everything observed from the same spot, it would have been excessively long, quite lacking in the clarity that comes from a methodical distribution of subject matter. Despite the efforts made to avoid these errors in this narration of my journey, I am aware that I have not always succeeded in separating the observations of detail from the general results that interest all educated minds. These results should bring together the influence of climate on organized beings, the look of the landscape, the variety of soils and plants, the mountains and rivers that separate tribes as much as plants. I do not regret lingering on these interesting objects for modern civilization can be characterized by how it broadens our ideas, making us perceive the connections between the physical and the intellectual worlds. It is likely that my travel journal will interest many more readers than my purely scientific researches into the population, commerce and mines in New Spain.

After dividing all that belongs to astronomy, botany,

zoology, the political description of New Spain, and the history of the ancient civilizations of certain New World nations into separate works, many general results and local descriptions remained left over, which I could still collect into separate treatises. I had prepared several during my journey; on races in South America; on the Orinoco missions; on what hinders civilization in the torrid zone, from the climate to the vegetation; the landscape of the Andes compared to the Swiss Alps; analogies between the rocks of the two continents; the air in the equinoctial regions, etc. I had left Europe with the firm decision not to write what is usually called the historical narrative of a journey, but just to publish the results of my researches. I had arranged the facts not as they presented themselves individually but in their relationships to each other. Surrounded by such powerful nature, and all the things seen every day, the traveller feels no inclination to record in a journal all the ordinary details of life that happen to him.

During my navigation up the South American rivers, and over land, I had written a very brief itinerary where I described on the spot what I saw when I climbed the summit of a volcano or any other mountain, but I did not continue my notes in the towns, or when busy with something else. When I did take notes my only motive was to preserve those fugitive ideas that occur to a naturalist, to make a temporary collection of facts and first impressions. But I did not think at the time that these jotted-down notes would form the basis of a work offered to the public. I thought that my journey might add something to science, but would not include those colourful details that are the main interest in journeys.

Since my return the difficulties I experienced trying to write a number of treatises and make certain phenomena known have overcome my reluctance to write the narrative of my journey. In doing this I have been guided by a number of respectable people. I realized that even scientific men, after presenting their researches, feel that they have not satisfied their public if they do not also write up their journal.

A historical narrative covers two quite different aims: whatever happens to the traveller; and the observations he makes during his journey. Unity of composition, which distinguishes good work from bad, can be sought only when the traveller describes what he has seen with his own eyes, and when he has concentrated on the different customs of people, and the great phenomena of nature, rather than on scientific observations. The most accurate picture of customs is one that deals with man's relationships with other men. What characterizes savage and civilized life is captured either through the difficulties encountered by a traveller or by the sensations he feels. It is the man himself we wish to see in contact with the objects around him. His narration interests us far more if a local colouring informs the descriptions of the country and its people. This is what excites us in the narrations of the early navigators who were driven more by guts than by scientific curiosity and struggled against the elements as they sought a new world in unknown seas.

The more travellers research into natural history, geography or political economy, the more their journey loses that unity and simplicity of composition typical of the earlier travellers. It is now virtually impossible to link so many different fields of research in a narrative so that what we may call the dramatic events give way to descriptive passages. Most readers, who prefer to be agreeably amused to being solidly instructed, gain nothing from expeditions loaded with instruments and collections.

To give some variety to my work I have often interrupted the historical narrative with straightforward descriptions. I begin by describing the phenomena as they appeared to me, then I consider their individual relations to the whole.

I have included details about our everyday life that might be useful to any who follow us in the same countries. I have retained only a few of those personal incidents that offer no interest to readers, and amuse us only when well written.

Concerning the country I have travelled through, I am fully aware of the great advantages enjoyed by those who travel to Greece, Egypt, the banks of the Euphrates, and the Pacific Islands over those who travel to America. In the Old World the nuances and differences between nations form the main focus of the picture. In the New World, man and his productions disappear, so to speak, in the midst of a wild and outsize nature. In the New World the human race has been preserved by a few scarcely civilized tribes, or by the uniform customs and institutions transplanted on to foreign shores by European colonists. Facts about the history of our species, different kinds of government and monuments of art affect us far more than descriptions of vast emptinesses destined for plants and wild animals.

If America does not occupy an important place in the history of mankind, and in the revolutions that have shattered the world, it does offer a wide field for a naturalist. Nowhere else does nature so vividly suggest general ideas on the cause of events, and their mutual interrelationships. I do not mean by this solely the overpowering vegetation and freshness of organic life, the different climates we experience as we climb the cordilleras and navigate those immense rivers, but also the geology and natural history of an unknown continent. A traveller can count himself lucky if he has taken advantage of his travels by adding new facts to the mass of those previously discovered!

Connected by the most intimate bonds of friendship over the five years of our travels (and since then), Bonpland and I have jointly published the whole of our work.[2] I have tried to explain what we both observed but, as this work has been written from my notes on the spot, all errors that might arise are solely mine. In this introduction I would also like to thank Gay-Lussac and Arago, my colleagues at the Institute, who have added their names to important work done, and who possess that high-mindedness which all who share a passion for science should have. Living in intimate friendship I have consulted them daily on matters of chemistry, natural history and mathematics.

Since I have returned from America one of those revolutions that shake the human race has broken out in the Spanish colonies, and promises a new future for the 14 million inhabitants spread out from La Plata to the remotest areas in Mexico. Deep resentments, exacerbated by colonial laws and maintained by suspicious policies, have stained with blood-shed areas that for three centuries once enjoyed not happiness but at least uninterrupted peace. Already in Quito the most educated citizens have been killed fighting for their country. While writing about certain areas I remembered the loss of dear friends.[3]

When we reflect on the great political upheavals in the New World we note that Spanish Americans are in a less fortunate position than the inhabitants of the United States, who were more prepared for independence by constitutional liberty. Internal feuds are inevitable in regions where civilization has not taken root and where, thanks to the climate, forests soon cover all cleared land if agriculture is abandoned. I fear that for many years no foreign traveller will be able to cross those countries I visited. This circumstance may increase the interest of a work that portrays the state of the greater part of the Spanish colonies at the turn of the nineteenth century. I also venture to hope, once peace has been established, that this work may contribute to a new social order. If some of these pages are rescued from oblivion, those who live on the banks of the Orinoco or Atabapo may see cities enriched by commerce and fertile fields cultivated by free men on the very spot where during my travels I saw impenetrable jungle and flooded lands.

Paris, February 1812.

CHAPTER I

FROM MY EARLIEST days I felt the urge to travel to distant lands seldom visited by Europeans. This urge characterizes a moment when our life seems to open before us like a limitless horizon in which nothing attracts us more than intense mental thrills and images of positive danger. I was brought up in a country that has no relations with either of the Indies, and I lived in mountains far from the sea and famous for their working mines, yet I felt an increasing passion for the sea and a yearning to travel far overseas. What we glean from travellers' vivid descriptions has a special charm; whatever is far off and suggestive excites our imagination; such pleasures tempt us far more than anything we may daily experience in the narrow circle of sedentary life. My taste for botanizing and the study of geology, with the chance of a trip to Holland, England and France accompanied by Georg Forster, who was lucky enough to travel with Captain Cook on his second world tour, helped determine the travel plans I had been hatching since I was eighteen years old. What attracted me about the torrid zone was no longer the promise of a wandering life full of adventures, but a desire to see with my own eyes a grand, wild nature rich in every conceivable natural product, and the prospect of collecting facts that might contribute to the progress of science. Personal circumstances prevented me from carrying out these absorbing plans, and for six years I had the leisure to prepare myself for the observations I would make in the New World by travelling through several European countries and exploring the Alps, whose structure I would later compare with the Andes between Quito and Peru.

During that time a voyage to explore the Pacific was being planned in France, under the direction of Captain Baudin.[4]

The early plan was daring and grand, and would have been better entrusted to a more enlightened man. The idea was to travel across the Spanish colonies in South America from the mouth of the River Plate to the kingdom of Quito and the Panama isthmus. The two corvettes would then proceed to New Holland through the Pacific archipelagoes, stopping at Madagascar and returning home round the Cape of Good Hope. I had arrived in Paris when the preparations for the voyage had just begun. I had little faith in Captain Baudin's character as he had given me cause to be suspicious in the Viennese Court when charged to accompany one of my friends to Brazil, but as I could never with my own resources have afforded such a far-reaching expedition, nor visited such a beautiful part of the earth, I decided to risk taking part in the expedition. I got permission to embark with my instruments on one of the corvettes destined for the Pacific, and I did this on the agreement that I could leave Captain Baudin whenever it suited me. Michaux, who had visited Persia and parts of North America, and Bonpland, who became and remained a close friend, were also to accompany this expedition as naturalists.

I met the Swedish Consul Skiöldebrand, who passed through Paris on his way to embark in Marseille on a mission to bring gifts to the Dey of Algiers. That respectable gentleman had lived for a long time on the African coast and, as he was well known in the Algerian Court, could get me authorization to visit the Atlas mountains. Every year he despatched a ship to Tunis, which brought pilgrims to Mecca, and he promised to let me go to Egypt that way. I did not hesitate to seize that chance and was convinced I could carry out the plan I had hatched before my arrival in France. Up until then no geologist had ever explored the high mountain ranges that in Morocco reach the perpetual snows. I quickly completed my collection of instruments and obtained books that dealt with the countries I was to visit. I said goodbye to my brother, whose example and advice had helped guide my thinking. He approved of my motives for wanting to abandon Europe; a secret voice told me we would see each other again. I left Paris eager to embark for Algeria and Egypt, and chance – so often playing a decisive role in human lives – had it that I would see my brother again after returning from the Amazon and Peru, without putting a foot on African soil.

The Swedish frigate that was to convey Skiöldebrand to Algeria was expected at Marseille towards the end of October. Bonpland and I rushed there in case we arrived late and missed the boat. We did not predict the new set-backs that were soon to crop up.

Skiöldebrand was as impatient as we were to reach his destination. Several times a day we would climb the Notre-Dame de la Garde mountain, which dominated a wide stretch of the Mediterranean. Every sail that appeared on the horizon excited us. But after two months of waiting we heard through the newspapers that the Swedish frigate had been badly damaged in a storm off Portugal, and had put into Cádiz to refit. Private letters then confirmed this news; the *Jaramas* (as it was called) would not reach Marseille before the spring.

We did not feel like prolonging our stay in Provence until the spring. The countryside, and especially the climate, were a delight, but the sight of the sea continuously reminded us of the failure of our plans. During a trip we made to Hyères and Toulon we came across the frigate *La Boudeuse*, bound for Corsica, which had been under the command of Bougainville[5] during his world voyage. This famous navigator had been particularly kind to me during my stay in Paris while I prepared to join Captain Baudin. I cannot describe the impression that this ship, which had carried Commerson to the Pacific, had on me. There are moments in our lives when painful feelings mingle with our experiences.

We resolved to spend the winter in Spain, hoping to embark from Cartagena or Cádiz in the spring, if the political situation in the east permitted this. We crossed the kingdoms of Catalonia and Valencia to reach Madrid. On the way we visited the ruins of Tarragona and ancient Saguntum. From Barcelona we made an excursion to Montserrat, whose elevated peaks are inhabited by hermits. The contrast between luxuriant vegetation and desolate, bare rocks forms a peculiar scenery.

Arriving at Madrid I soon congratulated myself on my

decision to visit the peninsula. Baron de Forell, Saxon Ambassador to the Spanish Court, received me in a friendly way that greatly favoured my project. To his knowledge of mineralogy he added a great interest in the progress of science. He let me know that under the patronage of an enlightened minister, Don Mariano Luis de Urquijo, I might be permitted to make a journey to the interior of Spanish America, at my own expense. After all the set-backs I had suffered I did not hesitate to take up this suggestion.

In March 1799 I was presented at the Court of Aranjuez and the King received me graciously. I explained the motives that prompted me to undertake a journey to the New World and the Philippines, and presented a memoir of my plans to the Secretary of State. Señor de Urquijo supported my petition and overcame every obstacle in my path, proceeding with commendable generosity given I had no personal relationship with him. The zeal with which he helped me can be due only to his love for science.

I obtained two passports; one from the Secretary of State, the other from the Council of the Indies. Never before had such concessions been granted to a traveller, and never had the Spanish Government shown such confidence in a foreigner. To waylay all the possible reservations that the viceroys and captain-generals might raise concerning the nature and finality of my work, it said in my safe conduct from the First Secretary of State that 'I was authorized to freely use my physical and geodesical instruments, that in all the Spanish possessions I could make astronomical observations, measure the height of mountains, collect whatever grew on the ground, and carry out any task that might advance the Sciences.'[6]

For the past year so many obstacles had crossed my path that I could hardly believe that at last my innermost desires would be fulfilled. We left Madrid in the middle of May and crossed Old Castile and the kingdoms of León and Galicia to La Coruña, where we were to embark for the island of Cuba. The winter had been long and hard but now, during our journey, we enjoyed the mild temperatures of spring that in the south usually begin in March or April. Snow still covered the tall granitic peaks of the Guadarrama but in the deep Galician valleys, which reminded me of the picturesque scenery of Switzerland and the Tyrol, the rocks were covered in flowering cistus and arborescent heaths. The traveller is happy to quit the Castilian plains devoid of vegetation and their intense winter cold and summers of oppressive heat.

The First Secretary of State had particularly recommended Brigadier Rafael Clavijo, recently appointed Inspector General of Maritime Couriers. This officer advised us to board the corvette *Pizarro*, bound for Havana and Mexico. This light frigate was not famed for its sailing speed, although during its long journey from the River Plate it had luckily just escaped English men-of-war. Clavijo sent instructions to the *Pizarro* to authorize the loading of our instruments, and to allow us to carry out atmospheric tests during the sea-voyage. The captain was ordered to stop at Tenerife and remain there as long as was needed for us to visit the port of Orotava and climb the Pico de Teide.

The harbours of Ferrol and La Coruña both communicate with the same bay, so a ship driven by foul weather towards the coast may anchor in either, according to the wind. Such an advantage is invaluable where the sea is almost always rough, as it is between Capes Ortegal and Finisterre, the promontories Trileucum and Artabrum of ancient geography. A narrow passage, flanked by perpendicular granite rocks, leads to the extensive bay of Ferrol. No port in Europe offers such an extraordinary anchorage, from its very inland position. The narrow and tortuous passage by which vessels enter this port has been opened, either by the pounding of waves or the reiterated shocks of very violent earthquakes. In the New World, on the coasts of New Andalusia, the Laguna del Obispo is formed exactly like the port of Ferrol. The most curious geological phenomena are often repeated at immense distances on the surface of different continents; and naturalists who have examined different parts of the globe are struck by the extreme resemblances observed in the fracturing of coasts, in the sinuosities of the valleys, in the appearance of mountains, and in their distribution by groups. The accidental concurrence of the same causes must everywhere have produced the same effects; and amidst the variety of nature an analogy of structure and form is observed in the arrangement of inanimate matter, as well as in the internal organization of plants and animals.

The moment of leaving Europe for the first time is impressive. We vainly recall the frequency of communications between the two worlds; we vainly reflect how, thanks to the improved state of navigation, we may now cross the Atlantic, which compared to the Pacific is but a shortish arm of the sea; yet what we feel when we begin our first long-distance voyage is none the less accompanied by a deep emotion, unlike any we may have felt in our youth. Separated from the objects of our dearest affections, and entering into a new life, we are forced to fall back on ourselves, and we feel more isolated than we have ever felt before.[7]

A thick fog that hid the horizon warned us at last – to our delight – that the weather was changing. On the evening of the 4th of June the north-east wind, so constant on the Galician coast at this time of year, began blowing. On the 5th the *Pizarro* set sail, despite the news, which had reached the watchtower at Sisarga a few hours previously, that an English squadron was bound for the Tagus river mouth. Those who came to watch our corvette weigh anchor warned us by shouting that within three days we would be captured and would have to follow our ship into Lisbon. This forecast worried us.

By two in the afternoon the *Pizarro* was under sail. The channel that ships follow to leave the port of La Coruña is long and narrow. As it opens towards the north, and as the wind blew against us, we had to tack eight times, three of which were useless. We manoeuvred very clumsily, and once dangerously, as the current dragged us close to some reefs against which waves noisily broke. We stared at the San Antonio castle where the luckless Malaspina[8] fretted in a State prison. At this moment of leaving Europe to visit those countries this illustrious traveller had so fruitfully visited, I would rather have thought about something less sad.

At half past six we passed the Tower of Hercules, which acts as the La Coruña lighthouse, at the top of which a coal light has been kept burning from remote times to guide ships. At around nine we spotted the light of a fisherman's hut at Sisarga, the last we would see on the European coast. Soon distance weakened that feeble light, which we began to confuse with stars on the horizon, but our eyes refused to stop staring at it. These impressions are never forgotten by those who begin a long ocean journey at an age when their feelings remain vivid and profound. So many memories are awoken in our imagination by a dot of light in a dark night, flickering on and off above the rough waves, signalling our home land!

At sunset on the 8th of June the look-out sighted from his crow's-nest a British convoy sailing along the coast towards the south-east. To avoid it we altered our course during the night. We were also given orders not to put our lights on in the great cabin so that we would not be seen from afar. We constantly had to use dark-lanterns to make our observations of the sea's temperature, or read the markings on our astronomical instruments. In the torrid zone, where twilight lasts a few minutes, we were condemned to inaction, in similar circumstances, from six in the evening. For me this was particularly irritating as I have never suffered from seasickness and no sooner am I on board than I feel the urge to work more than ever.[9]

From La Coruña to the 36th degree of latitude we had scarcely seen any living creature apart from sea swallows and a few dolphins. We searched in vain for seaweed and molluscs. On the 11th of June we were struck by a curious sight that later we would see often in the Pacific. We reached a zone where the sea seemed covered with an enormous amount of jellyfish. The boat could hardly move, though the jellyfish floated towards the south-east four times faster than the current. This procession lasted some forty-five minutes; then we saw a few scattered and exhausted ones struggling to follow the main bunch, as if tired of their journey.

Between Madeira and the African coast we were almost becalmed, which suited me perfectly as I could carry out my magnetic experiments. We never tired of admiring the magnificent nights; nothing approaches the clarity and serenity of the African sky. We were struck by the extraordinary number of shooting stars that crossed the night sky. The further south we advanced, the more we saw, especially near the Canary Islands. When we were about 40 leagues east of Madeira, a common swallow (*Hirundo rustica*) landed on the topmast. It was so exhausted we easily caught it. What drives a bird so far off its course at such a calm time of year?

The *Pizarro* had orders to anchor off the island of Lanzarote, one of the seven large Canary Islands, to find out if the English were still blockading the Santa Cruz bay. From the 15th we were dubious about which route to follow. Finally, on the 16th, at two in the afternoon, we sighted land, which looked like a little cloud stuck on the horizon. At five, with the sun very low, we could clearly see the island of Lanzarote before us.

The current dragged us towards the coast with more force than was safe. As we advanced we saw first the island of Fuerteventura, famous for the many camels that live there, and then later the small island of Lobos, in the channel that separates Fuerteventura from Lanzarote. We spent the night on deck; the moon illumined the island's volcanic peaks, whose slopes, covered in ash, shone like silver. The night was beautifully serene and fresh; although we were only a short distance from the African coast and the limit of the torrid zone, the thermometer recorded only 18 °C. It seemed as if the phosphorescence of the sea heightened the mass of light diffused in the air. After midnight great black clouds rose behind the volcano and intermittently covered the moon and the beautiful Scorpion constellation. On the shore we saw lights move in all directions; probably fishermen getting ready for work. During the voyage we had been reading the ancient Spanish navigators, and those moving lights reminded us of Pedro Gutiérrez,[10] Queen Isabel's page, who saw similar lights on Guanahani Island on the memorable night the New World was discovered.

The island of Lanzarote used to be called Titeroigotra. When the Spaniards arrived its inhabitants differed from those on the other islands by their superior culture. They built their houses with cut stones while the Guanches of Tenerife lived in caves like troglodytes. At that time a strange custom – repeated only in Tibet – prevailed. A woman had several husbands, who each took it in turn to exercise the rights of the head of the family. Each husband was known as such during a lunar month; then another took his place while he returned to being a servant in the house. In the fifteenth century the island of Lanzarote consisted of two states separated by a wall; a kind of monument, which outlives national enmities, found also in Scotland, Peru and China.

Guessing from some signs on an old Portuguese map, the captain of the *Pizarro* thought we were opposite a small fort built north of Teguise, the capital of Lanzarote. Mistaking some basaltic crags for a castle he saluted it properly by hoisting the Spanish flag and sending a boat with an officer to the supposed fort to find out if the English were lurking in these waters. We were not a little surprised to discover that the land we took for the coast of Lanzarote was the small island of Graciosa, and that for several leagues around there was not a sound of life.

We took the opportunity to use the boat to survey the land around the large bay. No words can evoke the feelings of a naturalist who first steps on soil outside Europe. So many objects call for his attention that it is hard to order his impressions. At each step he thinks he is coming across something new, and in his excitement he does not recognize things that commonly feature in botanical gardens and natural history collections. Two hundred yards off the coast we saw a man fishing with a rod. We turned the boat towards him but he fled and hid behind a rock. It took our sailors some effort to capture him. The sight of the corvette, the thunder of our cannons in such a solitary place – possibly visited only by pirates – the launching of our boat, all this terrified the poor fisherman. He informed us that the island of Graciosa on which we had landed was separated from Lanzarote by a small channel called El Río. He offered to guide us to Los Colorados harbour to find out about the blockade at Tenerife but, when the man assured us that for weeks he had not seen any ships out at sea, the captain decided to set sail for Santa Cruz.

We re-embarked at sunset and set sail, but the breeze was too weak to enable us to follow our route to Tenerife. The sea was calm; a reddish haze covered the horizon, seeming to magnify everything. In such solitudes, surrounded by so many uninhabited islands, we savoured the view of such a grandiose and wild nature. The black mountains of Graciosa had perpendicular walls some 500 to 600 feet high. Their shadows, projected across the sea, made the scene gloomy. The basalt rocks stuck out of the water like the ruins of a vast building. Their existence reminded us of that bygone age when underwater volcanoes gave birth to new islands, or destroyed continents. Everything around us spoke of destruction and sterility; yet beyond this scene the coast of Lanzarote seemed more friendly. In a narrow gorge, between two hills crowned with scattered trees, you could see some cultivated land. The last rays of sun lit up the ripe corn, ready for harvesting. Even the desert is animated when you see some trace of man's work in it.

On the morning of the 18th the wind freshened a little and we managed to pass through the channel. We lost sight of the small islands of Alegranza, Montaña Clara and Graciosa, which appear to have been inhabited by the Guanches. People visit them now only to gather archil,[11] but this is less sought after since so many north European lichens yield better dyes. Montaña Clara is noted for its beautiful canary-birds. There are also goats, proof that the interior of the island is not as desolate as the coast we had seen.[12]

CHAPTER 2

FROM THE TIME we left Graciosa the sky remained so consistently hazy that despite the height of the mountains of Gran Canaria we did not make out the island until the evening of the 18th. It is the granary of the archipelago of the Fortunate Islands and, remarkably for an area outside the Tropics, there are two wheat harvests a year, one in February, the other in June. Gran Canaria has never been visited before by a geologist, yet it is worth observing because its mountains differ entirely from those of Lanzarote and Tenerife.

On the morning of the 19th of June we caught sight of the point of Naga, but the Pico de Teide remained invisible. Land stood out vaguely because a thick fog effaced the details. As we approached the natural bay of Santa Cruz we watched the mist, driven by wind, draw near. The sea was very rough, as it usually is in this place. After much sounding we anchored. The fog was so thick that visibility was limited to a few cables' length. Just as we were about to fire the customary salute the fog suddenly dissipated and the Pico de Teide appeared in a clearing above the clouds, illuminated by the first rays of sun, which had not reached us yet. We rushed to the bow of the corvette not to miss this marvellous spectacle, but at that very same moment we saw four English warships hove to near our stern, not far out in the open sea. We had passed them closely by in the thick fog that had prevented us from seeing the peak, and had thus been saved from the danger of being sent back to Europe. It would have been distressing for naturalists to have seen the Tenerife coasts from far off and not to have been able to land on soil crushed by volcanoes. We quickly weighed anchor and the *Pizarro* approached the fort as closely as possible to be under its protection. Here, two years before in an attempted landing, Admiral Nelson lost his arm to a cannon-ball. The English ships left the bay; a few days earlier they had chased the packet-boat *Alcudia*, which had left La Coruña just before we did. It had been forced into Las Palmas harbour, and several passengers were captured while being transferred to Santa Cruz in a launch.

The location of the town of Santa Cruz is similar to La Guaira, the busiest port in the province of Caracas. The heat is excessive in both places, but Santa Cruz is sadder. On a deserted sandy beach, houses of a dazzling white with flat roofs and windows without panes lie close to a rocky cliff stripped of vegetation. A fine stone quay and public walk planted with poplars are the only attraction in that monotonous picture. From Santa Cruz the peak seems far less picturesque than it does from the port of Orotava. There a smiling and richly cultivated plain contrasts with the wild appearance of the volcano. From the groves of palm and banana trees on the shore to the region of strawberry trees, laurels and pine the volcanic rock is covered with luxuriant vegetation. It is easy to see why the inhabitants of the beautiful climates of Greece and Italy thought they had discovered one of the Fortunate Isles on the western part of Tenerife. The eastern Santa Cruz side is everywhere marked with sterility.

After answering tiresome questions about political events from those who came on board, we landed. The boat was straightaway sent back to the ship in case the surf, which in this bay is dangerous, should crush it against the wharf. Our attention was first caught by a tall woman, of a brownish complexion and badly dressed, called the *capitana*. She was followed by several other women, equally badly dressed. They tried to board the *Pizarro* but were refused. In this harbour, frequented by Europeans, licentiousness seems to be quite ordered. The *capitana* is chosen by her companions, she ensures that no injuries are done to sailors, and then sends them back on board at the right time. Officers seek her out if they think one of their crew might be hiding on land to desert later.

When we stepped into the streets of Santa Cruz the heat was suffocating, though the thermometer recorded only 25 °C. After breathing sea air for such a long time one suffers on land, not because the air contains more oxygen at sea but because it is less charged with the gases emanating from rotting animal and vegetable substances.

Santa Cruz, the Añaza of the Guanches, is a pretty town of some 8,000 people. I was not struck by the vast number of monks that travellers always find in the Spanish possessions, nor shall I bother to describe the churches, the Dominican library with its meagre 200 tomes; nor the quay where people meet in the evening to enjoy the fresh air, nor the famous 30-foot-high monument in Cararra marble dedicated to Our Lady of Candelaria in memory of the virgin's miraculous appearance in 1392 in Chimisay, near Güimar. The port of Santa Cruz is in fact a great caravanserai on the route to America and India. Every traveller who writes his adventures begins by describing Madeira and Tenerife, though the natural history of these islands remains quite unknown.

The recommendations from the Madrid Court assured us that we were always well received in all the Spanish possessions. The Captain-General immediately gave us permission to visit the island. Colonel Armiaga, in command of an infantry regiment, warmly welcomed us to his house. We did not tire of admiring the banana trees, the papaw trees, the *Poinciana pulcherrima* and other plants usually seen only in greenhouses.

Although the captain of the *Pizarro* had orders to remain long enough at Tenerife to allow us to climb the peak, snow permitting, he let us know that the English ships' blockade meant that we could not count on a stay of more than four or five days. So we hurried to the port of Orotava on the western slope of the volcano where we hoped to find guides. Nobody in Santa Cruz had ever climbed to the summit of the mountain.

On the 20th of June, before sunrise, we set off for the Villa de Laguna, some 350 toises[13] above Santa Cruz harbour. The narrow and tortuous path leading to La Laguna climbs along a torrent, which in the rainy season turns into fine cascades.

Near the town we met some white camels, barely laden. These animals are mainly used to transport goods from the customs house to the merchants. Camels are not numerous in Tenerife, while in Lanzarote and Fuerteventura there are thousands.

As we approached La Laguna the air cooled. This sensation delighted us as we found the air in Santa Cruz asphyxiating. As we tend to feel disagreeable sensations more strongly, we felt the change in temperature more as we returned from La Laguna to the port, as if we were approaching the mouth of a furnace.

The perpetual cool that prevails in La Laguna makes the city the favourite home for the inhabitants of the Canaries. The residential capital of Tenerife is magnificently placed in a small plain surrounded by gardens at the foot of a hill crowned with laurel, myrtle and strawberry trees. It would be a mistake to rely on some travellers who believe the town lies by a lake. The rain sometimes forms an enormous sheet of water, and a geologist who sees the past rather than the present state of nature in everything would not doubt that the whole plain was once a great lake, now dried up. La Laguna has fallen from its opulence since the erupting volcano destroyed the port of Garachico and Santa Cruz became the trading centre of the island. It has no more than 9,000 inhabitants, with nearly 400 monks distributed in six convents, though some travellers insist half the population wear cassocks. Numerous windmills surround the city, a sign that wheat is cultivated in this high country. The Guanches called wheat at Tenerife *tano*, at Lanzarote *triffa*; barley in Gran Canaria was called *aramotanoque*, and at Lanzarote *tamosen*. The flour of roasted barley (*gofio*) and goat's milk constituted the main food of these people about whose origins so many systematic fables have been written.

Many chapels, called *ermitas* by the Spaniards, surround La Laguna. Built on hillocks among evergreen trees, these chapels add a picturesque effect to the countryside. The interior of the town does not correspond at all to its outskirts. The houses are solid, but very ancient, and the streets sad. A botanist should not complain of the age of these houses for the roofs and walls are covered with *Sempervivum canariensis* and the pretty trichomanes, mentioned by every traveller. The plants are watered by the abundant mists.

The ground of the island rises to form an amphitheatre and, as in Peru and Mexico, contains in miniature all the possible climates, from African heat to alpine cold.[14] The mean temperatures of Santa Cruz, the port of Orotava, Orotava itself and La Laguna form a descending series. In southern Europe the change of seasons is too strongly felt to offer the same advantages. Tenerife on the other hand, on the threshold of the Tropics and a few days' journey from Spain, benefits from a good part of what nature has lavished in the Tropics. Its flora include the beautiful and imposing bananas and palms. He who is able to feel nature's beauty finds in this precious island a far more effective remedy than the climate. Nowhere else in the world seems more appropriate to dissipate melancholy and restore peace to troubled minds than Tenerife and Madeira. These effects are due not only to the magnificent situation and to the purity of air, but above all to the absence of slavery, which so deeply revolts us in all those places where Europeans have brought what they call their 'enlightenment' and their 'commerce' to their colonies.

The valley of Tacoronte leads one into a delicious country glowingly spoken of by all travellers. In the Tropics I found places where nature is more grand and richer in its varieties; but after crossing the Orinoco, the Peruvian cordilleras and the valleys of Mexico I admit that I have never seen a more attractive, more harmonious view in the distribution of greenery and rocks than the western coast of Tenerife.

The sea coast is fringed with date and coconut palms; above them groups of banana trees stand out from the dragon trees whose trunks are often rightly compared to snakes' bodies. The hills are covered in vines, which grow over high stakes. Orange trees loaded with blossom, myrtle and cypress surround chapels raised devotedly by the islanders on cleared hilltops. Land is divided by hedges made of agave and cactus. Innumerable cryptogamous plants, predominantly fern, cover the walls moistened by small clear-water springs. In winter when the volcano is covered with snow and ice this place enjoys an eternal spring. In summer, as the evening falls, a sea breeze freshens the air. The coastal population is very dense and appears to be even greater because the houses and gardens are scattered, increasing the picturesque aspect. Unhappily, the wealth of the inhabitants does not correspond with hard work or with nature's richness. Those who work the land are not its owners; the fruit of their labour belongs to the nobility and the feudal system that for so long was the shame of Europe and still prevents the people's progress here.

On our way to the port of Orotava we passed through the pretty villages of Matanza and Victoria. These names are found together in all the Spanish colonies and contrast in an ugly way with the peaceful feelings those countries inspire. Matanza signifies slaughter, and the word alone recalls the price at which victory was won. In the New World it generally indicates the defeat of the Indians; at Tenerife the village of Matanza was built in a place where the Spaniards were defeated by the Guanches, who were soon sold as slaves in Europe.[15]

By the morning of the 21st of June we were on our way to the volcano's summit. The day was not fine and the peak's summit, generally visible from Orotava from sunrise to ten at night, was covered in cloud. What links an excursion to the peak with similar ones to Chamonix or Etna is that one is obliged to follow guides, and sees only what has already been seen and described by previous travellers.

From a distance Villa de la Orotava pleases because of the many streams running down the main streets. The Agua Mansa spring, trapped in two large reservoirs, turns several mills and is then released in the nearby vineyards. The climate in the town is even more refreshing than in the port as a strong wind always blows from ten in the morning onwards. Because of the altitude water evaporates in the air and frequently precipitates to make the climate misty. The town lies 160 toises above sea-level; which is 200 toises lower than La Laguna; it was noted that plants flower a month later here.

Orotava, the ancient Taoro of the Guanches, lies on an abrupt slope of a hill. The streets seemed deserted; the houses solidly built but melancholic; they nearly all belong to a nobility accused of being too proud, presumptuously calling itself the Twelve Houses. We passed along a high aqueduct lined with luxuriant fern, and visited many gardens where northern European fruit trees grow along with orange, pomegranate and date trees. Even though we knew about Franqui's dragon tree[16] from previous travellers, its enormous thickness amazed us. We were told that this tree, mentioned in several ancient documents, served as a boundary mark and already in the fifteenth century was as enormous as it is today. We calculated its height to be about 50 to 60 feet; its circumference a little above its roots measured 45 feet. The trunk is divided into many branches, which rise up in the form of a chandelier and end in tufts of leaves similar to the Mexican yucca.

This tree, which grows only in cultivated areas in the Canaries, Madeira and Porto Santo, presents a curious phenomenon in plant migration. In Africa it has never been found in a wild state, and its country of origin is East India. How has this tree become acclimatized in Tenerife? Did the Guanches have contact with nations originally from Asia?

From Orotava, along a narrow and stony path through a beautiful chestnut forest (*el monte de castaños*), we reached an area covered with brambles, laurels and arboreal heaths. The trunks of the latter grow to an extraordinary size and their mass of flowers contrasts agreeably with the abundant *Hypericum canariensis*. We stopped under a solitary pine to fill up with water. This place commanded a magnificent panorama over the sea and the western part of the island.

We continued to climb from this pine to the crater of the volcano without crossing one valley, for the ravines do not merit this name. To the eyes of a geologist the whole of the island is one mountain whose oval base is prolonged to the north-east and in which several systems of volcanic rock, formed in different periods, may be distinguished.

Above the region of arborescent heaths, called Monte Verde, lies the region of ferns. Nowhere else have I seen such a profusion of pteris, blechnum and asplenium. The roots of the *Pteris aquilina* serve as food for the inhabitants of Palma and Gomera; they grate it to a powder and mix in a bit of barley flour, which when boiled is called *gofio*. The use of such a primitive food is proof of the misery of the peasants of the Canary Islands. Monte Verde is scored by several small and arid ravines. Above the zone of ferns we reached a juniper and pine wood, severely punished by storms.

We spent nearly two and a half hours crossing this plain, which is nothing but an immense sea of sand. Despite the altitude the thermometer indicated 13.8 °C in the evening, 3.7 °C higher than at noon. We suffered continuously from the pumice-stone dust. In the midst of this plain are tufts of broom, *Spartium nubigenum*. This beautiful shrub grows to a height of some 9 feet and is covered with aromatic flowers with which the goat hunters we met in our path decorated their hats. The dark, chestnut-coloured goats of the peak are supposed to be very tasty as they eat the leaves of this plant, and have run wild in these wastes from time immemorial.

As far as the rock of Gayta, that is, up to the beginning of the great retama plain, the Tenerife peak is covered in beautiful vegetation, with no traces of recent devastations. But hardly have you entered the plain littered with pumice-stone than the countryside changes dramatically; at every step you trip over enormous obsidian blocks thrown down by the volcano. Everything here betrays a deep solitude. A few goats and rabbits are the only signs of life in this high plain. From up here the island becomes an immense heap of burned matter surrounded by a narrow fringe of vegetation.

Above the region of *Spartium nubigenum* we passed through narrow defiles and small, old ravines cut by rainwater to a higher plateau and then on to the place where we intended to spend the night, some 1,530 toises above the coast. This place is called Estancia de los Ingleses (English Halt) because most of the travellers who have scaled the peak have been English. Two protruding rocks form a kind of cave, which offers shelter from the wind. This point, higher than the summit of Canigou, can be reached on mule: many a curious traveller hoping to reach the crater's edge from Orotava have had to wait here. Despite it being summer and there being a blue African sky above us that night we froze; the thermometer dropped to 5 °C. Our guides lit a bonfire with dried retama branches. Without a tent or coats, we had to lie down on calcinated scree, and the flames and smoke that the wind drove ceaselessly towards us made it an extremely uncomfortable night. We had never spent a night so high up and I had no idea that we would soon live in cities higher than the summit of this volcano. The further the temperature plummeted, the thicker the clouds round the peak grew. A strong north wind dissipated them; at intervals the moon appeared, its white disk shining against a blue backdrop. With the volcano in sight, that night scene was truly majestic. Suddenly the peak would disappear completely in the mist, then it would reappear worryingly close, casting its shadow over the clouds below us like some monstrous pyramid.

Around three in the morning, lit by the dismal light of a few pine torches, we set off for the summit of the Piton. We began the ascent from the northern side, which is extremely steep. After two hours we reached a small plateau, named Alta Vista because of its height. The *neveros*, those natives who collect ice and snow to sell in the nearby towns, reach as far as this point. Their mules, better trained to climb than those hired by travellers, reach Alta Vista. The *neveros* then have to carry the collected snow on their shoulders as they go down. Beyond this point the *malpaís* begins. This term, in use in Mexico, Peru and all places where there are volcanoes, refers to regions stripped of vegetation and covered in lava fragments.

We turned to the right to visit the ice cave situated at 1,728 toises, just under the perpetual snow altitude limit. During winter the grotto fills with ice and snow and, as the sun's rays do not penetrate its interior, summer heat is unable to melt the frozen water.

Day was breaking when we left the ice cave. A layer of white fleecy cloud blocked out the lower regions of the surrounding islands. The clouds were spread out so uniformly and in such a flat way that they looked like an immense plain covered in snow. The colossal pyramid of the peak, the volcanic summits of Lanzarote, Fuerteventura and La Palma stuck up like reefs

above a sea of fog. Their dark colour contrasted vividly with
the whiteness of the clouds.

We were forced to cut our own track across the *malpaís*. The
slope is very steep, and the volcanic blocks slipped under our
feet. The rubble on the peak's summit has sharp edges and
leaves gaps into which explorers risk falling up to their waists.
Unfortunately the laziness and bad temper of our guides made
this ascent more difficult. They were despairingly phlegmatic.
The night before they had tried to convince us not to pass
beyond the limit of the rocks. Every ten minutes they would
sit down to rest; they threw away pieces of obsidian and
pumice-stone that we had carefully collected. Finally we realized that none of them had ever visited the volcano's summit
before.

After three hours' walking we reached a small plain called
La Rambleta at the far end of the *malpaís*; from its centre rises
the Piton or Sugar Loaf. From the Orotava side this mountain
resembles those pyramids with steps found in Féjoun or Mexico. Here we found the air holes that locals call the Nostrils of
the Peak (Narices del Pico). Hot watery vapours seep out at
regular intervals from cracks in the rock, and the thermometer
marked 43.2 °C. I cannot, however, accept the daring hypothesis which states that the Nostrils of the Peak are vents of an
immense apparatus of distillation whose lower part is situated
below sea-level. Since we have been studying volcanoes with
more care, and since innate love for all that is marvellous is
less common in geological books, doubts have been expressed
about these constant and direct links between sea water and
volcanic fire. There is a far simpler explanation of this phenomenon. The peak is covered with snow part of the year; we
found snow still around on the Rambleta plain. This led us to
conclude that the Tenerife peak, like the Andes and Manila
islands' volcanoes, are filled with filtered water. The watery
vapours emitted by the Nostrils and cracks of the crater are
those same waters heated.

We had yet to climb the steepest part of the mountain, the
Piton, which forms the summit. The slope of this small cone,
covered with volcanic ashes and fragments of pumice-stone,

is so steep that it would have been impossible to reach the top had we not been able to follow an old lava current that seemed to have flowed down from the crater and whose remains have defied the ravages of time. The debris forms a wall of scoria, which reaches into the loose ash. We climbed to the Piton by clinging to this sharp-edged scoria, which, worn down by the weather, often broke off in our hands. It took us half an hour to reach the top, though it was only some 90 toises above us.

When we reached the Piton's summit we were surprised to find that there was barely enough room to sit down comfortably. We faced a small circular wall of porphyritic lava, with a base of pitch-stone, which prevented us from seeing the interior of the crater called La Caldera or the Cauldron. The wind blew so hard from the west that we could scarcely stand on our feet. It was eight in the morning and we were frozen though the temperature was just above freezing-point. We had become accustomed to heat, and the dry wind increased the sensation of cold.

The brink of the crater does not resemble any of the other volcanoes I have visited, such as Vesuvius, Jorullo or Pichincha. On the peak the wall, which surrounds the crater like a parapet, is so high that it would not let you reach La Caldera were it not for a breach on the eastern side caused by a very ancient lava overflow. We climbed down through this gap to the bottom of the elliptical funnel.

The external edges of La Caldera are almost perpendicular, rather like the Somma seen from the Atrio del Cavallo. We got to the bottom of the crater following a trail of broken lava from the eastern breach of the wall. We only felt the heat above the crevices, which exhaled watery vapours with a strange buzzing sound. Some of these crevices can be found on the outside of the crater, on the external parapet that surrounds it. A thermometer placed inside one of them rose suddenly from 68 °C to 75 °C. This would have risen higher, but we had to pull the thermometer out to prevent our hands from being burned. It might be thought that these vapours, which escape in puffs of air, contain muriatic or sulphuric acids, but when condensed they had no particular taste. Experiments showed that these chimneys exhale pure water only.

While on the spot I sketched a view[17] of the crater's interior edge as it is seen on the descent through the eastern wall's breach. Nothing is more striking than the superimposition of these lava strata, which reveals similar sinuosities to the calcareous rock of the Alps. These enormous ledges, sometimes horizontal and sometimes sloping or undulating, reminded us that long ago the entire mass had flowed, and that a combination of disruptive causes determined a particular flow. The crest of the wall exhibits the same strange ramifications we find in coke. The northern edge is the highest. Towards the south-west the wall has considerably subsided and an enormous amount of scoria seems glued to the outer edge. On the west the rock is perforated, and through a wide opening you can see the sea and horizon. Perhaps the force of the steam broke through here just when the lava overflowed from the crater.

The bottom of the crater is reached with danger. In a volcano such as Vesuvius, whose main activity is directed towards the summit, the depth of the crater varies with each eruption, but at the Tenerife peak the depth appears to have remained unchanged for a long time. Judging from what I could see, the actual site of the crater is properly speaking a solfatara; an area for interesting but not striking observations. The majesty of the site is due more to its height above sea-level, to the profound silence of these elevated regions, and to the immense space over which the eye ranges from the mountain's summit.

A journey to the Tenerife volcano's summit is not solely interesting for the amount of phenomena available for scientific research but far more for the picturesque beauties offered to those who keenly feel the splendours of nature. It is a hard task to describe these sensations for they work on us so much more powerfully the more they are vague. When a traveller must describe the highest peaks, the river cataracts, the tortuous Andes valleys, he risks tiring his readers with the monotonous expression of his admiration. It seems better suited to my intentions in this narrative of my journey to evoke the particular character of each zone. We get to know the features of each region better the more we indicate its varying characteristics by comparing it with others. This method enables us to discover the sources of the pleasures conferred by the great picture of nature.

Travellers know by experience that views from the summits of high mountains are neither as beautiful, picturesque, nor as varied as those from the heights of Vesuvius, Righi or the Puy-de-Dôme. Colossal mountains such as Chimborazo, Antisana or Monte Rosa compose such a huge mass that the richly cultivated plains are seen only at a great distance where a bluish and watery tint spreads over the landscape. The Tenerife peak, due to its narrow shape and local position, combines the advantages of the less high summits with those of the very high. From its top we can see not only the sea to the horizon, but also the forests of Tenerife and the inhabited coastal strips, which seem so close that their shapes and tones stand out in beautiful contrasts. It could be said that the volcano crushes the little island that serves as its base, and that it shoots up from the depths of the seas to a height three times higher than cloud level in summer.

Seated on the crater's external edge we turned our eyes towards the north-east where the coasts are decorated with villages and hamlets. At our feet masses of mist, continually tossed about by the winds, changed shape all the time. A uniform layer of cloud between us and the lower regions of the island had been pierced here and there by wind currents sent up from the heated earth. The Orotava bay, its vessels at anchor, the gardens and vineyards round the town, appeared in an opening that seemed to enlarge all the time. From these solitary regions our eyes dived down to the inhabited world below; we enjoyed the striking contrasts between the peak's arid slopes, its steep sides covered with scoriae, its elevated plains devoid of vegetation, and the smiling spectacle of the cultivated land below. We saw how plants were distributed according to the decreasing temperatures of altitudes. Below the peak lichens begin to cover the scorious and polished lava; a violet (*Viola cheiranthifolia*) similar to the *Viola decumbens* climbs the volcano's slopes up to 1,740 toises above all other herbaceous plants. Tufts of flowering broom decorate the valleys hollowed out by the torrents and blocked by the effects of lateral eruptions. Below the retama lies the region of ferns, and then the arborescent heaths. Laurel, rhamnus and strawberry-tree woods grow between the scrub and the rising ground planted with vines and fruit trees. A rich green carpet extends from the plain of brooms and the zone of alpine plants to groups of date palms and banana trees whose feet are bathed by the ocean.

The apparent proximity of the hamlets, vineyards and coastal gardens from the summit is increased by the surprising transparency of the air. Despite the great distance we could not only pick out the houses, the tree trunks and the sails on the vessels, but also the vivid colouring of the plain's rich vegetation. The Pico de Teide is not situated in the Tropics, but the dryness of the air, which rises continuously above the neighbouring African plains and is rapidly blown over by the eastern winds, gives the atmosphere of the Canary Islands a transparency which not only surpasses that of the air around Naples and Sicily, but also of the air around Quito and Peru. This transparency may be one of the main reasons for the beauty of tropical scenery; it heightens the splendours of the vegetation's colouring, and contributes to the magical effects of its harmonies and contrasts. If the light tires the eyes during part of the day, the inhabitant of these southern regions has his compensation in a moral enjoyment, for a lucid clarity of mind corresponds to the surrounding transparency of the air.

Despite the heat the traveller feels under his feet on the brink of the crater, the cone of ashes remains covered with snow for several months. The cold, angry wind, which had been blowing since dawn, forced us to seek shelter at the foot of the Piton. Our hands and feet were frozen, while our boots were burned by the ground we walked on. In a few minutes we reached the foot of the Sugar Loaf, which we had so laboriously climbed; our speed of descent was in part involuntary as we slipped down on the ashes. We reluctantly abandoned that solitary place where nature had magnificently displayed herself before us. We deluded ourselves that we might again visit the Canary Islands, but this, like many other plans, has never been carried out.

We crossed the *malpaís* slowly; for it is hard to walk securely on lava fragments. Nearer the Station of the Rocks the path down was extremely difficult; the short thick grass was so slippery that we were constantly forced to lean our bodies backwards in order not to fall. In the sandy plain of retama the thermometer rose to 22.5 °C; this heat seemed suffocating after the cold we had suffered on the summit. We had no more water; our guides had not only secretly drunk our small supply of malmsey wine but had also broken our water jugs.

In the beautiful region of the arborescent erica and fern we at last enjoyed some cool breezes, and we were wrapped in thick clouds, stationary at some 600 toises above sea-level.

Near the town of Orotava we came across great flocks of canaries. These birds, well known in Europe, were in general uniformly green; some had a yellowish tinge on their backs; their song was the same as that of the domesticated canary. It has been noted that those canaries captured in the island of Gran Canaria, and in the islet of Monte Clara, near Lanzarote, have a louder, more harmonious call. In every zone, among birds of the same species, each flock has its peculiar call. The yellow canaries are a variety now breeding in Europe; those we saw in cages had been bought at Cádiz and other Spanish ports. But the bird from the Canary Islands that has the most agreeable song is unknown in Europe. It is the *capirote*, which has never been tamed, so much does he love his freedom. I have enjoyed his sweet and melodious warbling in a garden in Orotava, but have never seen him close enough to judge what family he belongs to. As for the parrots supposedly seen during Captain Cook's stay at Tenerife, they never existed but in the narratives of some travellers who have copied from each other.

Towards sunset we reached the port of Orotava where we received the unexpected news that the *Pizarro* was not to sail until the 24th or 25th. Had we been warned of this delay we would have prolonged our stay on the peak, or made another journey to the volcano of Chahorra. The following day we visited the outskirts of Orotava and enjoyed the pleasant company that Cologan's house offered. We noticed that Tenerife had attractions not only for those who busy themselves with natural history; we found in Orotava several people who had a taste for literature and music, bringing their European sophistication with them to these distant islands. In this respect, with the exception of Havana, the Canary Islands bore no resemblance to any other Spanish colonies.

On the eve of Saint John's Day we were present at a country party in Little's garden. This gentleman, who greatly helped the Canarians during the last wheat famine, has cultivated a hill covered with volcanic debris. In this delicious place he has installed an English garden from which there is a magnificent view of the peak, of the villages along the coast, and of the island of Las Palmas on the edge of the great ocean. That view can only be compared to the views of Genoa and Naples bays; but Orotava is far superior to both in terms of the grandeur of its masses and the richness of its vegetation. As night fell the volcano's slopes presented us with a wonderful spectacle. Following a custom introduced by the Spaniards, though it dates back to remotest times, the shepherds lit the fires of Saint John. The scattered masses of fire and columns of smoke driven by the wind stood out from the deep green of the forests lining the peak. The shepherds' distant yells of joy were the only sounds that broke the silence of that night in those solitary places.[18]

Before we leave the Old World to cross over into the New there is a subject I must speak about because it belongs to the history of man, and to those fatal revolutions that have made whole tribes disappear from the earth. We ask in Cuba, in Santo Domingo and in Jamaica, where are the primitive inhabitants of these countries? We ask at Tenerife, what has become of the Guanches whose mummies alone, buried in caves, have escaped destruction? In the fifteenth century almost all the mercantile nations, especially the Spaniards and the Portuguese, sought slaves on the Canary Islands, as later they did on the Guinea coast. Christianity, which originally favoured the freedom of mankind, served later as a pretext for European cupidity.

A short time after the discovery of America, when Spain was at the zenith of her glory, the gentle character of the Guanches was the fashionable topic, just as in our times we praise the Arcadian innocence of the Tahitians. In both these pictures the colouring is more vivid than true. When nations are mentally exhausted and see the seeds of depravity in their refinements, the idea that in some distant region infant societies enjoy pure and perpetual happiness pleases them.

CHAPTER 3

CROSSING FROM TENERIFE TO THE COASTS OF
SOUTH AMERICA — SIGHTING OF TOBAGO —
ARRIVAL AT CUMANÁ

ON THE EVENING of the 25th of June we left Santa Cruz and set our course for South America. A strong north-westerly was blowing and tight, sharp waves were caused by strong currents. We soon lost sight of the Canary Islands above whose high peaks a reddish mist appeared; only the Pico de Teide reappeared briefly from time to time as the wind dispersed the clouds surrounding the peak. For the first time we realized how deeply we are stirred by the sight of land situated on the limits of the torrid zone, where nature appears so opulent, grandiose and marvellous. We had stayed at Tenerife for a few days only, yet we left the island feeling we had lived there for a long time.

The sea-crossing from Santa Cruz to Cumaná, the most eastern part of the New Continent, was indescribably beautiful. We cut the Tropic of Cancer on the 27th and, despite the *Pizarro* not being a fast sailer, took only twenty days to cover the 900 leagues that separate the African coast from the New World. Some land birds, blown out to sea by the strong wind, followed us for a few days.

We followed the same route as Columbus had taken on his first voyage out to the Antilles. It is well known that during the crossing from Santa Cruz to Cumaná, or from Acapulco to the Philippines, sailors barely have to worry about working the sails. We crossed the ocean as if descending a river, and would have been in no greater danger if we had made the voyage in an open boat.

The further we left the African coast behind the weaker the wind became: it was often completely calm for hours, followed regularly by electrical phenomena. Thick black perfectly shaped clouds formed in the east; it seemed as if a squall might force us to fasten the topsail; then the wind would rise again, a few large raindrops would fall, and the storm would vanish without a single clap of thunder. It is thanks to these squalls alternating with dead calms that you are able to cross the ocean from the Canaries to the West Indies during June and July.

Nothing equals the beauty and mildness of a tropical ocean's climate. While the trade wind blew strongly the thermometer remained steadily at 23 °C or 24 °C by day, and 22 °C to 22.5 °C by night. What a contrast between the tempestuous seas of the northern latitudes and those regions where the peace of nature is never disturbed! If the return journey from Mexico or South America was as quick and agreeable as the outgoing one the number of Europeans settled in the colonies would be considerably less than it is at the present. The seas that surround the Azores and Bermudas, which you cross when returning to Europe, are oddly called by Spaniards El Golfo de las Yeguas (Gulf of Mares). Settlers who are not used to the sea and who have lived isolatedly in Guianan forests, or in the savannahs of Caracas, or in the mountains of Peru, fear this gulf more than people fear Cape Horn. They exaggerate the dangers of a journey that is treacherous only in winter. They postpone this dangerous return year after year until death surprises them still planning.

To the north of the Cape Verde Islands we found great masses of floating seaweeds. They were the tropical sea-grape variety (*Fucus natans*), which grow on rocks below sea-level from the equator to the 40th degree of latitude. These seaweeds seem to indicate the presence of currents. These scattered weeds should not be confused with those banks of weeds that Columbus compared to great meadows, which terrified the crew of the *Santa María* on the 42nd degree of latitude.

From the 22nd degree of latitude the surface of the sea was covered with flying fish (*Exocoetuus volitans*); they threw themselves 12, 15 and even 18 feet into the air and fell on deck. I do not hesitate to speak on a subject as common in travelogues as dolphins, sharks, seasickness and the phosphorescence of the ocean. There is nothing that does not interest a naturalist as long as he makes a detailed study. Nature is an inexhaustible source of study, and as science advances so new facts reveal themselves to an observer who knows how to interrogate her.

I have mentioned flying fish in order to draw the attention of naturalists to the extraordinary size of their natatory bladder. As this bladder takes up more than half the fish's body volume it probably contributes to its lightness. One could say that this reservoir of air is more adapted for flying than swimming. Flying fish, like almost all animals with gills, enjoy the possibility of breathing for a long time with the same organs both in air and in water. They pass much of their time in the air, although flying does not make them less wretched. If they leave the sea to escape from the voracious dolphin they meet frigate-birds, albatrosses and other birds in the air, which seize them in mid-flight. Thus, on the Orinoco banks, herds of capybara (*Cavia capybara*) rush from the water to escape crocodiles and fall prey to jaguars waiting for them on the banks. I doubt that flying fish leap from the water solely to escape their predators. Like swallows they shoot forward in thousands in straight lines, always against the waves. In our climate, by a clear-water river struck by the sun's rays, we often see single fish, with no reason to fear anything, leap into the air as if they enjoyed breathing air. Why aren't these games more frequent and prolonged with flying fish who, thanks to their pectoral fins and extreme lightness, fly easily in the air?

On the 1st of July we came across the wreck of a sunken ship. We could distinguish its mast covered in floating seaweed. In a zone where the sea is perpetually calm the boat could not have sunk. Perhaps its remains came from the northerly stormy area and were dragged there by the extraordinary whirling of the Atlantic Ocean in the Southern hemisphere.

On the 3rd and 4th of July we crossed that part of the Atlantic Ocean where charts indicate the Maelstrom; at night we changed course to avoid the danger, though its existence is as dubious as that of the isles of Fonseco and Saint Anne.[19] The old charts are filled with rocks, some of which really exist, though most are due to optical illusions, which are more frequent at sea than on land.

From the time we entered the torrid zone we never tired of admiring, night after night, the beauty of the southern sky, which as we advanced further south opened up new constellations. A strange, completely unknown feeling is awoken in us when nearing the equator and crossing from one hemisphere to another; the stars we have known since infancy begin to vanish. Nothing strikes the traveller more completely about the immense distances that separate him from home than the look of a new sky. The grouping of great stars, some scattered nebulae that rival the Milky Way in splendour, and regions that stand out because of their intense blackness, give the southern sky its unique characteristics. This sight strikes the imagination of those who even, without knowledge of the exact sciences, like to stare at the heavens as if admiring a lovely country scene, or a majestic site. You do not have to be a botanist to recognize immediately the torrid zone by its vegetation. Even those with no inkling of astronomy know they are no longer in Europe when they see the enormous constellation of the Ship or the brilliant Clouds of Magellan rise in the night sky. Everything on earth and in the sky in the tropical countries takes on an exotic note.

On the night of the 4th of July, at about the 16th degree of latitude, we saw the Southern Cross clearly for the first time; it appeared strongly inclined and shone intermittently between clouds. When flashes of lightning passed across its centre it shone with a silvery light. If a traveller may be permitted to speak of his personal emotions, I will add that on that night I saw one of the dreams of my earliest youth come true.

When we first glance at geographical maps, and read the narratives of navigators, we feel a special charm for certain countries and climates, which we cannot explain when older. These impressions exercise a considerable hold over what we do in life, and we instinctively try to connect ourselves with anything associated with these places. When I first studied the stars to identify them I was disturbed by a fear unknown to those who love sedentary life. It was painful to me to have to renounce the hope of seeing the beautiful constellations near the South Pole. Impatient to explore the equatorial regions

I could not raise my eyes to the sky without dreaming of the Southern Cross and remembering a passage from Dante.[20] Our joy over discovering the Southern Cross was vividly shared by those sailors who had lived in the colonies. In the solitudes of the oceans you wave at a star as if it is a friend you haven't seen for ages. Portuguese and Spaniards are particularly susceptible to this feeling; religious sentiments attach them to a constellation whose shape recalls the sign of the faith planted by their ancestors in the deserts of the New World.

That the Cross is nearly perpendicular when it passes the meridian is known to all who inhabit the Tropics. It has been observed at which hour of the night, in different seasons, the Cross is erect or inclined. How often have we heard our guides exclaim in the savannahs of Venezuela or in the desert stretching from Lima to Trujillo, 'Midnight is past, the Cross begins to bend!' How those words reminded me of that moving scene where Paul and Virginie,[21] seated near the source of the river Lataniers, chat together for the last time, and where the old man, at the sight of the Southern Cross, warns them that it is time to separate!

The last days of our crossing were not as peaceful as the mild climate and calm ocean had led us to hope. We were not disturbed by the dangers of the deep, but by the presence of a malignant fever that developed as we approached the West Indies. Between the overcrowded decks the heat was unbearable; the thermometer stayed at 36 °C. Two sailors, several passengers and, strangely, two blacks from the Guinean coast and a mulatto child were attacked by an illness that threatened to turn into an epidemic. The symptoms were not as serious in all the sick; but some of them, even among the most robust, became delirious on the second day and lost all body strength. With that indifference which on passenger ships affects everything that is not to do with the ship's movements and speed, the captain did not for a moment think of applying the simplest remedies. He did not fumigate. A phlegmatic and ignorant Gallician surgeon prescribed bleedings, attributing the fever to what he called the heat and corruption of blood.

There was not an ounce of quinine on board and we, on boarding, had forgotten to bring a supply, more concerned for our instruments than for our health as we had not predicted that a Spanish ship would be without this Peruvian bark febrifuge.

On the 8th of July a sailor, near death, recovered his health in circumstances worthy of relating. His hammock had been strung in such a way that between his face and the ceiling there was not more than 10 inches. In such a position it was impossible to administer the sacraments; according to the custom on Spanish ships the Last Sacrament has to be brought down lighted by candles, followed by the crew. For this reason they had to take the sailor to a more airy place near the hatchway where they had made a little berth with flags and canvas. The man would stay there until his death. But hardly had he passed from an asphyxiating, noxious and humid atmosphere to the open air than he gradually began to recover from his lethargy. His convalescence began the day they moved him out from the middle deck. As is common in medicine the same facts are quoted in support of diametrically opposed systems; this recovery confirmed our doctor's ideas about bleeding and evacuation. We soon felt the fatal effects of this treatment and longed to reach the coast of America.

The pilots trusted the ship's log more than my time-keeper,[22] and smiled at my prediction that we would soon sight land, sure that we still had two to three days of sailing. It was with great satisfaction that on the 13th, at about six in the morning, high land was seen through the mist by someone from the mast. A strong wind blew and the sea was very rough. Every now and then heavy drops of rain fell. Everything pointed to a difficult situation. The captain intended to pass through the channel that separates the islands of Tobago and Trinidad and, knowing that our corvette was slow to turn, feared the south wind and the approach to the Boca del Dragón.

The island of Tobago presents an extremely picturesque scene. It is a heap of rocks skilfully cultivated. The dazzling whiteness of the rocks stands out from the green of the scattered trees. High cylindrical cacti crown the mountain tops and give a peculiar quality to the tropical countryside. Just this sight tells the traveller that he is looking at the American coast, because the cacti are as unique to the New World as heaths are to the Old.

We had left doubled the northern cape of Tobago and the small island of Saint Giles when the look-out pointed out the presence of an enemy squadron. We immediately changed course and the passengers began to fret as many of them had invested small fortunes in goods to sell in the Spanish colonies. The squadron did not appear to move and soon we saw that the look-out had confused ships with an isolated reef.

The epidemic on board the *Pizarro* spread rapidly as soon as we neared the coast of Terra Firma.[23] By night the thermometer regularly marked 22 °C or 23 °C, by day it rose to 24 °C and 27 °C. Congestion in the head, extreme dryness of skin and the failing of all strength became alarming symptoms but, having reached the end of the voyage, we flattered ourselves that the sick would recover their health as soon as we landed them on Margarita Island or at Cumaná harbour, both known for their salubrity.

This hope was not totally justified. The youngest passenger attacked by the malignant fever was unluckily the only victim. He was a nineteen-year-old Asturian, the only son of a widow without means. Several circumstances made the death of this sensitive and mild-tempered youth moving. He had embarked against his will; his mother, whom he hoped to help through his work, had sacrificed her tenderness and own interests in order to assure the fortune of her son in the colonies, helping a rich cousin in Cuba. The luckless youth had fallen from the start into a total lethargy, with moments of delirium, and died on the third day. Yellow fever, or black vomit as it is called at Veracruz, does not carry off the sick so frighteningly quickly. Another Asturian, even younger than he, never left his bedside and, more remarkably, never caught the illness. He was following his compatriot to Cuba, to be introduced into his relation's house, on whom they had based all their hopes. It was desperate to see this young man abandon himself to deep grief and curse the advice of those who had sent him to a distant land, alone and without support.

We were all on deck sunk in sad thoughts. There was no doubt that the fever raging on board had taken a pernicious turn. Our glances were fixed on a deserted mountainous coast, intermittently lit by the moon. The calm sea shone with a feeble phosphorescence. We heard only the monotonous cries of large sea birds seeking the shore. A deep calm reigned in these lonely places, but nature's calm contrasted with the painful feelings agitating us. Towards eight that night the dead man's knell was tolled; at this lugubrious signal the sailors stopped work and kneeled in short prayers in a touching ceremony, which, recalling the times when the early Christians saw themselves as members of the same family, brought us together in a common sorrow. At night the young Asturian's corpse was carried to the bridge, and the priest arranged to delay dropping him into the sea until dawn, according to the Roman Catholic rite. Everybody mourned the bad luck of this young man who but a few days before had seemed so fresh and healthy.

The passengers on board the *Pizarro* who had not yet noticed the symptoms of this malady[24] decided to leave the ship at the first port of call and await the arrival of another mail-boat to continue on to Cuba and Mexico. They felt the between decks were infected, and though it had not been proved that the fever was contagious I thought it more prudent to disembark at Cumaná. It would have been a pity to put into port at Cumaná and La Guaira without penetrating into a land so little explored by naturalists.

The decision we took on the night of the 14th of July had a happy influence on the direction of our travels. Instead of weeks, we spent a year in this part of the world. Had not the fever broken out on board the *Pizarro* we would never have explored the Orinoco, the Casiquiare and the frontiers with the Portuguese possessions on the Río Negro. We perhaps also owed to this circumstance the good health we enjoyed for such a long period in the equinoctial regions.

It is well known that during the first months that Europeans are exposed to the burning heat of the Tropics they live in great danger. The ease of acclimatization seems to be in the inverse ratio of the difference between the mean temperature of the torrid zone and that of the native country of the settler because the irritability of the organs and their vital actions are powerfully modified by the atmospheric heat. We were lucky enough for recently disembarked Europeans to spend that dangerous period in Cumaná, a very hot but dry place celebrated for its salubrity.

At around eleven in the morning we caught sight of a low-lying island with large sand dunes. We did not see any sign of life or farming through the telescope. Here and there rose the cylindrical cacti in the form of candelabra. The ground, devoid of vegetation, seemed to ripple due to the intense refraction of the sun's rays through the air above an intensely heated surface. All over the world deserts and beaches look like rough seas from the effect of mirage.

The sight of such a flat land did not match the ideas we had formed about the island of Margarita. While we tried hard to match what we saw with what appeared on our map a look-out sighted some small fishing-boats. The captain of the *Pizarro* called them with a cannon shot: but this signal is useless in places where the weak confront the strong only to be crushed. The boats escaped to the west. The coasts from a distance are like clouds, where each observer sees the form of the objects that occupy his imagination. Our readings on the chronometer contradicted our maps, and we were lost in useless conjectures. Some took dunes for Indian huts, and pointed out the place where the fort of Pampatar was situated; others saw herds of goats common in the dry valleys of Saint John; or the high mountains of Macanao, partly hidden by clouds. The captain decided to send a pilot ashore, and the men prepared to lower the longboat.

As we were about to go ashore we saw two pirogues sailing along the coast. The captain hailed them with a second burst of cannon fire, and though we hoisted the Spanish colours they drew near defiantly. Their pirogues, like all those used by Indians, were cut from one tree trunk. In each canoe there were eighteen Guaiquerí Indians, naked to the waist and very tall. They looked very muscular, with a skin colour between brown and coppery red. From afar, sitting still and standing out against the horizon, they could be taken for bronze statues. Their appearance did not correspond with the traits and extreme weakness described by previous travellers.

When we were close enough to the pirogues to shout to the Indians in Spanish they lost their suspicion and boarded. They informed us that the low-lying island opposite was called Coche, and had never been inhabited. Spanish ships sailing in from Europe usually sailed further north between this island and Margarita to take a coastal pilot aboard at Pampatar.

The Guaiquerí belong to a tribe of civilized Indians inhabiting the coast of Margarita and the surroundings of the town of Cumaná. They enjoy several privileges because they remained faithful to the Castilians from earliest times. Also the King names them in some decrees as 'his dear, noble and loyal Guaiquerías'. Those manning the two pirogues had left Cumaná harbour at night. They were searching for building timber from the cedar forests (*Cedrela odorata*, Linn.) that stretch from Cape San José beyond the mouth of the Carupano river. They offered us fresh coconuts and stunningly coloured fish from the *Chaetodon* genus. What riches these poor Indians held in their pirogues! Huge *vijao* (*Heliconia bihai*) leaves covered bunches of bananas; the scaly cuirass of an armadillo (*Dasypus, cachicamo*); the fruit of the calabash tree (*Crescentia cujete*), used by the Indians as a cup, quite common in European cabinets, vividly reminded us that we had reached the longed-for torrid zone.

The chief of one of the pirogues offered to stay on board to guide us as a coastal pilot. He was a most trustworthy Guaiquerí; a keen observer, and led by a genuine thirst for learning he had studied the produce of the sea and land around him. It was fortunate that the first Indian we met on arrival was a man whose knowledge was to prove extremely helpful for our journey's objectives. With great pleasure I record his name as Carlos del Pino, who accompanied us for sixteen months up and down the coast, and into the interior.

Towards evening the captain weighed anchor and sailed west. Soon we came within sight of the little island of Cubagua, now entirely deserted but once famous for its pearl fisheries. There the Spaniards, immediately after Columbus's and Ojeda's journeys, had built a city called Nueva Cádiz, of which there is now not a trace. At the beginning of the sixteenth century Cubagua pearls were known in Seville, Toledo and the great fairs at Augsburg and Bruges. Nueva Cádiz had no water, so it had to be conveyed there from the Manzanares river. For some reason this water was thought to cause eye diseases.

The wind hardly blew so the captain thought it safe to tack until dawn. He did not dare enter Cumaná harbour at night. An unfortunate incident that occurred a year before justified his prudence. A mail-boat had anchored without lighting its poop lanterns; it was taken for an enemy and fired on by the fort. A cannon-ball ripped the captain's leg off and he died a few days later in Cumaná.

We spent part of the night on deck as the Indian pilot entertained us with stories about the plants and animals of his land. We learned with great satisfaction that a few leagues from the coast there was a mountain range, inhabited by the Spaniards, where it was quite cold, and that in the plains there were two kinds of very different crocodile (*Crocodilus acutus* and *C. bava*), as well as boas, electric eels (*Gymnotus electricus*, *temblador*) and various species of jaguar. Though the words *bava*, *cachicamo* and *temblador* were entirely unknown to us the naïve descriptions of the forms and habits of the animals allowed us to identify them easily. Nothing excites a naturalist's curiosity more than marvellous tales of a country he is about to explore.

At dawn on the 16th of July 1799 we saw the green, picturesque coast. The mountains of Nueva Andalucía, hidden in clouds, bordered the horizon. The city of Cumaná, with its fort, stood in coconut groves. At nine in the morning, after forty-one days at sea, we anchored in the harbour. The sick crawled on deck to comfort themselves with the vision of a land where they hoped they would be cured.[25]

CHAPTER 4

OUR EYES WERE fixed on groups of coconut trees that bordered the river whose trunks, which were more than sixty feet high, dominated the landscape. The plain was covered with thickets of cassia, capers and arborescent mimosa, which, similar to Italian pines, spread their branches out like parasols. The pinnated leaves of the palms stood out against the blue sky, in which there was not a trace of mist. The sun was climbing rapidly towards its zenith; a dazzling light spread through the atmosphere on to the whitish hills covered in cylindrical cacti, as well as the becalmed sea and the shores populated with pelicans (*Pelicanus fuscus*, Linn.), flamingoes and herons. The intense luminosity of the day, the vivid colours and forms of the vegetation, the variegated plumage of the birds, all bore the grand seal of tropical nature.

The town of Cumaná, capital of New Andalusia, lies a mile from the landing-stage or the *boca* battery where we stepped ashore after crossing the bar of the Manzanares river. We had to traverse a vast plain (*el salado*) between the Guaiquerí dwellings and the coast. The reverberation from the parched land increased the intense heat. The thermometer, plunged into the white sand, reached 37.7 °C. The first plant we gathered from American soil was the *Avicennia tomentosa* (*Mangle prieto*), which scarcely reaches 2 feet high here. This shrub, with the sesuvium, the yellow gomphrena and the cacti, covered a ground saturated with soda salts; they belong to the scant social plants like European heaths, and in the torrid zone thrive only on the seashore and high in the Andean plateaux.

The Indian pilot led us across his garden, which seemed more a copse than cultivated land. As proof of the land's fertility he showed us a silk-cotton tree (*Bombax heptaphyllum*) whose trunk measured nearly 2.5 feet in diameter after only four years' growth. However, I think the Indian's estimate of the tree's age was somewhat exaggerated. Still on the Cumaná beach, in the Guaiquerí's garden, we saw for the first time a *guama* (*Inga spuria*) loaded with flowers, remarkable for the length and silvery brilliance of their numerous stamen. We passed the neatly arranged streets of the Indian quarters, bordered with small new houses of attractive design. This part of the town has just been rebuilt after the earthquake a year and a half before our arrival that destroyed Cumaná. Hardly had we crossed the wooden bridge over the Manzanares river, full of *bavas* or small crocodiles, than we saw traces of that terrible catastrophe everywhere; new buildings rose over the ruins of the old.

The *Pizarro*'s captain accompanied us to the provincial governor's residence to present Don Vicente Emparán with our passports granted by the First Secretary of State. He received us with that frankness and simplicity that have always characterized the Basques. Before he was appointed governor of Portobello and Cumaná he distinguished himself a captain in the Royal Navy. His name evokes one of the most notable and distressing episodes in the history of naval warfare. After the last break between Spain and England two of Governor Emparán's brothers, outside Cádiz, attacked each other's ships, thinking the other was the enemy. The battle was ferocious and both ships sunk at almost the same time. Only a few of the crew were saved, and the two brothers realized their mistake just before dying.

The Governor of Cumaná expressed great satisfaction at our decision to remain awhile in New Andalusia, a province scarcely known in Europe at the time, not even by name, and whose mountains and numerous river banks afford a naturalist a wonderful field for observations. The governor showed us cottons dyed with indigenous plants and beautiful furniture carved from local wood. He was interested in all branches of natural philosophy, and to our amazement asked us if we thought that the atmosphere in the beautiful tropical sky contained more nitrogen than that in Spain, or if the speed with which iron oxidated was due to the greater humidity shown by the hair hygrometer. The name of his native country pronounced on a distant shore could not please the ears of a traveller more than hearing the words 'nitrogen', 'oxidation of iron' and 'hygrometer'. We knew, despite the court orders and recommendations of an influential minister, that we would face innumerable unpleasant incidents if we did not manage to make good relations with those ruling these immense lands. Sr Emparán was far too enamoured of the sciences to think it odd that we had come so far to collect plants and determine specific places from astronomical observations. He did not suspect any other motives than those that figured in our safe conducts, and the proof of public esteem he gave us throughout our stay in his territory contributed to giving us a warm welcome in all the South American countries.

At nightfall we ordered our instruments to be disembarked; and to our relief none had been damaged. We hired a spacious and well-situated house for our astronomical observations. When the sea wind blew we enjoyed the cool air. The windows did not have glass panes, nor the paper squares that replace glass in most Cumaná houses. All the passengers on the *Pizarro* left the ship, but those with the malignant fever recovered very slowly. Some were still terribly pale and emaciated after a month of illness, despite the care lavished on them by their compatriots. In the Spanish colonies the hospitality is such that a European who arrives without money or recommendations is almost sure to find help should he disembark sick in any port. Catalans, Galicians and Basques maintain an intense trade with America, where they form three distinct bodies, and exercise a great influence on the customs, industry and commerce of the colonies. The poorest inhabitant of Sitges or Vigo may be assured of being received in the house of a Catalan or Galician merchant (*pulpero*[26]) whether in Chile or Mexico or the Philippines. I have witnessed moving examples where strangers are looked after assiduously for years. Some may say that hospitality is no virtue in a land with such a magnificent climate, with plenty of food, and where indigenous plants supply efficient medicines, and a sick person finds necessary refuge in a hammock under a covering. But does not the arrival of a stranger in a family imply more work? Are not the proofs of disinterested sympathy, the spirit of sacrifice in the women, the patience that long convalescence requires, worthy of note? It has been observed that, with the exception of some populated cities, hospitality has not really decreased since the arrival of the Spanish settlers in the New World. It distresses me to think that this change will happen as the colonial population and industry progress rapidly, and that the state of society that we have agreed to call advanced civilization might banish 'the ancient Castilian frankness'.

The hill of calcareous rocks on which Cumaná stands, once an island in an ancient gulf, is covered with candle-like cacti and opuntia, some of the most arresting reaching as much as 30 to 40 feet high, with their trunks branching out like candelabra and covered in lichen. Near Maniquarez, at Punta Araya, we measured a cactus (*Tuna macho*) whose trunk had a circumference of 1.54 metres. Europeans who do not know opuntia apart from those in hothouses will be surprised to learn that the wood of this plant hardens extraordinarily with age, that for centuries it resists both air and humidity, and that the Cumaná Indians use it for making oars and door-frames. Cumaná, Coro, Margarita Island and Curaçao are the places in South America where the nopals thrive most. Only after a long stay could a botanist write a monograph on the genus *Cactus*.

One place where spiky cacti of great size grow together is almost impossible to walk through. These areas, known as *tunales*, not only prevent bare-chested Indians from entering, but also anyone fully dressed. During our solitary walks we tried several times to penetrate the *tunal* that crowns the hill with the fort, along which runs a path. There we found thousands of examples of this strange plant. At times nightfall surprised us as there is no twilight. Then this place becomes dangerous, for the rattlesnake (*Crotalus cumanensis*), the coral and other poisonous snakes seek out these hot places to deposit their eggs in the sand.

The *tunal* is considered here and everywhere in the Spanish colonies as crucial to military defence; and when earthworks are raised the engineers propagate the thorny opuntia, as they keep crocodiles in the ditches. In regions where nature is so fertile, man uses the carnivorous reptile and a plant with an armour of thorns to his advantage.

The San Antonio fort, where the Castilian flag is hoisted on feast days, stands at some 30 toises above sea-level. From its bare calcareous site it dominates the town, and seen from sea as you enter the port it looks very picturesque. It is a wonderful place to enjoy the sunset and view the gulf as a fresh sea breeze reaches it.

The town of Cumaná itself stretches from the San Antonio fort to the small Manzanares and Santa Catalina rivers. The delta formed by the former is fertile, covered with mammees, sapotas (*achra*), banana trees and other plants cultivated by the Indians in their *charas*.[27] The town boasts no buildings of particular interest, and the frequency of earthquakes prevents such plans.

The outlying area of Cumaná is as densely populated as the old town. This includes Los Cerritos, where we met with attractive tamarind trees, San Francisco to the south-east, and the place where the Guaiquerí live. The name of this tribe was quite unknown before the conquest. The Indians who use this name used to belong to the Warao who still inhabit the marshy area of the Orinoco delta. Some old men assured me that the language of their ancestors was a Warao dialect, but in Cumaná and Margarita not one Indian has spoken anything but Castilian for over a century.

The word 'Guaiquerí', like the words 'Peru' and 'Peruvian', owes its origin to a simple mistake. When Christopher Columbus's companions reached Margarita Island, on whose northern tip these Indians still live, they found several Indians fishing with harpoons, throwing these sharp-pointed sticks tied with string at the fish. Columbus's men asked the Indians in the Haitian language what their name was, but the Indians thought the foreigners referred to their harpoons made of the hard and heavy wood of the macana palm and answered: 'Guaike, guaike', meaning 'pointed stick'. These Guaiquerí are an intelligent and civilized tribe of fishermen, notably different from the wild Guarano from the Orinoco who build their houses up in the mauritia palm trees.

The beach near the mouth of the small Santa Catalina river is lined with mangrove trees (*Rhizophora mangle*); but these mangroves (*manglares*) are not extensive enough to affect the salubrity of Cumaná's air. Otherwise the plain is partly bare and partly covered with tufts of plants including the *Avicennia tomentosa*, the *Scoparia dulcis*, a shrub-like mimosa with very sensitive leaves,[28] and especially cassias, so many of which can be found in South America that on our travels we gathered more than thirty new species.

On leaving the Indian suburbs and climbing the river towards the south we reached a little wood of cacti, and then a marvellous place shaded by tamarind trees, brazilettos, bombax and other trees remarkable for their leaves and flowers. Here the soil is rich enough for pasturing, and among the trees there are dairies built of reeds. The milk is kept fresh not in the calabashes, which are made of thick ligneous fibres, but in porous earthenware pots from Maniquarez. A prejudice current in northern countries led me to believe that cows in the torrid zone did not give buttery milk. However, during my stay in Cumaná, and especially while on a trip through the vast plains of Calabozo, covered in grasses and sensitive plants, I learned that European cows adapt perfectly to extreme heat provided they are given water and good fodder.

As the inhabitants of Cumaná prefer the freshness of the sea breeze to forests their favourite walk is along the open shore. The Castilians, accused of not being fond of trees or birdsong, have transported these tastes and prejudices into their colonies. In Terra Firma, Mexico and Peru it is rare to see a native plant a tree just to get some shade, and, excepting the great capitals, tree alleys are almost unknown. The arid plain of Cumaná provides an extraordinary phenomenon after violent rainstorms. After being drenched with rain the earth is heated by the sun and gives off that musky smell common to many different tropical animals like the jaguar, the small tiger-cat, the capybara (*Cavia capybara*), the gallinazo vulture (*Vultur aura*), the crocodile, viper and rattlesnake. These gases seem to emanate from mould containing innumerable reptiles, worms and insect remains. I have seen Indian children from the Chaima tribe pick out 18-inch millipedes from the earth and eat them.

The waters of the Manzanares river are very clear and do not resemble at all the Manzanares river in Madrid, made to seem even more narrow by its sumptuous bridge. It springs, like all the rivers of New Andalusia, from the llanos (plains) known as the plateaux of Jonoro, Amana and Guanipa. The construction of a dyke to irrigate the land has been several times proposed to the government, but without success for, despite the apparent sterility, the land is extremely productive wherever heat and humidity meet.

The banks of the Manzanares are very attractive, shaded by mimosas, erythrinas, ceibas and other gigantic trees. A river whose temperature descends during the floods to as low as 22 °C when the air is 30 °C to 35 °C is a blessing in a country where the heat is excessive all year round and one wants to bathe several times a day. Children spend a good part of their lives in this water; everybody, including the richest women, knows how to swim. In a country where people live so close to nature the most important question people ask each other on first meeting is whether the river water is fresher than it was the day before. There are several ways of bathing. Each evening we visited a group of respectable people in the Guaiquerí suburb. In the moonlight they would install chairs by the water; men and women were lightly dressed as if at European spas, and would spend hours smoking cigars and chatting with their families and strangers, according to the habits of the place, about the dryness, the heavy rains and the excessive luxury of Caracas and Havana ladies. Nobody worried about the small but rare crocodiles that approach humans without attacking, although dolphins swim upstream and scare bathers by spouting water.

Cumaná harbour has an anchorage in which all the fleets of Europe would fit. The whole of the Gulf of Cariaco, which is about 35 miles long and 6 to 8 miles wide, offers excellent anchoring. The hurricanes of the West Indies are never felt in this region, and you can sail about in an open boat. I have spent some time describing the location of Cumaná because it seemed important to make the place that has seen so many tremendous earthquakes known.

The city, dominated by the fort, lies at the foot of a hill without greenery. Not one bell-tower nor one dome attract the traveller from afar; just a few tamarind trees and coconut and date palms stand out above the flat-roofed houses. The surrounding plains, especially near the sea, appear sad, dusty and arid, while fresh, luxuriant vegetation marks out the winding river that divides the city from its outskirts and the European settlers from the copper-coloured Indians. The isolated, bare and white San Antonio mountain, with its fort, reflects a great mass of light and heat: it is made of breccia, whose strata contain fossil marine life. Far away towards the south you can make out a dark curtain of mountains. They are the high calcareous New Andalusian alps, topped with sandstone and other recent geological formations. Majestic forests cover this inland mountain chain linked along a forested valley with the salty, clayey and bare ground around Cumaná. In the gulf and on its shores you can see flocks of fishing herons and gannets, awkward, heavy birds, which, like swans, sail along the water with their wings raised. Nearer the inhabited areas, you can count thousands of gallinazo vultures, veritable flying jackals, ceaselessly picking at carcasses. A gulf whose depths contain hot thermal springs divides the secondary from the primary and schistose rocks of the Araya peninsula. The two coasts are bathed by a calm blue sea lightly rippled by a constant breeze. A dry, pure sky, only lightly clouded at sunset, lies above the sea, over a peninsula devoid of trees and above the Cumaná plains, while one sees storms building up and bursting into fertile downpours around the inland mountain peaks.

Another characteristic common to both the New Andalusian coast and Peru is the frequency of earthquakes and the limits nature seems to have prescribed for these phenomena. In Cumaná we ourselves felt violent seismic shocks; they were still rebuilding the ruined houses and so we were able to gather detailed information on the spot about the terrible catastrophe of the 14th of December 1797. These notions will be the more interesting as earthquakes have been considered up to now less from a physical and geographical point of view than from the way they disastrously affect the population and well-being of society.

On the Cumaná coast and on Margarita Island most share the opinion that the Gulf of Cariaco was formed as a consequence of a fracturing of the territory and a flooding from the sea. The memory of this powerful cataclysm had been preserved by the Indians up to the fifteenth century, and it is said that by Christopher Columbus's third voyage the Indians still talked about it as recent. In 1530 the inhabitants of the Paria and Cumaná coasts were terrified by new shocks. The sea flooded the land and a huge crack was created in the Cariaco mountains and in the gulf of the same name. A great body of salt water, mixed with asphaltum, burst out of the micaceous schist. At the end of the sixteenth century earthquakes were very common and, according to tradition, the sea flooded the shore several times, rising some 90 to 100 feet above normal. The inhabitants fled to the San Antonio hills, and to the hill where the San Francisco convent stands today.

Because there are no records kept in Cumaná, and thanks to the persistent destructive activity of the termites, the white ants, no documents older than 150 years remain in the archives, thus making it hard to know the exact dates for the earlier earthquakes. We know only that 1766 was most fatal for the settlers and most remarkable for the natural history of the country. There had been a drought for over fifteen months when on the 21st of October 1766 the city of Cumaná was completely destroyed. Every year that date is celebrated by a religious service and a solemn procession. All the houses collapsed in a few minutes, and every hour for fourteen months tremors were felt. In several areas in the province the earth opened up and vomited out sulphureous water. During 1766 and 1767 the Cumaná inhabitants camped out in the streets and began rebuilding only when the tremors slowed down to a few a month. While the earth continually rocked it felt as if the air was about to dissolve into water. Formidable rainstorms swelled the river; the year was extraordinarily fertile, and the Indians, whose frail shacks survive the most violent earthquakes, celebrated with dances of joy following an ancient superstition about the destruction of the old world and the birth of a new one.

According to tradition, during the quake of 1766 the earth moved in simple horizontal waves; only on the fatal day of the 14th of December did the earth rise up. More than four fifths of the city was completely destroyed, and the shock, accompanied by a loud subterranean noise, resembled the explosion of a mine placed deep in the ground. Fortunately the main shocks were preceded by light undulations thanks to which most of the inhabitants were able to reach the streets, and only a few who hid in the church died. It is generally believed in Cumaná that the worst earthquakes are preceded by weak oscillations in the ground, and by a humming that does not escape the notice of those used to this phenomenon. In those desperate moments you heard people everywhere shouting 'Misericordia! Tiembla! Tiembla!' ('Mercy! The earth is trembling!') The most faint-hearted attentively observe the dogs, goats and pigs. These last, with their acute sense of smell, and skill in poking around in the earth, give warnings of approaching dangers with frightened screams.

In Cumaná, on San Francisco hill with its convent, an intense stink of sulphur was smelled on the 14th of December 1797 half an hour before the great catastrophe. In this same place the underground noise was loudest. At the same time flames were seen on the Manzanares river banks near the Capuchin hospital, and in the Gulf of Cariaco near Mariguitar. This phenomenon, so strange in non-volcanic countries, happens frequently in the calcareous mountains near Cumanacoa, in the Bordones river valley, on Margarita Island and on the plains of New Andalusia. On these plains the sparks of fire rose to a considerable height and were seen for hours in the most arid places. Some asserted that when the ground through which the inflammable substances rose was examined not the smallest crack was found. This fire, which recalls the springs of methane or the Salse of Modena and the will-o'-the-wisp of our marshes, does not burn the grass. The people, though less superstitious here than in Spain, call these reddish flames by the odd name of The Soul of the Tyrant Aguirre; imagining that the ghost of Lope de Aguirre,[29] harassed by remorse, wanders over these countries sullied by his crimes.

We will not continue to describe in detail the local changes produced by the different earthquakes of Cumaná. In order to follow our original plan we shall try to generalize our ideas, and include in one section everything that relates to these frightening and difficult-to-explain phenomena. If men of science who visit the Alps of Switzerland or the coasts of Lapland should broaden our knowledge about glaciers and the aurora borealis, then a traveller who has journeyed through Spanish America should mainly fix his attention on volcanoes and earthquakes. Every part of the earth merits particular study. When we cannot hope to guess the causes of natural phenomena, we ought at least to try to discover their laws and, by comparing numerous facts, distinguish what is permanent and constant from what is variable and accidental.

The great earthquakes, which appear between long series of slight shocks, do not happen regularly at Cumaná. We have seen them take place at intervals of eighty, a hundred and sometimes less than thirty years, while on the Peruvian coasts, for example at Lima, a certain regularity has marked the complete ruin of the city. The local belief in this uniformity has luckily aided public tranquillity and encouraged industry. Most admit that a long period of time elapses before the same causes act with the same energy. But such reasoning counts only if the shocks are considered as a local phenomenon, and if one supposes that great catastrophes are caused at one particular place. When new buildings are raised on the ruins of the old we learn from those who refuse to rebuild that the destruction of Lisbon on the 1st of November 1755 was soon followed by a second and no less fatal quake on the 31st of March 1761.

A very ancient belief, still commonly held at Cumaná, Acapulco and Lima, establishes a perceptible connection between earthquakes and the state of the atmosphere that precedes these phenomena. On the coasts of New Andalusia people are alarmed when, in excessively hot weather and after long droughts, the breeze suddenly drops and the clear, cloudless sky turns reddish near the horizon. However, this way of predicting earthquakes is very uncertain, for when we gather together all the meteorological variations in times of earthquakes we find that violent shocks take place equally in dry and wet weather, whether when a cool wind blows or during a dead and suffocating calm. From the great number of earthquakes that I have witnessed on both sides of the equator, on the continent and at sea, on coasts and 2,500 toises high, it appears to me that the oscillations are quite independent of the previous state of the atmosphere. This opinion is shared by many educated people in the Spanish colonies whose experience of earthquakes, if not as extensive as mine, covers more years. Against this, scientific observers in Europe, where earthquakes are rare compared to America, tend to admit some close connections between the undulations of the ground and certain meteors that appear as if by chance at the same time. In Italy, for example, the sirocco and earthquakes are suspected to have some link; and in London, the frequency of shooting stars and those southern lights that have since often been observed by Dalton were considered as forerunners of those shocks felt from 1748 to 1756.

In the Tropics on those days when the earth is shaken by violent shocks the regularity of the barometer is not disturbed. I have verified this observation at Cumaná, at Lima and at Riobamba. Scientific observers should note this, for on Santo Domingo, in the town of Cape François, it has been asserted that a water barometer sank 2.5 inches just before the earthquake of 1770. It has also been related that a chemist, at the time of Oran's destruction, fled with his family a few minutes before the earthquake because he had noticed that the mercury in his barometer had sunk in an extraordinary manner. I do not know whether to believe his story. But as it is practically impossible to examine the variations of the weight of the atmosphere during the shocks, we must be satisfied with observing the barometer before and after.

We cannot question that the earth, when split open and shaken by shocks, sometimes emits gaseous substances into the atmosphere in places remote from active volcanoes. At Cumaná, as we have already observed, flames and vapours mixed with sulphureous acid rise from the most arid soil. In other parts of the same province the earth throws up water and petroleum. At Riobamba, a muddy, inflammable mass, called *moya*, issues from crevices that close up again and pile up into hills. Seven leagues from Lisbon, near Colares, during the terrible earthquake of the 1st of November 1755, flames and a column of thick smoke rose up from the rock face of Alvidras and, according to some witnesses, from the depths of the sea. This smoke lasted several days and was thicker when the underground noises accompanied the strongest tremors.

I am inclined to think that nothing escapes from the shaken earth during earthquakes and that when gases and steam are seen they precede as often as they follow or accompany the shocks. This last circumstance probably explains the mysterious influence in equinoctial America of earthquakes on the climate and seasons of rains and droughts. If the earth acts only on the air at the moment of shock we can see why a perceptible meteorological change so rarely predicts one of these great revolutions of nature.

The hypothesis that during the Cumaná earthquakes elastic fluids escape from the earth's surface seems confirmed by the dreadful noise heard during the shocks near the wells in the plain of Charas. Water and sand are sometimes thrown 20 feet high. Similar phenomena did not escape the ancients' notice in areas of Greece and Asia Minor, in caves, crevices and underground rivers. Nature, in its uniform progress, everywhere gives birth to the same ideas concerning the causes of earthquakes, and man, forgetting the measure of its force, tries to diminish the effect of underground explosions. What the great Roman naturalist Pliny said about how wells and caves are the cause is repeated by the most ignorant Indians of Quito when they show travellers the *guaicos*, or crevices, of Pichincha.

The underground noise so frequently heard during earthquakes is not usually related to the strength of the shocks. At

Cumaná the noise constantly preceded the shocks, while at Quito, and recently at Caracas and in the West Indies, a noise like the discharge of a battery of guns was heard a long time after the shocks had ended. A third kind of phenomenon, and the most remarkable of all of them, is the rolling of those underground thunders that last several months without being accompanied by the slightest tremors.

In every country subject to earthquakes the spot where the effects are most clearly felt, probably due to a particular disposition of the stony strata, is selected as the cause and focus of the shocks. Thus, at Cumaná, the hill of the San Antonio castle, especially where the San Francisco convent stands, is thought to contain an enormous amount of sulphur and other inflammable matter. We forget that the speed with which the undulations are propagated across great distances, even across the ocean, proves that the centre of action is very remote from the earth's surface. For this same reason earthquakes are not confined to certain types of rock, as some naturalists claim, for tremors pass through all kinds of rock. If I remain faithful to my own experiences I can here cite the granites of Lima and Acapulco, the gneiss of Caracas, the mica-slate of the Araya peninsula, the primitive schist of Tepecoacuilco in Mexico, the secondary limestones of the Apennines, Spain and New Andalusia, and finally the trappean porphyries of the provinces of Quito and Popayan. In these different places the ground is frequently shaken by the most violent shocks, but sometimes, in the same rock, the upper strata form invincible barriers to the propagation of the waves. In Saxony mines we have seen miners rush up frightened by oscillations that were not felt on the earth's surface.

If, in regions remote from each other, primitive, secondary and volcanic rocks conduct in equal ways the earth's convulsive movements, we have also to admit that within very limited areas certain classes of rock do not propagate shocks. At Cumaná, for example, before the great catastrophe of 1797, earthquakes were felt only along the southern calcareous coast of the Gulf of Cariaco as far as the town of the same name, while in the Araya peninsula and at the village of Maniquarez the ground did not move at all. The inhabitants of this northern coast composed of mica-slate built their huts on solid earth, and a gulf some 3,000 to 4,000 toises wide separated them from a plain covered with ruins and overturned by earthquakes. This security, based on the experience of several centuries, no longer exists, because since the 14th of December 1797 new underground communications have opened up. At the present moment the Araya peninsula is not only subject to the same shaking as at Cumaná, but the mica-slate promontory has become a particular centre of tremors.

In New Andalusia, as well as in Chile and Peru, shocks follow the shore line and hardly extend inland. This circumstance indicates, as we shall soon show, an intimate connection between the causes that produce earthquakes and volcanoes. If the earth were most shaken on coasts because they are the lowest part of the land, why do we not feel equally strong oscillations on those vast savannahs or plains scarcely 8 to 10 toises above sea-level?

The earthquakes at Cumaná are connected with those of the West Indies, and it has even been suspected that they are somehow connected with the volcanic activity of the Andean cordilleras. On the 4th of February 1797 the ground of the province of Quito suffered such a destructive upheaval that nearly 40,000 natives died buried in the ruins of their houses, sucked into crevices or drowned in suddenly formed lakes. At the same time, the inhabitants of the eastern Antilles were alarmed by shocks that lasted for eight months when the volcano of Guadeloupe threw out pumice-stone, ashes and gusts of sulphureous gases. This eruption of the 27th of September, during which constant underground roaring was heard, was followed on the 14th of December by the great Cumaná earthquake. Another volcano in the West Indies, at Saint Vincent, has recently given a fresh example of these extraordinary connections. This volcano has not been active since 1718, and it burst out again in 1812. The complete ruin of Caracas preceded this explosion by thirty-four days, and violent waves were felt both on the islands and on the coasts of Terra Firma.

It has long been noted that the effects of great earthquakes extend much further than phenomena arising from active volcanoes. In studying the physical revolutions of Italy and carefully examining the series of eruptions of Vesuvius and Etna, we can see scarcely any sign of simultaneous action, despite their proximity. But it is a fact that at the last two destructions of Lisbon (1755 and 1761) the sea was violently stirred as far away as Barbados in the New World, more than 1,200 leagues from Portugal.

Several facts seem to prove that the causes that produce earthquakes are connected with those that cause volcanic eruptions. The linking of these causes, already known by the ancients, struck Europeans again when America was discovered. This discovery not only brought new objects to satisfy man's curiosity, but also new ideas about physical geography, about the varieties of human species, and about the migrations of tribes. It is impossible to read the narratives of the first Spanish travellers, especially the Jesuit Acosta's,[30] without realizing the happy influence that the appearance of this great continent, the study of its marvellous nature, and the contact with men of different races has exerted on the progress of knowledge in Europe. The germ of a great number of physical truths can be found in these sixteenth-century works, and this germ would have given fruit had it not been crushed by fanaticism and superstition.

We learned at Pasto that the column of thick black smoke that, in 1797, issued from the volcano near the shore for several months, disappeared at the very moment when, 60 leagues south, the towns of Riobamba, Hambato and Tacunga were destroyed by an enormous shock. Thus, sitting in the interior of a burning crater near those hillocks formed by scoriae and ashes, we feel the ground move several seconds before each eruption takes place. We observed this phenomenon at Vesuvius in 1805 while the mountain threw out scoriae at white heat; we witnessed the same thing in 1802 on the brink of the immense crater of Pichincha, but this time only gases came out.

Everything in earthquakes seems to indicate the action of elastic fluids seeking an outlet to spread into the atmosphere.

Often on the Pacific coast the action is almost immediately communicated from Chile to the Gulf of Guayaquil, some 600 leagues distant. Remarkably the shocks seem to be stronger the further the country is from the active volcano. The granitic mountains of Calabria, covered with very recent breccias, the calcareous chain of the Apennines, the country of Pignerol, the coasts of Portugal and Greece, those of Peru and Terra Firma, all show striking proof of this claim. The earth, we might say, is shaken with greater force in proportion to the smaller number of funnels communicating the surface to caverns deep inside. At Naples and at Messina, at the foot of Cotopaxi and of Tungurahua, earthquakes are dreaded only if gases and flames do not burst out of the crater. The great catastrophes of Riobamba and Quito have led several well-informed people to think that this unfortunate country would be less often disturbed if the underground fires could break the porphyritic dome of Chimborazo and turn this gigantic mountain into an active volcano. Throughout the ages, similar facts have led to identical hypotheses. Like us, the Greeks attributed the ground's undulations to the tensions of elastic fluids, and quoted in support of their argument the fact that tremors on Elba ceased when a crevasse opened on the Levantine plain.

We have tried to collect at the end of this chapter the general phenomena of earthquakes in different climates. We have shown that subterranean gases are subjected to the same laws as those in the atmosphere. We have avoided discussing the nature of the chemical agents that cause the great earthquakes and volcanoes. It is sufficient to note that these causes are hidden at immense depths, and that we must seek them in what we call primitive rocks, perhaps below the earthy, and oxidized, crust, in the abysses that hold the metalloidal bases of silex, lime, soda and potash.

The phenomena of volcanoes and earthquakes have recently been seen as the effects of voltaic electricity, developed by a particular disposition of heterogeneous strata. It cannot be denied that when violent shocks often follow each other the electricity in the air increases the moment the ground is most shaken. But in order to explain this phenomenon it is not necessary to state a hypothesis which directly contradicts everything that has already been observed concerning the structure of our planet and the disposition of its strata.

CHAPTER 5

WE SPENT THE first weeks of our stay in Cumaná testing our instruments, botanizing in the nearby countryside, and investigating the traces of the earthquake of the 14th of December 1797. Dazzled by the sheer amount of different objects we found it awkward to stick to a systematic way of studying and observing. If everything that we saw around us excited us, our instruments in their turn awoke the curiosity of the local inhabitants. The numerous visitors disturbed us; in order not to disappoint all those who seemed so pleased to see the spots of the moon through Dollond's telescope,[31] the absorption of two gases in a eudiometrical tube, or the effects of galvanism on the motions of a frog, we had to answer many obscure questions and repeat the same experiments for hours.

This same situation repeated itself over the five years of our journey whenever we settled down in a place where people knew we had microscopes, telescopes and electrical apparatus. This was all the more tiresome as those who visited us held confused notions of astronomy or physics, two sciences that in the Spanish colonies are called by the bizarre name of new philosophy, *nueva filosofía*. The half-scientific looked at us scornfully when they heard we had not brought with us books like Abbé Pluche's *Spectacle de la nature* or Sigaud la Fond's *Cours de physique* or Valmont de Bomare's Dictionary. These, along with Baron Bielfeld's *Traité d'économie politique*, are the foreign works most admired in Spanish America. No one is deemed learned who cannot quote from them in translation. Only in the great capitals are the names of Haller, Cavendish and Lavoisier replacing those who have been famous for over fifty years.

Our house in Cumaná was magnificently situated for

observing the sky and meteorological phenomena; on the other hand, during the day, we witnessed scenes that disgusted us. A part of the great plaza is surrounded with arcades above which runs a long wooden gallery, common to all hot countries. This is where the slaves brought from Africa were once sold. Of all European countries Denmark was the first and for ages the only government to abolish the slave-trade; yet the first slaves we saw here were transported by a Danish slave-ship. What silences the speculations of vile interest in its struggle with the duties of humanity, national honour and the laws of the fatherland?

The slaves put up for sale were young people from fifteen to twenty years old. Every morning they were given coconut oil to rub into their bodies to make their skin black and shiny. All the time buyers would approach and, examining their teeth, would calculate their age and health; they forced open their mouths just as if dealing with horses at market. This debasing custom dates back to Africa as is faithfully shown in a play by Cervantes who, after a long captivity with the Moors, outlined the sale of Christian slaves in Algiers.[32] It is distressing to think that still today in the Spanish West Indies slaves are branded with hot irons to identify them in case they escape. This is how one treats those 'who save other men from the labour of sowing, working in the fields and harvesting'.[33]

The deep impression caused by our first sight of a slave sale in Cumaná was alleviated somewhat by the relief of finding ourselves with a people and on a continent where this spectacle is very rare, and the number of slaves, in general, insignificant. In 1800 there were not more than 600 slaves in the two provinces of Cumaná and New Barcelona, while the total population reached around 110,000. The trade in African slaves, never favoured by the Spanish Crown, has dwindled to almost nothing on these coasts where, in the sixteenth century, it reached a terrifying figure.

Our first excursion was to the Araya peninsula and those regions formerly so infamous for slave-trading and pearl fishing. On the 19th of August, at about two in the morning, we embarked on the Manzanares river, near the Indian settlement. Our main objectives on this short trip were to visit the ruins of the ancient Araya fort, the salt works and the mountains that form the narrow Maniquarez peninsula where we hoped to carry out some geological research. The night was deliciously cool, swarms of luminous insects (*Elater noctilucus*) shone in the air, on the ground covered with sesuvium, and in the mimosa (*Lampyris italica*) thickets bordering the river. We know how common glow-worms are in Italy and all southern Europe, yet the picturesque effect they produce cannot compare with these innumerable scattered and moving lights, which embellish the tropical nights all over the plains, repeating the spectacle of the stars in the sky on the ground.

Descending the river we passed the plantations or *charas* where negroes had lit bonfires for their fiestas. A light billowing smoke rose above the palm-tree tops, giving a reddish colour to the moon's disk. It was a Sunday night and the slaves danced to the monotonous and noisy music of guitars. A fundamental feature of the black African races is their inexhaustible store of vitality and joy. After working painfully hard all week, they prefer to dance and sing on their fiesta days rather than sleep for a long time. We should be wary of criticizing this mixture of thoughtlessness and frivolity for it sweetens the evils of a life of deprivations and suffering!

The boat in which we crossed the Gulf of Cariaco was very spacious. They had spread large jaguar skins out so that we could rest at night. We had been scarcely two months in the torrid zone, and already our organs were so sensitive to the slightest temperature changes that cold stopped us sleeping. To our surprise we saw that the thermometer marked 21.8 °C. This fact is familiar to those who have lived long in the Indies. During our stay at Guayaquil in January 1803, we watched the Indians cover themselves and complain of the cold when the temperature sank to 23.8 °C, while they suffocated with heat at 30.5 °C. A difference of 6 °C or 7 °C was sufficient to cause the opposite sensations of cold and heat. At Cumaná, during heavy showers, people in the streets are heard to complain 'Qué hielo! Estoy emparamado,'[34] though the thermometer exposed to the rain sinks only to 21.5 °C.

At about eight in the morning we landed at Araya point, near the new salt works. A solitary house (La Ranchería de la Salina Nueva) stood in the middle of an arid plain, next to a battery of three cannons, sole defence on this coast since the destruction of the Santiago fort. The salt-works' inspector spends his life in a hammock from where he passes on his orders to his workers, and a 'king's launch' (*la lancha del rey*) brings him his supplies from Cumaná every week. It is astonishing that a salt works which once made the English, Dutch and other powerful maritime countries jealous did not lead to the founding of a village or even a farm. Only a few miserable Indian fishermen's huts exist at the tip of Araya point.

The abundance of salt contained in the Araya peninsula was known to Alonso Niño when, following the tracks of Columbus, Ojeda and Amerigo Vespucci, he visited these countries in 1499. Though the Indians of South America consume the least salt of any people on the globe because they eat mainly vegetables, it appears that the Guaiquerí dug into the clayey and muriatic soil of Punta Arena for salt. The Spaniards, established first at Cubagua, then on the Cumaná coasts, worked the salt marshes from the beginning of the sixteenth century. As the peninsula had no settled population the Dutch availed themselves of the natural riches of a soil that to them seemed common property. In our days, each colony has its own salt works. Navigation has so improved that merchants in Cádiz can send salt, at little expense, from Spain to cure meat in Montevideo or Buenos Aires, some 1,900 leagues away. These advantages were unknown at the time of the conquest. Colonial industry has made so little progress that Araya salt was carried to Cartagena and Portobello.[35] In 1605 the Madrid Court sent armed ships to expel the Dutch by force. The Dutch continued furtively to gather salt until a fort was built in 1622 near the salt works, which became known as Santiago fort, or the Real Fuerza de Araya. These great salt mines are laid down on the oldest Spanish maps. In 1726 a violent hurricane destroyed the Araya salt works and made the expensively built fort useless. This sudden hurricane was very rare in a region where the sea is generally as calm as the water of our large rivers; the high waves penetrated far inland and transformed the salty lake into a gulf several miles long. Since then there have been artificial deposits or vasets to the north of the chain of hills that separate the fort from the northern coast of the peninsula.[36]

Having examined the salt works and finished our geodesical observations, we left at dusk with the intention of spending the night in an Indian hut near the ruins of the Araya fort. We sent our instruments and provisions on ahead as the extreme heat and irradiation from the ground so exhausted us that we only felt like eating in the cool of night and early morning. Going southward, we crossed first the bare plain covered in salty clay, and then two chains of hills formed with sandstone between which there was a lagoon. Night surprised us while following a narrow path bordered on one side by the sea, and on the other by a wall of perpendicular rock. The tide was rising fast, and at each step narrowed the path. When we reached the foot of the old Araya fort we saw before us a natural picture that was melancholic and romantic. Yet neither the freshness of the dark jungle nor the grandeur of the plants could enhance the beauty of the ruins. These ruins stand on a bare, arid hill, with nothing but agave, columnar cacti and thorny mimosa, and seemed less like the work of men than masses of rock torn apart during the early revolutions of the earth.

We wanted to linger and admire the superb spectacle, and to observe the setting of Venus, whose disk appeared now and then between the broken fragments of the fort; but our mulatto guide was parched with thirst and insistently begged us to return. For a long time he had thought that we were lost, and, trying to scare us, he talked of the dangers of tigers and rattlesnakes. It is true that venomous reptiles are very common near the fort, and that a few days before two jaguars had been killed near the entrance to the village of Maniquarez. Judging by the skins we saw they could not be much smaller than tigers from India. We vainly tried to calm our man by telling him that those animals do not attack humans on a coast where goats offer copious prey: but we had to give in and retrace our steps. When we had been walking for three quarters of an hour along a beach covered by high tide we met the negro who was carrying our food; on seeing that we had not returned he had got worried and set out to find us. He led us through a wood of nopal cacti to the hut of an Indian family. We were received with that frank hospitality common in these lands to people from all social classes. From the outside the hut where we slung our hammocks looked very clean. Inside we found fish, bananas and other edibles, and, something that in this arid zone is far more appreciated than delicious food, excellent fresh water.

At dawn the next day we realized that the hut where we had spent the night formed part of a group of huts situated on the banks of a salt lake. They are the few remains left of a considerable village formed long ago around the fort. The ruins of the church were half buried in sand and covered with brushwood. When in 1762 the Araya fort was completely dismantled, to save the expense of maintaining a garrison, the Indians and other coloured residents who lived around about emigrated one by one to Maniquarez, Cariaco and the Guaiquerí suburb at Cumaná. Only a few remained in the wild and desolate village, deeply attached to their native land. These poor people live from fishing on the coast and in neighbouring shoals rich in fish. They seemed content with their fate and found it strange that I asked them why they had no gardens to cultivate nutritious plants. 'Our gardens,' they replied, 'lie on the other side of the strait; we bring fish to Cumaná and they give us cassava, bananas and coconuts in return.' This economic system, which flatters laziness, is followed at Maniquarez and throughout the Araya peninsula. The principal wealth of these inhabitants consists of large, beautiful goats. They move freely about like the goats on the Tenerife peak; they are completely wild, and are branded like the mules because it would be difficult to recognize them from their colour or spots. These fawn goats do not vary in colour like domestic ones. When a settler out hunting shoots a goat that is not his, he brings it to whichever neighbour it belongs to.

Among the mulattos whose huts surround the salt lake we

found a shoemaker of Castilian descent. He received us with that gravity and self-sufficiency characteristic in those countries where the people feel they possess some special talent. He was stretching the string of a bow, and sharpening arrows to shoot birds. His trade of shoemaking could not be very lucrative in a country where the majority go barefoot; and he complained that the expense of European gunpowder reduced him to using the same weapons as the Indians. He was the sage of this place; he understood the formation of salt through the influence of the sun and full moon, the symptoms of earthquakes, the marks by which gold and silver mines are found, and the structure of medicinal plants, which he divided, like everybody in South America, into hot and cold. Having collected local traditions he gave us some curious accounts of the pearls of Cubagua, objects of luxury, which he treated with contempt. To show how familiar he was with the Bible he liked quoting Job, who preferred wisdom to all the pearls of the Indies. His philosophy was limited to the narrow circle of his vital needs. All he wanted was a strong ass to carry a load of bananas to the loading-wharf.

After a long speech on the vanity of human greatness he pulled a few small opaque pearls from out of his leather pouch and forced us to accept them, making us note down on our writing tablets that a poor shoemaker of Araya, white and of noble Castilian race, had given us something that, across the ocean,[37] was thought of as very precious.

The pearl-oyster (*Aviculidae*, *Meleagrina margaritifera*, Cuvier) abounds on the shoals that extend from Cape Paria to Cape La Vela. The islands of Margarita, Cubagua, Coche, Punta Araya and the mouth of the Hacha river were as famous in the sixteenth century as the Persian Gulf and the island of Taprobana were to the ancients.

Benzoni[38] relates the adventure of one Louis Lampagnano, to whom Charles V granted the privilege of proceeding with five caravels to the Cumaná coasts to fish for pearls. The settlers sent him back with the bold message that the Emperor, too liberal with what was not his own, had no right to dispose of the oysters living at the bottom of the sea.

The pearl fisheries diminished rapidly towards the end of the sixteenth century, and had long ceased by 1683. The industrious Venetians who imitated fine pearls perfectly, and the growing popularity of cut diamonds, made the Cubagua fisheries less lucrative. At the same time the oysters became scarcer, not because, according to popular legend, they were frightened by the sound of oars and moved away, but because the rash gathering of thousands at a time stopped them propagating themselves. To form an idea of the destruction of the shells caused by the divers, we must remember that a boat collects in two to three weeks more than 35,000 oysters. The animal lives but nine to ten years, and only in its fourth year do pearls begin to show. In 10,000 shells there is often not a single pearl of value.

On the morning of the 20th the son of our host, a young, robust Indian, led us to the village of Maniquarez, passing through Barigon and Caney. It was a four-hour walk. Because of the reverberation of the sun's rays on the sand the thermometer remained at 31.3 °C. The cylindrical cacti along the path made the landscape green, but without freshness or shade. We had walked barely a league when our guide decided, at every opportunity, to sit down and rest. When we got near to Casas de la Vela he even tried to lie down in the shade of a beautiful tamarind tree, to await nightfall. We observed this characteristic trait whenever we travelled with Indians; it has given rise to the most mistaken ideas about the physical constitutions of different races. The copper-coloured Indian, who is more used to the burning heat of these regions than a European, complains more because nothing stimulates his interest. Money is no bait, and if he is tempted by gain he repents of his decision as soon as he starts walking. This same Indian, who would complain when we loaded him with a box filled with plants while herborizing, would row his canoe against the strongest current for fourteen or fifteen hours in order to be back home.

We examined the remarkably solid ruins of Santiago. The 5-foot-thick walls of freestone have been toppled over by mines; but we still found huge sections with scarcely a crack in them. Our guide showed us a cistern (*el aljibe*), 30 feet deep, which though damaged furnishes water to the inhabitants of the Araya peninsula. This cistern was finished in 1681. As the basin is covered with an arched vault the excellent water remains very cool. Crossing the arid hills of Cape Cirial we detected a strong smell of petroleum. The wind blew from the place where the springs of petroleum, mentioned by the first chroniclers,[39] are to be found.

The Maniquarez potteries, famous from time immemorial, are a specialized industry completely run by Indian women. They work with the same method that was used before the conquest. This reveals both the infancy of this craft and that immobility of manners so characteristic of American Indians. Three hundred years have not sufficed to introduce the potter's wheel to a coast not more than forty days' sailing from Spain. The Indians have a vague idea that something of the sort exists, and surely would adopt one should it be shown to them. The quarries where they extract their clay lie half a league to the east of Maniquarez. This clay is produced by the decomposition of a mica-slate stained red by iron oxide. The Indian women prefer the part most loaded with mica; and very skilfully shape vessels of 2 to 3 feet in diameter with regular curves. As they do not know how to use kilns they place scrub from desmanthus, cassia and arborescent capparis around the pots and bake them in the open air.

At Maniquarez we met some creoles who had been hunting at Cubagua. Deer of a small variety abound in this uninhabited island, and one person may kill three or four a day. I do not know how these animals got to the island as chroniclers mention only the great amount of rabbits. The *venado* of Cubagua belong to one of those numerous species of small American deer long confused under the vague name of *Cervus mexicanus*. In the plains of Cari we were shown something very rare in these hot climates, a completely white deer. Albino varieties are found in the New Continent even among tigers. Azara[40] saw a completely white-skinned jaguar.

The most extraordinary, even most marvellous, object on the Araya coast is what the people call the 'eye stone' (*piedra de los ojos*). This calcareous substance is the subject of many conversations as it is, according to Indian science, both stone and animal. It is found in the sand, where it is motionless: but if it is picked up and placed on a polished surface, for example a pewter or pottery plate, it begins to move if you drip some lemon juice on it. If it is then placed in the eye this supposed animal will expel any other foreign substance that may accidentally get in there. At the new salt works, and in the village of Maniquarez, hundreds of eye stones were offered to us, and the Indians pressed us to test them with lemon juice. They wanted to put sand in our eyes to convince us of the virtues of this remedy. Very quickly we saw that these 'stones' are the thin and porous valves of diminutive univalve shells. They have a diameter of some 1 to 4 lines, with one surface plane, the other convex. These calcareous coverings effervesce with lemon juice and start moving as the carbonic acid is formed. When placed in eyes, these eye stones act as tiny round pearls and seeds, used by the Indians of America to stimulate the flow of tears. These explanations did not satisfy the inhabitants of Araya. For man nature seems more grand the more it is mysterious, and the physics of the people rejects any simple explanation.

Along the southern coast, east of Maniquarez, three strips of land run out to sea. In these parts the seabed is made of mica-slate, and from these orogenic rock formations, some 26 metres from the coast, issues a spring of petroleum whose smell reaches far inland. We had to wade into the water up to our waists to observe this interesting phenomenon. The waters are covered with zostera, and in the centre of a large bank of these plants you see a clear round patch, about 3 feet in diameter, across which float masses of *Ulva lactuca*. It is here that the springs are found. The bed of the bay is covered with sand, and the transparent and yellow petroleum resembles naphtha itself, bursting out in jets, accompanied by air bubbles. When we trod down the bottom with our feet we saw how these little springs changed place. The naphtha covers the sea for more than 1,000 feet from the shore line.

After exploring the outskirts of Maniquarez, we embarked in a fishing-boat for Cumaná. Nothing confirms how calm the sea is here as much as the tiny, badly kept boats with their one tall sail. Though we had picked the least damaged boat it leaked so much that the pilot's son had to continually bale out the water with a *tutumo*, or shell of the fruit of the *Crescentia cujete* (or calabash). In the Gulf of Cariaco, especially north of the Araya peninsula, canoes laden with coconuts often capsize because they sail too near the wind and against the waves. These accidents inspire fear only in those travellers who do not swim well; for when a pirogue is manned by an Indian fisherman and his son, the father turns the pirogue round and bales out the water while the son swims around, gathering all the coconuts. In less than a quarter of an hour the pirogue is sailing again without the Indian, with his boundless impassivity, having once complained.

The inhabitants of Araya, whom we visited a second time when returning from the Orinoco, have not forgotten that their peninsula is one of the places most anciently populated by the Castilians. They like talking about the pearl fisheries, the ruins of the Santiago fort, which they hope will be rebuilt one day, and all that they call the ancient splendour of these countries. In China and Japan inventions are called recent if they are more than 2,000 years old: in the European colonies an event seems extremely ancient if it is three centuries old, dating back to the discovery.

This absence of memories, which characterizes these new people in the United States of America and in the Spanish and Portuguese possessions, is worthy of attention. It is not only distressing to the traveller, who becomes deprived of the pleasures of the imagination, it also influences the bonds that tie a settler to the land he inhabits, the form of the rocks around his hut, the trees shading his cradle.

Most of these modern colonies are founded in a zone where the climate, the produce, the sky and landscape, all differ completely from Europe. The settler vainly tries to name the mountains, rivers and valleys with names that recall his motherland; these names soon lose their charm, and mean nothing to later generations. Under the influence of an exotic nature new habits are born for new needs; national memories are slowly effaced, and those remembered, like ghosts of our imaginations, are not attached to any time or place. The glories of Don Pelayo or the Cid Campeador have penetrated the forests and mountains of America; people sometimes pronounce these famous names, but they seem to come from an ideal world, from vague, fabulous times.

Moreover, the American colonies are founded in countries where the dead leave barely any trace of their existence. To the north of Gila river, on the banks of the Missouri, and in the Andean plain, traditions date back only a century. In Peru, Guatemala and Mexico, ruins, historic paintings and sculptured monuments attest, it is true, to ancient Indian civilizations, but throughout an entire province only a few families have precise notions about Inca history or Mexican princesses. The Indian has kept his language, his customs and national character; but the loss of *quipus*[41] and symbolic paintings, the introduction of Christianity, and other factors, have made the historic and religious traditions vanish. On the one hand the European settler scorns everything to do with the defeated Indians. Placed between memories of the metropolis and the actual country he was born in, he looks to both indifferently; in a climate where the equality of the seasons makes the succession of years almost indifferent he lives only for the pleasures of the moment and rarely looks to the past.

CHAPTER 6

OUR FIRST EXCURSION to the Araya peninsula was followed by another more important and instructive one to the mountain missions of the Chaima Indians. Such a variety of objects attracted our attention. We found ourselves in a country bristling with forests on our way to visit a convent shaded by palm trees and arborescent ferns in a narrow valley which was deliciously fresh, despite being in the middle of the torrid zone. In the surrounding mountains there are caves inhabited by thousands of nocturnal birds; and, what struck our imagination more than all the marvels of the physical world, even further up we found a people until recently still nomadic, hardly free from a natural, wild state, but not barbarians, made stupid more from ignorance than from long years of being brutalized. What we knew about history increased our interest in these people. The promontory of Paria was what Columbus first saw of this continent; these valleys ended there, devastated first by the warlike, cannibalistic Caribs, then by the mercantile and orderly European nations. If the Spaniards visited these shores it was only to get, either by violence or exchange, slaves, pearls, gold and dye-woods; they tried to dignify their motives for such an insatiable greed with the pretence of religious zeal.

The treatment of the copper-coloured Indians was accompanied by the same acts of inhumanity that later were meted out to the black Africans, with the same consequences of making both conquered and conquering wilder. From that time wars between the Indians became more common; prisoners were dragged from the interior to the coasts to be sold to whites who chained them to their boats. Yet the Spaniards at that period, and long after, were one of the most civilized nations of Europe. The light that art and literature shed over Italy was reflected on every nation whose language stemmed from the same source as that of Dante and Petrarch. One might have expected a general sweetening of manners as the natural consequence of this noble awakening of the mind, this soaring of the imagination. But across the seas, wherever the thirst for riches led to the abuse of power, the nations of Europe have always displayed the same characteristics. The noble century of Leo X was marked in the New World by acts of cruelty that belonged to a barbaric past.

The missionaries' privilege was to console humanity for a part of the evils committed by the conquistadores; to plead the cause of the Indians before kings, to resist the violence of the *comendadores*, and to gather nomadic Indians into small communities called missions[42] to help agriculture progress. And so, imperceptibly, following a uniform and premeditated plan, these vast monastic establishments were formed into extraordinary regimes, always isolating themselves, with countries four or five times larger than France under their administration.

But these institutions, useful at first in preventing the spilling of blood and establishing the basis of society, have become hostile to progress. The effect of their isolation has been such that the Indians have remained in the same state as they were found before their scattered huts were grouped around missions. Their number has considerably increased but not their mental development. They have progressively lost that vigour of character and natural vivacity which everywhere comes from independence. By subjecting even the slightest domestic actions to invariable rules the Indians have been kept stupid in an effort to make them obedient. Their subsistence is more certain, and their habits more pacific, but subject to constraints and the dull monotony of the missions. They show by their gloomy and abstracted looks that they have not sacrificed freedom for comfort without regret.

At five in the morning on the 4th of September we set out for the missions of the Chaima Indians and the high mountains crossing New Andalusia. Because of the road's extreme difficulties we had been advised to reduce our equipment as much as we could. Two mules sufficed to carry our provisions, our instruments and the paper necessary to dry plants. Our box contained a sextant, a dipping needle, an instrument to determine magnetic variation, thermometers and Saussure's hygrometer.[43] Choosing the instruments caused us most problems on the short journeys.

The morning was deliciously cool. The road, or rather path, that led to Cumanacoa follows the right bank of the Manzanares river, passing the Capuchin hospital situated in a small wood of lignum vitae and caper trees. After leaving Cumaná we reached the San Francisco hill during twilight and enjoyed an extensive view of the sea, the plain covered with golden-flowered bera (*Palo sano, Zygophyllum arboreum*), whose flowers smell of vanilla, and the Brigantín mountains.

At the Divina Pastora hospice the path turns to the northeast along a stretch without trees, formerly levelled by the waters. There we found not only cacti, tufts of cistus-leaved tribulus and the beautiful purple euphorbia, cultivated in Havana gardens under the odd name of *Dictamno real*, but also the avicennia, the allionia, the sesuvium, the thalinum and most of the portulaceous plants that grow on the banks of the Gulf of Cariaco. This geographical distribution of plants appears to designate the limits of the ancient coast and to prove that the hills along the southern side, which we were following, once formed islands separated from the continent by an arm of the sea.

After walking for two hours we reached the foot of the high inland mountain chain. There new rock formations begin, and with them another kind of vegetation. Everything seems more grand and picturesque. The soil, rich in springs, is furrowed by streams in every direction. Gigantic trees, covered with lianas, rise from the ravines; their black bark, burned by the sun and oxygen, contrasts with the fresh green of the pothos and dracontium, whose tough, shiny leaves reach as much as 2 metres in length.

We passed some huts inhabited by mestizos. Each hut stands in the centre of an enclosure containing banana trees, papaw trees, sugar cane and maize. The small extent of cultivated land might surprise us until we recall that an acre planted with bananas produces nearly twenty times as much food as the same space sown with cereals. In Europe our wheat, barley and rye cover vast spaces of land; in general arable lands border each other wherever inhabitants live on wheat. It is different in the torrid zone where man obtains food from plants that yield more abundant harvests more quickly. In these favoured climates the immense fertility of the soil corresponds to the heat and humidity. A large population can be fed from a small plot of land covered with banana, cassava, yams and maize. The isolation of huts dispersed in the forest indicates to the traveller how fertile nature is.

In Europe we calculate the number of inhabitants of a country by the extent of cultivation; in the Tropics, in the warmest and most humid parts of South America, very populated areas seem deserted because man cultivates but a small number of acres to feed himself. Without neighbours, virtually cut off from the rest of mankind, each family forms a different tribe. This isolated state retards the progress of civilization, which advances only as society becomes more populated and its connections more intimate and multiplied. But, on the other hand, solitude develops and strengthens liberty and independence; and has fed that pride of character which distinguishes the Castilian race.

For these reasons land in the most populated areas of tropical America still seems wild; a quality lost in temperate climates by the cultivation of wheat. Within the Tropics agriculture occupies less land; man has not extended his empire, and he appears not as the absolute master who alters the soil at his will but as a transient guest who peacefully enjoys the gifts of nature. There, near the most populated cities, land remains bristling with forests or covered with a tangle of plants, untouched by plough. Spontaneous vegetation still predominates over cultivated plants, and determines the aspect of nature. If in our temperate regions the cultivation of wheat contributes to the spreading of a dull uniformity over the cleared land, we cannot doubt that, even with an increasing population, the torrid zone will keep its majesty of plant life, those marks of an untamed, virgin nature that make it so attractive and picturesque.

As we entered the jungle the barometer showed that we were gaining altitude. Here the tree trunks offered us an extraordinary view: a gramineous plant with verticillate branches[44] climbs like a liana to a height of 8 to 10 feet, forming garlands that cross our path and swing in the wind. At about three in the afternoon we stopped on a small plain known as Quetepe, some 190 toises above sea-level. A few huts stand by a spring whose water is known by the Indians to be fresh and healthy. We found the water delicious. Its temperature was only 22.5 °C while the air was 28.7 °C.

From the top of a sandstone hill overlooking the Quetepe spring we had a magnificent view of the sea, Cape Macanao and the Maniquarez peninsula. From our feet an immense jungle stretched out as far as the ocean. The tree-tops, intertwined with lianas and their long tufts of flowers, formed an enormous green carpet whose dark tint increased the brilliancy of the light. This picture struck us more powerfully as it was the first time we had seen tropical vegetation. On the Quetepe hill, under the *Malpighia cocollobaefolia*, with its hard coriaceous leaves, we collected our first melastoma; especially that beautiful species that goes under the name of *Melastoma rufescens*, among thickets of *Polygala montana*. Our memory of this place will remain with us for a long time; the traveller pleasurably remembers those places where for the first time he finds a plant family never seen before in its wild state.

Further to the south-west the soil turns dry and sandy. We climbed a relatively high range that separates the coast from the great plains or savannahs bordering the Orinoco. That section of the mountains through which the road to Cumanacoa leads is devoid of vegetation and falls steeply both to the south and north. It has been called Imposible because this impenetrable mountain ridge would offer a refuge to the inhabitants of Cumaná during a hostile invasion. We reached the top just before sunset. I scarcely had the time to take a few

horary angles with my chronometer to calculate the geographic longitude of the place.

The view from Imposible is even more beautiful and extensive than that from the tableland of Quetepe. With our naked
eyes we could easily pick out the flattened top of the Brigantín,
whose exact geographic position must be verified, the landing-
place and Cumaná outer harbour. The rocky coast of Araya
stretched out before us. We were particularly struck by the
extraordinary structure of the harbour known as Laguna
Grande, or Laguna del Obispo. A vast basin, surrounded by
high mountains, communicates with the Gulf of Cariaco via a
narrow canal along which only one boat at a time may pass.
With our eyes we traced the sinuosities of this arm of sea,
which has dug a bed like a river between perpendicular rocks
stripped of vegetation. This extraordinary view reminded us
of the fantastic landscape that Leonardo da Vinci painted in
the background of his famous portrait of Mona Lisa.

We spent the night in a house occupied by a military post
of eight soldiers under a Spanish sergeant. It was a hospice,
built next to a powder-magazine. The summit of Imposible,
as far as I could make out, was covered with a sandstone rich
in quartz, without fossils. Here, as on the neighbouring hills,
the strata are lined regularly along a north-north-east, south-
south-west axis.

The *llaneros*, or inhabitants of the llanos (plains), send their
products – maize, hides and cattle – to Cumaná harbour by the
road over Imposible. We saw Indians or mulattos with mules
coming towards us, rapidly moving in single file.

Several parts of the vast forests that surround the mountains were on fire. The reddish flames, half hidden by clouds
of smoke, stunned us. The inhabitants set fire to the forests to
improve their pasturage and to destroy the shrubs that choke
the scant grass. Enormous forest fires are also caused by the
carelessness of the Indians who forget to put out their camp
fires. These accidents have diminished the old trees along the
Cumaná–Cumanacoa road, and inhabitants have justly
noticed that aridity has increased all over the province, not
only because the land has more crevices from earthquakes, but

also because it is less forested than it was before the conquest.

We left Imposible on the 5th of September before dawn. The descent is very dangerous for the pack-animals; the path is only some 15 inches wide, with precipices on either side. In 1796 a useful plan to build a road from the village of San Fernando to the mountain was conceived. A third of this route had already been finished, but unfortunately it ran only from the plain to the foot of Imposible. Work was halted for one of those reasons that makes all attempts at improvement in the Spanish colonies fail. Several authorities wanted to assume the rights of running the works. The people patiently paid their tolls for a route that did not exist until the Cumaná governor put an end to this abuse. As we descended we noticed that alpine limestone reappeared under the sandstone. As the strata generally incline to the south and south-east many springs well up along the southern side of the mountain. In the rainy season these springs become torrents that rush down under the hura, the cuspa and the silver-leafed cecropia, or trumpet trees.

The cuspa, common enough around Cumaná and Bordones, is still an unknown tree to European botanists. For a long time it was used only for building houses. Since 1797, under the name of the cascarilla or bark tree (cinchona), it has become rather famous. Its trunk barely reaches 15 to 20 feet high. Its thin, pale yellow bark is an excellent febrifuge. It is even more bitter than the bark of the real cinchona, but less disagreeable. Cuspa is administered with great success in both alcoholic extracts and watery infusions for both intermittent and malignant fevers.[45]

When we left the ravine that descends from the Imposible we entered a thick jungle cut by numerous rivers, which we easily forded. In the middle of the forest, on the banks of the Cedoño river, as well as on the southern slopes of the Cocollar, we found wild papaw and orange trees with large, sweet fruit. These are probably the remains of some *conucos*, or Indian plantations, because the orange is not a native tree; neither are the banana, papaw, maize, cassava and so many other useful plants whose countries of origin are unknown, though they have accompanied man in his migrations from remotest time.

When a traveller recently arrived from Europe steps into South American jungle for the first time he sees nature in a completely unexpected guise. The objects that surround him only faintly bring to mind those descriptions by famous writers of the banks of the Mississippi, of Florida and of other temperate regions of the New World. With each step he feels not at the frontiers of the torrid zone but in its midst; not on one of the West Indian Islands but in a vast continent where everything is gigantic; mountains, rivers and the masses of plants. If he is able to feel the beauty of landscape, he will find it hard to analyse his many impressions. He does not know what shocks him more: whether the calm silence of the solitude, or the beauty of the diverse, contrasting objects, or that fullness and freshness of plant life in the Tropics. It could be said that the earth, overloaded with plants, does not have sufficient space to develop. Everywhere tree trunks are hidden behind a thick green carpet. If you carefully transplanted all the orchids, all the epiphytes that grow on one single American fig tree (*Ficus gigantea*) you would manage to cover an enormous amount of ground. The same lianas that trail along the ground climb up to the tree-tops, swinging from one tree to another 100 feet up in the air. As these parasitical plants form a real tangle, a botanist often confuses flowers, fruit and leaves belonging to different species.

We walked for hours in the shade of these plant vaults that scarcely let us catch glimpses of the blue sky, which appeared to be more of a deep indigo blue because the green, verging on brown, of tropical plants seemed so intense. A great fern tree (perhaps *Aspidium caducum*) rose above masses of scattered rock. For the first time we saw those nests in the shape of bottles or small bags that hang from the lower branches. They are the work of that clever builder the oriole, whose song blends with the noisy shrieking of parrots and macaws. These last, so well known for their vivid colours, fly around in pairs, while the parrots proper fly in flocks of hundreds. A man must live in these regions, particularly the hot Andean valleys, to understand how these birds can sometimes drown the noise of waterfalls with their voices.

About a league from San Fernando village we left the jungle. A narrow winding path led to open but extremely humid country. In a more temperate climate this region would have been a vast meadow of grass and reeds: but here the ground was packed with aquatic plants with lanceolate leaves, especially basil plants among which we recognized the magnificent flowers of the costus, thalia and heliconia. These succulent plants reach some 8 to 10 feet high; in Europe their bunching together would be considered a small wood.

Near San Fernando the evaporation caused by the sun's rays was so intense that, although lightly dressed, we soon became as soaked as if we had had a steam bath. Along the road a kind of bamboo (*Bambusa gadua*[46]) that the Indians call *iagua* or *gadua* grows to a height of some 40 feet. It is hard to imagine anything more elegant than this arborescent grass. The form and disposition of its leaves give it a lightness that contrasts agreeably with its height. The smooth and shiny trunks of the *iagua* generally lean towards the river banks, swaying at the slightest breeze. However tall canes (*Arundo donax*) may grow in southern Europe they cannot compare with the arborescent grasses; and if I dare resort to my own experience I would say that the bamboo and fern tree are, of all tropical vegetation, what strikes the traveller's imagination most.

The bamboo-lined road led us to the small village of San Fernando, located in a narrow plain, surrounded by steep calcareous cliffs. It was the first mission we visited in America. The houses, or rather shacks, of the Chaima Indians are scattered about, and are without vegetable gardens. The straight narrow streets cut each other at right angles. The thin irregular walls are made of clay and bound with lianas. The monotony of the houses, the serious and taciturn aspect of the inhabitants and the extreme cleanliness inside their homes reminded us of the establishments of the Moravian Brethren.[47] Each family cultivates the *conuco de la comunidad*, which is outside the village, as are their own individual vegetable plots. Adults of both sexes work there an hour in the morning and an hour in the evening. In the missions near the coast, the communal garden is nearly always planted with sugar cane or indigo and

run by the missions. Their product, if the law is strictly
followed, can be used only for the upkeep of the church and
the purchase of whatever the priests may need. San Fernando's
great square, in the centre of the village, contains the church,
the missionary's house and the modest building that goes
pompously under the name of 'king's house' (*casa del rey*). This
is the official hostel for travellers and, as we often confirmed,
a real blessing in a land where the word 'inn' is unknown.
These *casas del rey* can be found all over Spanish colonies, no
doubt imitating the Peruvian *tambos* established by Manco
Capac's laws.[48]

The syndic in Cumaná had recommended us to the missionaries who run the Chaima Indian mission. This recommenda-
tion was all the more useful to us as the missionaries, zealous
for the purity of their parishioners' morals, and wary of the
indiscreet curiosity of strangers, tended to apply an ancient
rule of their order according to which no white secular person
could remain more than one night in an Indian village. In
general, to travel agreeably in Spanish missions it would not
be wise to trust solely to the passport issued by the Madrid
Secretary of State: you must arm yourself with recommendations from the ecclesiastical authorities, especially the custo-
dians of convents, or the generals of orders residing in Rome,
who are far more respected by missionaries than bishops. Missions have become, in reality, a distinct, almost independent,
hierarchy, despite being primitive or canonical institutions.

The missionary in San Fernando was an Aragonese Capuchin, well advanced in years but very strong and lively. His
obesity, his good humour and his interest in battles and sieges
contradicted the ideas held in northern countries concerning
the melancholic reveries and contemplative life of missionaries. Though extremely busy organizing the slaughter of a cow
for the following day he received us good-naturedly, and let
us hang our hammocks in a gallery of his house. Sitting in his
redwood armchair most of the day without doing anything, he
complained of what he called the laziness and ignorance of his
countrymen. He asked us thousands of questions about the
real purpose of our journey, which to him seemed hazardous

and quite useless. Here, as on the Orinoco, we grew weary of
the lively curiosity manifested by Europeans in the middle
of American jungles for the wars and political storms in the
Old World.

Our missionary, however, seemed quite satisfied with his
situation. He treated the Indians well; his mission prospered,
and he enthused about the water, the bananas and the milk of
this place. The sight of our instruments, our books and dried
plants made him smile sarcastically; and he acknowledged with
the naïvety peculiar to the inhabitants of these countries that
his greatest pleasure in life, even including sleep, was eating
good beef, *carne de vaca*; thus does sensuality triumph when
there is nothing to occupy the mind. Our host often enjoined
us to visit the cow he had bought, and the following day, at
dawn, we could not avoid watching his cow being slaughtered
in the manner of the country, that is, cutting its hamstrings
before plunging a long knife into the vertebra of its neck.
Disgusting as this was, it did teach us about the immense skill
of the Chaima Indians, who, numbering eight, managed to cut
the animal up into little pieces in less than twenty minutes.

The road from San Fernando to Cumanacoa passes through
small plantations in a humid, open valley. We forded numerous streams. In the shade the thermometer did not rise above
30 °C, but we were exposed to the sun's rays because the bamboos along the path gave only a feeble shade and we suffered
a lot from the heat. We passed through the village of Arenas,
inhabited by Indians of the same race as those at San Fernando. But Arenas is no longer a mission, and the Indians,
governed by a regular priest, are less naked and more civilized.
Their church is known in the area for the primitive paintings
on its walls. A narrow frieze encloses pictures of armadillos,
caymans, jaguars and other New World animals.

Francisco Lozano, a labourer who lived in this village, presented a curious physiological phenomenon that struck our
imagination, but did not contradict any laws of organic nature.
This man breast-fed a child with his own milk. When the
mother fell ill, the father, to pacify the child, took it to bed and
pressed it to his nipples. Lozano, then thirty-two years old,

had never noticed before that he had milk, but the irritation of the nipple sucked by the child caused liquid to accumulate. The milk was thick and very sweet. The father, astonished at how his breasts increased, suckled his child two or three times a day for five months. He attracted his neighbours' attention but, unlike someone living in Europe, never thought of exploiting this curiosity. We saw the certificate, drawn up on the spot, that attested this remarkable fact; eyewitnesses are still living. We were assured that during the breast-feeding the child received no other food but his father's milk. Lozano, away from Arenas when we visited, came to see us at Cumaná, accompanied by his son of already thirteen or fourteen. Bonpland carefully examined the father's breasts and found them wrinkled, like those of a woman who has suckled.[49]

Cumanacoa was founded in 1717 by Domingo Arias on his return from an expedition to the mouth of the Guarapiche river, undertaken in an attempt to destroy a settlement of French pirates. The new town was first called Baltasar de las Arias but the Indian name Cumanacoa prevailed; as did Caracas over Santiago de Leon, still to be found on our maps.

The plain, or rather tableland, on which Cumanacoa stands is only 104 toises above sea-level, three or four times lower than the inhabitants of Cumaná, who have an exaggerated view of how cold it is up there, think it is. The climatic difference between the two neighbouring towns is due less to the height of one of them than to local weather conditions. Among these causes are the proximity of the jungle, the frequency of rivers falling down narrow valleys, the amount of rain and those thick fogs that block out sunlight. The cool climate surprises us all the more because, as in the town of Cartago, at Tomependa on the Amazon, as in the Agarua valleys west of Caracas, very great heat is felt though the height varies between 200 and 480 toises above sea-level. In plains, as well as on mountains, isothermal lines are not constantly parallel to the equator or the surface of the earth. Meteorology's great problem will be to determine the direction of these lines and variations due to local causes, and to discover the constant laws in the distribution of heat.

The port of Cumaná lies some 7 leagues from Cumanacoa. It hardly ever rains in the former place, while in the latter the rainy season lasts seven months. In Cumanacoa the dry season stretches from the winter solstice to the spring equinox. Sporadic showers are common in April, May and June; then a drought begins again until the summer solstice or the end of August. Then the rainy season proper starts and lasts until November, and water pours down in torrents from the sky.

Our first day in the missions corresponded to the first day of the rainy season. Every night a thick mist covered the sky like a uniform veil; only through clearings did I manage to make any observations of the stars. The thermometer marked between 18.5 °C and 20 °C, which in this zone, and for a traveller arrived from the coast, appeared rather cold. In Cumaná I never saw the thermometer go lower than 21 °C. The hottest hours are from midday to three in the afternoon when the thermometer rises to 26 °C or 27 °C. During the hottest hour of the day, two hours before the sun passes over the meridian, a storm regularly built up and then exploded. Thick black low clouds dissolved in rain; the downpour lasted two to three hours while the thermometer sunk to 5 °C or 6 °C. At about five the rain stopped, the sun appeared just before sunset, and the hygrometer moved towards the point of dryness; by eight or nine at night we were again enveloped in a thick mist. These different changes follow successively – we were assured – day after day for months, yet not the slightest breeze was felt.

The vegetation in the plain surrounding the city is monotonous, although remarkably fresh due to the humidity. Its principal feature is an arborescent solanum, the *Urtica baccifera*, which reaches 40 feet tall, and a new species of the *Guettarda* genus. The ground is very fertile and could be easily watered if irrigation ditches were dug from the numerous rivers that do not dry up all year round. The most precious product in the zone is tobacco; it is solely to this plant that the small, badly built city owes its meagre fame. Since the introduction of the royal monopoly (Estanco Real de Tabaco) in 1799 the cultivation of this plant in the Cumaná province is limited

almost exclusively to the Cumanacoa valley. This mono-
polistic farming system is deeply hated by the people. The
entire tobacco harvest has to be sold to the government, and
to prevent or limit smuggling tobacco was concentrated in
only one place. Inspectors travel the country burning plantations found outside the authorized zone, and inform against
those wretches who dare to smoke their own home-made
cigars. These inspectors are mostly Spaniards, as insolent as
those doing the same job in Europe. This insolence has greatly
contributed to the maintenance of the hatred between the colonies and the metropolis.[10]

After tobacco the most important product of the Cumanacoa valley is indigo, whose intense colour makes it the equal
of Guatemalan indigo. All the indigo factories that we visited
are constructed along the same principles. Two vats, where the
plants 'rot', are placed together. Each one measures 15 feet
square and 2.5 feet deep. From these upper vats the liquid
passes into beaters where the water-mill is placed. The axle-
tree of the great wheel crosses the two beaters. It is nailed with
ladles, fixed to long handles, for the beating. From another
percolating vat the coloured starch passes to the drying-boxes,
spread on planks of Brazil-wood on small wheels so that they
can be pushed under a roof in case of sudden rain. These sloping and low roofs give the drying-boxes the appearance of
hothouses from a distance. In the Cumanacoa valley the fer-
mentation of the plant takes place amazingly quickly; usually
it does not take longer than four or five hours. This can be
attributed to the humidity and the absence of sun during the
plant's development.

The Cumanacoa plains, scattered with farms and tobacco
plantations, are surrounded by mountains, which are higher
in the south. Everything suggests that the valley is an ancient
seabed. The mountains that once formed its shores rise vertically from the sea. When excavating foundations near Cumanacoa, beds of round pebbles mixed with small bivalve shells
were found. According to many reliable people two enormous
femur bones were discovered, about thirty years ago. The
Indians took them, as do people today in Europe, for giant's

bones, while the semi-educated country people, who try to explain everything, seriously claimed that they are nature's sports, not worthy of consideration. They were probably the gigantic femur of elephants of a vanished species.

We frequently visited a small farm called the Conuco de Bermúdez, situated opposite the Cuchivano crevice. In its moist soil grow bananas, tobacco and several species of cotton trees, especially the one whose cotton is wild nankeen yellow, so common on Margarita Island. The owner told us that the ravine was inhabited by jaguars. These animals spend the day in caverns and prowl around human settlements at night. If well fed they reach some 6 feet in length. A year before, one of these cats had devoured a farm horse. In clear moonlight he dragged his prey across the savannah to the foot of an enormous ceiba. The neighing of the dying horse woke up the farm slaves. Armed with lances and machetes[11] they rushed out in the middle of the night. The jaguar, stretched over its victim, waited quietly, and was killed only after a long and stubborn fight. This fact, and many others verified on the spot, prove that the great jaguar of Terra Firma (*Felis onca*), like the jaguarete of Paraguay and the Asian tiger, does not run away when attacked by man, and is not scared by the number of his enemy. Naturalists today know that Buffon[12] completely failed to recognize the greatest of American cats. What this famous writer says about the cowardice of tigers in the New World relates to the small ocelots (*Felis pardalis*). In the Orinoco, the American jaguar sometimes leaps into the water to attack Indians in their canoes.

Opposite Bermúdez's farm two spacious caves open out of Cuchivano's crevice. At times flames, which can be seen from great distances, burst out. They illuminate the surrounding mountains, and from the mark left on the rocks by these burning gases we could be tempted to believe they reach some 100 feet high. During the last violent Cumaná earthquake this phenomenon was accompanied by long, dull, underground noises.

During a herborizing trip to Rinconada, we tried vainly to penetrate into the crevice. We wanted to closely study the rocks inside that seemed to cause those extraordinary fires. The thickness of the vegetation with its tangle of liana and thorny plants blocked the way. Fortunately the inhabitants of the valley took an active part in our researches, not out of fear of a volcanic eruption, but because their imagination was struck by the idea that the Risco de Cuchivano contained a gold mine. They would not listen to our explanation that there could be no gold in secondary limestone; they wanted to know 'what the German miner thought about the richness of the vein'. Since the times of Charles V and the government of the Welsers, the people of Terra Firma have retained a belief that Germans know all about exploiting mines. No matter where I was in South America, as soon as people knew where I had been born they brought me mineral samples. In the colonies all the French are doctors, and all Germans miners.

The farmers and their slaves cut a path through the jungle to the first Juagua river waterfall, and on the 10th of September we made our excursion to the Cuchivano crevice. Entering the cave we saw a disembowelled porcupine and smelled the stink of excrement, similar to that of European cats, and knew that a jaguar had been near by. For safety the Indians returned to the farm to fetch small dogs. It is said that when you meet a jaguar in your path he will leap on to a dog before a man. We did not follow the bank of the torrent, but a rocky wall overhanging the water. We walked on a very narrow ledge along the side of a precipice with a drop of some 200 to 300 feet. When it narrowed, so that we could not walk along it any further, we climbed down to the torrent and crossed it on foot, or on the backs of slaves, to climb up the other side. Climbing is very tiring, and you cannot trust the lianas, which, like thick rope, hang from tree-tops. Creepers and parasites hang loosely from the branches they grip; their stalks together weigh a lot, and if you slip and grab one of the lianas you risk bringing down a tangle of green branches. The vegetation became impenetrable the more we advanced. In some places the roots of trees grew in the existing cracks between strata and had burst the calcareous rock. We could hardly carry the plants we picked at each step. The canna, the heliconia with pretty purple flowers, the costus and other plants from the *Amomum* genus reach here the height of 8 to 10 feet. Their tender, fresh green leaves, their silky sheen and the extraordinary development of their juicy pulp contrast with the brown of the arborescent ferns whose leaves are so delicately jagged. The Indians made deep incisions in the tree trunks with their long knives to draw our attention to the beauty of the red- and gold-coloured woods, which one day will be sought after by our furniture makers. They showed us a plant with composite flowers that reaches some 20 feet high (*Eupatorium laevigatum*), the so-called 'Rose of Belveria' (*Brownea racemosa*), famous for the brilliance of its purple flowers, and the local 'dragon's blood', a species of euphorbia not yet catalogued, whose red and astringent sap is used to strengthen the gums. They distinguished species by their smell and by chewing their woody fibres. Two Indians, given the same wood to chew, pronounced, often without hesitation, the same name. But we could not take advantage of our guides' wisdom, for how could they reach leaves, flowers and fruit[33] growing on branches some 50 to 60 feet above the ground? We were struck in this gorge by the fact that the bark of the trees, even the ground, were covered in moss and lichen.

The supposed gold mine of Cuchivano, which was the object of our trip, was nothing but a hole that had been cut in one of the strata of black marl, rich in pyrites. The marly stratum crosses the torrent and, as the water washes out metallic grains, the people imagine that the torrent carries gold because of the brilliancy of the pyrites. We were told that after the great earthquake of 1765 the Juagua river waters were so filled with gold that 'men came from great distances and unknown countries' to set up washing places on the spot. They disappeared over night, having collected masses of gold. Needless to add that this is a fable. Some direct experiments made with acids during my stay at Caracas proved that the Cuchivano pyrites are not all auriferous. My disbelief upset our guides. However much I said and repeated that from the supposed gold mine the most that could be found was alum and sulphate of iron, they continued to gather secretly all the pyrite fragments they saw sparkling in the water. The fewer mines there are in a country, the more the inhabitants hold exaggerated ideas about how easily riches are extracted from the depths of the earth. How much time was lost during our five-year voyage exploring ravines, at the insistence of our hosts, where pyrite strata have for centuries been called by the pretentious name of *minas de oro*! We have smiled so often seeing men of all classes – magistrates, village priests, serious missionaries – all grinding amphibole or yellow mica with endless patience, desperate to extract gold by means of mercury! This rage for searching for mines amazed us in a climate where the earth needs only to be slightly raked in order to produce rich harvests.

After more tiring climbing, and soaked from crossing the torrent so often, we reached the foot of the Cuchivano caverns. A wall of stone rises perpendicularly 800 toises up. In a zone where the fertility of nature everywhere hides the ground and rocks, it is rare to see a great mountain revealing naked strata in a perpendicular section. In the middle of this unfortunately inaccessible cutting, the two caverns open out in the form of a crevice. We were assured that nocturnal birds, the same as those that lived in the Cueva del Guácharo at Caripe, lived there.

We rested at the foot of the caverns from which the flames have issued more and more frequently as the years have passed. Our guides and the farmer, equally familiar with the local terrain, discussed, in the manner of the creoles, the dangers to which Cumanacoa might be exposed if the Cuchivano became an active volcano and 'se veniesse a reventar' (might explode). It was obvious to them that since the great earthquakes of Quito and Cumaná in 1797 New Andalusia was every day more and more undermined by subterranean fires. They cited the flames that had been seen coming out of the ground at Cumaná, and the tremors in places where there had not been any before. They remembered that in Macarapán sulphureous smells had been noted over the last months. We were struck by these facts on which they had based their predictions, which nearly all turned out to be true. In 1812 enormous damage was done in Caracas, proof of the incredible instability of nature in the north-east of Terra Firma.

On the 12th we continued our journey to the Caripe monastery, centre of the Chaima Indian missions. Instead of the direct road, we chose the one that passes by the Cocollar[14] and Turimiquiri mountains. We passed the little Indian village of Aricagua, pleasantly located in wooded hills. From there we climbed up hill for four hours. This part of the route is very tiring; we crossed the Pututucuar, whose river bed is packed with blocks of calcareous rock, twenty-two times. When we had reached the Cuesta del Cocollar, some 2,000 feet above sea-level, we saw, to our surprise, that the jungle of tall trees had vanished. Then we crossed an immense plain covered in grass. Only mimosas, with hemispheric tops and trunks some 4 to 5 feet in diameter, break the desolate monotony of the savannahs. Their branches are bent towards the ground, or spread out like parasols.

After climbing the mountain for a long time we reached the Hato de Cocollar on a small plateau. This is an isolated farm on the crest of the tableland. We rested here in this lonely spot for three days, well looked after by its owner Don Mathias Yturburi from Biscay, who had accompanied us from Cumaná harbour. We found milk and excellent meat thanks to the rich grassland, and above all a wonderful climate.

From that high point, as far as the eye could see, there was only naked savannah; tufts of trees were scattered about in small ravines and, despite the apparent uniformity of the vegetation, we found a great number of extremely interesting plants. Here I shall limit myself to citing a magnificent lobelia with purple flowers (*Lobelia spectabilis*), the *Brownea coccinea*, which reaches almost 100 feet high, and above all the *pejoa* (*Gaultheria odorata*), famous in the country because when crushed between your fingers it gives off a delicious aroma. What enchanted us most about this solitary place was the beauty and silence of the nights. The owner stayed up with us; he seemed delighted that Europeans recently arrived in the Tropics never tired of admiring the fresh spring air enjoyed in these mountains when the sun sets.

Our host had visited the New World with an expedition that was set up to fell wood for the Spanish navy on the Paria Gulf shore. In the vast jungle of mahogany, cedar and Brazil-wood that borders the Caribbean Sea they wanted to select the largest trees, shape them in a rough way for the building of ships, and send them every year to the dockyard at Cádiz. White, unacclimatized men could not support the hard work, the heat, or the effect of the noxious air from the jungle. The same winds that are loaded with the perfume of flowers, leaves and wood also bring, so to speak, the germs of disease into our organs. Destructive fevers carried off not only the ship carpenter but also those who managed the business; so this bay, which the early Spaniards called Golfo Triste on account of the gloomy and wild aspect of its coasts, became the grave-yard of European seamen.

Nothing can compare to the majestic tranquillity of the stars in the sky in this solitary place. At nightfall, when we stared at the point where the horizon meets the meadows on this gently rolling plain, it seemed, as later in the Orinoco steppes, as if we were seeing the surface of an ocean support-ing the starry vault. The tree at whose feet we sat, the luminous insects dancing in the air, the shining constellations of the Southern hemisphere, everything reminded us that we were far from our homeland. And if, in the middle of this exotic nature, the sound of cow bells or the bellowing of a bull came from the small valleys, memories of our native land were sud-denly awoken. It was as if we heard distant voices echoing across the ocean, magically carrying us from one hemisphere to another. How strangely mobile is man's imagination, eternal source of his joys and pains!

In the cool of dawn we set off to climb the Turimiquiri. This is the name given to the Cocollar peak, which forms one large mountain range with the Brigantín, called before by the Indi-ans Sierra de los Tageres. We travelled a part of the way on the horses that run free on the savannahs, but are used to being saddled. Even when they look heavily laden they climb the slipperiest slopes with ease. Wherever the sandstone appears above ground the land is even and forms small plateaux succeeding each other like steps. Up to 700 feet, and even further, the mountain is covered with grass. On the Cocollar the short turf begins to grow some 350 toises above sea-level, and you continue to walk on this grass up to 1,800 toises high; above those strips of grassy land you find, on virtually inaccessible peaks, a little forest of cedrela, javillo (*Hura crepitans*) and mahogany. Judging by local conditions, the mountainous savannahs of the Cocollar and Turimiquiri owe their existence to the destructive custom of Indians burning the woods to make pasture land. Today, after a thick tangle of grass and alpine plants have been covering the ground for over three centuries, seeds of trees cannot root themselves in the ground and germinate, despite the wind and the birds that continually bring them from the distant jungle.

The climate of these mountains is so mild that at the Cocollar farm cotton trees, coffee trees and even sugar cane grow with ease. The Turimiquiri meadows lose their richness the higher they are. Wherever scattered rocks cast shade, lichen and various European mosses grow. *Melastoma guacito* (*Melastoma xanthostachyum*) and a shrub (*Palicourea rigida, chaparro bova*) whose large, leathery leaves rustle like parchment in the breeze rise here and there on the savannah. But the main attraction in the grass is a liliaceous plant with a golden-yellow flower, the *Marica martinicensis*.

The rounded Turimiquiri summit and the sharp peaks, or cucuruchos, stand out, covered with jungle where many tigers live and are hunted for the beauty of their skin. We found that this grassy summit stood at 707 toises above sea-level. A steep rocky ridge going west is broken after a mile by an enormous crevice that descends to the Gulf of Cariaco. In the place where the mountain ridge should have continued two mamelons or calcareous peaks rise, with the more northern one the highest. It is the Cucurucho de Turimiquiri proper, considered to be higher than the Brigantín, well known to sailors approaching the Cumaná coast.

On the 14th of September we descended the Cocollar towards the San Antonio mission. The road passes at first through savannahs strewn with huge calcareous blocks, and then enters a thick jungle. Having crossed two steep passes we saw before us a pretty valley, some 5 to 6 leagues long from east to west. Here lie the San Antonio and Guanaguana missions. The first is famous for its little brick church, with two towers and Doric columns, in a tolerable style. The prefect of the Capuchins finished building it in less than two summers, despite using only Indians from his village. The moulding of the capitals on the columns, the cornices and the frieze, decorated with suns and arabesques, were all modelled from clay mixed with ground brick. The provincial governor disapproved of such luxury in a mission and the church remained unfinished, much to the regret of the fathers. The Indians in San Antonio did not complain at all, indeed they secretly approved the governor's decision, as it favoured their natural laziness.

I stayed in the San Antonio mission long enough to open the barometer and take some measurements of the sun's altitude. The great square lies 216 toises above Cumaná. Beyond the village we crossed the Colorado and Guarapiche rivers, both of which rise in the Cocollar mountains and meet lower down in the east. The Colorado has a very fast current and its mouth is wider than the Rhine; the Guarapiche, joining the Areo river, is more than 25 fathoms deep. On their banks grow a beautiful grass (*lata o caña brava*), which I drew[55] two years later as I ascended the Magdalena river, whose silver-leafed stalks reach 15 to 20 feet. Our mules could hardly move through the thick mud along the narrow and flat road. Torrents of rain fell from the sky and turned the jungle into a swamp.

Towards evening we reached the Guanaguana mission, situated at about the same height as the village of San Antonio. We really had to dry ourselves. The missionary received us very cordially. He was an old man who seemed to govern the Indians intelligently. The village has been in this place for only thirty years – before it lay more to the south, against a hill. It is astonishing how easily Indian villages are moved about. In South America there are villages that in less than fifty years have changed places three times. Indians feel bound to the land with such weak ties that they indifferently accept orders to demolish their houses and build them again elsewhere. A village changes its site like a military camp. As long as there are clay, reeds, palm tree and heliconia leaves around they finish rebuilding their huts in a few days. These compulsory changes often have no other motive than the whim of a missionary who, recently arrived from Spain, fancies that the site of the mission is feverish, or not sufficiently exposed to the wind. Whole villages have been transported several leagues just because a monk did not like the view from his house.

Guanaguana still does not have a church. The old priest, who had lived for more than thirty years in the American jungles, pointed out that the community's money, meaning the product of the Indians' work, should first be spent on building the missionary house; secondly on building a church; and lastly on their clothes. He seriously insisted that this order could not be altered on any account. The Indians can wait their turn as they prefer walking around completely naked to wearing the scantiest clothes. The spacious padre's house had just been finished and we noted with surprise that the terraced roof was decorated with a great number of chimneys that looked like turrets. Our host told us that this was done to remind him of his Aragonese winters, despite the tropical heat. The Guanaguana Indians grow cotton for themselves, the church and the missionary. The produce is supposed to belong to the community; it is with this communal money that the needs of the priest and altar are looked after. They have simple machines that separate the seed from the plant. Wooden cylinders of tiny diameter between which the cotton passes are activated, like a spinning-wheel, by pedals. However, these primitive machines are very useful and other missions are beginning to imitate them. But here, as in all places where nature's fertility hinders the development of industry, only a few hectares are converted into cultivated land, and nobody thinks of changing that cultivation into one of alimentary plants. Famine is felt each time the maize harvest is lost to a long drought. The Guanaguana Indians told us an amazing story that happened the year before when they went off with their women and children and spent three months *al monte*, that is, wandering about in the neighbouring jungle and living off juicy plants, palm cabbages, fern roots and wild fruit. They did not speak of this nomadic state as one of deprivation. Only the missionary lost out because his village was left completely abandoned, and the community members, when they returned from the woods, appeared to be less docile than before.

The beautiful Guanaguana valley stretches towards the east, opening into the Punzera and Terecen plains. We would have liked to visit those plains to explore the petroleum springs that lie between the Guarapiche and Areo rivers, but the rainy season had started, and every day we had problems trying to dry and preserve our plant collections. Near Punzera we saw little bags woven in silk hanging from the lower branches of the savannah trees. It is the *seda silvestre*, or wild silk of the country, which has a lovely sheen but is rough to the touch. The moth that weaves these cocoons is perhaps the same as the one in the Guanajuato and Antioquia provinces that also makes a wild silk. In the beautiful Punzera forests grow two trees that are called *curucay* and *canela*; the first because it yields a resin much sought after by the *piaches*, or Indian sorcerers; the second because its leaves smell like proper cinnamon from Ceylon.

After struggling a while with our plan to descend the Guarapiche river to the Golfo Triste, we took the direct road to the mountains. The Guanaguana and Caripe valleys are separated by an embankment or calcareous ridge famous for miles around for its name Cuchilla de Guanaguana. We found this way tiring because we still had to climb the cordilleras, but it is by no means as dangerous as they claim in Cumaná. In many places the path is no more than 14 or 15 inches wide; the mountain ridge it follows is covered with a short slippery grass; its sides are both very steep and the traveller who fell could roll some 700 to 800 feet down over that grass. However, the mountain has abrupt slopes, not precipices. The local mules are so sure-footed that they inspire confidence. They behave just like mules from Switzerland or the Pyrenees. The wilder a country, the more acute and sensitive is instinct in domestic animals. When the mules glimpse a danger they stop and turn their heads from right to left and raise and lower their ears as if thinking. They delay making up their minds, but always choose the right course of action if the traveller does not distract them or make them continue. In the Andes, during journeys of six and seven months, in mountains furrowed with torrents, the intelligence of horses and beasts of burden develops in a surprising way. You often hear mountain people say: 'I will not give you a mule with a comfortable gait, but the one that reasons best (*la más racional*).' This popular expression, the result of long experiences, contradicts far more convincingly than speculative philosophy those who claim that animals are simply animated machines.

CHAPTER 7

AN ALLEY OF avocado trees led us to the Aragonese Capuchins' hospice. We stopped in front of a Brazil-wood cross, surrounded with benches on which the sick monks sit and say their rosaries, in the middle of a spacious square. The convent backs on to an enormous perpendicular wall of rock, covered with thick vegetation. Dazzling white stone appears every now and then through the foliage. It would be hard to imagine a more picturesque place. Instead of European beeches and maples you find here the imposing ceiba trees and the *praga* and *irasse* palms. Numerous springs bubble out from the mountainsides that encircle the Caripe basin and whose southern slopes rise to some 1,000 feet in height. These springs issue mainly from crevices or narrow gorges. The humidity they bring favours the growth of huge trees, and the Indians, who prefer solitary places, set up their *conucos* along these ravines. Banana and papaw trees grow around groves of arborescent ferns. This mixture of wild and cultivated plants gives a special charm to this place. From afar, on the naked mountainside, you can pick out the springs by the thick tangles of vegetation, which at first seem to hang from the rock, and then, as they descend into the valley, follow the meandering streams.

We were received with eagerness by the monks of the hospice. The father superior was away but, notified of our departure from Cumaná, he had taken great pains to ensure our comfort at the convent. There was an inner cloister, typical of all Spanish monasteries. We used this enclosed space to install our instruments and get them working. In the convent we discovered a varied company; young monks recently arrived from Spain before being sent out to different missions, while old, sick missionaries recuperated in the healthy air of the Caripe hills. I was lodged in the father superior's cell, which had a notable library. To my surprise I found Feijóo's *Teatro crítico*, the *Lettres édifiantes*, and L'abbé Nollet's *Traité d'électricité*. Science has progressed to even the American jungles. The youngest of the Capuchin monks had brought with him a Spanish translation of Chaptal's treatise on chemistry,[16] which he intended to study in the isolation of the mission where he was to be abandoned on his own for the rest of his days. I doubt that the desire to learn can be kept alive in a young monk isolated on the banks of the Tigre river; but what is certain, and an honour to the spirit of this century, is that during our long stay in South American missions we never saw the least sign of intolerance.

Experience has shown that the mild climate and light air of this place are very favourable to the cultivation of the coffee tree, which, as is known, prefers altitudes. The Capuchin father superior, an active, educated man, introduced this new plant into the province. Before, indigo was cultivated in Caripe, but this plant, which needs plenty of heat, gave off so little dye that its cultivation had to be stopped. In the communal *conuco* we found many culinary plants, maize, sugar cane and a large area of coffee trees promising a rich harvest. In Caripe the *conuco* looks like a large, beautiful garden: Indians are obliged to work there every morning from six to ten. The Indian *alcaldes* (or magistrates) and *alguaciles* (or bailiffs) watch over these tasks. They are the high functionaries, who alone have the right to carry a walking-stick, and are appointed by the convent superiors. They are extremely proud of their status. Their pedantic and taciturn seriousness, their cold and mysterious air, and the zeal with which they fulfil their role in the church and communal assemblies make Europeans smile. We were still unaccustomed to these nuances of Indian temperament, found equally on the Orinoco, in Mexico and in Peru, among people totally different from each other in customs and language. The *alcaldes* came to the convent every day, less to deal with the monks about mission matters than to learn about the health of those travellers who had just arrived. As we gave them brandy, they visited us more than the monks thought proper.

Apart from its exceptionally fresh climate the Caripe valley is also famous for the great *cueva*, or Guácharo grotto.[57] In a country so given to the marvellous, a cave that gives birth to a river, and is inhabited by thousands of nocturnal birds whose fat is used for preparing the food in the monastery, becomes an unending topic of discussions and arguments. Hardly has a foreigner disembarked at Cumaná than he hears such talk about the Araya eye stones, the Arenas father who breast-fed his child, and the Guácharo grotto said to be several leagues long, that he soon gets fed up. A keen interest in nature is maintained everywhere where society has no life, or lives in sad monotony, and things are seen in simple ways that do not stimulate curiosity.

The cave, known by the Indians as a 'mine of fat', is not in the Caripe valley itself, but some 3 leagues to the west-south-west. On the 18th of September we set out for that sierra, accompanied by the *alcaldes* and the majority of the monks. A narrow path led us first for an hour and a half south through an attractive plain covered with beautiful grass; then we turned west and ascended a rivulet that issues from the cave mouth. We followed this for three quarters of an hour, sometimes walking in the shallow water, or between the water and the rocky walls on very slippery and muddy ground. Many earthfalls and uprooted tree trunks, over which the mules laboured, and creeping plants made this stretch very tiring. We were surprised to find here, at barely 500 toises above sea-level, the cruciferous plant *Raphanus pinnatus*.

At the foot of the tall Guácharo mountain, and only 400 steps from the cave, we still could not make out its entrance. The torrent flows from a ravine, cut by the waters, under a ledge of rocks that blocks out the sky. The path follows the winding rivulet. At the last bend you suddenly come across the enormous grotto opening. This is an imposing scene, even for those used to the picturesque higher Alps. I had seen the caves of the Derbyshire peaks where, lying flat on a boat, we went down an underground stream under an arch 2 feet high. I had

visited the beautiful grotto of Treshemienshiz in the Carpath-
ian mountains, and the Hartz and Franconia caves, which are
vast cemeteries with bones of tigers and hyenas, and bears
as large as horses. Nature in every zone follows immutable
laws in the distribution of rocks, mountains and dramatic
changes in the planet's crust. Such uniformity led me to expect
that the Caripe caves would not differ from what I had previously seen in my travels. The reality far exceeded my
expectations.

The Guácharo cave is pierced into the vertical rock face.
The entrance opens towards the south. Gigantic trees grow
above the rock that serves as roof to the grotto. The mammee
tree and the genipap (*Genipa americana*), with its large shiny
leaves, raise their branches towards the sky while those of the
courbaril and the *poro*, or coral tree, stretch out to form a thick,
green vault. Pothos with succulent stems, oxalises and orchids
with strange shapes grow in the driest cracks in the rocks,
while climbing plants, swaying in the wind, knot themselves
into garlands at the cave entrance. Among these we saw a
violet-blue jacaranda, a dolichos with purple flowers, and for
the first time, that stunning solandra (*Solandra scandens*) with its
orange flower and fleshy tube some 4 inches long.

However, this luxuriant vegetation does not only embellish
the outer vault but also reaches into the vestibule of the grotto.
We saw, to our surprise, that superb heliconias 18 feet tall, with
banana-tree type leaves, *praga* palms and arborescent arums
bordered the rivulet's banks right into the cave. Vegetation
penetrates inside the Caripe cave some thirty to forty paces.
We measured the way in by means of a cord, and went about
430 feet without needing to light torches. Daylight reaches this
place because the cave forms one single gallery that stretches
south-east to north-west. In the spot where light begins to fail
we heard the hoarse screams of the nocturnal birds that,
according to the Indians, live only in these underground caves.

The *guácharo* is about the size of our chickens, with the
mouth of our goatsuckers and the gait of vultures, with silky
stiff hair around their curved beaks. The plumage is of a dark
bluish-grey with small streaks and black dots; great white

patches in the shape of a heart, bordered with black, mark its wings, head and tail. Its eyes are wounded by daylight; they are blue and smaller than those of the goatsuckers or flying frogs. The wing-span, seventeen or eighteen quill feathers, is 3.5 feet. The *guácharo* leaves the cave at nightfall when there is a moon. It is the only grain-eating nocturnal bird that we know of to date; the structure of its feet shows that it does not hunt like our owls. It eats hard seed, like the nutcracker (bullfinch). The Indians insist that the *guácharo* does not chase beetles or moths like the goatsucker. It is sufficient to compare their beaks to be convinced that they lead completely different lives.

It is difficult to give an idea of the dreadful noise made by thousands of these birds in the darkness of the cave. It cannot be compared to the noise of those crows who live together in nests in our northern pine forests. The *guácharo*'s piercing scream reverberates against the rocky vault and echoes in the depths of the cave. The Indians showed us their nests by tying torches on to long poles. They were some 50 to 60 feet above us in holes riddling the ceiling in the form of funnels. The further we penetrated into the cave with our copal torches the more the frightened birds screamed. If for a few moments the din around us quietened we heard the plaintive cry of other nesting birds in other parts of the cave. It was as if differing groups answered each other alternatively.

The Indians enter the caves once a year near midsummer with poles to destroy most of the nests. Several thousand birds are killed; the older ones hover over their heads to defend their young, screaming horribly. The young, called *los pollos del guácharo*, fall to the ground and are cut open on the spot. Their peritoneum is loaded with fat; a layer of fat reaches from the abdomen to the anus, forming a kind of wad between the bird's legs. During this period, called the *cosecha de la manteca* (oil harvest) in Caripe, the Indians build palm-leaf huts near the entrance and in the cave vestibule itself. We could see their remains. With a brushwood fire they melt the fat of the young birds just killed and pour it into clay pots. This fat is known as butter or *guácharo* oil; it is semi-liquid, clear and odourless, and so pure that it lasts for a year without going rancid. In the

Caripe convent kitchen they only use fat from this cave, and the food never had a disagreeable taste or smell thanks to this fat.

The race of *guácharo* would long ago have become extinct had not diverse circumstances combined to preserve them. The superstitious Indians rarely dare to penetrate deep into the grotto. It appears that these birds also nest in other nearby caves inaccessible to man. Perhaps this great cave is repopulated by colonies coming from smaller ones because the missionaries assured us that these birds had not diminished in numbers. When the gizzards of the young birds in the cave are opened they contain all kinds of hard and dried fruits, which, under the name of *semilla del guácharo*, are a famous remedy against intermittent fevers. The adult birds carry these seeds to their young. They are carefully collected and sent to the sick at Cariaco.

We entered into the cave following the rivulet, some 28 to 30 feet wide. We walked along the banks as far as the calcareous incrustations allowed us; frequently, when the current slipped between high clusters of stalactites, we were forced to walk along the river bed, only 2 feet deep. To our surprise we learned that this underground stream is the source to the Caripe river and becomes navigable for canoes a few leagues from here, after joining the Santa María river. Along the underground rivulet banks we found a quantity of palm-tree wood, remains of trunks used by Indians to climb to the cave's ceiling when searching for nests. The rings formed from the traces of the leaf stems are used as a perpendicular ladder.

The Caripe grotto measures exactly 472 metres and keeps the same width and height of 60 to 70 feet all through. It was difficult to persuade the Indians to penetrate any further into the grotto than where they usually went to collect the fat. We needed the padres' authority to make them go as far as the point where the ground rises suddenly at a 60-degree angle and where the rivulet forms a small underground cascade. This cave, home of nocturnal birds, is for the Indian a mystical place; they believe that the souls of their ancestors live in its depths. Man – they say – should fear these places not illumined by the sun (*zis*) or moon (*nuna*). To join the *guácharos* is synonymous with joining your ancestors, that is, to die. For this reason, the magicians (*piaches*) and the poisoners (*imorons*) cast their nocturnal spells to call up the supreme evil spirit Ivorokiamo. Thus, all over the earth similarities may be found in the early fictions of people, especially those concerning the two principles ruling the world: the abode of souls after death, the happiness of the virtuous and the punishment of the guilty. The most different and barbarous languages present a certain number of similar images because they have the same source in the nature of our intelligence and our sensations. Darkness is everywhere connected with death.

At the point where the river becomes an underground cascade, the ground located near the opening is covered in greenery and looks extremely picturesque. You can see the outside from the far end of the straight gallery, some 240 toises away. Stalactites hanging from the ceiling, like floating columns, stand out from this green background. We shot our guns aimlessly in the dark wherever the screaming birds or the beating of wings made us suspect their nests lay ahead. Bonpland at last managed to kill two *guácharos* dazzled by our torches. This is how I was able to sketch this bird, up to now completely unknown to naturalists. We struggled to climb the rise from which the rivulet fell. We saw that the grotto narrowed; its height shrunk to 40 feet as it followed a north-east direction, parallel to the Caripe valley.

In this part of the cavern the rivulet deposits blackish earth, a mixture of silex, clay and vegetable detritus. We walked in thick mud to a place where, to our shock, we discovered underground vegetation. The seeds that the birds bring into the grotto to feed to their chicks germinate wherever they fall on to earth covering the calcareous incrustations. Blanched stalks with rudimentary leaves rose to some 2 feet. It was impossible to identify the plants as the absence of light had completely transformed their form, colour and aspect. These traces of plant life in the dark struck the Indians, usually so stupid and difficult to impress. They examined the plants in a silence inspired by a place they fear. You could have said these pale, deformed, underground plants seemed like ghosts banished from the earth's surface. For me, however, they recalled one of the happiest days of my youth when during a long stay at the Freiberg mines I began my research into the effects of blanching plants.

Despite their authority the missionaries could not persuade the Indians to go any further on into the cavern. The lower the vault the more piercing the screaming of the *guácharos* became. Thanks to the cowardice of our guides we had to retreat. We found that a bishop of Saint Thomas of Guiana had gone further than us. He had measured 2,500 feet from the mouth to where he stopped, but the cavern went further. The memory of this feat was preserved in the Caripe convent, without precise dates. The bishop had used torches made from white Castile wax, while we had torches made of tree bark and resin. The thick smoke from our torches in the narrow underground passage hurt our eyes and made breathing difficult.

We found our way out by following the rivulet. Before daylight dazzled our eyes we saw the river water outside the grotto sparkle among the foliage. It looked like a painting, with the cave opening as a frame. Once outside we rested by the stream. We could hardly believe that this cave had remained unknown in Europe. The *guácharos* should have made it far more famous. The missionaries had ordered a meal to be prepared at the entrance. Banana and *vijao* (*Heliconia bihai*) leaves served as a tablecloth, following the custom of the country.[58]

CHAPTER 8

DEPARTURE FROM CARIPE — THE MOUNTAIN AND
VALLEY OF SANTA MARÍA — THE CATUARO MISSION —
CARIACO HARBOUR

DAYS PASSED QUICKLY in the Capuchin convent in the Caripe mountains, despite our simple but monotonous life. From sunrise to sunset we toured the forests and mountains near by looking for plants, and have never collected so many. When the heavy rain stopped us travelling far we visited Indian huts and the communal *conuco*, or attended the nightly meetings when the *alcaldes* handed out the work for the following day. We did not return to the convent until bells called us for meals in the refectory with the monks. At dawn we sometimes accompanied them to the church to attend *doctrina*, that is, religious classes for Indians. It was hard explaining dogma to people who hardly knew Spanish. The monks are almost completely ignorant of the Chaima Indian language, and the resemblance of sounds between the languages muddles the poor Indians so that strange ideas arise. One day we witnessed a missionary struggling to explain to his class that *invierno*, winter, and *infierno*, hell, were not the same thing, but as different as hot and cold. The Chaima Indians know winter only as the rainy season, and imagine that 'the white's hell' is a place where the evil are exposed to horrific rainstorms. The missionary lost his temper, but it was useless; the first impression caused by the almost identical words persisted; in the Indians' minds the images of rain and hell could not be separated.

After spending the whole day outdoors, we wrote down our observations in the convent at night, and dried our plants and sketched what we thought were new species. Unfortunately the misty sky of a valley where the forests give off an enormous amount of water into the air was not favourable for astronomic observations. The only annoyance experienced in the Caripe valley was the impossibility of observing stars due to the sky being continuously covered. I spent part of every night waiting for the moment when a star might be visible between clouds. I often shivered with cold, though the thermometer only sank to 16 °C.

This site has something wild and tranquil, melancholic and attractive about it. In the midst of such powerful nature we felt nothing inside but peace and repose. In the solitude of these mountains I was less struck by the new impressions recorded at each step than by the fact that such diverse climates have so much in common. In the hills where the convent stands palm trees and tree fern grow; in the afternoon, before the rainfalls, the monotonous screaming of the howler monkeys seems like a distant wind in the forests. Despite these exotic sounds, and the strange plant forms and marvels of the New World, everywhere nature allows man to sense a voice speaking to him in familiar terms. The grass carpeting the ground, the old moss and ferns covering tree roots, the torrent that falls over steep calcareous rocks, the harmonious colours reflecting the water, the green and the sky, all evoke familiar sensations in the traveller.

The natural beauties of the mountains absorbed us so completely that we did not notice we were becoming a weight on our good and hospitable padres. Their provisions of wine and wheat bread were small, and both are considered real luxuries in these lands, so it inhibited us to think that our hosts deprived themselves, on our account. Our ration of bread had been reduced to one quarter, yet the cruel rains delayed our departure for two days. How long that delay seemed; we dreaded the bell that called us for a meal!

We left finally on the 22nd of September, with four mules carrying our instruments and plants. Leaving the Caripe valley we first crossed a chain of hills running north-east from the convent. The road was uphill across a wide savannah towards the tableland of Guardia de San Agustín. We waited there for the Indian who carried our barometer. We stood at 533 toises above sea-level. The savannahs, or natural grasslands, excellent pasture for the monastery cows, were totally devoid of trees and shrubs. It is the kingdom of the mono-cotyledonous plants, with only a few maguey (*Agave americana*), whose flowers rise some 26 feet above the grass. On the high tableland of Guardia we felt we had been carried to an ancient lake flattened by the prolonged effect of the waters. You think you can recognize the curves of the ancient shore, the promi-nent tongues of land, the steep cliffs forming islands. Even the distribution of flora seems to refer to that primitive state. The bottom of the basin is a savannah, while its edges are covered with tall trees. It is sad that a place so favoured by its climate, and fit for wheat, should be totally uninhabited.

Leaving the tableland of Guardia we descended to the Indian village of Santa Cruz. First we reached a steep, extremely slippery slope that the missionaries strangely named Bajada del Purgatorio, or Descent of Purgatory. It consists of eroded slaty sandstone, covered with clay; the slope seems ter-ribly steep. To go down, the mules draw their hind legs to their forelegs, lower their rumps and trust their luck sliding down-hill. The rider has nothing to fear as long as he drops the reins and leaves the mule alone. From here to the left we saw the great pyramid of Guácharo. This calcareous peak looks very picturesque, but we soon lost it to view when we entered the thick jungle known as Montana de Santa María. We spent seven hours crossing it. It is hard to imagine a worse path; a veritable ladder, a kind of gorge where, during the rainy sea-son, torrent water rushes down the rocks step by step. The steps are from 2 to 3 feet high. The hapless animals first have to calculate how to pass their loads between the tree trunks, and then jump from one block to another. Scared of slipping they wait a few moments, as if studying the terrain, and then draw their four legs together like wild goats do. If the mule misses the nearest rock it sinks deep into the soft ochre clay that fills in the gaps between the rocks. When there are no rocks, the rider's feet and the mule's legs are supported by a tangle of enormous tree roots. The creoles have faith in the skill and instinct of their mules and remain in the saddle during the long dangerous descent. We preferred to dismount because we feared fatigue less than they do, and were more prepared to travel slowly as we never stopped collecting plants and examining the rocks.

The jungle that covers the steep slope of the Santa María mountain is one of the densest I have ever seen. The trees are amazingly tall and thick. Under the dark green and matted canopy of leaves it always seems far darker than under our pine, oak and beech woods. Despite the temperature, it would seem that the air cannot absorb all the water emanating from the ground, the leaves and trunks of the trees with their tangle of orchids, peperomias and other succulent plants. Mixed with the aromatic smells given off by the flowers, fruit and even wood there was something of our misty autumn forests. Among the majestic trees that reach 120 to 130 feet high our guides pointed out the *curucay*, which yields a whitish, liquid resin with a strong odour. The Cumanagoto and Tagire Indians used to burn it before their idols as incense. The young branches have an agreeable taste, though somewhat acid. Apart from the *curucay* and the enormous trunks of the hymenaea, from 9 to 10 feet in diameter, we noticed, above all others, the dragon (*Croton sanguifluum*), whose dark purple resin flows from its white bark; as well as the medicinal *calahuala* fern, and the *irasse, macanilla*, corozo and *praga* palm trees. This latter gives a tasty 'heart of palm' that we sometimes ate at the Caripe convent. These palm trees with pinnate and thorny leaves contrast pleasingly with the tree ferns. In the Caripe valley we discovered five new species of tree fern, while in Linnaeus's time botanists had not even found four in both continents.

We observed that fern trees are usually far rarer than palm trees. Nature has limited them to temperate, humid and shady places. They shun the direct rays of the sun and while the *pumos*, corypha of the steppes, and other American palms prefer the naked, burning plains these tree fern, which seen from afar look like palms, maintain the character and habits of cryptogams. They prefer solitary places, shade, humidity and damp. Sometimes you find them on the coast, but only when protected by thick shade.

As we descended the Santa María mountain fern trees became rarer and palms more frequent. Nymphales, the beautiful large-winged butterflies that fly at prodigious heights, became more and more common. Everything suggested that we were near the coast in a zone whose average temperature ranged between 28 °C and 30 °C.

The weather was cloudy, threatening one of those cloudbursts during which some 1 to 1.5 inches of rain may fall in a day. The sun shone on the tree-tops and, although we were not exposed to the rays, the heat was asphyxiating. Thunder rolled at a distance. The clouds hovered over the peaks of the high Guácharo chain, and the plaintive howling of the araguatoes, heard so often in Caripe at sunset, announced the imminent storm. For the first time we had an opportunity to see those howler monkeys that belong to the family Alouatta (*Stentor*, Geoffroy), whose different species have long been confused by zoologists close at hand. While the small American sapajous, who imitate sparrow song with a whistle, have a simple, thin tongue bone, the large monkeys, the alouates and spider monkeys (*Ateles*, Geoffroy), have a tongue that rests on a large bony drum. The sad howling typical of the araguato is produced by air penetrating violently into this drum. I sketched these organs[19] on the spot as they are not well known to European anatomists. If you think about the size of the alouatta's bony box and the number of howler monkeys that can gather in one tree in the Cumaná and Guianan jungles, you will be less surprised by the force and volume of their united voices.

The araguato, which the Tamanaco Indians call *aravata* and the Maypures *marave*, resembles a bear cub. From the top of its small and pointed head to the beginning of its prehensile tail it measures 3 feet; its coat is thick and reddish-brown; even its breasts and belly are covered in pretty fur. The araguato's face is blackish-blue, with wrinkled skin. Its beard is longish, and although its facial angle is no more than 30 degrees there is as much humanity in its look and facial expressions as in the marimonda (*Simia belzebuth*) and the capuchin (*Simia chiripotes*) of the Orinoco.

The araguato of the Caripe region is a new species of the

genus *Stentor* that I named *Simia ursina*. I prefer this name to the one referring to its colour. Its eyes, voice and gait make it appear sad. I have seen young araguatoes brought up in Indian huts. They never play like the little sagoins. Their seriousness was described naïvely by Lopez de Gomara at the start of the sixteenth century: 'The aranata of the Cumaneses has the face of a man, the beard of a goat, and a serious bearing, *honrado gesto*.' The closer they resemble man the sadder monkeys look.

We stopped to observe the howler monkeys, which move in lines across the intricate branches linking the jungle trees in packs of thirty and forty. While watching this new spectacle we met a group of Indians on their way to the Caripe mountains. They were completely naked, like most Indians in these lands. Behind them came the women, laden with heavy packs, while all the men and boys were armed with bows and arrows. They walked in silence, staring at the ground. We would have liked to ask them if the Santa Cruz mission, where we hoped to spend the night, was far off. We were exhausted, and thirsty. The heat was increasing as the storm approached, and we had not found any springs. As the Indians invariably answered *si padre* and *no padre* we thought they understood a little Spanish. In their eyes every white is a monk, a padre. In the missions the colour of the skin characterizes the monk more than the colour of his habit. When we asked those Indians if Santa Cruz was far off they answered *si* or *no* so arbitrarily that we could make no sense of their answers. This made us angry, for their smiles and gestures showed that they would have liked to direct us as the jungle became thicker and thicker. We had to leave them; our guides, who spoke the Chaima language, lagged behind as the loaded mules kept falling into ravines.

After travelling several hours downhill over scattered blocks of stone we suddenly found we had reached the end of the Santa María jungle. As far as our eyes could see a vast plain spread out, its grass revived by the rainy season. Looking down on to the tree-tops it seemed as if we were looking at a dark green carpet below us. The jungle clearings seemed like huge funnels in which we recognized the delicate pinnate leaves of the *praga* and *irasse* palms. The countryside is extremely picturesque due to the Sierra of Guacharo whose northern slopes are steep and form a rocky wall some 3,000 feet high. There is little vegetation on this wall, so you can follow the calcareous strata. The peak itself is flat.

The savannah we crossed to reach the Indian village of Santa Cruz is made up of various very flat plateaux lying one above another. This geological phenomenon seems to show that they were once basins where water poured from one to the other. On the spot where we last saw the limestone of the Santa María jungle we found nodules of iron ore, and, if I was not mistaken, a bit of ammonite, but we could not detach it. The Santa Cruz mission is situated in the middle of the plain. We reached it as night fell, half dead with thirst as we had been eight hours without water. We spent the night in one of those *ajupas* known as 'kings' houses', which serve as *tambos* or inns for travellers. As it was raining there was no chance of making any astronomical observations so, on the next day, the 23rd of September, we set off for the Gulf of Cariaco. Beyond Santa Cruz thick jungle reappears. Under tufts of melastoma we found a beautiful fern, with leaves similar to the *osmunda*, which belonged to a new genus (*Polybotria*) of the polypodiaceous order.

The Catuaro mission is situated in a very wild place. The church is surrounded by tall trees. At night jaguars hunt the Indians' chickens and pigs. We lodged in the priest's house, a monk of the Observance congregation, to whom the Capuchins had given this mission because they did not have enough priests in their own community. He was a doctor in theology, a little, dried-up and petulant man. He entertained us with stories about the trial he had had with the superior of his convent, with the enmity of his brothers and the injustice of the *alcaldes*, who, ignoring his privileges, once threw him in jail. Despite these set-backs he had conserved an unfortunate liking for what he called metaphysical questions. He wanted to know what I thought of free will, of how to raise the soul from the prison of the body, and, above all, about animal souls. When you have crossed a jungle in the rainy season you do not feel like these kind of speculations. Besides, everything about this little Catuaro mission was odd, even the priest's house. It had two floors, and had become the object of a keen rivalry between secular and ecclesiastical authorities. The priest's superior found it too luxurious for a missionary, and wanted the Indians to demolish it; the governor opposed this strongly, and his will prevailed.

There we met the district *corregidor*, Don Alejandro Mejía, an amiable and well-educated man. He gave us three Indians who would cut us a path through the jungle with machetes. In this country, where people rarely travel, the vegetation is so fertile that a man on horseback can barely make his way along the jungle paths tangled with liana and branches during the rainy season. To our great annoyance the Catuaro missionary insisted on leading us to Cariaco, and we could not decline his offer. He told us a dreadful story. The independence movement, which had nearly broken out in 1798, had been preceded and followed by trouble among the slaves at Cariaco. An unfortunate negro had been condemned to death and our host was going to Cariaco to give him some spiritual comfort. How tedious this journey became. We could not escape talking about 'the necessity of slavery, the innate wickedness of the blacks, and how slavery benefited Christians'!

The road through the Catuaro jungle resembles the descent through the Santa María mountain; the difficult parts are given odd names. You follow a narrow channel, scooped out by torrents and filled with a fine, sticky clay. In the steep parts the mules sit on their rumps and slide downhill. This descent is called Saca Manteca because the consistence of the mud is like butter. There is no danger in this descent as the mules are very skilled at sliding.

In Cariaco we found most of the inhabitants in their hammocks, ill with intermittent fevers that in autumn become malignant and lead to dysentery. If you think how extraordinarily fertile and humid the plain is, and of the amount of vegetation that rots there, it is easy to understand why the atmosphere here is not as healthy as it is at Cumaná. In the torrid zone the amazing fertility of the soil, the frequent and prolonged rainy season, and the extraordinary opulence of the vegetation are advantages outweighed by a climate dangerous for whites.

The fevers reigning in Cariaco forced us, to our regret, to shorten our stay there. As we were still not completely acclimatized, the inhabitants to whom we had been recommended warned us not to delay. In the town we met many people who, through a certain ease of behaviour, or through being more broad-minded and preferring a United States type government, revealed that they were in contact with foreigners. For the first time we heard the names of Franklin and Washington enthusiastically pronounced. With these shows of enthusiasm we heard complaints about the present state of New Andalusia, exaggerated enumerations of their natural wealth, and passionate and impatient hopes for a better future. This state of mind struck a traveller who had been witness to the great political upheavals in Europe.

We embarked at dawn hoping to cross the Gulf of Cariaco in a day. The sea is no rougher than any of our great lakes when a breeze blows. From the Cumaná wharf the distance is only 3 leagues. Leaving the small town of Cariaco behind us we went west towards the Carenicuar river, which, straight as an artificial canal, runs through gardens and cotton plantations. On the banks of the river we saw Indian women washing clothes with the fruit of the *parapara* (*Sapindus saponaria*). They say that this is very rough on their hands. The bark of this fruit gives a strong lather, and the fruit is so elastic that when thrown on to stone it bounces three or four times to the height of 6 feet. Being round, it is also used to make rosaries.

Once on board we had to contend with strong winds. It poured with rain, and near by thunder rolled. Flocks of flamingoes, egrets and cormorants flew past towards the shore. Only the alcatras, a large kind of pelican, continued to fish calmly in the gulf. We were eighteen on board, and the narrow pirogue, overloaded with sugar cane and bunches of bananas and coconuts, could hardly hold our instruments. The edge of the boat barely stood above the water-line.

Adverse winds and rain forced us to go on shore at Pericantral, a small farm on the southern coast of the gulf. The whole of this coast, covered in beautiful vegetation, is completely uncultivated. Only some 700 people live here, and, excepting in the village of Mariguitar,[60] we saw only coconut plantations, which produce oil for the people.

We did not leave the Pericantral farm until dark. We spent a very uncomfortable night in the narrow, overloaded pirogue. At three in the morning we found ourselves at the mouth of the Manzanares river. As the sun rose we saw the *zamuro* vultures (*Vultur aura*) perched in flocks of forty and fifty in the coconut palms. To sleep, these birds line up together on branches like fowl, and are so lazy that they go to sleep ages before sunset and do not wake up until the sun is up. It seems as if the trees with pinnate leaves share this laziness with the birds. The mimosas and tamarinds close their leaves when the sky is clear some twenty-five to thirty-five minutes before sunset, and in the morning do not open them again until the sun is high up.

CHAPTER 9

PHYSICAL CONSTITUTION AND CUSTOMS OF THE
CHAIMA INDIANS — THEIR LANGUAGE

IN THE CHRONICLE of our journey to the Caripe missions I did not wish to insert general considerations concerning the customs, languages and common origins of the different Indian tribes populating New Andalusia. Now, having returned to my starting-point, I will place in one section matters that concern the history of human beings. As we advance further into the interior of the continent this subject will become even more interesting than the phenomena of the physical world.

In the mountainous regions we have just crossed, Indians form half the population of the provinces of Cumaná and New Barcelona. Their number can be calculated at some 60,000, of which some 24,000 live in New Andalusia. The Indians of Cumaná do not all live in the mission villages. Some are dispersed around the cities, along the coasts, attracted by fishing, and some in the small farms on the llanos or plains. Some 15,000 Indians, all belonging to the Chaima tribe, live in the Aragonese Capuchin missions we visited. However, their villages are not as densely populated as in New Barcelona province. Their average population is only 500 to 600, while more to the west, in the Franciscan missions of Piritu, there are Indian villages with up to 3,000 inhabitants. If I calculated the Indian population in the provinces of Cumaná and New Barcelona to be some 60,000 I included only those living on Terra Firma, not the Guaiquerí on Margarita Island, nor the great number of independent Guaraunos living in the Orinoco delta islands. Their number is estimated, perhaps exaggeratedly, at some 6,000 to 8,000. Apart from Guaraunos families seen now and then in the marshes (Los Morichales), which are covered with moriche palms, for the last thirty years there have been no wild Indians living in New Andalusia.

I use the word 'savage' grudgingly because it implies a cultural difference between the tamed Indians living in missions and the free ones, which belies the facts. In the South American jungles there are Indian tribes who live peacefully in villages under their chiefs, who cultivate banana trees, cassava and cotton in large areas of land, and weave their hammocks with cotton fibres. They are not more barbarous than the naked Indians of the missions who have learned to make the sign of the cross. In Europe it is a common fallacy to assume that all Indians who are not tamed are nomadic hunters. In Terra Firma agriculture was known long before the arrival of the Europeans, and today is still practised between the Orinoco and Amazon rivers in jungle clearings never visited by missionaries. What the missionaries have achieved is to have increased the Indians' attachment to owning land, their desire for secure dwelling places, and their taste for more peaceful lives. It would be accepting false ideas about the actual condition of South American Indians to assume that 'Christian', 'tamed' and 'civilized' were synonymous with 'pagan', 'savage' and 'free'. The tamed Indian is often as little a Christian as the free Indian is an idolater. Both, caught up in the needs of the moment, betray a marked indifference for religious sentiments, and a secret tendency to worship nature and her powers.

If the independent Indians have almost disappeared over the last century in those areas north of the Orinoco, it must not be concluded that fewer Indians exist at present than in the time of the bishop of Chiapas, Bartolomeo de las Casas. I have already proved in my work on Mexico how mistaken it is to assume the destruction and diminution of Indians in the Spanish colonies, as Ulloa has written 'Es cosa constante irse disminuyendo por todas panes el numero de los Indios' (There is everywhere a constant decrease in the number of Indians). There are still more than 6 million copper-coloured races in both Americas, and though countless tribes and languages have died out it is beyond discussion that within the Tropics, where civilization arrived with Columbus, the number of Indians has considerably increased.[61]

As the missionaries struggle to penetrate the jungles and gain the Indian land, so white colonists try, in their turn, to invade missionary land. In this long-drawn-out struggle the secular arm continually tends to take over those Indians tamed by the missions, and missionaries are replaced by priests. Whites and mestizos, favoured by *corregidores*, have established themselves among the Indians. The missions are transformed into Spanish villages and the Indians soon forget even the memory of their own language. So civilization slowly works its way inland from the coast, sometimes hindered by human passions.

In the New Andalusia and Barcelona provinces, under the name of the Gobierno de Cumaná, there are more than fourteen tribes: in New Andalusia reside the Chaimas, the Guaiquerí, the Pariagotos, the Quaquas, the Araucans, the Caribs and the Guaraunos; in the province of New Barcelona, the Cumanagotos, the Palenques, the Caribs, the Piritus, the Tomuzas, the Topocuares, the Chacopotes and the Guarives. Nine to ten of these tribes consider themselves to be of entirely different races. Of the remaining tribes, the most numerous are the Chaimas in the Caripe mountains, the Caribs in the southern savannahs of New Barcelona, and the Cumanagotos in the Piritu missions. Some Guarauno families live on the left shore of the Orinoco where the delta begins, under missionary discipline. The most common languages are those of the Guaraunos, the Caribs, the Cumanagotos and the Chaimas.

The Indians in the missions dedicate themselves to agriculture, and, apart from those who live in the high mountains, all cultivate the same plants; their huts are arranged in the same manner; their working day, their tasks in the communal *conuco*, their relationship with the missionaries and elected functionaries, all run along fixed rules. However, we observe in the copper-coloured men a moral inflexibility, a stubbornness concerning habits and customs, which, though modified in each tribe, characterize the whole race from the equator to Hudson's Bay and the Strait of Magellan.

In the missions there are a few villages where families belong to different tribes, speaking different languages. Societies composed of such heterogeneous elements are difficult to govern. In general, the padres have settled whole tribes, or large parts of them, in villages not far from each other. The Indians see only those of their own tribe, for lack of communication and isolation are the main aims of missionary policy. Among the tamed Chaimas, Caribs and Tamanacs racial characteristics are retained if they are allowed to keep their respective languages. If man's individuality is reflected in his dialects, then these in their turn influence thoughts and feelings. This intimate link between language, national character and physical constitution ensures the differences and idiosyncrasies of the tribes, which in turn constitutes an unending source of movement and life at the mental level.

Missionaries have managed to rid the Indians of certain customs concerning birth, entering puberty and burying the dead; they have managed to stop them painting their skin or making incisions in their chins, noses and cheeks; they have banished the superstitious ideas that in many families are passed down mysteriously from father to son; but it was far easier to suppress practices and memories than it was to replace the old ideas with new ones. In the missions the Indian has a far more secure life than he had before. He is no longer a victim of the continuous struggle between man and the elements, and he leads a more monotonous and passive life than the wild Indian, but he is also less likely to animate his own spiritual development. His thinking has not increased with his contact with whites; he has remained estranged from the objects with which European civilization has enriched the Americas. All his acts seem dictated exclusively by wants of the moment. He is taciturn, without joy, introverted and, on the outside, serious and mysterious. Someone who has been but a short time in a mission could mistake his laziness and passivity for a meditative frame of mind.

I shall begin with the Chaimas, of whom some 15,000 live in the missions we visited. Their territory stretches over the high mountain range of the Cocollar and the Guácharo, the banks of the Guarapiche, the Colorado river, the Areo and the Caño de Caripe. According to a statistical survey made with great care by a father superior in the Aragonese Capuchin mission of Cumaná, nineteen mission villages, the oldest dating back to 1728, held 1,465 families, and a total of 6,433 people. From 1730 to 1736 the population was diminished by the ravages of smallpox, always more fatal for the copper-skinned Indians than for the whites.

The Chaimas are usually short and thickset, with extremely broad shoulders and flat chests, and their legs are rounded and fleshy. The colour of their skin is the same as that of all American Indians from the cold plateaux of Quito to the burning jungles of the Amazon.

Their facial expression is not hard or wild but rather serious and gloomy. Their foreheads are small and barely salient, which is why in various languages of their territory they say about a beautiful woman that 'she is fat, with a narrow forehead'; their eyes are black, deep set and very elongated. The Chaimas, and all South American Indians, resemble the Mongols in the shape of their eyes, their high cheekbones, their straight and smooth hair, and an almost total absence of beard; yet they differ in the form of their noses. These are rather long and broad at the nostril, which opens downwards like a Caucasian nose. Their mouths are wide, with full lips but not fleshy, and frequently show their good nature. Between the nose and mouth are two furrows that diverge from the nostrils to the corners of the mouth. The chin is very small and round; the jaws very strong and wide.

The Chaimas have attractive white teeth like all who lead a very simple life, but not as strong as negro teeth. The early explorers noted their custom of blacking their teeth with plant juices and quicklime; today this custom has disappeared. I doubt whether the custom of blacking their teeth had anything to do with odd ideas about beauty or a remedy against toothache. It could be said that Indians do not know toothache, and Spaniards who live in the Tropics do not suffer from this pain either.

Like all the Indian tribes that I know the Chaimas have small, slender hands. Contrary to this, their feet are large, and their toes remain extremely mobile. All the Chaimas resemble each other, as if they were all related, and this is all the more evident because between twenty and fifty years old, age is not indicated by wrinkling skin, white hair or body decrepitude. When you enter a hut it is hard to differentiate a father from a son, one generation from another. I think that this family resemblance has two different causes: the local position of the Indian villages, and the lack of intellectual culture. Indian nations are subdivided into an infinity of tribes, all hating each other, and never allied even if speaking the same language or living on the same river or nearby hill. This characteristic is preserved in the missions where marriages are made only within tribes. This blood link that unites a whole tribe is naïvely illustrated by those Spanish-speaking Indians who designate members of the same tribe as *mis parientes* (my relatives).

The Indians of the missions, remote from all civilization, are influenced solely by physical needs, which they satisfy very easily in their favourable climate, and therefore tend to lead dull, monotonous lives, which are reflected in their facial expressions.

The Chaimas, like all semi-wild people in hot climates, show a great aversion to clothes. In the torrid zone the Indians are ashamed – so they say – to wear clothes, and if they are forced to do so too soon they rush off into the jungle in order to remain naked. Despite the efforts of the monks the Chaima men and women walk around naked in their houses. When they go into villages they put on a kind of cotton shirt, which hardly reaches to their knees. Sometimes we met Indians outside the mission grounds, during a rainstorm, who had taken their clothes off and rolled them under their arms. They prefer to let the rain fall on their naked bodies than letting it wet their clothes. The older women hid behind trees and burst into loud fits of laughter when they saw us pass by fully dressed.

Chaima women are not pretty according to our ideas of beauty; however, the girls have a sweet, melancholic look, which softens their often hard and wild mouths. They wear their hair in two plaits and do not paint their skin; in their extreme poverty they use no ornaments apart from shell, bird-bone and seed necklaces and bracelets. Both women and men are very muscular, though plump and round. I saw no Indian with any natural deformity. In the wild state, which is a state of equality, nothing can induce a man to marry a deformed or ill woman. Such a woman, if she survives the accidents of life, dies childless.

The Chaimas hardly have any hair on their chins, like the Tongouses and other Mongolic races. They pluck out the few hairs that grow. In general it is erroneous to say that they cannot grow beards, because they pluck them out – though even without that custom, they would be mostly smooth-faced.

The Chaimas lead an extremely monotonous life. They go to bed regularly at half past seven in the evening, and get up long before dawn, at about half past four. Every Indian has a fire next to his hammock. Women suffer the cold greatly; I have even seen a woman shiver at church when the temperature was above 18 °C. Their huts are very clean. Their hammocks and reed mats, their pots full of cassava or fermented maize, their bow and arrows, all are kept in perfect order. Men and women wash every day, and as they walk around naked do not get as dirty as people who wear clothes. Apart from their village hut they also have in the *conuco*, next to a spring or at the entrance to a small valley, a hut roofed with palm- or banana-tree leaves. Though life is less comfortable in the *conuco* they prefer living there as much as possible. I have already alluded to their irresistible drive to flee and return to the jungle. Even young children flee from their parents to spend four or five days in the jungle, feeding off wild fruit, palm hearts and roots. When travelling through the missions it is not rare to find them empty as everyone is either in their garden or in the jungle, *al monte*. Similar feelings account for civilized people's passion for hunting: the charm of solitude, the innate desire for freedom, and the deep impressions felt whenever man is alone in contact with nature.

Among the Chaimas, as among all semi-barbarous people, the state of women is one of privation and suffering. The hardest work falls to them. In the evening when we saw the Chaimas return from their gardens the men carried only their machetes to cut their way through the undergrowth. The women walk loaded with bananas, a child in their arms and two others sometimes perched on top of their load. Despite this social inequality South American Indian women seem, in general, happier than North American ones. In the missions men work in the fields as much as women.

Nothing matches the difficulty that Indians have in learning Spanish. As long as they are distanced from white men they have an aversion to be called civilized Indians or, as the missions call them, *indios muy latinos*. But what struck me most, not only among the Chaimas, but among all the isolated missions that I later visited, was the extreme difficulty they have in co-ordinating and expressing the simplest ideas in Spanish, even if they know the meaning of the single words and sentences.

You would think their mental stupidity greater than that of children when a white asks them questions about objects that have surrounded them since birth. Missionaries assured us that this is not due to timidity, and that among the missionary Indians in charge of public works this is not an innate stupidity but a block they have concerning the mechanisms of a language so different to their mother tongue. The Indians affirmed or denied whatever pleased the monks, and laziness, accompanied by that cunning courtesy common to all Indians, made them sometimes give the answers suggested by the questions. Travellers cannot be wary enough of this over-obliging approbation when they want to find out what Indians think. To test an Indian *alcalde* I asked him 'if he did not think that the Caripe river that comes from the Guacharo caves might not return there by some unknown entrance after climbing up the hill'. He looked as if he gave it serious thought for a while and answered in support of my theory: 'If it did not do this how else is there always water in the river?'

The Chaimas have extreme difficulty in coping with numerical relationships. I did not meet one who could tell me whether he was eighteen or sixty years old. The Chaima language has words to express high numbers, but few Indians know how to use them. As they need to count the more intelligent ones count in Spanish up to thirty or forty, and even that seems a great mental strain. In their own language they cannot count up to six. Since European savants have dedicated themselves to the study of the structure of American languages we cannot attribute the imperfection of a language to what appears to be the stupidity of a people. We recognize that everywhere languages offer greater richnesses and more nuances than can be supposed from the lack of culture of the people speaking them.

The American languages have a structure so different from Latin that the Jesuits, who look carefully to anything that might favour a quick establishing of missions, introduced the richer Indian languages, especially Quechua and Guarani, instead of Spanish, to their converts because these languages were systematic and already widespread. They tried to substitute these poorer, coarser dialects with irregular constructions. They found this substitution easy; Indians from different tribes docilely learned them, and these languages became a medium of communication between missionary and Indian. Through these languages the Jesuits found it easier to link the various tribes until then separated from each other by language.

In America, from the Eskimos to the Orinoco banks, from the burning plains to the icy Strait of Magellan, mother tongues, quite different in terms of their roots, share the same physiognomy. We recognize striking analogies in grammatical structure, not only in the more learned languages like that of the Incas, the Aymara, the Guaranu, Cora and Mexican, but also in the more primitive ones. It is thanks to this structural analogy rather than words in common that the mission Indian learns another American language more easily than a metropolitan one. In the Orinoco jungle I have met the dullest Indians who speak two or three languages.

If the Jesuit system had been followed, languages that cover a large amount of the continent would have become almost general. In Terra Firma and on the Orinoco, Carib and Tamanaco alone would be spoken, and in the south and south-west,

Quechua, Guarani, Omagua and Araucan. By appropriating these languages with regular grammatical forms, the missionaries would have had a more intimate contact with their Indians. The numberless difficulties arising from missions with a dozen different tribes would have vanished with the confusions of their languages, and the Indian, by preserving an American language, would have retained individuality and national identity.

At the Capuchin hospice in Caripe I collected, with Bonpland's help, a small list of Chaima words. The three languages most common in this province are Chaima, Cumanagoto and Carib. Here they have been seen as separate languages and a dictionary of each has been compiled for mission use. The few grammars printed in the seventeenth century passed into the missions and have been lost in the jungle. Damp air and voracious insects (termites known as *comején*) make preserving books in these hot lands almost impossible, and they are soon destroyed.

On the right bank of the Orinoco, south-east of the Encaramada mission, 100 leagues from the Chaimas, live the Tamanacos. Despite the distance and numerous local obstacles it is clear that Chaima is a branch of Tamanaco. I discovered the link between these languages years after my return to Europe when I compared data collected in a grammar book of an old missionary on the Orinoco, printed in Italy.[62]

CHAPTER 10

WE STAYED ANOTHER month at Cumaná. The river journey
we intended to take up the Orinoco and the Río Negro
demanded all kinds of preparation. We had to choose the easi-
est instruments to carry on narrow canoes; we had to provide
ourselves with the funds for a ten-month trip inland across a
country without communications with the coast. As astronomic determination of places was the main aim of our undertaking I did not want to miss the solar eclipse that would be
visible at the end of October. I chose to wait until then in Cumaná where the sky is usually beautiful and clear. It was too late
to reach the Orinoco river banks, and the high Caracas valley
offered less favourable chances due to the mists that gather
round the neighbouring mountains. Having precisely fixed the
Cumaná longitude I had a starting-point for my chronometric
determinations, the only ones I could count on when usually
I did not remain long enough to take lunar distances or to
observe Jupiter's satellites.

A dreadful accident almost made me put off my Orinoco
journey, or postpone it for a long time. On the 27th of
October, the night before the eclipse, we were strolling along
the gulf shore as usual, to take some fresh air and observe high
tide. Its highest point in this area was no more than 12 to 13
inches. It was eight at night and the breeze had not begun. The
sky was overcast and during this dead calm it was extremely
hot. We were crossing the beach that separates the landing-
stage from the Guaiquerí Indian village. I heard somebody
walking behind me; as I turned I saw a tall man, the colour of
a mulatto, and naked to the waist. Just above my head he was
holding a macana, a huge stick made of palm-tree wood,
enlarged at the end like a club. I avoided his blow by leaping

to the left. Bonpland, walking at my right, was less lucky. He had noticed the mulatto later than I had; he received the blow above his temple and fell to the ground. We were alone, unarmed, some half a league from any houses, in a vast plain bordered by the sea. The mulatto, instead of attacking me, turned back slowly to grab Bonpland's hat, which had softened the blow and fallen far from us. Terrified at seeing my travelling companion on the ground and for a few seconds unconscious I was worried only about him. I helped him up; pain and anger doubled his strength. We made for the mulatto who, either due to that cowardice typical of his race or because he saw some men far off on the beach, rushed off into the *tunal*, a coppice of cacti and tree aviccenia. Luck had him fall as he was running, and Bonpland, who had reached him first, began fighting with him, exposing himself to great danger. The mulatto pulled out a long knife from his trousers, and in such an unequal fight we would surely have been wounded if some Basque merchants taking the fresh air on the beach had not come to our aid. Seeing himself surrounded the mulatto gave up all idea of defending himself: then he managed to escape again and we followed him for a long time through the thorny cacti until he threw himself exhausted into a cow shed from where he let himself be quietly led off to prison.

That night Bonpland had a fever; but being brave, and gifted with that good character which a traveller should rank higher than anything else, he took up his work the next morning. The blow from the macana reached the crown of his head; he felt it for two to three months, up to our stay in Caracas. When he bent down to pick up plants he was several times made dizzy, which made us worry that some internal damage might have been done. Luckily our fears had no base and these alarming symptoms slowly vanished. The Cumaná inhabitants showed us the greatest kindness. We discovered that the mulatto came from one of the Indian villages round the great Maracaibo lake. He had served on a pirate ship from the island of Santo Domingo and, after a quarrel with the captain, had abandoned ship on the Cumaná coast. Why, after knocking one of us down, did he then try to steal a hat? In an interrogation his answers were so confused and stupid that we were unable to clear this matter up.

Despite Bonpland's tiresome accident I found myself the next day, the 28th of October, at five in the morning, on the roof terrace of our house, preparing to observe the eclipse. The sky was clear and beautiful. The crescent of Venus and the constellation of the Ship, so dazzling because of the proximity of their enormous nebulae, were soon lost by the rays of the rising sun. I congratulated myself for such a fine day, as during the last weeks storms had built up regularly in the south and south-east two or three hours after the sun passed the meridian and had prevented me setting the clocks with the corresponding heights. At night one of those reddish vapours, which hardly affect the hygrometer in the lower levels of the atmosphere, covered the stars. This phenomenon was all the more extraordinary as in previous years it often happened that for three or four months one did not see the least trace of cloud or vapour. I observed the complete progress and end of the eclipse.

The days before and after the eclipse were accompanied by strange atmospheric phenomena. We were in the season called winter here, that is, when clouds build up and release short stormy downpours. From the 10th of October to the 3rd of November the horizon is covered over each night by a reddish mist, quickly spreading across the sky-blue vault in a more or less thick veil. When this reddish mist lightly covered the sky not even the brightest stars could be seen even at their highest points. They twinkled at all altitudes as if after a rainstorm.

From the 28th of October to the 3rd of November the reddish mist was thicker than usual: at night the heat was stifling yet the thermometer did not rise beyond 26 °C. The sea breeze, which usually refreshed the air from eight to nine at night, was not felt at all. The air was sweltering hot, and the dusty, dry ground started cracking everywhere. On the 4th of November, around two in the afternoon, extraordinarily thick black clouds covered the tall Brigantín and Tataraqual mountains, and then reached the zenith. At about four it began to thunder way above us without rumbling; making a cracking noise, which often suddenly stopped. At the moment that the greatest electrical discharge was produced, twelve minutes past four, we felt two successive seismic shocks, fifteen seconds from each other. Everybody ran out into the street screaming. Bonpland, who was examining some plants, leaning over a table, was almost thrown to the floor, and I felt the shock very clearly in spite of being in my hammock. The direction of the earthquake was from north to south, rare in Cumaná. Some slaves drawing water from a well, some 18 to 20 feet deep next to the Manzanares river, heard a noise comparable to artillery fire, which seemed to rise up out of the well; a surprising phenomenon, though quite common in American countries exposed to earthquakes.

A few minutes before the first shock there was a violent gust of wind, accompanied by flashes of lightning and large raindrops. The sky remained covered; after the storm the wind died down, staying quiet all night. The sunset was extraordinarily beautiful. The thick veil of clouds tore open into strips just above the horizon, forming shreds, and the sun shone at 12 degrees of altitude against an indigo-blue sky. Its disk appeared incredibly swollen, distorted and wavy at its edges. The clouds were gilded, and clusters of rays coloured like the rainbow spread in every direction from its centre. A great crowd had congregated in the main square. This phenomenon, the accompanying earthquake, thunder rolling as the earth shook, and that reddish mist lasting so many days were blamed on the eclipse.

Hardly twenty-two months had passed since a previous earthquake had nearly destroyed the city of Cumaná. The people regard the reddish mist veiling the sky and the absence of a sea breeze at night as infallible ill omens. Many people came to see us to ask if our instruments predicted any further quakes. Their anxiety increased greatly when on the 5th of November, at the same time as the day before, there was a violent gust of wind, accompanied by thunder and a few raindrops. But no shock was felt.

The earthquake of the 4th of November, the first I had experienced, made a great impression on me, heightened, perhaps accidentally, by remarkable meteorological variations. It was also a movement that went up and down, not in waves. I would never have thought then that, after a long stay in Quito and on the Peruvian coast, I would get as used to these often violent ground movements as in Europe we get used to thunder. In Quito we never considered getting out of bed when at night there were underground rumblings (*bramidos*), which seemed to announce a shock from the Pichincha volcano. The casualness of the inhabitants, who know that their city has not been destroyed in three centuries, easily communicates itself to the most frightened traveller. It is not so much a fear of danger as of the novelty of the sensation that strikes one so vividly when an earthquake is felt for the first time.

When shocks from an earthquake are felt, and the earth we think of as so stable shakes on its foundations, one second is long enough to destroy long-held illusions. It is like waking painfully from a dream. We think we have been tricked by nature's seeming stability; we listen out for the smallest noise; for the first time we mistrust the very ground we walk on. But if these shocks are repeated frequently over successive days, then fear quickly disappears. On the Peruvian coasts we got as used to the earth tremors as sailors do to rough waves.

The night of the 11th was cool and exceptionally beautiful. A little before dawn, at about half past two in the morning, extraordinarily luminous meteors were seen. Bonpland, who had got up to get some fresh air in the gallery, was the first to notice them. Thousands of fire-balls and shooting stars fell continually over four hours from north to south. According to Bonpland, from the start of this phenomenon there was not a patch of sky the size of three quarters of the moon that was not packed with fire-balls and shooting stars. The meteors trailed behind them long luminous traces whose phosphorescence lasted some eight seconds.

Almost all Cumaná's inhabitants witnessed this phenomenon as they got up before four in the morning to go to first mass. The sight of these fire-balls did not leave them indifferent, far to the contrary; the older ones recalled that the great 1766 earthquake was preceded by a similar manifestation.[63]

CHAPTER 11

CROSSING FROM CUMANÁ to La Guaira by sea our plan was
to stay in Caracas until the end of the rainy season; from there
we would go to the great plains, the llanos, and the Orinoco
missions; then we would travel upstream on the great river
from south of the cataracts to the Río Negro and the Brazilian
frontier, and return to Cumaná through the capital of Spanish
Guiana, called Angostura[64] or Straits. It was impossible to calculate how long this journey of some 700 leagues would take
in canoes. On the coasts only the mouth of the Orinoco is
known. No trading is carried out with the missions. What lies
beyond the plains is unknown country for the inhabitants of
Caracas and Cumaná. In a land where few travel, people enjoy
exaggerating the dangers arising from the climate, animals and
wild men.

The boat that took us from Cumaná to La Guaira was one
of those that trade between the coasts and the West Indies
Islands. They are 30 feet long, and not more than 3 feet above
the water, without decks. Although the sea is extremely rough
from Cape Codera to La Guaira, and although these boats have
large triangular sails, not one of them has been lost at sea in a
storm. The skill of the Guaiquerí pilots is such that voyages
of 120 to 150 leagues in open sea, out of sight of land, are done
without charts or compasses, as with the ancients. The Indian
pilot guides himself by the polar star or the sun.

When we left the Cumaná coast we felt as if we had been
living there for a long time. It was the first land that we had
reached in a world that I had longed to know from my childhood. The impression produced by nature in the New World
is so powerful and magnificent that after only a few months in

these places you feel you have been here years. In the Tropics everything in nature seems new and marvellous. In the open plains and tangled jungles all memories of Europe are virtually effaced as it is nature that determines the character of a country. How memorable the first new country you land at continues to be all your life! In my imagination I still see Cumaná and its dusty ground more intensely than all the marvels of the Andes.

As we approached the shoal surrounding Cape Arenas we admired the phosphorescence of the sea. Bands of dolphins enjoyed following our boat. When they broke the surface of the water with their broad tails they diffused a brilliant light that seemed like flames coming from the depths of the ocean. We found ourselves at midnight between some barren, rocky islands in the middle of the sea, forming the Caracas and Chimanas groups. The moon lit up these jagged, fantastic rocks, which had not a trace of vegetation. All these islands are uninhabited, except one where large, fast, brown goats can be found. Our Indian pilot said they tasted delicious. Thirty years back a family of whites settled here and grew maize and cassava. The father outlived his children. As he had become rich he bought two black slaves, who murdered him. Thus the goats ran wild, but not the maize. Maize appears to survive only if looked after by man. Birds destroy all the seeds needed to reproduce. The two slaves escaped punishment, as nothing could be proved. One of the blacks is now the hangman at Cumaná. He betrayed his companion, and obtained pardon by accepting being hangman.

We landed on the right bank of the Neveri and climbed to the little fort of El Morro de Barcelona, built some 60 to 70 toises above sea-level. We remained five hours in this fort guarded by the provincial militia. We waited in vain for news about English pirates stationed along the coast. Two of our fellow travellers, brothers of the Marquis of Toro in Caracas, came from Spain. They were highly cultivated men returning home after years abroad. They had more reason to fear being captured and taken as prisoners to Jamaica. I had no passport from the Admiralty, but I felt safe in the protection given by the English Government to those who travel for the progress of science.

The shock of the waves was felt in our boat. My fellow travellers all suffered. I slept calmly, being lucky never to suffer seasickness. By sunrise of the 20th of November we expected to double the cape in a few hours. We hoped to arrive that day at La Guaira, but our Indian pilot was scared of pirates. He preferred to make for land and wait in the little harbour of Higuerote[65] until night. We found neither a village nor a farm but two or three huts inhabited by mestizo fishermen with extremely thin children, which told us how unhealthy and feverish this coast was. The sea was so shallow that we had to wade ashore. The jungle came right down to the beach, covered in thickets of mangrove. On landing we smelled a sickly smell,[66] which reminded me of deserted mines.

Wherever mangroves grow on the seashore thousands of molluscs and insects thrive. These animals love shade and half light, and in the scaffolding of the thick intertwined roots find shelter from the crashing waves, riding above the water. Shellfish cling to the network of roots; crabs dig into the hollow trunks, and seaweeds, drifting ashore, hang from branches and bend them down. Thus, as the mud accumulates between the roots, so dry land moves further and further out from the jungly shores.

When we reached the high seas my travelling companions got so scared from the boat's rolling in a rough sea that they decided to continue by land from Higuerote to Caracas, despite having to cross a wild and humid country in constant rain and flooding rivers. Bonpland also chose the land way, which pleased me as he collected numerous new plants. I stayed alone with the Guaiquerí pilot as I thought it too dangerous to lose sight of the precious instruments that I wanted to take up the Orinoco.

La Guaira is more a bay than a harbour; the sea is always rough, and boats are exposed to dangerous winds, sandbanks and mist. Disembarking is very difficult as large waves prevent mules from being taken ashore. The negroes and freed mulattos who carry the goods on to the boats are exceptionally muscular. They wade into the water up to their waists and, sur-prisingly, are not scared of the sharks that teem in the harbour. The sharks are dangerous and bloodthirsty at the island oppo-site the coast of Caracas, although they do not attack anybody swimming in the harbour. To explain physical phenomena simply people have always resorted to marvels, insisting that here a bishop had blessed the sharks in the port.

We suffered much from the heat, increased by the rever-beration from the dry, dusty ground. However, the excessive effect of the sun held no harmful consequences for us. At La Guaira sunstroke and its effects on the brain are feared, espe-cially when yellow fever is beginning to appear. One day I was on the roof of our house observing the meridian point and the temperature difference between the sun and shade when a man came running towards me and begged me to take a drink he had brought along with him. He was a doctor who had been watching me for half an hour out in the sun from his window, without a hat on my head, exposed to the sun's rays. He assured me that coming from northern climes such imprudence would undoubtedly lead that night to an attack of yellow fever if I did not take his medicine. His prediction, however seriously argued, did not alarm me as I had had plenty of time to get acclimatized. But how could I refuse his argument when he was so polite and caring? I swallowed his potion, and the doc-tor must now have included me in the list of people he had saved from fever that year.[67]

From La Venta the road to Caracas rises another 150 toises to El Guayabo, the highest point; but I continued to use the barometer until we reached the small fort of Cuchilla. As I did not have a pass – for over five years I only needed it once, when I first disembarked – I was nearly arrested at an artillery post. To placate the angry soldiers I transformed the height of the mountains into Spanish *varas*. They were not particularly interested in this, and if I had anyone to thank for my release it was an Andalusian who became very friendly the moment I told him that the Sierra Nevada of his home were far higher than any of the mountains around Caracas.

When I first travelled the high plateaux towards Caracas I

met many travellers resting mules at the small inn of Guayabo. They lived in Caracas, and were arguing over the uprising that had recently taken place concerning the independence of the country. Joseph España had died on the scaffold.[68] The excitement and bitterness of these people, who should have agreed on such questions, surprised me. While they argued about the hate mulattos have for freed blacks, about the wealth of monks, and the difficulties of owning slaves, a cold wind, which seemed to blow down from La Silla, enveloped us in a thick mist and ended the animated discussion. Once inside the inn, an old man who before had spoken with great equanimity, said to the others that it was unwise to deal with political matters at a time when spies could be lurking around, as much in the mountains as in the cities. These words, spoken in the emptiness of the sierra, deeply impressed me; I was to hear them often during our journeys.

Caracas is the capital of a country almost twice the size of Peru and only a little smaller than Nueva Granada (Colombia). This country is officially called in Spanish the Capitanía-General de Caracas or the Capitanía-General de las Provincias de Venezuela, and has nearly a million inhabitants, of whom some 60,000 are slaves. The copper-coloured natives, the *indios*, form a large part of the population only where Spaniards found complex urban societies already established. In the Capitanía-General the rural Indian population in the cultivated areas outside the missions is insignificant. In 1800 I calculated that the Indian population was about 90,000, which is one ninth of the total population, while in Mexico it rose to almost 50 per cent.

Among the races making up the Venezuelan population blacks are important – seen both compassionately for their wretched state, and with fear due to possible violent uprisings – because they are concentrated in limited areas, not so much because of their total number. Of the 60,000 slaves in the Venezuelan provinces, 40,000 live in the province of Caracas. In the plains there are only some 4,000 to 5,000, spread around the haciendas and looking after the cattle. The number of freed slaves is very high as Spanish legislation and custom favour emancipation. A slave-owner cannot deny a slave his freedom if he can pay 300 piastres,[69] even if this would have cost the slave-owner double because of the amount of work the slave might have done.

After the blacks I was interested in the number of white *criollos*, who I call Hispano-Americans,[70] and those whites born in Europe. It is difficult to find exact figures for such a delicate issue. People in the New World, as in the Old, hate population censuses because they think they are being carried out to increase taxation. The number of white *criollos* may reach some 200,000 to 210,000 people.[71]

I remained two months in Caracas. Bonpland and I lived in a large virtually isolated house in the elevated part of the city. From the gallery we could see the La Silla peak, the serrated crest of the Galipano, and the cheerful Guaire valley whose leafy fields contrasted with the curtain of the mountains around. It was the dry season. To improve the land the savannah and grass on the rocks were set on fire. Seen from far off, these great fires created surprising light effects. Wherever the savannah climbed up the slopes and filled the gorges cut by torrential waters these strips of land on fire seemed at night like lava hanging above the valley.

If we had reasons to be pleased with the location of our house we had even more for the way we were welcomed by people from all classes. I have had the advantage, which few Spaniards can share with me, of having successively visited Caracas, Havana, Bogotá, Quito, Lima and Mexico, and of making contact with men of all ranks in these six capitals. In Mexico and Bogotá it seemed to me that interest in serious scientific studies predominated; in Quito and Lima people seemed more inclined to literature and all that flatters a lively imagination; in Havana and Caracas, there predominated a broader culture in political matters, more open criteria about the state of the colonies and metropolis. Intense commerce with Europe and the Caribbean Sea have powerfully influenced the social evolution of Cuba and the beautiful provinces of Venezuela. Nowhere else in Spanish America does civilization appear so European.

In the colonies skin colour is the real badge of nobility. In Mexico as well as in Peru, at Caracas as in Cuba, a barefoot man with a white skin is often heard to say: 'Does that rich person think himself whiter than I am?' Because Europe pours so many people into America, it can easily be seen that the axiom 'Todo blanco es caballero' (All whites are gentlemen) must wound the pretensions of many ancient and aristocratic European families. We do not find among the people of Spanish origin that cold and pretentious air which modern civilization has made more common in Europe than in Spain. Conviviality, candour and great simplicity of manner unite the different classes in the colonies.[72]

In several families I found a feeling for culture. They know about the great works of French and Italian literature; music pleases them, and is played with talent, which like all of the arts unites the different social classes. The exact sciences, and drawing and painting, are not as well established here as they are in Mexico and Bogotá, thanks to the liberality of the government and the patriotism of the Spanish people.

In a country with such ravishing views I hoped to find many people who might know about the high mountains in the region; and yet we could not find one person who had climbed to La Silla's peak. Hunters do not climb high enough, and in these countries nobody would dream of going out to look for alpine plants, or to study rock strata, or take barometers up to high altitudes. They are used to a dull domestic life, and avoid fatigue and sudden changes in climate as if they live not to enjoy life but to prolong it.

The Captain-General, Sr Guevara, lent us guides; they were negroes who knew the way that led to the coast along the sierra ridge near the western peak. It is the path used by smugglers, but neither our guides nor the most experienced militia, formed to chase the clandestine traffickers, had ever climbed to the eastern La Silla peak.

We set off before sunrise, at five in the morning, with the slaves carrying our instruments. Our party consisted of eighteen people, and we advanced in Indian file along a narrow path on a steep grassy slope. From La Puerta the path becomes steep. You have to lean forward to climb. The thick grass was very slippery because of the prolonged drought. Cramp-irons and iron-tipped sticks would have been very useful. Short grass covers the gneiss rocks; it is impossible to grip it or dig steps into it as in softer soil. More tiring than dangerous, the climb soon disheartened the men accompanying us who were not used to mountain climbing. We wasted a lot of time waiting for them, and did not decide to continue alone until we saw them returning down the mountain instead of climbing up after us. Bonpland and I foresaw that we would soon be covered in thick fog. Fearing that our guides would use the fog to abandon us we made those carrying the instruments go ahead of us. The familiar chatting of the negroes contrasted with the taciturn seriousness of the Indians who had accompanied us up to then. They joked about those who had spent hours preparing for the ascent, and then abandoned it straightaway.

After four hours walking through savannah we reached a little wood composed of shrubs called *el pejual*, perhaps because of the amount of *pejoa* (*Gaultheria odorata*) there, a plant with strong-smelling leaves. The mountain slope became more gentle and we could pleasurably study the plants of the region. Perhaps nowhere else can so many beautiful and useful plants be discovered in such a small space. At 1,000 toises high the raised plains of La Silla gave place to a zone of shrubs that reminded one of the *páramos* and *punas*.

Even when nature does not produce the same species in analogous climates, either in the plains of isothermal parallels or on tablelands whose temperature resembles that of places nearer the poles,[73] we still noticed a striking resemblance of appearance and physiognomy in the vegetation of the most distant countries. This phenomenon is one of the most curious in the history of organic forms. I say history, for reason cannot stop man forming hypotheses on the origin of things; he will always puzzle himself with insoluble problems relating to the distribution of beings.

A grass from Switzerland grows on the granitic rocks of the Magellan Strait.[74] New Holland contains more than forty

European phanerogamous plants. The greater amount of these plants, found equally in the temperate zones of both hemispheres, are completely absent in the intermediary or equinoctial regions, on plains and on mountains. A hairy-leafed violet, which signifies the last of the phanerogamous plants on Tenerife, and long thought specific to that island, can be seen 300 leagues further north near the snowy Pyrenean peaks. Grasses and sedges of Germany, Arabia and Senegal have been recognized among plants collected by Bonpland and myself on the cold Mexican tablelands, on the burning Orinoco banks and on the Andes, and at Quito in the Southern hemisphere. How can one believe that plants migrate over regions covered by sea? How have the germs of life, identical in appearance and in internal structure, developed at unequal distances from the poles and from the oceans, in places that share similar temperatures? Despite the influence of air pressure on the plants' vital functions, and despite the greater or lesser degree of light, it is heat, unequally distributed in different seasons, that must be considered vegetation's most powerful stimulus.

The amount of identical species in the two continents and in the two hemispheres is far less than early travellers once led us to think. The high mountains of equinoctial America have their plantains, valerians, arenarias, ranunculuses, medlars, oaks and pines, which from their features we could confuse with European ones, but they are all specifically different. When nature does not present the same species, she repeats the same genera. Neighbouring species are often found at enormous distances from each other, in low regions of a temperate zone, and on mountains on the equator. And, as we found on La Silla at Caracas, they are not the European genera that have colonized mountains of the torrid zone, but genera of the same tribe, which have taken their place and are hard to distinguish.

The more we study the distribution of organized life on the globe, the more we tend to abandon the hypothesis of migration. The Andes chain divides the whole of South America into two unequal longitudinal parts. At the foot of this chain, on both east and west, we found many plants that were specifically identical. The various passes on the Andes would not let any vegetation from warm regions cross from the Pacific coast to the Amazon banks. When a peak reaches a great height, whether in the middle of low mountains and plains, or in the centre of an archipelago raised by volcanic fires, its summit is covered with alpine plants, many of which are also found at immense distances on other mountains under similar climates. Such are the general phenomena of plant distribution.

There is a saying that a mountain is high enough to reach the rhododendron and befaria limit, in the same way one says one has reached the snow limit. In employing this expression it is tacitly assumed that under identical temperatures a certain kind of vegetation must grow. This is not strictly true. The pines of Mexico are absent in the Peruvian Andes. The Caracas La Silla is not covered with the same oaks that flourish in New Granada at the same height. Identity of forms suggests an analogy of climate, but in similar climates the species may be very diversified.

The attractive Andean rhododendron, or befaria, was first observed by Mutis[75] near Pamplona and Bogotá, in the 4th and 7th degree of latitude. It was so little known before our expedition up La Silla that it was not to be found in any European herbal. The learned editors of *The Flora of Peru* had even described it under another name. The two species of befaria we brought down from La Silla are specifically different from those at Pamplona and Bogotá. Near the equator the Andean rhododendrons cover the mountains right up to 1,600 and 1,700 toises. Going further north on La Silla we find them lower, below 1,000 toises. Befaria recently discovered in Florida, in latitude 30, grow on low hills. Thus, within 600 leagues in latitude, these shrubs descend towards the plains in proportion as their distance from the equator increases.

Due to the thickness of the vegetation, made up of a plant of the Musaceae family, it was hard to find a path. We had to make one through that jungle of musaceous plants; the negroes led us, cutting a path with machetes. We saw the peak at intervals through breaks in the cloud, but soon we were covered in a thick mist and could only proceed using the compass; with each step we risked finding ourselves at the edge of a precipice, which fell 6,000 feet down to the sea. We had to stop, surrounded by cloud down to the ground, and we began to doubt if we would reach the eastern peak before sunset. Luckily the negroes carrying the water and the food had arrived, so we decided to eat something. But the meal did not last long because either the Capuchin father had not calculated our numbers properly or the slaves had already eaten everything. We found only olives and some bread. We had been walking for nine hours without stopping or finding water. Our guides seemed to lose heart, and wanted to go back. Bonpland and I had difficulty in persuading them to stay with us.

To reach the peak we had to approach as near as possible to the great cliff that falls to the coast. We needed three quarters of an hour to reach the top. While sitting on the peak observing the inclination of the magnetic needle I saw a great number of hairy bees, somewhat smaller than the northern European ones, crawling all over my hands. These bees nest in the ground and rarely fly. Their apathy seemed to derive from the cold mountain air. Here they are called *angelitos* (little angels) because they hardly ever sting. Until you are sure about the harmlessness of these *angelitos* you remain suspicious. I confess that often during astronomic observations I almost dropped my instruments when I realized my face and hands were covered with these hairy bees. Our guides assured us that these bees only attacked when you annoyed them by picking them up by their legs. I did not try.

It was half past four in the afternoon when we finished our observations. Satisfied with the success of our journey we forgot that there might be dangers descending steep slopes covered with a smooth, slippery grass in the dark. We did not arrive at the valley bottom until ten at night. We were exhausted and thirsty after walking for fifteen hours, practically without stopping. The soles of our feet were cut and torn by the rough, rocky soil and the hard, dry grass stalks, for we had been forced to pull our boots off as the ground was too slippery. We spent the night at the foot of La Silla. Our friends at Caracas had been able to follow us on the summit with binoculars. They liked hearing our account of the expedition but were not happy with the result of our measurements, for La Silla was not as high as the highest mountains in the Pyrenees.

CHAPTER 12

WE LEFT CARACAS on the 7th of February, on a fresh afternoon, ready to begin our journey to the Orinoco. The memory of this period is today more painful than it was years ago. In those remote countries our friends have lost their lives in the bloody revolutions that gave them freedom and then alternatively deprived them of it.[76] The house where we lived is now a heap of rubble. Terrible earthquakes have transformed the shape of the ground; the city I described has disappeared. On the same spot, on the fissured ground, another city is slowly being built. The ruins, tombs for a large population, have already turned into shelter for human beings.

I reckoned that it was my duty in this book to record all the data obtained from reliable sources concerning the seismic shocks that on the 26th of March 1812 destroyed the city of Caracas; in all the province of Venezuela more than 20,000 people perished. As a historian of nature, the traveller should note down the moment when great natural calamities happen, and investigate the causes and relations, and establish fixed points in the rapid course of time, in the transformations that succeed each other ceaselessly so that he can compare them with previous catastrophes.[77]

On my arrival at Terra Firma I was struck by the correlation between two natural phenomena: the destruction of Cumaná on the 14th of December 1797 and volcanic eruptions in the smaller West Indian Islands. Something similar happened at Caracas on the 26th of March 1812. In 1797 the volcano on Guadeloupe Island, on the Cumaná coast, seemed to have reacted; fifteen years later another volcano on San Vincente also reacted, and its effects were felt as far as Caracas and the banks of the Apure. Probably both times the centre of the eruption was at an enormous depth in the earth, equidistant from the points on the earth's surface that felt the movement. The shock felt at Caracas in December 1811 was the only one that preceded the terrible catastrophe of the 26th of March 1812. In Caracas, and for 90 leagues around, not one drop of rain had fallen for five months up to the destruction of the capital. The 26th of March was a very hot day; there was no wind and no cloud. It was Ascension Day and most people had congregated in the churches. Nothing suggested the horrors to come. At seven minutes past four the first shock was felt. 'It was so violent that the church bells rang, and lasted five to six seconds. It was followed immediately by another lasting ten to twelve seconds when the ground seemed to ripple like boiling water. People thought the quake was over when an infernal din came from under the ground. It was like thunder but louder and longer than any tropical storm. Following this there was a vertical movement lasting three seconds followed by undulations. The shocks coming from these contrary movements tore the city apart. Thousands of people were trapped in the churches and houses.'[78]

On the 8th of February we set off at sunrise to cross Higuer-ote, a group of tall mountains separating the valleys of Caracas and Aragua. Descending the woody slopes of Higuerote towards the south-west we reached the small village of San Pedro, 584 toises high, located in a basin where several valleys meet. Banana trees, potatoes and coffee grow there. In an inn (*pulpería*) we met several European Spaniards working at the Tobacco Office. Their bad temper contrasted with our mood. Tired by the route, they vented their anger by cursing the wretched country ('estas tierras infelices') where they were doomed to live, while we never wearied of admiring the wild scenery, the fertile earth and mild climate. From Las Lagu-netas we descended into the Tuy river valley. This western slope is called Las Cocuyzas, and is covered with two plants with agave leaves; the maguey of Cocuzza and the maguey of Cocuy. The latter belongs to the *Yucca* genus. Its sweet fer-mented juice is distilled into an alcohol, and I have seen people eat its young green leaves. The fibres of the full-grown leaves are made into extremely long cords. At Caracas cathedral a maguey cord has suspended the weight of a 350-pound clock for fifteen years. We spent two very agreeable days at the plantation of Don José de Manterola who, when young, had been attached to the Spanish Legation in Russia. Brought up and protected by Sr de Xavedra, one of the more enlightened administrators in Caracas, de Manterola wanted to leave for Europe when that famous man became minister. The governor of the province, fearing de Manterola's prestige, arrested him in the harbour and when the order from Spain finally arrived to release him from such an unjust arrest the minister had fallen from grace.

The farm we lodged at was a fine sugar-cane plantation. The ground is smooth like the bed of a dried lake. The Tuy river winds through land covered with banana trees and a little wood of *Hura crepitans*, *Erythrina corallodrendron*, and figs with nymphae leaves. The river is formed with quartz pebbles. I can think of no more pleasant bathe than that in the Tuy. The crystal-clear water remains at 18.6 °C. This is cool for the climate; the sources of the river are in the surrounding mountains. The owner's house is situated on a hillock surrounded by huts for the negroes. Those who are married provide their own food. They are given, as everywhere in the Aragua valleys, a plot of land to cultivate, which they work on their Saturdays and Sundays, the free days of the week. They have chicken, and sometimes a pig. The owner boasts of their contentment in the same way that northern European landowners boast about the happy peasants on their land. The day we arrived three runaway negroes had been captured; newly bought slaves. I dreaded witnessing those punishments that ruin the charm of the countryside wherever there are slaves. Luckily, the blacks were treated humanely.

In this plantation, as in all the provinces of Venezuela, you can distinguish, from afar, three kinds of sugar cane by the colour of their leaves; the old Creole cane, Otaheite cane and Batavia cane. The first has a darker green leaf, a thinner stalk with knots close together. It was the first sugar cane introduced from India to Sicily, the Canaries and the West Indies.

The second is lighter green; its stalk is fatter, more succulent. The whole plant seems more luxuriant. It arrived thanks to the voyages of Bougainville, Cook and Bligh. Bougainville brought it to Mauritius, where it went to Cayenne, Martinique and from 1792 to the rest of the West Indies. Otaheite sugar cane, the *to* of the islanders, is one of the most important agricultural acquisitions due to the voyages of naturalists. On the same plot of land it gives a third of *vezou* (juice) more than Creole cane, but due to the thickness of its stalk and strength of its ligneous fibres furnishes much more fuel. This is an advantage in the West Indian Islands where the destruction of the forests has forced planters to use the bagasse as fuel for their furnaces. The third species, the violet sugar cane, is called Batavia or Guinea cane, and certainly comes from Java. Its leaves are purple and large and it is preferred in Caracas for making rum.[79] At Tuy they were busy finishing a ditch to bring irrigation water. This enterprise had cost the owner 7,000 piastres to build and 4,000 piastres in lawsuits with his neighbours. While the lawyers argued over the canal, which was only half finished, de Manterola had already begun to doubt the worth of his project. I took the level of the ground with a *lunette d'épreuve* placed on an artificial horizon and found that the dam had been placed 8 feet too low. What sums of money have not been uselessly spent in the Spanish colonies founding constructions on poor levelling!

The Tuy valley has its 'gold mine', as do nearly all the places near mountains inhabited by white Europeans. I was assured that in 1780 foreign gold seekers had been seen extracting gold nuggets and had set up a place for washing the sand. The overseer of a nearby plantation had followed their tracks and after his death a jacket with gold buttons was found among his belongings, which according to popular logic meant that they came from the gold seam, later covered by a rock fall. It was no use my saying that from simply looking at the ground, without opening up a deep gallery, I would not be able to decide if there once had been a mine there – I had to yield to my host's entreaties. For twenty years the overseer's jacket had been the talking-point of the area. Gold dug out from the ground has, in the people's eyes, a special lure unrelated to the diligent farmer harvesting a fertile land under a gentle climate.

Our guides led us to the 'mine'. We turned west, and finally reached the Quebrada de Oro. On the hillside there was hardly a trace of a quartz seam. The landslide, caused by rain, had so transformed the ground that we could not even think of exploring it. Huge trees now grew where twenty years before gold seekers had worked. It is likely that there are veins in the mica-slate containing this venerable metal, but how could I judge if it was worth exploiting or if the metal was to be found in nodules? To compensate our efforts, we set to botanizing in the thick wood around the Hato.

We left the Manterola plantation on the 11th of February at sunrise. A little before reaching Mamon we stopped at a farm belonging to the Monteras family. A negress, more than a hundred years old, was sitting outside a mud-and-reed hut. Her age was known because she had been a creole slave. She seemed to enjoy amazing good health. 'I keep her in the sun' (*La tengo al sol*), said her grandson. 'The heat keeps her alive.' This treatment seemed rather harsh as the sun's rays fell vertically on to her. Blacks and Indians reach very advanced ages in the torrid zone. Hilario Pari, a native of Peru, died at the extraordinary age of one hundred and forty-three, having been married ninety years.

Beyond the village of Turmero, towards Maracay, you can observe on the distant horizon something that seems to be a tumulus covered in vegetation. But it is not a hill, nor a group of trees growing close together, but one single tree, the famous *zamang de Guayre*, known through the country for the enormous extent of its branches, which form a semi-spherical head some 576 feet in circumference. The zamang is a fine species of the mimosa family whose twisted branches are forked. We rested a long time under this vegetable roof. The branches extend like an enormous umbrella and bend towards the ground. Parasitical plants grow on the branches and in the dried bark. The inhabitants, especially the Indians, venerate this tree, which the first conquerors found in more or less the same state as it is in today. We heard with satisfaction that the present owner of the zamang had brought a lawsuit against a cultivator accused of cutting off a branch. The case was tried and the man found guilty.

We reached Maracay late. The people who had been recommended to us were away, but no sooner had the inhabitants realized our worries than they came from everywhere to offer us lodging for our instruments and mules. It has been said a thousand times, but the traveller always feels the need to repeat that the Spanish colonies are the authentic land of hospitality, even in places where industry and commerce have created wealth and a little culture. A Canarian family warmly invited us to stay, and cooked an excellent dinner. The master of the house was away on a business trip and his young wife had just given birth. She was wild with joy when she heard that we were due to pass through Angostura where her husband was. Through us he would learn about the birth of his first child. As we were about to leave we were shown the baby; we had seen her the night before, asleep, but the mother wanted us to see her awake. We promised to describe her features one by one to the father, but when she saw our instruments and books the good woman worried: 'On such a long journey, and with so many other things to think about, you could easily forget the colour of my baby's eyes!'

We spent seven agreeable days at the Hacienda de Cura in a small hut surrounded by thickets; the house itself, located in a sugar plantation, was infected with bubos, a skin disease common among slaves in the valleys. We lived like the rich; we bathed twice a day, slept three times and ate three meals in twenty-four hours. The lake water was warm, some 24 °C to 25 °C. The coolest bathing place was under the shade of ceibas and zamangs at Toma in a stream that rushes out of the granite Rincón del Diablo mountains. Entering this bath was fearsome, not because of the insects but because of the little brown hairs covering the pods of the *Dolichos pruriens*. When these small hairs, called *pica pica*, stick to your body they cause violent irritations. You feel the sting but cannot see what stung you.

During our stay at Cura we made numerous excursions to

the rocky islands in the middle of Lake Valencia, to the hot springs at Mariara, and the high mountain called El Cucurucho de Coco. A narrow, dangerous path leads to the port of Turiamo and the famous coastal cacao plantations. Throughout all our excursions we were surprised not only by the progress of culture but also by the increase in the numbers of the free, hard-working population, used to manual work and too poor to buy slaves. Everywhere whites and mulattos had bought small isolated farms. Our host, whose father enjoyed an income of 40,000 piastres a year, had more land than he could farm; he distributed plots in the Aragua valley to poor families who wanted to grow cotton. He tried to surround his enormous plantation with free working men, because they wanted to work for themselves, or for others. Count Tovar was busy trying to abolish slavery and hoped to make slaves less necessary for the important estates, and to offer the freed slaves land to become farmers themselves. When he left for Europe he had broken up and rented land around Cura. Four years later, on returning to America, he found fine cotton fields and a little village called Punta Samuro, which we often visited with him. The inhabitants are all mulatto, *zambow*[80] and freed slaves. The rent is ten piastres a *fanega* of land; it is paid in cash or cotton. As the small farmers are often in need, they sell their cotton at modest prices. They sell it even before harvest, and this advance is used by the rich landowners to make the poor dependent on them as day workers. The price of labour is less than it is in France. A free man is paid five piastres a month without food, which costs very little as meat and vegetables are abundant. I like quoting these details about colonial agriculture because they prove to Europeans that there is no doubt that sugar, cotton and indigo can be produced by free men, and that the miserable slaves can become peasants, farmers and landowners.

CHAPTER 13

LAKE TACARIGUA — HOT SPRINGS OF MARIARA — THE
TOWN OF NUEVA VALENCIA — DESCENT TO THE PUERTO
CABELLO COASTS

THE ARAGUA VALLEYS form a basin, closed between granitic
and calcareous mountain ranges of unequal height. Due to the
land's peculiar configuration, the small rivers of the Aragua
valleys form an enclosed system and flow into a basin blocked
off on all sides; these rivers do not flow to the ocean but end
in an inland lake, and thanks to constant evaporation lose
themselves, so to speak, in the air. These rivers and lakes determine the fertility of the soil and agricultural produce in the
valleys. The aspect of the place and the experience of some
fifty years show that the water-level is not constant; that the
balance between evaporation and inflow is broken. As the lake
lies 1,000 feet above the neighbouring Calabozo steppes, and
1,332 feet above sea-level, it was thought that the water filtered
out through a subterranean channel. As islands emerge, and
the water-level progressively decreases, it is feared the lake
might completely dry out.

Lake Valencia, called Tacarigua by the Indians, is larger
than Lake Neuchâtel in Switzerland; its general form
resembles Lake Geneva, situated at about the same altitude.
Its opposite banks are notably different: the southern one is
deserted, stripped of vegetation and virtually uninhabited; a
curtain of high mountains gives it a sad, monotonous quality;
in contrast, the northern side is pleasant and rural, and has rich
plantations of sugar cane, coffee and cotton. Paths bordered
with cestrum, azedaracs, and other perpetually flowering
shrubs cross the plain and link the isolated farms. All the
houses are surrounded by trees. The ceiba (*Bombax hibiscifol-
ius*), with large yellow flowers, and the erythrina, with purple
ones, whose overlapping branches give the countryside its

special quality. During the season of drought, when a thick mist floats above the burning ground, artificial irrigation keeps the land green and wild. Every now and then granite blocks pierce through the cultivated ground; large masses of rocks rise up in the middle of the valley. Some succulent plants grow in its bare and cracked walls, preparing mould for the coming centuries. Often a fig tree, or a clusia with fleshy leaves, growing in clefts, crowns these isolated little summits. With their dry withered branches they look like signals along a cliff. The shape of these heights betrays the secret of their ancient origins; for when the whole valley was still submerged and waves lapped the foot of the Mariara peaks (El Rincón del Diablo) and the coastal chain, these rocky hills were shoals and islands.

But the shores of Lake Valencia are not famed solely for their picturesque beauties: the basin presents several phenomena whose interpretation holds great interest for natural historians and for the inhabitants. What causes the lowering of the lake's water-level? Is it receding faster than before? Will the balance between the flowing in and the draining out be restored, or will the fear that the lake might dry up be proved justified?

I have no doubt that from remotest times the whole valley was filled with water. Everywhere the shape of the promontories and their steep slopes reveals the ancient shore of this alpine lake. We find vast tracts of land, formerly flooded, now cultivated with banana, sugar cane and cotton. Wherever a hut is built on the lake shore you can see how year by year the water recedes. As the water decreases, you can see how islands begin to join the land while others form promontories or become hills. We visited two islands still completely surrounded by water and found, under the scrub, on small flats between 4 and 8 toises above the water-level, fine sand mixed with helicites deposited by waves. On all these islands you will discover clear traces of the gradual lowering of the water.

The destruction of the forests, the clearing of the plains, and the cultivation of indigo over half a century has affected the amount of water flowing in as well as the evaporation of the soil and the dryness of the air, which forcefully explains why the present Lake Valencia is decreasing. By felling trees that cover the tops and sides of mountains men everywhere have ensured two calamities at the same time for the future: lack of fuel, and scarcity of water. Trees, by the nature of their perspiration, and the radiation from their leaves in a cloudless sky, surround themselves with an atmosphere that is constantly cool and misty. They affect the amount of springs by sheltering the soil from the sun's direct actions and reducing the rainwater's evaporation. When forests are destroyed, as they are everywhere in America by European planters, with imprudent haste, the springs dry up completely, or merely trickle. River beds remain dry part of the year and are then turned into torrents whenever it rains heavily on the heights. As grass and moss disappear with the brushwood from the mountainsides, so rainwater is unchecked in its course. Instead of slowly raising the river level by filtrations, the heavy rains dig channels into the hillsides, dragging down loose soil, and forming sudden, destructive floods. Thus, the clearing of forests, the absence of permanent springs, and torrents are three closely connected phenomena. Countries in different hemispheres like Lombardy bordered by the Alps, and Lower Peru between the Pacific and the Andes, confirm this assertion.

Until the middle of the last century the mountains surrounding the Aragua valley were covered in forests. Huge trees of the mimosa, ceiba and fig families shaded the lake shore and kept it cool. The sparsely populated plain was invaded by shrubs, fallen tree trunks and parasitical plants, and was covered in thick grass so that heat was not lost as easily as from cultivated ground, which is not sheltered from the sun's rays. When the trees are felled, and sugar cane, indigo and cotton are planted, springs and natural supplies to the lake dry up. It is hard to form a fair idea of the enormous amount of evaporation taking place in the torrid zone, especially in a valley surrounded by steep mountains where maritime breezes blow, and whose ground is completely flat as if levelled by water. The heat prevailing on the lake shore is comparable to that in Naples and Sicily.

Lake Valencia is full of islands, which embellish the countryside with the picturesque form of their rocks and by the kind of vegetation that covers them. Tropical lakes have this advantage over alpine ones. The islands, without counting Morro and Cabrera, which are already joined to the mainland, are fifteen in number. They are partially cultivated, and very fertile due to the vapours rising from the lake. Burro, the largest island, some 2 miles long, is inhabited by mestizo families who rear goats. These simple people rarely visit the Mocundo coast. The lake seems gigantic to them: they produce bananas, cassava, milk and fish. A hut built of reeds, some hammocks woven with cotton grown in neighbouring fields, a large stone on which they build their fires, and the ligneous fruit of the *tutuma* to draw water with are their sole household needs. The old mestizo who offered us goat's milk had a lovely daughter. We learned from our guide that isolation had made him as suspicious as if he lived in a city. The night before our arrival some hunters had visited the island. Night surprised them and they preferred to sleep out in the open rather than return to Mocundo. This news spread alarm around the island. The father forced his young daughter to climb a very tall zamang or mimosa, which grows on the plain at some distance from the hut. He slept at the foot of this tree, and didn't let his daughter down until the hunters had left.

The lake is usually full of fish; there are three species with soft flesh, which are not very tasty: the *guavina*, the *bagre* and the *sardina*. The last two reach the lake from streams. The *guavina*, which I sketched on the spot, was some 20 inches long and 3 to 5 inches wide. It is perhaps a new species of Gronovius's *Erythrina*. It has silver scales bordered with green. This fish is extremely voracious and destroys other species. Fishermen assured us that a little crocodile, the *bava*, which often swam near as we bathed, contributed to the destruction of the fish. We never managed to catch this reptile and examine it close up. It is said to be very innocent; yet its habits, like its shape, clearly resemble the alligator or *Crocodilus acutus*. It swims so that only the tips of its snout and tail show: it lies at midday on deserted beaches.

The island of Chamberg is a granitic outcrop some 200 feet high, with two peaks linked by a saddle. The sides of the rock are bare; only a few white flowering clusia manage to grow there. But the view of the lake and surrounding plantations is magnificent, especially at sunset when thousands of heron, flamingo and wild duck fly over the water to roost on the island.

It is thought that some of the plants that grow on the rocky islands of Lake Valencia are exclusive to them because they have not been discovered elsewhere. Among these are the papaw tree of the lake (*papaya de la laguna*), and a tomato[81] from Cura Island; this differs from our *Solanum lycopersicum* in that its fruit is round and small but very tasty. The papaw of the lake is common also on Cura Island and at Cabo Blanco. Its trunk is slenderer than the ordinary papaw, but its fruit is half the size and completely round, without projecting ribs. This fruit, which I have often eaten, is extremely sweet.

The areas around the lake are unhealthy only in the dry season when the water-level falls and the mud bed is exposed to the sun's heat. The bank, shaded by woods of *Coccoloba barbadensis* and decorated with beautiful lilies, reminds one, because of the similar aquatic plants found there, of the marshy banks of our European lakes. Here we find pondweed (potamogeton), chara and cat's-tails 3 feet high, hardly different from the *Typha angustifolia* of our marshes. Only after very careful examination do we recognize each plant to be a distinct species, peculiar to the New World. How many plants from the Strait of Magellan to the cordilleras of Quito have once been confused with northern temperate ones owing to their analogy in form and appearance!

Some of the rivers flowing into Lake Valencia come from thermal springs, worthy of special note. These springs gush out at three points from the coastal granitic chain at Onoto, Mariara and Las Trincheras. I was only able to carefully examine the physical and geological relations of the thermal waters of Mariara and Las Trincheras. All the springs contain small amounts of sulphuretted hydrogen gas. The stink of rotten eggs, typical of this gas, could only be smelled very close to the spring. In one of the puddles, which had a temperature of 56.2 °C, bubbles burst up at regular intervals of two to three minutes. I was not able to ignite the gas, not even the small amounts in the bubbles as they burst on the warm surface of the water, nor after collecting it in a bottle, despite feeling nausea caused more by the heat than by the gas. The water, when cold, is tasteless and quite drinkable.

South of the ravine, in the plain that stretches to the lake shore, another less hot and less gassy sulphureous spring gushes out. The thermometer reached only 42 °C. The water collects in a basin surrounded by large trees. The unhappy slaves throw themselves in this pool at sunset, covered in dust after working in the indigo and sugar-cane fields. Despite the water being 12 °C to 14 °C warmer than the air the negroes call it refreshing. In the torrid zone this word is used for anything that restores your strength, calms nerves or produces a feeling of well-being. We also experienced the salutary effects of this bath. We had our hammocks slung in the trees shading this pond and spent a whole day in this place so rich in plants. Near this *baño de Mariara* we found the *volador* or gyrocarpus. The winged fruits of this tree seem like flying beings when they separate from the stem. On shaking the branches of the *volador*, we saw the air filled with its fruits, all falling together. We sent some fruit to Europe, and they germinated in Berlin, Paris and Malmaison. The numerous plants of the *volador*, now seen in hothouses, owe their origin to the only tree of its kind found near Mariara.

While following the local custom of drying ourselves in the sun after our bath, half wrapped in towels, a small mulatto approached. After greeting us in a serious manner, he made a long speech about the properties of the Mariara waters, the many sick people who over the years have come here, and the advantageous position of the spring between Valencia and Caracas, where morals became more and more dissolute. He showed us his house, a little hut covered with palm leaves in an enclosure near by, next to a stream that fed the pool. He assured us that we would find there all the comforts we could imagine; nails to hang our hammocks, oxhides to cover reed beds, jugs of fresh water, and those large lizards (iguanas) whose flesh is considered to be a refreshing meal after a bathe. From his speech we reckoned that this poor man had mistaken us for sick people wanting to install themselves near the spring. He called himself 'the inspector of the waters and the *pulpero* of the place'. He stopped talking to us as soon as he saw we were there out of curiosity – 'para ver no más' as they say in these colonies, 'an ideal place for lazy people'.

On the 21st of February, at nightfall, we left the pretty Hacienda de Cura and set off for Guacara and Nueva Valencia. As the heat of the day was stifling we travelled by night. We crossed the village of Punta Zamuro at the foot of Las Viruelas mountain. The road is lined with large zamangs, or mimosa trees, reaching some 60 feet high. Their almost horizontal branches meet at more than 150 feet distance. I have never seen a canopy of leaves so thick and beautiful as these. The night was dark: the Rincón del Diablo and its dentated rocks appeared every now and then, illuminated by the brilliance of the burning savannahs, or wrapped in clouds of reddish smoke. In the thickest part of the brush our horses panicked when they heard the howl of an animal that seemed to be following us. It was an enormous jaguar that had been roaming these mountains for three years. It had escaped from the most daring hunters. It attacked horses and mules, even when they were penned in, but not lacking food had not yet attacked human beings. Our negro guide screamed wildly to scare off the beast, which he obviously did not achieve.

We spent the 23rd of February in the marquis of Toro's house, in the village of Guacara, a large Indian community. The Indians live a life of ease because they have just won a legal case restoring lands disputed by whites. An avenue of carolineas leads from Guacara to Mocundo, a rich sugar plantation belonging to the Moro family. We found a rare garden there with an artificial clump of trees, and, on top of a granitic outcrop near a stream, a pavilion with a *mirador* or viewpoint. From here you see a splendid panorama over the west of the lake, the surrounding mountains and a wood of palm trees. The sugar-cane fields with their tender green leaves seem like a great plain. Everything suggests abundance, although those who work the land have to sacrifice their freedom.

The preparation of sugar, its boiling, and the claying, is not well done in Terra Firma because it is made for local consumption. More *papelón* is sold than either refined or raw sugar. *Papelón* is an impure sugar in the form of little yellowish-brown loaves. It is a blend of molasses and mucilaginous matter. The poorest man eats *papelón* the way in Europe he eats cheese. It is said to be nutritious. Fermented with water it yields *guarapo*, the favourite local drink.

The city of New Valencia occupies a large area of ground, but its population is of some 6,000 to 7,000 souls. The roads are very wide, the market place (*plaza mayor*) is disproportionately large. As the houses are few the difference between the population and the land they occupy is greater even than at Caracas. Many of the whites of European stock, especially the poorest, leave their town houses and live for most of the year in their cotton and indigo plantations. They dare to work with their own hands, which, given the rigid prejudices in this country, would be a disgrace in the city. The industriousness of the inhabitants has greatly increased after freedom was granted to business in Puerto Cabello, now open as a major port (*puerto mayor*) to ships coming directly from Spain.

Founded in 1555, under the government of Villacinda, by Alonso Díaz Moreno, Nueva Valencia is twelve years older than Caracas. Some justifiably regret that Valencia has not become the capital of the country. Its situation on the plain, next to a lake, recalls Mexico City. If you consider the easy communications offered by the Aragua valleys with the plains and rivers entering the Orinoco; if you accept the possibility of opening up navigation into the interior through the Pao and Portuguesa rivers as far as the Orinoco mouth, the Casiquiare and the Amazon, you realize that the capital of the vast Venezuelan provinces would have been better placed next to the superb Puerto Cabello, under a pure, serene sky, and not next to the barely sheltered bay of La Guaira, in a temperate but always misty valley.

Only those who have seen the quantity of ants that infest the countries of the torrid zone can picture the destruction and the sinking of the ground caused by these insects. They abound to such a degree in Valencia that their excavations resemble underground canals, which flood with water during the rains and threaten buildings. Here they have not used the extraordinary means employed by the monks on the island of Santo Domingo when troops of ants ravaged the fine plains of La Vega. The monks, after trying to burn the ant larvae and fumigate the nests, told the inhabitants to choose a saint by lot who would act as an Abogado contra las Hormigas. The choice fell on Saint Saturnin, and the ants disappeared as soon as the saint's festival was celebrated.

On the morning of the 27th of February we visited the hot springs of La Trinchera, 3 leagues from Valencia. They flow more fully than any we had seen until then, forming a rivulet, which in the dry season maintains a depth of some 2 feet 8 inches of water. The carefully taken water temperature was 90.3 °C. We had breakfast near the spring: our eggs were cooked in less than four minutes in the hot water. The rock from which the spring gushes is of real coarse-grained granite. Whenever the water evaporates in the air, it forms sediments and incrustations of carbonate of lime. The exuberance of the vegetation around the basin surprised us. Mimosas with delicate pinnate leaves, clusias and figs send their roots into the muddy ground, which is as hot as 85 °C. Two currents flow down on parallel courses, and the Indians showed us how to prepare a bath of whatever temperature you want by opening a hole in the ground between the two streams. The sick, who come to La Trinchera to take steam baths, build a kind of framework with branches and thin reeds above the spring. They lie down naked on this frame, which, as far as I could see, was not very strong, perhaps even dangerous.

As we approached the coast the heat became stifling. A reddish mist covered the horizon. It was sunset but no sea breeze blew. We rested in the lonely farm called both Cambury and House of the Canarian (Casa del Isleño). The hot-water river, along whose bank we travelled, became deeper. A 9-foot-long crocodile lay dead on the sand. We wanted to examine its teeth and the inside of its mouth, but having been exposed to the sun for weeks it stank so bad we had to climb back on to our horses.

More than 10,000 mules are exported every year from Puerto Cabello. It is curious to see these animals being embarked. They are pulled down with lassos and lifted on board by something akin to a crane. In the boat they are placed in double rows, and with the rolling and pitching of the boat can barely stand. To terrify them, and keep them docile, a drum is beaten day and night.

From Puerto Cabello we returned to the Aragua valley, and stopped again at the Barbula plantation through which the new road to Nueva Valencia will pass. Weeks before we had been told about a tree whose sap is a nourishing milk. They call it the 'cow tree', and assured us that negroes on the estates drank quantities of this vegetable milk. As the milky juices of plants are acrid, bitter and more or less poisonous, it seemed hard to believe what we heard, but during our stay in Barbula we proved that nobody had exaggerated the properties of *palo de vaca*. This fine tree is similar to the *Chrysophyllum cainito* (broad-leafed star-apple). When incisions are made in the trunk it yields abundant glutinous milk; it is quite thick, devoid of all acridity, and has an agreeable balmy smell. It was offered to us in *tutuma*-fruit – or gourd – bowls, and we drank a lot before going to bed, and again in the morning, without any ill effects. Only its viscosity makes it a little disagreeable. Negroes and free people who work on the plantations dip their maize and cassava bread in it. The overseer of the estate told us that negroes put on weight during the period that the *palo de vaca* exudes milk. This notable tree appears to be peculiar to the cordillera coast. At Caucagua the natives called it the 'milk tree'. They say they can recognize the trunks that yield most juice from the thickness and colour of the leaves. No botanist has so far known this plant.

Of all the natural phenomena that I have seen during my voyages few have produced a greater impression than the *palo de vaca*. What moved me so deeply was not the proud shadows of the jungles, nor the majestic flow of the rivers, nor the mountains covered with eternal snows, but a few drops of a vegetable juice that brings to mind all the power and fertility of nature. On a barren rocky wall grows a tree with dry leathery leaves; its large woody roots hardly dig into the rocky ground. For months not a drop of rain wets its leaves; the branches appear dry, dead. But if you perforate the trunk, especially at dawn, a sweet nutritious milk pours out.[82]

It was Carnival Tuesday, and everywhere people celebrated. The amusements, called *carnes tollendas* (or 'farewell to the flesh'), became at times rather wild: some paraded an ass loaded with water, and whenever they found an open window pumped water into the room; others carried bags full of hair from the *pica pica* (*Dolichos pruriens*), which greatly irritates skin on contact, and threw it into the faces of passers-by.

From La Guaira we returned to Nueva Valencia, where we met several French *émigrés*, the only ones we saw in five years in the Spanish colonies. In spite of the blood links between the Spanish and French royal families, not even French priests could find refuge in this part of the New World, where man finds it so easy to find food and shelter. Beyond the Atlantic Ocean, only the United States of America offers asylum to those in need. A government that is strong because it is free, and confident because it is just, has nothing to fear in granting refuge to exiles.

Before leaving the Aragua valleys and its neighbouring coasts, I will deal with the cacao plantations, which have always been the main source of wealth in this area. The cacao-producing tree does not grow wild anywhere in the forests north of the Orinoco. This scarcity of wild cacao trees in South America is a curious phenomenon, yet little studied. The amount of trees in the cacao plantations has been estimated at more than 16 million. We met no tribe on the Orinoco that prepared a drink with cacao seeds. Indians suck the pulp of the pod and chuck the seeds, often found in heaps in places where Indians have spent the night. It seems to me that in Caracas cacao cultivation follows the examples of Mexico and Guatemala. Spaniards established in Terra Firma learned how to cultivate the cacao tree – sheltered while young by the leaves of the erythrina and banana, making *chocolatl* cakes, and using the liquid of the same name, thanks to trade with Mexico, Guatemala and Nicaragua whose people are of Toltec and Aztec origin.

As far back as the sixteenth century travellers have greatly differed in their opinions about *chocolatl*. Benzoni said, in his crude language, that it is a drink 'fitter for pigs than humans'. The Jesuit Acosta asserts that 'the Spaniards who inhabit America are fond of chocolate to excess . . .' Fernando Cortez highly praised chocolate as being an agreeable drink if prepared cold and, especially, as being very nutritious. Cortez's page writes: 'He who has drunk one cup can travel all day without further food, especially in very hot climates.' We shall soon celebrate this quality in chocolate in our voyage up the Orinoco. It is easily transported and prepared: as food it is both nutritious and stimulating.[83]

CHAPTER 14

MOUNTAINS SITUATED BETWEEN THE ARAGUA VALLEYS
AND THE CARACAS PLAINS — VILLA DE CURA —
PARAPARA — LLANOS OR STEPPES — CALABOZO

THE CHAIN OF mountains limited on the south by Lake Tacarigua forms, you could say, the northern boundary of the great
basin of the plains or savannahs of Caracas. From the Aragua
valleys you reach the savannahs over the Guigue and Tucut-
enemo mountains. Moving from a region peopled and
embellished by agriculture you find a vast desert. Accustomed
to rocks and shaded valleys, the traveller contemplates with
astonishment those plains without trees, those immense tracts
of land that seem to climb to the horizon.[84]

We left the Aragua valleys before sunset on the 6th of
March. We crossed a richly cultivated plain, bordering the
south-westerly banks of Lake Valencia, along ground recently
uncovered by receding water. The fertility of the earth, planted
with gourds, water melons and bananas, amazed us. The distant howling of monkeys announced dawn. Opposite a clump
of trees in the middle of the plain we caught sight of several
bands of araguatoes (*Simia ursina*) who, as if in procession,
passed very slowly from one branch to another. After the male
followed several females, many with young on their backs.
Due to their life-style howling monkeys all look alike, even
those belonging to different species. It is striking how uniform
their movements are. When the branches of two trees are too
far apart, the male that guides his troop hangs on his prehensile tail and swings in the air until he reaches the nearest branch.
Then all the band repeat the same operation in the same place.
It is almost superfluous to add how dubious Ulloa's[85] assertion
is that the araguatoes form a kind of chain in order to reach
the opposite bank of a river. During five years we had ample
opportunity to observe thousands of these animals: for this

reason we have no confidence in statements possibly invented by Europeans themselves, although missionary Indians repeat them as if they come from their own traditions. The further man is from civilization, the more he enjoys astonishing people while recounting the marvels of his country. He says he has seen what he imagines may have been seen by others. Every Indian is a hunter and the stories of hunters borrow from the imagination the more intelligent the hunted animal appears to be. Hence so many fictions in Europe about the foxes, monkeys, crows and condors in the Andes.

The Indians claim that when howler monkeys fill the jungles with their howls there is always one that leads the howling. Their observation is correct. You generally hear one solitary and intense voice, replaced by another at a different pitch. Indians also assert that when an araguato female is about to give birth, the chorus of howling stops until the new monkey is born. I was not able to prove this, but I have observed that the howling ceases for a few minutes when something unexpected happens, like when a wounded monkey claims the attention of the troop. Our guides seriously assured us that 'To cure asthma you must drink out of the bony drum of the araguato's hyoid bone.' Having such a loud voice this animal is thought to impart a curing effect from its larynx to the water drunk out of it. Such is the people's science, which sometimes resembles the ancients'.

We spent the night in the village of Guigue. We lodged with an old sergeant from Murcia. To prove he had studied with the Jesuits he recited to us the history of the creation in Latin. He knew the names of Augustus, Tiberius and Diocletian, and while enjoying the agreeably cool nights on his banana plantation interested himself in all that had happened in the times of the Roman emperors. He asked us for a remedy for his painful gout. 'I know,' he said, 'that a *zambo* from Valencia, a famous *curioso*, could cure me, but the *zambo* would expect to be treated as an equal, and that I cannot do with a man of his colour. I prefer to remain as I am.'

San Luis de Cura or, as it is more usually called, Villa de Cura, lies in a very barren valley. Apart from a few fruit trees the region is without vegetation. The *meseta* is dry and several rivers lose themselves in cracks in the ground. Cura is more a village than a town. We lodged with a family that had been persecuted by the government after the 1797 revolution in Caracas. After years in prison, one of their sons had been taken to Havana, where he lived locked in a fort. How pleased his mother was when she heard that we were bound for Havana after visiting the Orinoco. She handed me five piastres – 'all her savings'. I tried to hand them back, but how could I wound the delicacy of a woman happy with her self-imposed sacrifice! All the society in the village met in the evening to look at a magic lantern showing sights of the great European cities, the Tuileries palace and the statue of the Great Elector in Berlin. How odd to see our native city in a magic lantern some 2,000 leagues away!

After bathing in the fresh clear water of the San Juan river at two in the morning, we set off on the road for Mesa de Paja. The llanos at that time were infested with bandits, so other travellers joined us to form a kind of caravan. The route was downhill for several hours.

At Mesa de Paja we entered the basin of the llanos. The sun was almost at its highest point. On the ground we recorded a temperature of 48 °C to 50 °C in the sterile parts without vegetation. At the height of our heads, as we were riding the mules, we did not feel the slightest breath of air; but in the midst of that apparent calm small dust whirls were continually raised by air currents arising from the difference in temperature between the bare sand and the grass. These sand winds increased the suffocating heat. The plains surrounding us seemed to reach the sky and looked to us like an ocean covered with seaweed. Sky and land merged. Through the dry mist and vapours you could make out, in the distance, trunks of palm trees. Stripped of their leaves these trunks looked like ship masts on the horizon.

The monotony of these steppes is imposing, sad and oppressive. Everything appears motionless; only now and then from a distance does the shadow of a small cloud promising rain move across the sky. The first glimpse of the plains is no less surprising than that of the Andean chain. It is hard to get accustomed to the views on the Venezuelan and Casanare plains, or to the pampas of Buenos Aires and the *chaco* when, for twenty to thirty days without stopping, you feel you are on the surface of an ocean. The plains of eastern and northern Europe can give only a pallid image of the immense South American llanos.

The llanos and pampas of South America are really steppes. During the rainy season they appear beautifully green, but in the dry season they look more like deserts. The grass dries out and turns to dust; the ground cracks, crocodiles and snakes bury themselves in the dried mud waiting for the first rains of spring to wake them from prolonged lethargy.

Rivers have only a slight, often imperceptible fall. When the wind blows, or the Orinoco floods, the rivers disembouging in it are pushed backward. In the Arauca you often see the current going the wrong way. Indians have paddled a whole day downstream when in reality they have been going upstream. Between the descending and ascending waters lie large stagnant tracts, and dangerous whirlpools are formed.

The most typical characteristic of the South American savannahs or steppes is the total absence of hills, the perfect flatness of the land. That is why the Spanish conquistadores did not call them deserts, savannahs or meadows but plains, *los llanos*. Often in an area of 600 square kilometres no part of the ground rises more than 1 metre high.

Despite the apparent uniformity of the ground the llanos offer two kinds of inequalities that cannot escape the attentive traveller. The first are called *bancos* (banks); they are in reality shoals in the basin of the steppes, rising some 4 to 5 feet above the plains. These banks can reach some 3 to 4 leagues in length; they are completely smooth and horizontal, and can only be recognized when you examine their edges. The second inequality can only be detected by geodesical or barometric measurements, or else by the flow of a river; they are called *mesa*, or tables. They are small flats, or convex elevations, that rise imperceptibly some metres high to divide the waters between the Orinoco and the northern Terra Firma coast.

Only the gentle curvature of the savannah forms this division.

The infinite monotony of the llanos; the extreme rarity of inhabitants; the difficulties of travelling in such heat and in an atmosphere darkened by dust; the perspective of the horizon, which constantly retreats before the traveller; the few scattered palms that are so similar that one despairs of ever reaching them, and confuses them with others further afield; all these aspects together make the stranger looking at the llanos think they are far larger than they are.[86]

After spending two nights on horseback, and having vainly looked for shade under tufts of the mauritia palms, we arrived before nightfall at the small farm called Alligator (El Cayman), also called La Guadalupe. It is a *hato de ganado*, that is, an isolated house on the steppes, surrounded by small huts covered in reeds and skins. Cattle, oxen, horses and mules are not penned in; they wander freely in a space of several square leagues. Nowhere do you see any enclosures. Men, naked to the waist, and armed with lances, ride the savannahs to inspect the animals, to bring back those that have strayed too far off, and to brand with a hot iron those still not branded with the owner's mark. These coloured men, called *peones llaneros*, are partly freed and partly enslaved. There is no race more constantly exposed to the devouring fire of the tropical sun than this one. They eat meat dried in the sun, and barely salted. Even their horses eat this. Always in the saddle, they do not ever try to walk a few paces. On the farm we found an old negro slave in charge while his master was away. We were told about herds of several thousand cows grazing the steppes, and yet it was impossible to get a bowl of milk. We were offered a yellowish, muddy and fetid water drawn from a nearby stagnant pool in bowls made of *tutuma* fruit. The laziness of the llano inhabitants is such that they cannot be bothered to dig wells, even though they know that 9 feet down you can everywhere find fine springs under a stratum of conglomerate or red sandstone. After suffering half a year of flooding, you are then exposed to another half of painful drought. The old negro warned us to cover the jug with a cloth and to drink the water through a filter so as not to smell the stink, and not to swallow the fine yellowish clay in the water. We did not know then that we would follow his instructions for months on end. The Orinoco waters are just as charged with particles of earth, and are even fetid in creeks, where dead crocodiles rot on sandbanks, half buried in the slime.

We had hardly unpacked our instruments before we freed our mules and let them, as is said here, 'find water on the savannah'. There are small pools around the farm and animals find them guided by instinct, by the sight of scattered tufts of mauritia palms, by the sensation of humidity that gives rise to small air currents in an otherwise calm atmosphere. When these stagnant ponds are far off, and the farm-hands are too lazy to lead the animals to their natural watering-holes, they are locked for five or six hours in a very hot stable, and then released. Excessive thirst increases their instinctive cleverness. As soon as you open the stable doors you see the horses, and especially the mules, far more intelligent than horses, rush off into the savannah. Tails in the air, heads back, they rush into the wind, stopping for a while to explore around them, following less their sight than their sense of smell, until they finally announce by neighing that water has been found. All these movements are more successfully carried out by horses born on the llanos who have enjoyed the freedom of wild herds than by those coming from the coast, descendants of domestic horses. With most animals, as with man, the alertness of the senses diminishes after years of work, after domestic habits and the progress of culture.

We followed our mules as they sought one of these stagnant ponds that give muddy water, which hardly satisfied our thirst. We were covered in dust, and tanned by the sand wind, which burns the skin more than the sun. We were desperate to have a bathe but we found only a pool of stagnating water surrounded by palms. The water was muddy, but to our surprise cooler than the air. Used as we were on this long journey to bathing every time we could, often several times a day, we did not hesitate to throw ourselves into the pool. We had hardly begun to enjoy the cool water when we heard a noise on the far bank that made us leap out. It was a crocodile slipping into the mud. It would have been unwise to spend the night in that muddy place.

We had gone scarcely more than a quarter of a league away from the farm, yet we walked for more than an hour on our way back without reaching it. Too late we saw that we had been going in the wrong direction. We had left as the day ended, before the stars had come out, and had proceeded haphazardly into the plains. As usual we had our compass. It would have been easy to find our direction from the position of Canopus and the Southern Cross; but the means were useless because we were uncertain whether we had gone east or south when we left the small farm. We tried to return to our bathing place, and walked for another three quarters of an hour without finding the stagnant pond. We often thought we saw fire on the horizon; it was a star rising, its image magnified by vapours. After wandering for a long time on the savannah we decided to sit down on a palm trunk in a dry place surrounded by short grass; for Europeans who have recently arrived fear water snakes more than they do jaguars. We did not fool ourselves into believing that our guides, whose indolence we well knew, would come looking for us before preparing and eating their food. The more unsure we were about our situation, the more pleasing it was eventually to hear horse hooves approaching from afar. It was an Indian, with his lance, doing his *rodeo*, that is, rounding up cattle. The sight of two white men saying they were lost made him think it was a trick. It was hard to convince him of our sincerity. He eventually agreed to lead us to the Alligator farm, but without slowing down his trotting horse. Our guides assured us that 'they were already getting worried about us', and to justify their worry had made a long list of people who had been lost in the llanos and found completely worn out. It is clear that danger exists only for those far from any farm or, as had happened recently, for those robbed by bandits and tied to a palm tree.

To avoid suffering the heat of day we left at two in the morning, hoping to reach Calabozo, a busy little town in the middle of the llanos, by midday. The appearance of the countryside remained always the same. There was no moon, but the great mass of stars decorating the southern skies lit up part of our path. This imposing spectacle of the starry vault stretching out over our heads, this fresh breeze blowing over the plains at night, the rippling of the grass wherever it is long, all reminded us of the surface of an ocean. This illusion increased especially (and we did not tire of the repetition of this sight) when the sun's disk showed on the horizon, doubling itself through refraction, and soon losing its flattened form, rising quickly towards the zenith.

As the sun rose the plains came alive. Cattle, lying down at night by ponds or at the foot of moriche and rhopala palms, regrouped, and the solitudes became populated with horses, mules and oxen that live here not like wild animals but free, without fixed abode, scorning man's care. In this torrid zone the bulls, although of Spanish pedigree like those on the cold tablelands of Quito, are tame. The traveller is never in danger of being attacked or chased, contrary to what often happened during our wanderings in the Andes. Near Calabozo we saw herds of roebucks grazing peacefully with the horses and oxen. They are called *matacanes*; their meat is very tasty. They are larger than our deer and have a very sleek skin of a dark brown with white spots. Their horns seem to be simple points and they are not shy. We saw some completely white ones in the groups of thirty to forty that we observed.

Besides the scattered trunk of the *palma de cobija* we found real groves (*palmares*) in which the corypha is mixed with a tree of the proteaceous family called *chaparro* by the Indians, which is a new species of rhopala, with hard, crackling leaves. The little groves of rhopala are called *chaparrales* and it is easy to see that in a vast plain where only two or three kinds of tree grow that the *chaparro*, which gives shade, is deemed of great value. South of Guayaval other palms predominate: the *piritu* (*Bactris speciosa*) and the mauritia (*Mauritia flexuosa*), celebrated as the *árbol de la vida*. This last is the sago tree of America: it gives flour, wine, fibres to weave hammocks, baskets, nets and clothes. Its fruit, shaped like a pine-cone and covered in scales, tastes rather like an apple, and when ripe is yellow inside and red outside. Howler monkeys love them, and the Guaramo

Indians, whose existence is closely linked to this palm, make a fermented liquor that is acid and refreshing.

On the La Mesa road, near Calabozo, it was extremely hot. The temperature of the air rose considerably as soon as the wind blew. The air was full of dust, and when there were gusts the thermometer reached 40 °C and 41 °C. We moved forward slowly as it would have been dangerous to leave the mules transporting our instruments behind. Our guides advised us to line our hats with rhopala leaves to mitigate the effect of the sun's rays on our heads. In fact it was quite a relief, and later we bore this in mind.

It is hard to formulate exactly how many cattle there are on the llanos of Caracas, Barcelona, Cumaná and Spanish Guiana. Monsieur Depons, who has lived longer in Caracas than I have, and whose statistics are generally correct, calculates that in these vast plains, from the mouth of the Orinoco to Lake Maracaibo, there are 1,200,000 oxen, 180,000 horses and 90,000 mules. He worked out a value of 5 million francs for the produce of these herds, including exportation and the price of leather in the country. In the Buenos Aires pampas there are, so we believe, some 12 million cows and 3 million horses, not counting the animals without owners.

I shall not hazard any general evaluations as they are too vague by nature; but I will observe that in the Caracas llanos owners of the great *hatos* have no idea how many animals they have. They count only the young animals branded every year with the sign of their herd. The richer owners brand up to 14,000 animals a year, and sell 5,000 to 6,000. According to official documents the export of leather in all the Capitanía-General of Caracas reaches 174,000 oxhides and 11,500 goat hides. When one remembers that these figures come from custom registers and do not include contraband one is tempted to think that the calculation of 1,200,000 oxen wandering in the llanos is far too low.

In Calabozo, in the middle of the llanos, we found an electric machine with great disks, electrophori, batteries and electrometers; an apparatus as complete as any found in Europe. These objects had not been bought in America but made by a man who had never seen any instruments, who had never been able to consult anybody, and who knew about electricity only from reading Sigaud de la Fond's *Traité* and Franklin's *Mémoires*. Carlos del Pozo, this man's name, had begun by making cylindrical electrical machines using large glass jars, and cutting off their necks. Years later he managed to get two plates from Philadelphia to make a disk machine to obtain greater electric effects. It is easy to guess how difficult it must have been for Sr Pozo to succeed once the first works on electricity fell into his hands, and how he managed to work everything out for himself. Up to then he had enjoyed astonishing uneducated people with his experiments, and had never travelled out of the llanos. Our stay in Calabozo gave him altogether another kind of pleasure. He must have set some value on two travellers who could compare his apparatus with European ones. With me I had electrometers mounted in straw, pith-balls and gold leaf, as well as a small Leyden jar that could be charged by rubbing, following Ingenhousz's method, which I used for physiological tests. Pozo could not hide his joy when for the first time he saw instruments that he had not made but which appeared to copy his. We also showed him the effects of the contact of different metals on the nerves of frogs. The names of Galvani and Volta had not yet echoed in these vast solitudes.

After the electric apparatus, made by a clever inhabitant of the llanos, nothing interested us more in Calabozo than the gymnoti, living electric apparatuses. I had busied myself daily over many years with the phenomenon of Galvanic electricity and had enthusiastically experimented without knowing what I had discovered; I had built real batteries by placing metal disks on top of each other and alternating them with bits of muscle flesh, or other humid matter, and so was eager, after arriving at Cumaná, to obtain electric eels. We had often been promised them, and had always been deceived. Money means less the further from the coast you go, and there was no way to shake the imperturbable apathy of the people when even money meant nothing!

Under the name of *tembladores* ('which make you tremble')

Spaniards confuse all electric fish. There are some in the Caribbean Sea, off the Cumaná coast. The Guaiquerí Indians, the cleverest fishermen in the area, brought us a fish that numbed their hands. This fish swims up the little Manzanares river. It was a new species of ray whose lateral spots are hard to see, and which resembles Galvani's torpedo. The Cumaná torpedo was very lively, and energetic in its muscular contractions, yet its electric charges were weak. They became stronger when we galvanized the animal in contact with zinc and gold. Other *tembladores*, proper electric eels, live in the Colorado and Guarapiche rivers and several little streams crossing the Chaima Indian missions. There are many of them in the great South American rivers, the Orinoco, Amazon and Meta, but the strength of the currents and the depths prevent Indians from catching them. They see these fish less often than they feel their electric shocks when they swim in the rivers. But it is in the llanos, especially around Calabozo, between the small farm of Morichal and the *missions de arriba* and *de abaxo*, that the stagnant ponds and tributaries of the Orinoco are filled with electric eels. We wanted first to experiment in the house we lived in at Calabozo but the fear of the eel's electric shock is so exaggerated that for three days nobody would fish any out for us, despite our promising the Indians two piastres for each one. Yet they tell whites that they can touch *tembladores* without shock if they are chewing tobacco.

Impatient of waiting, and having only obtained uncertain results from a living eel brought to us, we went to the Caño de Bera to experiment on the water's edge. Early in the morning on the 19th of March we left for the little village of Rastro de Abaxo: from there Indians led us to a stream, which in the dry season forms a muddy pond surrounded by trees, clusia, amyris and mimosa with fragrant flowers. Fishing eels with nets is very difficult because of the extreme agility with which they dive into the mud, like snakes. We did not want to use *barbasco*, made with roots of *Piscidia erythrina*, *Jacquinia armillaris* and other species of phyllanthus which, chucked into the pond, numbs fish. This would have weakened the eel. The Indians decided to fish with their horses, *embarbascar con caballos.*[87] It was hard to imagine this way of fishing; but soon we saw our guides returning from the savannah with a troop of wild horses and mules. There were about thirty of them, and they forced them into the water.

The extraordinary noise made by the stamping of the horses made the fish jump out of the mud and attack. These livid, yellow eels, like great water snakes, swim on the water's surface and squeeze under the bellies of the horses and mules. A fight between such different animals is a picturesque scene.[88] With harpoons and long pointed reeds the Indians tightly circled the pond; some climbed trees whose branches hung over the water's surface. Screaming and prodding with their reeds they stopped the horses leaving the pond. The eels, dazed by the noise, defended themselves with their electrical charges. For a while it seemed they might win. Several horses collapsed from the shocks received on their most vital organs, and drowned under the water. Others, panting, their manes erect, their eyes anguished, stood up and tried to escape the storm surprising them in the water. They were pushed back by the Indians, but a few managed to escape to the bank, stumbling at each step, falling on to the sand exhausted and numbed from the electric shocks.

In less than two minutes two horses had drowned. The eel is about 5 feet long and presses all its length along the belly of the horse, giving it electric shocks. They attack the heart, intestines and the *plexus coeliacus* of the abdominal nerves. It is obvious that the shock felt by the horse is worse than that felt by a man touched on one small part. But the horses were probably not killed, just stunned. They drowned because they could not escape from among the other horses and eels.

We were sure that the fishing would end with the death of all the animals used. But gradually the violence of the unequal combat died down, and the tired eels dispersed. They need a long rest and plenty of food to recuperate the lost galvanic energy. The mules and horses seemed less frightened; their manes did not stand on end, and their eyes seemed less terrified. The eels timidly approached the shore of the marshy pond where we fished them with harpoons tied to long strings.

While the string is dry the Indians do not feel any shocks. In a few minutes we had five huge eels, only slightly wounded. Later, more were caught.

The water temperature where these animals live is 26 °C to 27 °C. We are assured that their electric energy decreases in colder water. It is remarkable that these animals with electromotive organs are found not in the air but in a fluid that conducts electricity.

The eel is the largest of the electric fish; I have measured one that is 5 feet 3 inches long. Indians say they have seen even longer. A fish 3 feet 6 inches weighed 12 pounds. The eels from the Caño de Bera are of a pretty olive green, with a yellow mixed with red under their heads. Two rows of small yellow stains are placed symmetrically along their backs from the head to the tail. Each stain has an excretory opening. The skin is constantly covered with a mucus, which, as Volta has shown, conducts electricity twenty to thirty times more efficiently than pure water. It is odd that none of the electric fish discovered here are covered in scales.

It would be dangerous to expose yourself to the first shocks from a large excited eel. If by chance you get a shock before the fish is wounded, or exhausted by a long chase, the pain and numbness are so extreme that it is hard to describe the nature of the sensation. I do not remember ever getting such shocks from a Leyden jar as when I mistakenly stepped on a gymnotus just taken out of the water. All day I felt strong pain in my knees and in all my joints. Torpedoes and electric eels cause a twitching of the tendon in the muscle touched by the electric organ, which reaches one's elbow. With each stroke you feel an internal vibration that lasts two or three seconds, followed by a painful numbness. In the graphic language of the Tamanac Indians the electric eel is called *arimna*, which means 'something that deprives you of movement'.

While European naturalists find electric eels extremely interesting, the Indians hate and fear them. However, their flesh is not bad, although most of the body consists of the electric apparatus, which is slimy and disagreeable to eat. The scarcity of fish in the marshes and ponds on the llanos is blamed on the eels. They kill far more than they eat, and Indians told us that when they capture young alligators and electric eels in their tough nets the eels do not appear to be hurt because they paralyse the young alligators before they themselves can be attacked. All the inhabitants of the waters flee the eels. Lizards, turtles and frogs seek ponds free of eels. At Uritici a road had to be redirected as so many mules were being killed by eels as they forded a river.

On the 24th of March we left Calabozo. At about four in the afternoon we found a young naked Indian girl stretched out on her back in the savannah; she seemed to be around twelve or thirteen. She was exhausted with fatigue and thirst, with her eyes, nose and mouth full of sand, and breathing with a rattle in her throat. Next to her there was a jar on its side, half full of sand. Luckily we had a mule carrying water. We revived her by washing her face and making her drink some wine. She was scared when she found herself surrounded by so many people, but she slowly relaxed and talked to our guides. From the position of the sun she reckoned she had fainted and remained unconscious for several hours. Nothing could persuade her to mount one of our mules. She wanted to return to Uritici where she had been a servant on a hacienda whose owner had sacked her after she had suffered a long illness because she could not work as well as before. Our threats and requests were useless; she was hardened to suffering, like all of her race, and lived in the present without fear of the future. She insisted on going to one of the Indian missions near Calabozo. We emptied her jar of sand and filled it with water. Before we had mounted our mules she had set off, and was soon a cloud of sand in the distance.

During the night we forded the Uritici river, home of numerous voracious alligators. We were told that we should not let our dogs drink from the river as alligators often leave the banks and chase dogs. We were shown a hut, or a kind of shed, where our host in Calabozo had had an extraordinary adventure. He was sleeping with a friend on a bench, covered with skins, when at dawn he was woken by a noise and violent shaking. Bits of earth flew about the hut, and suddenly a young alligator climbed up from under their bed and tried to attack a dog sleeping in the doorway; but it could not catch it, and ran to the bank and dived into the water. When they examined the ground under their bed they found it excavated; it was hardened mud where the alligator had spent its summer asleep, as they all do in the llano dry season. The noise of the men and horses, and the smell of dogs, had woken it up. The Indians often find enormous boas,[89] which they call *uji*, or water snakes, in a similar state of lethargy. To revive them they sprinkle the boas with water. They kill them and hang them in a stream, and after they have rotted they make guitar strings from the tendons on their dorsal muscles, which are far better than strings made from howler-monkey guts.

CHAPTER 15

UNTIL THE SECOND half of the eighteenth century the great
Apure, Payare, Arauca and Meta rivers were hardly known in
Europe by their names, and were obviously far less known
than in preceding centuries when the valiant Felipe de Urre[90]
and the conquerors of Tocayo crossed the llanos seeking the
great city of El Dorado and the rich country of Omagua, the
Timbuktu of the New World, beyond the Apure river. Such
daring expeditions could take place only on a war footing. The
weapons meant to protect the new colonizers were ceaselessly
turned against the unhappy Indians. Following that period of
violence and misery two Indian tribes, the Cabres and the Orinoco Caribs, became masters of those parts no longer being
devastated by the Spaniards. Only poor monks were allowed
to advance south of the steppes. The Venezuelan coast became
isolated and the slow conquest of the Jesuit missionaries
followed the banks of the Orinoco. It is hard to believe that
the city of San Fernando de Apure, some 50 leagues from the
coast, was not founded until 1789.

The position of San Fernando on a great navigable river,
near the mouth of another river that crosses the whole province of Varinas, is extremely useful for trade. All that is
produced in this province, the leathers, cocoa, cotton and
top-quality Mijagual indigo, is washed down past this town to
the Orinoco mouth. During the rainy season big ships come
upstream from Angostura to San Fernando de Apure and
along the Santo Domingo river as far as Torunos, the harbour
for the town of Barinas. During this season the flooded rivers
form a labyrinth of waterways between the Apure, Arauca,
Capanaparo and Sinaruco rivers, covering a country of

roughly 400 square leagues. At this point the Orinoco, deviating from its course, due not to neighbouring mountains but to
the rising counter-slopes, turns east instead of following its
ancient path in the line of the meridian. If you consider the
surface of the earth as a polyhedron formed of variously
inclined planes you will see by simply consulting a map that
between San Fernando de Apure, Caycara and the mouth of
the Meta the intersection of three slopes, higher in the north,
west and south, must have caused a considerable depression.
In this basin the savannahs can be covered by 12 to 14 feet of
water and turned into a great lake after the rains. Villages and
farms look as though they are on shoals, rising barely 2 to 3
feet above the water surface. The flooding of the Apure, Meta
and Orinoco rivers is also periodic. In the rainy season horses
that roam the savannah do not have time to reach the plateaux
and they drown in their hundreds. You see mares followed by
foals, barely sticking up out of the water, swimming part of
the day to eat grass. While swimming they are chased by crocodiles, and some carry crocodile tooth marks on their hides.
Horse, mule and cow carcasses attract numberless vultures.

San Fernando is infamous for its suffocating heat throughout most of the year. This western part of the llanos is the
hottest because the air from all the arid steppes reaches here.
During the rainy season the heat of the llanos increases considerably, especially in July when the sky is covered with cloud.
The thermometer reached 39.5 °C in the shade.

On the 28th of March I was on the river bank trying to
measure the width of the Apure river, which was 206 toises.
It was thundering everywhere; the first storm and rains of
the rainy season. The river was whipped up by an east wind
into large waves, then it suddenly calmed down, and then many
large cetaceans, resembling the dolphins of our seas, began to
play in long lines on the river surface. The slow and lazy crocodiles seemed to fear these noisy and impetuous animals as they
dived underwater when these animals approached. It is extraordinary to find these mammals so far from the coast. The
mission Spaniards call them *toninas*, as they do dolphins; their
Tamanaco name is *orinucna*. They are 3 to 4 feet long, and on

bending their backs and whipping the water with their tails they reveal part of their back and dorsal fins. I did not succeed in catching any of them, though I often paid Indians to shoot at them with arrows.

The electrometer gave no sign of electricity. As the storm gathered the blue of the sky changed to grey. The thermometer rose 3 °C, as is usual in the Tropics, and a heavy rain fell. Being sufficiently adapted to the climate not to fear the effect of a tropical downpour we stayed on the shore to observe the electrometer. I held it more than twenty minutes in my hand, 6 feet above the ground. For several minutes the electric charge remained the same, and then I noticed that the electricity in the atmosphere was first positive, then nil, then negative. I have gone into these details on the electric charge in the atmosphere because newly arrived European travellers usually describe just their impressions of a tropical storm. In a country where the year is divided into two halves, the dry and the wet season, or as the Indians say in their expressive language, 'of sun and rain', it is interesting to follow meteorological phenomena as one season turns into the next.

The look of the sky, the movement of electricity, and the downpour of the 28th March announced the start of the rainy season: we were still advised to go to San Fernando de Apure by San Francisco de Capanaparo, along the Sinaruco river and the San Antonio *hato* to the Otomac village recently founded on the banks of the Meta river, and to embark on the Orinoco a little above Carichana. This land road crosses an unhealthy, fever-ridden country. An old farmer, Don Francisco Sanchez, offered to lead us. His clothes revealed how simply people live in these far-off countries. He had made a fortune of 100,000 piastres yet he rode on horseback barefoot with large silver spurs. We knew from several weeks' experience how sad and monotonous the llanos are and so we chose the longer route along the Apure river to the Orinoco. We chose one of the long pirogues that the Spaniards call *lanchas*. A pilot and four Indians were sufficient to drive it. On the poop a cabin covered with corypha leaves was built in a few hours. It was so spacious that it could have held a table and benches. They used oxhides stretched and nailed to frames of Brazil-wood. I mention these minute details to prove that our life on the Apure river was very different from the time when we were reduced to the narrow Orinoco canoes. We packed the pirogue with provisions for a month. You find plenty of hens, eggs, bananas, cassava and cacao at San Fernando. The good Capuchin monk gave us sherry, oranges and tamarinds to make fresh juices. We could easily tell that a roof made of palm leaves would heat up excessively on the bed of a large river where we would be always exposed to the sun's perpendicular rays. The Indians relied less on our supplies than on their hooks and nets. We also brought some weapons along, whose use was common as far as the cataracts. Further south the extreme humidity prevents missionaries from using guns. The Apure river teems with fish, manatees[91] and turtles whose eggs are more nourishing than tasty. The river banks are full of birds, including the *pauxi* and *guacharaca*, that could be called the turkey and pheasant of this region. Their flesh seemed harder and less white than our European gallinaceous family as they use their muscles more. We did not forget to add to our provisions fishing tackle, fire-arms and a few casks of brandy to use as exchange with the Orinoco Indians.

We left San Fernando on the 30th of March at four in the afternoon. The heat was suffocating; the thermometer marked 34 °C in the shade despite a strong south-east wind. This wind prevented us from setting our sails. During our journey along the Apure, the Orinoco and the Río Negro we were accompanied by the brother-in-law of the governor of the Barinas province, Don Nicolás Soto, recently arrived from Cádiz. To get to know land worthy of a European's curiosity he decided to spend seventy-four days with us in a narrow *lancha*, invaded by mosquitoes. The right bank of the Apure is somewhat better cultivated than the left bank where the Yaruro Indians have built huts with reeds and palm-leaf stalks. They live from hunting and fishing, and are skilled in hunting the jaguar whose skins, called 'tiger skins', reach Spain thanks to them. Some of these Indians have been baptized, but they never go to church. They are considered to be wild because they want to remain independent. Other Yaruro tribes accept missionary discipline. The people of this tribe look like a branch of the Mongol family. Their look is serious; their eyes elongated, their cheek-bones high and with a prominent nose.

During our voyage from San Fernando to San Carlos on the Río Negro, and from there to the town of Angostura, I made the effort to note down in writing, every day, whether in the canoe or at night camps, anything that happened which was worthy of note. The heavy rain and incredible amount of mosquitoes crowding the air on the Orinoco and Casiquiare obviously left gaps in my chronicle, but I always wrote it up a few days later. The following pages are taken from this journal. What is noted down while actually viewing the described objects keeps a semblance of truth (dare I say 'individuality'), which gives charm even to insignificant things.

March 31st.[92] A contrary wind forced us to stay on the river bank until midday. We saw a part of the cane fields devastated by a fire spreading from a nearby forest. Nomadic Indians set the forest alight everywhere they set up camp for the night; during the dry season vast provinces would be in flames if it was not for the extreme hardness of the wood, which does not completely burn. We found trunks of desmanthus and mahogany (*cahoba*) that were hardly burned more than 2 inches deep.

Only after Diamante do you enter territory inhabited by tigers, crocodiles and *chiguires*, a large species of Linnaeus's genus *Cavia* (capybara). We saw flocks of birds pressed against each other flash across the sky like a black cloud changing shape all the time. The river slowly grew wider. One of the banks is usually arid and sandy due to flooding. The other is higher, covered with full-grown trees. Sometimes the river is lined with jungle on both sides and becomes a straight canal some 150 toises wide. The arrangement of the trees is remarkable. First you see the *sauso* shrubs (*Hermesia castaneifolia*), a hedge some 4 feet high as if cut by man. Behind this hedge a brushwood of cedar, Brazil-wood and *gayac*. Palms are rare; you see only scattered trunks of corozo and thorny *piritu*. The large quadrupeds of these regions, tigers, tapirs and peccaries, have opened passages in the *sauso* hedge. They appear through these gaps to drink water. They are not frightened of the canoes, so we see them skirting the river until they disappear into the jungle through a gap in the hedge. I confess that these often repeated scenes greatly appeal to me. The pleasure comes not solely from the curiosity a naturalist feels for the objects of his studies, but also to a feeling common to all men brought up in the customs of civilization. You find yourself in a new world, in a wild, untamed nature. Sometimes it is a jaguar, the beautiful American panther, on the banks; sometimes it is the hocco (*Crax alector*) with its black feathers and tufted head, slowly strolling along the *sauso* hedge. All kinds of animals appear, one after the other. 'Es como en el paraíso' ('It is like paradise') our old Indian pilot said. Everything here reminds you of that state of the ancient world revealed in venerable traditions about the innocence and happiness of all people; but when carefully observing the relationships between the animals you see how they avoid and fear each other. The golden age has ended. In this paradise of American jungles, as everywhere else, a long, sad experience has taught all living beings that gentleness is rarely linked to might.

Where the shore is very wide, the line of *sausos* remains far from the river. In the intermediate zone up to ten crocodiles can be seen stretched out in the sand. Immobile, with their jaws wide open at right angles, they lie next to each other without the least sign of sociability, unlike those animals that live in groups. The troop separates as soon as it leaves the shore; however, it consists probably of one male and numerous females as males are rare due to the rutting season when they fight and kill each other. There were so many of these great reptiles that all along the river we could always see at least five or six of them, although the fact that the Apure had not yet flooded meant that hundreds more of these saurians remained buried in the savannah's mud. The Indians told us that not a year went by without two or three people, mainly women going to fetch water, being torn apart by these carnivorous lizards. They told us the story of an Indian girl from Uritici who by her intrepidity and presence of mind had saved herself from the jaws of one of those monsters. As soon as she felt herself seized she poked her fingers so violently into the animal's eyes that pain forced it to drop its prey after slicing off one arm. Despite the copious bleeding the little Indian girl swam ashore with her remaining arm. In those lonely places where man lives in constant struggle with nature he must resort to any means to fight off a jaguar, a boa (*tragavenado*) or a crocodile; everyone is prepared for some sort of danger. 'I knew,' said the young Indian girl coolly, 'that the crocodile would let go when I stuck my fingers in its eyes.'

The Apure crocodiles find enough food eating *chiguires* (*Cavia capybara*), which live in herds of fifty to sixty on the river banks. These unhappy animals, as big as our pigs, cannot defend themselves. They swim better than they run, but in the water they fall to crocodiles and on land to jaguars. It is difficult to understand how, exposed to such formidable enemies, they remain so numerous; it can be explained only by how quickly they reproduce.

We stopped by the mouth of the Caño de la Triguera, in a bay called Vuelta de Jobal, to measure the speed of the current, which was 2.56 feet an hour. We were again surrounded by *chiguires*, who swim like dogs with their heads and necks out of the water. On the beach opposite we saw an enormous crocodile sleeping among these rodents. It woke when we approached and slowly slipped into the water without disturbing the rodents. Indians say that their indifference is due to stupidity, but perhaps they know that the Apure and Orinoco crocodile does not attack prey on land, only when it comes across one in its way as it slips into the water.

Near the Jobal nature takes on a more imposing and wild character. It was there we saw the largest tiger we have ever seen. Even the Indians were surprised by its prodigious size; it was bigger than all the Indian tigers I have seen in European zoos. The animal lay under the shade of a great zamang. It had just killed a *chiguire*; but it had not yet touched its victim, over which it rested a paw. *Zamuros*, a kind of vulture, had gathered in flocks to devour what was left over from the jaguar's meal. It was a strange scene, mixing daring with timidity. They hop to within 2 feet of the jaguar, but the slightest movement and they rush away. To observe their movements more closely we climbed into the small canoe accompanying our pirogue. It is very rare for a tiger to attack a canoe by swimming out to it, and it will only do this if it has been deprived of all food for a long time. The noise of our oars made the animal slowly get up and hide behind the *sauso* shrub along the bank. The vultures wanted to profit from this momentary absence to devour the dead *chiguire*. But the tiger, despite our proximity, jumped into their midst; and in a fit of anger, expressed by the movement of its tail, dragged his prey into the jungle. The Indians lamented not having their lances to leap ashore and attack the tiger with. They are used to this weapon and did not trust our rifles, which in the humidity refused to fire.

Going on down the river we met the large herd of *chiguires* that the tiger had scattered after choosing his victim. These animals watched us come ashore without panicking. Some sat and stared at us like rabbits, moving their upper lips. They did not seem to fear man, but the sight of our big dog put them to flight. As their hindquarters are higher than their front they run with little gallops but so slowly that we managed to capture two of them. The *chiguire*, who swims well, lets out little groans when it runs as if it had difficulty breathing. It is the largest of the rodents; it defends itself only when it is surrounded or wounded. As its grinding teeth, particularly those at the back, are very strong and long it can, simply by biting, tear the paw off a tiger or the leg off a horse. Its flesh smells disagreeably of musk, yet local ham is made from it. That explains the name, 'water pig', given to it by ancient naturalists. Missionary monks do not hesitate to eat this ham during Lent. According to their classification they place the armadillo, the *chiguire* and the manatee near the turtles; the first because it is covered with a hard armour, like a kind of shell; the other two because they are amphibious. On the banks of the Santo Domingo, Apure and Arauca rivers, and in the marshes of the flooded savannahs, the *chiguires* reach such numbers that the pasture lands suffer. They graze the grass that fattens the horses, called *chiguirero*. They also eat fish. These animals, scared by the approach of our boat, stayed for eight to ten minutes under water.

We spent the night as usual in the open air, though we were in a plantation whose owner was hunting tigers. He was almost naked, and brownish-black like a *zambo*; this did not stop him believing that he was from the caste of whites. He called his wife and daughter, as naked as he was, Doña Isabela and Doña Manuela. Without ever having left the Apure river bank they took a lively interest 'in news from Madrid, of the unending wars, and that kind of thing from over there (*todas las cosas de allá*)'. He knew that the King of Spain would soon come and visit 'the great Caracas country', yet he added pleasingly, 'As people from the court eat only wheat bread they would never go beyond the town of Victoria so we would never see them here.' I had brought a *chiguire* with me that I wanted to roast; but our host assured me that '*Nosotros caballeros blancos* (white men like he and I) were not born to eat Indian game.' He offered us venison, killed the evening before with an arrow, as he did not have powder or firearms.

We supposed that a small wood of banana trees hid the farm hut; but this man, so proud of his nobility and the colour of his skin, had not bothered to build even an *ajupa* with palm leaves. He invited us to hang our hammocks near his, between two trees; and promised us, in a satisfied way, that if we returned up river during the rainy season we would find him under a roof. We would soon be complaining of a philosophy that rewards laziness and makes man indifferent to life's comforts. A furious wind rose after midnight, lightning crossed the sky, thunder groaned, and we were soaked to the bone. During the storm a bizarre accident cheered us up. Doña Isabela's cat was perched on the tamarind tree under which we were spending the night. He let himself fall into the hammock of one of our companions who, wounded by the cat's claws and woken from deepest sleep, thought he had been attacked by a wild animal. We ran up to him while he was screaming, and with embarrassment told him of his confusion. While the rain poured down on our hammocks and instruments Don Ignacio congratulated us on the good fortune of not having slept on the beach but on his land with well-bred white people, 'entre gente blanca y de trato'. As we were soaked it was hard to convince ourselves of this better situation, and we listened impatiently to the long story that our host told of his expedition to the Meta river, the bravery he had displayed in a bloody battle with the Guahibo Indians, and of the 'favours he had rendered to God and his King in kidnapping children (*los indiecitos*) from their parents to distribute them around the missions'. What an odd experience it was to find ourselves in these vast solitudes with a man who believed he was European, with all the vain pretensions, hereditary prejudices and mistakes of civilization, but whose only roof was a tree.

April 1st. At sunrise we said goodbye to Don Ignacio and Doña Isabela, his wife. We passed a low island where thousands of flamingoes, pink pelicans, herons and moorhens nested, displaying the most varied colours. These birds were so packed together that they gave the impression that they could not move. The island was called Isla de Aves.

We stopped on the right bank in a small mission inhabited by Indians of the Guamo tribe. There were some eighteen to twenty huts made of palm leaves, but in the statistics sent annually to the court by the missionaries this grouping of huts was registered under the name Pueblo de Santa Bárbara de Arichuna. The Guamo tribe refuse to be tamed and become sedentary. Their customs have much in common with the Achagua, Guahibo and Otomac, especially their dirtiness, their love for vengeance and their nomadic life-style, but their languages are completely different. These four tribes live principally from fishing and hunting on the often flooded plains between the Apure, Meta and Guaviare rivers. Nomadic life has been imposed by the physical conditions. The Indians of the Santa Bárbara mission could not offer us supplies as they grow only a little cassava. However, they were friendly, and when we entered their huts they gave us dried fish and water kept in porous jars where it stayed fresh.

We spent the night on a dry, wide beach. The night was silent and calm and the moon shone marvellously. The crocodiles lay on the beach so that they could see our fire. We thought that maybe the glow of the fire attracted them, as it did fish, crayfish and other water creatures. The Indians showed us tracks in the sand from three jaguars, two of them young; doubtless a female with cubs come to drink water. Finding no trees on the beach we stuck our oars in the sand and hung our hammocks. All was peaceful until about eleven when a dreadful noise began in the jungle around us that made sleep impossible. Among the many noises of screeching animals the Indians could recognize only those that were heard separately; the fluted notes of the *apajous*, the sighs of the alouate apes, the roar of the jaguar and puma; the calls of the peccary, sloth, hocco, *parraka* and other gallinaceous birds. When the jaguars approached the edge of the jungle our dog, who up to then had been barking continuously, began to growl and hid under our hammocks. Sometimes, after a long silence, we again heard the tiger's roar from the tops of trees, and then the din of monkeys' whistles as they fled from danger.

The confidence of the Indians helped to make us feel braver. One agrees with them that tigers fear fire, and never attack a man in his hammock. If you ask the Indians why jungle animals make such a din at certain moments of the night they say, 'They are celebrating the full moon.' I think that the din comes from deep in the jungle because a desperate fight is taking place. Jaguars, for example, hunt tapir and peccaries, who protect themselves in large herds, trampling down the vegetation in their way.

April 3rd. Since leaving San Fernando we had not met one boat on the beautiful river. Everything suggested the most profound solitude. In the morning the Indians had caught with a hook the fish called *caribe* or *caribito* locally as no other fish is more avid for blood.[93] It attacks bathers and swimmers by biting large chunks of flesh out of them. When one is slightly wounded it is difficult to leave the water without getting more wounds. Indians are terrified of the *caribe* fish and several showed us wounds on their calfs and thighs, deep scars made by these little fish that the Maypure call *umati*. They live at the bottom of rivers, but as soon as a few drops of blood are spilled in the water they reach the surface in their thousands.

When you consider the numbers of these fish, of which the most voracious and cruel are but 4 to 5 inches long, the triangular shape of their sharp, cutting teeth, and the width of their retractile mouths you cannot doubt the fear that the *caribe* inspires in the river inhabitants. In places on the river when the water was clear and no fish could be seen we threw bits of bloodied meat in, and within minutes a cloud of *caribes* came to fight for their food. I described and drew this fish on the spot. The *caribito* has a very agreeable taste. As one does not dare bathe when it is around you can regard it as the greatest scourge of this climate where mosquito bites and skin irritation make a bath so necessary.

At midday we stopped at a deserted spot called Algodonal. I left my companions while they beached the boat and prepared the meal. I walked along the beach to observe a group of crocodiles asleep in the sun, their tails, covered with broad scaly plates, resting on each other. Small herons, as white as snow, walked on their backs, even on their heads, as if they were tree trunks. The crocodiles were grey-green, their bodies were half covered in dried mud. From their colour and immobility they looked like bronze statues. However, my stroll almost cost me my life. I had been constantly looking towards the river, and then, on seeing a flash of mica in the sand, I also spotted fresh jaguar tracks, easily recognizable by their shape. The animal had gone off into the jungle, and as I looked in that direction I saw it lying down under the thick foliage of a ceiba, eighty steps away from me. Never has a tiger seemed so enormous.

There are moments in life when it is useless to call on reason. I was very scared. However, I was sufficiently in control of myself to remember what the Indians had advised us to do in such circumstances. I carried on walking, without breaking into a run or moving my arms, and thought I noted that the wild beast had its eye on a herd of capybaras swimming in the river. The further away I got the more I quickened my pace. I was so tempted to turn round and see if the cat was chasing me! Luckily I resisted this impulse, and the tiger remained lying down. These enormous cats with spotted skins are so well fed in this country well stocked with capybara, peccaries and deer that they rarely attack humans. I reached the launch panting and told my adventure story to the Indians, who did not give it much importance.

In the evening we passed the mouth of the Caño del Manati, named after the immense amount of manatees caught there every year. This herbivorous animal of the Cetacea family is called by the Indians *apcia* and *avia*, and reaches 10 to 12 feet long. The manatee is plentiful in the Orinoco. We dissected one that was 9 feet long while at Carichana, an Orinocan mission. The manatee eats so much grass that we found its stomach, divided into several cavities, and its intestines (108 feet long) filled with it. Its flesh is very savoury, though some prejudice considers it to be unwholesome and fever-producing. Its flesh when dried can last for a year. The clergy consider this mammal a fish, so they eat it at Lent.

We spent the night on Isla Conserva. The Indians had lit a camp-fire near the water. Again we confirmed that the glow of the flames attracted crocodiles and dolphins (*toninas*) whose noise stopped us sleeping until we decided to put the fire out. That night we had to get up twice. I mention this as an example of what it means to live in the jungle. A female jaguar approached our camp-site when it brought a cub to drink water. The Indians chased it away, but we heard its cub's cries, like a cat's, for hours. A little later our large dog was bitten, or stung as the Indians say, by some enormous bats[94] that flew around our hammocks. The wound in its snout was tiny and the dog howled more from fear than pain.

April 4th. It was our last day on the Apure river. During several days a plague of insects had been torturing our hands and faces. They were not mosquitoes but *zancudos*, which are really gnats. They appear after sunset; their proboscises are so long that they can pierce your hammock, your canvas and your clothes from the other side.

CHAPTER 16

ON LEAVING THE Apure river we found ourselves in a vastly different countryside. An immense plain of water stretched out in front of us like a lake as far as the eye could see. White-topped waves rose several feet high from the clash between the breeze and the current. We no longer heard the cries of the herons, flamingoes and spoonbills flying in long lines from one bank to the other. We vainly looked out for those diving birds whose busy tricks vary according to their species. Nature herself seemed less alive. Only now and then did we see between waves some large crocodiles breaking the water with their tails. The horizon was lined with a ribbon of jungle; but nowhere did the jungle reach the river. Vast beaches burned by the sun were as deserted and arid as sea beaches and, thanks to mirages, resembled stagnant marshes from afar. Rather than limiting the river these sandy banks blurred it. The banks drew near or receded according to the play of the sun's rays.

These scattered features of the countryside, this trait of solitude and grandeur, characterizes the course of the Orinoco, one of the greatest New World rivers. Everywhere water, like land, displays its unique characteristics. The Orinoco bed has no similarities with the Meta, Guaviare, Río Negro or Amazon beds. These differences do not depend solely on the width or speed of the current; they derive from a combination of relations easier to grasp on the spot than to define precisely. In the same way, the shape of the waves, the colour of the water, the kind of sky and clouds, all help a navigator guess whether he is in the Atlantic, the Mediterranean or in the equinoctial part of the Pacific.

A fresh east-north-east wind blew, allowing us to sail up the Orinoco towards the Encaramada mission. Our pirogue rode the waves so badly that the rocking of the boat caused those who suffered from seasickness to feel sick on the river. The lapping of the waves arises from two rivers meeting. We passed the Punta Curiquima, an isolated mass of quartzite granite, a small promontory composed of rounded blocks. It is there, on the right bank of the Orinoco, that Father Rotella founded a mission for the Palenka and Viriviri or Guire Indians. During flooding the Curiquima rock and village at its foot are completely surrounded by water. This serious inconvenience, and the innumerable mosquitoes and *niguas*,[95] made the suffering missionaries abandon their damp site. It is entirely deserted today while on the left bank the low Coruato mountains have become the retreat for those nomadic Indians either expelled from missions or from tribes not subject to the monks.

In the port of Encaramada we met some Caribs of Panapa with their cacique on their way up the Orinoco to take part in the famous fishing of turtle eggs. His pirogue was rounded towards the bottom like a *bongo*, and followed by a smaller canoe called a *curiara*. He was sitting under a kind of tent (*toldo*) built, like the sails, of palm leaves. His silent, cold reserve, and the respect others gave him, denoted an important person. The cacique was dressed like his people. All were naked, armed with bows and arrows, and covered in annatto, the dye made from *Bixa orellana*. The chief, the servants, the furniture, the sail and boat were all painted red. These Caribs are almost athletic in build and seemed far taller than any Indians we had seen up to now. Smooth, thick hair cut in a fringe like choir boys', eyebrows painted black, and a lively and gloomy stare give these Indians an incredibly hard expression. Having seen only skulls of these Indians in European collections we were surprised to see that their foreheads were more rounded than we had imagined. The fat, disgustingly dirty women carried their children on their backs. Their thighs and legs were bound by knotted cotton ligatures, leaving space for flesh to bulge out between the strands. It is noticeable that the Caribs are as careful about their exterior and dress as naked, painted men can be. They attach great importance to the shapes of certain parts of their bodies. A mother would be accused of indifference to her children if she did not artificially bind their calves in the fashion of the country. As none of our Apure Indians spoke the Carib language we could not ask the chief where he was going to camp to gather the turtle eggs.

The Indians of this area have preserved the belief that 'during the great flood, when their ancestors had to take to the canoes to escape, the sea waves beat against the Encaramada rocks'. This tradition is found in nearly all the tribes of the Upper Orinoco. When the Tamanaco are asked how the human race survived that great catastrophe they answer: 'A man and a woman saved themselves on a high mountain called Tamanacu and there threw seed from the mauritia palm over their heads, and little men and women were born from the seeds who repopulated the world.' Among wild tribes we find a simple version of a legend that the Greeks had embellished with their great imagination! A few leagues from Encaramada a rock called Tepu-mereme (Painted Rock) rises in the middle of the savannah. It is covered with animal drawings and symbolic signs. The representations that we have found on rocks in uninhabited places – stars, suns, jaguars, crocodiles – do not seem to be related to religious cults. These hieroglyphic figures are frequently carved so high up that only scaffolding could reach them. When we asked the Indians how they could have carved those images, they answered, smiling, as if only whites could ignore such an obvious answer: 'During *the great waters*, their ancestors reached those rocks in their canoes.'

The fresh north-east wind blew us at full sail towards the *boca de la tortuga*. At eleven in the morning we landed on an island, which the Indians of the Uruana mission regard as their own, situated in the middle of the river. This island is famous for the fishing of turtles or, as is said here, the *cosecha*, or annual harvest of eggs. We found a group of Indians camping in palm-leaf huts. This camp-site had over 300 people in it. As we had been used, since San Fernando de Apure, to seeing only deserted beaches, we were struck by the bustle. Apart from Guamos and Otomacs, seen as two wild and untamed tribes, there were Caribs and other Indians from the Lower Orinoco.

Each tribe camped separately, and could be recognized only by the different paints on their skins. We also found, among this noisy reunion, some white men, mainly *pulperos*, the small traders from Angostura, who had come upstream to buy turtle-egg oil from the Indians. The Uruana missionary, from Alcalá de Henares, came to meet us, extremely surprised to see us there. After inspecting our instruments, he exaggeratedly described the hardships we would suffer going further upstream beyond the cataracts. The purpose of our journey seemed very mysterious to him. 'How is anyone to believe,' he said, 'that you left your homeland to come up this river to be eaten by mosquitoes and measure lands that do not belong to you?' Luckily we were armed with recommendations from the guardian father of the Franciscan missions, while the brother-in-law of the Barinas governor accompanying us soon resolved the doubts that the whites there had about our dress, accent and arrival on the island. The missionary invited us to share a frugal meal of bananas and fish with him. He told us he had come to camp with the Indians during the harvesting of the eggs 'to celebrate open-air mass every day, to get oil for the lights in his church, and above all to govern this Republica de Indios y Castellanos where individuals wanted to profit selfishly with what God had given to everybody'.

We walked round the island with the missionary and a *pulpero* who boasted that he had been visiting the Indians' camp and the *pesca de tortugas* for over ten years. People come to this part of the Orinoco in the same way we visit fairs in Frankfurt or Beaucaire. We were on a plain of perfectly smooth sand. 'As far as the eye can see,' they told us, 'a layer of sand covers the turtle eggs.' The missionary had a long pole in his hand. He showed us that by sounding with this pole (*vara*) he could determine the depth of the stratum of eggs in the same way a miner discovers the limits of a bed of marl, bog iron or coal. By thrusting the pole perpendicularly into the sand he immediately feels, by the lack of resistance, that he has penetrated into the cavity hiding the eggs. We saw that the stratum is generally spread with such uniformity that the pole finds it everywhere in a radius of 10 toises around any given spot. People speak of 'square poles of eggs'; it is like a minefield divided into regularly exploited lots. The stratum of eggs is far from covering the whole island; it is no longer found where land rises abruptly because the turtles cannot climb to these plateaux. I reminded my guides that Father Gumilla's vivid descriptions assured us that the Orinoco beaches have less grains of sand than turtles, and that they were so numerous that if men and tigers did not annually kill thousands of them the turtles would stop boats sailing upstream. 'Son cuentos de frailes,' the *pulpero* from Angostura whispered; for the only travellers in these lands are poor missionaries and what one calls monks' tales here are what in Europe would be called travellers' tales.

Indians assured us that upstream on the Orinoco, from its mouth to its junction with the Apure, not one island nor one beach could be found to harvest eggs. The large *arrau* turtle fears inhabited places where there are many boats. It is a shy and suspicious animal, which raises its head above the water and hides on hearing the slightest noise. The beaches where nearly all the Orinoco turtles seem to annually gather is situated between the junction of the Orinoco and Apure and the Great Cataracts or Raudales between Abruta and the Atures mission. It seems that *arrau* turtles cannot climb up the cataracts, and that beyond Atures and Maypures you only find *terekay* turtles.

The three camps formed by the Indians are set up during the end of March and first days of April. The harvesting of the eggs is carried out in the regular way that characterizes all monastic institutions. Before the arrival of the monks up the river Indians profited far less from an abundant harvest supplied by nature. Each tribe dug in the beach wherever they felt like it and broke innumerable eggs because they did not dig carefully, and they unearthed more eggs than they needed. It was like amateurs exploiting a mine. Jesuit fathers have the merit of having regularized the exploitation, and although the Franciscans, who succeeded the Jesuits, boast that they follow their predecessors' examples they do not do all that prudence dictates. Jesuits did not allow the whole beach to be dug up; they kept a small part intact, for fear of seeing the race of *arrau* turtles destroyed or diminished. Today the whole beach is dug up. It has been noticed that the harvests are getting smaller and smaller each year.

Once the camp has been set up the Uruana missionary designates his representative or superintendent, who divides the beach into lots according to the number in each tribe who are to harvest. They are all mission Indians, as naked and stupid as jungle Indians: they are called *reducidos* and *neofitos* because they attend church when the bells toll, and kneel during Communion. With a long pole made of wood or bamboo, he examines the extent of the stratum of eggs. According to our calculations this reaches 120 feet from the shore, and 3 feet deep. The Indians dig with their hands, put the harvested eggs in baskets called *mappiri*, and bring them to the camp to throw them into great wooden troughs filled with water. The eggs are smashed with sticks, shaken about and exposed to the sun until the yolk, the oily floating part, thickens out. This oily substance collecting on the surface is scooped off and cooked on a hot fire. The animal oil turns into what is called *manteca de tortuga* by the Spaniards (turtle fat), and keeps better the longer it is cooked. If it is well done it is completely clear, without smell and barely yellow. Missionaries compare it with the best olive oil and not only use it for burning in lamps but also for cooking, as its taste does not spoil good food. However, we could never obtain the pure oil. Generally it stinks because the eggs are mixed up with the already formed but dead baby turtles.

I acquired some statistical notions on the spot by consulting the Uruana missionary and the traders. The three beaches furnish annually some 5,000 *botijas*, or jars of oil. Two hundred eggs yield enough oil to fill a bottle, and 5,000 eggs to fill the jar. If we estimate the number of eggs laid by each turtle as 116, and reckon that one third are destroyed, we can calculate that 330,000 *arrau* turtles must lay 33 million eggs on the three shores. But this calculation is far too low. For example, the number of eggs that hatch before the *cosecha* is so prodigious that near the Uruana camp I saw the whole beach swarming with little turtles escaping from the Indian children.

The Indians who go harvesting take thousands of dried or lightly cooked eggs away to their villages. Our rowers always had some in baskets or cotton bags. When they are well preserved the taste is not too bad. They showed us large turtle shells emptied by jaguars, who wait for the turtles on the beach where the eggs are laid. They attack them on the sand. To eat them they turn them upside down so that the undershell is right-side up. In this position the turtles cannot right themselves, and as jaguars turn many more over than they can eat in one night the Indians avail themselves of the cats' greed and cunning. If you think how hard it is for a travelling naturalist to pull the turtle's body out without separating it from the cuirass of the shell you can only admire the litheness of the jaguar's paw as it empties the two-sided shield of the *arrau* as if the muscular ligaments had been severed by a surgeon. The jaguar chases turtles into the water, even digs up the eggs, and, along with the crocodile, heron and gallinazo vulture, is one of the cruellest enemies of the newborn turtles. When the first rains come – called 'turtle rains' (*peje canepori*) – the wild Indians go along the Orinoco banks with their poisoned arrows and kill the turtles as they warm themselves in the sun.

Our pilot had tied up the pirogue at the Playa de Huevos to buy provisions as our stores were running out. We found fresh meat; Angostura rice and even biscuits made of wheat. Our Indians filled the boat with live young turtles and sundried eggs for their own use. After saying goodbye to the missionary who had been so friendly to us we continued our journey upstream. There was a fresh wind that turned into squalls. Since we had entered the mountainous part of the country we had begun to notice that our boat sailed poorly, but the pilot wanted to show the Indians gathered on the bank that by sailing close to the wind he could reach the middle of the stream without tacking. Just as he was boasting of his skill and the daring of his manoeuvre the wind gusted against the sail with such violence that we nearly sank. One of the boat's sides was submerged. Water poured in so suddenly that we were soon knee-deep in water. It washed over a table I was writing on in the stern. I just managed to rescue my diary, and then saw our books, dried plants and papers floating away. Bonpland was sleeping in the middle of the boat. Woken by the flooding water and the shrieking Indian he immediately took control of the situation with that coolness which he always showed in danger.[96] As one side of the boat rose up out of the water he did not think the boat would sink. He thought that if we had to abandon boat we could swim ashore as there were no crocodiles about. Then the ropes holding the sails broke, and the same gust of wind that almost sank us now helped us recover. We baled the water out with gourds, mended the sail, and in less than half an hour we were able to continue our journey. When we criticized our pilot for having sailed too close to the wind he resorted to that typical Indian phlegmatic attitude: 'that the whites would find plenty of sun on the beaches to dry their papers'. We had lost only one book overboard – the first volume of Schreber's *Genera plantarum*. Such losses are particularly painful when you are able to take so few scientific books.

As night fell we camped on a deserted island in the middle of the river. We dined in the moonlight sitting on scattered empty turtle shells. How pleasing it was to be safe and together! We imagined how it would be if one man had saved himself alone, wandering these deserted banks, meeting more and more tributaries and unable to swim because of the crocodile and *caribe* fish. We pictured this sensitive man never knowing what had happened to his companions, more worried about them than himself. If you like surrendering to these sad thoughts it is because escaping from danger makes you feel the need for strong emotions.

We landed in the middle of the Strait of Baraguan to measure the river's breadth. In this excessively hot place we looked in vain for plants in the clefts of rocks. The stones were covered with thousands of iguanas and geckos with spreading, membranous fingers. The thermometer placed against the rock rose to 50.2 °C. The ground appeared to undulate in the mirages, without a breath of wind in the air. How vivid is the calm of nature at midday in these burning zones. The wild animals retire to the thickets; birds hide under leaves. Yet in this silence, if you listen carefully, you hear slight sounds, a dull vibration, a hum of insects. Nothing makes you sense the extent and power of organic life more keenly than this.

We spent the night on the left bank of the Orinoco, at the foot of a granite hill. In this deserted place there had once stood the San Regis mission. We dearly wanted to find a spring in Baraguan for the river water smelled of musk and had a sweetish, unpleasant taste. The Indians said, 'It is due to the bark' – they meant coriaceous skin – 'of the rotting crocodiles. The older they are, the more bitter their bark is.'

April 9th. We reached the Pararuma beach early in the morning where we found a camp of Indians, like those we had seen before. They had come to dig up the sand and harvest turtle eggs for their oil but unluckily they had arrived several days too late. The young turtles had broken out of their eggs before the Indians had set up camp. Crocodiles and *garzas*, a kind of white heron, had benefited from this mistake because they devour quantities of these young. They hunt at night as the young turtles do not break the surface of the sand until it is dark.

Among the Indians gathered at Pararuma we found some whites who had come from Angostura to buy turtle butter. After wearying us with their complaints about the 'poor harvest' and about the harm done by the jaguars as the turtles laid their eggs, they led us under an *ajupa* raised in the middle of the Indian camp. There we found the missionary monks from Carichana and the cataracts sitting on the ground playing cards and smoking tobacco in long pipes. These poor priests received us in a very friendly manner. They had been suffering from tertiary fever for months. Pale and emaciated, they had no trouble convincing us that the countries we were about to visit were dangerous for our health.

The Indian pilot who had led us from San Fernando de Apure up to the Pararuma beach did not know his way through the Orinoco rapids, and no longer wanted to sail our boat. We had to accept his decision. Luckily the Carichana missionary agreed to loan us a fine pirogue quite cheaply. Father Bernardo Zea, missionary from Atures and Maypures near the Great Cataracts, even offered to accompany us himself to the

Brazilian border. The number of Indians willing to carry the canoes along the cataracts was so few that without this monk's presence we risked waiting weeks in that humid and unhealthy area. Father Zea hoped to recover his health by visiting the Río Negro missions. He talked of those places with the enthusiasm that all those in the colonies feel when talking about far-off places.

The gathering of Indians at Pararuma again afforded a fascinating chance for civilized men to study the development of our intellectual faculties in savages. It is hard to recognize in this infancy of society, in this gathering of dull, silent, impassive Indians, the primitive origins of our species. We do not see here a human nature that is sweet and naïve as described by our poets. We would like to persuade ourselves that these Indians, squatting by the fire, or sitting on huge turtle shells, their bodies covered in mud and grease, fixing their eyes stupidly for hours on the drink they are preparing, belong to a degenerate race rather than being a primitive type of our own species that, having been dispersed for ages in jungles, have fallen back into barbarism.

Red paint is – we could say – the only clothing the Indians use. Two kinds may be distinguished according to how prosperous they are. The common decoration of the Caribs, Oto- macs and Yaruros is annatto, which Spaniards call *achote*. It is the colouring matter extracted from the pulp of *Bixa orellana*. To prepare this annatto Indian women throw the seeds of the plant into a tub filled with water. They beat this for an hour and then leave the mixture to deposit the colouring fecula, which is an intense brick-red. After pouring off the water they take out the fecula, dry it in their hands and mix it with turtle oil, after which it is shaped into rounded cakes. Another more precious pigment comes from a plant of the Bignoniaceae family, which Bonpland has made known by the name *Bignonia chica*. It climbs up the tallest trees by attaching its tendrils. Its bilabiate flowers are an inch long and of a pretty violet colour. The fruit is a pod filled with winged seeds, some 2 feet long. This bignonia grows wild and abundantly near Maypures. The red chica dye does not come from the fruit but from the leaves when soaked in water. The colouring matter separates itself as a light powder. It is gathered, without being mixed with turtle oil, into little loaves. When heated they give off a pleasant smell of benzoin. Chica, which was not known until our voyage, could even be used in the arts. The chemistry practised by the savage is essentially the preparation of pigments and poisons, and the neutralization of amylaceous roots.

Most missionaries on the Upper and Lower Orinoco let their Indians paint their skin. It is painful to say that some missionaries make a profit from the nakedness of Indians. Unable to sell them cloth or clothes the monks trade in red pigment. I have often seen in their huts, pompously called *conventos*, stores of chica cakes, sold for up to four francs. To give an exact idea of what Indians mean by luxury I would say that here a man of large stature hardly earns for two weeks' work enough chica to paint himself red. Just as in temperate climates we say of a poor man that 'he does not earn enough to dress himself' so I have heard Indians say that 'a man is so miserable he cannot even paint half his body'.

Some Indians are not content with colouring themselves evenly all over. They sometimes imitate European clothes by painting them on. We saw one at Parurama who had painted a blue jacket with black buttons on to his skin.

We were struck to see in the Parurama camp that old women were more preoccupied in painting themselves than young ones. We saw an Otomac woman having her hair rubbed with turtle oil and her back painted with annatto by her two daughters. The ornaments consisted of a kind of lattice-work in crossed black lines on a red background. It was work needing incredible patience. We came back from a long herborization and the painting was still only half done. It is all the more amazing that this research into ornament does not result in tattooing, for the painting done so carefully washes off if the Indian exposes herself to a downpour. Some nations paint themselves to celebrate festivals; others are covered in paint all year round. With these Indians annatto is seen as so indispensable that men and women have less shame in appearing without a *guayuco*[97] than without paint. The Orinoco *guayucos* are made from bark and cotton. Men wear larger ones than women who, according to the missionaries, seem to feel less shame than men. Shouldn't we attribute this indifference, this lack of shame in the women in tribes that are not depraved, to the state of numbness and slavery to which the female sex has been reduced in South America by the injustice and power of men?

When one speaks in Europe of a Guianan Indian we imagine a man whose head and waist are decorated with beautiful macaw, toucan and hummingbird feathers. Our painters and sculptors have for a long time seen these ornaments as typical of the native Americans. We were surprised not to find, on any of the Orinoco and Casiquiare banks, these fine feathers that travellers so frequently reported from Cayenne and Demerara. Most of the Guianan Indians, even those with the most developed intellectual faculties, who cultivate food and weave with cotton, are naked and poor. Extreme heat and sweating make clothes unbearable.

In the Pararuma camp we saw for the first time some live animals that we had only previously seen stuffed in European cabinets. Missionaries trade with these little animals. They exchange tobacco, a resin called *mani*, chica pigment, *gallitos* (cock-of-the-rocks), titi monkeys, capuchin monkeys, and other monkeys appreciated on the coast, for cloth, nails, axes, hooks and needles. These Orinoco animals are bought at disgustingly low prices from the Indians who live in the monks' missions. These same Indians then have to buy from the monks at very high prices what they need for fishing and farming with the money they get from the egg harvest. We bought various little animals, which travelled with us for the rest of our voyage upriver, enabling us to study their way of life.

The *gallitos*, or cock-of-the-rocks, sold at Pararuma in pretty cages woven from palm leaves, are far rarer on the Orinoco banks and in all northern and western tropical America than in French Guiana. They have been spotted only here in the Raudales. This bird chooses its nest in hollows in the granite rocks of the cataracts. We saw it a few times in the middle of the foaming river, calling its females and fighting like our cocks while folding back the mobile double crest on top of its head.

The titi of the Orinoco (*Simia sciurea*) is very common south of the cataracts. Its face is white, with a blue-black spot covering its mouth and the tip of its nose. No other monkey reminds you more of a child than the titi; the same innocent expression, the same cheeky smile, the same sudden shifts from joy to sadness. Its large eyes fill with tears the moment it is frightened. It is avid for insects, especially spiders. The cleverness of this little monkey is such that one we brought in our boat could perfectly distinguish different plates in Cuvier's *Tableau élémentaire d'histoire naturelle*.[98] Though the engravings are not coloured yet the titi tried to catch a grasshopper or a wasp with its small hand every time we showed a plate with these insects represented. When several of these little monkeys are shut up in the same cage and exposed to rain they twist their tails round their necks and hug each other to warm themselves. The titis are delicate and timid little animals. They become sad and dejected when they leave the jungle and enter the llanos.

The *macavahu*, called by the missionaries *viuditas*, or 'widows in mourning', has soft glossy black hair. Its face is a kind of whitish-blue square mask, which contains its eyes, nose and mouth. Its ears have an edge; are small, pretty and hairless. Its neck has a white area in two rings. Its feet, or hind legs, are black like its body, but its forehands are white outside and black inside. These white spots led the missionaries to recognize a veil, a neck scarf and the gloves of a widow in mourning. The character of this little monkey, which sits up on its hind legs to eat, is not related to its appearance. It has a wild and shy air, and often refuses food even when ravenous. We have seen it remain motionless for hours without sleeping, attentive to everything happening around it. The *viudita*, when alone, becomes furious at the sight of a bird, and climbs and runs with astonishing speed, and, like a cat, leaps on to its prey and eats all it can. The *viuditas* accompanied us throughout our entire voyage on the Casiquiare and Río Negro. It is an advantage to study animals for several months in the open air, and not indoors where they lose their natural vivacity.

We began to load the new pirogue. It was, like all Indian canoes, made from one tree trunk, hollowed out by axe and fire. It was 40 feet long and 3 feet wide. Three people could not squeeze together from one side to the other. These pirogues are so unstable that the weight must be distributed very equally and if you want to stand up for a second you must warn the rowers (*bogas*) to lean over the other side. Without this precaution water would pour in on the lopsided side. It is difficult to form an idea of the inconveniences of these miserable boats.

The missionary from the Raudales looked after the preparations for our journey rather too well. He worried that there might not be enough Maco and Guahibo Indians on hand who knew the labyrinth of small canals and rapids that form the *raudales* and cataracts, so at night he put two Indians in the *cepo*, that is, they were tied to the ground and fastened together between two pieces of wood with a padlock. In the morning we were awoken by the shouts of a young Indian who was being brutally beaten with a whip of manatee skin. His name was Zerepe, an extremely intelligent Indian who later served us well, but at the time refused to travel with us. He had been born in the Atures mission; his father was from the Maco tribe and his mother from the Maypure; he had run off to the jungle (*al monte*) and lived with wild Indians for years. He had learned several languages, and the missionary used him as an interpreter. Not without difficulty did we obtain his pardon. 'Without severity,' we were told, 'you would get nothing.'

April 10th. We were unable to set sail until ten in the morning. It was hard to adapt to the new pirogue, which we saw as a new prison. To make it wider at the back of the boat we made branches into a kind of trellis, which stuck out on both sides. Unfortunately the leaf roof of this lattice-work was so low that you either had to lie down, and consequently saw nothing, or you had to stay hunched over. The need to transport pirogues across rapids, and even from one river to another, and the fear of giving too much hold to the wind by raising the *toldo* made this construction necessary for the little boats going up the Río Negro. The roof was designed for four people stretched out on the deck or lattice-work, but your legs stuck far out, and when it rained half your body got wet. Worse still, you lie on oxhides or tiger skins, and the branches under the skins hurt you when you lie down. The front of the boat was filled with the Indian rowers, armed with 3-foot-long paddles in the form of spoons. They are all naked, sitting in twos, and row beautifully together. Their songs are sad and monotonous. The little cages with our birds and monkeys, increasing as we went on, were tied to the *toldo* and the prow. It was our travelling zoo. Despite losses due to accidents and sunstroke, we counted fourteen little animals when we came back from the Casiquiare. Every night when we established camp, our zoo and instruments occupied the middle; around them we hung our hammocks, then the Indians' hammocks and, outside, the fires we thought indispensable to scare off jaguars. At sunrise our caged monkeys answered the cries of the jungle monkeys.

In the overloaded pirogue, which was only 3 feet deep, there was no other room for the dried plants, trunks, sextant, compass and meteorological instruments but under the lattice of branches on which we were obliged to lie down for most of our trip. To take the smallest object from a trunk, or to use an instrument, we had to moor up and get ashore. To these inconveniences can be added the torment of mosquitoes that accumulate under the low roof, and the heat coming from the palm leaves continually exposed to the burning sun. We tried everything to improve our situation, without any results. While one of us hid under a sheet to avoid insects, the other insisted on lighting greenwood under the *toldo* to chase off the mosquitoes with the smoke. Pain in our eyes and increasing heat in a climate that was already asphyxiating made both these means impractical. With some gaiety of temper, with looking after each other and taking a lively interest in the majestic nature of these great river valleys, the travellers put up with the evils that became habitual. I have entered into such minute details in order to describe how we navigated on the Orinoco, and to show that despite our goodwill, Bonpland and I were not able to multiply our observations during this section of the journey.

April 11th. To avoid the effect of flooding, so harmful to health, the Carichana mission was installed some three quarters of a league from the river. The Indians belonged to the Saliva tribe, and speak with a disagreeable nasal pronunciation. They are mild, shy and sociable, easier to discipline than other tribes on the Orinoco. To escape the dominating Caribs the Saliva readily congregated in the early Jesuit missions. These fathers praised the intelligence of these tribes, and their keenness to learn. The Saliva show a natural talent for music; from remote times they have played a trumpet, some 4 or 5 feet long, made of baked earth, with several large globular cavities joined by narrow pipes. The sound is mournful. Since the dispersion of the Jesuits missionaries have continued to stimulate their beautiful religious music. Not long ago a traveller was surprised to see how Indians played the violin, violoncello, guitar and flute.

Among the Saliva Indians we found a white woman, the sister of a Jesuit from New Granada. After having lived with people who did not understand us, it is hard to describe the joy we felt on meeting somebody with whom we could converse without an interpreter. Each mission has at least two interpreters, *lenguarazes*. These Indians are rather less stupid than the others through whom the missionaries, who do not bother to learn the languages any more, communicate with neophytes. These interpreters accompanied us when we went out botanizing; they understood Spanish but spoke it badly. With their usual apathy they would arbitrarily answer any questions with a smiling 'yes father' or 'no father'. You will understand that after months of this kind of dialogue you lose patience without managing to get the information that you urgently require. It was not rare for us to use several interpreters, and sometimes we had to translate several times the same sentence in order to begin to understand the Indians. 'After leaving my mission,' said the goodly monk at Uruana, 'you will be travelling as mutes.' This prediction was exact. To get something even from the most primitive Indians we met, we turned to sign language. As soon as the Indian realizes you do not need him as an interpreter but are asking him something directly by pointing it out, he drops his usual apathy and shows a special skill in making himself understood. He varies his signs, pronounces his words slowly, and seems flattered by your interest.

April 12th. We left Carichana at about two in the afternoon and found our way obstructed with granite blocks that break the river current. We passed close to the great reef called Piedra del Tigre. The river is so deep that sounding with a line of 22 fathoms did not touch the bottom. Towards the evening the sky covered over and squalls of wind announced a coming storm. It began to pour so hard with rain that our leafy roof hardly protected us. Luckily the rain scared off the mosquitoes that had been tormenting us all day. We were opposite the Cariven cataract, and the current was so strong that we had great difficulty in reaching land. Time and time again we were pushed back to the middle of the river until two Salivas, excellent swimmers, threw themselves into the water and swam ashore, pulling the boat in until it could be tied to a rock where we spent the night. Thunder rolled all night; the river swelled under our eyes, and we often worried that the furious waves would sink our fragile boat.

From the mouth of the Meta, the Orinoco seemed freer of shoals and rocks. We navigated in a canal 500 toises wide. The Indians stayed in the pirogue, rowing without towing or pushing it with their hands, tiring us with their wild screams. It was already dark when we found ourselves by the Raudal de Tabaje. The Indians did not want to risk crossing the cataract and so we spent the night on land on a site that was extremely uncomfortable, on a rock bench with a steep slope sheltering a cloud of bats in crevices. All night we heard the cries of jaguars. Our dog answered by howling back. The deafening noise of the Orinoco waterfalls contrasted with the thunder grumbling over the jungle.

April 13th. Early in the morning we passed the Tabaje rapids and landed again. Father Zea, who accompanied us, wanted to say mass in the new San Borja mission established two years before. We found six huts inhabited by uncatechized Indians. They were no different from wild Indians. Only their large black eyes showed more liveliness than those living in older missions. They refused our brandy without even trying it. The young girls had their faces marked with round black spots. The rest of their bodies were not painted. Some of the men had beards, and they seemed proud. Holding our chins they showed through signs that they were made like us. I was again struck by how similar all the Orinoco Indians are. Their look is sombre and sad, not hard or ferocious. Without any notions about the practices of the Christian religion they behaved quite decently in the church. Indians like representations; they submit themselves momentarily to any nuisance provided they are sure of being stared at. Just before the moment of communion they make signs to show that the priest was about to bring the chalice to his lips. Apart from this gesture they stay immobile, in their imperturbable apathy.

AS THE ORINOCO runs from south to north it crosses a chain
of granite mountains. Twice checked in its course the river
breaks furiously against rocks that form steps and transversal
dykes. Nothing can be grander than this countryside. Neither
the Tequendama Falls[99] near Bogotá, nor the magnificent cordilleras surpassed my first impressions of the Atures and Maypures rapids. Standing in a position that dominates the
uninterrupted series of cataracts it is as if the river, lit by the
setting sun, hangs above its bed like an immense sheet of foam
and vapours. The two great and famous cataracts of the Orinoco are formed as the river breaks through the Parima mountains. Indians call them Mapara and Quituna, but missionaries
have substituted these names with Atures and Maypures,
named after tribes living in two villages near by. On the Caracas coast the two Great Cataracts are simply called the two
Raudales, from the Spanish *raudo*, 'rushing'.[100]

   Beyond the Great Cataracts an unknown land begins. This
partly mountainous and partly flat land receives tributaries
from both the Amazon and the Orinoco. No missionary writing about the Orinoco before me has passed beyond the Maypures *raudal*. Up river, along the Orinoco for a stretch of over
100 leagues, we came across only three Christian settlements
with some six to eight whites of European origin there. Not
surprisingly, such a deserted territory has become the classic
place for legends and fantastic histories. Up here serious missionaries have located tribes whose people have one eye in the
middle of their foreheads, the heads of dogs, and mouths
below their stomachs. It would be wrong to attribute these
exaggerated fictions to the inventions of simple missionaries

because they usually come by them from Indian legends. From his vocation, a missionary does not tend towards scepticism; he imprints on his memory all that the Indians have repeated and when back in Europe delights in astonishing people by reciting facts he has collected. These travellers' and monks' tales (*cuentos de viajeros y frailes*) increase in improbability the further you go from the Orinoco forests towards the coasts inhabited by whites. When at Cumaná you betray signs of incredulity, you are silenced by these words, 'The fathers have seen it, but far above the Great Cataracts *más arriba de los Raudales.*'

April 15th. At dawn we passed the Anaveni river, a tributary river that comes down from mountains in the east. The heat was so excessive that we stayed for a long time in a shaded place, fishing, but we could not carry off all the fish we hooked. Much later we reached the foot of the Great Cataract in a bay, and took the difficult path – it was night by then – to the Atures mission, a league away. We found this mission in a deplorable state. At the time of Solano's boundary expedition[101] it contained 320 Indians. Today it has only forty-seven. When it was founded Atures, Maypures, Meyepures, Abanis and Uirupas tribes lived there, but now there were only Guahibos and a few families from the Macos left. The Atures have completely disappeared; the little known about them comes from burial caves in Ataruipe.

Between the 4th and 8th degrees of latitude the Orinoco not only divides the great jungles of Parima from the bare savannahs of the Apure, Meta and Guaviare but also separates tribes of very different customs. On the west the Guahibo, Chiricoa and Guamo tribes wander through treeless plains. They are filthy, proud of their independence, wild, and hard to settle in a fixed place to do regular work. Spanish missionaries call them *indios andantes* (wandering Indians). On the east of the Orinoco live the Maco, Saliva, Curacicana and Pareca tribes; they are tame, peaceful farmers who easily adapt to missionary discipline.

In the Atures mission both types of tribe can be found. With the missionary we visited huts of the Macos. The independent Macos are orderly and clean. They have their *roch-elas*, or villages, two or three days' journey away. They are very numerous and like all wild Indians cultivate cassava, not maize. Thanks to these peaceful relations some *indios monteros*, or nomadic Indians, had established themselves in the mission a short time before. They insistently asked for knives, hooks and coloured glass beads, which they sewed on to their *guayucos* (*perizomas*). Once they got what they wanted they slipped back to the jungle because missionary discipline was not to their liking. Epidemics of fever, so common at the start of the rainy season, contributed to the desertion. Jungle Indians have a horror of the life of civilized man and desert when the slightest misfortune befalls them in the mission.

Smallpox, which has so devastated other areas of America that Indians burn their huts, kill their children and avoid any grouping of tribes, is not one of the reasons for the depopulation of the Raudales. In the Upper Orinoco this plague is almost unknown. Desertion from Christian missionaries must be sought more in the Indian's hate for the discipline, the poor food, the awful climate, and the unpardonable custom that Indian mothers have of using poisonous herbs to avoid pregnancy. Many of the women do not want to have babies. If they do have children they are not only exposed to jungle dangers but also to absurd superstitions. When twins are born family honour demands that one be killed. Indians say: 'To bring twins into the world is to be exposed to public scorn, it is to resemble rats, sarigues and the vilest animals.' And, 'Two children born at the same time cannot belong to the same father.' If a newborn child shows some physical deformity the father kills it immediately. They want only well-formed, robust children because deformities indicate some evil spell. Among the Orinoco Indians the father returns home only to eat or sleep in his hammock; he shows no affection for his children or his wife, who are there only to serve him.

While we unloaded the pirogue we investigated the impressive spectacle of a great river squeezed and reduced to foam. Instead of just describing my own sensations I shall try to paint an overall view of one of the most famous spots in the

New World. The more imposing and majestic a scene, the more important it is to capture it in its smallest details, to fix the outline of the picture that you want to present to the reader's imagination, and to simply describe the particular characteristics of the great monuments of nature.

Throughout his entire journey through the Lower Orinoco the traveller faces only one danger: the natural rafts formed by drifting trees uprooted by the river. Woe to the canoes that at night strike one of these rafts of tangled lianas and tree trunks! When Indians wish to attack an enemy by surprise they tie several canoes together and cover them with grass to make it seem like a tangle of trees. Today Spanish smugglers do the same to avoid customs in Angostura.

Above the Anaveni river, between the Uniana and Sipapu mountains, you reach the Mapara and Quituna cataracts, commonly called by missionaries the Raudales. These natural weirs crossing from one side to the other offer the same picture: one of the greatest rivers in the world breaks into foam among many islands, rocky dykes and piles of granite blocks covered in palms.[102]

April 16th. Towards evening we heard that our boats had passed both rapids in less than six hours, and arrived in good condition at the Puerto de Arriba. 'Your boat will not be wrecked because you are not carrying goods, and you travel with the monk of the Raudales,' a little brown man said to us bitterly. By his accent we recognized him as a Catalan. He traded in tortoise oil with the mission Indians, and was not a friend of the missionaries. 'The frail boats belong to us Catalans who, with permission from the Guianan Government, but not from the president of the mission, try to trade above the Atures and Maypures. Our boats are wrecked in the Raudales, key to all the missions beyond, and then Indians take us back to Carichana and try to force us to stop trading.' What is the source of this deep hatred of the missions in the Spanish colonies? It cannot be because they are rich in the Upper Orinoco. They have no houses, no goats and few cows. The resentment is aimed at the ways the missionaries obstinately close their territories off to white men.

In the little Atures church we were shown remains of the
Jesuits' wealth. A heavy silver lamp lay half buried in sand. This
object did not tempt the Indians; the Orinoco natives are not
thieves, and have a great respect for property. They do not
even steal food, hooks or axes. At Maypures and Atures locks
on doors are unknown.

The missionary told us a story about the jaguars. Some
months before our arrival a young jaguar had wounded a child
while playing with him. I have verified the facts on the spot; it
should interest those who study animal behaviour. Two Indian
children, a boy and a girl of about eight and nine years of age,
were sitting on the grass near the village when a jaguar came
out from the jungle and ran round the children, jumping and
hiding in the high grass, like our cats. The little boy sensed
danger only when the jaguar struck him with its paw until
blood began to flow. The little girl chased it off with branches
from a tree. The intelligent little boy was brought to us. The
jaguar's claw had ripped skin from his forehead. What did this
playfulness mean in the jaguar? If the jaguar was not hungry,
why did it approach the children? There is something mysterious in the sympathies and hatreds of animals.

In this area there are several species of peccaries, or pigs
with lumbar glands, only two of which are known to naturalists in Europe. The Indians call the little peccary a *chacharo*.
Reared in their houses they become tame like our sheep and
goats. Another kind is called the *apida*, which is also domesticated and wanders in large herds. These animals announce
themselves from a long way off because they break down all
the shrubs in their way. During a botanical excursion Bonpland was warned by his Indian guides to hide behind a tree
trunk as these *cochinos*, or *puercos del monte*, passed by. The flesh
of the *chacharo* is flabby and disagreeable, but the Indians hunt
them nevertheless, with small lances tied to cords. We were
told at Atures that jaguars dread being surrounded by herds
of wild pigs and climb trees to save themselves. Is this a
hunters' tale, or a fact?

Among the monkeys we saw at the Atures mission we
found one new species, which the creoles call *machis*. It is the

ouavapavi,[103] with grey hair and a bluish face. This little animal is as tame as it is ugly. Every day in the missionary courtyard it would grab a pig and sit on its back all day. We have also seen it riding a large cat brought up in Father Zea's house.

It was at the cataracts that we first heard talk about the hairy man of the jungle, called *salvaje*, who rapes women, builds huts, and sometimes eats human flesh. Neither Indians nor missionaries doubt the existence of this man-shaped monkey, which terrifies them. Father Gili seriously related the story of a lady from San Carlos who praised the gentle character of the man of the jungle. She lived several years with him in great domestic harmony, and only asked hunters to bring her back home because she and her children (rather hairy also) 'were tired of living far from a church'. This legend, taken by missionaries, Spaniards and black Africans from descriptions of the orang-utang, followed us for the five years of our journey. We annoyed people everywhere by being suspicious of the presence of a great anthropomorphic ape in the Americas.

After two days near the Atures cataract we were happy to load the canoe again and leave a place where the temperature was usually 29 °C by day and 26 °C at night. All day we were horribly tormented by mosquitoes and *jejenes*, tiny venomous flies (or *simuliums*), and all night by *zancudos*, another kind of mosquito feared even by the Indians. Our hands began to swell, and this swelling increased until we reached the banks of the Temi. The means found to escape these insects are often quite original. The kind missionary Father Zea, all his life tormented by mosquitoes, had built a small room near his church, up on a scaffolding of palm trunks, where you could breathe more freely. At night we climbed up a ladder to dry our plants and write our diary. The missionary had correctly observed that the insects preferred the lower levels, that is, from the ground up to some 15 feet. At Maypures the Indians leave their villages at night and sleep near the cataracts because the mosquitoes seem to avoid air loaded with vapours.

Those who have not travelled the great rivers of tropical America, like the Orinoco or the Magdalena, cannot imagine how all day long, ceaselessly, you are tormented by mosquitoes that float in the air, and how this crowd of little animals can make huge stretches of land uninhabitable. However used to the pain you may become, without complaining; however much you try to observe the object you are studying, the mosquitoes, *jejenes* and *zancudos* will tear you away as they cover your head and hands, pricking you with their needle-like suckers through your clothes, and climbing into your nose and mouth, making you cough and sneeze whenever you try to talk. In the Orinoco missions the *plaga de las moscas*, or plague of mosquitoes, is an inexhaustible subject of conversation. When two people meet in the morning the first questions they ask each other are, 'Que le han parecido los zancudos de anoche?' and 'Como estamos hoy de mosquitos?' ('How were the *zancudos* last night?' and 'How are we for mosquitoes today?').

The lower strata of air, from the ground to some 20 feet up, are invaded by poisonous insects, like thick clouds. If you stand in a dark place, such as a cave formed by granite blocks in the cataracts, and look towards the sunlit opening you will see actual clouds of mosquitoes that get thicker or thinner according to the density of insects. I doubt that there is another country on earth where man suffers more cruelly during the rainy season than here. When you leave latitude 5 the biting lessens, but in the Upper Orinoco it becomes more painful because it is hotter, and there is absolutely no wind so your skin becomes more irritated. 'How good it would be to live on the moon,' a Saliva Indian said. 'It is so beautiful and clear that it must be free of mosquitoes.'[104]

Whoever lives in this region, whether white, mulatto, black or Indian, suffers equally from insect stings. People spend their time complaining of the *plaga, del insufrible tormento de las moscas*. I have mentioned the curious fact that whites born in the Tropics can walk about barefoot in the same room where a recently arrived European runs the risk of being bitten by *niguas*, or chigoes (*Pulex penetrans*). These hardly visible animals dig under toenails and soon reach the size of a pea as they develop their eggs, situated in little sacs under their abdomens. It seems as if the *nigua* is able to distinguish the cellular membrane and blood of a European from those of a white *criollo*, something that the most detailed chemical analysis has been unable to do. It is not the same with mosquitoes, despite what is said on South American coasts. These insects attack Indians as much as Europeans; only the consequences of the bites vary with race. The same venomous liquid applied to the skin of a copper-coloured Indian and to a recently arrived white does not cause inflammations to the first, while to the second it causes hard, inflamed blisters that last for various numbers of days.

All day, even when rowing, Indians continually slap each other hard with the palm of the hand to scare off mosquitoes. Brusque in all their movements they continue to slap each other mechanically while they sleep. At Maypures we saw young Indians sitting in a circle, cruelly scratching each other's back with bark dried by the fire. With that patience only known in the copper-coloured race, some Indian women busied themselves by digging small lumps of coagulated blood from each bite with a sharp, pointed bone. One of the wildest Orinoco tribes, the Otomacs, use mosquito nets woven from fibre from the moriche palm. In villages on the Magdalena river Indians often invited us to lie down on oxhides near the church in the middle of the *plaza grande* where they had herded all the cattle, as the proximity of cattle gives you some respite from bites. When Indians saw that Bonpland was unable to prepare his plants because of the plague of mosquitoes they invited him into their 'ovens' (*hornitos*), as they call these small spaces without doors or windows, which they slide into on their bellies through a low opening. Thanks to a fire of greenwood, which gives off plenty of smoke, they expel all the insects and then block the 'oven' door. Bonpland, with a praiseworthy courage and patience, dried hundreds of plants shut up in these Indian *hornitos*.

The trouble an Indian takes to avoid the insects proves that despite his different skin colour he is just as sensitive to mosquito bites as any white. Irritability is increased by wearing warm clothes, by applying alcoholic liquors, by scratching the wounds, and – and this I have observed myself – by taking too many baths. By bathing whenever we could Bonpland and I observed that a bath, though soothing for old bites, made us more sensitive to new ones. If you take a bath more than twice a day the skin becomes nervously excited in a way nobody in Europe could understand. It seems as if all one's sensitivity has become concentrated in the epidermic layers. Today the dangers that prevent Spaniards navigating up the Orinoco do not come from wild Indians or snakes or crocodiles or jaguars but, as they naïvely say, from 'el sudar y las moscas' (sweating and mosquitoes).

I have shown that winged insects which live in society and whose suckers contain a liquid that irritates skin make vast territories virtually uninhabitable. Other insects, just as small, called termites (*comején*) create insuperable obstacles to the progress of civilization in several hot countries. They rapidly devour paper, cardboard and parchment, and thus destroy archives and libraries. Whole provinces of Spanish America do not have any document that dates back more than a hundred years.

CHAPTER 18

OUR BOAT WAS waiting for us in the Puerto de Arriba above the Atures cataract. On the narrow path that led to the *embarcadero* we were shown the distant rocks near the Ataruipe caves. We did not have time to visit that Indian cemetery though Father Zea had not stopped talking about the skeletons painted red with *onoto* inside the great jars. 'You will hardly believe,' said the missionary, 'that these skeletons and painted vases, which we thought unknown to the rest of the world, have brought me trouble. You know the misery I endure in the Raudales. Devoured by mosquitoes, and lacking in bananas and cassava, yet people in Caracas envy me! I was denounced by a white man for hiding treasure that had been abandoned in the caves when the Jesuits had to leave. I was ordered to appear in Caracas in person and journeyed pointlessly over 150 leagues to declare that the cave contained only human bones and dried bats. However, commissioners were appointed to come up here and investigate. We shall wait a long time for these commissioners. The cloud of mosquitoes (*nube de moscas*) in the Raudales is a good defence.'

April 17th. After walking for three hours we reached our boat at about eleven in the morning. Father Zea packed provisions of clumps of bananas, cassava and chicken with our instruments. We found the river free of shoals, and after a few hours had passed the Garcita *raudal* whose rapids are easily crossed during high water. We were struck by a succession of great holes, more than 180 feet above the present water-level, that appeared to have been caused by water erosion. The night was clear and beautiful but the plague of mosquitoes near the ground was such that I was unable to record the level of the artificial horizon and lost the opportunity of observing the stars.

April 18th. We set off at three in the morning in order to reach the cataracts known as the Raudal de Guahibos before nightfall. We moored at the mouth of the Tomo river, and the Indians camped on the shore. At five in the afternoon we reached the *raudal*. It was extremely difficult to row against the current and the mass of water rushing over a bank several feet high. One Indian swam to a rock that divided the cataract in two, tied a rope to it, and began hauling our boat until, halfway up, we were able to get off with our instruments, dried plants and bare provisions. Surprisingly we found that above the natural wall over which the river fell there was a piece of dry land. Our position in the middle of the cataract was strange but without danger. Our companion, the missionary father, had one of his fever fits, and to relieve him we decided to make a refreshing drink. We had taken on board at Apures a *mapire*, or Indian basket, filled with sugar, lemons and grenadillas, or passion-fruit, which the Spaniards call *parchas*. As we had no bowl in which to mix the juices we poured river water into one of the holes in the rock with a *tutuma*, and then added the sugar and acid fruit juices. In a few seconds we had a wonderfully refreshing juice, almost a luxury in this wild spot, but necessity had made us more and more ingenious. After quenching our thirst we wanted to have a swim. Carefully examining the narrow rocky dyke on which we sat, we saw that it formed little coves where the water was clear and still. We had the pleasure of a quiet bathe in the midst of noisy cataracts and screaming Indians. I enter into such detail to remind those who plan to travel afar that at any moment in life pleasures can be found.

After waiting for an hour we saw that our pirogue had safely crossed the *raudal*. We loaded our instruments and provisions and left the Guahibo rock. We began a journey that was quite dangerous. Above the cataract the river is some 800 toises wide and must be crossed obliquely at the point where the waters start rushing towards the fall. The men had been rowing for over twenty minutes when the pilot said that instead of advancing we were drifting back to the falls. Then there was a storm and heavy rain fell. Those anxious moments seemed to last for ever. The Indians whisper as they always do when in danger; but they rowed very hard and we reached the port of Maypures by nightfall.

The night was very dark and it would take us two hours to reach the village of Maypures. We were soaked to the skin, and after it stopped raining the *zancudos* returned. My companions were undecided as to whether to camp in the harbour or walk to the village. Father Zea insisted on going to the village where, with help from Indians, he had begun to build a two-floored house. 'You will find there,' he said naïvely, 'the same comforts as you have out of doors. There are no tables or chairs but you will suffer less from mosquitoes because in the mission they are not as shameless as down by the river.' We followed the missionary's advice. He ordered torches of copal to be lit. These are tubes of bark filled with copal resin. At first we passed beds of slippery rock, then a thick palm grove. We twice had to cross streams over tree trunks. The torches burned out. They give off more smoke than light, and easily extinguish. Our companion, Don Nicolás Soto, lost his balance in the dark crossing a marsh and fell off a tree trunk. For a while we had no idea how far he had fallen, but luckily it was not far and he was not hurt. The Indian pilot, who spoke Spanish quite well, did not stop saying how easy it would be to be attacked by snakes or jaguars. This is the obligatory topic of conversation when you travel at night with Indians. They think that by frightening European travellers they will become more necessary to them, and will win their confidence.

The Maypures cataracts[105] appear like a cluster of little waterfalls following each other, as if falling down steps. The *raudal*, the name given by Spaniards to these kinds of cataracts, is made up of a veritable archipelago of small islands and rocks which narrow the river so thoroughly that there is often less than 18 to 21 feet for boats to navigate through.

At the confluence of the Cameji and Orinoco we unloaded our baggage, and the Indians, familiar with all the shoals in the *raudal*, led the empty pirogue to the mouth of the Toparo river where the water is no longer dangerous. Each rock forming the falls of the *raudal* has a different name. As long as they are not more than 1.5 to 2 feet above water the Indians do not mind letting the current take their canoes; but to go up river they swim ahead and after much struggling tie cables to rocks and pull the boats up.

Sometimes, and it's the only accident the Indians fear, the canoes break against rocks. Then, their bodies bloodied, the Indians try to escape the whirlpools and swim ashore. In those places where the rocks are very high, or the embankment they are going up crosses the whole river, they roll the boat up on tree trunks.

The most famous cataracts, with the most obstacles, are called Purimarimi and Manimi and are about 3 metres wide. The difficulties involved in reaching these places, and the foul air filled with millions of mosquitoes, made it impossible to take a geodesical levelling, but with the aid of a barometer I was amazed that the whole fall of the *raudal* from the mouth of the Cameji to the Toparo was only some 27 to 30 feet. My surprise was related to the terrible din and foam flying from the river.

From the Manimi rock there is a marvellous view. Your eyes survey a foaming surface that stretches away for almost 2 leagues. In the middle of the waves rocks as black as iron, like ruined towers, rise up. Each island, each rock, is crowned by trees with many branches; a thick cloud floats above the mirror of the water and through it you see the tops of tall palms. What name shall we give these majestic plants? I guess that they are *vadgiai*, a new species, more than 80 feet high. Everywhere on the backs of the naked rocks during the rainy season the noisy waters have piled up islands of vegetation. Decorated with ferns and flowering plants these islands form flower-beds in the middle of exposed, desolate rocks. At the foot of the Man-imi rock, where we had bathed the day before, the Indians killed a 7.5-foot snake, which we examined at leisure. The Macos called it a *camudu*. It was beautiful, and not poisonous. I thought at first that it was a boa, and then perhaps a python. I say 'perhaps' for a great naturalist like Cuvier appears to say that pythons belong to the Old World, and boas to the New.

I shall not add to the confusions in zoological naming by proposing new changes, but shall observe that the missionaries and the latinized Indians of the mission clearly distinguish the *tragavenado* (boa) from the *culebra de agua*, which is like the *camudu*.

In the time of the Jesuits the Maypures *raudal* mission was well known and had as many as 600 inhabitants including several families of whites. Under the government of the fathers of the Observance this has shrunk to some sixty. Those who still live there are mild and moderate, and very clean. Most of the wild Indians of the Orinoco are not excessively fond of strong alcohol like the North American Indian. It is true that Otomacs, Yaruros, Achaguas and Caribs often get drunk on *chicha* and other fermented drinks made from cassava, maize and sugared palm-tree fruit. But travellers, as usual, have generalized from the habits of a few villages. We often could not persuade the Guahibos who worked with us to drink brandy even when they seemed exhausted.[106]

They grow banana and cassava, but not maize. Like the majority of Orinoco Indians, those in Maypures also make drinks that could be called nutritious. A famous one in the country is made from a palm called the *seje*, which grows wild in the vicinity. I estimated the number of flowers on one cluster at 44,000; the fruit that fall without ripening amount to 8,000. These fruit are little fleshy drupes. They are thrown into boiling water for a few minutes to separate the pulp, which has a sweet taste, from the skin, and are then pounded and bruised in a large vessel filled with water. Taken cold, the infusion is yellowish and tastes like almond milk. Sometimes *papelón* (unrefined sugar) or sugar cane is added. The missionary said that the Indians become visibly fatter during the two or three months when they drink this *seje* or dip their cassava cakes in it. The *piaches*, or Indian shamans, go into the jungle and sound the *botuto* (the sacred trumpet) under *seje* palm trees 'to force the tree to give a good harvest the following year'.

'Tengo en mi pueblo la fábrica de loza' (I have a pottery works in my village), Father Zea told us and led us to the hut of an Indian family who were baking large earthenware vessels, up to 2.5 feet high, out in the open on a fire of shrubs. This industry is characteristic of the diverse branches of the May-pures tribes, cultivated since time immemorial. Wherever you dig up the ground in the jungle, far from any human habita-tions, you find bits of painted pottery. It is noteworthy that the same motifs are used everywhere. The Maypures Indians painted decorations in front of us that were identical to those we had seen on the jars from the Ataruipe caves, with wavy lines, figures of crocodiles, monkeys and a large quadruped that I did not recognize but which was always crouched in the same position.

With the Maypures Indians, it is the women who decorate the vessels, clean the clay by washing it several times; then they shape it into cylinders and mould even the largest jars with their hands. The American Indians never discovered the pot-ter's wheel.

It was fascinating to see *guacamayos*, or tame macaws, flying around the Indian huts as we see pigeons in Europe. This bird is the largest and most majestic of the parrot species. Including its tail it measures 2 feet 3 inches. The flesh, which is often eaten, is black and rather tough. These macaws, whose feathers shine with tints of purple, blue and yellow, are a grand ornament in Indian yards, and are just as beautiful as the pea-cock or golden pheasant. Rearing parrots was noticed by Col-umbus when he first discovered America.

Near the Maypures village grows an impressive tree some 60 feet high called by the colonists the *fruta de burro*. It is a new species of annona. The tree is famous for its aromatic fruit whose infusion is an efficient febrifuge. The poor missionaries of the Orinoco who suffer tertian fevers most of the year rarely travel without a little bag of *fruta de burro*.

April 21st. After spending two and a half days in the little village of Maypures near the Great Cataracts, we embarked in the canoe that the Carichana missionary had got for us. It had been damaged by the knocks it had received in the river, and by the Indians' carelessness. Once you have passed the Great Cataracts[107] you feel you are in a new world; that you have stepped over the barriers that nature seems to have raised between the civilized coasts and the wild, unknown interior. On the way to the landing-stage we caught a new species of tree frog on the trunk of a hevea. It had a yellow belly, a back and head of velvety purple, and a narrow white stripe from its nose to its hind parts. This frog was 2 inches long; probably allied to the *Rana tinctoria* whose blood, so it is said, makes the feathers that have been plucked out of a parrot grow again in frizzled yellow and red if poured on to its skin.

The Indians told us that the jungles which cover the banks of the Sipapo abound in the climbing plant called *bejuco de maimure*. This species of liana is very important for the Indians as they weave baskets and mats from it. The Sipapo jungles are completely unknown. It is there that the missionaries place the Rayas tribe, whose mouths are said to be in their navels, perhaps due to the analogy with rays, whose mouths appear to be halfway down their bodies. An old Indian we met at Carichana, who boasted that he had often eaten human flesh, had seen these headless people 'with his own eyes'.

At the mouth of the Zama river we entered into a fluvial network worthy of attention. The Zama, Mataveni, Atabapo, Tuamini, Temi and Guianai rivers have *aguas negras*, that is, seen as a mass they appear brown like coffee, or greenish-black. These waters are, however, beautifully clear and very tasty. I have observed that crocodiles and mosquitoes, but not the *zancudos*, tend to avoid the black waters.

April 24th. A violent rainstorm forced us to embark before dawn. We left at two in the morning and had to abandon some books, which we could not find in the dark. The river runs straight from south to north, its banks are low and lined with thick jungle.

CHAPTER 19

SAN FERNANDO DE ATABAPO — SAN BALTASAR — THE
TEMI AND TUAMINI RIVERS — JAVITA — JOURNEY ON
FOOT FROM THE TUAMINI RIVER TO THE RÍO NEGRO

DURING THE NIGHT we had left the Orinoco waters almost
without realizing it. At sunrise we found ourselves in a new
country, on the banks of a river whose name we had hardly
heard mentioned, and which would lead us after a foot journey
over Pimichín to the Río Negro on the Brazilian frontier. The
father superior of the San Fernando mission said to us: 'First
you must go up the Atabapo, then the Temi, and finally the
Tuamini. If the black-water current is too strong to do this the
guides will take you over flooded land through the jungle. In
that deserted zone between the Orinoco and the Río Negro
you will meet only two monks established there. In Javita you
will find people to carry your canoe over land in four days to
Caño Pimichín. If the canoe is not wrecked go straight down
the Río Negro to the fort of San Carlos, then go up the
Casiquiare and in a month you will reach San Fernando along
the Upper Orinoco.' That was the plan drawn up for us, which
we carried out, without danger, in thirty-three days. The bends
are such in this labyrinth of rivers that without the map which
I have drawn it would be impossible to picture the route we
took. In the first part of this journey from east to west you
find the famous bifurcations that have given rise to so many
disputes, and whose location I was the first to establish
through astronomic observations. One arm of the Orinoco,
the Casiquiare,[108] running north to south, pours into the Guainia or Río Negro, which in turn joins the Marañon or Amazon.

No astronomical instruments had been brought along during the frontier expedition in this region, so with my chronometer, and by the meridional height of the stars, I established
the exact location of San Baltasar de Atabapo, Javita, San

Carlos de Río Negro, the Culimacarai rock and the Esmeralda mission. The map I drew has resolved any doubts about the reciprocal distances between the Christian outposts. When there is no other road but the tortuous and intricate river; when little villages lie hidden in thick jungle; when in a completely flat country with no mountains visible, you can read where you are on earth only by looking up to the sky.

The San Fernando missionary, with whom we stayed two days, lived in a village that appears slightly more prosperous than others we had stayed in on our journey, yet still had only 226 inhabitants.[109] We found some traces of agriculture; every Indian has his own cacao plantation, which gives a good crop by the fifth year but stops fruiting earlier than in the Aragua valleys. Around San Fernando there are some savannahs with good pasture but only some seven or eight cows remain from a vast herd left behind by the frontier expedition. The Indians are a little more civilized than in the other missions. Surprisingly, we came across an Indian blacksmith.

In San Fernando we were most struck by the *pihiguado* or *pirijao* palm, which gives the countryside its peculiar quality. Covered with thorns, its trunk reaches more than 60 feet high. The fruit of this tree is extraordinary; each bunch has some fifty to eighty; they are yellow, like apples, but turn purple on ripening, when they are 2 or 3 inches thick. Generally they fall off before the kernel develops. Of the eighty to ninety palm trees peculiar to the New World that I have described in my *Nova Genera plantarum aequinoctialem* (1815–25) none has such a fleshy fruit. The *pirijao* fruit yields a substance rather like flour, as yellow as egg yolk, slightly sweet and very nutritious. It is eaten like banana or sweet potato, cooked or baked in ashes, and is as healthy as it tastes good. Indians and missionaries vie in praising this magnificent palm, which could be called the peach palm. In these wild regions I was reminded of Linnaeus's assertion that the country of palm trees was man's first abode, and that man is essentially palmivorous.[110] When we examined what food the Indians stored in their huts we noticed that their diet depends as much on the fruit of the *pirijao* as on cassava and banana.

At San Fernando, and in the neighbouring villages of San Baltasar and Javita, the missionaries live in attractive houses, covered in liana and surrounded by gardens. The tall *pirijao* were the most decorative part of the plantation. In our walks the head of the mission told us about his incursions up the Guaviare river. He reminded us how these journeys, undertaken for the 'conquest of souls', are eagerly anticipated by the Indians. All the Indians enjoy taking part, even old men and women. Under the pretext of recovering neophytes who have deserted the village, children of eight to ten are kidnapped and distributed among the missionary Indians as serfs, or *poitos*.

As soon as you enter the basin of the Atabapo river everything changes: the air, the colour of the water, the shape of the river-side trees. By day you no longer suffer the torment of mosquitoes; and their long-legged cousins the *zancudos* become rare at night. Beyond the San Fernando mission these nocturnal insects disappear altogether. The Orinoco waters are turbid, full of earthy matter, and in the coves give off a faint musky smell from the amount of dead crocodiles and other putrefying animals. To drink that water we had to filter it through a linen cloth. The waters of the Atabapo, on the other hand, are pure, taste good, are without smell, and appear brownish in reflected light and yellow under the sun.

The extreme purity of the black waters is confirmed by their transparency, and by the way they clearly reflect all the surrounding objects. The minutest fish are visible at a depth of 20 or 30 feet. It is easy to see the river bottom, which is not muddy but composed of a dazzlingly white granite or quartz sand. Nothing can be compared to the beauty of the Atabapo river banks, overloaded with vegetation, among which rise the palms with plumed leaves, reflected in the river water. The green of the reflected image seems as real as the object seen with your eyes.

Contrary to geographers, the Indians of San Fernando claim that the Orinoco rises from two rivers, the Guaviare and the Paragua. This latter name they give to the Upper Orinoco. Following their hypothesis they say the Casiquiare is not a branch of the Orinoco, but of the Paragua. If you look at my map you will see these names are quite arbitrary. It does not matter if you do not call the Orinoco the Paragua as long as you trace the rivers as they actually are in nature and do not separate rivers that form part of the same river system with mountain chains. The Paragua, or that part of the Orinoco east of the mouth of the Guaviare, has clearer, purer, more transparent water than the part of the Orinoco below San Fernando. The waters of the Guaviare are white and turbid and have the same taste, according to the Indians whose sense organs are very delicate and well tested, as the Orinoco waters near the Great Cataracts. 'Give me water from three or four great rivers of this country,' an old Indian from the Javita mission said, 'and I will tell you by tasting them where they come from; whether it is a white or black river, whether it is the Atabapo, Paragua or Guaviare.' European geographers are wrong not to admit to seeing things as Indians do, for they are the geographers of their own country.

April 26th. We advanced only 2 or 3 leagues, and spent the night on a rock near the Indian plantations or *conucos* of Guapasoso. As the river floods and spills over into the jungle, you lose sight of the banks and can moor only to a rock or small tableland rising above the water. In these granite rocks I found no cavity (druse), no crystallized substance, not even rock crystal, and no trace of pyrites or other metallic substances. I mention this detail on account of the chimerical ideas that have spread following Berrio's and Raleigh's voyages about 'the immense riches of the great and fine empire of Guiana'.[111]

In the Atabapo, above San Fernando, there are no longer any crocodiles; every now and then you come across some *bavas*, numerous freshwater dolphins, but no manatees. You would not find tapirs, nor araguato monkeys, nor howler monkeys, *zamuros*, or *guacharacas*, a kind of crested pheasant. However, enormous water snakes similar to boas are very common and endanger Indian bathers. From the first day we saw them swimming past our canoes, reaching 14 feet in length.

April 27th. The night was beautiful; black clouds crossed the sky with surprising speed. Guapasoso's latitude was 3.53′ 55″. The black waters served as my horizon. I was all the more delighted to make this observation as in the white-water rivers from the Apure to the Orinoco we had been cruelly bitten by mosquitoes, as Bonpland recorded the hours with the chronometer, and I myself adjusted the horizon. At two we left the Guapasoso *conucos*, going south and upstream as the river, at least that part of it free of trees, began to narrow. At sunrise it started to rain. In these forests we no longer heard the cries of the howler monkeys. Dolphins, or *toninas*, played by the side of our boat. At about midday we passed the mouth of the Ipur-ichapano river, and a little later the granite rock called Piedra del Tigre. We later regretted not resting near this rock as we had some problems trying to find a spot of dry land large enough upon which to light a fire and set up our hammocks and instruments.

April 28th. It poured with rain as soon as the sun set and we were worried about the damage to our collections. The poor missionary suffered one of his fever attacks and begged us to leave before midnight. After passing the Guarinuma rapids the Indians pointed out the ruins of the Mendaxari mission, abandoned some time back. On the east bank of the river, near the little rock of Kemarumo in the middle of Indian plantations, we saw a gigantic ceiba (the *Bombax ceiba*). We landed to measure it; it was some 120 feet high, with a diameter of 14 or 15 feet.

April 29th. The air was cooler, and without *zancudos*, but the clouds blocked out all the stars. I begin to miss the Lower Orinoco as the strong current slowed our progress. We stopped for most of the day, looking for plants. It was night when we reached the San Baltasar mission or, as the monks call it, *la divina pastora de Baltasar de Atabapo*. We lodged with a Catalan missionary, a lively and friendly man who, in the middle of the jungle, displayed the activities of his people. He had planted a wonderful orchard where European figs grew with persea, and lemon trees with mamey. The village was built with a regularity typical of Protestant Germany or America. Here we saw for the first time that white and spongy substance which I have made known as *dapicho* and *zapis*. We saw that this stuff was similar to elastic resin. But through sign language the

Indians made us think that it came from under ground so we first thought that maybe it was a fossil rubber. A Poimisano Indian was sitting by a fire in the missionary hut transforming *dapicho* into black rubber. He had stuck several bits on to thin sticks and was roasting it by the fire like meat. As it melts and becomes elastic the *dapicho* blackens. The Indian then beat the black mass with a club made of Brazil-wood and then kneaded the *dapicho* into small balls some 3 to 4 inches thick, and let them cool. The balls appear identical to rubber though the surface remains slightly sticky. At San Baltasar they are not used for the game of pelota that Indians play in Uruana and Encaramada but are cut up and used as more effective corks than those made from cork itself. In front of the Casa de los Solteros – the house where unmarried men lived – the missionary showed us a drum made from a hollow cylinder of wood. This drum was beaten with great lumps of *dapicho* serving as drumsticks. The drum has openings that could be blocked by hand to vary the sounds, and was hanging on two light supports. Wild Indians love noisy music. Drums and *botutos*, the baked-earth trumpets, are indispensable instruments when Indians decide to play music and make a show.

April 30th. We continued upstream on the Atabapo for 5 miles, then instead of following this river to its source, where it is called the Atacavi, we entered the Temi river. Before reaching this tributary, near the Guasacavi mouth, a granite outcrop on the west bank fixed our attention: it is called the rock of the Guahiba Indian woman, or the Mother Rock, the Piedra de la Madre. Father Zea could not explain its bizarre name, but a few weeks later another missionary told us a story that stirred up painful feelings. If, in these deserted places, man leaves hardly any traces behind him, it is doubly humiliating for a European to see in the name of a rock a memory of the moral degradation of whites that contrasts the virtue of a wild Indian with the barbarity of civilized men!

In 1797 the San Fernando missionary had led his men to the banks of the Guaviare river on one of those hostile incursions banned both by religion and Spanish law. They found a Guahiba mother with three children in a hut, two of whom were not yet adults. They were busy preparing cassava flour. Resistance was impossible; their father had gone out fishing, so the mother tried to run off with her children. She had just reached the savannah when the Indians, who hunt people the way whites hunt blacks in Africa, caught her. The mother and children were tied up and brought back to the river bank. The monks were waiting for this expedition to end, without suffering any of the dangers. Had the mother resisted the Indians would have killed her; anything is allowed in this hunting of souls (*conquista espiritual*), and it is especially children that are captured and treated as *poitos* or slaves in the Christian missions. They brought the prisoners to San Fernando, hoping that the mother would not find her way back by land to her home. Separated from those children who had gone fishing with their father the day she was kidnapped, this poor woman began to show signs of the deepest despair. She wanted to bring those children in the power of the missionaries back home, and several times ran off with them from the San Fernando village but the Indians hunted her down each time. After severely punishing her the missionary took the cruel decision of separating the mother from her two infants. She was led alone to a mission on the Río Negro, up the Atabapo river. Loosely tied up, she sat in the bow of the boat. She had not been told where she was going; but she guessed by the sun's position that she was being taken away from her house and native land. She managed to break her bonds and jumped into the water and swam to the river bank. The current pushed her to a bank of rock, which is named after her today. She climbed up and walked into the jungle. But the head of the mission ordered his Indians to follow and capture her. She was again caught by the evening. She was stretched out on the rock (the Piedra de la Madre) where she was beaten with manatee whips. Her hands tied up behind her back with the strong cords of the *mavacure*, she was then dragged to the Javita mission and thrown into one of the inns called *casas del rey*. It was the rainy season and the night was very dark. Impenetrable forests separate the Javita and San Fernando missions some 25 leagues apart in a straight line. The only known route was by river. Nobody ever tried to go by land from one mission to another, even if only a few leagues away. But this did not prevent a mother separated from her children. Her children were at San Fernando so she had to find them, rescue them from Christians, and bring them back to their father on the Guaviare. The Guahiba woman was not closely supervised in the inn. As her hands were bloodied the Javita Indians had loosened her bindings. With her teeth she managed to break the cords, and she disappeared into the night. On the fourth day she was seen prowling round the hut where her children were being kept at the San Fernando mission. 'This woman had just carried out,' added the monk telling us this sad story, 'something that the toughest Indian would not have even considered.' She had crossed the jungle in a season when the sky is continuously covered with cloud, when the sun appears only for a few minutes for days on end. Had she followed the flow of water? But flooding had forced her to walk far from the river, in the middle of jungles where the river is imperceptible. How many times must she have been blocked by thorny liana growing round trees! How many times must she have swum across streams! What on earth could this luckless woman have eaten during her four days' walk? She said that she had eaten only those large black ants called *vachacos* that climb up trees and hang resinous nests from branches. We pressed the missionary to tell us whether the Guahiba woman had finally enjoyed peace and happiness with her family. He did not want to satisfy our curiosity. But on our return from the Río Negro we learned that this Indian woman was not even left to recover from her wounds before she was again separated from her children, and sent to a mission on the Upper Orinoco. She died by refusing to eat food, as do all Indians when faced with great calamities.[112]

Such is the memory attached to this fatal rock called the Piedra de la Madre. If I have dawdled over this touching story of maternal love in an often vilified race, it is because I wanted to make public this story heard from monks to prove that even missions should obey laws.

Wherever the Temi forms bays the jungle is flooded for

more than half a square league. To avoid the bends and shorten our journey the Indians leave the river bed and go south along paths or *sendas*, that is, canals, some 4 or 5 feet wide. The depth of the water rarely exceeds half a fathom. These *sendas* are formed in the flooded jungle like paths in dry land. Whenever they could the Indians crossed from one mission to another along the same path in their pirogues. But as the passage is narrow the thick vegetation sometimes leads to surprises. An Indian stands in the bow with his machete, incessantly cutting branches blocking the canal. In the thickest part of the jungle we heard an odd noise. As the Indian cut at some branches a school of *toninas* – freshwater dolphins – surrounded our boat. The animals had hidden under branches of a ceiba and escaped through the flooded jungle, squirting up water and compressed air, living up to their name of 'blowers'. What a strange sight, inland, 300 to 400 leagues from the Orinoco and Amazon mouths!

May 1st. The Indians wanted to leave long before sunrise. We got up before them because we had hoped to see some stars, but in this humid, thick-jungled zone the nights were getting darker and darker as we approached the Río Negro and the interior of Brazil. We stayed in the river until dawn, fearing to get lost in the trees. But as soon as the sun rose we went through the flooded jungle to avoid the strong current. We reached the confluence of the Temi and Tuamini and went upstream on the latter south-west, reaching the Javita mission on the banks of the Tuamini at about eleven in the morning. It was at this Christian mission that we hoped to find help in carrying our pirogue to the Río Negro. A minor accident shows how fearful the little sagouin monkeys are. The noise of the 'blowers' scared one of them and it fell into the water. These monkeys can hardly swim, and we just managed to save it.

At Javita we had the pleasure of meeting a cultured, reasonable monk. We had to stay in his house the four or five days it took to carry our canoe along the Pimichín portage. Delay allowed us to visit the region, as well as rid us of an irritation that had been annoying us for the last two days: an intense itching in the articulations of our fingers and the backs of our hands. The missionary said this came from *aradores* (literally, 'ploughers') encrusted under our skin. With the aid of a magnifying glass we saw only lines, or whitish parallel furrows, which show why it is called an *arador*. The monks called for a mulatta who knew how to deal with all the little insects that burrow into human skin, from *niguas*, *nuches* and *coyas* to the *arador*. She was the *curandera*, the local doctor. She promised to remove all the insects irritating us, one by one. She heated the tip of a little stick on the fire and dug it into the furrows in our skin. After a long examination she announced, with that pedantic gravity peculiar to coloured people, that she had found an *arador*. I saw a little round bag that could have been the egg of the acaride. I should have been relieved when this clumsy mulatta poked out three or four more of these *aradores*. But as my skin was full of acarides I lost all patience with an operation that had already lasted until well into the night. The next day a Javita Indian cured us incredibly quickly. He brought a branch of a shrub called *uzao*, which had little shiny leathery leaves similar to the cassia. With its bark he prepared a cold bluish infusion that smelled of liquorice. When he beat it it became very frothy. Thanks to a washing with this *uzao* infusion the itching caused by the *aradores* disappeared. We were never able to find flowers or fruit of this *uzao*; the shrub seemed to belong to the leguminous family. We dreaded the pain caused by these *aradores* so much that we took various branches with us right up to San Carlos.

The mission of San Antonio was usually named after its Indian founder Javita. This captain, Javita, was still living when we arrived at the Río Negro. He was an Indian with a lively mind and body, and spoke Spanish with great ease. As he accompanied us on all our herborizations we obtained very useful information directly from him. In his youth he had seen all the Indian tribes of the region eat human flesh, and the Daricavanos, Puchirinavis and Manitibitanos seemed to him to be the greatest cannibals.[113] He believed that cannibalism was the effect of a system of vengeance; they only eat enemies captured in battle. It was very rare for an Indian to eat a close relation like a wife or an unfaithful mistress.

The climate of the Javita mission is extremely rainy. Rains fall all year round and the sky is constantly clouded. The missionary assured us that he had seen it rain for four and five months without stopping. I measured the rainfall on the 1st of May over five hours and registered 46.4 millimetres.

The Indians in Javita number about 160 and come from the Poimisano, Echinavis and Paraganis tribes. They make canoes out of the trunks of sassafras (*Ocotea cymbatum*), hollowing them out with fire and axes. These trees grow over 100 feet high, their wood is yellow, resinous, and never rots in water. It gives off a rich smell.

The jungle between Javita and Caño Pimichín holds a quantity of gigantic trees: ocoteas, laurels, *curvana, jacio, iacifate,* with a red wood like Brazil-wood, *guamufate,* the *Amyris caraña* and the *mani.* All these trees top 100 feet. As their trunks throw out branches more than 100 feet high we had trouble getting flowers and leaves. Though the ground was strewn with foliage we could not rely on the Indians to tell us from which tree or liana they came. In the midst of such natural riches, our herborizations caused us more regret than satisfaction. What we managed to collect seemed without interest in comparison with what we might have collected. It rained without a break for several months and Bonpland lost the greater part of the specimens he had dried with artificial heat. Usually Indians name trees by chewing the bark. They distinguish leaves better than flowers or fruit. Busy in locating timber for canoes they are inattentive to flowers. 'None of those tall trees have flowers or fruit,' they continually repeated. Like the botanists of antiquity, they denied what they had not bothered to observe. Tired by our questions they, in turn, made us impatient.

Every day we went into the jungle to see how our canoe was advancing over land. Twenty-three Indians were dragging it by placing logs as rollers. Usually this takes a day and a half, but our canoe was very large. As we also had to pass the cataracts a second time it was necessary to be very careful about not scraping it on the ground.

In this same jungle we at last were able to solve the problem of the supposed fossil rubber that the Indians call *dapicho*. The old Indian captain Javita led us to a small stream that runs into the Tuamini. He showed us how to dig some 2 to 3 feet deep into the muddy ground between the roots of two trees: the *jacio* and the *curvana*. The first is the hevea or siphonia of modern botany, which yields rubber; the second has pinnate leaves; its juice is milky but very diluted and barely sticky. It appears that *dapicho* is formed when the latex oozes out from the roots, especially when the tree is very old and begins to decay inside its trunk. The bark and sapwood crack to achieve naturally what man himself must do to gather latex.

Four days had passed and our boat still had not reached the Pimichín river landing-stage. 'There is nothing you lack in my mission,' Father Cerezo said to us. 'There are bananas and fish; at night mosquitoes do not bite; and the longer you stay the more likely it is that you will be able to observe stars. If your boat is wrecked during the portage we will get you another one and I will enjoy living a few more weeks *con gente blanca y de razón* (with white and rational people).' Despite our impatience, we listened with interest to this missionary's stories confirming all that we had been told about the spiritual state of the Indians in that region. They live in isolated clans of forty to fifty people under a chief. They recognize a common cacique only in times of war with neighbours. Between these clans mutual mistrust is great, as even those who live near each other speak different languages. Such is the labyrinth of these rivers that families settled themselves without knowing what tribe lived nearest to them. In Spanish Guiana a mountain or a jungle just half a league wide separates clans who would need two days navigating along rivers to meet. In the impenetrable jungle of the torrid zone rivers increase the dismemberment of great nations, favour the transition of dialects into separate languages, and nourish distrust and national hatred. Men avoid each other because they do not understand each other, and hate because they fear.

When we carefully examine this wild part of America we imagine how it was in primitive times when the land was peopled in stages, and seem to be present at the birth of human societies. In the New World we do not see the progressive developments of civilization, those moments of rest, those stations in the lives of a people. Such is the wonderful fertility of nature that the Indian's field is a patch of land. To clear it means setting fire to branches. To farm means dropping a few seeds into the ground. However far back in time you go in thought in these dense jungles the Indians have got their food from the earth, but as this earth produces abundantly on a small patch, without much work, these people often change their homes along the river banks. Still today, the Orinoco Indians travel with their seeds, transporting what they cultivate (*conucos*), like the Arab does his tents.

The tribes of the Upper Orinoco, the Atabapo and the Inirida, worship only the forces of nature. The principle of good is called Cachimana; it is the *manitu*, the great spirit, that controls the seasons and ripens fruit. Next to Cachimana there is the principle of evil, Jolokiamo, less powerful but more astute and, especially, more dynamic. When the jungle Indians go to missions it is difficult for them to conceive of a church or an image. 'These good people,' said our missionary, 'like only outdoor processions. Recently when I celebrated the village's saint's day the Inirida Indians came to mass. They told me: "Your god is locked into a house as if he was old and sick; our god is in the jungle, in fields, in the Sipapu mountains from where the rains come."' In the larger, and thus more barbarous tribes, peculiar religious societies are formed. Some of the older Indians claim to be better initiated in divine matters and guard the famous *botuto* that they play under palm trees to make the fruit ripen. On the Orinoco banks no images or idols can be found, but the *botuto*, the sacred trumpet, is worshipped. To be initiated into the mysteries of the *botuto* you must be pure and celibate. The initiated are subject to flagellations, fasting and other disciplinarian practices. There are few sacred trumpets. The most famous is found on a hill at the confluence of the Tomo and Guainia rivers. It is said it can be heard at a distance of 10 leagues. Father Cerezo assured us that Indians talk of this *botuto* as the object of a cult common to several neighbouring tribes. Fruit and alcoholic drinks are placed round this sacred trumpet. Sometimes the great spirit Cachimana himself blows the *botuto*, sometimes he speaks through whoever guards the instrument. As these tricks are very ancient (the fathers of our fathers, the Indians say) you should not be surprised that there are many believers. Women are not allowed to see the marvellous trumpet, and are excluded from all religious service. If one has the misfortune to see it she is mercilessly killed. The missionary told us that in 1798 he was lucky enough to save a young girl whom a jealous lover had accused of having followed the Indians who sounded the *botuto*. 'They would have murdered her publicly,' said Father Cerezo. 'How could she have protected herself from Indian fanaticism, in a country where it is so easy to be poisoned? I sent her away to one of the missions on the Lower Orinoco.'

On the evening of the 4th of May we were told that an Indian carrying our boat by the Pimichín portage had been bitten by a poisonous snake. The tall, strong man was brought to the mission, seriously ill. He had lost consciousness; nausea, giddiness and headaches followed his collapse. Many Indians ran to the sick man's hut, and gave him infusions of *raíz de mato*. We cannot say exactly what plant is used for this antidote. I really regret that travelling botanists are often unable to see the fruit or flower of plants useful to man when so many other plants can be seen daily in flower. This root is probably an apocynacea, perhaps the *Cerbera tevethia* that people in Cumaná call *lengua de mato* or *contra-culebra*, used against snake bites.

In the snake-bitten Indian's hut we found balls, some 2 to 3 inches thick, of an earthy, dirty salt called *chivi*, which Indians prepare meticulously. In Javita they make salt by burning the spadix and fruit of the *seje* palm. As well as this they also distil the ashes of the famous *cupana*, a liana. A missionary seldom travels without seeds prepared from the *cupana*. This preparation requires great care. The Indians break up the seeds and mix them with cassava flour wrapped in banana leaves and leave the mixture to ferment in water until it becomes a saffron-yellow colour. This yellow paste is dried in the sun and taken in the morning as a tea. The drink is bitter and stom-achic, though I found it repulsive.

May 5th. We set off on foot following our boat, which had reached Caño Pimichín by portage. We had to wade through numerous streams. This journey demands caution because water snakes teem in the marshes. Indians pointed out tracks in the wet clay left by the small black bears that are so common on the Temi banks. They are different in size from the *Ursus americanus*: missionaries call them *oso carnicero* to differentiate them from the *oso palmero* or tamanoir (*Myrmecophaga jubata*) and the *oso hormiguero* or tamandua ant-eater. Two of these animals, which are good to eat, defend themselves by rising up on to their hind legs. Buffon's tamanoir is called *uaraca* by the Indians: they are irascible and brave, which is strange given that they are without teeth. As we advanced we came across some accessible clearings in the jungle. We picked new species of *coffea*, a *Galega piscatorum*, which Indians use like the jacqui-nia, and a composite plant of the Temi river, as a kind of *bar-basco* to stun fish; and a large liana known locally as *bejuco de mavacure*, which gives the famous curare poison.

Towards night we reached a small farm in the port of Caño Pimichín. We were shown a cross near the river, which marked a spot 'where a poor Capuchin missionary had been killed by wasps'. Here people talk a lot about poisonous wasps and ants, but we were not able to find any. It is well known that in the torrid zone tiny bites bring on intense fevers. The death of the luckless monk was more likely the result of exhaustion and dampness than the poison in the wasps' stings, which the Indi-ans also dread.

The Pimichín landing-stage is surrounded by a small cacao plantation. The trees are very robust and loaded with fruit all year round. When you think that the cacao tree is native to the Parima jungle, south of latitude 6, and that the humid climate of the Upper Orinoco suits this precious tree far more than the Caracas and New Barcelona air, which each year gets drier, then one regrets that this beautiful part of the world is in monks' hands as they discourage agriculture. We spent the night in a recently abandoned hut. An Indian family had left behind fishing tackle, earthen jars, mats woven with palm-tree petioles: all the household goods of these carefree people who are indifferent to property. Large amounts of *mani* (a mixture of the resins *moronobea* and *Amyris caraña*) lay in piles around the hut. This is used by Indians to pitch their canoes and to fix the bony ray spines on to their arrows. We found several jars filled with a vegetable milk, which is used as a varnish, called in the missions *leche para pintar* (milk for painting). They coat their furniture with this viscous juice. It leaves it a fine white; it thickens in contact with air to appear glossy. The more we study vegetable chemistry in the torrid zone the more we shall discover in remote spots still accessible to European trade, and already half prepared by the plants themselves, products that we believed belonged to the animal kingdom. These discoveries will be multiplied when, as the political state of the world now seems to show, European civilization flows towards the equinoctial regions of the New World.

As I have already written, the marshy plains between Javita and the Pimichín landing-stage are infamous for the quantity of poisonous snakes inhabiting them. Before we installed ourselves in the hut some Indians killed two *mapanares* snakes, about 5 feet long. It is a beautiful animal, with a white belly and red and black spots on its back, and very poisonous. As we could not hang our hammocks, and as there was lots of grass inside the hut, we were nervous about sleeping on the floor. In the morning as we lifted up a jaguar skin that one of our servants had slept on, another large snake appeared. Indians say these reptiles move slowly while not being chased, and approach man seeking his heat. I do not want to defend snakes, but I can assure you that if these poisonous animals were as aggressive as some think, in some places in America, like the Orinoco and the damp mountains of Choco, man would long ago have died out faced with the infinite number of snakes.

May 6th. We set off at dawn after inspecting the bottom of our canoe. We counted on our boat surviving another 300 leagues of navigation down the Río Negro, up the Casiquiare and back down the Orinoco again to Angostura. The Pimichín is about as wide as the Seine in Paris but little trees that like water narrow the river so much that only a canal of some 15 to 20 toises remains. This *caño* is navigable all year round. After following it for four hours we at last reached the Río Negro.

The morning was fresh and beautiful. For thirty-six days we had been locked up in a narrow canoe which was so unsteady that standing up suddenly from your seat would have capsized it. We had cruelly suffered from insect bites, but we had survived this unhealthy climate, and had crossed the many waterfalls and dykes that block the rivers and make the journey more dangerous than crossing the seas, without sinking. After all that we had endured, it gives me pleasure to speak of the joy we felt in having reached a tributary of the Amazon, of having passed the isthmus that separates the two great river systems. The uninhabited banks of the Casiquiare, covered in jungle, busied my imagination. In this interior of a new continent you get used to seeing man as not essential to the natural order. The earth is overloaded with vegetation: nothing prevents its development. An immense layer of mould manifests the uninterrupted action of organic forces. Crocodile and boa are the masters of the river; jaguar, peccary, the dante and monkeys cross the jungle without fear or danger, established there in an ancient heritage. This view of a living nature where man is nothing is both odd and sad. Here, in a fertile land, in an eternal greenness, you search in vain for traces of man; you feel you are carried into a different world from the one you were born into.

CHAPTER 20

IF YOU COMPARE the Río Negro with the Amazon, the River
Plate or the Orinoco it is but a river of the second order.
Possessing it has been, for centuries, of great political interest
for the Spanish Government because it affords its rivals, the
Portuguese, easy access into the Guianan missions to worry
the Capitanía-General of Caracas in its southern limits. Three
hundred years have passed in pointless territorial disputes. In
different times, according to their degree of civilization,
people have leaned either on papal authority or on astronomy.
As they have generally been keener to prolong this dispute
rather than solve it, only nautical science and geography have
gained anything. When the affairs of Paraguay and the possession of the Sacramento colony became important for the two
Courts of Madrid and Lisbon, commissioners were sent out
to study the boundaries of the Orinoco, Amazon and River
Plate. Besides the idle, who filled archives with their complaints and lawsuits, there were a few educated engineers and
some naval officers acquainted with the means of determining
the position of a place. The little we knew up to the end of the
last century about the geography of the interior of the New
Continent is due to these hard-working men. It is pleasing to
remind ourselves that the sciences gained accidentally from
these border commissions, often forgotten by the states that
sent them out.

When one knows how unreliable the maps of America are,
and when one has closely seen these uncultivated lands
between the Jupura, the Río Negro, the Madeira, the Ucayale,
the Branco river and the Cayenne coast that have been seriously disputed in Europe up until today, one is surprised how
these litigations over who owns a few square leagues have so
perseveringly dragged on.

The Río Negro and the Jupura are two tributaries of the Amazon, comparable in length to the Danube, whose upper parts belong to Spain and whose lower reaches are occupied by Portugal. In these majestic rivers people have gathered in those places where civilization is most ancient. The banks of the Upper Jupura or Caqueta have been cultivated by missionaries who came down from the mountains of Popayan and Neiva. From Mocoa to the confluence with Caguan there are many Christian settlements, while in the Lower Jupura the Portuguese have founded hardly a few villages. Along the Río Negro, on the other hand, the Spaniards have not been able to rival their neighbours. How can they rely on a people so distanced from the province of Caracas? Steppes and virtually deserted jungle some 160 leagues thick separate the cultivated parts of the river bank from the four missions of Maroa, Tomo, Davipe and San Carlos.

When I was in Spanish Río Negro the conflict between the Courts of Lisbon and Madrid – even in peaceful times – had heightened the mistrust of the commanders of petty neighbouring forts. A commander with sixteen to eighteen soldiers tired 'the garrison' with his measures for safety, dictated by 'the important state of affairs'. If he were attacked he hoped 'to surround the enemy'. A people who have preserved a national hatred through the ages loves any excuse to vent it. We enjoy all that is passionate and dynamic, as much in our feelings as in the rival hatreds built up on age-old prejudices. On the banks of the Río Negro the Indians in the neighbouring Portuguese and Spanish villages hate each other. These poor people speak only their Indian languages and have no idea what happens 'on the other bank of the ocean, beyond the great salt pond', but the gowns of the missionaries are of different colours and this enrages them.

The rivalry between Spain and Portugal has contributed to the poor geographical knowledge about the tributary rivers of the Amazon. The Indians are excellent geographers and can outflank the enemy despite the limits on the maps and the forts. Each side prefers to conceal what it knows, and the love of what is mysterious, so common among ignorant people, perpetuates doubt. It is also known that different Indian tribes in this labyrinth of rivers give rivers different names that all mean 'river', 'great water' and 'current'. I have often been puzzled trying to determine synonyms after examining the most intelligent Indians through an interpreter. Three or four languages are spoken in the same mission, it is hard to make witnesses agree. Our maps are full of arbitrary names. The desire to leave no void in maps in order to give them an appearance of accuracy has caused rivers to be created whose names are not synonymous.[114]

After entering the Río Negro by the Pimichín, and passing the small cataract at the confluence of the two rivers, we saw the mission of Maroa a quarter of a league off. This village of 150 Indians appeared prosperous and cheerful. We bought some beautiful live toucans (*piapoco*); birds whose 'intelligence' can be trained, like our ravens. Above Maroa we passed the mouths of the Aquio and of the Tomo. We did not enter the Tomo mission, but Father Zea told us with a smile that the Indians of Tomo and Maroa had been in full insurrection because monks had tried to force them to dance the famous 'dance of the devils'. The missionary had wanted to hold the ceremony in which the *piastres* (who are shamans, doctors and conjurors) evoke the evil spirit Jolokiamo, but in a burlesque way. He thought that the 'dance of the devils' would show the neophytes that Jolokiamo no longer had any power over them. Some young Indians, believing the missionary's promises, agreed to act as devils; they were decked out in black and yellow feathers and jaguar skins with long tails. The church square had been surrounded by soldiers from other missions to make the missionary more redoubtable. Indians who were unsure about the dance and the impotence of the evil spirits were brought along. But the oldest of the Indians managed to imbue all the younger ones with a superstitious dread and they decided to flee *al monte*. The missionary had to postpone his project of mocking the Indian demon.

After two hours' navigation we reached the mouth of the Tomo and the small mission of Davipe, founded in 1755 by an army lieutenant, and not by monks. Father Morillo, the missionary on the spot, with whom we stayed a few hours, received us with great hospitality, and even offered us some Madeira wine. As far as luxury foods go we would have preferred wheat bread; the absence of bread is felt far more over a long time than any alcoholic drink. Every now and then the Portuguese bring small quantities of Madeira wine to the Río Negro. But the word *madera* in Spanish means 'wood', so some monks, poorly versed in geography, were reluctant to celebrate mass with Madeira wine; they took it for a fermented liquor from some local tree, like palm-tree wine, and asked the superior of their order to decide if the *vino de Madera* was in fact a wine made from grapes or the sweet juice from a tree (*de algún palo*). Already, from the beginning of the conquest, the question of whether priests could celebrate mass with another fermented liquor similar to wine had been raised. The question, predictably, was decided negatively.

At Davipe we bought provisions, including chicken and a pig. This purchase greatly interested the Indians, who had not eaten meat for ages. They urged us to leave for Dapa Island where the pig was to be killed and roasted overnight. In the convent we just had time to examine great piles of the *mani* resin and rope from the *chiquichiqui* palm, which deserves to be better known in Europe.

A little above the Davipe mission the Río Negro receives a branch of the Casiquiare whose existence is a remarkable phenomenon in the history of river branching. This branch emerges from the Casiquiare, north of Vasiva, under the name Itinivi; and after crossing a flat, virtually uninhabited country some 25 leagues long, pours into the Río Negro under the name of Río Conorichite. It seemed to me, near its mouth, to be 120 toises wide, and added large quantities of white waters to the black waters. Even though the Conorichite current is very fast, you shorten the journey from Davipe to Esmeralda by three days using this canal. It is not surprising to find a double communication between the Casiquiare and the Río Negro when you recall that so many American rivers form deltas when they meet other rivers. In this way the Branco and the Jupura pour into the Río Negro and Amazon through many branches. At the confluence with the Jupura there is another more extraordinary phenomenon. Before joining the Amazon this river, which is its main recipient, sends three branches called Uaranapu, Manhama and Avateprana to the Jupura, which is none other than its tributary. The Amazon thus sends its waters into the Jupura before receiving the waters of the latter back.

The Río Conorichite played an important role in the time when the Portuguese traded in slaves in Spanish territory. The slave-traders went up the Casiquiare and the Caño Mee to Conorichite; then they carried their canoes over land to the Rochuelas de Manuteso, and thus reached the Atabapo. This abominable trade lasted until about 1756. The Caribs, a warrior and trading people, received knives, hooks, mirrors and glass objects from the Dutch and Portuguese. In exchange, they urged Indian caciques to fight each other, and then bought their prisoners of war, or cunningly grabbed them, or used force to get them. These Carib incursions covered an enormous region.

We left the Conorichite mouth and the Davipe mission and at sunset reached the island of Dapa, picturesquely situated in the middle of the river. We were amazed to find cultivated ground and, on top of a hill, an Indian hut. Four Indians sat round a small brushwood fire eating a kind of white paste spotted with black that aroused our curiosity. These black spots proved to be *vachacos*, large ants, whose abdomens resemble lumps of grease. They had been dried and blackened by smoking. We saw several bags of ants hanging above the fire. These good people paid little attention to us, yet there were more than fourteen Indians lying completely naked in hammocks hung one above the other in the hut. When Father Zea arrived they received him joyously. Two young Indian women came down from their hammocks to make cassava cakes for us. Through an interpreter we asked them if the land on the island was fertile. They answered saying that cassava grew poorly but that it was a good place for ants. *Vachacos* were the subsistence diet of Río Negro and Guianan Indians. They are not eaten out of greed but because, in the missionary's terms, the fat is very nutritious. When the cakes were ready, Father Zea, whose fever seemed to increase rather than decrease his appetite, asked for a bag of smoked ants to be brought to him. Then he mixed these crushed insects into the cassava flour and urged us to taste. It tasted rather like rancid butter mixed with breadcrumbs. The cassava was not acid, but vestiges of our European prejudices restrained us from praising what the missionary called 'an excellent ant pâté'.

As rain was pouring down we had to sleep in the overcrowded hut. The Indians slept only from eight at night to two in the morning; the rest of the time they chatted and prepared their bitter *cupana* drink, poking the fire and complaining of the cold, even though the temperature was 21 °C. This custom of staying awake, even of getting up four or five hours before dawn, is common to the Guiana Indians.

Despite the speed of the current and the effort of our rowers it took us twelve hours on the river to reach the San Carlos fort on the Río Negro. We left the mouth of the Casiquiare on our left, and the little island of Cumarai on our right. Here they believe that the fort lies on the equator itself, but after my observations made on the Culimacari rock, it lies on 1.54′ 11″.

At San Carlos we lodged with the fort commander, a lieutenant in the militia. From a gallery in the house we enjoyed an agreeable view on to three long islands covered in thick vegetation. The river lies straight from north to south, as if it had been dug by man. The constantly covered sky gives these countries a solemn, sombre quality. In the village we found some *juvia* trunks: it is the majestic tree that gives what in Europe are called Brazil-nuts. We made it known under the name *Bertholletia excelsa*.[115] The trees reach 30 feet in eight years.

The military establishment of this frontier consists of seventeen soldiers, ten of whom are detached in neighbouring missions. The humidity is such that hardly four rifles work. The Portuguese have twenty-five better-dressed and better-armed men in the fort of San Jose de Maravitanos. In the San Carlos mission we found a *garita*, or square house, built with unbaked bricks, with six rooms. The fort, or as they prefer to call it, the Castillo de San Felipe, is on the right bank of the

Río Negro, *vis-à-vis* San Carlos. The commander showed some scruples, and refused to allow Bonpland and myself to visit the fort as our passports clearly stated we could measure mountains and perform trigonometric operations on land, but we could not see inside fortified places. Our fellow traveller, Don Nicolás Soto, a Spanish officer, was luckier, and was allowed to cross the river.

The passage from the mouth of the Río Negro to Grand Para took only twenty to twenty-five days, so we could have gone down the Amazon as far as the Brazilian coast just as easily as returning by the Casiquiare to Caracas. We were told at San Carlos that political circumstances made it difficult to cross from Spanish to Portuguese colonies, but we did not know until our return to Europe what danger we would have been exposed to had we gone as far as Barcellos. It was known in Brazil, probably through newspapers, whose indiscretion is not helpful for travellers, that I was going to visit the Río Negro missions and examine the natural canal uniting the two river systems. In these deserted jungles the only instruments ever seen had been carried by the boundary commissioners. The Portuguese Government agents could not conceive how a sensible man could exhaust himself 'measuring lands that did not belong to him'. Orders had been issued to arrest me, seize my instruments, and especially my astronomical observations, so dangerous to the safety of the State. We were to be led along the Amazon to Grand Para, and then back to Lisbon. Fortunately, the Lisbon Government instantly ordered that I should not be disturbed but rather encouraged.

In the lands of the Río Negro Indians we found several of those green stones known as 'Amazon stones' because Indians claim that they come from a country of 'women without men', or 'women living alone'. Superstition attaches great importance to these stones, which are worn as amulets round the neck as popular belief claims they protect wearers from nervous diseases, fevers and poisonous snake bites. Because of this they have for centuries been traded between the Indians of the northern Orinoco and those in the south. The Caribs made them known on the coast. Up to a few years ago during debates about quinine these green stones were considered an efficient febrifuge in enlightened Europe; if we can count on the credulity of Europeans, there is nothing odd about Spanish colonizers appreciating these amulets as much as the Indians, or that these stones are sold at high prices. Usually they are shaped into cylinders with holes down the sides, and covered in inscriptions and figures. But it is not today's Indians who have perforated holes in such hard stones or carved animals and fruit. This work suggests another, older culture. The actual inhabitants of the torrid zone are so ignorant of how to carve hard stone that they think the green stone comes from soft earth, and that it hardens when carved.

The history of the jade, or green Guianan stones, is intimately linked with that of the warlike women named Amazons by sixteenth-century travellers. La Condamine has produced many testimonies in favour of this tradition. Since returning from the Orinoco and Amazon I have often been asked in Paris if I agreed with that learned man, or thought that he said what he said to satisfy a public eager for novelties. A taste for the marvellous and a wish to describe the New World with some of the tones of antiquity no doubt contributed to the reputation of the Amazons. But this is not enough to reject a tradition shared by many isolated tribes. I would conclude that women, tired of the state of slavery in which men have held them, united together and kept their independence as warriors. They received visits once a year from men, and probably killed off their male babies. This society of women may have been quite powerful in one part of Guiana. But such is the disposition of man's mind that, in the long succession of travellers discovering and writing about the marvels of the New World, each one readily declared that he had seen what earlier ones had announced.

We passed three nights in San Carlos. I counted the nights because I stayed awake hoping to be able to observe stars. But I had to leave the place without ever once being able to effect a trusty observation of the geographical latitude of the place.

May 10th. Overnight our canoe was loaded and we set off a little before dawn to go up the Río Negro to the mouth of the Casiquiare and begin our researches on the true course of this river linking the Orinoco and Amazon. The morning was beautiful, but as the heat rose the sky began to cloud over. The air is so saturated with water in these forests that water bubbles become visible at the slightest increase of evaporation on the earth's surface. As there is no breeze the humid strata are not replaced and renewed by drier air. This clouded sky made us gloomier and gloomier. Through this humidity Bonpland lost the plants he had collected; for my part I feared finding the same Río Negro mists in the Casiquiare valley. For more than half a century nobody in the missions has doubted the existence of communications between the two great river systems: the important aim of our journey was reduced to fixing the course of the Casiquiare by astronomic means, especially at its point of entry into the Río Negro, and its bifurcation with the Orinoco. Without sun or stars this aim would have been frustrated, and we would have been uselessly exposed to long, weary deprivations. Our travelling companions wanted to return by the shortest journey, along the Pimichín and its small rivers; but Bonpland preferred, like myself, to persist in the original plan we had traced out while crossing the Great Cataracts. We had already travelled by canoe from San Fernando de Apure to San Carlos along the Apure, Orinoco, Atabapo, Temi, Tuamini and Río Negro for over 180 leagues. In entering the Orinoco by the Casiquiare we still had some 320 leagues to cover from San Carlos to Angostura. It would have been a shame to let ourselves be discouraged by the fear of a cloudy sky and the Casiquiare mosquitoes. Our Indian pilot, who had recently visited Mandavaca, promised us sun and 'those great stars that eat up clouds' once we had left the black waters of the Guaviare. So we managed to carry out our first plan and returned to San Fernando along the Casiquiare. Luckily for our researches the Indian's prediction was fulfilled. The white waters brought us a clear sky, stars, mosquitoes and crocodiles.

Having reached the south of the Caravine *raudal* we saw that the winding Casiquiare again approached San Carlos. By land the distance from the San Francisco Solano mission, where we slept, is only 2.5 leagues, but by river it was 7 or 8. I spent part of the night outside, vainly waiting for stars to appear.

The San Francisco mission, situated on the left bank of the Casiquiare, was named after one of the leaders of the boundary expedition, Don Joseph Solano. This educated officer never got any further than San Fernando de Atabapo; he had never seen the Río Negro waters or the Casiquiare, or the Orinoco east of the Guaviare. Ignorance of the Spanish language drove geographers to locate erroneously on the famous La Cruz Olmedilla map the 400-league route made by Joseph Solano to the sources of the Orinoco. The San Francisco mission was founded not by monks but by military authorities. Following the boundary expedition, villages were built wherever an officer or a corporal stopped with his soldiers. Some of the Indians withdrew and remained independent; others, whose chiefs were caught, joined the missions. Where there was no church they were happy to raise a great red wooden cross, and to build a *casa fuerte*, that is, a house with long beams placed horizontally on top of each other, next to it. This house had two floors; upstairs were placed small cannons; downstairs two soldiers lived, served by Indian families. Tamed Indians established themselves around the *casa fuerte*. In the event of an attack soldiers would gather the Indians together by sounding the horn, or the baked-earth *botuto*. These were the nineteen so-called Christian establishments founded by Don Antonio Santos. Military posts had no effect in civilizing the Indians living there. They figured on maps and in mission works as *pueblos* (villages) and as *reducciones apostólicas*.

The Indians we found at San Francisco Solano belong to two different tribes: the Pacimonales and the Cheruvichanenas. The latter came from a prestigious tribe living on the Tomo river, near the Manivas of the Upper Guiana, so I tried to find out from them about the upper course of the Río Negro, and where I could find its sources; but my interpreter could not make them understand the true sense of my question. They just repeated over and over again that the sources of the Río Negro and the Inirida were as close together as 'two fingers on a hand'. In one of the Pacimonales's huts we bought two great, beautiful birds: a toucan (*piapoco*), similar to the *Ramphastos erythrorynchos*, and an *ana*, a kind of macaw, with purple feathers like the *Psittacus macao*. In our canoe we already had seven parrots, two cock-of-the-rocks (*pipra*), a motmot, two guans or *pavas del monte*, two *manaviris* (cercoleptes or *Viverra caudivolvula*), and eight monkeys, of which three were new species. Father Zea was not too happy about the rate our zoological collection increased day by day, although he kept that to himself. The toucan resembles the raven in its habits and intelligence; it is a brave creature and easy to tame. Its long, strong beak serves as its defence. It becomes master of the house; steals whatever it can, frequently takes a bath, and likes fishing on the river bank. The one we bought was very young, yet throughout our journey it took malicious delight in molesting the sad, irritable monkeys. The structure of the toucan's beak does not oblige it to swallow food by throwing it into the air as some naturalists claim. It is true that it does have problems lifting food from the ground, but once food is seized in its long beak it throws back its head so that it swallows perpendicularly. When this bird wants to drink it makes an odd gesture; monks say it makes the sign of the cross over the water. Because of this creoles have baptized the toucan with the strange name of Diostedé (May God give it to you).

Most of our animals were locked in small reed cages, but some ran freely about the boat. When it threatened to rain the macaws started a terrible racket, the toucan tried to fly to the shore to fish, and the titi monkeys ran to hide under Father Zea's long sleeves. These spectacles were common, and allowed us to forget the torment of mosquitoes. To camp at night we built a kind of leather box (*petaca*), which held our provisions; next to it we placed our instruments and the animal cages; around this we hung our hammocks and a little further out the Indians' hammocks. Around the outside we lit fires to scare off jungle jaguars. The Indians often spoke of a small nocturnal animal with a long snout, which traps young parrots in their nests and uses its hands to eat like monkeys. They call it *guachi*; it is doubtless a coati. Missionaries forbid the eating of *guachi* flesh. Superstition claims that it is an aphrodisiac.

May 11th. We went on shore. A few steps from the beach Bonpland discovered an *almendrón*, a majestic *Bertholletia excelsa*. The Indians assured us that this tree on the Casiquiare banks was unknown at San Francisco Solano, Vasiva and Esmeralda. They did not think that this 60-foot-high tree could have been accidentally planted by some traveller. Experiments made at San Carlos have shown how rare it is to make a bertholletia germinate because of its ligneous pericarp, and the oil in the nut, which turns the seed rancid. Perhaps this was part of a forest of inland bertholletia.[116]

May 12th. We set off from the Culimacari rock at half past one in the morning. The plague of mosquitoes was intensifying as we left the Río Negro. In the Casiquiare valley there are no *zancudos*, but insects from the Simulium and the Tipulary families are all the more numerous and poisonous. Before reaching the Esmeralda mission we still had eight more nights to spend out in the open in this unhealthy, humid country. Our pilot was happy to count on the hospitality of the Mandavaca missionary and shelter in the village of Vasiva. We struggled against the current, which flowed at some 8 miles an hour. Where we aimed to rest was only some 3 leagues away, yet we took fourteen hours to make this short journey, despite the effort of our rowers.

We crossed some violent rapids before reaching the Mandavaca mission. The village, also called Quirabuena, has only sixty inhabitants. Most of these Christian settlements are in such a deplorable condition that over a stretch of 50 leagues we counted barely 200 people. The river banks were more populated before the arrival of the missionaries. The Indians retreated into the jungle towards the east as the plains on the west are uninhabited. They live for part of the year off the large ants I have already described. In Mandavaca we met a good missionary who had spent 'over twenty years of mosquitoes in the Casiquiare jungles' and whose legs were so spotted by mosquito bites that you could hardly see he was a white. He spoke of his isolation, and the sad necessity that forced him to witness how the most atrocious crimes went unpunished.

In Vasiva a few years before an Indian chief had eaten one of his wives after taking her from her *conuco* and fattening her up with plenty of food. If the Guiana Indians eat human flesh it is not because of privations, or during rituals, but out of vengeance after a victory or, as the missionaries say, 'out of their perverted greed'. Victory over an enemy horde is celebrated with a feast where parts of prisoners' corpses are eaten. During the night an enemy family is attacked, or an enemy found by chance in the jungle is killed by a poisoned arrow. The corpse is cut up and brought home like a trophy. Civilization has led man to sense the unity of the human race, the bonds that link him to customs and languages which he does not know. Wild Indians hate all those who do not belong to their tribe or family. Indians who are at war with a neighbouring tribe hunt them as we would animals in the wood. When they see unknown jungle Indians arrive at their mission they say: 'They must be related to us as we understand what they say.' They recognize only their own family: a tribe is but a reunion of relations. They recognize family and kin ties, but not those of humanity in general. No feelings of compassion prevent them from killing women or children of an enemy tribe. These latter are their favourite food after a skirmish or ambush.

The hate that Indians show for nearly all human beings who speak another language, and are considered to be barbarians of an inferior race, often erupts in the missions after years of slumber. A few months before our arrival at Esmeralda, an Indian born in the jungle behind the Duida was travelling with another who previously, having been captured by the Spaniards on the banks of the Ventuario, had lived peacefully in the village or, as they say, 'under the sound of a bell' (*debajo de la campana*). This latter Indian had to walk slowly because of a fever he had caught in the mission, usually due to a sudden change in diet. Annoyed by this delay his companion killed him and hid the corpse under some thickets near Esmeralda. The crime, like so many others committed among the Indians, would not have been discovered if the murderer had not proposed to celebrate a feast the following day. He tried to persuade his sons, who were born in the mission and were

Christians, to accompany him to the jungle and fetch bits of the corpse to eat. The boys had difficulty in stopping him. The family squabble alerted a soldier who found out what the Indians had tried to conceal.

'You cannot imagine,' said the old Mandavaca missionary, 'how perverse this *familia de indios* (family of Indians) is. You accept individuals from another tribe into your mission; they seem tame, honest, good workers; you let them out on a foray (*entrada*) to capture wild Indians and you can scarcely stop them throttling all they can and hiding pieces of the corpses.' We had with us in our pirogue an Indian who had escaped from the Guaisia river. In a few weeks he had become very civilized. At night he helped us prepare our astronomical instruments. He was as cheerful as he was intelligent, and we were ready to employ him. Imagine our disappointment when through an interpreter we heard him say that 'Marimonda monkey meat, although blacker, had the same taste as human meat.' He assured us that 'his *relations* – that is, his tribal brothers – preferred to eat the palms of human hands, as well as those of bears'. As he spoke he gestured to emphasize his brutal greed. We asked this young, pacifistic man through our interpreter if he still felt a desire to 'eat a Cheruvichanena Indian' and he answered calmly that 'in the mission he would eat only what he saw *los padres* (the fathers) eating'. It is no point reproaching Indians about this abominable practice. In the eyes of a Guaisia Indian, a Cheruvichanena Indian is totally alien to him; to kill one was not morally very different from killing a jaguar. Eating what the fathers ate in the mission was simply convenience. If Indians escape to rejoin their tribes, or are driven by hunger, they quickly fall back into cannibalism.

The Casiquiare Indians, though easily reverting to barbaric customs, show some intelligence in the missions, work well and learn Spanish. As most missions have two or three tribes speaking different languages the language of the missionaries lets them communicate with each other. I saw a Poignave Indian talk in Castilian with a Guahibo, though both had left the jungle only three months before. Every quarter of an hour one spoke a carefully prepared phrase in which the verb, following the grammar of their own languages, was always a gerund ('When me seeing the father, the father me saying ...').

Both here and in the Río Negro the humidity and consequent quantity of insects make all agriculture impossible. Everywhere you see large ants, which march in packed columns and devour all cultivated plants that are soft and juicy, while in the jungle they can find only woody stalks. If a missionary wants to plant lettuce, or any other European vegetable, he has to hang his garden in the air. He fills an old canoe with good earth and hangs it 4 feet above the ground with rope made from *chiquichiqui* palm or, more commonly, rests it on some scaffolding.

May 13th. We left Mandavaca at half past two in the morning. After six hours of travelling we passed the mouth of the Idapa or Siapa on the east. It rises on the Uturan mountain. It has white waters. Its upper course has been strangely misrepresented on La Cruz's and Surville's maps, which all later maps have imitated. We stopped near the Cunuri *raudal*. The noise of the little cataract got much louder during the night. Our Indians said that meant certain rain. It fell before sunrise. However, the araguato monkeys' continuous wails had warned us that rain was approaching.

May 14th. Mosquitoes and ants chased us from the river bank before two in the morning. We thought that ants could not climb the ropes on which we hung our hammocks; but whether this was inexact, or whether they fell on top of us from branches, we struggled to rid ourselves of these annoying insects. The more we advanced the narrower the river became. Its banks were so muddy that Bonpland could only reach the trunk of a *Carolinea princeps* covered with enormous purple flowers with extreme effort. This tree is the most beautiful in these jungles.

From the 14th to the 21st of May we slept out in the open air; but I cannot point out where exactly we camped. This country is so wild and so deserted that, apart from a few rivers, the Indians could not name anything from my compass bearings. No observations of stars could reassure me about our latitude. After passing the place where the Itinivini separates from the Casiquiare to go west towards the granite Daripabo hills, we found the muddy banks covered with bamboo. These arborescent *gramina* rise up to 20 feet; their stalks arch towards the top. It is a new species of long-leafed bamboo. Bonpland rejoiced to find one in flower. Nothing is more rare in the New World than seeing these gigantic *gramina* in flower. Mutis[117] herbalized for over twenty years without ever finding one in flower.

Our first camp, above the Vasiva, was easily set up. We found a corner of dry land free from shrubs at the south of the *caño* Curamuni in a place where we saw capuchin monkeys, so easily identified with their black beards and sad, wild look, as they climbed along horizontal branches of a genipap. The next five nights became more and more uncomfortable as we approached the Orinoco bifurcation. The exuberance of the vegetation increases to such a point that it is hard to imagine, even when you have got used to the Tropics. There is no beach; a palisade of bunched trees becomes the river bank. You see a channel some 200 toises wide bordered with two enormous walls carpeted with leaves and liana. We tried to get ashore but could not even get out of the canoe. Sometimes at sunset we would follow the bank for an hour to reach, not a clearing, but a less overgrown patch where our Indians with their machetes could cut down enough to let thirteen or fourteen people camp. We could not spend the night in the pirogue. The mosquitoes that tormented us during the day crowded towards evening under the *toldo*, that is, the roof made of palm leaves that sheltered us from rain. Never were our hands or faces more swollen. Even Father Zea, boasting that in his cataract missions he had the biggest and bravest (*los más valientes*) mosquitoes, agreed that these Casiquiare bites were the most painful he had ever felt. In the middle of thick jungle it was difficult to find any wood to light our fire; the branches are so full of sap in this equatorial region where it always rains that they hardly burn. Where there are no arid beaches we hardly ever came across that old wood which Indians say has been 'cooked in the sun'. A fire was only necessary to scare away jungle animals: we had such a low stock of food that we did not need wood to cook.

On the evening of the 18th of May we reached a place on the bank where wild cacao trees grew. The seed of these cacao trees is small and bitter; the Indians suck the pulp and throw away the seed, which is then picked up by mission Indians who sell it to those who are not too fussy about how to prepare cocoa. 'This is Puerto del Cacao (Cacao Port)', said our pilot. 'Here the Fathers sleep on their way to Esmeralda to buy *sarbacans* (blowpipes to shoot poison arrows) and *juvias* (Brazilnuts).' Only five boats a year pass along the Casiquiare. Since Maypures, that is, for a month, we had not met anyone on the rivers outside the missions. We spent the night south of Lake Duractumuni in a forest of palm trees. It poured with rain, but the pothoses, arums and lianas made such a thick trellis that we sheltered underneath.

Of all body complaints those that persist without change are the worst; against them the only cure is patience. It is likely that the emanations of the Casiquiare jungle infected Bonpland with such a serious disease that he almost died when we reached Angostura. Luckily neither he nor I suspected this at the time. The view of the river and the hum of insects became monotonous; but our natural good temper did not snap, and helped us survive this long journey. We discovered that eating small bits of dry cacao ground without sugar and drinking a lot of river water appeased our hunger for several hours. Ants and mosquitoes annoyed us more than hunger and humidity.

We passed the night of the 20th of May, the last on the Casiquiare, near the bifurcation with the Orinoco. We hoped to make some astronomical observations as we saw extraordinary shooting stars visible through the mist. Indians, who do not embellish their imagination through words, call shooting stars the 'piss of the stars', and dew the 'spit of the stars'. But the clouds thickened and prevented us from seeing both meteors and stars.

We had been warned that we would find the insects at Esmeralda 'even more cruel and voracious' than in this branch of the Orinoco; despite this we looked forward to sleeping in an inhabited place, and botanizing a little at last. At our last camp on the Casiquiare we had quite a fright. I presume to describe something that might not greatly interest a reader, but should be part of a journal of incidents on a river in such wild country. We slept on the edge of the jungle. At midnight the Indians warned us that they had heard a jaguar growl very close to us; it seemed to be up a nearby tree. The jungle is so thick here that only animals who climb trees exist. As our fires gave off plenty of light, and as we had become hardened to fear, we did not worry too much about the jaguar's cries. The smell and barking of one of our dogs had attracted the jaguar. This dog, a large mastiff, had barked at the start, but when the jaguar approached the dog howled and hid under our hammocks. Since the Apure we had been used to this alternating bravery and fear in a young, tame and affectionate dog. We had a terrible shock the next morning. When getting ready to leave, the Indians told us that our dog had disappeared! There was no doubt that the jaguar had killed it. Perhaps when it no longer heard the roars it had wandered off along the shore, or perhaps we slept so deeply we never heard the dog's yelps. We were often told that on the Orinoco and the Magdalena old jaguars were so clever that they hunted their prey in the very camps, and twisted their victims' necks so that they could not shout. We waited a long while in case the dog was merely lost. Three days later we returned to the same place and again heard a jaguar roar. So the dog, which had been our companion from Caracas, and had often swum away from crocodiles, had ended up being devoured in the jungle.

On the 21st of May we again entered the bed of the Orinoco, 3 leagues above the Esmeralda mission. It had been a month since we had left this river near the mouth of the Guaviare. We still had 750 leagues to navigate as far as Angostura, but it was downstream, and this made the thought less painful. Going downstream you follow the middle of the river bed where there are less mosquitoes. Going upstream you are forced to stick close to the banks, to benefit from eddies and counter-currents, where the jungle and organic detritus thrown up on the beaches attract insects of the Tipulary family. The point where the Orinoco bifurcates is incredibly imposing. High granitic mountains rise on the northern shore, among them the Maraguaca and the Duida. There are no mountains at all on the left bank, or to the west or east as far as the mouth of the Tamatama.[118]

CHAPTER 21

THE UPPER ORINOCO FROM ITS CONFLUENCE WITH THE
GUAVIARE — SECOND CROSSING OF THE ATURES AND
MAYPURES CATARACTS — THE LOWER ORINOCO
BETWEEN THE MOUTH OF THE APURE RIVER AND
ANGOSTURA, CAPITAL OF SPANISH GUIANA

I STILL HAVE to refer to the most isolated of the Christian colonies of the Upper Orinoco. Opposite the point where the Orinoco bifurcates there is a granite mass called Duida, in the form of an amphitheatre. The missionaries call this mountain of nearly 8,000 feet a volcano. Because its slopes on the south and west are very steep it looks grand. The peak is bare and stony; but everywhere else in the less steep slopes earth has collected and jungles seem to hang from the air. At the foot of the Duida lies the Esmeralda mission, a small village of eighty people, surrounded by a lovely plain, and fed by little black-watered but limpid streams; a proper prairie with groups of mauritia palms, the American breadfruit. As you approach the mountain the marshy plain becomes a savannah that stretches along the lower reaches of the chain. There you find enormous, delicious pineapples. These bromelia always grow solitary among the grasses.

There is no missionary at Esmeralda: the monk appointed to celebrate mass here lives in Santa Bárbara, some 50 leagues away. To come upstream takes him four days and he only appears five or six times a year. An old soldier welcomed us in a friendly way; he took us for Catalan shopkeepers come to trade with the missions. When he saw our wads of paper for drying plants he laughed at our naïve ignorance: 'You have come to a land where nobody is going to buy such a thing. Here few write. We use dried maize, banana and *vijaho* (heliconia) leaves, as you do paper in Europe, to wrap up small objects like needles, hooks and other things you have to look after carefully.' This old soldier was both the civil and spiritual authority. He taught children, if not the catechism, then at least how to say the rosary, and he tolled the bells as a hobby. Sometimes he used the sacristan's stick in ways that did not amuse the Indians.

Despite the size of the Esmeralda mission three languages are spoken: Catarpen, Idapaminare and Maquiritare. This last is the dominant language of the Upper Orinoco, like Carin in the Lower, Otomac near the Apure, and Tamanac and Maypure at the Great Cataracts. It was strange to see many *zambos*, mulattos and other coloured people who, through vanity, call themselves Spaniards, and think that they are white because they are not red like the Indians. These people lead a miserable life; most of them had been banished to here (*desterrados*). To found a territory in the interior as quickly as possible, in order to keep the Portuguese out, Solano had rounded up as many vagabonds and criminals as he could and sent them to the Upper Orinoco where they lived with the unhappy Indians lured from the jungle. A mineralogical error had made Esmeralda famous. The Duida and Maraguaca granite holds superficial seams of a pretty rock crystal, sometimes quite transparent and sometimes coloured by chlorite or mixed with actonite and mistaken for diamonds and emeralds. In those mountains, so close to the sources of the Orinoco, everybody dreamed of El Dorado, which could not be far off, with Lake Parime and the ruins of the great city of Manoa.

The vagabonds of the plains had as little interest in working as the Indians, who were obliged to live 'under the sound of the church bell'. The former used their pride to justify their indolence. In the missions every coloured person who is not completely black like an African, or copper-coloured like an Indian, calls himself a Spaniard; belongs to the *gente de razón*, that is, gifted with reason, and this 'reason', which is both arrogant and lazy, tells the whites and those who think themselves white that agriculture is work for slaves, *poitos* and newly converted Indians. As these American colonists were separated from their homelands by jungles and savannahs they soon dispersed, some going north to Caura and Caroní, and others south to the Portuguese possessions. Thus, the fame of the emerald mines of Duida died out, and Esmeralda became a cursed place of banishment for monks where the dreadful cloud of mosquitoes darkens the atmosphere all year round. When the father superior of the mission wants to upbraid his monks he threatens to send them to Esmeralda: 'That is,' say the monks, 'to be condemned to mosquitoes, to be devoured by *zancudos gritones* (shouting flies), which God seems to have created to punish man.'

Esmeralda is the most famous place on the Orinoco for the making of the active poison that is used in war, out hunting and, surprisingly, as a remedy against gastric illnesses. The poison of the Amazonian Tikuna, the *upas-tieuté* of Java and the Guianan curare are the most poisonous substances known. Already by the sixteenth century Raleigh had heard the word *urari* spoken, signifying a vegetable substance used to poison arrows. However, nothing was known for sure in Europe about this poison.[119]

When we arrived in Esmeralda, most of the Indians were returning from an excursion they had made beyond the Pad- amo river to pick *juvias*, the fruit of the bertholletia, and a liana that gives curare. Their return was celebrated with a feast called in this mission the *fiesta de las juvias*, which resembles our harvest festivals. Women had prepared plenty of alcohol and for two days you met only drunk Indians. Among people who attach importance to palm-tree fruits and other useful trees, the period when these are harvested is marked by public cel- ebrations. We were lucky to find an Indian slightly less drunk than others, who was making curare with the recently picked plants. He was the chemist of the locality. Around him we saw large clay boilers used to cook the vegetable juices, as well as shallow vessels used for evaporation, and banana leaves rolled into filters to separate the liquid from the fibres. The Indian who was to teach us was known in the mission as master of the poison, *amo del curare*; he had that same formal and pedantic air that chemists were formerly accused of in Europe. 'I know,' he said, 'that whites have the secret of making soap, and that black powder which scares away the animals you hunt when you miss. But the curare that we prepare from father to son is superior to all that you know over there. It is the sap of a plant that "kills silently", without the victim knowing where it comes from.'

The chemical operation, whose importance is exaggerated by the master of the curare, seemed to us very simple. The *bejuco* used to make the poison in Esmeralda has the same name as in the Javita jungles. It is the *bejuco de mavacure*, which is found in abundance east of the mission on the left bank of the Orinoco. Although the bundles of *bejuco* that we found in the Indian's hut were stripped of leaves, there was no doubt that they came from the same plant of the *Strychnos* genus that we examined in the Pimichín jungles. They use either fresh *mavacure* or *mavacure* that has been dried for several weeks. The sap of a recently cut liana is not considered as poisonous; perhaps it only really works when it is very concentrated. The bark and part of the sapwood contain this terrible poison. With a knife they grate some *mavacure* branches; the bark is crushed and reduced to thin filaments with a stone like those used to make cassava flour. The poisonous sap is yellow, so all this matter takes on that colour. It is thrown into a funnel some 9 inches high and 4 inches wide. Of all the instruments in the Indian's laboratory, this funnel is the one he was most proud of. He several times asked if *por allá* (over there, in Europe) we had seen anything comparable to his *embudo*. It was a banana leaf rolled into a trumpet shape, and placed into another rolled trumpet made of palm leaves; this apparatus was held up by a scaffolding made of palm-leaf stalks. You begin by making a cold infusion, pouring water on the fibrous matter that is the crushed bark of the *mavacure*. A yellow water filters through the leafy funnel, drop by drop. This filtered water is the poisonous liquid; but it becomes strong only when concentrated through evaporation, like molasses, in wide clay vessels. Every now and then the Indian asked us to taste the liquid. From its bitterness you judge whether the heated liquid has gone far enough. There is nothing dangerous about this as curare only poisons when it comes into contact with blood. The steam rising from the boiler is not noxious, whatever the Orinoco missionaries might say.

The most concentrated sap from the *mavacure* is not thick enough to stick on arrows. It is thus only to thicken the poison that another concentrated infusion of vegetable sap is added. This is an extremely sticky sap taken from a tree with long leaves called *kiracaguero*. As this tree grows a long way off, and at this period is without flowers or fruit like the *bejuco de mavacure*, we were not able to name it botanically. I have often spoken of the ill fate that prevents travellers from studying the most interesting plants. When you travel quickly you hardly see an eighth of the trees that offer the essential parts of their fructification, even in the Tropics where flowers last so long.

The moment the sticky sap of the *kiracaguero* tree is poured into the poisonous and concentrated liquid, kept boiling, it blackens and coagulates to become rather like tar or a thick syrup. This mass is the curare that is sold inside crescentia fruit; but as its preparation is in the hands of a few families, first-class curare from Esmeralda and Mandavaca is sold at high prices. When dried this substance looks like opium, but it attracts humidity if exposed to air. It tastes agreeably bitter, and Bonpland and I have often swallowed little bits. There is no danger as long as you make sure your gums and lips are not bleeding. The Indians regard curare taken by mouth as an excellent stomachic. The way the poison is made is rather similar everywhere, but there is no certainty that different poisons sold under the same name in the Orinoco and Amazon are identical or from the same plant.

In the Orinoco the curare made from the *raíz* (root) is differentiated from that made from the *bejuco* (the liana or bark from branches). We saw only the latter prepared; the former is weaker and less sought after. On the Amazon we learned to identify poisons made by the Tikuna, Yagua, Pevas and Jibaros tribes, which, coming from the same plant, differ only due to more or less care spent in their elaboration. The Tikuna poison, made famous in Europe by M. de la Condamine, and which is becoming known as *tikuna*, is taken from a liana that grows on the Upper Marañon. This poison is partly due to the Tikuna Indians, who have remained independent in Spanish territory, and partly to Indians of the same tribe in missions. As poisons are indispensable to hunters in this climate, the Orinoco and Amazon missionaries have not interfered with their production. The poisons just named are completely different from those made by the Peca, the Lamas and Moyobambas. I convey such details because the fragments of plants that we examined have proved (contrary to common opinion) that the three poisons of the Tikuna, Peca and Moyobambas do not come from the same species, not even the same family. Just as curare is simple in its composition, so the fabrication of the Moyobamba poison is long and complicated. You mix the sap of the *bejuco de ambihuasca*, the main ingredient, with pepper (capsicum), tobacco, *barbasco* (*Jacquinia armillaris*), *sanango* (*Tabernae montana*) and the milk of some apocyneae. The fresh sap of the *ambihuasca* is poisonous if it touches blood; the sap of the *mavacure* is deadly only when it is concentrated by heating, and boiling eliminates the poison from the root of the *Jatropha manihot* (*Yucca amarca*). When I rubbed the liana, which gives the cruel poison of the Peca, for a long time between my fingers on a very hot day, my hands became numb.

I will not go into further details about the physiological properties of these New World poisons that kill so quickly without ever making you sick if taken in the stomach, and without warning you of death by violently exciting the marrow in your spine. On the Orinoco river banks you cannot eat chicken that has not been killed by a poison arrow. Missionaries claim that animal flesh is only worth eating if killed in this way. Though ill with tertiary fever Father Zea insisted every morning that a poison arrow and the live chicken due to be eaten by us be brought to his hammock. He did not want anybody else to kill the bird, despite his weakness. Large birds like the guan (*pava de monte*) or the curassow (*alector*), pricked in their thighs, die in two to five minutes; but it takes ten to twelve minutes for a pig or peccary to die. Bonpland found that the same poison bought in different villages revealed enormous differences.

I placed very active curare on the crural nerves of a frog

without noticing any change, measuring the degree of its organs' irritability with an arc formed of heterogeneous metals. But these Galvanic experiments hardly worked on birds a few minutes after they had been shot with poison arrows. Curare works only when the poison acts on the vascular system. At Maypures, a coloured man (a *zambo*, a cross between Indian and negro) was preparing one of those poison arrows that are shot in blowpipes, to kill small monkeys or birds for M. Bonpland. He was a carpenter of extraordinary strength. He stupidly rubbed the curare beween slightly bleeding fingers and fell to the ground, dizzy for half an hour. Luckily it was a weak curare (*destemplado*), used for small animals, which may be revived later by placing muriate of soda in the wound. During our journey back from Esmeralda to Attires I escaped from danger myself. The curare had attracted humidity and become liquid and spilled from a poorly closed jar on to our clothes. We forgot to check the inside of a sock filled with curare when washing our clothes. Just touching this sticky stuff with my hand I realized I should not pull on the poison sock. The danger was all the greater as my toes were bleeding from chigoe wounds.

There is exciting chemical and physiological work to be done in Europe with the effects of New World poisons once we are sure that different poisons from different areas are properly distinguished. As far as our botanical knowledge about these poisonous plants is concerned we could sort out the differences only very slowly. Most Indians who make poison arrows completely ignore the nature of poisonous substances used by other tribes. A mystery surrounds the history of toxics and antidotes. Among wild Indians the preparation is the monopoly of *piaches*, who are priests, tricksters and doctors all at once; it is only with Indians from the missions that you can learn anything certain about such problematic matters. Centuries passed before any Europeans learned, thanks to Mutis's researches, that the *bejuco del guaco* is the most powerful antidote to snake bites, and which we were the first to describe botanically.

It is well established in the missions that there is no cure for curare that is fresh and concentrated and that has remained long enough in the wound for it to enter the bloodstream. Indians who have been wounded in wars by arrows dipped in curare described to us symptoms that resembled those of snake bites. The individual feels a congestion in his head, and giddiness makes him sit down. He feels nausea, vomits several times, and is tortured by thirst as the area around his wound becomes numb.

The old Indian called 'master of the poison' was flattered by our interest in his chemical procedures. He found us intelligent enough to think that we could make soap; for making soap, after making curare, seemed to him the greatest of human inventions. Once the poison was poured into its jars, we accompanied the Indian to the *juvias* fiesta. They were celebrating the Brazil-nut harvest, and became wildly drunk. The hut where the Indians had gathered over several days was the strangest sight you could imagine. Inside there were no tables or benches, only large smoked and roasted monkeys lined up symmetrically against the wall. These were marimondas (*Ateles belzebuth*) and the bearded capuchins. The way these animals, which look so like human beings, are roasted helps you understand why civilized people find eating them so repulsive. A little grill made of a hard wood is raised about a foot from the ground. The skinned monkey is placed on top in a sitting position so that he is held up by his long thin hands; sometimes the hands are crossed over his shoulders. Once it is fixed to the grill a fire is lit underneath; flames and smoke cover the monkey, which is roasted and smoked at the same time.[120] Seeing Indians eat a leg or arm of a roasted monkey makes you realize why cannibalism is not so repugnant to Indians. Roasted monkeys, especially those with very round heads, look horribly like children. Europeans who are forced to eat them prefer to cut off the head and hands before serving up the rest of the monkey. The flesh of the monkey is so lean and dry that Bonpland kept an arm and a hand, roasted in Esmeralda, in his Paris collections. After many years it did not smell in the least.

We saw the Indians dancing. These dances are all the more

monotonous as women do not dare take part. The men, both young and old, hold hands, form a circle, and for hours turn around to the right, then the left, in utter silence. Usually the dancers themselves are the musicians. Weak notes blown from reeds of different sizes make it all seem slow and sad. To mark the time the leading dancer bends both knees rhythmically. The reeds are tied together in rows. We were surprised to see how quickly young Indians could cut reeds and tune them as flutes when they found them on the banks.

In the Indian huts we found several vegetable productions brought from the Guiana mountains that fascinated us. I will mention only the fruit of the *juvia* or Brazil-nut, some extremely long reeds, and shirts made from marima bark. The *almendrón* or *juvia*, one of the most impressive trees in the New World jungles, was virtually unknown before our journey to the Río Negro.

This Brazil-nut tree is usually not more than 2 to 3 feet in diameter, but reaches up to 120 feet in height. The fruit ripens at the end of May and, as they are as big as a child's head, make a lot of noise when they fall from so high up. I usually found between fifteen and twenty-two nuts in one fruit. The taste is very agreeable when the nuts are fresh; but its copious oil – its main use – quickly goes rancid. In the Upper Orinoco we often ate quantities of these nuts for want of food, and no harm came to us. According to trustworthy Indians only small rodents can break into this fruit, thanks to their teeth and incredible tenacity. But once the fruit have fallen to the ground all kinds of jungle animals rush to the spot: monkeys, *manaviris*, squirrels, cavies, parrots and macaws fight over the booty. All are strong enough to break the woody seed case, pick out the nut and climb back up the trees. 'They too have their fiestas,' the Indians say as they return from the harvest. To hear them complain about these animals you would think that the Indians alone are masters of the jungle.[121]

One of the four canoes that the Indians had used for their expedition was filled with a kind of reed (*carice*) used to make blowpipes. The reeds measured 15 to 17 feet without a sign of a knot for leaves and branches. They are quite straight, smooth and cylindrical. Known as 'reeds of Esmeralda' they are very sought after beyond the Orinoco. A hunter keeps the same blowpipe all his life; he boasts of its lightness, precision and shine as we might our firearms. What monocotyledonous plant do these magnificent reeds come from? I was unable to answer this question, as I was unable to say what plant was used in making the marima shirts. On the slopes of the Duida mountain we saw trunks of this tree reaching 50 feet high. The Indians cut off cylindrical pieces 2 feet in diameter and peel off the red fibrous bark, careful not to make longitudinal incisions. This bark becomes a kind of garment, like a sack, of a coarse material without seams. You put your head through a hole at the top and your arms through two holes cut in the sides. Indians wear these marima shirts when it rains; they look like cotton ponchos. In these climates the abundance and beneficence of nature are blamed for the Indians' laziness. Missionaries do not miss the opportunity of saying: 'In the Orinoco jungles clothes are found readymade on trees.'

In the fiesta women were excluded from dancing and other festivities; their sad role was reduced to serving men roast monkey, fermented drinks and palm-tree hearts, which tasted rather like our cauliflowers. Another more nutritious substance comes from the animal kingdom: fish flour (*mandioca de pescado*). Throughout the Upper Orinoco Indians roast fish, dry them in the sun and crush them into powder, along with the bones. When eaten it is mixed with water into a paste.

In Esmeralda, as in all missions, the Indians who refuse to be baptized but who live in the villages have remained polygamous. The number of wives differs according to the tribe; those who have most are the Caribs and those tribes that still carry young girls off from enemy tribes. Women live as slaves. As men exert absolute authority no women dare to complain in their presence. In the homes an apparent peace reigns, and the women vie to anticipate the whims of their demanding and bad-tempered master. They look after children, whether their own or another's. Missionaries say that this peace, the result of collective fear, breaks down when the master is away for a long time. The squabbling does not end until he returns and silences them just with the sound of his voice, or with a simple gesture, or by some other more violent means. As these unhappy women do all the work, it is not strange that in some tribes there are few women. Then you find a sort of polyandry. With the Avanos and Maypures several brothers share one wife. When an Indian with several wives becomes a Christian the missionaries force him to choose the one he wants to keep and to reject the others. The moment of separation is critical: the new convert finds that each wife has some special quality: one knows about plants, another how to make *chicha*, the drink made from cassava root. Sometimes an Indian would rather keep his wives than become a Christian; but usually the man lets the missionary choose for him, as part of his fate.

According to my careful trigonometric calculations the Duida mountain rises 2,179 metres above the Esmeralda plain, some 2,530 metres, more or less, above sea-level. I say more or less because I had the bad luck to break my barometer before our arrival in Esmeralda. The rain had been so heavy that we could not protect this instrument from the damp and, with the unequal expansion of the wood, the tubes snapped. This accident especially annoyed me as no barometer had ever lasted so long on such a journey. The granite summit of the Duida falls so steeply that Indians have not managed to climb it. Though the mountains are not as high as people think, it is the highest point of the chain that stretches from the Orinoco to the Amazon.

Between the mouths of the Padamo and the Mavaca the Orinoco receives the Ocamo from the north, into which flows the Matacona river. At the source of this last river live the Guainare Indians, far less copper-coloured or brown than others in this region. This tribe belongs to what missionaries call 'fair Indians' or *Indios blancos*. Near the mouth of the Ocamo travellers are shown a rock that is the local marvel. It is granite passing into gneiss, characterized by its black mica, which forms little ramified veins. Spaniards call this rock Piedra Mapaya (Map Rock). I chipped off a bit.[122]

We left the Esmeralda mission on the 23rd of May. We were not exactly ill, but emaciated and weak thanks to the torment of mosquitoes, the bad food and the long journey on that narrow and damp pirogue. We did not go further up the Orinoco than the mouth of the Guapo; had we wanted to reach the Orinoco sources we would have gone beyond this point, but private travellers are not authorized to leave pacified areas. From the Guapo river to the Guaharibo cataract there are only 15 leagues. But the cataract is crossed by a liana bridge where Indians armed with bows and arrows stop whites from entering their lands. Up to the present time the Orinoco posed two distinct problems for geographers: its sources, and the nature of its communications with the Amazon. This latter was the aim of our journey.

Our canoe was not ready until nearly three in the afternoon. During our trip up the Casiquiare countless ants had nested in its *toldo* and hulk where we would have to lie for another twenty-two days, and it was difficult to clear them out. We spent the morning trying again to find out from those who lived in Esmeralda whether they knew about a lake towards the east. When shown maps the old soldiers laughed at the idea of a supposed link between the Orinoco and Iapa, as much as they laughed at the idea of its being linked to the 'white sea'. What we politely call geographers' fictions they call *mentiras de por allá* ('Lies from over there, the Old World'). These good men could not understand how people could draw maps of unseen countries and know precise things without ever having visited the country, things that even those who do live there have never heard about.

On the point of leaving we were surrounded by those inhabitants who called themselves whites and Spaniards. They begged us to ask the Angostura Government to let them return to the llanos, or at least to the Río Negro missions. 'However serious our crimes,' they said, 'we have expiated them after twenty years of hell in this swarm of mosquitoes.' I pleaded their case in a report to the government on the industrial and commercial state of these countries.

All I could say about our journey from Esmeralda to the mouth of the Atabapo would be merely a list of rivers and uninhabited places. From the 24th to the 27th of May we slept only twice on land; the first at the confluence with the Jao river and the second below the Santa Bárbara mission on Minisi island. As the Orinoco has no shoals the Indian pilot let the canoe drift all night with the current. It took us only thirty-five hours to reach Santa Bárbara. The Santa Bárbara mission is located a little to the west of the mouth of the Venturari river. We found in this small village of 120 inhabitants some traces of industry; but what the Indians produce is of little use to them; it is reserved for the monks or, as they say, for the church and the convent. We were told that a great silver lamp, bought at the expense of the neophytes, was expected from Madrid. Let us hope that after this lamp arrives they will think of clothing the Indians, buying them agricultural instruments, and schooling their children. The few oxen in the savannahs round the mission are not used to turn the mill (*trapiche*) to crush the juice from the sugar cane. This the Indians do and, as happens whenever Indians work for the church, they are not paid.

We spent only one day at San Fernando de Atabapo, despite the village, with its *pirijao* palms and their peach-like fruit, promising us a delightful refuge. Tame *pauxis* (*Crax alector*) ran round the Indian huts; in one of which we saw a very rare monkey that lives on the banks of the Guaviare. It is called the caparro, which I have made known in my *Observations on Zoology and Comparative Anatomy*.[123] Its hair is grey and extremely soft to touch. It has a round head, and a sweet, agreeable expression.

Over night the Orinoco had swollen and its faster current took us in ten hours the 13 leagues from the mouth of the Mataveni to the higher Maypures cataract, reminding us where we had camped coming up river. From the mouth of the Atabapo to that of the Apure we enjoyed travelling through a country in which we had long lived. We were just as squashed in the canoe and were stung by the same mosquitoes, but the certainty that in a few weeks our suffering would end kept our spirits up.

On the 31st of May we passed the Guahibo and Garcita rapids. The islands in the middle of the river were covered in a brilliant green. The winter rains had unfolded the spathes of the *vadgiai* palms whose leaves pointed up to the sky. Just before sunset we landed on the eastern bank of the Orinoco, at the Puerto de Expedición, in order to visit the Ataruipe cavern, apparently the burial-ground of a tribe that was destroyed.

We had a tiring and dangerous climb up a bald granite hill. It would have been impossible to have kept our balance on the steep slippery surface of the rock had it not been for large feldspar crystals that stuck out and supported us. At the summit we were amazed at the extraordinary panorama. An archipelago of islands covered with palm trees filled the foamy river bed. The setting sun seemed like a ball of fire hanging over the plain. Birds of prey and goatsuckers flew out of reach above us. It was a pleasure to follow their shadows over the wall of rocks.

The most remote part of the valley is covered with thick jungle. In this shady place lies the opening to the Ataruipe cavern, less a cavern than a deep vault formed by an overhanging rock, and scooped out by water when it reached this height. This is the cemetery of an extinct race. We counted some 600 well-preserved skeletons, lined in rows. Each skeleton is enclosed in a basket made of palm-leaf petioles. These baskets, called *mapires* by the Indians, are a kind of square sack whose dimensions vary according to the age of the dead. Children who die at birth also have their *mapires*. The skeletons are so intact that not even a rib or a phalanx is missing.

The bones are prepared in three different ways; they are whitened, or coloured red with annatto, a dye from *Bixa orellana*, or varnished with a scented resin and wrapped like mummies in banana leaves. Indians insisted that as soon as somebody died the corpse was left for months in damp earth so that the flesh rotted away; then it was dug up and the remains of the flesh scraped off with a sharp stone. Some tribes in Guiana still practise this method. Next to the baskets or *mapires* we also found half-baked clay urns with the remains of whole families. The largest urns are almost 3 feet high and 5.5 feet wide. They are greenish, and of a pleasing oval shape. Some have crocodiles and snakes drawn on them. The top edges are decorated with meanders and labyrinths. These are very similar to the decorations covering the walls of the Mexican palace at Mitla; they are found everywhere, even among the Greeks and Romans, as on the shields of the Tahitians and other Pacific Islanders.

Our interpreters could give us no details about the age of these baskets and vessels. However, the majority of the skeletons did not seem to be more than a hundred years old. Among the Guareca Indians there is a legend that the brave Atures, chased by the cannibalistic Caribs, hid in the cataract rocks, where they died out, leaving no trace of their language. The last survivor of the Atures could not have lasted much longer, for at Maypures you can still see an old parrot that 'nobody understands because', so the Indians say, 'it speaks the language of the Atures'.[124]

Despite the indignation of our guides we opened various *mapires* to study the skulls. They were all typical of the American race, with one or two Caucasian types. We took several skulls with us, as well as a skeleton of a six- or seven-year-old child, and two Atures adults. All these bones, partly painted red, and partly covered in resin, lay in the baskets already described. They made up the whole load of one mule and, as we knew all about the superstitious aversions that Indians have about corpses once they have been buried, we covered the baskets with newly woven mats. But nothing could fool the Indians and their acute sense of smell. Wherever we stopped Indians ran to surround our mules and admire the monkeys we had bought on the Orinoco. But hardly had they touched our luggage than they announced the certain death of the mule that 'carried the dead'. In vain we tried to dissuade them and said the baskets contained crocodile and manatee skeletons. They insisted that they smelled the resin that covered the bones 'of their old relations'. One of the skulls we brought from the Ataruipe cavern has been painted by my old master Blumenbach.[125] But the skeletons of the Indians have been lost with much of our collection in a storm off Africa, where our travelling companion and friend the Franciscan monk Juan Gonzalez also drowned. We left the burial-ground of this extinct race in a sad mood.

We stayed in the Atures mission just the time needed to have the canoes taken down the cataracts. The bottom of our small boat was so worn that we took great care to prevent it cracking. We said goodbye to Father Bernardo Zea who, after two months of travelling with us, sharing all our sufferings, remained in Atures. The poor man continued to have fits of tertian fever, a chronic condition that did not worry him at all. During this second stay in Atures other fevers raged. Most of the Indians could not leave their hammocks; to get some cassava bread we had to ask the independent Piraoas tribe to find some for us. Up to now we had escaped fevers, which I believe are not always contagious.

We dared to cross the last half of the Atures *raudal* in our boat. We landed every now and then on rocks, which act as dykes, forming islands. Sometimes water crashes over them, sometimes it falls into them with a deafening noise. It was here that we saw one of the most extraordinary scenes. The river rolled its waters over our heads, like the sea crashing against reefs, but in the entrance to a cavern we could stay dry as the large sheet of water formed an arch over the rocks. We had the chance to view this bizarre sight for longer than we wished. Our canoe should have passed around a narrow island on the eastern bank and picked us up after a long detour. We waited for several hours as night and a furious storm approached. Rain poured down. We began to fear that our fragile boat had smashed against some rocks and that the Indians, as indifferent as ever to the distress of others, had gone off to the mission. There were only three of us, soaked to the skin and worrying about our pirogue, as well as thinking about spending the night in the Tropics, sleeping in the din of the cataracts. M. Bonpland proposed to leave me alone on the island with Don Nicolás Soto and swim the bit of the river between the granite dykes. He hoped to reach the jungle and seek help from Father Zea at Atures. We finally managed to dissuade him. He had no idea about the labyrinth of canals that split up the Orinoco or of the dangerous eddies. Then what happened under our noses as we were discussing this proved that the Indians had been wrong to say there were no crocodiles in the cataracts. We had placed our little monkeys on the tip of our island. Soaked by the rain, and sensitive to any fall in temperature, they began to howl, attracting two very old lead-grey crocodiles. Seeing them made me realize how dangerous our swim in this same *raudal* on our way up had been. After a long wait our Indians turned up just as the sun was setting.

We continued to travel part of the night, and set up camp on Panumana island, passing the Santa Bárbara mission by without stopping. Only days later did we hear that the little colony of Guahibo Indians there had fled *al monte* because they thought we had come to capture them and sell them as *poitos* or slaves. In Carichana Bonpland was able to dissect a 9-foot-long manatee. It was a female and its meat tasted of ox. The Piraoas Indians at this mission so hate this animal that they hid so as not to have to touch its flesh as it was being carried to our hut. They claim 'that people from their tribe die if they eat its flesh'.

Our stay in Carichana let us gather our strength. Bonpland was carrying the germs of a serious illness, and needed rest. But as the delta of the rivers Horeda and Paruasi is covered with dense vegetation he could not resist a long botanical excursion and soaked himself several times a day in the water. Fortunately in the missionary's house we were supplied with bread made from maize flour, and even milk.

In two days we went down the Orinoco from Carichana to the Uruana mission, again passing the famous Baraguan Strait. The Uruana mission is situated in a very picturesque place. The little Indian village backs on to a high granite mountain. Rocks rise like pillars above the highest jungle trees. Nowhere else is the Orinoco more majestic than when viewed from Father Ramón Bueno's missionary hut. It is more than 2,600 toises wide and runs in a straight line east like a canal. The mission is inhabited by Otomacs, a barbaric tribe who offered us an extraordinary physiological phenomenon. The Otomacs eat earth; every day for several months they swallow quantities of earth to appease their hunger without any ill effect on their health. This verifiable fact has become, since my return to Europe, the object of lively disputes. Though we could stay only one day in Uruana it was sufficient to find out how the *poya* (balls of earth) are prepared, to examine the reserves of this the Indians keep, and how much is eaten in twenty-four hours. I also found traces of this perverse appetite among the Guamos, between the Meta and the Apure. Everybody speaks of earth eating or *geophagie* as anciently known. I shall limit myself to what I saw and heard from the missionary, doomed to twelve years among this wild, unruly Otomac tribe.

The Uruana inhabitants belong to those people of the savannah (*Indios andantes*), harder to civilize than those from the jungle (*Indios del monte*). They show a great aversion to agriculture and live exclusively from hunting and fishing. The men are tough, ugly, wild, vindictive and passionately fond of alcohol. They are 'omnivorous animals' in every sense. That is why other Indians consider them as barbarians and say, 'There is nothing, however disgusting it is, that an Otomac will not eat.' While the Orinoco and its waters are low the Otomacs live on fish and turtles. They kill fish with astounding skill, shooting them with arrows when they surface. The river floods stop all fishing: it becomes as hard as fishing in deep sea. During the period of floods the Otomacs eat earth in prodigious amounts. We found pyramids of earth balls in their huts. The earth they eat is a fine oily clay, of a greyish-yellow; they cook it slightly so that its hard crust turns red due to the iron oxide in it.

The Otomacs do not eat all clays indiscriminately: they choose alluvial beds where the earth is oilier and smoother to touch. They do not mix the clay with maize flour or turtle fat or crocodile fat. In Paris we analysed a ball of earth brought back from the Orinoco and found no trace of organic matter. The savage will eat anything as long as it satisfies his hunger. Earth becomes his staple diet, for it is hard to find even a lizard or a fern root or a dead fish floating on the water. Surprisingly, during the flood season, the Otomac does not get thin; in fact he remains very tough, and without a swollen belly.

The following are the true facts, which I verified. The Otomacs, over months, eat three quarters of a pound of slightly baked clay daily. Their health is not affected. They moisten the clay to swallow it. It was not possible to find out what other vegetable or animal matter the Indians ate at the same time; but it is clear that the sensation of a full stomach came from the clay, and not from whatever else they might eat. Everywhere in the torrid zone I noticed women, children, even full-grown men, show a great desire to swallow earth. Not an alkaline or calcareous earth to neutralize acid juices, but a fat, oily clay with a strong smell. They often have to tie children's hands to prevent them from eating earth when it stops raining. In the village of Banco, on the Magdalena, I saw Indian women potters continually swallowing great lumps of clay. They were not pregnant, and said, 'Earth is food that does not harm us.' It could be asked why this mania for eating earth is so rare in the cool, temperate zones, compared to the Tropics; and why in Europe it is confined to pregnant women and sick children.[126]

The little village of Uruana is harder to govern than most other missions. The Otomacs are restless, noisy, and extreme in their passions. They not only adore the fermented liquors of cassava, maize and palm wine, but also get very drunk, to the point of madness, with *niopo* powder. They gather the long pods of a mimosa, which we have made known as *Acacia niopo*; they cut them into little pieces, dampen them and let them ferment. When the macerated plants turn black they are crushed into a paste and mixed with cassava flour and lime obtained from burning the shell of a helix. They cook this mass on a grill of hardwood above a fire. The hardened pâté looks like little cakes. When they want to use it they crumble it into a powder and put it on a small plate. The Otomac holds this plate with one hand while through his nose, along the forked bone of a bird whose two extremities end up in his nostrils, he breathes in the *niopo*. I sent some *niopo* and all the necessary instruments to Fourcroy in Paris.[127] *Niopo* is so stimulating that a tiny portion produces violent sneezing in those not used to it. Father Gumilla wrote: 'The diabolic powder of the Otomacs makes them drunk through their nostrils, deprives them of reason for several hours, and makes them mad in battle.'

The proper herbaceous tobacco[128] (for missionaries call *niopo* 'tree-tobacco') has been cultivated from time immemorial by all the Orinoco tribes: from the time of the conquest smoking had spread to all the Americas. The Tamanacs and Maypures wrap their cigars in maize leaves, as the Mexicans had done when Cortés arrived. Imitating them, the Spaniards substituted maize leaf for paper. The poor Indians of the Orinoco jungles know as well as the great lords in Montezuma's Court that tobacco smoke is an excellent narcotic. They use it not only to take siestas but also to reach that quiet state they naïvely call 'a dream with your eyes open, or day-dream'.

It is neither from Virginia nor South America that Europe received in 1559 the first tobacco seeds, as is erroneously stated in most botanical books, but from the Mexican province of Yucatán. The man who boasted most about the fertility of the Orinoco banks, the famous Raleigh, also introduced smoking tobacco to the northern peoples. Already by the end of the sixteenth century there were bitter complaints in England 'of this imitation of wild Indian manners'. They thought that by smoking tobacco 'Englishmen would degenerate into a barbarous state'.

After the Otomacs of Uruana take *niopo* (their tree-tobacco), or their fermented liquors, they fall into a drunken stupor lasting days on end, and they kill each other without using weapons. The most vicious put poisonous curare on a fingernail, and according to the missionary a scratch from this fingernail can kill if the curare is very active. At night, after a brawl, when they murder someone they chuck the corpse into the river in case signs of violence can be seen on the body. 'Each time,' Father Bueno said, 'I see women fetching water from a part of the river bank that is not their usual place I guess that someone has been murdered.'

In the Uruana huts we found that vegetable substance called *yesca de hormigas* (ant tinder) already seen at the cataracts, used to stop bleeding. This tinder, which should be called 'ant's nest', is much needed in a region where there is so much violence. A new species of ant (*Formica spinicollis*), of a pretty emerald green, gathers this soft cotton-like down from the leaves of a melastomacea to make its nest.

On the 7th of June we sadly left Father Ramón Bueno. Alone among all the missionaries we met he cared for the Indians. He hoped to return to Madrid to publish the result of his researches into the figures and characters that cover the Uruana rocks. In this area between the Meta, Arauca and Apure, Alonso de Herrera,[129] during the first 1535 expedition to the Orinoco, found mute dogs (perros mudos). We cannot doubt that this dog is indigenous to South America. Different Indian languages have words for this dog that cannot be related to European languages. Early historians all speak of mute dogs, and this same dog was eaten in Mexico and on the Orinoco.

We took nine days to travel the 95 leagues from the island of Cucuruparu to the capital of Guiana, commonly called Angostura. We rarely spent the night on land, but the plague of mosquitoes was diminishing. On the morning of the 9th of June we met many boats filled with merchandise going up the Orinoco by sail towards the Apure. It is a much frequented trade route between Angostura and Torunos. Our travelling companion, Don Nicolás Soto, brother-in-law of the governor of Barinas, took this route to return to his family. During the great floods months are lost struggling against the currents. Boatmen are forced to moor to tree trunks and haul themselves up river. In this winding river they can take days just to advance 200 to 300 toises.

How hard it is to express the pleasure we felt arriving at Angostura, capital of Spanish Guiana. The discomforts felt at sea in small boats cannot be compared to those felt under a burning sky, surrounded by swarms of mosquitoes, cramped for months on end in a pirogue that does not let you budge an inch because of its delicate balance. In seventy-five days we had travelled along the five great rivers of the Apure, the Orinoco, the Atabapo, the Río Negro and the Casiquiare for 500 leagues, rarely sighting inhabited places. Although, after our life in the jungle, our clothes were not in good order, we hurried to present ourselves to the provincial governor Don Felipe de Ynciarte. He received us in the most considerate way, and lodged us in the house of the Secretary of the Intendencia. Coming from such deserted places we were struck by the bustle of a town of only 6,000 people. We appreciated what work and trade can do to make life more civilized. Modest houses seemed luxurious: anybody who spoke to us seemed witty. Long deprivations make small things pleasurable: how can I express the joy we felt on seeing wheat bread on the governor's table. I may be wrong in repeating what all travellers feel after long journeys. You enjoy finding yourself back in civilization, though it can be short-lived if you have learned to feel deeply the marvels of tropical nature. The memory of what you endured soon fades; as you reach the coasts inhabited by European colonists you begin to plan to make another journey into the interior.

A dreadful circumstance forced us to stay a whole month in Angostura. The first days after our arrival we felt tired and weak, but completely healthy. Bonpland began to study the few plants that he had managed to protect from the humidity while I was busy determining the longitude and latitude of the capital and observing the dip of the magnetic needle. All our work was interrupted. On almost the same day we were struck by an illness that took the form of a malignant typhus in my travelling companion. At that time the air in Angostura was quite healthy and, as the only servant we had brought from Cumaná showed the same symptoms, our generous hosts were sure that we had caught the typhus germs somewhere in the damp Casiquiare jungles. As our mulatto servant had been far more exposed to the intense rains, his illness developed with alarming speed. He got so weak that after eight days we thought he was dead. However, he had only fainted, and he later recovered. I too was attacked by a violent fever; I was given a mixture of honey and quinine from the Caroní river (*Cortex angosturae*), a medicine recommended by the Capuchin monks. My fever continued to rise, but vanished the following day. Bonpland's fever was more serious, and for weeks we worried about his health. Luckily he was strong enough to look after himself; and took medicines that suited him better than the Caroní river quinine. The fever continued and, as is usual in the Tropics, developed into dysentery. During his illness Bonpland maintained his strength of character and that calmness which never left him even in the most trying circumstances. I was tortured by premonitions. It was I who had chosen to go up-river; the danger to my companion seemed to be the fatal consequence of my rash choice.

After reaching an extraordinary violence the fever became less alarming. The intestinal inflammation yielded to emollients obtained from malvaceous plants. But the patient's recuperation was very slow, as happens with Europeans not thoroughly acclimatized to the Tropics. The rainy season continued. To return to the Cumaná coast meant crossing the llanos, which would be flooded. So as not to expose Bonpland to a dangerous relapse we decided to stay in Angostura until the 10th of July. We spent part of the time in a nearby plantation, which grew mangoes and breadfruit (*Artocarpus incisa*).[130]

CHAPTER 22

THE LLANOS OF PAYO, OR THE EASTERN VENEZUELAN
PLAINS — CARIB MISSIONS — LAST VISIT TO THE NUEVA
BARCELONA, CUMANÁ AND ARAYA COASTS

IT WAS ALREADY dark when we crossed the Orinoco bed for the last time. We meant to spend the night near the small San Rafael fort and begin the journey across the Venezuelan steppes at dawn. Nearly six weeks had passed since our arrival at Angostura; we dearly wanted to reach the Cumaná or Nueva Barcelona coasts to find a boat to take us to Cuba and then on to Mexico. After several months on mosquito-infested rivers in small canoes, a long sea journey excited our imaginations.

Our mules waited for us on the left bank of the Orinoco. The plant collections and geological specimens brought from Esmeralda and the Río Negro had greatly increased our baggage. It would have been dangerous to leave our herbals behind, but this added weight meant we now faced a tediously slow journey across the llanos. The heat was excessive due to the bare ground's reverberations. The thermometer by day recorded between 30 °C and 34 °C, and at night 27 °C to 28 °C. Like everywhere in the Tropics it was less the actual degree of heat than its duration that affected our bodies. We spent thirteen days crossing the steppes, resting a little in the Carib missions and in the village of Payo.

Soon after entering the Nueva Barcelona llanos we spent the night in a Frenchman's house. He welcomed us very cordially. He came from Lyon, and had left home when still very young. He seemed quite indifferent to all that was happening across the ocean or, as they scornfully say here, 'del otro lado del charco' ('on the other side of the pond'). He was busy sticking large bits of wood together with a glue called *guayca*, used by carpenters in Angostura. It is as good as any glue made from animal matter. It is found ready-made between the bark and sap of a creeper of the Combretaceae family (*Combretum guayca*). It resembles birdlime made from mistletoe berries and the inner bark of the holly. An astonishing amount of this glue pours out from the twining branches of the *bejuco de guayca* when they are cut.

It took us three days to reach the Can Carib missions. The ground was not as cracked by the drought as in the Calabozo plains. A few showers had revived the vegetation. We saw a few fan palms (*Corypha tectorum*), rhopalas (*Chaparro*) and malpighias with leathery, shiny leaves growing far apart from each other. From far off you recognize where there might be water from groups of mauritia palms. It was the season in which they are loaded with enormous clusters of red fruit looking like fircones. Our monkeys loved this fruit, which tasted like overripe apples. The monkeys were carried with our baggage on the backs of mules and did all they could to reach the clusters hanging over their heads. The plains seemed to ripple from the mirages. When, after travelling for an hour, we reached those palms standing like masts on the horizon, we were amazed to realize how many things are linked to the existence of one single plant. The wind, losing its force as it strikes leaves and branches, piles sand round the trunks. The smell of fruit and the bright green of the leaves attract passing birds that like to sway on the arrow-like branches of the palms. All around you hear a murmur of sound. Oppressed by the heat, and used to the bleak silence of the llanos, you think you feel cooler just by hearing the sound of branches swaying. Insects and worms, so rare in the llanos, thrive here so that even one stunted tree, which no traveller would have noticed in the Orinoco jungles, spreads life around it in the desert.

On the 13th of July we reached the village of Cari, the first of the Carib missions dependent on the Observance monks from the Piritu college. As usual we stayed in the convent, that is, with the parish priest. Apart from passports issued by the Captain-General of the province, we also carried recommendations from bishops and the director of the Orinoco missions. From the coasts of New California to Valdivia and the mouth of the River Plate, along 2,000 leagues, you can overcome all obstacles by appealing to the protection of the American clergy. Their power is too well entrenched for a new order of things to break out for a long time. Our host could hardly believe how 'people born in northern Europe could arrive in his village from the frontiers with Brazil by the Río Negro, and not by the Cumaná coast'. Although affable, he was also extremely curious, like everyone who meets travellers who are not Spanish. He was sure that the minerals we carried contained gold, and that the plants we had dried were medicinal. Here, as in many parts of Europe, sciences interest people only if they bring immediate and practical benefit.

We counted more than 500 Caribs in the Cari village; and many more in the surrounding missions. It is curious to meet a once nomadic tribe only recently settled, whose intellectual and physical powers make them different from other Indians. Never have I seen such a tall race (from 5 feet 9 inches to 6 feet 2 inches). As is common all over America the men cover their bodies more than the women, who wear only the *guayuco* or *perizoma* in the form of narrow bands. The men wrap the lower part of their bodies down to their hips in a dark blue, almost black, cloth. This drapery is so ample that when the temperature drops at night the Caribs use it to cover their shoulders. Seen from far off against the sky, their bodies, dyed with annatto, and their tall, copper-coloured and picturesquely wrapped figures, look like ancient statues. The way the men cut their hair is typical: like monks or choirboys. The partly shaved forehead makes it seem larger than it is. A tuft of hair, cut in a circle, starts near the crown of the head. The resemblance of the Caribs with the monks does not come from mission life, from the false argument that the Indians wanted to imitate their masters, the Franciscan monks. Tribes still independent like those at the source of the Caroní and Branco rivers can be distinguished by their *cerquillo de frailes* (monks' circular tonsures), which were seen from the earliest discovery of America. All the Caribs that we saw, whether in boats on the Lower Orinoco or in the Piritu missions, differ from other Indians by their height and by the regularity of their features; their noses are shorter and less flat, their cheekbones not so prominent, their physiognomy less Mongoloid. Their eyes, blacker than is usual among the Guiana hordes, show intelligence, almost a capacity for thought. Caribs have a serious manner and a sad look, common to all the New World tribes. Their severe look is heightened by their mania for dyeing their eyebrows with sap from the *caruto*, then lengthening and joining them together. They often paint black dots all over their faces to make themselves look wilder. The local magistrates, governors and mayors, who alone are authorized to carry long canes, came to visit us. Among these were some young Indians aged between eighteen and twenty, appointed by the missionaries. We were struck to see among these Caribs painted in annatto the same sense of importance, the same cold, scornful manners that can be found among people with the same positions in the Old World. Carib women are less strong, and uglier than the men. They do nearly all the housework and fieldwork. They insistently asked us for pins, which they stuck under their lower lips; they pierce their skin so that the pin's head remains inside the mouth. It is a custom from earlier savage times. The young girls are dyed red and, apart from their *guayuco*, are naked. Among the different tribes in the two continents the idea of nakedness is relative. In some parts of Asia a woman is not allowed to show a fingertip, while a Carib Indian woman wears only a 2-inch-long *guayuco*. Even this small band is seen as less essential than the pigment covering her skin. To leave her hut without her coat of annatto dye would be to break all the rules of tribal decency.

The Indians of the Piritu mission intrigued us because they belonged to a tribe whose daring, and warrior and mercantile skills, have exerted a big influence on a vast part of the land. All along the Orinoco we came across records of the hostile excursions of the Caribs. Also the Carib language is one of the more widely spread.

The fine Carib tribes inhabit only a small part of the country they once occupied before the discovery of America. European cruelty ensured that they completely vanished from the West Indies and Darien coasts. Once subdued they lived in populous villages in Nueva Barcelona province and Spanish

Guiana. I think you could count more than 35,000 Caribs living in the Piritu llanos and on the banks of the Caroní and Cuyuni. If you add the independent Caribs living in the Cayenne and Pacaraymo mountains between the Essequibo and Branco river sources they would reach a total of 40,000 pure-blooded Indians. I linger on this point because the Caribs, before my voyage, had been supposed to have become extinct.

I first found the word 'Carib' in a letter from Pierre Martyr d'Anghiera.[131] It derives from 'Calina' and 'Caripuna', the l and p transformed into r and b. It is noteworthy that this word, heard by Columbus from people on Haiti, is also found on other islands and on the mainland. From Carina, or Calina, Galibi (Caribi) was formed. This is how a tribe in French Guiana are still known, though they are shorter and speak a Carib dialect. Those on the islands called themselves in men's language Calinago; and in women's language Callipinan. This difference between the languages of the two sexes is more marked than among other American tribes. This is possibly due to the women living so cut off from men that they have adopted ways of speaking that men refuse to follow. But the contrast in Carib tribes between the dialects of the two sexes is so great, and surprising, that a more satisfying explanation must be sought. It could be found in the Caribs' barbarous custom of killing all male prisoners and making the women slaves. When the Caribs burst into the archipelago of the smaller West Indian Islands they arrived as warriors, not as colonizers with their families. The female language was formed slowly by these conquerors living with foreign women, learning words alien to Carib.

The Caribs on the mainland admit that the smaller West Indian Islands were inhabited by Arowaks, a warlike tribe still found on the unhealthy banks of the Surinam and Berbice rivers. They say that all the Arowaks were exterminated by Caribs coming from the Orinoco mouth, except for the women. They quote as evidence the similarities between Arowak and Carib women's languages.

The Caribs have so dominated such a large part of the continent that the memory of their ancient grandeur has left them with a dignity and national superiority that is obvious in their manners and way of speaking. 'We alone are a tribe,' they say proverbially, 'the others (*oquili*) are here to serve us.' This scorn that Caribs have for their old enemies is so accentuated that I have seen a ten-year-old child froth with rage when called a Cabre or a Cavere. Yet he had never seen anyone from such a tribe, decimated by the Caribs after a long resistance. Among half-civilized tribes, as much as in civilized Europe, we find similar deep-seated hates where the names of enemy people have passed into language as the worst kind of insult.

The missionary led us into several ordered and extremely clean Indian huts. It was painful to see how Carib mothers forced their children from the earliest age to enlarge the calves of their legs, as well as mould their flesh in stripes from the ankle to the top of the thigh. Bands of leather or cotton are tied tightly 2 inches apart and pulled hard so that the muscles in between swell out. Our swaddled children suffer far less than the Carib children, who are meant to be closer to nature. The monks, ignorant of Rousseau's works[132] and even of his name, are unable to prevent this ancient physical education; man from the jungle, whom we believed to be so simple in customs, is far from docile when it comes to his dress and ideas about beauty and well-being. I was also surprised to see that the torture imposed on these children in no way hindered their blood circulation or their muscular movements. There is no tribe that is stronger or runs faster than the Caribs.

When you travel through Carib missions and observe the order and submission there it is hard to remind yourself that you are among cannibals. This American word, of doubtful origin, probably comes from the Haitian or Puerto Rican language. It passed into European languages from the fifteenth century as a synonym for anthropophagy. I do not doubt that the conquering island Caribs were cruel to the Ygneris and other West Indian inhabitants, who were so weak and unwarlike; but their cruelty has been exaggerated because the first discoverers listened only to stories from conquered tribes. All the missionaries that I asked assured me that the Caribs are perhaps the least cannibalistic of the New World tribes. Perhaps the desperate way in which the Caribs fought the Spaniards, which led in 1504 to a royal decree declaring them to be slaves, contributed to their fame for ferocity. It was Christopher Columbus who first decided to attack the Caribs and deny them their freedom and natural rights; he was a fifteenth-century man, and less humane than is thought today. In 1520 Rodrigo de Figueroa was appointed by the Spanish Court to decide which South American tribes were Caribs, or cannibals, and which were Guatiaos, or peaceful and friendly to Spain. His ethnographic piece, called *El auto de Figueroa*, is one of the most curious records of the early conquistadores' barbarism. Without paying attention to languages, any tribe that was accused of eating prisoners was called Carib. All the tribes that Figueroa called Carib were condemned to slavery; they could be sold at will or exterminated. It was after these bloody wars, and the death of their husbands, that Carib women, d'Anghiera says, became known as Amazons.

On feast days, after celebrating mass, the whole community assembles in front of the church. Young girls leave bundles of firewood, maize, bananas and other foodstuff at the missionary's feet. At the same time the governor, mayor and other municipal officers, all pure Indians, exhort the Indians to work, arrange who will do what, scold the lazy and, it has to be said, cruelly beat those who refuse to obey. These strokes are received with the same impassivity with which they are given. These acts of justice last a long time and are frequently seen by any traveller who crosses the llanos. It would be better if the priest did not impose corporal punishment as soon as he left the altar; he should not witness the punishment of men and women in his priestly robes; but his abuse arises from the bizarre principles on which missions are based. The most arbitrary civil powers are tightly linked to the rights exercised by priests; yet, though the Caribs are not cannibals, and you would like them to be treated gently, you do realize that some violence is necessary to maintain order in a new society.

When we were about to leave the Cari mission we had an argument with our Indian muleteers. To our amazement they had discovered that we were transporting skeletons from the Ataruipe caves, and were sure that the mule carrying 'the corpses of our ancient relatives' would die on the journey. All our precautions to hide the bones had been useless; nothing escapes the Carib's sense of smell. We needed the missionary's authority to be able to leave. We had to cross the Cari river in a boat and ford, or perhaps I should say swim, the Río de Agua Clara. Quicksand on the bottom made the crossing during the floods very tiring. You are surprised to find such strong currents in flat land. We spent unpleasant nights out at Matagorda and Los Riecitos. Everywhere we saw the same things: small huts made of reed and roofed with leather, men on horseback with lances, guarding the cattle, semi-wild herds of horned cattle all the same colour, fighting for grass with horses and mules. Not a goat or a sheep in these immense steppes!

On the 15th of July we reached the fundación, or the Villa de Pao, established in 1744 and well situated as a depot between Nueva Barcelona and Angostura. Many geographers have mistaken its position, confusing it with other small towns. Though it was cloudy I was able to determine the latitude and the longitude from the sun. The astronomical fixing of Calabozo and Concepción del Pao are very important to the geography of this country where there are so few fixed points in the savannahs. Around about we saw some fruit trees, quite rare in the steppes. We also noticed coconut palms, despite the distance from the sea. I insist on this observation as some have doubted the veracity of travellers describing coconut palms, a coastal plant, in Timbuktu and in the heart of Africa.

It took us five long days from the Villa de Pao to the port of Nueva Barcelona. As we got closer the sky became clearer, the ground more dusty and the air more burning hot. This oppressive heat does not arise from the temperature but from fine sand floating in the air, which irradiates heat in all directions, and whips your face and the ball of the thermometer. In fact I never saw the mercury rise above 45.8 °C once in this sand wind in America.

We spent the night of the 16th of July in the Indian village of Santa Cruz de Cachipo, founded in 1749 when several Carib families from the unhealthy, flooding Orinoco gathered together. We lodged in the missionary's house. In the parish register we discovered how rapidly the mission had progressed thanks to his zeal and intelligence. From the middle of the plains the heat had become almost unbearable so we thought of travelling by night; but we were not armed and the llanos were infested with numberless robbers who murdered all whites who fell into their hands in atrociously cunning ways. Nothing can be worse than the administration of justice in these colonies. Everywhere we found the prisons filled with criminals who had waited up to eight years for a trial. About one third escape from prison and find refuge in the llanos, where nobody but cattle live. They attack on horseback, like Bedouin Arabs. The dirt in the prisons would be intolerable if prisoners were not allowed to escape every now and then. It is also common that the death penalty cannot be carried out because there are no executioners. When this happens they pardon one of the guilty if he agrees to hang the others. Our guides told us about a *zambo*, famous for his violence, who, just before our arrival at Cumaná, chose to avoid his execution by turning executioner. The preparations broke his will, and he was horrified at what he was about to do, preferring death to the shame of saving his own life. He asked for his irons to be put back on. He did not stay in prison much longer, as cowardice in another prisoner saw that he was executed. This awakening of honour in a murderer is psychologically very interesting. A man who has spilled so much blood robbing travellers on the steppes hesitates to inflict a punishment that he feels he himself has deserved.

If in the peaceful times when Bonpland and myself travelled through both Americas the llanos were the refuge of criminals from the Orinoco missions, or who had escaped from coastal prisons, how much worse it must be following the bloody Independence struggles! Our wastes and heaths are but a poor image of the New World savannahs, which for over 8,000 to 10,000 square leagues are as smooth as the sea. Their immensity makes it easy for vagabonds to remain free.

After three days' journey we finally glimpsed the Cumaná

mountains between the llanos or, as they say here, 'the great sea of green' ('los llanos son como un mar de yerbas'), and the Caribbean coast. Although some 800 toises high, the Brigantín is visible from over 27 leagues away; however, the atmosphere prevented us from seeing that attractive curtain of mountains. At first it appeared as a layer of mist; gradually this mass of mist turned blue and took on its fixed outline. What a sailor sees on approaching new land is what a traveller experiences on the borders of the llano. A *llanero*, or llano inhabitant, only feels at ease when, so the popular saying goes, 'he can see all around him'. What appears to us as covered in vegetation, a rolling land with slight hills, is for him a terrible region bristling with mountains. After having lived for months in the thick Orinoco jungles where you see stars as if from a well, a gallop across the steppes is quite agreeable. The novelty of all you feel strikes you, and like a *llanero* you too feel happy 'to see everywhere around you'. But this new pleasure (which we ourselves experienced) does not last long. To contemplate an immense horizon is imposing whether from Andean summits or the Venezuelan plains. Limitless space reflects a similar quality inside us (as poets in all languages have written); it suggests higher matters, and elevates the minds of those who enjoy solitary meditation. However, there is also something sad and monotonous about the dusty and cracked steppes. After eight to ten days' journey you get used to the mirages and the brilliant green of the tufts of mauritia palms, and seek more variety, like seeing tall jungle trees or wild cataracts or cultivated lands.

On the 23rd of July we entered the town of Nueva Barcelona, less affected by the heat on the llanos than by the sand wind that painfully chapped our skin. We were well received at the house of Don Pedro Lavié, a wealthy French merchant. He had been accused of hiding the unfortunate España[133] on the run in 1796. He was arrested by order of the *audiencia*. But his friendship with the Cumaná governor, and his services as a merchant, got him released. We had visited him in prison before and now found him back with his family, but very ill. He died without seeing the independence of America that his friend Don José España had predicted just before his execution.

The climate of Nueva Barcelona is not as hot as that of Cumaná, but it is humid and unhealthy during the rainy season. Bonpland had survived the crossing of the llanos and had recovered his strength to work as hard as before. I myself felt worse in Nueva Barcelona than I had in Angostura after our long river trip. One of those tropical downpours, with those enormous raindrops that fall far apart from each other, made me so ill I thought I had typhus. We spent a month in Neuva Barcelona, enjoying all the comforts of the town.

Two leagues south-east of Nueva Barcelona there is a high chain of mountains backing on the Cerro Brigantín known as the Aguas Calientes (Hot Waters). When I felt my health had returned we made an excursion there. This trip ended with an unfortunate accident. Our host had lent us his best saddle horses. We had been warned not to cross the Narigual river on horseback so we crossed on a kind of bridge made of tree trunks; the animals swam across as we held the bridles. Suddenly my horse disappeared and struggled under water. There was no way I could find out what had pulled it under. Our guides guessed that it must have been a cayman, common in this region, that had seized its legs.

The mail-boats (*correos*) that cross from La Coruña to Havana and Mexico had been due for over three months. It was thought they had been attacked by English ships near by. I was in a hurry to reach Cumaná and cross to Veracruz so on the 26th of August I hired an open boat called a *lancha*. This *lancha* smuggled cocoa to the island of Trinidad, so its owner was not afraid of the enemy ships blockading the Spanish ports. We loaded our plants, instruments and monkeys and hoped that it would be but a short journey from the mouth of the Neveri river to Cumaná. But no sooner were we in the narrow canal that separates the mainland from the rocky islands of Borracha and Chimanas than we bumped into an armed ship, which ordered us to stop, and fired a round at us from far off. The boat belonged to a pirate from Halifax. By his accent and build I recognized a Prussian from Memel among his crew. Since

I had been in America I had not once spoken my mother
tongue, and would have preferred a more peaceful opportunity to do so. But my protests were to no avail, and we were
led aboard the pirate ship. They ignored the passports issued
by the governor of Trinidad allowing cocoa smuggling, and
considered us a lawful prize. As I spoke English fairly well
I was able to bargain with the captain, and stopped him from
taking us to Nova Scotia by persuading him to put us ashore
on the nearest coast. While I was arguing about our rights in
the cabin I heard a noise on deck. A sailor rushed in and whispered something to the captain, who left quite upset. Luckily
for us an English warship (the *Hawk*) was also passing by. It
had signalled the pirate boat, but on receiving no answer had
shot a round of artillery and sent a midshipman aboard. He
was a polite young man who led me to hope that our *lancha*
with its cocoa would be released. He invited me to accompany
him, assuring me that Captain John Garnier of the Royal Navy
could offer better accommodation than the ship from Halifax.

I accepted, and was very politely welcomed by Captain
Garnier. He had been as far to the north-west as Vancouver,
and was fascinated by all that I told him about the great Atures
and Maypures cataracts, about the Orinoco bifurcation and
its link with the Amazon. He had followed my progress from
reading English newspapers.[134] He introduced me to several
of his officers. For over a year I had not met so many well-
informed people in one gathering. I was very well treated, and
the captain gave me his state room. When you have come from
the Casiquiare jungles, with nothing but the company of a narrow circle of missionaries for months, it is a joy to talk to men
who have travelled round the world and broadened their
minds by seeing so many different things. I left the boat, blessing the career I had devoted my life to.

It was moving to see the beach where we had first arrived,
and where Bonpland had nearly lost his life. Among the cacti
stood the Guaiquerí Indian huts. Every part of the landscape
was familiar to us, from the forest of cacti to the huts and the
giant ceiba, which grew near where we had swum every evening. Our Cumaná friends came to meet the *lancha*; botanizing

had enabled us to meet people from all social classes. They were relieved as there had been news that Bonpland had died of fever on the banks of the Orinoco, and that we had sunk in a storm near the Urana mission.

The port of Cumaná was closely blockaded, and we had to wait there two and a half months longer. We spent our time completing our collection of the flora of Cumaná, geologizing along the eastern part of the Araya peninsula, and observing numerous planetary eclipses. The live animals we had brought from the Orinoco intrigued all the Cumaná inhabitants. We wanted to send them to the zoo in Paris. The arrival of a French squadron gave us an unexpected opportunity to send the monkeys and birds on, but they all died in Guadeloupe.

Having given up hope of the mail-boat from Spain we boarded an American ship loaded with salt for Cuba. We had spent sixteen months on this coast and in the interior of Venezuela. On the 16th of November we left our Cumaná friends to cross the Gulf of Cariaco for Nueva Barcelona for the third time. The sea breeze was strong and after six hours we anchored off the Morro of Nueva Barcelona, where a ship was waiting to take us to Havana.[135]

CHAPTER 23

CUBA TO CARTAGENA

I TWICE VISITED the island of Cuba, living there first for three months, and then for six weeks. Bonpland and I visited the neighbourhood of Havana, the beautiful Guines valley, and the coast between Batabanó and the port of Trinidad.

The way Havana looks as you enter the port makes it one of the most pleasant and picturesque places on the American equinoctial coasts.[136] Celebrated by travellers from all over the world, this site is not like the luxurious vegetation along the Guayaquil banks, nor the wild majesty of Rio de Janeiro's rocky coasts, but the charms that in our climates embellish cultivated nature are here joined to the power and organic vigour of tropical nature. In this sweet blend of impressions, the European forgets the dangers that threaten him in crowded West Indian cities; he tries to seize all the diverse elements in this vast countryside and contemplate the forts that crown the rocks to the east of the port, the inland basin surrounded by villages and farms, the palm trees reaching amazing heights, a town half hidden by a forest of ships' masts and sails. You enter Havana harbour between the Morro fort (Castillo de los Santos Reyes) and the San Salvador de la Punta fort: the opening is barely some 170 to 200 toises wide, and remains like this for one fifth of a mile. Leaving this neck, and the beautiful San Carlos de la Cabaña castle and the Casa Blanca to the north, you reach the basin shaped like a clover whose great axis, stretching south-south-west to north-north-east, is about 2.2 miles long. This basin links up with three creeks, one of which, the Mares, is supplied with fresh water. The city of Havana, surrounded by walls, forms a promontory limited to the south by the arsenal; to the north by the Punta fort. Passing some sunken ships, and the Luz shoals, the water becomes some 5 to 6 fathoms deep. The castles defend the town from the west. The rest of the land is filled with suburbs (*arrabales* or *barrios extra muros*), which year by year shrink the Field of Mars (Campo de Marte). Havana's great buildings, the cathedral, the Casa del Gobierno, the admiral's house, the arsenal, the *correo* or post office, and the tobacco factory are less remarkable for their beauty than for their solidity; most of the streets are very narrow and are not yet paved. As stones come from Veracruz, and as transporting them is expensive, someone had recently come up with the strange idea of using tree trunks instead of paving-stones. This project was quickly abandoned, though recently arrived travellers could see fine *cahoba* (mahogany) tree trunks sunk into the mud. During my stay, few cities in Spanish America could have been more unpleasant due to the lack of a strong local government. You walked around in mud up to your knees, while the amount of four-wheeled carriages or *volantes* so typical of Havana, carts loaded with sugar cane, and porters who elbowed passers-by made being a pedestrian annoying and humiliating. The stench of *tasajo*, or poorly dried meat, stank out the houses and tortuous streets. I have been assured that the police have now remedied these inconveniences, and cleaned up the streets. Houses are more aerated; but here, as in ancient European cities, correcting badly planned streets is a slow process.

There are two fine walks, one (the Alameda) between the Paula hospital and the theatre, redecorated by an Italian artist in 1803 in fine taste; the other between the Punta fort and the Puerta de la Muralla. This last one, also called the Paseo Extra Muros, is a deliciously fresh walk: after sunset many carriages come here. Near the Campo de Marte there is a botanical garden, and something else, which disgusts me – the huts in front of which the slaves are put to be sold. It is along this walk that a marble statue of Charles III was meant to be erected. Originally this site was meant for a monument to Columbus, whose ashes were brought from Santo Domingo to Cuba. Fernando Cortés's ashes had been transferred the same year to Mexico from one church to another. At the end of the eighteenth century the two greatest men in the history of the conquest of America were given new tombs.

The most majestic palm tree of its tribe, the *palma real*, gives the countryside around Havana its special character. It is the *Oreodoxa regia* in our description of American palms; its tall trunk, swelling slightly in the middle, rises 60 to 80 feet high; its upper part shines with a tender green, newly formed by the closing and dilation of the petioles, and contrasts with the rest, which is whitish and fissured. It looks like two columns, one on top of the other. The Cuban *palma real* has feathery leaves rising straight up towards the sky, curving only at the tips. The form of this plant reminded us of the *vadgiai* palm covering the rocks on the Orinoco cataracts, balancing its long arrows above the mist of foam. Here, like everywhere, as the population increases so vegetation diminishes. Around Havana, in the Regla amphitheatre, these palms that so delighted me are now disappearing year by year. The marshy places covered with bamboos have been cultivated and are drying out. Civilization progresses; and today I am told that the land offers only a few traces of its former savage abundance. From the Punta to San Lázaro, from the Cabaña to Regla, from Regla to Atares, everything is covered with houses: those circling the bay are lightly and elegantly built. The owners draw a plan and order a house from the United States, as if ordering furniture. As long as yellow fever rages in Havana, people will retire to their country houses and enjoy fresher air. In the cool nights, when ships cross the bay and leave long phosphorescent tracks in the water, these rural sites become a refuge for those who flee a tumultuous, overpopulated city.[137]

At the end of April Bonpland and I had completed the observations we intended to make at the northern extreme of the torrid zone and were about to leave for Veracruz with Admiral Ariztizabal's fleet. But we were misled by false information concerning Captain Baudin's journey and decided to forgo our plan of passing Mexico on our way to the Philippine Islands. A newspaper announced that the two French sloops, the *Géographie* and the *Naturaliste*, had set sail for Cape Horn and would call in at Chile and Peru on their way to New Holland. This news shook me. I was reminded of my original intention in Paris when I had asked the Directorate to hasten Captain Baudin's departure.[138]

On leaving Spain I had promised to join his expedition wherever I could reach it. Bonpland, as active and optimistic as usual, and I immediately decided to split our herbals into three lots to avoid the risk of losing what had taken so much trouble to collect on the banks of the Orinoco, Atabapo and Río Negro. We sent one collection by way of England to Germany, another via Cádiz to France, and the third we left in Havana. We had reason to congratulate ourselves on this prudence. Each collection contained virtually the same species; if the cases were taken by pirates there were instructions to send them to Sir Joseph Banks or to the natural history museum in Paris. Luckily I did not send my manuscripts to Cádiz with our friend and fellow traveller Father Juan Gonzalez, who left Cuba soon after us but whose vessel sank off Africa, with the loss of all life. We lost duplicates of our herbal collection, and all the insects Bonpland had gathered. For over two years we did not receive one letter from Europe; and those we got in the following three years never mentioned earlier letters. You may easily guess how nervous I was about sending a journal with my astronomical observations and barometrical measurements when I had not had the patience to make a copy. After visiting New Granada, Peru and Mexico I happened to be reading a scientific journal in the public library in Philadelphia and saw: 'M. de Humboldt's manuscripts have arrived at his brother's house in Paris via Spain.' I could scarcely suppress an exclamation of joy.

While Bonpland worked day and night dividing our herbal collections, thousands of obstacles prevented our departure from Havana. No ship would take us to Porto Bello or Cartagena. People seemed to enjoy exaggerating the difficulties faced crossing the isthmus and the time it takes to go by ship from Guayaquil to Lima. They reproached me for not continuing to explore those vast rich Spanish American lands that for over fifty years had not been open to any foreign travellers. Finding no boat I had to hire a Catalonian sloop anchored at Batabanó to take me to Porto Bello or Cartagena, depending on how the Santa Marta gales might blow. The prosperity of Havana, and its mercantile links with pacific ports, allowed me to procure funds for several years. I was able to exchange my revenues in Prussia for a part of General Don Gonzalo O'Farrill's, who was Minister to the Spanish Court in Prussia. On the 6th of March the sloop I had hired was ready to sail.

The road from Río Blanco to Batabanó crossed uncultivated land, half covered in jungle, with wild indigo and cotton trees in the clearings. Several friends, including Señor de Mendoza, captain of Valparaíso harbour, and brother of the famous astronomer who had lived so long in London, accompanied us to Potrero de Mopox. While herborizing we found a new palm tree with fan leaves (*Corypha maritima*).

Batabanó was then a poor village, and its church had only just been finished. The *ciénaga* begins about half a league from the village, a marsh stretching about 60 leagues from west to east. At Batabanó it is thought that the sea is encroaching on the land. Nothing is sadder than these marshes. Not even a shrub breaks the monotony; a few stunted palm trees rise like broken masts among tufts of reeds. As we stayed only one night there I regretted not being able to investigate the two species of crocodile, or *cocodrilo*, infesting the *ciénaga*. One the locals call a cayman. The crocodile is said to be very daring, and even climbs into boats when it can. It often wanders a league inland just to devour pigs. It reaches some 15 feet long, and even chases (so they say) men on horseback, while the caymans are so shy that people can bathe in the water when they are around.

On my second visit to Havana in 1804[139] I could not return to the Batabanó *ciénaga* and so I had these two species brought to me at great expense. Two crocodiles arrived alive. The eldest was 4 feet 3 inches long. They were captured with great difficulty and arrived on mules with their snouts muzzled and bound. They were lively and ferocious. In order to observe them we let them loose in a great hall, and from high pieces of furniture watched them attack large dogs. Having lived on the Orinoco, the Apure and the Magdalena for six months among crocodiles we enjoyed observing this strange animal before leaving for Europe, as they change from immobility to frenzied action quite suddenly. I counted thirty-eight teeth in the upper jaw and thirty in the lower. In the description that Bonpland and I made on the spot we deliberately marked that the lower fourth tooth rises over the upper jaw. The cayman sent from Batabanó died on the way and stupidly was not brought to us, so we could not compare the two species.

We set sail on the 9th of March before dawn, nervous about the uncomfortable narrow boat in which we had to sleep on deck. The cabin (*cámara de pozo*) had no light or air and was merely a hold for provisions; we could only just fit our instruments in there. These inconveniences lasted only twenty days.

Batabanó Gulf, surrounded by a low marshy coast, looks like a vast desert. The sea is a greenish-brown. Our sloop was the only boat in the gulf, for this sea route is used only by smugglers or, as they are politely called here, 'traders' (*los tratantes*). One large island called Isla de Pinos, with mountains covered with pines, rises in this bay. We sailed east-south-east to clear the archipelago that Spanish pilots called Jardines (Gardens) and Jardinillos (Bowers), reaching the rocky island of Cayo de Piedras. Columbus named them the Queen's Gardens in 1494 when on his second voyage he struggled for fifty-eight days with the winds and currents between Pinos Island and the eastern cape of Cuba. A part of these so-called gardens is indeed beautiful; the scene changes all the time and the green contrasts with the white, barren sands. The sand seems to undulate in the sun's heat as if it were liquid.

Despite the small size of our boat, and the boasted skill of our pilot, we often ran aground. The bottom was soft so there was no danger of sinking. At sunset we preferred to lie at anchor. The first night was beautifully serene, with countless shooting stars all falling in the same direction. This area is completely deserted, while in Columbus's time it was inhabited by great numbers of fishermen. These Cuban inhabitants used a small fish to catch the great sea-turtles. They tied this fish to a long cord of the *revés* (the Spanish name for the echeneis). This 'fisher-fish' fixed itself on the shell of the turtle by means of its suckers. The Indians pulled both sucker fish and turtle ashore. It took three days to pass through this labyrinth of Jardines and Jardinillos. As we moved east the sea got rougher.

We visited the Cayo Bonito, which deserves its name (pretty) as it is covered with lush vegetation. On a layer of sand and shells 5 to 6 inches thick rises a forest of mangroves. From their shape and size they look from afar like laurels. What characterizes these coral islands is the wonderful *Tournefortia gnaphalioides* of jacquin, with silvery leaves, which we found here for the first time. This is a shrub some 4 to 5 feet high that gives off a pleasing scent. While we were botanizing our sailors looked for lobsters among the rocks. Irritated at not finding any they took revenge by climbing into the mangroves and slaughtering young alcatras nesting in pairs. This alcatras builds its nest where several branches meet, and four or five nest on the same trunk. The younger birds tried to defend themselves with their long beaks, while the older ones flew above our heads making hoarse, plaintive cries. Blood streamed from the trees for the sailors were armed with long sticks and machetes. We tried to prevent this pointless cruelty but sailors, after years at sea, enjoy slaughtering animals. The ground was littered with wounded birds struggling against death. When we arrived on the scene it was strangely silent, as if saying, 'man has passed this way'.

On the 14th of March we entered the Guaurabo river at one of Trinidad de Cuba's two ports, to put our *práctico*, or pilot, who had steered us through the Jardinillos and run us aground, ashore. We also hoped to catch a *correo marítimo* (mailboat) to Cartagena. Towards evening I landed and began to set up Borda's azimuth compass and the artificial horizon to observe the stars when a party of *pulperos*, or small traders, who had dined on board a foreign ship cheerfully invited us to accompany them into town. These good people asked us to mount two each to a horse; as it was excessively hot we accepted their offer. The road to Trinidad runs across a plain covered with vegetation where the *miraguama*, a silver-leafed palm tree, stands out. This fertile soil, although of *tierra colorada*, needs only to be tilled to yield rich harvests. After emerging from a forest we saw a curtain of hills whose south-ern slope was covered with houses. This is Trinidad, founded in 1514 on account of the 'rich gold mines' said to lie in the Armani river valley. The streets of Trinidad are all very steep and again show why people complain, as they do over all Span-ish America, of how badly the conquistadores chose the sites of new towns.

We spent a very agreeable evening in the house of Don Antonio Padrón, one of the richest inhabitants, where we found all Trinidad society gathered in a *tertulia*. We were again struck by how vivacious Cuban women are. Though lacking the refinements of European civilization, the primitive simpli-city of their charms pleased us. We left Trinidad on March the 15th. The mayor had us driven down to the mouth of the Guaurabo river in a fine carriage lined with old crimson dam-ask. To add to our confusion a priest, the local poet, dressed in a velvet suit despite the heat, celebrated our voyage to the Orinoco with a sonnet.

On the road to the harbour we were struck by the countless phosphorescent insects (*Cocuyo, Elater noctilucus*). The grass, the branches and the leaves of trees all shone with that reddish, flickering light. It seemed as if the stars had fallen on to the savannah! In the poorest hut in the country fifteen *cocuyos*, placed in a gourd pierced with holes, give sufficient light to look for things at night. Shaking the gourd excites the animals and increases the luminous disks on their bodies. A young woman at Trinidad told us that during a long passage from the mainland she used the phosphorescent *cocuyos* when she wanted to nurse her baby at night. The captain of the ship would use only *cocuyos* lights so as not to attract pirates.

Our journey from Cuba to the South American coast near the Sinu river took sixteen days. On the 30th of March we doubled Punta Gigantes, and made for the Boca Chica, the present entrance to Cartagena harbour. From there to our anchorage the distance is 7 or 8 miles. We took a *práctico* to pilot us but repeatedly touched sandbanks. On landing I learned with great satisfaction that M. Fidalgo's coastal surveying expedition[140] had not yet set out to sea. This enabled me to fix astronomical positions of several towns on the shore. The passage from Cartagena to Porto Bello, and the isthmus along the Chagres and Cruces rivers, is short and easy. But we were warned that we might stay in Panama a while before finding a boat for Guayaquil, and then it would take ages to sail against the winds and currents. I reluctantly gave up my plan to level the isthmus mountains with my barometer, though I never guessed that as I write today (1827) people would still be ignorant of the height of the ridge dividing the waters of the isthmus.[141] Everybody agreed that a land journey via Bogotá, Popayán, Quito and Cajamaraca would be better than a sea journey, and would enable us to explore far more. The European preference for the *tierras frías*, the cold, temperate climate of the Andes, helped us make our decision. The distances were known, but not the time we finally took. We had no idea it would take us eighteen months to cross from Cartagena to Lima. This change in our plan and direction did allow me to trace the map of the Magdalena river, and astronomically determine eighty points inland, collect several thousand new plants and observe volcanoes.

The result of my labours have long since been published. My map of the Magdalena river appeared in 1816. Till then no traveller had ever described New Granada, and the public, except in Spain, knew how to navigate the Magdalena only from some lines traced by Bouguer.[142] Travel books have multiplied, and political events have drawn travellers to countries with free institutions who publish their journals too hurriedly on returning to Europe. They have described the towns they visited and stayed in, as well as the beautiful landscape; they give information about the people, the means of travel in boat, on mule or on men's backs. Though these works have familiarized the Old World with Spanish America, the absence of a proper knowledge of Spanish and the little care taken to establish the names of rivers, places and tribes have led to extraordinary mistakes.[143]

During our six-day stay at Cartagena, our most interesting excursions were to the Boca Grande and the Popa hill with its fine view. The port, or *bahía*, is 9.5 miles long. The unhealthiness of Cartagena comes from the great marshes surrounding the town on the east and north. The Ciénaga de Tesca is more than 15 miles long. A sad vegetation of cactus, *Jatropha gossypifolia*, croton and mimosa covers the arid slopes of Cerro de la Popa. While botanizing on these wild spots our guides pointed out a thick *Acacia cornigera* bush infamous for a deplorable event. This acacia is armed with very sharp thorns, and extraordinarily large ants live on it. A woman, annoyed by her husband's well-founded jealousy, planned a barbarous revenge. With the help of her lover she tied her husband up with rope, and at night chucked him into this *Acacia cornigera* bush. The more violently he struggled the more the sharp thorns tore his skin. His screams were heard by some passers-by who found him after several hours covered with blood and dreadfully stung by ants. This crime is without example in the history of human perversion; the violence of its passion derives from the coarseness of manners, not from the Tropics. My most important work at Cartagena was comparing my observations with the astronomical positions fixed by Fidalgo's officers.

We prolonged our stay in Cartagena as long as our work and my comparisons with Fidalgo's astronomical observations demanded. The company of this excellent sailor and Pombo and Don Ignacio Cavero (once Secretary to Viceroy Góngora) taught us a lot about statistics. I often quoted Pombo's notes about trade in *quinquina* and the state of the province of Cartagena's population and agriculture. We also came across a curious collection of drawings, machine models and minerals from New Granada in an artillery officer's house. The Pascua (Easter) processions enabled us to see how civilized the customs of the lower classes are. The temporary altars are decorated with thousands of flowers, including the shiny *Plumeria alba* and *Plumeria rubra*. Nothing can be compared with the strangeness of those who took the main parts in the procession. Beggars with crowns of thorns asked for alms, with crucifixes in their hands. They were covered in black cloth and went from house to house having paid the priest a few piastres for the right to collect. Pilate was dressed in a suit of striped silk; the apostles sitting round a long table laid with sweet foods were carried on the shoulders of *zambos*. At sunset you saw dummies of Jews dressed as Frenchmen, filled with straw and rockets, hanging from strings like our own street lights. People waited for the moment when these *judíos* (Jews) would be set on fire. They complained that this year the Jews did not burn as well as they had in others because it was so damp. These 'holy recreations' (the name given to this barbarous spectacle) in no way improve manners.

Frightened about being exposed too long to the unhealthy Cartagena airs we moved to the Indian village of Turbaco (once called Tarasco) on the 6th of April. It is situated in a delicious place where the jungle begins some 5 leagues south-south-east of Pipa. We were happy to leave a foul inn *(fonda)* packed with soldiers left over from General Rochambeau's unfortunate expedition.[144] Interminable discussions about the need to be cruel to the blacks of Santo Domingo reminded me of the opinions and horrors of the sixteenth-century conquistadores. Pombo lent us his beautiful house in Turbaco, built by Archbishop Viceroy Góngora. We stayed as long as it took us to prepare for our journey up the Magdalena, and then the long land trip from Honda to Bogotá, Popoyán and Quito. Few stays in the Tropics have pleased me more. The village lies some 180 toises above sea-level. Snakes are very common and chase rats into the houses. They climb on to roofs and wage war with the bats, whose screaming annoyed us all night. The Indian huts covered a steep plateau so that everywhere you can view shady valleys watered by small streams. We especially enjoyed being on our terrace at sunrise and sunset as it faced the Sierra Nevada de Santa Marta, some 35 leagues distant. The snow-covered peaks – probably San Lorenzo – are clearly seen from Turbaco when the wind blows and brings cooler air. Thick vegetation covers the hills and plains between the Mahates dyke and the snowy mountains: they often reminded us of the beautiful Orinoco mountains. We were surprised to find, so close to the coast in a land frequented by Europeans for over three centuries, gigantic trees belonging to completely unknown species, such as the

Rhinocarpus excelsa (which the creoles call *caracoli* because of its spiral-shaped fruit), the *Ocotea turbacensis* and the *mocundo* or *Cavanillesia platanifolia*, whose large fruit resemble oiled paper lanterns hanging at the tip of each branch.

Every day we went botanizing in the Turbaco forests from five in the morning until dark: these long walks would have been a delight in this fertile marshy soil if we had not been devoured by mosquitoes, *zancudos*, chigoes and numberless insects already described in the Orinoco part of this narrative. In the midst of these wonderful forests, smelling the flowers of the *Crinum erubescens* and *Pancratium littorale*, we often came across Indian *conucos*, little banana and maize plantations where Indians, ever ready to flee from whites, live during the rainy season. This taste for the jungle and isolation typifies the American Indian. Though the Spanish population has mixed with the Indian population in Turbaco, the latter display the same lack of culture as in the Guianan missions. Examining their farming tools, the way they build their bamboo huts, their clothes and crude arts, I ask myself what the copper race has earned by contact with European civilization.

People in Turbaco out botanizing with us often spoke of a marshy land in the middle of a palm-tree forest that they called 'little volcanoes', *los volcancitos*. A village tradition claims that this land had once been in flames but that a good priest, known for his piety, cast holy water and put the underground fire out, changing the volcano of fire into a volcano of water, *volcán de agua*. This tale reminded me of the geological disputes between Neptunists and Vulcanists of the last century. The local wise man, the Turbaco priest, assured us that the *volcancitos* were simply thermal waters swimming with sulphur, erupting during storms with 'moans'. We had been too long in the Spanish colonies not to doubt these marvellous fantasies coming more from superstitious whites than from Indians, half-castes and African slaves. We were led to the *volcancitos* in the jungle by Indians and found *salses*, or air volcanoes.

In the Turbaco forest, full of palm trees, there is a clearing about 800 square feet in size without any vegetation, bordered by tufts of *Bromelia karatas*, whose leaf is like a pineapple's. The surface of the ground was composed of layers of cracked grey-black clay. What they call *volcancitos* are fifteen to twenty small truncated cones rising in the middle of the clearing. They are some 3 to 4 toises high. The high edges are filled with water and they periodically release large air bubbles. I counted five explosions in two minutes. The force of the rising air makes you think of a powerful pressure deep in the earth. Indian children who came with us helped us block some of the smaller craters with clay, but the gas always pushed the earth away. According to the Indians the number and shape of the cones near the path had not changed for over twenty years, and they remain full of water even in droughts. The heat of the water was the same as that of the air. With long sticks we could reach some 6 to 7 feet down inside a cone. Leaving the water in a glass it became quite clear, and tasted slightly of alum.

Our stay in Turbaco was extremely agreeable, and useful for our botanical collection. Even today those bamboo forests, the wild fertility of the land, the orchids carpeting the old ocotea and Indian fig-tree trunks, the majestic view of the snowy mountains, the light mist covering the valleys at sunrise, bunches of gigantic trees like green islands above a sea of mist, all return incessantly to my imagination. Our life at Turbaco was simple and hard-working; we were young, linked by similar tastes and characters, always full of hope in the future, on the eve of a journey that would take us to the highest Andean peaks, and volcanoes on fire in a country where earthquakes are common. We felt happier than at any other moment in our expedition. The years that have passed since then, not without bitterness and hardships, have added to the charms of these impressions; I would like to think that in his exile in the Southern hemisphere, in the isolation of Paraguay, my unfortunate friend Bonpland[145] might still recall our delightful herborizings.

As Bonpland's health had cruelly suffered during our journey on the Orinoco and Casiquiare we decided to follow the advice of the locals and supply ourselves with all the comforts possible on our trip up the Magdalena. Instead of sleeping in hammocks or lying on the ground on skins, exposed to the nightly torment of mosquitoes, we did what was done in the country, and got hold of a mattress, a country-bed that was easy to unfold, as well as a *toldo*, a cotton sheet, which could fold under the mattress and make a kind of closed-off tent that no insects could penetrate. Two of these beds, rolled into cylinders of thick leather, were packed on to a mule. I could not praise this system more; it is far superior to the mosquito net.

We had as travelling companions a Frenchman, Dr Rieux from Carcassonne, and the young son of the ill-fated Nariño. The bad luck of these two moved us, reminding us of the state of oppression in this unhappy country. Dr Rieux, a charming, educated man, had come from Europe as doctor to Viceroy Ezpeleta. He was accused of interfering in politics, dragged out of his house in Honda in 1794, clapped in irons and taken to the inquisition prison in Cartagena. This damp place caused him a chronic blindness. For more than a year his wife had no news of his whereabouts. His belongings were dispersed and, as nothing could be proved, he was sent (*bajo partido de registro*) to Cádiz prison where his case would be forgotten. He managed to escape off the African coast.

We left Turbaco on a fresh and very dark night, walking through a bamboo forest. Our muleteers had difficulty finding the track, which was narrow and very muddy. Swarms of phosphorescent insects lit up the tree-tops like moving clouds, giving off a soft bluish light. At dawn we found ourselves at Arjona where the bamboo forest ends and arborescent grasses begin.

We waited nearly the whole day in the miserable village of Mahates for the animals carrying our belongings to the landing-stage on the Magdalena river. It was suffocatingly hot; at this time of year there is not a breath of wind. Feeling depressed we lay on the ground in the main square. My barometer had broken and it was the last one I had. I had anticipated measuring the slope of the river and fixing the speed of its current and the position of different stages through astronomical observations. Only travellers know how painful it is to suffer such accidents, which continued to dog me in the

Andes and in Mexico; each time this happened I felt the same. Of all the instruments a traveller should carry the barometer is the one, despite all its imperfections, that caused me the most worry and whose loss I felt the most. Only chronometers, which sometimes suddenly and unpredictably change their rates, give rise to the same sense of loss. Indeed, after travelling thousands of leagues over land with astronomical and physical instruments, you are tempted to cry out: 'Lucky are those who travel without instruments that break, without dried plants that get wet, without animal collections that rot; lucky are those who travel the world to see it with their own eyes, trying to understand it, and recollecting the sweet emotions that nature inspires!'

We saw several beautiful species of large *aras* (*guacamayos*) in the hands of Indians who had killed them in the nearby jungle to eat them. We began to dissect their enormous brains, though they are far less intelligent than parrots. I sketched the parts while Bonpland cut them apart; I examined the hyoid bone and the lower larynx, which cause this bird's raucous sounds. It was the kind of research that Cuvier had recently instigated in anatomy and it appealed to me. I began to console myself for the loss of my barometer. Night did not allow me to determine our latitude through the stars. On the 20th of April at three in the morning, while it was still delightfully fresh, we set off for the Magdalena river landing-stage in the village of Barancas Nuevas. We were still in the thick jungle of bamboos, *Palma amarga* and mimosas, especially the inga with purple flowers. Halfway between Mahates and Barancas we came across some huts raised on bamboo trunks inhabited by *zambos*. This mixture of negro and Indian is very common around here. Copper-coloured women are very attracted to African men and many negroes from Choco, Antioquia province and Simitarra, once they gained their freedom by working hard, have settled in this river valley. We have often reminded you how the wisdom of the oldest Spanish laws favoured the freeing of black slaves while other European nations, boasting of a high degree of civilization, have hindered and continue to hinder this absurd and inhuman law.[146]

NOTES

1. Relation historique: The full title in French was *Relation historique du voyage aux régions équinoxiales du nouveau continent*, which I have translated as *Personal Narrative of Travels to the Equinoctial Regions of America*.

2. *jointly published ... our work:* Humboldt generously attributed all the thirty volumes to Bonpland and himself, though Bonpland actually authored only one of the two volumes of *Monographie des melastomacées* (1816).

3. *loss of dear friends:* For example, Humboldt's young aristocratic friend Carlos Montúfar and the young botanist José de Caldas were executed by the Spaniards in 1816.

4. *Captain Baudin:* Captain Thomas Nicolas Baudin (?1750–1803) was sent on a scientific expedition to the West Indies and on to Australia in year VI of the French Revolutionary calendar. Humboldt wrote to Baudin from La Coruña saying that he intended to join his round-the-world voyage. In 1801 in Cuba he read in an American newspaper that Baudin had left Le Havre. So Humboldt hired a boat from Cuba to Portobello and journeyed south as far as Quito before discovering that Baudin had gone via the Cape of Good Hope. False news made Humboldt travel over 800 leagues (some 2,400 miles) out of his way. Part of Baudin's voyage was published as *Voyage dans les quatre principales îles des mers d'Afrique ... avec l'histoire de la traversée jusqu'au Port-Louis de l'île de France* in 1804, followed by the Australian part, *Voyage de découverte aux terres australes* in 1841.

5. *Bougainville:* Louis Antoine de Bougainville (1729–1811) sailed round the world in the frigate *La Boudeuse* from 1766 to 1769 and published his influential account *Voyage autour du monde* in 1771. Humboldt met him in Paris. See Louis Constant's edition and introduction (Paris, 1980).

6. '*I was authorized ... advance the Sciences*': Humboldt included the whole document in Spanish in a footnote, dated 7 May 1799.

7. This section is followed by Humboldt's meticulous list of instruments brought with him on his journey. It should be noted in passing that when Humboldt refers to his barometer he meant a mercury barometer with glass tubes some 30 inches long, both delicate and easily broken.

8. *Malaspina:* Alejandro Malaspina (1754–1810), a Sicilian, sailed round the world in the frigate *Astrea* from 1782 to 1784. In 1789 he was in charge of a fleet hired to map the north-western coast of America but could not find the north-west passage. In 1795 he was arrested as politically suspect and imprisoned without trial. Humboldt refers to him in his *Essai politique sur le royaume de la Nouvelle-Espagne* (1811), vol. I, p. 338. See Edward J. Goodman, *The Explorers of South America* (New York, 1972), pp. 209–20; and Iris H.W. Engstrand, *Spanish Scientists in the New World: The Eighteenth-Century Expeditions* (London, 1981), pp. 44–75.

9. As an example of Humboldt's digressions this last passage is followed by thirty quarto pages of detailed speculation on ocean currents and their origins.

10. *Gutiérrez:* Pedro Gutiérrez, chief steward on Columbus's first voyage and formerly butler of the King's dais, was murdered by the cacique of Maguara on Hispaniola. Guanahani, named San Salvador by Columbus, was the first sight of the 'Indies', seen on 12 October 1492. It is one of the Bahamas. See Samuel Eliot Morison, *The Great Explorers: The European Discovery of America* (Oxford, 1978).

11. *archil:* Archil is a name given to various species of lichen (like *Roccella tinctoria*), which yield a violet dye and the chemical test substance litmus. It is also the colouring-matter prepared from these lichens.

12. The chapter ends with Humboldt speculating on the visibility of mountain peaks from a distance.

13. *toises:* 1 toise (a French lineal measure) = 1.946 metres or 6.25 feet. Humboldt also uses leagues: the Spanish land league = 4.2 kilometres or 2.6 miles (the English land league = *c.* 3 miles). The metric system, sometimes used by Humboldt,

was introduced by a French Revolutionary decree of 1795.

14. *African heat to alpine cold:* Humboldt initiated 'plant geography', especially linking latitudinal vegetation zones with altitudinal ones as seen in his famous cross section or profile of the Andes, covered with plant names. See Malcolm Nicolson, 'Alexander von Humboldt and the Geography of Vegetation' in Andrew Cunningham and Nicholas Jardine (eds.), *Romanticism and the Sciences* (Cambridge, 1990).

15. Humboldt goes on to describe the establishing of a botanical garden at Tenerife.

16. *Franqui's dragon tree:* Humboldt's *Atlas pittoresque* (1810) includes a sketch of Franqui's dragon tree made in 1776. Marianne North painted several dragon trees, which can be seen at Kew Gardens. Humboldt saw his *Atlas* as a companion volume to his travels. In a note Humboldt describes the dragon tree's astringent juice, called dragon's blood, which nuns at La Laguna soak toothpicks in, which are praised for preserving gums.

17. *sketched a view:* In Humboldt's *Atlas pittoresque* (1810).

18. Humboldt continues: 'So as not to interrupt the narrative of my journey to the summit of the Pico I have been silent about my geological observations,' and then offers a detailed 'tableau physique' of the Canary Islands from quarto pp. 148 to 197. Clearly written, it is based on much extra reading after his return home. The basis of this section is Humboldt's boast that he has formed his ideas by actually being there on the spot to compare volcanoes in both the Old and New Worlds. Travel and new observations had changed his fixed ideas about nature. He sees himself as the first scientist to look at the whole earth 'dans son ensemble'.

19. *existence is as dubious as that of the isles of Fonseco and Saint Anne:* Humboldt's note: 'Jeffery's and Van-Keulen's charts indicate four islands, which are only imaginary dangers: Garca, Saint Anne, the Green Island and Fonseco. How is it possible to believe in the existence of four islands in latitudes crossed by thousands of ships?'

20. *passage from Dante:* Humboldt cites in Italian:

Right-hand I turned, and, setting me to spy
    That alien pole, beheld four stars, the same
    The first men saw, and since, no living eye;

Meseemed the heavens exulted in their flame –
    O widowed world beneath the northern Plough,
    For ever famished of the sight of them!
                        Dante's *Purgatory*, Canto 1, 22–7

21. *Paul and Virginie:* Humboldt virtually knew Jacques-Henri Bernadin de Saint-Pierre's novel *Paul et Virginie* by heart.

22. *time-keeper.* Humboldt's time-keeper or chronometer was a Lewis Berthoud, No. 27, and had belonged to 'the celebrated Borda'; Jean Louis Borda (1733–99), a French sailor and mathematician who tested various measuring instruments.

23. *Terra Firma:* Terra Firma refers to the northern coasts of South America (Venezuela/Colombia) as distinct from the West Indies.

24. *this malady:* Humboldt identifies the disease in a note: '*Typhus*, Sauvages; *Febris nervosa*, Frank.'

25. Humboldt closes this chapter by saying that he has avoided interrupting the narrative of his voyage by giving detailed physical observations. He then fully explains, from quarto pp. 224 to 266, with tables and speculations, all his experiments on board ship concerning the temperature of the air, the colour of the sky and sea, the dip of the magnetic needle, and his log with time and latitudes all noted. These pages exemplify his ceaseless activity.

26. pulpero: Humboldt notes that a *pulpero* is the owner of a *pulpería*, or little shop, where food and drinks are sold.

27. charas: Humboldt notes that *chara* is corrupted from *chacra*, meaning a hut surrounded by a garden.

28. Scoparia dulcis ... *sensitive leaves:* Humboldt notes that Spaniards called these plants *dormideras* (sleeping plants) and that he and Bonpland discovered three new species previously unknown to botanists.

29. *Lope de Aguirre:* Humboldt's note:

When at Cumaná, or on the island of Margarita, people say the word 'el tirano' it is always to denote the hated Lopez d'Aguire (Lope de Aguirre), who, after taking part in the 1560 revolt led by Fernando de Guzmán against Pedro de Ursúa, governor of the Omeguas and Dorado, voluntarily took the title of *traidor*, or traitor. He descended the Amazon river with his band and reached the island of Margarita along the Guianan rivers. The port of Paraguache is still called the tyrant's port.

30. *Acosta's:* José Acosta, Jesuit priest, was born *c.* 1539 in Spain, went out to Peru in 1571, and died in 1600. He wrote *Historia natural y moral de las Indias* in Spanish in 1590, translated into English in 1604.

31. *Dollond's telescope:* Humboldt used the English-made 3-foot achromatic Dollond telescope, strong enough to see Jupiter's moons. Luigi Galvani (1737–98) was an Italian experimenter with electricity who published in 1791 his *De Viribus electricitatis in motu musculari* after discovering that electricity made a frog's legs twitch. He made a device with two different metal contacts that made muscles contract. Humboldt, with his brother Wilhelm, experimented with Galvanism in Jena in 1795; in 1797 he published a paper on his Galvanic experiments.

32. *debasing custom … shown in a play by Cervantes … Algiers:* Miguel de Cervantes Saavedra (1547–1616) was captured at sea by the Turks and taken to Algiers as a slave for five years until 1580. He wrote an early play called *El trato de Argel*, discovered in manuscript in 1784.

33. *'who save … harvesting':* Humboldt quotes from La Bruyère's *Caractères* (1765).

34. *'Qué hielo! Estoy emparamado':* In a note Humboldt translates, 'What an icy cold! I shiver as if I was on top of a mountain.' The provincial word *emparamarse* he derives from *páramo*, in Peruvian *puna*, which signifies a mountainous place covered with stunted trees, exposed to the winds, where a damp cold prevails.

35. *abundance of salt … Portobello:* Humboldt notes that he unearthed these facts from an archive in Cumaná; another example of his industriousness.

36. Humboldt continues with a digression over salt and its uses, especially salted beef, or *tasajo*, and then the geology of the region.

37. *across the ocean:* Humboldt's note explains the Spanish 'por allá' and 'del otro lado del charco' – 'over there' and 'across the pond' – as figurative expressions used by colonists to denote Europe.

38. *Benzoni:* According to Humboldt Benzoni was related to the Duke of Milan's assassin, Galeazzi Maria Sfonza, and could not pay back the capital advanced to him by Sevillian traders; he stayed five years at Cubagua, and died in a fit of madness.

39. *petroleum, mentioned by the first chroniclers:* Humboldt quoted from Oviedo (Fernández de Oviedo y Valdés (1478–1557), official historian of the Indies who published in 1534 his *Historia general y natural de las Indies*) who called it a 'resinous, aromatic and medicinal liquor'.

40. *Azara:* Félix de Azara (1746–1821) spent many years mapping frontiers in Paraguay, and wrote in French his *Voyage dans l'Amérique méridionale* (Paris, 1809). See Edward J. Goodman, *The Explorers of South America* (New York, 1972), pp. 238–42.

41. quipus: The *quipu* was an Inca record knot, a mnemonic device of coloured knotted strings. The Incas had not developed writing.

42. *missions:* Humboldt notes that in the Spanish colonies a *misión*, or *pueblo de misiónes*, is a cluster of huts round a church run by a missionary monk. Indian villages, governed by priests, are called *pueblos de doctrina*. One differentiates the *cura doctrinario*, who is the priest in charge of Indians, from the *cura rector*, who is the priest of a village inhabited by whites or half-castes.

43. *Saussure's hygrometer:* Humboldt carried two instruments perfected by Horace Saussure (1740–99), a Swiss mountaineer and botanist whose *Voyage dans les Alpes* (1779–96) and *Traité d'hygrométrie* were famous in his day. The hygrometer (an instrument measuring humidity) was made of hair and whalebone. Humboldt also had Saussure's magnetometer.

44. *gramineous plant with verticillate branches:* Humboldt in his note calls it *carice*, excellent fodder for mules. He refers the reader to his forthcoming *Nova Genera et species plantatum* that he is preparing with Bonpland, though W. Kurth later replaced Bonpland. It came out in seven folio volumes between 1815 and 1825. See William T. Stearn (ed.), *Humboldt, Bonpland, Kurth and Tropical American Botany* (Stuttgart, 1968).

45. Humboldt digresses here to explore the cinchona-cuspa found here. He describes its taste but confesses he did not see its flower, and says, 'and we know not what genus it belongs to'. He reflects on all febrifuge plants by listing them and even tries experiments to find out whether the antifebrile virtues lie in the tannin or in its resinous matter.

46. Bambusa gadua: Illustrated by Humboldt in *Plantes équinoxiales*, vol. 2 (1808–9), plate 20.

47. *Moravian Brethren:* A Protestant sect founded in Saxony by emigrants from Moravia who followed the doctrines of John Huss, a fifteenth-century Bohemian martyr and religious reformer. The Brethren were active as missionaries.

48. tambos … *Manco Capac's laws:* Manco Capac was the first Inca emperor from about AD 1200, a demigod, and founder of the Inca dynasty. *Tambos*, or rest houses, were built along the Inca highways and used exclusively for those travelling on official business.

49. Humboldt digresses on male animals whose breasts contain milk, like Corsican billy-goats. After numerous researches, he found two or three examples of breast-feeding men. He concludes that this ability is not confined to American Indians, and is not more common in the New World than in the Old. Lozano was of European stock. Humboldt's other examples came from Syria and Cork, Ireland. He finally speculates on the purpose of the male nipple.

50. Humboldt continues by claiming that Cumaná tobacco is the most aromatic after Cuban and Río Negran. He details its culture – the *cura seca* – as it differs from the Virginian technique.

51. *machetes:* In a note Humboldt describes a machete as a large knife with a long blade, like a hunting knife. No one enters the jungles in the torrid zone without a machete, not only to cut through liana and branches but also as defence against wild animals.

52. *Buffon:* George Louis Leclerc, known as Count Buffon (1707–88), a prestigious Enlightenment figure, was elected to the Académie Royale des Sciences in 1739 and then to Director of the Jardin du Roi. His bestselling *Histoire naturelle* began to appear in 1749 and ran to thirty-six volumes by 1788, but covered only minerals, quadrupeds and birds. Humboldt set out to correct Buffon's erroneous views about Latin America, for Buffon, never having visited the New World, had accused Latin American nature of being immature, and of producing small, weak animals (and no elephants). See Germán Arciniegas, *América en Europa* (Buenos Aires, 1975); and H.R. Hays, *Birds, Beasts and Men: A Humanist History of Zoology* (London, 1973).

53. *leaves, flowers and fruit:* Botanical nomenclature requires leaves, flowers and fruit.

54. *Cocollar:* In a note Humboldt wonders if the former name is of Indian origin. 'At Cumaná I heard it derived, in a far-fetched manner, from the Spanish *cogollo*, meaning the heart of oleraceous plants.'

55. *beautiful grass … which I drew:* In Humboldt's *Plantes équinoxiales*, see note 46.

56. *Feijóo's* Teatro crítico … *Chaptal's treatise on chemistry:* Benito Jerónimo Feijóo (1676–1764), a Spanish Benedictine 'natural philosopher' who set out to eradicate superstition. L'Abbé Nollet (1700–70), member of the Académie Royale des Sciences, famous for his work on electricity. Jean Antoine Chaptal (1756–1832), a French chemist who rose to become Interior Minister in 1800. His *Eléments de chimie* came out in 1790.

57. *Guácharo grotto:* Humboldt notes the etymology. *Guácharo* is 'one who cries and laments'. The birds in the Caripe caves and the *guacharaca* are very noisy. The Latin name today is *Steatornis caripensis*. Humboldt follows 'M. Cuvier' (see note 98) in placing this bird with the Passeres, and noted it under the genus *Steatornis* in the second volume of his *Recueil d'observations de zoologie et d'anatomie comparée* (1805–33), which Humboldt had dedicated to Cuvier in 1811.

58. Humboldt adds: 'Before leaving the grotto, let us throw a

last glance on the phenomena presented by the Guácharo cave
. . .' and continues for nine quarto pages.

59. *I sketched these organs:* In Humboldt, *Recueil d'observations de zoologie et d'anatomie comparée*, vol. 1 (1805), plate 4. Humboldt read a paper on the new species of monkey – *Simia leonina* – that he had found on the Orinoco to the Institut National in Paris on 21 January 1805. He published a separate paper on all the monkeys he had observed, with colour prints, in 1810, which was later included in his *Recueil d'observations de zoologie* in 1811.

60. *Mariguitar:* Humboldt notes here that in Raynal's *Geographic Atlas* a town called Verina was drawn in between Cariaco and Cumaná. 'The most recent maps of America are loaded with names of rivers, places and mountains which are erroneous, and handed down from age to age.'

61. *independent Indians. . . Ulloa . . . considerably increased:* See Mary Maples Dunn's abridged edition of John Black's 1811 translation of Humboldt's *Political Essay on the Kingdom of New Spain* and the fascinating chapter on the Indians. Minguet claimed that Humboldt was the first to calculate the Indian population in the Spanish American colonies where whites were only 19 per cent of the total population, compared to 60 per cent in the USA. Antonio de Ulloa (1716–95) was sent with Jorge Juan by the Spanish Crown to accompany and report on the French Académie Royale des Sciences expedition. Ulloa wrote his *Relación histórica del viaje a la América meridional* in 1747, translated into English as *A Voyage to South America* in 1758. He also prepared a secret report, *Noticias secretas de América*, which was suppressed but finally published in England in 1826.

62. Over the next twenty-four quarto pages Humboldt 'succintly exposes his investigations' into the Chaima language. He lists words, tenses ('an enormous complication of tenses'), grammatical analogies and roots. He outlines other languages. He also lists American words passed into Spanish (*hamaca, tabaco*, etc.) and ends with a list of the grammar books of Indian languages he brought back with him, along with a basic word list. Humboldt brought an Indian servant back from Caripe to Europe. His elder brother Wilhelm was a celebrated philologist. See his *On Language: The Diversity of Human Language-Structure and Its Influence on the Mental Development of Mankind*, trans. Peter Heath (Cambridge, 1988).

63. Humboldt closes the chapter with a section on the causes of bolides and shooting stars.

64. *Angostura:* Today, Ciudad Bolívar.

65. *Higuerote:* In a letter to his mentor Willdenow (21 February 1801) Humboldt complains that there were so many mosquitoes in Higuerote that he had to bury himself in the sand to sleep.

66. *mangrove ... sickly smell:* Humboldt collected mangrove roots and branches. In Caracas, he tried to imitate the coastal tides in his room, to see what happened and what gases they gave off as they decomposed.

67. Humboldt continues with pages speculating on yellow fever – *calentura amarilla* or *vómito negro* – whose 'mysterious' cause was unknown in Humboldt's time, though he, like others, blamed miasma. In 1881, in Havana, Carlos Finlay thought the virus was transmitted by mosquitoes (*Aedes aegypti*); his view was confirmed in 1900 by Major Walter Reed; an inoculation was introduced in 1937.

68. *Joseph España had died on the scaffold:* España was executed in Caracas in 1799. He was the *corregidor* of Macuto and participated in the San Blas conspiracy in Spain in 1796, affirming the equality of races. See Charles Minguet, *Alexandre de Humboldt: Histories et géographe de l'Amérique espagnole (1799–1804)* (Paris, 1969), p. 252.

69. *piastres:* A piastre, or peso, a Spanish dollar, broke down into eight *reales*, small silver coins.

70. *Hispano-Americans:* Humboldt imitated the word 'Anglo-American'. He adds that in the Spanish colonies whites born in America are called Spaniards while real Spaniards are called Europeans, *gachupines* or *chapetones*.

71. Following the excerpts about population that I have included Humboldt goes on with a physical description of Caracas, its mean temperatures, rainfall, etc.

72. *peoples of Spanish origin ... in the colonies:* In letters home Humboldt praised their hospitality and simplicity, and did not

mind their ignorance. In a letter (1800) to Baron Forrel in Madrid he wrote: 'On returning to Europe I will very reluctantly de-Spanishify myself.'

73. *analogous climates ... the poles:* Humboldt's long note:

Plant geography does not merely examine analogies observed in the same hemispheres, like that between Pyrenean vegetation and Scandinavian plains, or that between the cordillera of Peru and Chilean coasts. It also investigates relations between alpine plants in both hemispheres. It compares plants on the Alleghanies and Mexican cordilleras with those in Chile and Brazil ...

74. *grass from Switzerland ... Magellan Strait:* Humboldt's note: '*Phleum alpinium*, examined by Mr Brown. The investigations of this great botanist prove that a certain number of plants are at once common to both hemispheres.' See D.J. Mabberley, *Jupiter Botanicus: Robert Brown of the British Museum* (Braunschweig, 1985).

75. *Mutis:* Father José Celestino Mutis, born in Cádiz in 1732, died in 1808. Appointed director of the botanical expedition to New Granada (1783–93), he was living in Bogotá from 1761, and warmly received Humboldt. He gave many of his plates to Humboldt, who dedicated his *Plantes équinoxiales*, vol. 2 (1808–9) to him. Humboldt called Mutis 'one of the century's greatest botanists'. Mutis's monumental *Flora de Bogotá* comprised 5,393 plates (2,495 coloured); they lay forgotten until recently when a joint project by the Spanish and Colombian Governments began to reprint them. Mutis gave Humboldt one hundred plates (now in the Institut National, Paris). See Edward J. Goodman, *The Explorers of South America* (New York, 1972), pp. 223–7.

76. *our friends ... bloody revolutions ... deprived them of it:* Humboldt wrote this in Paris in 1859. Bolívar was in Venezuela in 1808 when Napoleon invaded Spain. The first junta of Caracas was created in 1810, sending Bolívar to London. In 1811 independence was formally declared and a Republican constitution invoked. By 1812 Venezuela was back in Royalist hands. A year later, 1813, Bolívar, the 'libertador', was back in charge, only to lose out to the Spaniards a second time. By 1819 he was back in control. See J.P. Rippy and E.R. Brann, 'Alexander von Humboldt and Simón Bolívar', *American Historical Review*, 52 (July 1947), pp. 503–697.

77. *my duty ... compare them with previous catastrophes:* Humboldt admits he follows M. de la Condamine's example, who wrote about the eruptions of Cotopaxi long after his departure from Quito. La Condamine's *Voyage à l'équateur* (1751) was a model for Humboldt's own narrative. La Condamine, Voltaire's friend, was a scientist, a keen observer, and remained in South America for ten years (1735–44). He travelled down the Amazon, speculated on the myth of the Amazon women, the Casiquiare canal joining the Amazon and Orinoco rivers (later proved by Humboldt), Indian languages, and back in Paris read a memoir to the Académie Royale des Sciences on the rubber trees. See Helen Minguet's edition of his 1745 *Voyage sur l'Amazone* (Paris, 1981).

78. *'It was so violent ... churches and houses':* Humboldt quoted from a manuscript by Delpeche, *Sur le tremblement de terre de Venezuela en 1812*, with purple passages about mothers, groaning victims in the moonlight, etc. Humboldt's Romantic sympathy for catastrophes is followed by a long 'study of volcanoes', epitomizing his comparative approach, and his meticulous lists.

79. *In this plantation ... rum:* Humboldt repeats all this in his popular *Anschiten der Natur* (1808, in English, *Views of Nature or Contemplation on the Sublime Phenomena of Creation*, trans. E.C. Otté (London, 1850), pp. 22–4). This was Humboldt's first report back to Europe of his South American odyssey, and was immensely influential in securing his fame as far south as Argentina where this opening chapter served as Domingo Sarmiento's authority in *Facundo* (1845) for analysing the pampas in Humboldtian terms of civilization and barbarism.

80. zambo: *Zambos*, as Humboldt notes far later on, are descendants of Indians and negroes.

81. *papaw tree of the lake ... tomato:* Humboldt sent the seeds of the lake's papaw and tomato to the Berlin botanical garden. Willdenow called the tomato *Solanum humboldtii*. In a later note

Humboldt adds: 'They are said to lead to constipation, and are called by the locals *tapaculo*, that is, "arse blockers".'

82. *nutritious milk pours out:* Humboldt spends pages on plants that exude milky substances. He complains: 'It can scarcely be imagined in Europe how difficult it is to obtain accurate information in a country where nobody ever travels.'

83. Humboldt continues with pages of a detailed study of cacao.

84. *plains without trees … climb to the horizon:* Humboldt described the llanos in his popular *Anschiten der Natur* (1808).

85. *Ulloa's:* See note 61.

86. Humboldt interpolates a long description of the continent's llanos, comparing them with others in the world. He adds in these principal features 'to make the narrative of my journey across such a monotonous plain more interesting'; a touch of Humboldtian humour.

87. embarbascar con caballos: In a note Humboldt translates: 'to set to sleep, or intoxicate the eels by means of horses'.

88. *A fight … picturesque scene:* Humboldt had first introduced Europeans to electric eels in a paper read at the Institut de France (20 October 1806), then in his *Anschiten der Natur* (1808) where he offered the same 'picturesque' spectacle as here. The electric eel (*Electrophorus electricus*, family Gymnotidae) gives off an alternating electric current that passes from the electrically positive tail to the negative head, reaching 500 volts at 2 amperes to immobilize its prey. Humboldt had one sent back live to Paris where he continued experiments with his friend Gay-Lussac.

89. *enormous boas:* In his *Anschiten der Natur* Humboldt described the boas. The creoles call them *tragavenado*, and found one with antlers stuck in its throat after it had swallowed a stag. They supposedly attain 48 feet, though in Europe the longest actually measured reached only 23 feet.

90. *Felipe de Urre:* Humboldt refers to Philip von Hutten, known as Urre, a German born in 1511 who sailed as an adventurer to Venezuela under a concession granted by Charles V in 1528. He searched for treasure in the interior, and became Captain-General of Venezuela in 1540. He returned inland to

seek gold; after having been away for five years he was captured and executed in 1541.

91. *manatees:* Humboldt's notes on the manatee can be found
in his *Recueil d'observations de zoologie,* vol. 2 (1833). It is today
an endangered species.

92. *March 31st:* From here Humboldt dates his entries, copying
down from his actual diary.

93. caribe ... *avid for blood: Caribe* are the carnivorous piranha
of the Characidae family, genus *Serrasalmus,* with massive jaws
and razor-sharp teeth. They were called *caribe* after the fierce
Carib Indians, warriors from whom we derive the word 'canni-
bal'. According to Robin Furneaux, *The Amazon: The Story of a
Great River* (London, 1969) Humboldt was the first naturalist
to notice the piranha.

94. *our large dog was bitten ... by some enormous bats:* In Humboldt's
Anschiten der Natur (E.C. Otté's translation, 1850) we read:
'Huge bats now attack the animals during sleep and, vampire-
like, suck their blood.'

95. niguas: Humboldt's note: 'The chigoe (also jigger), *Pulex
penetrans,* which digs under the nails of toes in men and monkeys and lays its eggs there.'

96. *Bonpland ... took control ... in danger:* In a letter to his brother
(17 October 1800) Humboldt praised Bonpland's 'amazing
courage' and 'devotion', and tells how he calmed Humboldt
down, and baled out the boat, as if he had saved his life. Humboldt did not know how to swim.

97. guayuco: A narrow loincloth usually worn by Indian
women.

98. *Cuvier's* Tableau élémentaire d'histoire naturelle: There are
letters extant from Humboldt to Cuvier. Georges Cuvier
(1769–1832) was Professor of Natural History at Paris, and
Secretary of the Académie Royale des Sciences. An important
zoologist and comparative anatomist, his law of 'the correlation of parts' led to new means of classifying fossil remains.
See J. Théodorides, 'Humboldt and Cuvier', *Biologie médicale,*
LIX (1961), pp. 50–71; and Dorinda Outram, *Georges Cuvier:
Vocation, Science and Authority in Post-Revolutionary France* (Manchester, 1984).

99. *Tequendama Falls:* Illustrated by Humboldt in his *Atlas pitto-resque* (1810).

100. The following section on the rapids was first published in Humboldt's *Anschiten der Natur* (1808) in a more exaggerated way. 'Few Europeans' had visited these cataracts. Here Humboldt is explicit about how the physical world is reflected on the inner, susceptible mental world, a mysterious communion. Here also Humboldt mentions his famous parrot of May-pures; the last speaker of the language of the Atures tribe had vanished, so nobody could understand the parrot.

101. *Solano's boundary expedition:* José Solano y Boto (1726–1806), a member of the frontier expedition to the Orinoco.

102. Humboldt continues here with details on the phenom-enon of cataracts. Describing the moon, Humboldt felt trans-ported to Bernardin de Saint-Pierre's Ile de France (today Mauritius). Saint-Pierre 'knew how to depict nature, not because he had studied it scientifically, but because he felt it in all its harmonious analogies of forms, colours and inner powers'.

103. ouavapavi: Humboldt refers his reader to his monograph on the Orinoco monkeys, *Recueil d'observations de zoologie*, vol. 1 (1805). The *ouavapavi*, from the Guaiquerí language, is Humboldt's *Simia albifrons*.

104. Humboldt continues here with a discussion on the geo-graphical distribution of venomous insects, according to white and black waters 'in this labyrinth of rivers'. He laments that an entomologist cannot live on the spot. He gives a note in Latin of the five new species of culex he found. Later H.W. Bates, an entomologist, did live there from 1848 to 1859. See his *The Naturalist on the Amazons* (London, 1863). See also Vic-tor W. von Hagen, *The Green World of the Naturalists: A Treasury of Five Centuries of Natural History in South America* and *South America Called Them: Condamine, Humboldt, Darwin, Spruce* (New York, 1948 and London, 1949; and Edward J. Goodman, *The Explorers of South America* (New York 1972).

105. *Maypures cataracts:* Humboldt sketched this *raudal* for the Governor-General of Caracas in his *Atlas géographique* (1811). He remained three days in Maypures. He describes the geography; pointing out new species. 'No traveller has yet described this place.'

106. Following this Humboldt notes down as much as he can about the Maypures language and beliefs.

107. *Once you have passed the Great Cataracts:* In a note to the Governor-General of Caracas (see note 105) Humboldt suggested building a canal bypassing the cataracts.

108. *whose location I was the first to establish ... the Casiquiare:* Sailing down the Casiquiare was Humboldt's greatest exploratory achievement. The Casiquiare canal was known to La Condamine, but not actually explored by him. A.R. Wallace followed Humboldt's 'illustrious' trail from Brazil in 1851; see *Travels on the Río Negro* (1853), chs. 8–10. For a modern trip, accompanied by Humboldt's travelogue, see Redmond O'Hanlon, *In Trouble Again: A Journey between the Orinoco and the Amazon* (London, 1988).

109. Here Humboldt interrupts his narrative by gathering together all his observations and readings about the San Fernando mission.

110. *Linnaeus's assertion ... palmivorous:* Humboldt refers to Linnaeus, *Systema naturae*, in Latin, vol. 1 (1735), p. 24.

111. *Berrio's and Raleigh's ... Guiana:* Humboldt cites Raleigh's 'pompously' titled *The Discovery of the Large, Rich and Beautiful Empire of Guiana* (London, 1596). Raleigh sailed for the Orinoco in 1595 and again in 1616. Antonio de Berrio's first expedition up the Orinoco in search of El Dorado was in 1586. He was guided by a Spanish soldier who had been taken there blindfolded, so he could not remember the way back. In 1590 Berrio, now governor of El Dorado, tried again. See Edward J. Goodman, *The Explorers of South America* (New York, 1972), p. 80.

112. *Piedra de la Madre ... great calamities:* Humboldt in this tale airs his age's sentimentalities about the 'sanctity of motherhood'. Redmond O'Hanlon retells this story in Helen Maria Williams's words in *In Trouble Again* (London, 1988), pp. 134–6.

113. *the greatest cannibals:* In a letter to Willdenow in 1801 back home Humboldt exaggerated these tales of cannibalism:

'We found in some huts disgusting remains of cannibalism!'
114. Humboldt digresses twenty quarto pages to research into the sources of the Río Negro, and in passing praises La Condamine, whose 'voyage has thrown so much light on different parts of America'.

115. Bertholletia excelsa: Humboldt made the *Bertholletia excelsa* (*almendrón* and *juvia* in text) known in Europe. He named the Brazil-nut after Claude Louis Berthollet, a French chemist (1748–1822) who was active on scientific committees during the Revolution, went with Napoleon to Egypt, and ran meetings of distinguished scientists from 1807 to 1817 known as the Society of Arcueil – see Maurice Crosland, *The Society of Arcueil: A View of French Science at the Time of Napoleon I* (London, 1967). Humboldt published a paper on isothermal lines in the journal *Mémoires de la société d'Arcueil* run by Berthollet. According to Helmut de Terra, *Humboldt: The Life and Times of Alexander van Humboldt (1769–1859)* (New York, 1955), Berthollet said of Humboldt: 'Cet homme réunit toute une académie en lui.' The Brazil-nut tree grows straight up to some 98 feet. The fruit is the size of a croquet ball and its shell is harder than a coconut, with twenty-five to thirty seeds inside. A.R. Wallace in *Travels on the Amazon* (London, 1853) says they fall like cannon-balls, sometimes even killing people. See also Redmond O'Hanlon, *In Trouble Again* (London, 1988), pp. 33–4.

116. Humboldt continues here with details about fixing the boundary between the Spanish and Portuguese colonies. In a note he quotes from his own 1800 memoir in Spanish to Mariano de Urquijo (1768–1817; a Spanish statesman who had granted Humboldt his travel permit), arguing for free trade between the colonies. This would lessen the anger of *americanos* in their demand for natural rights. This note shows that Humboldt was aware of American grievances against the central Spanish Government.

117. *Mutis:* See note 75.

118. Humboldt moves out of his narrative at this point to consider the Orinoco, Río Negro and Amazon river systems over twenty-five quarto pages.

119. urari ... *poison:* Humboldt was the first to accurately report back to Europe on this secret poison curare, used by Indians to hunt animals by causing neuromuscular relaxation or paralysis, although Walter Raleigh had brought a little back in the seventeenth century. Only in 1937 were the majority of plants used to make up curare identified. Charles Waterton's *wourali* is the same. See A.R. McIntyre, *Curare: Its History, Nature and Clinical Use* (Chicago, 1947).

120. *monkey ... roasted and smoked at the same time:* Humboldt in a note describes a drawing made by Schick in Rome representing one of their camps in the Orinoco with Indians roasting monkeys.

121. Humboldt goes on to give details about the *juvia*, or the 'chestnut of Brazil' (see note 115), and traces earlier references to it in previous travellers' accounts.

122. Humboldt goes on to give details about tribes of dwarves and fair Indians.

123. *caparro ... made known in my* Observations on Zoology and Comparative Anatomy: Vol. 1 (1805), pp. 322 and 354. According to Humboldt, Geoffroy Saint-Hilaire thought it a new genus. Humboldt wrote letters to Geoffroy Saint-Hilaire, a 'Goethian' scientist.

124. *parrot ... language of the Atures:* See note 100.

125. *my old master Blumenbach:* J.F. Blumenbach (1752–1840) was Professor of Natural History at Göttingen, and a friend of Humboldt's.

126. Humboldt continues with a description of his researches into earth eating all round the world. This section caused controversy in Paris, as Humboldt notes.

127. *Fourcroy in Paris:* Fourcroy (1755–1809) was Professor of Chemistry at the Museum d'Histoire Naturelle, Paris. He was very active in education during the Revolution. Humboldt wrote at least two letters to him from South America addressing him as 'citizen'.

128. *tobacco:* In a note Humboldt derives the word 'tobacco', like the words 'savannah', 'maize', 'cacique', 'maguey' and 'manatee', from the ancient languages of Haiti. It did not refer to the plant but the tube through which it was smoked.

129. *Alonso de Herrera:* Humboldt read the historian Herrera's account of his expedition up the Orinoco with 'astonishment' and gives details of where he stayed. Herrera was killed in battle by an arrow poisoned with curare in 1535.

130. Humboldt wrote: 'I will end this chapter with a succinct description of Spanish Guiana,' and then researches into the El Dorado myth, and the search for that 'imaginary country', for over sixty quarto pages.

131. *Pierre Martyr d'Anghiera:* Pierre Martyr d'Anghiera (1455–1526), an Italian historian who wrote about Columbus in *De Rebus oceanicis et de orbe novo decades* (1494). This is a good example of how on his return to Europe Humboldt read voraciously and 'with attention the Spanish sixteenth-century authors' to document his own voyage.

132. *Carib children . . . closer to nature . . . Rousseau's works:* This is a critical reference to Jean-Jacques Rousseau, who described the Caribs as 'closest to the state of nature'. Rousseau claimed that they 'are precisely the most peaceful in their loves, and the least subject to jealousy, despite their living in the kind of hot climate that always seems to inflame those passions' (*A Discourse on Inequality*, trans. Maurice Cranston (Harmondsworth, 1984), p. 103). Rousseau's ideas on infant education come from his novel *Émile* (1762).

133. *the unfortunate España:* See note 68.

134. *He had followed my progress from reading English newspapers:* On Humboldt in English papers see Calvin P. Jones, 'The Spanish American Works of Alexander von Humboldt as Viewed by Leading British Periodicals, 1800–1830', *The Americas*, 29 (April 1973), pp. 442–8.

135. Before continuing his narrative Humboldt adds in a long chapter (ch. 26, quarto pp. 56–321) on the political state of the Venezuelan provinces, their population, natural productions and commerce, as well as research on the difficulties of communications in the Republic of Colombia. This is followed by a brief chapter (ch. 27, quarto pp. 322–41) factually describing Bonpland's and Humboldt's crossing from New Barcelona on 24 November 1801, arriving in Havana on 19 December 1801.

136. *The way Havana looks . . . coasts:* For a modern view of

Havana see Nissa Torrents, *La Habana* (Barcelona, 1989).

137. Humboldt here includes his *Essai politique sue l'île de Cuba* (quarto pp. 351–457), also published separately in Paris. It was translated in 1856 by J.S. Thrasher as *The Island of Cuba*, but Humboldt was furious that Thrasher cut out the chapter on the horror of slavery. As Louis Agassiz pointed out, Humboldt died pained that slavery (not abolished until 1865) had not been abolished in the United States during his lifetime.

138. *Captain Baudin's departure:* See note 4.

139. *On my second visit to Havana in 1804:* The travellers left Veracruz and arrived in Havana on 29 March 1804, and left for Philadelphia on the ship *La Concepción* on 29 April 1804.

140. *M. Fidalgo's coastal surveying expedition:* Joaqúin Francisco Fidalgo (?–1820), a Spanish sailor in charge of measuring the Caribbean coasts.

141. *waters of the isthmus:* Humboldt was the first to seriously propose a canal across the 'isthmus of Panama'.

142. *Bouguer:* Pierre Bouguer, Professor of Hydrography, accompanied Godin and La Condamine to Peru in 1736, and published his *Traité de la figure de la terre* (1749).

143. *Travel books have multiplied ... extraordinary mistakes:* Humboldt's writing up of his South American travels was so diversified into other disciplines that the third volume of his *Relation historique* came out in 1825, eleven years after the first. He complained to his reader: 'In the late publication of my *Personal Narrative*, which was preceded by more scientific tomes, I have been pre-empted by travellers who crossed America twenty-five years after me.' According to Miguel Wionczek, Humboldt's thirteen original diary volumes in French from his 1799–1804 trip remained unedited until 1986 when Margot Faak published *Alexander von Humboldt: Reise auf dem Rio Magdalena, durch die Anden und Mexico. Aus seinen Reisetagebuchern zusammengestellt und erlautert* (Berlin, 1986), which corresponds to the countries not covered by his *Personal Narrative*.

144. *General Rochambeau's unfortunate expedition:* Donatien Rochambeau (1750–1813) was sent out to Santo Domingo in 1792; chased the English from Martinique in 1793, and helped defeat Toussaint L'Ouverture in Haiti in 1802. But his troops were decimated by malaria and he was captured by the British in 1803 and imprisoned until 1811.

145. *in his exile ... my unfortunate friend Bonpland:* Bonpland was imprisoned by Dr Francia in Paraguay; see my essay, 'The Strange Fate of Aimé Bonpland', *London Magazine* (April–May 1994), pp. 36–48.

146. Humboldt's narrative ends in May 1801. He supposedly destroyed the final fourth volume, which was ready for press. A reader may follow his trip to Lima, his climbing of Chimborazo, his first sight of the Pacific in his *Anschiten der Natur* (1808), as well as in Margot Faak (1986) (see note 143).

From

ESSAY ON THE
GEOGRAPHY OF PLANTS

ALEXANDER VON HUMBOLDT AND AIMÉ BONPLAND
1807

Translated by Sylvie Romanowski

PREFACE

HAVING LEFT EUROPE five years ago, and having traveled through some countries never seen before by naturalists, I might have hastened to publish earlier an abridged account of my travels in the tropics and the various phenomena that I studied one after another. Perhaps I might have flattered myself that such a publication would be received by the public, some of whom showed warm interest for my personal well-being as well as for the success of my expedition. But I thought that before talking about myself and the obstacles that I had to overcome during my work, I should draw the physicists' attention to the broader phenomena exhibited by nature in the regions through which I have traveled. What I offer here is a comprehensive view of these phenomena. This essay gives the results of the observations that are developed in greater detail in other works that I am preparing for publication.

Here I bring together all the physical phenomena that one can observe both on the surface of the earth and in the surrounding atmosphere. The physicist who is acquainted with the current state of science, especially that of meteorology, will not be surprised to see that so many topics are discussed in so few pages. If I could have worked on this book for a longer time, it would have been even shorter; for a tableau must contain only the general physical qualities and results that are certain and able to be expressed in exact numbers.

I conceived of this book during my earliest years. I gave a first sketch of a *Geography of Plants* in 1790 to Cook's famous colleague, Mr. Georges Forster, with whom I had close ties of friendship and gratefulness. My later research in various areas of physics helped me reach a wider understanding of my initial ideas. My voyage in the tropics furnished me with precious materials for the physical history of the earth. I wrote the major part of this work in the very presence of the objects I was going to describe, at the foot of the Chimborazo, on the coasts of the South Sea. I thought it best to keep the title *Essay on the Geography of Plants*, because any less modest title might have revealed its imperfections and rendered it less worthy of the public's indulgence.

I must plead for this indulgence especially for the style: having been obliged to use several languages that just like French are not my own, I cannot hope to express myself in as pure a style as might be expected if I used my own language.

The tableau that I offer here is the result of my own observations and those of Mr. Bonpland. We are linked by the closest of friendships, having worked together for six years, and sharing the same troubles to which the traveler is necessarily exposed in uncivilized lands: for these reasons we decided that all the works resulting from our expedition would be published under our two names.

In revising these works, as I have been doing since my return from Philadelphia, I have had recourse to famous men who honor me with their kindness. Mr. Laplace, whose fame is beyond my ability to praise him, was kind enough to show his interest, thus flattering greatly the work I brought back as well as the work I believed I had to write after my return from Europe. His genius illuminates and enlivens, so to speak, everything that surrounds him, so that his kindness has become as useful to me as to all the young people who come to him.

It is a great pleasure to bring him the tribute of my admiration and my gratitude, and it is no less a sacred duty to fulfill the duties of friendship. Mr. Biot was kind enough to honor me with his advice in the writing of this book. Since he is as wise a physicist as he is profound a geodesist, my relationship with him has become for me a fertile source of learning: in spite of the large number of his engagements, he was kind enough to calculate the tables of the horizontal refractions and of the extinction of light which are appended to my tableau.

The facts that I state on the history of fruit trees come from the work of Mr. Sickler, containing both great erudition and very philosophical views, which are rarely found together.

Mr. Decandolle furnished me with interesting materials relating to the Geography of Plants in the upper Alps; Mr. Ramond gave me materials on the flora of the Pyrenees; I found others in the classic works of Mr. Wildenow. It was important to compare the phenomena of equinoctial vegetation with those found in our European soil. Mr. Delambre was kind enough to enrich my tableau with several measurements of altitudes which have never been published. A large number of my barometric observations were calculated by Mr. Prony according to Mr. Laplace's formula, taking into account the influence of gravity. This worthy scientist took his kindness so far as to have more than four hundred of my measurements of altitude calculated under his personal supervision.

At this moment, I am writing about the astronomical observations that I made during my expedition, a great number of which were presented at the Bureau des Longitudes in order to determine their exactitude. Before this is done, it would be unwise to publish the maps I drew up of the interior of the continents, or even the account of my travels, since the position of the sites and their altitude influence all the phenomena in the regions I visited. I am hopeful that especially the observations that I made during my navigations on the Orinoco, the Casiquiare, and the Río Negro will be of interest to those who study the geography of South America. Despite Father Caulin's precise description of the Casiquiare, modern geographers have expressed new doubts on the link between the Orinoco and the Amazon Rivers. Having worked in this location, I did not expect that I would encounter bitter opposition[1] to my having found in nature very different river flows than those indicated by the Cruz map; but it is the fate of travelers that they may displease others when they observe facts that are contrary to received ideas.

After I have written the book on astronomy, I will be able to proceed faster with my other works; only after having

1. *Géographie moderne* [Modern Geography], by Pinkerton, trans. Walkenaer; vol. 6, pp. 174–77.

published the results of my latest voyage will I undertake a new project, which may shed much light on meteorology and magnetic phenomena.

I cannot publish this essay, the first fruit of my research, without expressing my profound and respectful gratitude to the government that honored me with its generous protection during my travels: enjoying a permission never granted before to any individual, I lived for five years in the midst of an honest and loyal nation, and never encountered in the Spanish colonies any obstacles other than those of physical nature itself. The memory of the government's kindness will remain permanently in my soul, as will the interest and affection on the part of people from all classes who honored me during my stay in the two Americas.

Alex. de Humboldt

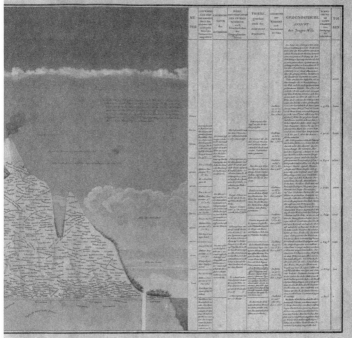

en in den Tropen-Ländern;

lde der Anden,

bis zum 10ten Grade südlicher Breite angestellt worden sind, in den Jahren 1799 bis 1803.

BOLDT und A. G. BONPLAND.

ESSAY ON THE GEOGRAPHY
OF PLANTS[1]

BOTANISTS USUALLY DIRECT their research towards objects that encompass only a very small part of their science. They are concerned almost exclusively with the discovery of new species of plants, the study of their external structure, their distinguishing characteristics, and the analogies that group them together into classes and families.

This knowledge of the forms which make up organized beings is no doubt the principal basis for descriptive natural history. It must be regarded as indispensable for the advancement of the sciences that concern the medical properties of plants, their cultivation, or their applications in the arts; even if this knowledge is worthy of occupying a great number of botanists, even if it can be considered from a philosophical point of view, it is no less important to understand the Geography of Plants, a science that up to now exists in name only, and yet is an essential part of general physics.

This is the science that concerns itself with plants in their local association in the various climates. This science, as vast as its object, paints with a broad brush the immense space occupied by plants, from the regions of perpetual snows to the bottom of the ocean, and into the very interior of the earth, where there subsist in obscure caves some cryptogams that are as little known as the insects feeding upon them.

The upper limit of vegetation varies, like that of perpetual snows, according to the distance of the location from the poles or the slant of the sun's rays. We do not know the lower limit of vegetation: but some precise observations carried out on subterranean vegetation in both hemispheres prove that the

1. Read in the Physics and Mathematics Class at the Institut National, 17th of Nivôse Year XIII [January 7, 1805].

interior of the earth supports life wherever organic seeds have found a place adequate for their development and the appropriate sustenance for their organism. The rocky and icy peaks above the clouds, barely discernible to the eye, are covered only with mosses and lichenous plants. Similar cryptogams, sometimes pale, sometimes colorful, branch out on the roofs of mines and underground caves. Thus the opposite limits of plant life produce beings with a similar structure and a physiology equally unknown to us.

The geography of plants does not merely categorize plants according to the various zones and altitudes where they are found; it does not consider them merely in relation to the conditions of atmospheric pressure, temperature, humidity, and electrical tension in which they live; it can discern, just as in animals, two classes having a very different kind of life, and, so to speak, very different habits.

One class of plants grows in an isolated and sparse fashion: such are, in Europe, *Solanum dulcamara*, *Lychnis dioica*, *Polygonum bistorta*, *Anthericum liliago*, *Crataegus aria*, *Weissia paludosa*, *Polytrichum piliferum*, *Fucus saccharinus*, *Clavaria pistillaris*, *Agaricus procerus*; in the tropics, *Theophrasta americana*, *Lysianthus longifolius*, *Cinchona*, *Hevea*. Another class of plants live in an organized society like the ants and the bees, and occupy immense terrains from which they exclude any heterogeneous plants. Such plants are strawberry plants (*Fragaria vesca*), bilberry plants (*Vaccinium myrtillus*), *Polygonum aviculare*, *Cyperus fuscus*, *Aira canescens*, *Pinus sylvestris*, *Sesuvium portulacastrum*, *Rhizophora mangle*, *Crotum argenteum*, *Convolvulus brasiliensis*, *Brathys juniperina*, *Escallonia myrtilloides*, *Bromelia karatas*, *Sphagnum palustre*, *Polytrichum commune*, *Fucus natans*, *Sphaeria digatata*, the lichen *Haematomma*, *Cladonia paschalis*, *Thelephora hirsuta*.

These socially organized plants are more common in temperate zones than in the tropics, where the vegetation is less uniform and thereby more picturesque. From the banks of the Orinoco to those of the Amazon and the Ucayali Rivers, for over five hundred leagues the entire surface of the land is covered with thick forests; and if the rivers did not break up this continuum, the monkeys who are almost the sole inhabitants of these solitary places could travel from the boreal to the austral hemisphere by leaping from branch to branch. But these immense forests do not offer a uniform kind of socially organized plant life; each part produces different kinds. Here one finds mimosas, *Psychotria*, or melastomes, there one finds laurel, Caesalpinaceae, *Ficus*, *Carolinea*, and *Hevea*, that interlace their branches: no one plant dominates over the others. This is not the case in the tropical region close to New Mexico and in Canada. From the 17th degree to the 22nd degree of latitude, the entire Anahuac region, the entire plateau lying from 1,500 to 3,000 meters above sea level, is covered with oaks and with a kind of pine tree that is close to *Pinus strobus*. On the eastern slope of the Cordillera, in the valleys of Jalapa, one finds a large forest of liquidambars: the soil, the vegetation, and the climate are like those of temperate regions; this is not observed in any other part of South America at a similar altitude.

The reason for this phenomenon seems to depend on the structure of the American continent. This continent widens out towards the north pole and continues in this direction much more than the European continent; this makes the Mexican climate much colder than it would be according to its latitude and its height above sea level. The plants in Canada and those in the more northerly regions spread towards the south, and the volcanic mountains in Mexico are covered with the same pine trees that would seem to belong only to the sources of the Gila and the Missouri.

In Europe, on the contrary, the great catastrophe which opened up the Strait of Gibraltar and fashioned the Mediterranean seabed prevented the plants in Africa from spreading since then into northern Europe: thus very few such plants are found north of the Pyrenees. But the oaks that crown the heights of the valley of Tenochtitlan are identical to the species at the 45th degree, and if a painter traveled through this tropical region to study its vegetation, he would not find the beauty and variety found in equinoctial plants. In the parallel of Jamaica, he would find forests of oaks, pines, *Cupressus disticha* and *Arbutus madronno*; these forests are very similar and just as monotonous as the social plants in Canada, Europe, and northern Asia.

It would be interesting to show on botanical maps the areas where these groupings of similar species of plants live. These maps would show long bands, whose irresistible extension causes the population of states to decrease, the nations to be separated, and creates stronger obstacles to communication than do mountains and seas. Heath, an association of *Erica vulgaris*, *Erica tetralix*, the lichens *Icmadophila* and *Haematomma*, spreads from the most northerly extremity of Jutland, through Holstein and Luneburg, up to the 52nd degree of latitude. From there it spreads towards the west, through the granitic sands of Munster and Breda, and to the Ocean coasts.

For a long stretch of centuries, these plants have made the soil sterile and have dominated these regions completely: despite man's efforts and his fight against an almost unconquerable nature, he has been able to claim only small areas for agriculture. These cultivated fields, the only fruits of hard work to be beneficial for humanity, are like small islands in the middle of the heath; they recall to the traveler's imagination those oases in Libya, so green and fresh in contrast to the surrounding desert sands.

A moss common to tropical and European marshes, *Sphagnum palustre*, used to cover a large part of Germania. This very moss made large areas of land uninhabitable for the nomadic peoples described by Tacitus. A geological feature explains this phenomenon. The oldest peat bogs, which have a mélange of sodium chloride and marine shells, arose from ulvae and *Fucus*; the most recent ones and the most widespread, on the contrary, arise from *Sphagnum* and *Mnium serpillifolium*; their existence thus proves how abundant these cryptogams once were on the earth. In cutting down the forests, agricultural peoples caused a decrease in the humidity of the climate; the marshes dried up, and useful plant life spread little by little over the plains that used to be occupied exclusively by cryptogams unfavorable to agriculture.

Even though the phenomenon of socially organized plant life seems to belong primarily in temperate zones, the tropics can also furnish several examples of this. Along the top of the long Andean chain of mountains, at an elevation of 3,000 meters, one can find *Brathys juniperina, Jarava* (a type of grass close to *Papporophorum*), *Escallonia myrtilloides*, several species of *Molina*, and especially *Tourrettia*, whose marrow provides a food that the impoverished Indian sometimes has to wrestle away from the bears. In the plains separating the Amazon River from the Chinchipe, one can find together *Croton argentum, Bougainvillea*, and *Godoya*; just as in the savannas of the Orinoco, one can find the palm tree *Mauritia*, herbaceous sensitive plants, and *Kyllingia*. In the kingdom of New Grenada, the *Bambusa* and the *Heliconia* occur in long uniform bands that are not interrupted by other plants: but these associations of the same species of plants are less consistently extensive, less numerous, than in temperate climates.

In order to determine the ancient link between neighboring continents, geology bases itself on the analogy of the coastal structures, on the ocean beds, and on the types of animals living there. The geography of plants can furnish precious materials for this kind of research: up to a point, it can show how islands that were previously linked are now separated; it can show that the separation of Africa from South America occurred before the development of organized forms of beings. This same science can determine which plants are common to east Asia and to the coasts of Mexico and California; it can determine whether there are any plants which live in every zone and in every elevation above sea level. The geography of plants can assist us in going back with some degree of certainty to the initial state of the earth: it can determine if, after the initial retreat of the waters which were abundant and agitated as attested by rocks filled with sea shells, the entire surface of the globe was covered at once with various plants, or whether, as traditional accounts of various peoples say, the earth, now stilled, produced plants only in one area, from which they were transported by sea currents in a progressive march to far-flung regions over the course of centuries.

This same science can examine whether among the immense variety of plant forms one can recognize some primitive forms, and whether the diversity of species can be considered to be an effect of the degeneration that over time transformed accidental varieties into permanent ones.

If I may draw some general conclusions from the phenomena I observed in both hemispheres, it seems to me that the seeds of cryptogams are the only ones that nature develops spontaneously in all climates. *Dicranium scoparium* and *Polytrichum commune*, *Verrucaria sanguinea* and *Verrucaria limitata* of Scopoli are found in all latitudes, in Europe as well as at the equator, and not only in the tallest mountain ranges, but even at sea level, wherever there is shade and humidity.

On the banks of the Magdalena, between Honda and the Egyptiaca, in a plain where the centigrade thermometer hovers almost constantly between 28 and 30 degrees, at the base of *Macrocnemum* and *Ochroma* trunks, mosses form lawns as green and as beautiful as those in Norway. Other travelers did affirm that cryptogams were very rare in the tropics, but this assertion was no doubt based on the fact that they went only near dry coasts or in small cultivated areas, without going far enough into the interior of the continents. Lichenous plants are found in every latitude: their shape seems as independent of the influence of the climates as is the kind of rocks they live on.

We do not yet know of any phanerogamous plant whose organs are flexible enough to adapt to all zones and all altitudes. In vain has it been asserted that *Alsine media*, *Fragaria vesca*, and *Solanum nigrum* enjoyed this advantage, a capacity shared only by man and a few mammals that he maintains around him. The strawberry of the United States and Canada is different from the one in Europe. Mr. Bonpland and I thought we had discovered a few of these plants in the Andean Cordillera while passing from the valley of the Magdalena to the Cauca valley through the snows of Quindiu. The solitary nature of these forests composed of styrax, passiflora trees and wax palm trees, the lack of agriculture in the environs, and other circumstances, seemed to exclude the possibility that these strawberry plants were brought here by man or by birds; but perhaps had we seen this plant in bloom, we would have found specific differences with *Fragaria vesca*, just as there are very slight nuances between *Fragaria elatior* and *Fragaria virginiana*: in any case, in the five years that we studied plants in both hemispheres, we never encountered any European plant produced spontaneously by the South American soil. We must be content with believing that *Alsine media*, *Solanum nigrum*, *Sonchus oleraceus*, *Apium graveolens*, and *Portulaca oleracea* are plants that, like the peoples of the races in the Caucasus, are very widespread in the northern part of the Old Continent. We know so little about what is produced in the interior of the lands that we must abstain from any general conclusion: we might fall into the error of those geologists who construct the entire earth according the shape of the nearest hills surrounding them.

In order to solve the great problem of the migration of plants, the geography of plants delves into the interior of the earth: it looks at the ancient monuments that nature has left behind in petrifications, in wood fossils, and in coal strata that are the tomb of the initial plant life of our planet. This science can discover petrified fruits in India, and palm trees, tree ferns, scitaminales, and tropical bamboos buried in the ice-covered lands in the north; it can consider whether these equinoctial productions, as well as the bones of elephants, tapirs, crocodiles, and marsupials which have been found recently in Europe, can have been carried to these temperate zones by the strength of currents in a submerged world, or whether these same climates formerly sustained the palm trees and the tapir, the crocodile and the bamboo. One can lean towards the latter supposition, when one considers the local circumstances that occur in Indian petrifications. But can one accept that such great changes in the atmosphere's temperature occurred without having recourse to a displacement of planets, or a change in the earth's axis – unlikely suppositions given our current knowledge of astronomy? Considering that the most striking geological phenomena show that the whole crust of the earth was once in a liquid state; that the stratification and differentiation of rocks indicate that the formation of mountains and the crystallization of the great land masses around a common nucleus did not happen at the same time on the whole surface of the earth; then one can conceive that the passage from liquid to solid states must have liberated an immense quantity of heat, and thereby increased the temperature of a region independently of solar heat: but would this local increase in temperature have lasted long enough to explain the nature of these phenomena?

Changes observed in the light of celestial bodies have led to the suspicion that the one which is at the center of our system undergoes similar variations. Would an increase in the intensity of the sun's rays have spread in certain periods tropical heat to the zones near the poles? Do such variations, which would enable equinoctial plants, elephants, and tapirs to live in Lapland, occur periodically? or are they the result of some temporary disturbances in our planetary system?

These are topics by which the geography of plants is related to geology. By shedding light on the prehistory of our planet, it offers to the human imagination a field to cultivate that is as rich as it is interesting.

Though plants are very analogous to animals regarding the irritability of their fibers and the stimuli that excite them, they are essentially different from animals as regards their mobility. Most animals leave their mother only when they reach adulthood. On the contrary, plants, being fixed in the soil after their development, can move only when still contained in the egg, whose structure favors mobility. But winds, currents, and birds are not the only ones that help plants migrate; the primary factor is man.

When man abandons the wandering life, he gathers around him the plants and animals that can feed and clothe him. This passage from nomadic life to agriculture occurs late in the northern peoples. In equinoctial regions, between the Orinoco and the Amazon, the density of the forest prevents the savage from living solely by means of hunting: he has to grow a few plants, some *Jatropha*, banana trees, and *Solanum*, for subsistence. Peach trees, the fruit of palm trees, and some small farms (if such a small group of cultivated plants can be so called), these are the basis for the South American Indians' food. The character of the savage is modified everywhere by the nature of the climate and the soil where he lives. These modifications alone accounted for the differences between the first inhabitants of Greece and the Bedouin herders, and between these and the Indians in Canada.

A few plants grown in gardens and farms since times immemorial accompanied man from one end of the planet to the other. In Europe, the Greeks took with them vines, the Romans, wheat, and the Arabs, cotton. In America, the Toltecs carried maize with them: potatoes and quinoa are found wherever went the inhabitants of the ancient Cundinamarca. The migration of these plants is obvious; but the land of their origin is as unknown as the origin of the various human races found all over the earth in the remotest times according to traditional accounts. South and east of the Caspian Sea, on the banks of the Amu Darya, in the ancient Colchis and especially in the province of Kurdistan, whose mountains are perpetually covered with snow and are hence over 3,000 meters, there the land is covered with lemon trees, pomegranate trees, cherry trees, pear trees, and all the fruit trees that we grow in our gardens. We do not know if these trees are native to those regions or whether they were formerly cultivated and became wild, and thereby attest to the antiquity of their cultivation in these regions. Situated between the Euphrates and the Indus, between the Caspian Sea and the Persian Gulf, these fertile lands gave Europe its most precious products. Persia gave us the walnut tree and the peach tree; Armenia, the apricot tree; Asia Minor, the cherry tree and the chestnut tree; Syria, the fig tree, the pear tree, the pomegranate tree, the olive tree, the plum tree, and the mulberry tree. In Cato's time, the Romans did not yet know the cherry, the peach, or the mulberry.

Hesiod and Homer already mention the cultivation of the olive tree in Greece and in the islands of the Archipelago. In the reign of Tarquinius the Ancient, this tree did not yet exist in Italy, Spain, or Africa. During Appius Claudius's consulate, oil was still very scarce in Rome; but by Pliny's time the olive tree had already spread to France and Spain. The vines that we grow today are not indigenous to Europe: they grow wild on the coasts of the Caspian Sea, in Armenia, and in Caramania. From Asia they spread to Greece and from there to Sicily. The Phoceans carried them to southern France: the Romans planted them on the banks of the Rhine. The *Vites* species growing wild in North America that gave its name (Vinland) to the first part of the land discovered by the Europeans is very different from our *Vitis vinifera*.

A cherry tree laden with fruit adorned Lucullus's triumph; it was the first tree of its kind ever seen in Italy. The dictator took it from the province of Pontus when he was victorious over Mithridates. In less than a century, the cherry tree became widespread in France, Germany, and England. So does man change at will the surface of the earth, gathering around him plants coming from the most distant climates. In the European colony of the two Indies, one small cultivated plot may contain coffee from Arabia, sugar cane from China, indigo from Africa, and a host of other plants belonging to both hemispheres. This variety of plants is interesting in that it recalls to one's imagination a series of events that caused the human race to spread over the entire surface of the earth and to appropriate all its productions.

In this manner, man, being restless and industrious, traveled in all the earth's regions and thereby forced a certain number of plants to live under many climates and in many altitudes; but the domination that he exercised over these organized beings did not modify their primitive structure. Grown in Chile at an altitude of 3,600 meters (1,936 toises), potatoes have the same blossoms as the ones introduced in the Siberian plains. Barley that was used to feed Achilles' horses is no doubt the same as the one grown today. The characteristic forms of the plants and animals that occupy the earth today do not seem to have undergone any changes since the remotest times. The ibis buried in the Egyptian catacombs, a bird that goes back almost to the time of the pyramids, is identical to the one fishing today on the banks of the Nile; this identity shows that the huge amounts of animal fossils found in the interior of the earth do not belong to varieties of current species, but to a very different order of things from ours, and too ancient for any of the traditions to remember.

Having introduced new plants, man preferred to cultivate these and made them dominant over the indigenous ones; but this preponderance of new plants, which makes the European cultures seem so monotonous and hopelessly dull to the botanist during his excursions, prevails only in a small part of the planet where civilization perfected itself and where consequently population increased the most. In the lands near the equator, man is too weak to tame a vegetation that hides the ground from view and leaves only the ocean and the rivers to be free. There nature demonstrates its wildness and majesty that render impossible all efforts of cultivation.

The origin and the first homeland of the plants most useful to man and living with him since the remotest times is as impenetrable a secret as that of the land of origin of domestic animals. We do not know the homeland of the grasses that are the primary subsistence for the peoples of the Mongolian race and of the Caucasus; we do not know in which region the cereals spontaneously arose, such as wheat, barley, oats, and rye. This latter species of grasses does not seem to have been grown even by the Romans. Some have maintained that these plants were found to grow wild, barley on the banks of the Samara in the land of the Tartars, *Triticum spelta* in Armenia, rye in Crete, wheat in Bashkiria in Asia: but these facts do not seem to be very well ascertained; it is too easy to confuse plants growing spontaneously with plants that fled from man's domination and regained their original freedom. Birds eating the seeds of cereals can easily disseminate them throughout the forests. Plants constituting the native wealth of all the tropics' inhabitants – the banana tree, *Carica papaya, Jatropha manihot*, and maize – have never been found in a wild state. I have seen a few such plants on the banks of the Casiquiare and the Río Negro: but the savages of this region, both melancholy and distrustful, cultivate small plots of land in the most solitary places; they abandon them a short while later, and the plants they left behind thus seem indigenous to the soil where they grow. The potato, so beneficial in feeding large populations in the most sterile regions of Europe, shares the same characteristics as the banana tree, maize, and wheat. However much research I conducted on location, I never learned that any traveler found it growing wild either on the summit of the Peruvian Cordillera or in the kingdom of New Grenada, where this plant is grown together with the *Chenopodium quinoa*.

Such are the characteristics found in agriculture and its various products, varying with their latitude or with the origin and needs of the peoples. The impact of food that can be more or less stimulating to the character and strength of the passions, the history of navigations and wars carried out over the products of the plant kingdom; such are the factors that link the geography of plants to the political and intellectual history of mankind.

These relationships would be no doubt sufficient to show how extended is the science which I am attempting to outline here; but the man who is sensitive to the beauty of nature will also find here the explanation for the influence exerted by nature on the peoples' taste and imagination. He will delight in examining what is called the character of vegetation, and the variety of effects it causes in the soul of the observer. These considerations are important in that they are closely related to the means by which imitative arts and descriptive poetry can affect us. Merely looking at nature, at its fields and forests, causes a pleasure that is essentially different from the impression given by studying the specific structure of an organized being. In the latter, the details interest us and excite our curiosity; in the former, the large picture, the ensemble, excites our imagination. How different is the aspect of a vast prairie surrounded with a few clumps of trees from that of a dense, dark forest of oaks and pines? How different are the forests of temperate zones from those of the equator where the naked and thin trunks of palm trees soar above the flowering mahogany trees and resemble majestic porticos? What is the intellectual cause of these feelings? Are they produced by nature, by the large size of these ensembles, by the outline of their shapes, or by the plants' posture? How does this posture, this more or less rich or cheerful aspect of nature influence the habits and sensibilities of peoples? What is the character of tropical vegetation? What features distinguish the African plants from those of the New World? What are the analogies in shape that link the alpine plants of the Andes with those of the high peaks of the Pyrenees? These questions have hardly been debated till now and are without a doubt worthy of the physicist's attention.

Among the variety of plants covering the surface of our planet, one can easily distinguish certain general forms under which the others can be subsumed, and which can be arranged into families or groups that are more or less analogous to each other. I will name only fifteen of these groups, whose aspect is most interesting to the painter of landscapes: (1) the scitaminales form (*Musa, Heliconia, Strelitzia*); (2) the palms; (3) the tree-ferns; (4) the form of *Arum, Pothos,* and *Dracontium;* (5) the pines (*Taxus, Pinus*); (6) heaths *folia acerosa;* (7) the tamarind form (*Mimosa, Gleditsia, Porlieria*); (8) the Malvaceae form (*Sterculia, Hibiscus, Ochroma, Cavanillesia*); (9) the lianas (*Vitis, Paullinia*); (10) the orchids (*Epidendrum, Seratis, Paullinia*); (11) the prickly-pears (*Cactus*); (12) the casuarines and *Equisetum;* (13) the grasses; (14) the mosses; (15) lastly, the lichens.

These divisions based on physiognomy have almost nothing in common with those made by botanists who have hitherto classified them according to very different principles. Only the outlines characterizing the aspect of vegetation and the similarities of impressions are used by the person contemplating nature, whereas descriptive botany classifies plants according to the resemblance of their smallest but most essential parts, those relating to fructification. An artist of distinction would find it worthwhile to study, not in greenhouses or in botany books but in nature itself, the physiognomy of the plant groups that I have enumerated. How very interesting for a tableau would be the antique trunk of a palm tree, with its variegated leaves swaying above a group of *Heliconia* and banana trees! How interesting would be the picturesque contrast of a tree-fern surrounded by Mexican oaks!

The absolute beauty of these shapes, their harmony, and the

contrast arising from their being together, all this makes what is called the character of nature in various regions. Some shapes, indeed, and the most beautiful ones (the scitaminales, palm trees, and bamboos), are missing entirely from our temperate regions; others, such as trees with pinnate leaves, are very rare and less elegant. Arborescent species are very few, not so tall, and less laden with flowers pleasing to the eye. Thus the number of social plants, as described earlier, and man's cultivation make the aspect of the land more monotonous. In the tropics, on the contrary, nature delighted in combining every possible shape. The shapes of pines seem to be missing at first glance; but in the Andes of Quindiu, in the temperate forests of Oxa and in Mexico, there are cypress, pines, and junipers.

In general near the equator plant shapes are more majestic and more imposing; the leaves shine more brilliantly, and the texture of the parenchyma is looser and more succulent. The tallest trees are consistently adorned with flowers that are more beautiful, bigger, and more perfumed than those of herbaceous plants found in temperate zones. The singed bark of their ancient trunks makes a most agreeable contrast with the tender green leaves of the lianas, the pothos, and especially the orchids, whose flowers imitate the shape and the feathers of the birds feeding upon their nectar. However, in the tropics, we almost never see the breadth of the green prairies that lie along the rivers in northern countries; we almost never feel there the sweet feeling of springtime awakening the vegetation. Nature, beneficial to all beings, apportioned its specific gifts for each region. There are fibers that are more or less loose, plant colors that are more or less vivid according to the chemical nature of their elements and the strength of the sun's stimulation: these are some of the causes of the varieties of plants that give each zone of the planet its particular character. The great elevation of the lands near the equator presents to the inhabitants of the tropics a curious spectacle where the plants have the same shapes as those of Europe.

The valleys in the Andes are adorned with banana and palm trees; at a higher elevation one can find a beneficial tree whose bark is the fastest and healthiest fever reducer. In this temperate elevation where quinquinas are found, and in higher elevations where there are *Escallonia*, there one finds oaks, pines, *Berberis*, *Alnus*, *Rubus*, and a host of genera that we think belong only in the northern lands. Thus the inhabitants of equinoctial regions know all the species that nature placed around them: the earth offers to their eyes a spectacle as varied as the azure vault of the heavens which hides none of its constellations from view.

The Europeans do not enjoy such a spectacle. The frail plants that people, out of love of science or refined luxury, grow in their hothouses are mere shadows of the majestic equinoctial plants; many of these shapes will remain forever unknown to the Europeans; but the richness and perfection of the languages, the imagination and sensitivity of the poets and the painters give some compensation in Europe. The varied spectacles of the equinoctial regions are given to us by the imitative arts. In Europe, a man isolated on an arid coast can enjoy in thought the picture of faraway regions: if his soul is sensitive to works of art, if he is educated enough in spirit to embrace the broad concepts of general physics, he can, in his utter solitude and without leaving his home, appropriate everything that the intrepid naturalist has discovered in the heavens and the oceans, in the subterranean grottos, or on the highest icy peaks. This is no doubt how enlightenment and civilization have the greatest impact on our individual happiness, by allowing us to live in the past as well as the present, by bringing to us everything produced by nature in its various climates, and by allowing us to communicate with all the peoples of the earth. Sustained by previous discoveries, we can go forth into the future, and by foreseeing the consequences of phenomena, we can understand once and for all the laws to which nature subjected itself. In the midst of this research, we can achieve an intellectual pleasure, a moral freedom that fortifies us against the blows of fate and which no external power can ever reach.

PHYSICAL TABLEAU OF
EQUATORIAL REGIONS

Based on measurements and observations performed on location, from the tenth degree of boreal latitude to the tenth degree of austral latitude in the years 1799, 1800, 1801, 1802, and 1803.

WHEN ONE ASCENDS from sea level to the peaks of high mountains, one can see a gradual change in the appearance of the land and in the various physical phenomena in the atmosphere. The plants in the plains are gradually replaced by very different ones: woody plants decrease little by little and are replaced by herbaceous and alpine plants; higher still, one finds only grasses and cryptogams. Rocks are covered with a few lichens, even in the regions of perpetual snow. As the appearance of the vegetation changes, so does the form of the animals: the mammals living in the woods, the birds flying in the air, even the insects gnawing at the roots in the soil are all different according to the elevation of the land.

By looking carefully at the nature of rocks of the earth's crust, the observer can also see changes in them as he climbs above sea level. Sometimes, the more recent formations covering the granite in the plains reach only a certain altitude; and near the mountain peaks this same primitive rock reappears that is the basis for all the others, and which constitutes the interior of our planet, so far as our feeble endeavors have allowed us to penetrate it.[1] Sometimes, this granitic rock remains hidden under other more recent formations. Peaks over 4,000 meters (2,053 toises) above today's sea level contain strata of shells and petrified corals. Sometimes, small scattered

---

1. The greatest vertical depth of mines in Europe is 408 meters (209 toises): the large mine in Valenciana in Mexico has a depth of 516 meters (266 toises).

cones made of basalt, greenstone (*Grünstein*), and porphyric schist crown the tops of high mountains, thus posing difficult enigmas for geologists. The mineralogist can see variations according to the elevation of the ground, just as the naturalist can see variations in the plants and the animals: furthermore, the air, this mixture of gaseous fluids of unknown size enveloping our planet, is no less subject to striking variations. As we go further away from sea level, the temperature and pressure of the air diminish; at the same time, its dryness and its electrical tension increase: the blue of the sky seems deeper according to one's altitude. This same altitude also influences the decrease of gravity, the temperature of boiling water, the intensity of the sun's rays traversing the atmosphere, and the refraction of the rays as they travel through it. Thus the observer who leaves the center of the earth by an infinitely small amount compared to the radius can reach a new world, so to speak, and he can observe more variations in the aspect of the soil and more modifications in the atmosphere than he would if he were to pass from one latitude to another.

These variations are found in every region where nature made mountain ranges and high plateaus above sea level; but they are less prominent in temperate zones than at the equator where the Cordilleras have an altitude of 5,000 to 6,000 meters (2,565 to 3,078 toises), and where there is a uniform and constant temperature at each elevation. Near the north pole there are mountains almost as colossal as those found in the Quito kingdom, and whose grouping has all too often been attributed to the earth's rotation. Mount Saint Elias, situated on the American coast opposite the Asian coast, at 60°21′ of boreal latitude, is 5,512 meters high (2,829 toises); Mount Fairweather, situated at the 59th degree of boreal latitude, is 4,547 meters high (2,334 toises).[1] In our average latitude of 45 degrees, the Mont-Blanc has a height of 4,754 meters (2,440 toises), and one can consider it to be the highest mountain in the Old Continent, until brave explorers can measure the

---

1. *Viaje al estrecho de Fuca* [Voyage to the Straight of Fuca], by Don Dionisio Galeano y Don Cajetano Valdes; p. lxv.

range of mountains in northwest China, which some have affirmed to be higher than Chimborazo. But in the northern regions, in the temperate zones at 45 degrees, the limit of permanent snow, which is also the limit for all organized life, is only at 2,533 meters above sea level (1,300 toises). The result is that on mountains in temperate zones, nature can develop the variety of organized beings and meteorological phenomena on only half the surface offered by tropical regions, where vegetation ceases to exist only at 4,793 meters (2,460 toises). In our northern latitudes, the slant of the sun's rays and the unequal length of the days raise the temperature in the mountain air so much that the difference between the temperature in the plains and the temperature at 1,500 meters is often imperceptible: for this reason, many plants that grow at the foot of our Alps are also found at great heights. The rigors of the cold temperature during autumn nights does not destroy their organization; they would undergo the same decrease in temperature a few months later in the plains. A few alpine plants in the Pyrenees grow at very low elevations in the valleys; there they find a temperature to which they might be exposed sometimes also at a higher elevation.

In the tropics, on the contrary, on the vast surface of up to 4,800 meters, on this steep surface climbing from the ocean level to the perpetual snows, various climates follow one another and are superimposed, so to speak. At each elevation the air temperature varies only slightly; the pressure of the atmosphere, the hygroscopic state of the air, its electrical charge, all these follow unalterable laws that are all the more easy to recognize because the phenomena are less complicated there. As a result, each elevation has its own specific conditions, and therefore produces differently according to these circumstances, so that in the Andes of Quito in a region with a breadth of 2,000 meters (1,000 toises) one can discover a greater variety of life forms than in an equal zone on the slopes of the Pyrenees.

I have attempted to gather in one single tableau the sum of the physical phenomena present in equinoctial regions, from the sea level of the South Sea to the very highest peak of the Andes. This tableau contains:

The vegetation;

The animals;

Geological phenomena;

Cultivation;

The air temperature;

The limit of perpetual snow;

The chemical composition of the atmosphere;

Its electrical tension;

Its barometric pressure;

The decrease in gravity;

The intensity of the azure color of the sky;

The weakening of light as it passes through the strata
    of the atmosphere;

The horizontal refractions, and the temperature of
    boiling water at various altitudes.

In order to facilitate the comparison of these phenomena with those of temperate zones, we have added a great number of elevations measured at various locations on the planet, along with the distance at which these elevations can be seen from the sea, not taking into account the earth's refraction.

This tableau contains almost the entirety of the research I carried out during my expedition in the tropics. It is the result of a large number of works that I am preparing for the public and in which I will develop what I can only outline here. I dared to think that this essay would be interesting not only for physicists but even more for all those interested in general physics, to whom it may suggest further comparisons and analogies. This science, no doubt one of the highest achievements of human knowledge, can progress only by individual studies and by connecting together all the phenomena and productions on the surface of the earth. In this great chain of causes and effects, no single fact can be considered in isolation. The general equilibrium obtaining in the midst of these disturbances and apparent disorder is the result of an infinite number of mechanical forces and chemical attractions which balance each other; and while each series of facts must be examined separately in order to recognize a specific law, the study of nature, which is the main problem of general physics, demands the gathering together of all the knowledge dealing with modifications of matter.

I thought that if my tableau were capable of suggesting unexpected analogies to those who will study its details, it would also be capable of speaking to the imagination and providing the pleasure that comes from contemplating a beneficial as well as majestic nature. So many objects are capable of seizing our imagination and lifting us to the most sublime considerations: the multitude of forms developed on the slopes of any one of the Cordilleras; the variety of living structures adapted to the climate of each elevation and to its barometric pressure; the layer of perpetual snow that poses insurmountable obstacles to the spreading of vegetation, but whose limit at the very equator is at 2,300 meters (1,200 toises) higher than under our climates; the volcanic fire that sometimes makes its way to the surface in low hills like Mount Vesuvius, sometimes at elevations five times higher, like the cone of Cotopaxi; the petrified shells found on the peaks of the highest mountains recalling the great catastrophes of our planet; finally, those elevated regions of the atmosphere where the aeronautical physicist went,[1] guided by his bold courage and his noble zeal. By speaking both to our imagination and our spirit at the same time, a physical tableau of the equatorial regions could not only be of interest to those in the field of physical sciences, but could also stimulate people to study it who do not yet know all the pleasures associated with developing our intelligence.

In stating these ideas, I have been concerned not so much with the tableau that I am presenting here, the imperfections of which I am well aware, but more with the breadth of which this kind of work is capable. The public, who is so well disposed towards me, will be indulgent toward this work which has been written in the midst of many very heterogeneous occupations. If the new projects I am preparing leave me enough time, I hope to be able eventually to bring this tableau

1. Mr. Gay-Lussac.

to a higher degree of perfection: for botanical maps are like the ones we call exclusively geographical; we can make them more exact only inasmuch as we accumulate a greater number of good observations.

I sketched out this tableau for the first time in the port of Guayaquil, in February 1803, when I was returning from Lima by way of the South Sea, and was preparing myself for the Acapulco navigation. I sent a first draft of this sketch to Mr. Mutis, who is well disposed toward me, in Santa Fé de Bogotá. No one was more qualified than he to ascertain the accuracy of my observations, and to take them further by means of those he conducted himself in the course of his travels throughout the kingdom of New Grenada for over forty years. Mr. Mutis, a great botanist who followed the results of our science despite his being far away from Europe, observed tropical plants at every elevation. He botanized in the plains of Cartagena, on the banks of the Magdalena River, and in the hills of Turbaco that are adorned with *Gustavia augusta*, *Anacardium caracoli*, and *Nectandra sanguinea*. He lived for a long time on the high plateaus of Pamplona, of Mariquita, and Ibagué, whose serene skies and delicious climate will always bring back to me the most pleasant of memories. He climbed the snowy peaks of the Andes, those icy regions where grow *Escallonia myrtilloides*, *Wintera granatensis*, and *Befaria*, which is constantly laden with flowers and which one could call the rose of the Alps of these regions. Mr. Mutis, whose barometric measurements enabled him to ascertain the elevation of these stations, was better able than any other botanist to gather together interesting observations on the geography of plants. Mr. Haenke, who accompanied the unfortunate Malaspina in his navigations, must have made a large number of observations similar to mine: this indefatigable botanist has been living for the past ten years in the high mountain chain of the Andes of Cochabamba that links the Potosí mountains to those in Brazil. Messrs Sessé and Mocinô, who brought to Europe the abundant plant life of Mexico, will no doubt have observed the great variety of plants growing in the soil of New Spain, from the coast of Yucatán and Vera Cruz to the snowy peaks of Citlaltépetl

(Orizaba peak) and Popocatépetl. But my stay in the United States and in Mexico as well as a few other circumstances prevented me from benefiting from the advice of these distinguished scientists whose insights could have been very useful to me.

The sketch that I drew in Guayaquil was executed in Paris by Mr. Schoenberger, whose rare talent is known in France and in Germany and who has bestowed on me for many years a special friendship. Having little free time, he was not able to execute it in all the detail necessary for engraving, and so Mr. Turpin was kind enough to take on the task of doing this tableau that I am now offering to the public. Equally distinguished as a painter and as a botanist, he executed this geography of plants with the good taste characterizing all his work. A drawing that by nature is bound to respect scales cannot be done in a very picturesque fashion: all the demands of geodetic precision are contrary to this. Vegetation should be seen as a mass, similar to that depicted in a military map. However, I thought that in the regions closest to the sea, one could represent a grove of scitaminales and palm trees with their slim trunks rising upwards. In this tableau, the eye can see the limits of these regions: there are fewer and fewer palm trees among the other trees, and the trees are gradually replaced by herbaceous plants, and these are displaced by grasses and cryptogams. Some persons of taste might have wished not to see observations surrounding the picture of the Cordillera and to have all these observations relegated near the scales in the margins of the tableau; but in a work of this kind, one must consider two conflicting interests, appearance and exactitude. The public will judge whether we have succeeded in any way in overcoming the difficulties hindering the execution of this sketch.

The tableau of the equatorial regions contains all the physical phenomena occurring on the surface of the earth and in the atmosphere from the 10th degree of boreal latitude to the 10th degree of austral latitude. Extending this zone closer to the borders of the tropical regions would have resulted in less exactitude, because of the great difference one observes not

only in the productions of the soil but especially in meteorological phenomena, between the 10th and 23rd degrees of
latitude.[1]

According to the geodetic measurements I executed in
Mexico, the limit of perpetual snow goes down only as far as
4,600 meters (2,400 toises) at the 19th degree of boreal latitude, that is, 200 meters (100 toises) lower than at the equator.
But many factors give to the regions situated between 20 and
23 degrees of boreal latitude a climate and a type of vegetation that one could not expect to find in the tropics: the
proximity of temperate zones, the currents maintaining
themselves in the atmosphere, the direction of the trade
winds according to the hemisphere where they blow, and
many other reasons due to the configuration of the continents. In New Spain the pine trees found at an altitude of as
much as 3,934 meters (2,019 toises), and 1,000 meters (500
toises) below the limit of perpetual snow, can still have trunks
one meter thick; while under the 5th and 6th degrees of latitude, the taller trees stop growing already at 3,508 meters of
altitude (1,800 toises). On the island of Cuba, the temperature
sometimes goes down to zero in winter, often for several
days. At sea level, it stays only at 7 degrees centigrade, while
in Vera Cruz and Santo Domingo, in somewhat more austral
latitudes, it does not go below 17 degrees. In the kingdom of
New Spain, snow has been known to fall in the capital of
Mexico, and even in the Michoacán province, in Valladolid,
although these cities' altitude is only 2,264 meters (1,163
toises), and 1,870 meters (959 toises) above sea level. From
the equator up to the 4th degree of latitude, it snows only
above 4,000 meters (2,000 toises).

Given these data regarding the vegetation and the climate
of the regions near the temperate zones, it would not be prudent to show in the same tableau the phenomena occurring in

1. It will be useful to note here that throughout this work, unless otherwise indicated, the centigrade thermometer scale has been used, and, for linear measurement,
the meter, but for time measurements and degrees of latitude, the older terms have
been used.

the entire tropical region. Beyond the 10th degree of latitude, north or south, the ground and the atmosphere no longer have the same character as in the equatorial regions.

In my picture, these regions are represented by a vertical cross-section that traverses the high Cordillera of the Andes from east to west. On one side, on the west, one can see the level of the South Sea, which in these regions deserves the name of Pacific Ocean; for from the 12th degree of austral latitude to the 5th degree of boreal latitude, and only within this range, its tranquility is never disturbed by impetuous winds. From the western coast to the Cordillera a long plateau stretches out that is very long from north to south, but only 20 to 30 leagues wide from west to east: this is the Peruvian valley that, north of 4°50′ of boreal latitude, has a vegetation as rich as it is majestic, but is arid and devoid of plants south of this parallel. Covered with granitic sand, sea shells, and rock salt, the soil shows all the characteristics of a land that was submerged by ocean waters for a long time. In this valley, from the hills of Amotape to Coquimbo, the inhabitants have never known either rain or thunder, while north of these hills it rains abundantly and thunderstorms are as furious as frequent. I placed the cross-section of the Andes Cordillera through the highest peak, situated at 1°27′ of austral latitude and 0°19′ west of the city of Quito: this is the peak of Chimborazo, measured only approximatively by French scientists. Mr. de La Condamine, whose travel narrative contains the most beautiful descriptions of geology and general physics, says that Chimborazo is about 6,274 meters high (3,220 toises); the Spanish geodesist Don Jorge Juan found it to be 6,586 meters high (3,380 toises): this is a considerable difference, since it amounts to 312 meters (160 toises). According to the beautiful map of the Peruvian coasts published by Depósito Hydrográfico in Madrid, Malaspina's expedition judged Chimborazo's height to be 7,496 varas (6,352 meters or 3,258 toises). A geodetic measurement that I did near the new city of Riobamba in the large volcanic plain of Tapia, gives to Chimborazo, supposing a refraction of one-fourteenth of the arc, an altitude of 3,640 meters (1,868 toises) above the Tapia plateau; however, Mr. Gouilly, using Mr. Laplace's formula to calculate the barometric observations, found that this plateau is 2,896 meters (1,485 toises) above sea level: consequently, the total height of Chimborazo would be 6,536 meters (3,354 toises). Using the new formula for refraction that Mr. Laplace was kind enough to furnish me and that he will publish very soon, I found the result of my geodetic measurements changing to 3,648 meters (1,872 toises), and the total height of Chimborazo to be 6,544 meters (3,358 toises). This figure is closer to Don Jorge Juan's estimate than to Mr. de La Condamine's; but one must remember that the latter geodesist perhaps used Bouguer's barometric formula[1] and did not correct for temperature, and so had to find the height to be 180 meters (92 toises) less than my measurements for which I used these corrections. Thus the difference in the assumptions relative to the height of the barometer above sea level leads us further away from being able to measure absolute height. Measurements carried out in the Andes Cordillera can be only half geodetic and half barometric, and this complication prevents a comparison between two sets of measurements carried out by very different methods. The length of my base, 1,702 meters (873 toises), the care taken to level it out, and the nature of my angles, should give some confidence in the result of my measurement. Chimborazo's summit is a large segment of a circle, a dome that somewhat resembles the Mont-Blanc. It was impossible to show its shape properly on the plate accompanying this volume; but I am preparing a picturesque image of this colossal mountain whose contours

1. The great differences found between the measurements of the same mountains carried out by French and Spanish scientists, differences that are greater than the ones that might result from the uncertainty regarding the Caraburu signal, leads one to suppose that the estimates of Chimborazo's height were modified by different hypotheses about barometric calculation. If, however, the absolute height of all peaks depends on the geodetic measure of the Ilinissa pyramid carried out from Niguas, as the *Figure de la Terre* [Description of the Earth] by Bouguer indicates, then these differences will be even less surprising. I will discuss elsewhere the sources of the errors occurring in this complicated operation.

I measured with a sextant, and which I will publish some day.

In this tableau, behind Chimborazo rises a cone 5,752 meters high (2,952 toises); this is the Cotopaxi summit, one of the most active volcanoes in the Quito province along with Tungurahua and Sangay. It is almost five times the height of Mount Vesuvius, which is only 1,197 meters high (615 toises); but it is not the highest volcano on the planet; higher still is Antisana, 5,832 meters high (2,993 toises), with several small mouths, from one of which I saw smoke rise in 1802. In reality, Cotopaxi is not as close to Chimborazo as it seems in my picture. If one had wanted to preserve the true horizontal distances, and if, as in the *Geographical Atlas* that I will soon publish, one wanted to represent the irregularity of the ground in a given region, one would have had to show the Cariguairazo volcano instead of Cotopaxi, for Cariguairazo is a mountain that leans against Chimborazo after having collapsed on July 19, 1698. Cariguairazo is not very interesting today, showing only the ruins of its former grandeur; but I had a very powerful reason for preferring Cotopaxi. I heard the underground groans of this volcano when I was in the port of Guayaquil undertaking the first sketch of this tableau. The mouth of Cotopaxi[1] was at a distance of 42 nautical leagues, yet its explosions sounded like repeated artillery gunfire. In 1744, this volcano was heard as far away as Honda and Monpós, cities 220 leagues hence. If Vesuvius had had the same volcanic intensity, one would have been able to hear it as far away as Dijon or Prague. The height reached by the smoke above Cotopaxi is not arbitrary; it is congruent with the measurements done by Mr. de La Condamine, who estimated that in 1738 the flames reached an altitude of over 900 meters (461 toises) above the mountain peak. During these same explosions, this volcano, like others in the kingdom of Quito, vomited immense quantities of fresh hydro-sulfuric water, carbonated clay with sulfur, and fish, barely disfigured by the

---

1. Cotopaxi's crater is almost 930 meters wide (478 toises); Rucupichincha's has a diameter of about 1,463 meters (751 toises), while Mount Vesuvius's crater is only 606 meters wide (312 toises).

heat and which comprised a new species¹ of the genus *Pimelodus*.

It is almost superfluous to add that the projection of the Cordillera is represented to scale only for heights, but that this same scale cannot be used for distances. The highest mountains are so small compared to distances that, for example, Chimborazo would be only 4 millimeters (2 lines) high on an in-folio picture that should represent a terrain 200 leagues long; a mountain as high as Mount Vesuvius would even become completely invisible. Furthermore, in order to use the same scale for distance as the one I have chosen for height, and to represent not the whole of South America, but just the small valley contained between the South Sea and the eastern slope of the Andes, one would need a sheet of paper 40 times as long as the format of this book; consequently when one represents a large part of the planet in profile, the scales for height and distance cannot be identical: this factor makes it impossible to show the nature of the terrain because it makes the slopes appear much steeper than they are in reality. I will soon have the opportunity of discussing the advantages and disadvantages of these projections, either in my *Essai sur la pasigraphie minéralogique* [Essay on the System of Mineralogy] or in the *Atlas géologique* [Geological Atlas] that I intend to publish as soon as my astronomical and geodetic observations are sufficiently verified.

The eastern slope of the Andes appears in this tableau a bit less steep than the western slope: thus nature has built this part of the Cordillera through which the cross-section was made. I am quite unconvinced that this general shape is as widespread as Buffon and other famous physicists have believed. When one considers how little known is the eastern slope of the Andes, and how easy it is to confuse the lateral ranges with the high ridges separating the immense plains of the Beni, Purús, and Ucayali Rivers from the narrow Peruvian valley,

---

1. I described *Pimelodus cyclopum* in a separate memoir. See the first notebook of my *Observations de zoologie et d'anatomie comparée* [Observations on Zoology and Comparative Anatomy].

one must abstain from drawing any general conclusion about the relative incline of the two slopes. When I passed through the Andes Cordillera by the Páramo of Guamani where the Inca had a palace at an elevation of 3,300 meters (1,704 toises) and sketched some constructions similar to Cyclopean ones, when I went down toward the Amazon River and climbed from the province of Jaén of Bracamorros to Micuipampa, I ascertained that at the 3rd and 6th degrees of austral latitude the eastern slope is much less gentle than the one facing the South Sea. Mr. Haenke made the same observation in the Cochabamba province and in the fertile mountains of Chiquitos. Near Santa Fé de Bogotá, the eastern slope of the Cordillera is so steep that no Indian has been able to reach the plains of the Casanare River by way of the Chingasa Páramo.

The crevasse that I showed on the eastern slope of the Cordillera recalls to the observer's imagination one of those narrow valleys that earthquakes seem to have opened in the Andes. Some of them are so deep that Mount Vesuvius, Schneekoppe in Silesia, and the Puy-de-Dôme in Auvergne could be placed there without their peak reaching the height of the mountains nearest to the valley. The Chota valley, in the kingdom of Quito, is 1,566 meters deep (804 toises); the Río Cutacu valley in Peru has a perpendicular depth of over 1,364 meters (700 toises): and yet their floor is still higher above sea level by an equal distance. Their width is often under 1,200 meters (500 toises), and geologists can observe immense seams that nature did not fill with metallic substances. In the Pyrenees also, the Ordesa crevasse near the Mont-Perdu has an average depth of 896 meters (459 toises), according to Mr. Ramond.

At the easternmost extremity of the profile one can see the coasts of the Atlantic ocean, the plains of the Para River, and Brazil. In order to indicate how much longer this part of the picture should be than the rest, a break was made in this immense plain in which flow the Amazon and the Río Negro.

So far I have described the geological phenomena that I have attempted to show in this profile's contours. Let us now cast our eyes toward the interior. Here the geography of the equinoctial vegetation is represented in as great a detail as is possible within the limits of a single plate. Mr. Bonpland and I brought back collections containing over 6,000 species of tropical plants that we gathered ourselves during the course of our botanizing. Since we were also carrying out at the same time astronomical observations as well as geodetic and barometric measurements, our manuscripts contain materials that can determine exactly the position and elevation of these plants. We can show the breadth of the latitudinal zone occupied by these plants, their maximum and minimum elevation, the nature of the soil in which they grow, and the temperature of the plants' native soil.

Following my observations, I placed on the tableau, holding a compass in my hand, the names of the plants that nature put between two specific limits. Each name was entered according to the scale in meters given next to the picture. In order to indicate that the plant is situated on a certain stretch of the Cordillera's slope, the name was often written on a slant. We gave only the generic name when all the known species of the same genus grow at about the same height. Thus, *Escallonia*, *Wintera*, *Befaria*, and *Brathys* are found at the equator only at very great elevations; while *Avicennia*, *Coccoloba*, *Caesalpinia*, and *Bombax* are found only in places near sea level. The restricted framework in which I have given these results allowed me to name only a small number of species: if the public shows some interest in this work, I will follow up with more specialized maps for which all the materials are now ready. How could one show, in one general tableau, 150 species of *Melastoma*, 58 *Psychotria*, 38 *Passifloras*, and over 400 grasses that we brought back from equatorial regions, and which for the most part grow only at specific elevations designated by nature? Often, I was forced to repeat the name of the same genus in order to indicate that some species grow at 500 meters (256 toises) and others at 3,000 meters (1,539 toises). After being back in Europe for a few months, I did not dare to add to this tableau a large number of new genera which we will publish but whose names we are not yet sure about: I have indicated only a few curious plants that are being engraved at this moment and which will be published in the first and second sections of our *Equinoctial Plants*, such as *Cusparia febrifuga* (the valuable tree that gives the *Cortex angosturae* [angostura bark], a new genus with dull and alternate leaves); *Matisia cordata*, and the wax palm tree (*Ceroxylon andicola*) that Mr. Bonpland described in a separate publication.

In order to bring together the notions one should have about the situation of these plants from a perspective that is more general and more worthy of physics, I have divided this botanical map into regions, according to the analogy existing between forms occurring at different elevations. The names of these regions were engraved in larger letters, as one does for provinces on ordinary maps. Thus, in climbing up from the interior of the earth or from the interior of mines to the icy peaks of the Andes, one can see first *the region of subterranean plants*. These are the cryptogams with an often bizarre structure first studied by Scopoli, and on which I published a separate work (*Florae fribergensis Prodromus, plantas cryptogamicas, praesertim subterraneas, recensens* [Preliminary study of the Freiburg flora, listing the cryptogam plants, especially the subterranean ones] 1790). These are different in specific ways from the cryptogams found on the surface of the earth, and like a great number of them, they seem independent of latitude and climate. Growing in a profound and perpetual darkness, they blanket the walls of subterranean caves and the framework that supports the structures built by miners. I saw the same species (*Boletus ceratophora, Lichen verticillatus, Boletus botrytes, Gymnodermea sinuata, Byssus speciosa*) in the mines of Germany, England, and Italy, as in those of those of New Grenada and Mexico, and, in the southern hemisphere, in the mines of Hualgayoc in Peru.

At the same level as these underground cryptogams and in as intense a darkness, some *Fucus* and a few species of *Ulva* also grow, which can be removed with a probe and whose green color presents an interesting problem for physics to account for.

If we leave this multitude of underground plants, we find ourselves in a region where nature took pleasure in bringing together the most majestic forms and grouped them together in a most pleasant sight for the eyes: this is the region where palm trees and scitaminales grow, a region stretching from sea level to an altitude of 1,000 meters (513 toises); this is the homeland of *Musa, Heliconia, Alpinia*, of the most strongly scented liliaceae, and of palm trees. In this sizzling climate grow *Theophrasta, Plumeria, Mussaenda, Caesalpinia, Cecropia peltata, Hymenaea*, the balsam of Tolu, and the cusparia or quinquina tree of Carony. On the arid sea coasts, in the shade of coconut trees, of *Laurus persea* and *Mimosa inga*, one can find *Allionia, Conocarpus, Rhizophora mangle, Convolvulus littoralis* and *brasiliensis, Talinum, Avicennia, Cactus, Pereskia*, and *Sesuvium portulacastrum*.

Some plants in this region show striking particularities and are remarkable exceptions to the general laws of plant life. Palm trees in southern America, like those of the Old Continent, cannot withstand the cold temperatures of high mountains and cannot grow above an elevation of 1,000 meters (513 toises). One sole Andean palm tree has the extraordinary characteristic of being able to grow only at an elevation equal to that of the Mont-Cenis, and can even be found at altitudes equal to the Canigou. The only palm tree known till now to grow in the Alps, *Ceroxylon andicola*, grows in the Andes of Quindiu and Tolima, at a boreal latitude of 4°25', at an elevation ranging from 1,860 up to 2,870 meters (954 to 1,472 toises). Its trunk, covered with a wax just analyzed by Mr. Vauquelin, can reach a length of 54 meters.

In the accounts of Admiral Córdoba's expedition, it has been stated that a palm tree was found in the ravines at the Strait of Magellan, i.e. at the 53rd degree of austral latitude. This statement is all the more striking because it is impossible to mistake another plant for the palm tree, unless it is a treefern, the existence of which in that Strait would be no less curious. In Europe, *Chamaerops* and the date tree grow only up to 43°40' of latitude.

Scitaminales, and especially the species of *Heliconia* already described, grow at heights only up to 800 meters (410 toises). Near the Silla of Caracas, at an elevation of 2,150 meters (1,103 toises) above sea level, we found a kind of scitaminales 3 to 4 meters high (9 to 12 feet) and in such abundance that we had great difficulty carving out a path through it: we did not see its blossoms, but according to its overall appearance, it was a new species of *Heliconia* resistant to the low temperatures of these altitudes. *Sesuvium portulacastrum* covers the coasts of Cumaná and grows abundantly in the Perote plain east of the city of Mexico, at an elevation of 2,340 meters (1,200 toises) in a terrain saturated with carbonate and with sodium chloride. Plants in salt marshes seem to me in general to be less sensitive to differences in temperature and barometric pressure.

Above the regions where palm trees and scitaminales are found, are the regions with arborescent ferns and *Cinchona*. The latter is much more widespread than the tree-ferns that grow only in temperate climates, at elevations between 400 and 1,600 meters (205 and 820 toises). Quinquina trees, on the contrary, can grow at an altitude of up to 2,900 meters (1,487 toises) above sea level. The *Cinchona* species that bear up the best in cold temperatures are *Cinchona lancifolia* and Mr. Mutis's *Cinchona cordifolia*: those that grow at the lowest elevations in the plains are *Cinchona oblongifolia* and *Cinchona longiflora*. I found some beautiful trees of the latter species even at an elevation of 740 meters (379 toises). The famous Loja quinquina tree growing in the Caxanuma and Uritucinga forests, very different from the orange-colored quinquina tree of Santa Fé, grows at elevations from 1,900 to 2,500 meters (975 to 1,282 toises). It is a species that presents some analogies with the *Cinchona glandulifera* of the Peruvian flora, but is essentially different. It has so far been discovered only near Loja between the Río Zamora and the Río Cachiyaco, in the Jaén de Braca-morros province, near the village of Sagique, and in a small section of Peru near Huancabamba. It grows on micaceous schists; and in order to set aside completely the inexact name of *Cinchona officinalis*, we will call it henceforth *Cinchona condaminea*, because the illustrious astronomer Mr. de La Condamine first sketched it in that location.

Some travelers stated that they had discovered quinquina trees at elevations of 4,600 meters (2,360 toises), very close to the limit of perpetual snow; but they did not recognize *Wintera* and a few species of *Weinmannia*, whose bark contain abundant tannins and are also used with success as a febrifuge. We saw no true *Cinchona* trees above 2,900 meters nor below 700 meters (1,487 and 359 toises); the quinquina tree in the Philippines described by Cavanilles, and the one recently discovered on the Island of Cuba in the Guines valley, seem to belong to a different genus.

Rubber is produced by plants that have few similarities, by *Ficus, Hevea, Lobelia, Castilloa*, and several euphorbia. Camphor is also found in plants that do not belong to the same genus: in Asia one finds it in a laurel tree; in Peru, in the fertile Cochabamba province, one can find it in a didynamous bush that Mr. Haenke discovered growing abundantly near Ayopaya. The fruit of *Myrica* and the trunk of a palm tree produce wax. Some substances whose chemical properties are the same are furnished by plants with very different structures: the same applies to the fever-reducing capacities of the quinquina tree that exist in plants not belonging to the same genus.

The cusparia of the Caroní River plains near the city of Upatu, that majestic tree that gives *Cortex angosturae*, belongs to a very different genus from the *Cinchona*. *Cuspa* or *Cumaná quina*, whose blossoms we have not been able to obtain till now, has alternate leaves without stipules: it does not belong to the genus *Cinchona*, even though it would be difficult for a chemist to tell a *Cuspa* infusion from one of the yellow quinquina of Santa Fé. On the coasts of the South Sea west of Popayán near Atacamez, a tree grows having the properties of *Cinchona* and *Wintera*, and which no doubt is different from both of these genera. The cusparia in Guyana, the *Cuspa* of New Andalusia, and the *Cascarilla* of Atacamez all grow at sea level, and nature prepares in their sap a substance analogous to that of the true quinquina trees growing at an elevation of 2,800 meters (1,436 toises).

In the narrative of my journey to the tropics, I will publish a *botanical map of the Cinchona genus*. It will show the places in both hemispheres where this interesting tree is found. It will show that it grows in the Andes Cordillera in an area over 700 leagues long. One will be able to see the *Cinchona* trees in an area from the Potosí region and the Plata River, situated at the 20th degree of austral latitude, up to the snow-covered mountains of Santa Marta at the 11th degree of boreal latitude. The entire eastern slope of the Andes, south of Huánuco, near the Tipuani mines, in the environs of Apollobamba and Yuracarées, is an uninterrupted forest of quinquina trees. Mr. Haenke saw that it stretches almost up to Santa Cruz of the Sierra. It does not seem that this tree grows any further to the east; it has not been found up till now in the Brazilian mountains, even though the Chiquitos Cordillera seems to link them with the Peruvian Andes. From La Paz on, *Cinchona* continue to grow throughout the provinces of Gualias and Gumalias, and into Huancabamba and Loja. In the east, they grow in the province of Jaén de Bracamorros, and even crown the hilltops near the Amazon River, near the famous Pongo de Manseriche. From Loja on, the quinquina tree goes as far as Cuenca and Alausi in the Quito kingdom: it is abundant east of Chimborazo; but it seems to be missing entirely in the whole high plateau of Riobamba and Quito, as in the Pasto province up to Almaguer. Have the great volcanic catastrophes that frequently wrack this country decreased the number of species? In general, we have observed that vegetation is less varied there than in other regions with the same elevation above sea level. North of Almaguer, which I found to be at 1°51′57″ of boreal latitude in the province of Popayán, quinquina trees are again abundant. They grow almost without interruption throughout the Andes of Quindiu, the Vega-de-Supia, the fertile hills of Mariquita, Guaduas, and Pamplona, up to the mountains of Mérida and Santa Marta, where waters of boiling hydro-sulfuric springs mingle with those of melting snows.

Silla-de-Caracas and a few mountains in the Cumaná province (Tumiriquiri, the environs of the Caripé convent, and the Guanaguana mountain pass) have an elevation of 1,300 to 2,500 meters (667 to 1,282 toises), and consequently they provide cool enough temperatures for *Cinchona* to grow there. The same applies to the kingdom of New Spain, whose high plateau has a climate quite similar to Peru's. However, up till now, no one has discovered any *Cinchona* either in the Cumaná province nor in Mexico. Could this phenomenon be accounted for by the scarcity of mountains surrounding the high peaks of the Santa Marta and those of Guamoco? The ridge of the Andes Cordillera disappears almost entirely between the Cupica Gulf and the delta of the Río Atracto. The Panama isthmus is below the lower limit of *Cinchona*. Has this plant, in its migration to the north, encountered obstacles in the too great heat of the climate in those regions? or in time, will not the quinquina tree be found in the beautiful Jalapa forests east of Vera Cruz, where the nature of the soil, the tree-ferns, the melastome trees, the temperate climate, and the humid air all seem to proclaim to the botanist that he will find this beneficial tree he has so far vainly searched for in this region?

In the temperate regions of the *Cinchona*, some Liliaceae grow, for example *Cypura* and *Sisyrinchium*, *Melastoma* with large purple flowers, passiflora trees that are as tall as our northern oaks, *Bocconia frutescens*, *Thibaudia*, *Fuchsia*, and *Alstroemeria* of rare beauty. This is where the *Macrocnemum*, *Lysianthus*, and cucullaires soar majestically. The ground there is covered with *Koelreutera*, *Weissia*, *Dicranum*, *Tetraphis*, and other mosses that are always green. In the ravines hide *Gunnera*, *Dorstenia*, *Oxalis*, and a multitude of unknown *Arum*. At an elevation of about 1,700 meters (872 toises) one finds *Porlieria hygrometrica*, which has been identified thanks to Messrs Ruiz and Pavon, *Citrosma* with scented leaves and fruit, *Eroteum*, *Hypericum baccatum* and *cayenense*, and many species of *Symplocos*. Above 2,200 meters (1,129 toises), we have not found any mimosas whose irritable leaves fold upon contact: the cool temperatures of these elevated regions set this limit to their irritability. Above 2,600 meters (1,334 toises) and especially at an altitude of 3,000 meters (1,539 toises), *Acaena*, *Dichondra*, *Nierembergia*, *Hydrocotile*, *Nerteria*, and *Alchemilla* make a thick lawn. This is the region of *Weinmannia*, oaks, *Vallea stipularis*, and *Spermacoce*. There *Mutisia* climbs on the tallest trees.

In equatorial regions, oaks (*Quercus granatensis*) grow only at an elevation above 1,700 meters (872 toises). In Mexico, under the 17th and 22nd degrees of latitude, I have seen them grow at altitudes as low as 800 meters (410 toises). Sometimes these oak trees indicate in springtime the changing of the seasons at the equator: they lose all their leaves, and one can see new leaves replacing them, whose young green color mingles with that of *Epidendrum* growing on their branches.

A new genus of malvaceae, *Cheirosthemon*, on which Mr. Cervantes, a botany professor in Mexico, published an interesting monograph, is also found in these elevated regions; but its flower, with its bizarre structure, has not been discovered up till now in the Peruvian Andes. For a long time, only one example was known, in the suburbs of the city of Toluca in Mexico. It grows wild in the Guatemala kingdom, and the famous hand-tree of Toluca was most likely planted there by some Rointztèques peoples. The gardens in Iztapalapan, whose remains Hernandez was able to glimpse, are a witness to the taste that the peoples whom we call savage and barbarians had for cultivation and for the beauties of the plant kingdom.

Near the equator, tall trees whose trunk exceeds 20 to 30 meters (10 to 15 toises) do not grow above an elevation of 2,700 meters (1,385 toises). From the level of the city of Quito on, the trees are not as tall and their height is not comparable to that of the same species growing in the most temperate climates. Above 3,500 meters (1,796 toises) there are almost no trees; but at this elevation, bushes are all the more common: this is the region of berberis, of *Duranta ellisii* and *mutisii*, and *Barnadesia*. The plateaus of Pasto and Quito are characterized by such plants, just as the region of Santa Fé is characterized by *Polymnia* and *Datura* trees. *Castelleja integrifolia* and *fissifolia*, *Columella*, the beautiful *Embothryum emarginatum*, and *Clusia* with four anthers are common in this region. The ground is covered with a multitude of calceolaria, whose gold-colored corolla makes a pleasing contrast with the green color of the lawn where they grow. Nature assigned them a particular zone: this zone begins at one degree of boreal latitude. Messrs Ruiz and Pavon, who conducted scientific research in Chile, will be able to indicate how far calceolaria extend in the austral hemisphere. Higher, on the summit of the Cordillera, from 2,800 meters to 3,300 meters (1,436 toises to 1,693 toises), lies the region of *Wintera* and *Escallonia*. The climate of these regions, cold but constantly humid, called *páramos* by the natives, produces bushes whose short, carbon-covered trunks divide into a multitude of branches covered with tough and shiny green leaves. A few orange quinquina trees, *Embothryum*, and *Melastoma* with purple, almost scarlet flowers, can grow at these elevations. *Alstonia*, whose dried leaves make a beneficial tea, *Wintera granatensis*, and *Escallonia tubar* which stretches out its leaves like an umbrella, grow in scattered groups. Underneath them grow some small *Lobelia*, bassella, and *Swertia quadricornis*.

Still higher, at 3,500 meters (1,796 toises), trees cease to grow, as I stated previously. Only on the Pichincha volcano, in a narrow valley going down from the Guagua Pichincha, have we discovered a group of [singenèses en arbre], with trunks 7 or 8 meters high (21 or 24 feet). From 2,000 meters to 4,100 meters (1,026 to 2,103 toises), this is the region of alpine plants: *Staehelina*, gentians, and *Espeletia frailexon*, whose furry leaves are often used as shelter by unfortunate Indians surprised by night in these regions. The carpet is adorned with *Lobelia nana*, *Sida pichinchensis*, *Ranunculus gusmani*, *Ribes frigidum*, *Gentiana quitensis*, and many other new species of plants that we will describe in our *Plantes équinoxiales* [Equinoctial Plants]. *Molina* are smaller bushes that we encountered at their greatest altitude on the Puracé volcano, near Popayán, and on the Antisana volcano.

At an altitude of 4,100 meters (2,103 toises), alpine plants make way for grasses,[1] whose region stretches up to 4,600 meters (2,360 toises). *Jarava*, *Stipa*, a multitude of new species of *Panicum*, *Agrostis*, *Avena*, and *Dactylis* cover the ground. From afar it looks like a golden carpet, called by the inhabitants of the region *pajonal*. From time to time snow falls on this region of grasses.

At an altitude of 4,600 meters (2,360 toises), there are no more phanerogams at the equator. From this elevation to that

1. La Condamine, *Voyage à l'Équateur* [Voyage to the Equator], p. 48.

of perpetual snow, only lichenous plants cover the rocks. Some seem to hide even under the perpetual ice; for at 5,554 meters (2,850 toises) of altitude, near the Chimborazo summit, I found on a rocky ridge *Umbilicaria pustulata* and *Verrucaria geographica*: those are the last organized beings we found in the ground at these great heights.

These are the principal characteristics of vegetation in the physical tableau of equatorial regions; it would be desirable to have a similar one for Europe. There are so many data not given in the classic works of Messrs Pallas, Jacquin, Wulfen, Lapeyrouse, Schranck, Villars, Host, and a great number of traveling naturalists. The famous botanists who traveled through the Alps of Salzburg, the Tyrol, and Styria, those who saw the high peaks of Switzerland and Savoy, would be able to furnish botanical maps much more complete than the one I am offering today to the public. Who has more precious materials for this work than the one[1] who, on the peaks of the Pyrenees, discovered that immense deposit of organic debris, who, equally knowledgeable in geology and botany, possesses both the art of observing well and the talent of speaking to the imagination?

I have already discussed the reasons why the phenomena of the geography of plants cannot be as varied nor as constant at the 45th degree of latitude as they are at the equator. Despite this disadvantage, a *Tableau physique des climats tempérés* [Physical Tableau of Temperate Climates] would nevertheless be very interesting. At its center, one would see the Mont-Blanc in the high European mountain range rise to 4,775 meters (2,448 toises). The slopes of this range would stretch on one side toward the Atlantic, and on the other toward the Mediterranean basin, where *Chamaerops*, date trees, and several plants on the Atlas mountains foreshadow the proximity of Africa. In this depiction, perpetual snow would descend to an altitude of 2,550 meters (1,307 toises) above sea level, that is to say, at an altitude where, at the equator, grow wax palm trees,

1. The author of *Observations faites dans les Pyrénées* [Observations Made in the Pyrenees], and of the *Voyages au Mont-Perdu* [Voyages to the Mont-Perdu], Mr. Ramond.

quinquina, and the most vigorous trees. Thus the zone in Europe between the level of the ocean and perpetual snow is half as narrow as in the tropical regions; but the snowcap covering the highest peaks of Europe, the Mont-Blanc and the Mont-Rose, is wider by 600 meters (308 toises) than the one covering Chimborazo. On the craggy rocks that rise above the limits of perpetual snow and remain bare because of the steepness of their slopes, in the Alps surrounding the Mont-Blanc at more than 3,100 meters (1,590 toises) of altitude, the following plants grow: *Androsace chamaejasma*, Jacq.; *Silene acaulis*, growing as low as 1,500 meters (769 toises) that Saussure found growing at 3,468 meters (1,778 toises); *Saxifraga androsacea*, *Cardamine alpina*, *Arabis caerulea*, Jacq., and *Draba hirta* of Villars, which is *Draba stellata*, Wild. At these great heights *Myosotis perennis* also grows, and *Androsace carnea*, whose stems become gradually smaller. The latter finally has only a single blossom and is found above 1,000 meters up to 3,100 meters (513 to 1,590 toises). In the Pyrenees, the highest regions from 2,400 to 3,400 meters (1,231 to 1,744 toises) are adorned with *Cerastium lanatum*, Lam., *Saxifraga groenlandica*, *Saxifraga androsacea*, *Aretia alpina*, and *Artemisia rupestris*. *Cerastium lanatum* does not even grow below 2,600 meters (1,333 toises). In the Alps, from 2,500 meters to 3,100 meters (1,282 to 1,590 toises), on the debris of rocks and gravel surrounding the permanent snow, and on the highest glaciers, the following plants grow: *Saxifraga biflora*, Allion., *Saxifraga oppositifolia*, *Achillea nana*, *Achillea atrata*, *Artemisia glacialis*, *Gentiana nivalis*, *Ranunculus alpestris*, *Ranunculus glacialis*, and *Juncus trifidus*. In the high mountain range of the Pyrenees at 3,000 meters (1,539 toises) and even at 1,500 meters lower (769 toises) are found: *Potentilla lupinoides*, Wild., *Silene acaulis*, *Sibbaldia procumbens*, *Carex curvula*, and *Carex nigra*, Allion., *Sempervivum montanum* and *Sempervivum arachnoideum*, *Arnica scorpioides*, *Androsace villosa*, and *Androsace carnea*. In the Alps, between 2,300 and 2,500 meters (1,180 and 1,282 toises), at the height reached by the edge of snows and glaciers, these plants grow not on stones but in a fertile soil, in fields moistened by highly oxygenated waters from melting snow, on a lawn of *Agrostis alpina*: *Saxifraga aspera* and *bryoides, Soldanella alpina, Viola biflora, Primula farinosa, Primula viscosa, Alchemilla pentaphyllea, Salix herbacea* that grows higher than any other woody plant, *Salix reticulata*, and *Salix retusa. Tussilago farfara* and *Statice armeria* also grow from the plains up to 2,600 meters (1,333 toises) of elevation. In the Pyrenees are found at these elevations *Scutellaria alpina, Senecio persicifolius, Ranunculus alpestris, Ranunculus parnassifolius, Galium pyrenaicum,* and *Aretia vitaliana.* Above the lower limit of perpetual snow, between 1,500 and 2,500 meters (769 and 1,028 toises), in the Savoy Alps, grow the following: *Eriophorum scheuchzeri, Eriophorum alpinum, Gentiana purpurea, Gentiana grandiflora, Saxifraga stellaris, Azalea procumbens, Tussilago alpina. Passerina geminiflora, Passerina nivalis, Merendera bulbocodium, Crocus multifidus, Fritillaria meleagris,* and *Anthemis montana* grow in the Pyrenees at the same elevation. *Genista lusitanica, Ranunculus gouani, Narcissus bicolor, Rubus saxatilis,* and a number of gentians are found lower. *Rhododendrum ferrugineum* usually prefers elevations between 1,500 and 2,500 meters (769 to 1,282 toises); however, Mr. Decandolle, to whom I owe these observations on the Alps, also saw it in the Jura mountains, at the bottom of Creux-du-Vent at 970 meters (498 toises) above sea level.

Linnaea borealis, which grows at sea level near Berlin, in Sweden, in the United States, and in the Nootka Sound, grows in the Swiss Alps at 500 and 700 meters (256 and 359 toises) of elevation. One can find it in the Valais along the edges of the torrent flowing under the Tête Noire; on the Saint-Gothard, where Haller saw it first; near Geneva on the Voirons mountain, according to Saussure; and even in France, near Montpellier, on the Espinouse.

Trees whose trunks exceed 5 meters (2.5 toises) grow at the equator at elevations barely up to 3,500 meters (1,796 toises). In the kingdom of New Spain at the 20th degree of latitude, a pine tree similar to *Pinus strobus* grows as high as 3,934 meters (2,018 toises); oaks grow as high as 3,100 meters (1,590 toises). The naturalist who is not aware of this phenomenon of plant geography would believe, simply from looking at them, that these mountains covered with pines at very high altitudes cannot be equal in height to the Tenerife peak. In the Pyrenees, Mr. Ramond observed that the two trees growing at the highest altitudes on the mountain peaks are *Pinus sylvestris* and *Pinus mugho*; they are found at altitudes between 2,000 and 2,400 meters (1,026 and 1,231 toises). *Abies taxifolia* and *Taxus communis* begin at 1,400 meters (718 toises) and go as far as 2,000 meters (1,026 toises). *Fagus sylvatica* occupies an intermediate region, from 600 to 1,800 meters (308 to 923 toises): but *Quercus robur*, found in the plains, can go only as far as 1,600 meters (821 toises); it stops growing 200 meters (102 toises) higher than the inferior limit for *Pinus mugho*.

Mr. Ramond[1] also furnished me with very interesting observations on the maximum and minimum altitudes at which species belonging to the same genus are found. Choosing the genera *Primula, Ranunculus, Daphne, Erica, Gentiana,* and *Saxifraga*, I present here a table showing the altitudes where each of the species making up these genera grows in the Pyrenees:

		Meters	Toises
Gentiana	*pneumonanthe*	0 to 800	0 to 400
	verna	600−3000	300−1540
	acaulis	1000−3000	500−1540
	campestris	1000−2400	500−1200
	ciliata	1200−1800	600−900
	lutea	1200−1600	600−800
	punctata, Villars	1600−2000	800−1000
Daphne	*laureola*	300−2000	150−1000
	mezereum	1000−2000	500−1000
	cneorum	2000−2400	1000−1200
Primula	*eliator*	0−2200	0−1100
	integrifolia	1500−2000	750−1000
	villosa	1800−2400	900−1200

1. See also his botanical observations in his *Voyage au sommet du Mont-Perdu* [Voyage to the Summit of Mont-Perdu], 1803, p. 21; and his *Mémoire sur les plantes alpines* [Memoir on Alpine Plants] in the *Annales d'histoire naturelle* [Annals of Natural History].

		Meters	Toises
Ranunculus	*aquatilis*	0–2100	0–1050
	gouani	500–2000	250–1000
	thora	1400–2000	700–1000
		1500–2400	750–1200
	alpestris	1800–2600	900–1300
	amplexicaulis	1800–2400	900–1200
	nivalis	2000–2800	1000–1400
	parnassifolius	2400–2800	1200–1400
	glacialis	2400–3200	1200–1640
Saxifraga	*tridactylides*	0– 40	0– 20
	geum	400–1600	200– 800
	longifolia	800–2400	400–1200
	aizoon	800–2400	400–1200
	pyramidalis	1200–2000	600–1000
	exarata	1400–1800	700– 900
	cespitosa	1600–3000	800–1540
	oppositifolia	1600–3400	800–1740
	umbrosa	1400–1800	700– 900
	granulata	1200–1600	600– 800
	groenlandica	2400–3400	1200–1740
	androsacea	2400–3400	1200–1740
Erica	*vagans*	0– 900	0– 450
	vulgaris	0–2000	0–1000
	tetralix	500–2400	250–1200
	arborea	550– 700	270– 350

The saxifrages in Tyrol present the same characteristics as those of the Pyrenees. Count Sternberg, who botanized in these mountains and on the Baldo and to whom we owe a description of its geology, communicated to me an interesting note on the Rhododendrums and other alpine plants. I owe it to these botanists and to the physicists to insert this note here in its entirety. Mr. Sternberg writes:

Unless there is a particular local circumstance, the region where *Rhododendrum* grows is hardly ever below 876 to

974 meters (450 to 500 toises). I did not find them lower than 100 meters (50 toises) above the Wallersee in Bavaria, which is 817 meters (420 toises) above sea level. *Rhododendrum chamaecistus* does go as low as *ferrugineum* and *hirsutum*. Besides, I have found them growing equally on primary limestone and on secondary limestone, in the *Sette communi* and on Mount Sumano that is 1,277 meters high (656 toises): they accompanied me up to an altitude of 1,950 meters (1,000 toises).

The most extensive region of alpine saxifrages appears to me to be in the Tyrolean Alps. I found *Saxifraga cotyledon* and *aizoon* in the Eiszach valley between Brixen and Botzen at 360 meters (184 toises) of altitude. They accompanied me till the Grappa summit, near Bassano, at 1,684 meters (865 toises). *Saxifraga caesia, aspera*, and *androsacea* are found in the intermediate region; above, one finds *Saxifraga autumnalis, mucosa, moschata*, and *petraea*; the highest-growing ones are usually *Saxifraga burseriana* and *bryoides* that cover the Baldo summit at 2,225 meters (1,143 toises). Primulas, especially *farinosa, auricula, marginata*, and *viscosa*, are not found in the Tyrolean Alps below 801 meters (417 toises). Representing a singular anomaly, *Primula farinacea* grows in the Regensburg plain. As for *Ranunculus glacialis* and *Ranunculus seguierii*, I never observed them growing below 1,950 meters (1,000 toises) of elevation.

However, in order to complete the geography of plants, it would not suffice to compose tableaux of the regions near the poles, the ones with temperate climates from 40 to 50 degrees of latitude, and the equatorial ones; it would not suffice to describe the austral and the boreal hemispheres, because the plants in Chiloé and Buenos Aires are very different from the ones in Spain and Greece: one would also have to furnish separate tableaux for the New and the Old Continents. Madagascar with its high granitic peaks perpetually covered in snow according to Commerson, with its coasts so well researched by Mr. du Petit-Thouars, the Adam peak on Ceylon, the island

of Sumatra, where the Ophyr cone rises, according to
Marsden, to an altitude of 3,949 meters (2,027 toises), all these
could furnish precious materials for the tableaux of the equatorial regions of Africa and the East Indies. The illustrious
Pallas might be able to determine the geography of plants in
the temperate climates in Asia. Mr. Barton, who is equally
versed in zoology, botany, and the study of Indian languages,
is currently conducting this type of research in the temperate
zones of the United States. There the mountains are no higher
than 2,000 meters (1,026 toises);[1] the height of 3,100 meters
(1,582 toises) attributed to the White Mountain in New
Hampshire by Messrs Cutler and Belknap is no doubt exaggerated. Mr. Barton does not find in his homeland the same
variety of phenomena present in the highest of the Cordilleras;
but this lack is largely compensated by the great variety of
arborescent plants found in the beautiful plains of Pennsylvania, Carolina, and Virginia. In the United States, there are
almost three times the number of oak species as the number
of different species of large trees present in all of Europe. The
aspect of vegetation in the New Continent is more varied and
more pleasant than in the old at the same latitude. *Gleditschia*,
tulip trees, and magnolias contrast in a most picturesque
manner with the dark foliage of *Thula* and the pines: one can
imagine that nature took pleasure in adorning a soil that would
be inhabited one day by an energetic and industrious people
worthy of enjoying peacefully all the benefits given to them
by a free society.

But the physical tableau of the equinoctial regions is useful
not only for developing new ideas regarding the geography of
plants; I believe that it could also help us understand the total-
ity of our knowledge about everything that varies with the altitudes rising above sea level. This consideration encouraged
me to bring together in 14 scales many numbers resulting from
the large quantity of research conducted in various branches
of general physics. These scales being self-explanatory, it will

---

1. See the work of Mr. Volney containing a broad description of the structure of
the planet in the northern part of the New Continent.

be sufficient to add only few words on their composition. The scales indicating the temperature, the air's hygroscopic state and its electrical tension, the blue color of the sky, the geological aspects, the cultivation of the soil, and the diversity of animals according to altitude, all these are based on my observations made during my expedition, which will be developed in further detail in the account of my travel to the equator.

From

VIEWS OF NATURE

1849

Translated by Mark W. Person

PREFACE TO THE FIRST EDITION

I HUMBLY EXTEND to the public a series of works that came into being within the contemplation of great objects in Nature, upon the ocean, in the forests of the Orinoco, in the steppes of Venezuela, in the wilderness of the Peruvian and Mexican mountains. Individual fragments were recorded at the place and time and only later forged together as a whole. A far-reaching overview of Nature, proof of the cooperation of forces, and a renewal of the delight that direct experience of the tropics gives to a person of feeling are the goals to which I strive. Each essay should of itself constitute a complete whole, but in each should be the equal expression of one and the same tendency. This aesthetic treatment of matters of natural history, despite the wonderful power and flexibility of the language of our native land, carries with it tremendous difficulties of composition. The richness of Nature encourages an agglomeration of individual images that disturbs the calmness and the overall impression of the portrait. In appealing to feeling and fancy, style easily degenerates into poetic prose. These ideas are here in need of no development, as the following pages offer manifold examples of such aberrations, of such a lack of composure.

May my *Views of Nature*, in spite of these flaws which I, myself, can more easily criticize than improve, provide the reader with but a portion of the enjoyment that a receptive mind finds in immediate inspection. Since this enjoyment is increased with insight into the interconnectedness of natural forces, each essay is accompanied by scientific annotations and additions.

Throughout, I have indicated the eternal influence that physical Nature exerts upon the moral disposition of Humanity and upon its fate. To embattled minds particularly, these pages are dedicated. '*Who saves himself from life's stormy wave*' will follow me gladly into the thickets of the forest, into the immeasurable steppes, and out upon the spine of the Andes range. Unto him speaks the world-directing chorus:

> In the mountains is freedom! The breath of the tomb
> Cannot climb up to the purest air's home,
> The world is perfect anywhere,
> If Humanity's anguish has not entered there.

PREFACE TO THE SECOND
AND THIRD EDITIONS

THE DUAL DIRECTION of this text (a painstaking effort to heighten the enjoyment of Nature through living depictions, while simultaneously increasing insight into the harmonious cooperative effect of forces according to the state of scientific understanding of the time) was delineated in the preface to the first edition nearly a half-century ago. The manifold hindrances inherent in the aesthetic treatment of great scenes in Nature were already indicated then. The combination of a literary with a purely scientific goal, the desire to occupy the imagination and at the same time, through the increase of knowledge, to enrich life with ideas, renders the ordering of the individual parts and the demands of unity of composition difficult to achieve. Despite these unfavorable conditions, the public has long granted the imperfect execution of my undertaking their charitable goodwill.

I oversaw the second edition of *Views of Nature* in Paris in the year 1826. Two articles – an essay 'Concerning the Structure and Action of Volcanoes in Various Regions of the Earth' and 'The Life Force, or The Rhodian *Genius*' – were added at that time. During my long stay in Jena, Schiller, in memory of the medical studies of his youth, enjoyed discussing physiological matters with me. My work on the disposition of stimulated muscle and nerve fibers through contact with chemically differing materials often led our discussions in a more serious direction. The short article on life force originates from this time. Schiller's fondness for the 'Rhodian *Genius*', which he accepted for publication in his journal *Die Horen*, gave me the courage to have it printed again. In a letter that has just recently been published (Wilhelm von Humboldt's *Briefe an eine Freundin*, part II, p. 39), my brother gently touches upon the same matter, but aptly adds: 'The development of a physiological idea is the goal of the entire essay. At the time in which it was written, there was more love than one would find now for such half-poetic adornment of serious truths.'

In my eightieth year I have had the joy of completing a third edition of my book and completely recasting it in accordance with the needs of the time. Nearly all scientific annotations have been either amended or replaced by new, more comprehensive ones. It has been my hope thereby to enliven the drive to study Nature such that, even in the smallest of spaces, the most diverse results of thoroughgoing observation might be concentrated, that the importance of exact numerical data and the thoughtful collation thereof be recognized and steered toward the dogmatic half-truths as well as the proper skepticism that have long had their place among the so-called higher circles of society.

The expedition to northern Asia (in the Urals, the Altai, and to the banks of the Caspian Sea) that I undertook in 1829 in cooperation with Ehrenberg and Gustav Rose at the command of the Emperor of Russia falls between the epochs of the second and third editions of my book. It contributed substantially to the broadening of my views in all matters concerning surface formation, the course of mountain ranges, the connection between steppes and deserts, and the proliferation of plant life in relation to measured temperature influences. The ignorance that has so long prevailed regarding the two great snow-covered mountain ranges between the Altai and the Himalayas, the Tien-Shan and the Kunlun, along with the unjustified disregarding of Chinese sources, has obscured understanding of the geography of inner Asia and, in widely read texts, has passed off fantasy as the result of observation. In just the last few months, important and rectifying elucidations have come back which were nearly unexpected in the hypsometric comparison of the culminating peaks of both continents and which will be presented for the first time in the following work (*Concerning the Steppes and Deserts*, notes 5 and 10). Now free of earlier error, the height measurements of two mountains in the eastern Andes range of Bolivia, the Sorata and the Illimani, have not yet with certainty

restored to Chimborazo its standing among the highest mountains of the new continent, while in the Himalayas, new trigonometric measurement of Kinchinjinga (26,438 Parisian feet)
open for this peak the next place behind Dhawalagiri, which
now has also been measured with greater trigonometric
accuracy.

To ensure numerical consistency with the two earlier editions of *Views of Nature*, the temperature data in this work,
unless specifically stated otherwise, are expressed in the 80-
degree Réaumurian thermometer. The foot measure is the old
French, where the toise counts as 6 Parisian feet. The miles
are geographical, 15 of which constitute one equatorial degree.
Longitude is reckoned from the first meridian of the Paris
Observatory.

Berlin, March 1849

I

CONCERNING THE STEPPES
AND DESERTS

AT THE FOOT of the high granite spine that, in the early days of our planet, defied the incursion of the waters during the formation of the Antillean Gulf, there begins a broad, immeasurable plain. Upon leaving behind the valleys of Caracas and the island-rich Lake Tacarigua, which reflects in its surface the trunks of the pisang trees, leaving behind fields resplendent with the delicate light green of Tahitian sugarcane or the solemn shade of cacao plants, one's gaze toward the South comes to rest upon steppes that, seeming to climb, dwindle into the distant horizon.

From the luxuriant fullness of organic life, the astonished wanderer comes to the barren edge of a sparse and treeless desert. No hill, no cliff rises as an island in this incalculable space. Only broken, stratified slabs two hundred square miles in area, lying here and there, show themselves visibly higher than the parts bordering them. The natives call these phenomena 'banks,' indicating instinctively through the half-awareness of language the state of things that once were, for these elevations were the shallows, and the steppes themselves the bed, of a great inland sea.

Even now, the disguise of night often calls back these pictures of the past. When the guiding celestial bodies in their rapid rising and setting illuminate the edge of the plain, or when they create a quivering double image of it in the lower layer of the undulating haze, one believes he sees before him the boundless oceans. Like the ocean, the steppe fills the mind with the feeling of infinity, and through this feeling, as if pulling free of sensory impression, with intellectual and spiritual inspiration of a higher order. But while the clear ocean surface in which ripples the graceful, softly foaming wave is a friendly sight, dead and stiff lies the steppe, stretched out like the naked rocky crust of a desolate planet.

In all zones of the globe, Nature offers this phenomenon of immense plains; each has a character of its own, a physiognomy determined by the individuality of its terrain, by its climate, and by its distance above sea level.

One can view as true steppes the heathlands of Northern Europe, which, covered by one single, all-supplanting variety of flora, stretch from the point of Jutland to the outlet of the Scheldt, although smaller and hillier than the Llanos and Pampas of South America or the grassy plains near the Missouri and Coppermine Rivers, on which the shaggy Bison and the small Musk-ox abound.

The plains of the African interior offer a greater and more serious vista. As with the broad expanses of the Pacific Ocean, only recently have attempts to explore them begun. These plains are part of an ocean of sand that in the east separates fertile strips of land from one another, or encompasses them, forming islands, like the deserts below the basalt mountain range of Harutsch, where the ruins of the Ammon Temple in the date-rich Oasis of Siwa mark the noble spot of early human civilization. No dew, no rain moistens these desolate areas to nurture the germination of plant life in the glowing womb of the earth. For everywhere, columns of heated air climb upward, dispelling the vapors and chasing away the fleeing clouds.

Where the desert approaches the Atlantic Ocean, as between *Wadi Nun* and the White Cape, the moist sea air streams in to fill the emptiness created by these upward winds. Even the mariner who steers for the mouth of the Gambia through a sea covered like a meadow with kelp senses, when the tropical east wind suddenly leaves him, the nearness of the sand, expansive and radiant with heat.

Herds of gazelle and fleet-footed ostrich run about the immeasurable space. Except for the recently discovered groups of water-rich islands in this ocean of sand, upon whose green shores swarm the nomadic Tibbos and Tuaryks, the remainder of the African desert may be viewed as uninhabitable by Man. Indeed, the civilized peoples of bordering regions only periodically dare to enter it. Upon paths that trade traffic has inalterably determined for millennia moves the long caravan from Tafilet to Timbuktu or from Murzuk to Bornu: bold undertakings whose very possibility depends upon the existence of the camel, the Ship of the Desert, as he is called in the old legends of the Eastern world. These African expanses fill an area that surpasses that of the nearby Mediterranean Sea threefold. They lie in part within the tropics themselves, in part near them, and this situation gives rise to the individual character of their nature. But in the eastern half of the Old Continent, this same geognostic phenomenon is more typical of the temperate zone.

Upon the ridge of Central Asia between the Golden Mountains, or Altai, and the Kunlun, from the Chinese Wall to the far side of the Celestial Mountains and around the Aral Sea to the northwest, over a length of several thousand miles, are scattered the largest, if not the highest, steppes in the world. I myself have had the opportunity to see, full thirty years after my South American journey, a part of these: the Kalmykian and the Kyrgyz steppes, which lie between the Don, the Volga, the Caspian Sea, and the Chinese Lake Dsaisang, that is to say, over a stretch of almost 700 geographical miles. The occasionally hilly Asiatic Steppes, interrupted now and again by forests of spruce, have a vegetation that, grouped in different areas, is much more variegated than that of the Llanos and Pampas of Caracas and Buenos Aires. The fairer part of the plain, populated by Asiatic shepherd folk, is adorned with shrubs of abundantly blooming white Rosaceae, with Crown Imperial (Fritillaria), tulips, and Cypripedia. Just as the torrid zone is consistently distinguished by the striving of all vegetation to grow in arborescent form, so too are some steppes of the Asiatic temperate zone characterized by the wondrous heights reached by their blooming herbs: Saussureae and other Synanthereae, leguminous plants, especially a host of various types of Astragalus. When one travels in the low-slung Tartar carriages over the trackless parts of these

herb-covered steppes, only by standing upright can one orient oneself and thus see the densely packed forest of plants
that bow before the wheels. Some of these Asiatic steppes
are grass plains; others are covered with succulent, evergreen
articulated alkali plants, many of them gleaming with salts
that sprout up like lichens, unevenly covering the clay-rich
soil like new-fallen snow.

These Mongolian and Tartar steppes, interrupted by
numerous mountain ranges, separate the long-civilized
humanity of Tibet and Hindustan from the barbarous peoples
of Northern Asia. The existence of these steppes has been of
tremendous influence on the changing fate of the human race.
They have forced human population southward; they have
hindered the intercourse of nations more than the Himalayas,
more than the snow-peaked ranges of Srinigar and Gorka, and
they have set unchallengeable limits in Northern Asia to the
dissemination of milder customs and the creative artistic
spirit.

But history must not view the plain of Inner Asia only as an
impeding barrier. It has also on numerous occasions brought
calamity and devastation across the globe. Shepherd peoples
of these steppes – the Mongols, the Getae, the Alani, and the
Uysyn – have shaken the world. Over the course of the centuries, whenever early intellectual culture has traveled like
revitalizing sunlight from east to west, so too have barbarism
and rawness of custom subsequently threatened to creep over
Europe like a fog. A brown shepherd tribe (Tukiuish, i.e.,
Turkic), the Xiongnu, populated the high steppes of the Gobi
in leather tents. Long a threat to the might of the Chinese, part
of the tribe was forced southward into Inner Asia. These dislodged people spread inexorably as far as the old home of the
Finns on the Ural. From there poured forth Huns, Avars,
Chasars, and numerous mixed Asiatic races. Hunnish armies
first appeared on the Volga, then in Pannonia, then on the
Marne and on the banks of the Po: ravaging the cultivated
farmlands where, since the time of Antenor, creative humanity
had heaped monument upon monument. Thus blew forth
from the Mongolian deserts a pestilential breath of wind that

choked the tender, long-cultivated blossoms of art in lands south of the Alps.

From the salt steppes of Asia, from the European heathlands, resplendent in summer with red, honey-rich flowers, and from the greenless deserts of Africa, we return to the plains of South America, whose portrait I have already begun to sketch with crude strokes. The interest, however, that such a portrait can provide the viewer is purely an interest in Nature. Here no oasis evokes memories of earlier inhabitants; no chiseled stone, no fruit tree gone wild reminds one of the efforts of bygone races. As though foreign to the fates of humanity, latching only to the present, there lies in this corner of the globe a wild showplace of free animal and plant life.

From the coastal range of Caracas, the steppe extends to the forests of Guyana, and from the snowy peaks of Mérida (on whose slopes salty Lake Urao is an object of religious superstition for the natives), it reaches down to the great delta that the Orinoco forms at its mouth. To the southwest, it stretches like a long, narrow gulf beyond the banks of the Meta and the Vichada to the unseen sources of the Guaviare, and thence to the lonely massif that the Spanish warriors, giving free rein to their active imagination, dubbed the *Paramo de la Suma Paz*, the beautiful spot, as it were, of eternal peace.

This steppe covers an expanse of 16,000 square geographical miles. Due to ignorance of the geography, it has often been described as extending, uninterrupted and with a consistent breadth, as far as the Strait of Magellan, disregarding the level, forested region of the Amazon River which is bordered north and south respectively by the grassy steppes of Apure and the River Plate. Between the Chiquitos Province and the isthmus of Villabella, the Andes range of Cochabamba and the mountain groups of Brazil extend individual spurs toward one another. A narrow plain joins the hylaea of the Amazon River with the Pampas of Buenos Aires. These latter surpass the area of the Llanos of Venezuela threefold. Indeed, their expanse is so extraordinarily great that they are bordered on the north by palm groves, while their southern reaches are almost covered

with eternal ice. The tuyu (*Struthio rhea*), similar to the casso-
wary, is unique to these Pampas, as are the colonies of feral
dogs that live sociably together in underground burrows, yet
often launch bloodthirsty attacks on the very humans for
whose defense their ancestors fought.

Like the greatest portions of the Sahara Desert, the Llanos,
or the northern plains of South America, lie in the Earth's torrid zone. Nevertheless, each half-year they appear in a different
form: first desolate, like the sand ocean of Libya; then as a
grassy expanse, like so many of the steppes of Central Asia.

It is a rewarding (if difficult) exercise in general regional
geography to compare the natural properties of remote
regions to one another and to describe the results of this comparison in concise terms. Many diverse and to some extent still
unestablished causes diminish the aridity and warmth of the
New Continent.

A great number of conditions provide the flat parts of
America with a climate that, in terms of moisture and coolness, contrasts marvelously with that of Africa: the nar-
rowness of the extensively indented mainlands in the northern
part of the tropics, where a liquid surface presents to the
atmosphere a cooler, ascending current of air; a great latitudinal distance from both ice-capped poles; an open ocean, over
which the cooler tropical seawinds blow; flatness of the eastern coasts; currents of cold ocean water from the Antarctic
region which, though originally directed from southwest to
northeast, strike the coast of Chile below the 35th parallel of
south latitude and advance northward along the coast of Peru
up to Cabo Parina, turning then suddenly to the west; the number of mountain ranges rich in water sources whose snow-
covered peaks aspire to heights above all cloud strata, and
upon whose flanks begin descending currents of air; the abundance of rivers of enormous width which, after many windings, always seek the most distant coast; sandless and thus less
heat-retaining steppes; the impassable forests that fill the
plains at the equator and in the land's interior, where mountains and ocean are farthest apart, protecting the ground from
the sun's rays or dispersing heat by the breadth of their leaves

and exhaling colossal amounts of water, some of which they have drawn in from outside and some of which originates within them – in these characteristics lies the cause of that luxuriant, succulent flora, that frondosity which is the peculiar characteristic of the New Continent.

If one side of our planet is thus said to be more humid than the other, then the observation of the present state of things is sufficient to solve this problem of inequality. The physical scientist need not wrap the explanation of such natural phenomena in the garb of geologic myths. It is not necessary to assume that the destructive battle of the elements upon the ancient earth was settled at different times in the Eastern and Western Hemispheres, or that America emerged from the chaotic covering of water later than the other parts of the world, as a swampy island, home to alligators and snakes.

Certainly South America, by the shape of its outline and the direction of its coasts, has a conspicuous similarity to the southwest peninsula of the Old Continent. But the inner structure of the land and its location relative to bordering landmasses gives rise in Africa to that astonishing aridity which in immeasurable spaces stands opposed to the development of organic life. By contrast, four-fifths of South America lies beneath the equator, in a hemisphere that, due to greater proportions of water and to many other causes, is cooler and more humid than is our Northern Hemisphere. To the latter hemisphere, however, belongs the greater part of Africa.

The South American steppes, the Llanos, when measured east to west, are only one-third as extensive as the African deserts. The former receive the tropical sea winds; the latter, lying beneath a latitudinal circle with Arabia and Southern Persia, are touched by layers of air that move over hot, radiating continents. Indeed, the honorable and long-unappreciated Father of History, Herodotus, in the true spirit of a broad view of Nature, depicted all the deserts of North Africa, in Yemen, Kerman and Mekran (the Gedrosia of the Greeks), even to Multan in Upper India, as a single connected ocean of sand.

Associated with the effect of hot land breezes in Africa, to the extent that we are familiar with it, is the lack of large rivers, of forests that exhale water vapor and create a cooling effect, and of high mountains. One may find ice year round only on the western portion of the Atlas range, whose narrow spine, when viewed from the side, appeared to ancient travelers along the coast as a single lonely and airy pillar beneath the heavens. The range runs easterly up to the area near Dakul, where, now sunk in rubble, Carthage once lay, commanding the sea. As a chain stretched along the coast, as a Gætulean outer wall, the mountains hold back the cool north winds and with them the mists that rise from the Mediterranean.

Once imagined to soar above the lower limit of the snow are the Mountains of the Moon, Djebel-al-Komr, which were said to form a mountainous parallel between that 'African Quito,' the high plain of Habesh, and the sources of the Séné-gal. Even the cordillera of Lupata, which stretches along the eastern coast of Mozambique and Monomotapa, like the Andes chain on the western coast of Peru, is capped with eternal ice in gold-rich Machinga and Mocanga. But these water-rich ranges lie far distant from the tremendous desert that stretches out from the southern flank of the Atlas and on to the Niger flowing eastward.

Perhaps all of these enumerated causes of aridity and heat would not be sufficient to convert such considerable portions of the African plains into a terrible sea of sand, had not some sort of revolution in Nature, perhaps the irrupting ocean, once robbed this flat region of its covering of vegetation and nutrient topsoil. Exactly when this occurrence took place, what force might have brought it about, is cloaked deep in the darkness of prehistory. Perhaps it was an effect of the great rotational current that drives the warmer Mexican waters over the bank of Newfoundland and onward to the Old Continent, and by which coconuts of the West Indies and other tropical fruits are able to reach Ireland and Norway. At least an arm of this ocean current is still present, directed southeast from the Azores on and striking the western dune shore of Africa, bringing calamity to mariners. For all seacoasts (the Peruvian coast between Amotape and Coquimbo comes to mind) show how centuries, indeed millennia, pass before the mobile sand, in hot, rainless stretches of the Earth, where neither lecidea nor other lichens sprout, is able to provide the roots of vegetation a secure purchase.

These observations are sufficient to explain why, in spite of the superficial similarity of the shape of the lands, Africa and South America feature the most divergent climatic conditions, the most differing characteristics of vegetation. Even though the South American steppe is covered with but a thin crust of fertile soil, it is also periodically saturated with pouring rain and then bedizened by luxuriantly growing grass; it was, however, unable to entice the neighboring tribes to leave the beautiful valleys of Caracas, the seacoast, and the river world of the Orinoco, to lose themselves in this treeless, springless waste. Thus the steppe, upon the arrival of European and African settlers, was found to be nearly devoid of people.

Certainly the Llanos are suitable for raising livestock; but the care of milk-giving animals was nearly unknown to the original inhabitants of the New Continent. Hardly any of the American tribes knew to make use of the advantages that Nature had also afforded them in this regard. The Native American race (all one and the same from 65° north to 55° south latitude, excepting possibly the Eskimos) moved from a hunting existence directly to an agricultural, skipping the stage of a herding life. Two types of native cattle graze in the grasslands of Western Canada and in Quivira, as well as around the colossal ruins of the Aztec Castle, which (like an American Palmyra) rises abandoned in the desert near the Gila River. A long-horned mouflon, similar to the so-called father of the sheep, abounds on the dry and naked limestone cliffs of California. To the southern peninsula belong the vicuñas, guanacos, alpacas, and llamas. But of these useful South American animals, only the first two mentioned have preserved for millennia their natural freedom. The enjoyment of milk and cheese, like the possession and cultivation of grasses that yield meal or flour, is a differentiating characteristic of the nations of the Old World.

If, from among these, some groups passed via Northern Asia to the west coast of America and, preferring the cold, pursued the ridge of the Andes to the south, this migration must have taken place along pathways upon which neither herds nor grains could accompany the newcomers. Could it be, perhaps, that when the long-unstable empire of the Xiongnu collapsed, the rolling forth of this mighty race set in motion migrations from Northeastern China and Korea, through which civilized Asians passed over to the New Continent? If these newcomers had been inhabitants of the steppes, where agriculture was not pursued, then this bold hypothesis, which through language comparison has heretofore garnered little favor, would at least explain the conspicuous absence of actual cereal grains in America. Perhaps there landed on the coasts of New California, battered by storms, one of those Asiatic priest colonies whose mystic reveries induced them to venture on long sea voyages, and of whom the history of the populating of Japan at the time of Qin Shi Huang-ti provides a memorable example.

If the pastoral life, this beneficial middle stage that binds throngs of nomadic hunters to the grass-covered lands while preparing them for agricultural life, thus remained unknown to the ancient Americans, then the reason for the sparse presence of humanity on the South American steppes lies in this ignorance. All the more freely, then, the forces of Nature manifested themselves upon the steppes in many diverse types of animal life: free and limited only by themselves, like the vegetation in the forests of the Orinoco, where the *Hymenaea* and the huge-trunked bay tree are never threatened by the hand of Man, but only by the luxuriant crush of entwining growth. Agoutis; small bright-spotted harts; plated armadillos that, like rats, frighten the hares from their subterranean burrows; herds of lethargic capybara; beautifully striped civet-cats that befoul the air; the great maneless lion; spotted jaguars (usually called tigers), which are capable of dragging a young steer they have killed to a hilltop – these and many other creatures wander the treeless plain.

Inhabitable by almost none but these animals, the plains would not have been able to keep hold of any of the nomadic human throngs who, in any case (in the Indo-Asiatic way), prefer vegetable nourishment, had not the fan palms, *Mauritia*, stood scattered here and there. The virtues of this beneficial Tree of Life are widely known. At the mouth of the Orinoco, north of the Sierra de Imataca, it alone sustains the unvanquished nation of the Guarani. When they were more numerous and densely populated, they not only elevated their huts on posts hewn from the palms, which bore a horizontal platform as a floor, but also (so legend tells) artfully stretched hammocks woven from the leaf-stalks of the Mauritia from trunk to trunk, so that during the rainy season when the delta is flooded, they might live in the trees in the manner of the monkeys. These suspended huts were partially covered with clay. On the damp lower level, the women stoked fire for household use. Those who passed by the river at night saw the fires blazing in rows, high in the air, detached from the earth. Even now, the Guarani owe the preservation of their physical and perhaps even their moral independence to the loose, semi-fluid bog soil across which they light-footedly move about, and to their residing in the trees: a high refuge to which religious enthusiasm would likely never lead an American Stylite.

The Mauritia, however, provides not only safe living quarters but abundant food as well. Before the tender blossom spathe bursts forth on the male palm, and only in this phase of the plant's metamorphosis, the pulp of the trunk contains a meal similar to sago, which, like the meal of the Jatropha root, is dried into thin, breadlike wafers. The fermented juice of the tree is the sweet, intoxicating palm wine of the Guarani. Like pisang and the juice of all fruits of the tropical world, this fruit, covered in small scales and looking like reddish pine cones, provides nourishment in different ways, depending on whether one partakes of it after the full development of its sugar content or earlier, in its meal-rich state. Thus do we find, at this most basic level of human intellectual development, the existence of an entire people bound (like the insect that is restricted to certain parts of a blossom) almost solely to a single tree.

Since the discovery of the New Continent, the Llanos have become inhabitable to humans. In order to ease the traffic

between the coast and Guyana (the Orinoco country), cities
have been built here and there on the rivers of the steppes. All
across the immeasurable space, animal husbandry has begun.
Single huts, woven from reeds and cords and covered in cow
hides, stand a day's journey from one another. Innumerable
bands of wild bulls, horses, and mules (estimated, at the peaceful time when I made my trip, at one and a half million head)
swarm about on the steppe. The enormous procreation of
these Old World animals is even more extraordinary given the
many dangers with which they must contend in this place.

When the charred grass falls to dust under the vertical rays
of the sun, the hardened earth gapes open as if shaken by
powerful tremors. Should it then be touched by opposing air
currents whose conflict equalizes in circular motion, the plain
takes on a curious appearance. In the form of funnel clouds
with their tips gliding across the earth, the sand rises like steam
through the airless, electrically charged center of the vortex,
like the hissing waterspouts feared by experienced boatmen.
A hazy, almost straw-colored half-light is thrown by the seemingly low-hanging heavens upon the desolate plain. The horizon draws suddenly nearer. It constricts the steppe and the
mood of the wanderer as well. The smothering heat of the air
is increased by the hot, dusty earth floating in the atmosphere,
which is veiled as if by fog. Instead of cooling, the east wind
brings only more warmth as it blows across the long-heated
ground.

The pools that the yellow-bleached fan palms protected
from evaporation also gradually disappear. As animals in the
North become dormant with the cold, so do the crocodile and
the boa snake slumber motionlessly here, buried deep in dry
clay. Everywhere the drought announces death; and yet everywhere, in the play of distorted light-rays, the illusion of the
waving surface of water hounds those who thirst. A narrow
strip of air separates the distant grove of palms from the
ground. Through the contact of layers of air of differing temperature and density, it floats, lifted by the mirage. Hidden in
darker clouds of dust, spooked by hunger and burning thirst,
ramble horses and cattle, the cows lowing hollowly, the horses

with outstretched necks snuffling the wind, that through the moisture in the air current they might guess the nearness of a water hole not yet completely evaporated.

More deliberate and wily, the mule seeks to relieve his thirst in a different way. A spherical and many-ribbed plant, the melon cactus, encloses within its prickly exterior a pulp rich in water. With his forefoot the mule strikes the needles away and only then dares to bring his lips carefully nearer and drink the cool cactus juice. But drawing drink from this living vegetable spring is not without danger; one often sees animals lamed in the hoof by cactus needles.

When the burning heat of the day is followed by the cooling of the night, which here is always of the same duration, even then the cattle and horses can enjoy no peace. Monstrous bats, vampirelike, suck the blood from them while they sleep or attach themselves firmly to their backs, where they irritate ulcerous sores in which mosquitoes, horseflies, and a host of biting insects settle. Thus do the animals live a painful life when the water disappears from the ground under the blaze of the sun.

When, after the long drought, the beneficent rainy season arrives, the scene on the steppe suddenly changes. The deep blue of the previously cloudless sky grows lighter. By night, one hardly recognizes the black space in the constellation of the Southern Cross. The gentle, seemingly phosphorescent shimmer of the Magellanic Clouds goes out. Even the stars of Aquila and Ophiuchus directly overhead glow with a trembling, less planetary light. In the South, like a remote mountain, a single cloud rises vertically from the horizon. Gradually, the many vapors spread like fog across the zenith. The distant thunder announces the coming of the invigorating rain.

The surface of the Earth is hardly moistened before the fragrant steppe becomes covered with Kyllinga, with many-panicled Paspalum and a number of diverse grasses. Enticed by the light, herbaceous Mimosas unfold their leaves sunken in slumber and greet the rising sun like the morning song of the birds and the opening blossoms of the water plants. Horses and cattle graze in glad enjoyment of life. The grass shooting upward hides the beautifully spotted jaguar. Keeping watch from a safe hiding place and carefully measuring the length of his spring, he snatches passing animals, catlike as the Asiatic tiger.

Occasionally one sees (so say the natives) the now-wet clay on the edge of the swamps slowly lift itself in clods. With a fierce roaring, as with the eruption of a mud volcano, the churned-up earth is flung high in the air. Those familiar with the sight flee at its occurrence, for a gigantic water snake or an armored crocodile is climbing forth from its crypt, awakened from seeming death by the first rainfall.

As the rivers that border the plain to the south (the Arauca, the Apure, and the Payara) gradually begin to swell, so then does Nature force the same animals that during the first half of the year languished in thirst on the waterless, dusty ground to live now as amphibians. The steppe now has the appearance of a vast inland sea. The mares move with their foals back to the higher banks, which protrude in the form of islands above the surface of the sea. With each day, the dry spaces grow smaller; without pasture, the huddled animals swim about for hours and meagerly nourish themselves on the grass panicles that lift themselves above the brown-colored, bubbling water. Many foals drown; many are taken by crocodiles, shattered by their serrated tails, and swallowed. One often sees horses and cattle that, having escaped the jaws of these bloodthirsty, gigantic lizards, bear on their haunches the scars of those pointed teeth.

Such a sight irresistibly reminds the serious observer of the flexibility with which all-providing Nature has endowed certain animals and plants. Like the farinaceous fruits of Ceres, so have the cow and horse followed man around the entire globe: from the Ganges to the Rio Plata, from the African sea-coast to the mountainous plain of Antisana, which lies higher than the cone peak of Tenerife. Here the northern birch, there the date palm protect the exhausted bull from the rays of the sun. The same animal species that in Eastern Europe battle with bears and wolves are threatened under another patch of sky by the attacks of the tiger and the crocodile!

But not only crocodile and jaguar prey upon the South American horses; among the fishes they also have a dangerous enemy. The swamp waters of Bera and Rastro are filled with innumerable electric eels whose slimy, yellow-flecked bodies can, from every part, discharge the jolting energy at will. These gymnotids have a length of 5 to 6 feet. They are powerful enough to kill the largest animals if they can discharge their nerve-laden organs all at once in a propitious direction. The road across the steppe at Uritucu once had to be changed because the gymnotids had massed together in a small river in such numbers that each year, several horses drowned in the ford after being stunned. All other fish in the area also flee these terrible eels. They even frighten anglers on the high banks when the wet line conducts the shock to them from afar. Thus does the electrical fire erupt from the bosom of the waters.

The capturing of the gymnotids affords a picturesque spectacle. Mules and horses, encircled by Indians, are driven into a swamp, until the bold fish are excited by the unaccustomed noise into attacking. One sees them swimming like snakes in the water and slyly crowding under the bellies of the horses. Of these, many succumb to the power of invisible strikes. With bristling mane and snorting, wild panic in their eyes, others flee from the raging storm. But the Indians, armed with poles of bamboo, drive them back to the middle of the pool.

Gradually, the rage of the mismatched fight abates. Like empty clouds, the exhausted fish disperse. They need long rest and plenty of food to regain the galvanic energy they have spent. The jolt of their strikes grows gradually weaker and weaker. Frightened by the noise of the stamping horses, they timidly draw near to the banks, where they are wounded by harpoons and pulled onto the steppe with dry, nonconductive sticks of wood.

This is the wondrous struggle of the horses and fish. That which, invisible, is the living weapon of this denizen of the water; which, awakened by the contact of moist and dissimilar parts, races through all organs of animals and plants; which thunderingly inflames the broad roof of the heavens, binds

iron to iron, and steers the silent, returning motion of the guiding needle – all, like the colors of the refracted beam of light,
flow forth from One Source; all melt together in an eternal,
all-encompassing power.

I could close here this bold attempt at a Nature-portrait of
the steppe. But as one's fancy likes to occupy itself while on
the ocean with pictures of distant shores, so too shall we,
before the great plain vanishes, cast a fleeting glance upon the
regions that border the steppe.

Africa's northern desert separates two races of humanity
who originally belonged to the same part of the globe and
whose evenly matched feud seems to be as old as the myth of
Osiris and Typhon. North of the Atlas live tribes of yellow hue
with straight, long hair and Caucasian facial features. South of
Senegal, in the area of the Sudan, however, live negro tribes,
who may be found at many various stages of civilization. In
Central Asia, Siberian barbarism is separated by the Mongolian steppe from the ancient human civilization found on
the peninsula of Hindustan.

The South American plains, too, set the boundary of the
region of European semi-culture. To the north, between the
mountain ranges of Venezuela and the Antillean seas, lie
industrious cities, tidy villages, and carefully cultivated crop
fields, one after the other. Aesthetic sensibility, scientific education, and the noble love of civil liberty have long since
awoken there. To the south, the steppe is bordered by a formidable wilderness. Thousand-year-old forests and impenetrable undergrowth fill this damp part of the world between
the Orinoco and the Amazon. Mighty, lead-colored granite
massifs enclose the beds of foaming rivers. Mountains and forests echo with the thunder of the crashing waters, the roar of
the tigerlike jaguar, the hollow howls of the bearded monkeys,
heralding the rain.

Where the shallow stream allows a sandbar to remain, there
lie stretched out, with open jaws and motionless as slabs of
stone, the hulking bodies of the crocodiles, often covered with
birds. The chessboard-patterned boa snake, its tail anchored
to a tree trunk and certain of its quarry, lies in wait coiled on

the bank. Quickly uncoiled and thrusting forth, it seizes the young bull or the weaker deer and forces its prey, covered in saliva, laboriously down its expanding throat.

Within this great and wild place of Nature live many and various races of humanity. Separated by a marvelous variety of languages, some, such as the Ottomaks and Jarures, are nomadic strangers to farming, outcasts who eat ants, rubber, and earth; others, such as the Maquiritares and Macos, are settled, knowledgeable, and of gentler customs, fed by fruits of their own cultivation. Large expanses between the Casiquiare and the Atabapo are inhabited not by men but only by tapirs and colonies of monkeys. Pictures carved in stone are evidence that these wastelands too were once places of higher culture. These images give witness to the changing fates of peoples, as do the variously developed and pliable languages that belong among the oldest and most everlasting historical monuments of humanity.

Though tiger and crocodile battle horses and cattle in the steppe, we see on its forested bank, in the wildernesses of Guyana, man forever armed against man. With unnatural desire, some tribes here drink the blood drained from their enemies; others, seemingly unarmed and yet equipped for murder, strangle the enemy with a poisoned thumbnail. The weaker tribes, when they take to the sandy bank, carefully brush away the traces of their timid steps with their hands.

Thus does man, at the lowest level of animal brutality or in the vainglory of his elevated civilization alike, ever make for himself a wearisome life. Thus is the wanderer pursued across the wide world, over land and sea, like all historians throughout the centuries, by the monotonous, comfortless spectacle of the sundered human race.

He who seeks spiritual peace amidst the unresolved strife between peoples therefore gladly lowers his gaze to the quiet life of plants and into the inner workings of the sacred force of Nature, or, surrendering to the instinctive drive that has glowed for millennia in the breast of humanity, he looks upward with awe to the high celestial bodies, which, in undisturbed harmony, complete their ancient, eternal course.

II

CONCERNING THE WATERFALLS
OF THE ORINOCO NEAR ATURES
AND MAYPURES

IN THE PREVIOUS chapter, which I used as the subject of an academic lecture, I described the immeasurable flatlands, the natural characteristics of which are so diversely modified by climatic conditions, appearing in one instance as deserts devoid of vegetation and in another as steppes or as far-reaching grassy plains. In contrast to the Llanos in the southern portion of the New Continent are the terrible oceans of sand that lie in the African interior; in contrast to these are the steppes of Central Asia, home to invading shepherd peoples who, driven from the East, once spread barbarism and desolation over the face of the Earth.

While I dared at that time (1806) to unify great land masses into a single portrait of Nature and to discourse before the public upon subjects of a complexion that bespoke the somber disposition of our minds, I will now, restricting myself to a narrower variety of phenomena, attempt to sketch the friendlier picture of luxuriant vegetation and effervescent river valleys. I refer to two nature scenes from the wilderness of Guyana: Atures and Maypures, the waterfalls of the Orinoco – of wide renown, and yet visited by few Europeans before me.

The impression that the sight of Nature leaves within us is determined less by the properties of the region than by the light in which mountain and meadow appear – now in ethereal sky-blue, now in the shadow of low-hanging clouds. In the same way, descriptions of Nature more strongly or weakly affect us depending upon the greater or lesser extent to which they correspond to the needs of our feelings. For in the innermost receptive mind, the physical world is reflected, living and true. That which designates the character of a landscape – the profile of the mountains that border the horizon in the hazy distance, the darkness of the fir forests, the roaring forest river that plummets between overhanging cliffs – all of it stands in an ancient and mysterious association with the disposition of human temperament.

Upon this association rests the nobler part of the enjoyment that Nature provides. Nowhere does she more completely fill us with the sense of her greatness, nowhere does she address us more mightily, than in the world of the tropics – under 'the Indian sky,' as the climate of the torrid zone was called in the early Middle Ages. If I may thus dare entertain this audience anew with a description of those regions, so might I hope that their inherent charm will not remain unfelt. The memory of a distant and richly endowed land, the sight of a free and powerful growth of vegetation, refreshes and fortifies the mind, much as the upwardly striving spirit, embattled by the present, gladly takes joy from the early age of humanity and its simple grandeur.

Westward currents and tropical winds facilitate the voyage across the peaceful arm of the ocean that fills the broad valley between the New Continent and West Africa. Even before the coast rises from the vaulted ocean bed, one notices a churning of foaming waves cutting across and through one another. Mariners unfamiliar with the region would assume the proximity of shallows or an astonishing eruption of freshwater springs, as may be found in the ocean between the Antillean Islands.

Nearer to the granite coast of Guyana appears the wide estuary of a mighty river that breaks forth like a shoreless sea and covers the ocean around it with freshwater. The river's waves of green, or milky-white in the shallows, contrast with the ocean's indigo blue, which forms a sharp perimeter around the river waves.

The name Orinoco, which was given to the river by its first discoverers and which probably owes its existence to a linguistic confusion, is unknown deep in the country's interior. Primitive peoples distinguish with particular geographical names only such objects as can be confused with others. The Orinoco, the Amazon, and the Magdalena Rivers are simply called 'the river,' or at best 'the great river' or 'the great water,' while the inhabitants of the banks differentiate the smallest streams with individual names.

The current that is created by the Orinoco between the South American continent and the bitumen-rich island of Trinidad is so powerful that ships sailing into it with a fresh west wind and sails unfurled can hardly overcome it. This bleak and fearsome region is called the 'Gulf of Sadness' (*Golfo Triste*). The entrance is the 'Dragon's Mouth' (*Boca del Drago*). Here individual cliffs rise up like towers amidst the raging flood, indicating the ancient dam of rock that, now penetrated by the current, once connected the island of Trinidad with the Paria Coast.

The view of this region first convinced the bold explorer Columbus of the existence of an American continent. 'Such a gigantic amount of freshwater,' concluded this man learned in the ways of Nature, 'could come together only in a river of great length. The land that gives forth these waters would have to be a continent, not an island.' Just as the companions of Alexander on crossing the snow-covered Parapanisus believed, according to Arrian, that they were seeing in the crocodile-filled Indus a part of the Nile, so did Columbus, unaware of the physiognomic similarities of all products of tropical climates, imagine the coast of the New Continent to be the eastern coast of far-reaching Asia. The mild coolness of the evening air, the ethereal purity of the starry firmament, the balsam scent of blossoms carried on the land wind: all led him to suspect (so says Herrera in the *Décadas*) that he was approaching here the Garden of Eden, the sacred home of the first generation of humanity. To him, the Orinoco seemed to be one of the four rivers that, according to the venerable myth of the world's origin, flowed down from Paradise to divide and water the Earth, now newly adorned with plant life. This poetic passage from Columbus's travel report, or rather, a letter to Ferdinand and Isabella, sent from Haiti (October 1498), is of singular psychological interest. It instructs us once more that the creative imagination of the poet expresses itself in the explorers of the world, as in any of humanity's great characters.

When one considers the amount of water that the Orinoco carries to the Atlantic Ocean, the question arises: which of the South American rivers, the Orinoco, the Amazon, or the Plata, is the largest? The question is ambiguous, as is the concept of size. The broadest estuary is that of the Rio de la Plata, with a width that covers 23 geographical miles. But this river, like those of England, is relatively short. Its insufficient depth already hinders shipping even at the city of Buenos Aires. The Amazon is the longest of all rivers. From its source at Lauricocha Lake to its mouth, its course covers 720 geographical miles. On the other hand, its breadth at the cataract of Rentama in the province of Jaen de Bracamoros, where I measured it beneath the picturesque mountains of Patachuma, is barely equal to the breadth of our Rhine at Mainz.

The Orinoco is narrower at its mouth than either the Plata or Amazon River, and its length, according to my astronomical observations, is only 280 geographical miles. Deep in the interior of Guyana, however, 140 geographical miles from its mouth, I found the river at high water to be over 16,200 feet wide. Its periodical rising lifts the water level annually 28 to 34 feet above the low-water mark. There is as yet insufficient information for an exact comparison of the tremendous rivers that cut across the South American continent. To accomplish this, one would have to become familiar with the profile of each river's bed and with its speed, which can vary so greatly in every area.

The delta that is embraced by the Orinoco's many separate and as yet unexplored arms shows manifold similarities with the Nile in terms of the regularity of its rising and falling and the number and size of its crocodiles. The two rivers are also analogous insofar as both wind their way for a long distance between granite and syenite mountains as rushing sylvan streams and then flow slowly forth, contained now by treeless banks, onto virtually level plains. From the celebrated mountain lake at Gondar in the alpine mountains of Gojam in

Abyssinia, an arm of the Green Nile (*Bahr el Azraq*) rolls through the mountains of Shangalla and Sennar down to Syene and Elephantine. In the same way, the Orinoco originates on the southern slope of the mountain range that, stretching along the 4th and 5th degrees of northern latitude, reaches westward from French Guyana toward the Andes of New Granada. The sources of the Orinoco have never been seen by a European; indeed, they have never been seen by a native who has had dealings with Europeans.

When we paddled up the Upper Orinoco in the summer of 1800, we reached, beyond the Esmeralda Mission, the mouths of the Sodomoni and Guapo. Jutting above the clouds here is the summit of Yeonnamari or Duida: a mountain that rises, according to my trigonometric measurements, to 8,278 feet above sea level, and whose aspect is one of the most superb nature scenes that the tropical world has to offer. Its southern slope is a treeless, grassy meadow. There the scent of pineapple fills the humid evening air. Amongst the low-growing meadow herbs rise the bromeliads, their stalks bursting with juices. Beneath the blue-green crown of leaves, the golden-yellow fruit may be seen glowing from afar. Where the mountain waters break forth from the covering grasses, there stand isolated groups of fan palms. In this hot region, their foliage is never moved by cooling currents of air.

East of Duida begins a thicket of wild cacao plants that surround the admirable almond tree *Bertholletia excelsa*, the mightiest product of the tropical world. The Indians collect the materials for their blowguns here – colossal grass stalks, which have segments of more than 17 feet from knot to knot. Some Franciscan monks have penetrated as far as the mouth of the Chiguire, where the river is already so narrow that the natives have woven a bridge of tendrillar plants across it near the waterfall of the Guaharibes. The Guaicas, a people with whitish skin but small in stature, arm themselves with poisoned arrows to defend against further eastward incursions.

Everything that has been proposed about the Orinoco originating in a lake is therefore fantasy. In vain does one seek in Nature the *Laguna Dorada*, which Arrowsmith's maps still show as an inland sea 20 geographical miles long. Could the small, reed-covered Amucu Lake, where the Pirara (a branch of the Mayu) originates, have given rise to this myth? This swamp, however, lies 4 degrees farther east than the region in which it is presumed the source of the Orinoco lies. Erroneously placed within it was the Island of Pumacena, a rock of mica schist, the glittering of which has played since the 16th century a memorable and, to a misguided humanity, often ruinous role in the legend of El Dorado.

According to the legends of many natives, the Magellanic Clouds of the southern sky (the patches of fog that accompany the ship-constellation Argo) are a reflection of the metallic gleam of those silver mountains of the Parima hills. It is also an ancient custom of dogmatic geographers to have every river of considerable size on the planet originate in an inland sea.

The Orinoco belongs among those remarkable rivers that, after a great number of turns to the west and the north, finally runs back to the east in such a manner that its mouth lies on almost the same parallel as its source. From the Chiguire and Gehette to the Guaviare, the course of the Orinoco runs westward, as though it wishes to take its waters to the Pacific. In this stretch it puts forth the Cassiquiare, an unusual arm little known in Europe which joins the Rio Negro (as the natives call it) or Guainia. This is the only example of a bifurcation in the deepest interior of a continent, a natural connection between the two great river valleys, the Orinoco and the Amazon. The nature of the ground surface and the influx of the Guaviare and the Atabapo into the Orinoco cause the latter to turn suddenly to the north. Due to ignorance of the geography, it was for a long time erroneously believed that the Guaviare, flowing from the west, was the true source of the Orinoco. The doubts regarding the possibility of a connection with the Amazon, which were engendered since 1797 by a famous geographer, Mr. Buache, have, I hope, been completely refuted by my expedition. On an uninterrupted boat trip of 230 geographical miles, by way of an extraordinary network of rivers, I succeeded in traveling across the interior of the continent – from the Rio Negro via the Cassiquiare to the Orinoco – from the Brazilian border to the coast of Caracas.

In this upper portion of the river region between the 3rd and 4th degrees of northern latitude, Nature has several times repeated the curious phenomenon of the so-called black water. The Atabapo, with its banks bejeweled by Carolinias and arborescent Melastomas, the Temi, the Tuamini, and the Guainia are rivers of a coffee-brown color. In the shade of the palms, this color changes to a nearly inky black. In a transparent container, the water is golden-yellow. With marvelous clarity the southern constellations are reflected in these black rivers. Where the water flows smoothly, they offer the astronomer who observes with reflective instruments a most excellent artificial horizon.

Scarcity of crocodiles, and fish as well, greater cooling, fewer plagues of the biting mosquitos, and salubrity of the air characterize the region of the black rivers. They probably owe their unusual color to a solution of carbonized hydrogen, the luxuriance of the tropical vegetation, and the abundance of plants in the ground over which they flow. Indeed, I have noted that on the western slope of Chimborazo, inclining toward the Pacific coast, the waters that spill over from the Rio de Guayaquil gradually take on a golden-yellow or almost coffee-brown color after they have covered the meadows for weeks.

Not far from the shared mouth of the Guaviare and the Atabapo can be found one of the noblest forms of all palm plants, the piriguao, whose 60-foot trunk is adorned with tender, reedy foliage with rippled edges. I know of no palms that bear fruit as large and as beautifully colored. These fruits are similar to peaches, yellow mixed with purplish-red. Seventy to eighty of them form bunches like enormous grapes, of which each trunk will produce three per year. One might call this magnificent plant a 'peach palm.' The fleshy fruits are for the most part seedless, thanks to the great luxuriance of the vegetation. They thus provide the natives with a nourishing and farinaceous food that, like pisangs and potatoes, may be prepared in a great many ways.

Up to this point, that is, up to the mouth of the Guaviare, the Orinoco runs parallel to the southern slope of the Parima range; but from its left bank southward to far beyond the equator approaching the 15th degree of southern latitude, stretches the tree-covered basin of the Amazon River. The Orinoco now suddenly turns northward at San Fernando de Atabapo, piercing a part of the range itself. Here are found the great waterfalls of Atures and Maypures. The riverbed here is narrowed everywhere by colossal rocks and at the same time broken into separate reservoirs by natural dams.

Before the mouth of the Meta there stands in a mighty whirlpool an isolated cliff, which the natives very aptly refer to as the 'Stone of Patience,' for at times of low water, it can cost those attempting to ship upstream a delay of two full days. Pressing deep into the countryside, the Orinoco here forms scenic, rocky bays. Across from the Indian mission of Carichana, the traveler is surprised by a remarkable sight. The eye is drawn irresistibly to a craggy granite cliff, el Mogote de Cocuyza, a great block that thrusts 200 vertical feet upward and has upon its flat top a forest of deciduous trees. Like a cyclopean monument of simple grandeur, this cliff rises far above the tops of the surrounding palms. It stands out in sharp relief against the blue of the sky: a forest above the forest.

Upon navigating farther downstream from Carichana, one comes to the point where the river has cut a way through the narrow pass of Baraguan. Here one can discern signs of chaotic devastation all around. Farther to the north toward Uruana and Encaramada rise granite masses of a grotesque appearance. Broken into jagged points and of a brilliant white, they blaze upward from the forest.

In this region, from the mouth of the Apure on, the river leaves the granite range. Moving eastward all the way to the Atlantic Ocean, it separates the impenetrable forests from the grasslands, upon which, at an inconceivable distance, the vault of the heavens rests. Thus does the Orinoco surround on three sides – to the south, the west, and the north – the high Parima mountain range that fills the broad region between the sources of the Jao and the Caura. The river also remains free of cliffs and whirlpools from Carichana all the way to its mouth, with the exception of Hell's Mouth (*Boca del Infierno*) near Muitaco, a whirlpool brought about by rocks that, however, do not dam the entire riverbed as they do at Atures and Mayapures. In this region near the sea, the boatmen know of no other danger than that of the natural rafts, upon which their canoes are often dashed, especially at night. These rafts consist of forest trees from the banks that are pulled up at the roots and borne away by the swelling current. Covered like meadows with blooming water plants, these rafts are reminiscent of the floating gardens of the Mexican lakes.

After this quick overview of the course of the Orinoco and the general circumstances around it, I turn to the description of the waterfalls of Maypures and Atures.

From the high mountain mass of Cunavami, between the sources of the rivers Sipapo and Ventuari, a granite spine thrusts westward toward the Uniama Mountains. From this spine, four streams flow down, confining the cataracts of Maypures: on the east bank of the Orinoco the Sipapo and the Sanariapo, on the west bank, the Cameji and the Toparo. Where the mission town of Maypures lies, the mountains form a sort of wide bay that opens on the southwest.

The river now flows foaming down the eastern slope of the mountain. Far to the west, one can recognize the old, abandoned bank. A wide grassland stretches out between the two ranges of hills. Upon this the Jesuits built a small church of palm trunks. The plain is raised barely 30 feet above the high-water mark of the river.

The geognostic appearance of this region, the insular form of the cliffs Keri and Oco, the hollows that the flood washed out in the first of these hills and that lie at exactly the same height as the holes in the island of Uivitari standing opposite: all of these phenomena indicate that the Orinoco once filled this entire, now dry, bay. The waters probably formed a wide lake for as long as the northern dam provided resistance. Upon the penetration of this dam, the grassy plain now inhabited by the Guarequena Indians emerged, first as an island. It may be that the river for a long time enclosed the Keri and Oco cliffs, which, rising like mountain castles from the old riverbed, provide a splendid sight. As the waters gradually receded, they withdrew completely in the direction of the eastern mountain range.

This assumption is supported by many circumstances. For example, the Orinoco possesses the remarkable characteristic, like the Nile at Philae and Syene, of changing the color of the granite masses around which it has flowed for thousands of years from reddish-white to black. As far as the waters reach, there appears on the rocky banks a lead-colored coating containing manganese and perhaps carbon penetrating the rock surface to a depth of barely one-tenth of a line. This blackening and the hollowing mentioned above are indications of the old water level of the Orinoco. In the Keri cliff, in the islands of the cataracts, in the gneisslike Cumadaminari hill chain that runs above the Island of Tomo, and at the mouth of the Jao, those black cavities may be found 150 to 180 feet above the current water level. Their existence teaches us (as may also be observed, by the way, in all riverbeds in Europe) that the watercourses whose size arouses our admiration today are but weak remnants of the tremendous bodies of water of ages past.

Even the primitive natives of Guyana did not fail to make these simple observations. Everywhere, the Indians brought to our attention the signs of the ancient presence of water. Indeed, in the midst of a grassy plain near Uruana there lies an isolated granite rock into which (according to the narratives of credible men) pictures of the sun, the moon, and many various animals, especially crocodiles and boa snakes, are carved almost in rows at a height of 80 feet. Without scaffolding, no one today can climb up this vertical wall, which deserves the most attentive investigation of future travelers. This is the remarkable position in which are found the hieroglyphic stone-carvings in the mountain regions of Uruana and Encaramada.

If one asks the natives how these pictures can have been carved, they answer: It happened in the time of the high water, for their ancestors then piloted boats at that height. Such a water level was thus contemporaneous with these rude memorials of human artistic endeavor. It is indicative of a former time of very different distribution of water and land, of an earlier stage of the Earth's surface; it is a stage, however, that may not be confused with that time during which the first adorning plants of our planet, the gigantic bodies of extinct land animals, and the pelagic creatures of a chaotic prehistoric world found their graves in the then-hardening crust of the Earth.

The northernmost outflow of the cataracts draws attention to itself through the so-called natural pictures of the sun and the moon. The Keri cliff, to which I have already referred several times, gets its name from a white spot that can be seen from far away, in which the Indians believe they see a conspicuous similarity to the disc of the full moon. I was not able to climb this sheer cliff face myself, but the white spot is probably a very large chunk of quartz formed by converging veins in the gray-black granite.

Across from the Keri cliff on the basaltlike twin mountain of the island of Uivitari, the Indians indicate with mysterious awe a similar disc which they revere as the image of the sun, *Camosi*. Perhaps the geographical juxtaposition of the two cliffs contributed to this appellation, for I did, in fact, find Keri oriented toward the evening and Camosi toward morning. Etymologizing language scholars have thought to discern in the American word *Camosi* some similarity to Camosh, the sun name in one of the Phoenician dialects, along with Apollo Chomeus, or Beelphegor, and Ammon.

Unlike the 140-foot Niagara Falls, the cataracts of Maypures do not consist of a single plunge of a great mass of water. They are also not narrows – passes through which the stream is forced with accelerated speed – like the Pongo de Manseriche in the Amazon River. The cataracts of Maypures appear as a multitude of small cascades that follow one another in a series of steps. The *raudal* (as the Spanish call this sort of cataract) is formed by an archipelago of islands and cliffs that narrow the 8,000-foot-wide riverbed to such an extent that often an opening of barely 20 feet is left for the water to pass through. The eastern side is at the present far more impassable and dangerous than the western.

At the mouth of the Cameji, goods are unloaded so that the empty canoe, or as they say here, the *piragua*, may be piloted by the Indians familiar with the *raudal* to the mouth of the Toparo, where the danger is considered to be past. If the individual cliffs or steps (each of which has been given its own name) are not more than 2 to 3 feet in height, the Indians venture to pilot the canoe down over them; should the direction be upstream, however, they swim ahead and, after many fruitless efforts, manage to get a line around the points of rock that jut out of the swirling waters and then use this line to pull the craft upward. In the course of this strenuous work, the canoe is often filled with water or capsized.

Occasionally, and only in this case do the natives show concern, the canoe is shattered upon the rocks. With bloodied body, the pilots attempt to escape the maelstrom and swim to the riverbank. Where the steps are high, or where the dam of rock has crossed the entire riverbed, the light boat is brought to land and pulled along the near bank on top of cut tree trunks like rollers.

The most celebrated and difficult steps are Purimarimi and Manimi. They have a drop of 9 feet. I was astonished to find through barometric measurements (it is impossible to conduct a geodetic leveling because of the inaccessibility of the location and the pestilential and mosquito-filled air) that the entire vertical drop of the *raudal*, from the mouth of the Cameji to that of the Toparo, amounts to only 28 to 30 feet. I say 'astonished' for it becomes clear from this that the terrible roaring and wild foaming of the river are the result of the narrowing of the bed by innumerable rocks and islands, the result of the back current brought about by the form and positioning of the masses of stone. The most convincing way to see the truth of this assertion of the small drop of the entire system of falls is to climb down from the village of Maypures over the Manimi cliff to the riverbed.

This is the spot where one may enjoy a marvelous view. All at once, a roiling mile-long surface offers itself to the eye. From this surface, iron-black cliffs tower like ruins and fortresses. Each island, each stone is adorned by lushly thriving forest trees. Thick fog drifts eternally over the water's surface. Through the steaming cloud from the foam the tops of the tall palms emerge. When a ray of the glowing evening sun penetrates the damp vapors, there begins an optical magic. Colorful rainbows disappear and then return. The ethereal image fluctuates in the play of the airs.

Here and there on the naked rock, the trickling waters of the long rainy season have heaped up islands of topsoil. Bedecked with *Melastoma* and *Drosera*, with small, silver-leaved mimosas and ferns, they form flowerbeds on the desolate stone. To the European, they call to mind the memory of those plant groups that the people of the Alps call *Courtils*: blocks of granite that protrude, lonely and adorned with flowers, out of the Savoyan glaciers.

In the blue distance, the eye comes to rest upon the Cunavami mountain range, a long mountain ridge that ends in a steep and truncated cone. This last (which has the Indian name *Calitamini*) we saw glowing like red fire in the setting sun. This spectacle returns daily. No one has ever been close to this mountain. Perhaps its gleam arises from a reflective decomposition of talc or mica slate.

During the five days that we spent in the area around the cataracts, it was striking how one perceived the roaring of the rushing stream to be three times louder by night than by day. The same phenomenon may be noted at all European waterfalls. What might the cause for this be in a remote area where nothing disturbs the peace of Nature? It is probably the currents of warm rising air which, through the disparate admixture of the elastic medium, impede the propagation of sound, continually breaking up the sound waves, and which then cease this action during the nightly cooling of the Earth's crust.

The Indians showed us traces of wagon tracks. They speak with amazement of the horned animals (oxen) that pulled the canoes on wagons along the left bank of the Orinoco from the mouth of the Cameji to that of the Toparo in the days when the Jesuits were pursuing their business of proselytizing. In those days, the canoes remained loaded and, unlike today, were not worn away by the continual beaching and dragging along on the rough cliffs.

The plan of the surrounding area that I drew up shows that a canal could be opened up from the Cameji to the Toparo. The valley in which those water-rich streams flow is smoothly flat. The canal, the building of which I have recommended to the governor general of Venezuela, would serve as a navigable adjacent arm of the river and would thus render the old, dangerous riverbed unnecessary.

The *raudal* of Atures is quite similar to the *raudal* of Maypures: again, an island world through which the river presses on for a distance of three to four thousand toises, a grove of palms rising right from the middle of the foaming water's surface. The best-known steps of the cataract lie between the islands of Avaguri and Javariveni, between Suripamana and Uirapuri.

When we, Mr. Bonpland and I, returned from the banks of the Rio Negro, we decided to risk navigating the last or lower half of the *raudal* of Atures in the laden canoe. Several times we climbed out onto the rocks, which, like causeways, join island to island. Sometimes the water crashes over these rocks; other times it falls into the hollows in the rocks with a dull roar. Thus whole stretches of riverbed are often dry, for the stream now makes its way through subterranean canals. The golden-yellow cliff hens (*Piprarupicola*) nest here – one of the most beautiful birds of the tropics, with a double-rowed crest of movable feathers, and as aggressive as the East Indian rooster.

In the Canucari *raudal*, piles of granite boulders form the rock dam. There we crawled into the interior of a cavity, the damp walls of which were covered with conferva and luminescent *Byssus*. With a dreadful roaring, the river rushed on above us. By chance we were presented with the opportunity to observe this great nature scene longer than we could have wished. The Indians left us there in the middle of the cataract. The canoe was supposed to navigate in a long detour around a narrow island, in order to pick us up again. For one and a half hours we waited under a fearful rainstorm. Night fell, and in vain we sought shelter between the cloven masses of granite. The plaintive cries of the little monkeys in woven cages that we had carried with us for months enticed the crocodiles, whose size and lead-gray color indicated great age. I would not mention this occurrence, so common in the Orinoco, had the Indians not assured us that a crocodile had never been seen in the cataracts; indeed, trusting in their assertion, we had even dared several times to bathe in this section of the river.

Meanwhile, the worry increased with each passing moment that we, soaked to the skin and deafened by the thundering of the crashing water, would have to wait through a sleepless tropical night in the middle of the *raudal* – until the Indians finally appeared with our canoe. They had found the step down which they had intended to ride impassable due to the water's being far too low. The pilots were thus compelled to seek a more navigable passage through the labyrinth of channels.

At the southern entrance to the *raudal* of Atures, on the right bank of the river, is the cavern of Ataruipe, famed far and wide amongst the Indians. The surrounding region is Nature of a great and solemn character, making it a suitable place for a national cemetery. One must laboriously scale a sheer wall of granite, not without danger of a great fall. It would hardly be possible to gain a firm foothold on the flat surface were it not for the large feldspar crystals that protrude an inch or more from the stone, defying the erosive effects of weather.

Immediately upon gaining the summit, one is surprised by a wide vista of the surrounding region. Rising from the foaming riverbed are hills ornamented with forest. On the opposite side of the river, beyond the western bank, one's view falls upon the immense grassland of Meta. Looming on the horizon like a bank of growing, threatening clouds are the Uniama mountain group. Such is the distant view; nearer at hand, all is bleak and closed in. In the deeply furrowed valley soar the lonely vulture and the cawing Caprimulgiformes.

Their retreating shadows glide across the bare rock walls.

This kettle-shaped valley is surrounded by mountains whose rounded summits support granite boulders of monstrous size. The diameter of these boulders is around 40 to 50 feet. They appear to touch the ground below them with but a single point, as if they would come rolling down upon even the smallest tremor of the Earth.

The rear side of the rocky valley is covered in dense deciduous forest. In this shady spot is the opening of the cavern of Ataruipe – actually not a cavern but a sort of vault, a cliff with a very large overhang, a bight of sorts that the waters wore out in the days when they reached this height. This place is the tomb of an extinct tribe. We counted approximately 600 well-preserved skeletons, each in a basket woven from the stalks of palm fronds. These baskets, which the natives call *mapires*, are in the shape of a sort of four-cornered sack, in different sizes depending upon the age of the deceased. Even newborn children have their own *mapire*. The skeletons are so complete that neither a rib nor a phalange is missing.

The bones are prepared in three ways: some are bleached, some are colored red with *Onoto*, the pigment of the *Bixorellana*, and some, in the manner of mummies, are rubbed with aromatic resins in pisang leaves. The Indians affirm that the fresh corpse is buried for some months in moist earth that gradually absorbs the muscle tissue; it is then exhumed, and any remaining tissue is scraped from the bones with sharp stones. This is still the practice of some tribes in Guyana. Next to the *mapires* or baskets, there are also half-fired clay urns that seem to contain the bones of entire families.

The largest of these urns are 3 feet high and $5\frac{1}{2}$ feet long, of an attractive oval shape, greenish, with handles in the shapes of crocodiles and snakes, and decorated around the rim with twining or labyrinthine designs. These decorations are quite similar to those that cover the walls of the Mexican palace of Mitla. Indeed, they are to be found in all zones, and at the most differing stages of human civilization: among the Greeks and Romans, as well as on the shields of the Tahitians and other Pacific Islanders – everywhere, the rhythmic repetition of

regular forms is pleasing to the eye. The causes of these similarities, as I develop further in another work, rest on psychological bases, upon the inner nature of our mental faculties,
more than being indicative of shared ancestry and ancient
intercourse between the different peoples.

Our interpreters were unable to give us any reliable information regarding the age of these vessels. But the majority of
skeletons appeared to be no more than one hundred years old.
There is a legend among the Guarequena Indians that relates
that the courageous people of Atures, pursued by cannibalistic
Caribs, saved themselves on the cliffs of the cataracts – a sad
place to settle, where the persecuted tribe and with them their
language died out. In the most inaccessible parts of the *raudal*
there are similar tombs; it is indeed possible that the last of the
Atures people did not die out until recently. For in Maypures
(a curious fact), there lives an old parrot, of which the natives
maintain that no one can understand him because he is speaking the language of the Atures people.

We left the cavern at nightfall, after collecting several skulls
and the complete skeleton of an older man, much to the great
irritation of our Indian guides. One of these skulls has been
copied by Blumenbach and included in his excellent work on
craniology. The skeleton, however, like a great portion of our
collection of natural specimens (especially the entomological
ones), was lost in a shipwreck on the African coast that also
took the life of our friend and former traveling companion,
the young Franciscan monk Juan Gonzalez.

As though with a premonition of this painful loss, it was in
a somber mood that we left behind us this tomb of an extinct
tribe. It was one of those serene and cool nights so common
in the tropics. Surrounded by colorful rings, the disc of the
moon stood high at the zenith. It illuminated the edge of
the fog that, in sharp outline, covered the foaming river like
clouds. Innumerable insects poured out their reddish phosphorescent light over the verdant earth. The ground glowed
with this living fire, as though the starry roof of the heavens
had laid itself down upon the grassland. Twining begonias, fragrant vanilla, and yellow-blossomed Banisteria adorned the

entrance to the cavern. Over the graves, the tops of the palm trees rustled.

Thus do the races of men die away. The admirable lore of the different peoples fades away. But with the wilting of each blossom of the spirit, whenever, in the storm of the times, the works of creative art are scattered, so forever will new life sprout forth from the womb of the Earth. Restlessly, procreative Nature opens her buds: unconcerned whether outrageous humanity (a forever discordant race) should trample the ripening fruit.

THE NOCTURNAL WILDLIFE OF
THE PRIMEVAL FOREST

ONE MAY ASSERT that the many forms of active appreciation of Nature among different peoples, and the characteristics of the countries these peoples have inhabited or transmigrated, have to varying degrees enriched language. They have enriched it with sharply indicative words for the shapes of mountains, the properties of vegetation, aspects of atmospheric motion, and the form and grouping of clouds. It is also true, however, that many of these descriptive terms, through long use and the vagaries of literature, have abandoned their original meaning. Things that should remain distinct are gradually considered synonymous, and language loses some of the grace and power with which it was able to depict, in its descriptions of Nature, the physiognomic character of the landscape. To show the linguistic richness that intimacy with Nature and the privations of the strenuous nomadic lifestyle can bring forth, I cite the innumerable characteristic terms by which plains, steppes, and deserts are differentiated in Arabic and Persian, according to whether they are completely bare, or covered with sand, or interrupted by cliffs, whether they have isolated pasture areas or feature long stretches of socially growing plants. Almost equally remarkable are the many expressions in Old Castilian dialects for the physiognomy of those mountainous masses whose formations appear everywhere under the sun and indicate, even at great distances, the nature of the stone of which they are composed. Since peoples of Spanish extraction inhabit the slopes of the Andes chain, the mountainous portion of the Canary Islands, the Antilles, and the Philippines, and because the contours of the ground in these places influence the lives of the inhabitants to a greater

degree than anywhere else on Earth (with the possible exception of the Himalayas and the Tibetan Plateau), the different
terms for mountains in the trachyte, basalt, and porphyry
regions, as well as in the slate, limestone, and sandstone mountains, have fortunately remained in daily use. New forms, too,
enter the common treasury of language. The speech of
humans is enlivened by everything indicative of natural truth,
be it in the representation of sensory impressions received
from the outer world or of profoundly stirred thought and
inner feelings.

The goal of all descriptions of Nature is the ceaseless striving after this truth, both in understanding phenomena and in
choosing the descriptive expression. It is most easily achieved
by simple narration of what has been observed and experienced directly, through the limiting individualization of the
situation on which the narrative hangs. Generalization of
physical appearances and enumeration of results belong to the
study of the Cosmos, which admittedly remains for us an
inductive science. But the living description of organisms, of
animals and of plants, within the context of their natural local
relationship to the many-faceted surface of the Earth (as a
small part of the Earth's collective life) presents the material
of that study. Wherever this description can examine great
natural phenomena in an aesthetic manner, it excites the mind.

Included among these great natural phenomena is surely
the immeasurable forest region in the tropical zone of South
America that fills the conjoined river systems of the Orinoco
and the Amazon. In the strictest sense of the word, this region
earns the name of 'primeval' forest, a term that has of late
suffered considerable misuse. Phrases using *primeval*, whether
describing a forest, a period, or a people, are inexact and for
the most part subjective. If every wild forest of densely growing trees upon which man has not yet laid his destructive hand
is called a primeval forest, then the phenomenon is native to
many parts of the temperate and frigid zones. But if the character lies in impenetrability, in the impossibility, over long
stretches, of cutting a path with an ax through trees with a
diameter of 8 to 12 feet, then the primeval forest belongs

exclusively to the tropics. And it is by no means only the rope-like, tendrillar climbing vines or *lianas* that are, as in the tales told in Europe, the cause of this impenetrability. The lianas make up only a small part of the total mass of the under-growth. The primary hindrance is created by the bushy growth that fills every open space – in a zone where everything that covers the ground becomes woody. When travelers who have just landed in a tropical region, even perhaps on an island, already think (while still near the coast) that they have pushed their way into a primeval forest, this misconception probably lies in their longing for the fulfillment of a long-cherished wish. Not every tropical forest is a primeval forest. I have almost never used this latter term in my travel works – yet I believe myself to be among those living explorers of Nature, like Bonpland, Martius, Pöppig, and Robert and Richard Schomburgk, who have lived the longest in the primeval for-ests of the deepest interior of a great continent.

In spite of the conspicuous wealth of terms descriptive of Nature in the Spanish language, which I mention above, one and the same word, *monte*, is employed for both mountain and forest, for *cerro* (*montaña*) and *selva*. In a work on the true breadth and the longest eastward extension of the Andes chain, I showed how that dual meaning of the word *monte* was the reason behind a beautiful and widely distributed English map of South America having displayed rows of high moun-tains, rather than forests, standing on the plains. For whereas the Spanish map of La Cruz Olmedilla, which has served as the basis for so many others, had depicted cacao forest, *montes de cacao*, cordilleras sprang up on the English map, even though cacao trees seek only the hottest depressions.

If one looks with a general overview upon the forested region that constitutes all of South America between the grass steppes of Venezuela (*los Llanos de Caracas*) and the Pampas of Buenos Aires, i.e., between 8° north and 19° south latitude, one will recognize that this continuous hylaea forest of the tropical zone is equaled in scope by no other on Earth. It pos-sesses a surface area approximately 12 times that of Germany. Crisscrossed in all directions by rivers and streams, whose branches and tributaries of primary and secondary order occasionally surpass our Danube and Rhine in water volume, this forest owes the extraordinarily luxuriant growth of its trees to the dual beneficial effects of great humidity and heat. In the temperate zone, especially in Europe and Northern Asia, forests can be named after the species of trees that form them by growing together as social plants (*plantae sociales*). In the oak, fir, and birch forests of the North, in the linden forests of the East, a single species of Amentaceae, conifer, or Tiliaceae usually predominates; occasionally one coniferous species will be mixed together with a hardwood. Such homogeneity of species is unknown in the tropical forests. The immense diversity of blossoming forest flora forbids the question 'What makes up the primeval forest?' An inconceivable number of families grow side by side here; even in small spaces, few species are found exclusively among their own kind. With each day, with each change of stopping-place, the traveler is met with new forms; often he sees blossoms that, though his attention is drawn by the shape of their leaves and their manner of branching, are simply beyond his reach.

The rivers, with their innumerable smaller arms, are the only paths through this country. Astronomical observations, or, lacking these, compass readings of the river bends, have on many occasions shown, in the region between the Orinoco, the Cassiquiare, and the Rio Negro, how there can be two lonely mission villages lying within the space of some few miles whose monks, following the windings of small streams in canoes fashioned from hollowed-out tree trunks, require one and a half days to go and visit one another. But the most conspicuous evidence of the impenetrability of certain parts of the forest is illustrated by the habits of the great American tiger, the pantherlike jaguar. These predators, thanks to the introduction of European cattle, horses, and mules, have been able to find bountiful nourishment in the Llanos and Pampas, those vast, treeless grasslands of Varinas, of the Meta, and of Buenos Aires, and thanks to this uneven conflict with the cattle herds they have, since the discovery of America, greatly increased their numbers there. But some individuals of this same breed lead a demanding life within the thicket of the forests, near to the sources of the Orinoco. The painful loss of a large dog of the German mastiff variety (our most faithful and friendly travel companion) at a bivouac near where the Cassiquiare flows into the Orinoco would later compel us, as we were returning from the insect swarms to the Esmeralda Mission, to spend a second night there, searching for the dog in vain and uncertain as to whether he had been savaged by a tiger. Quite nearby, we heard again the cry of the jaguar, probably the very one to which we could attribute the dreadful deed. Since the cloudy skies hindered astronomical observation, we had the interpreter (*lenguaraz*) repeat to us what the natives, our oarsmen, told about the tigers of the area.

Not uncommon among these is the so-called black jaguar, the largest and most bloodthirsty variation, with black, barely visible spots on a dark brown coat. It lives at the foot of the mountains Maraguaca and Unturan. 'The jaguars,' an Indian of the Durimund tribe related, 'through their desire to wander and hunt, lose themselves in such impenetrable parts of the forest that they cannot hunt on the ground, and so live long in the trees, a terror to the monkey families and the Kinkajou with the curling tail [*Cercoleptes*].'

My German journals, from which I take this information, were not completely exhausted in the French travelogue that I published. They also contain a detailed depiction of the nocturnal wildlife – I could say the nocturnal animal voices – of the tropical forests. I consider this depiction especially well suited for a book that will have the title *Views of Nature*. Words that are written down in the presence of the phenomenon, or shortly afterward, can lay claim to more freshness of life than the echoes of later remembrance.

Traveling from west to east by way of the Rio Apure, whose flooding I discussed in the essay concerning steppes and deserts, we were able to reach the bed of the Orinoco. It was at the time of low water. The Apure's average width was barely 1,200 feet, while I found that of the Orinoco at its confluence with the Apure (not far from the granite Curiquima cliff, where I was able to take a line of bearing) to still be over 11,430 feet.

But the Curiquima cliff is still, if measured in a straight line, a hundred geographical miles from the sea and from the delta of the Orinoco. One part of the plains, through which the Apure and the Payara flow, is inhabited by tribes of Yaruros and Achaguas. In the mission towns of the monks they are called savages because they desire to live independently. As for the degree to which their morality is primitive, they are quite on the same level as those who, while baptized and living 'under the bell (*baxo la campana*),' nevertheless remain strangers to all instruction and to any doctrine.

Onward from the isle *del Diamante*, upon which the Spanish-speaking Zambos cultivate sugarcane, one enters a great and wild Nature. The air was filled with countless flamingos (*Phoenicopterus*) and other waterfowl that, like a dark cloud with an ever-changing outline, lifted themselves into the blue vault of the heavens. The riverbed narrows to a width of 900 feet and forms a perfectly straight canal that is hemmed in on both sides by thick forestation. The edge of the forest presents an unusual sight: before the nearly impenetrable wall of the gigantic trunks of *Caesalpinia*, *Cedrela*, and *Desmanthus*, there arises with great regularity from the sandy bank of the river a low *sauso* hedge. It stands only 4 feet high and consists of a small shrub, *Hermesia castaneifolia*, which constitutes a new species of the family of Euphorbiaceae. Next to the hedge stand a few slender, thorny palms (varieties, perhaps, of the Martinezeia or Bactris), called Piritu and Corozo by the Spaniards. The whole resembles a trimmed garden hedge with gate-like openings at great distances from one another. The large quadrupeds of the forest undoubtedly created these openings for easy access to the stream. One may observe emerging from them, especially in the early morning and at sundown, the American tiger, the tapir, and the peccary (*Pecari*, *Dicotyles*) taking their young to water. Should they wish, upon being disturbed by the passing canoe of an Indian, to withdraw again to the forest, they do not attempt to penetrate the hedge by mere force; instead, one is treated to the sight of the wild animal running some four to five hundred paces between the riverbank and the hedge before disappearing into the next opening. While making our 74-day voyage, during which we were confined, with but few interruptions, to a narrow canoe for 380 geographical miles upon the Orinoco, the Casiquiare, and the Rio Negro, the same spectacle repeated itself for us at many points, each time, I dare say, renewing our delight. There appeared in groups, whether to drink, bathe, or fish, creatures of the most disparate classes: along with the large mammals were multicolored herons, *Palamedeae*, and the proudly strutting *Cracidae* (*Crax alector*, *C. pauxi*). Our pilot, an Indian who had been raised in the home of a clergyman, uttered with a pious expression, 'It is like being in Paradise here [*es como en el paraiso*].' But the sweet peace of the primeval golden age does not reign in the Paradise of the American animal world. Instead, the creatures watch for and avoid one another. The capybara, the 3- to 4-foot 'water swine' – a colossal version of the common Brazilian guinea pig (*Cavia aguti*) – is eaten in the water by the crocodile and on land by the tiger. And yet it runs so poorly that we were able several times to overtake and capture individuals from the numerous herds.

We camped one night below the Mission of Santa Barbara de Arichuna, under the open sky as usual, lying on a stretch of sand on the bank of the Apure. The area was closely surrounded by the impenetrable forest. We had difficulty finding dry wood for the fires with which, according to local custom, every bivouac is surrounded to discourage jaguar attacks. The night was mildly humid with a bright moon. Several crocodiles approached the bank. What I observed, I believe, is that the sight of the fire actually attracts them, much as it does our crabs and other water creatures. The oars of our small boats were carefully planted into the ground so that we might attach our hammocks to them. Quiet reigned; one heard only the occasional snorting of the freshwater dolphins, which are native both to the Orinoco river system and (according to Colebrooke) to the Ganges as far as Benares, following one another in long processions.

After 11 o'clock there arose in the forest nearby such a clamor that we were forced to abandon all hope of sleep for the rest of the night. The cries of wild beasts thundered

through the woods. Among the many voices that simultaneously gave cry, the Indians could identify only those that
might be heard singly after a short pause. There were the
monotonous, plaintive howls of the alouattae (howler monkeys), the whining, finely piping tone of the little sapajous, the
quavering grumble of the striped night monkeys (*Nyctipithecus
trivirgatus*, which I first described), the sporadic cries of the
great tiger, the cougar or maneless American lion, the peccary,
the sloth, and a host of parrots, parraquas (*Ortelida*), and other
pheasantlike birds. Whenever the tigers came near to the forest edge, the dog (that we later lost), who had been barking
without interruption, would whiningly seek refuge under our
hammocks. Occasionally, the tiger's cry would come down
from the top of a tree. In these instances it would always be
accompanied by the piping tones of the monkeys, who sought
to escape this unusual pursuit.

Should one ask the Indians why this incessant noise should
arise on certain nights, they would answer with a smile, 'The
animals are enjoying the beautiful moonlight; they are
celebrating the full moon.' To me, the scene appeared to originate merely by chance, developing into a long-extended and
ever-amplifying battle of the animals. The jaguar pursues the
peccaries and tapirs, who, driven together, crash through the
arborescent shrubbery, which hinders their flight. Frightened
by this, the monkeys in the treetops add their cries to those
of the larger beasts below. Together, they awaken the various
breeds of fowl roosting together, and so, gradually, the entire
animal world joins in the uproar. Long experience has taught
us that in no way is it always the 'celebrated moonlight' that
disturbs the quiet of the forests. The voices were loudest during times of heavy rainfall, or when, with cracks of thunder,
the lightning illuminated the forest interior. Good-natured
despite several months of fever-sickness, the Franciscan monk
who accompanied us past the cataracts of Atures and Maypures to San Carlos of the Rio Negro and onward to the Brazilian border used to say at nightfall, whenever he feared a storm
was coming, 'May Heaven grant a quiet night to us, and likewise to the wild beasts of the forest!'

In marvelous contrast to the Nature scenes that I describe here, which were played out for us time and again, stands the midday silence that reigns on unusually hot tropical days. From the same journal I now borrow a memory of the Baraguan strait. Here the Orinoco makes its way through the Parima mountain group. That which is referred to in this peculiar pass as a strait (*Angostura del Baraguan*) is really a water basin, the width of which is still 890 toises (5,340 feet). Aside from an old dry stem of the *aubletia* (*Apeibati bourbou*) and a new apocyne, *Allamanda salicifolia*, there was nothing to be found on the bare cliffs but a very few silvery croton shrubs. A thermometer, observed in the shade but within a few inches of the towering granite cliffs, climbed to over 40° Réaumur. All distant objects had wavelike, shimmering outlines, a result of reflection or optical displacement (*mirage*). Not a breath of air moved the dusty sand. The sun stood at zenith, and the tremendous light that it poured down upon the river, which the river in turn reflected back, sparkling in the gentle motion of its waves, intensified the hazy reddish blush that lay over the distance. All the blocks of stone and naked boulders were covered with innumerable large, thick-scaled iguanas, geckos, and colorfully speckled salamanders. Immobile, their heads lifted and mouths opened wide, they seem to inhale the hot air with delight. The larger animals are hiding now in the thickets of the forest, the birds under the foliage of the trees or within the clefts of the cliffs; if one were to listen now, however, for the quietest tones that come to us in this apparent stillness of Nature, then one perceives close to the ground and in the lower layers of the atmosphere a muffled sound, a whirring and buzzing of insects. Everything announces a world of active, organic powers. In every shrub, in the cracked bark of the trees, in the loose earth where live the hymenoptera, Life audibly stirs. It is one of the many voices of Nature, discernible to the solemn, receptive mind of humanity.

V

IDEAS FOR A PHYSIOGNOMY
OF PLANTS

WHEN A PERSON possessed of an active mind explores
Nature, or ponders in imagination the broad range of organic
creation, no single one among the manifold impressions that
occur to him has so deep and powerful an effect as that of the
ubiquitous abundance of life. Everywhere, even near the ice-
capped poles, the air rings with the songs of birds or the drone
of buzzing insects. Not only the lower layers of the air, where
the denser vapors hang, but the upper, ethereally pure layers
are inhabited as well. For each time that someone has
ascended to the spine of the Peruvian cordilleras or to the
summit of the White Mountain south of Lake Léman, animals
were discovered even in these desolate spots. On Chimborazo,
nearly eight thousand feet higher than Aetna, we saw butterflies and other winged insects. Even if, driven by vertical
air currents, they had merely gone astray to such places as the
restive thirst for discovery had led the tentative footsteps of
humans, their presence there still demonstrates that the more
adaptable nature of animals endures where vegetation has long
since met its limits. Higher than the cone of Tenerife, were it
set atop the snow-covered spine of the Pyrenees, higher than
all of the peaks of the Andes chain, there often soared above
us the condor, the giant among the vultures. Ravenous desire
to prey upon the soft-wooled vicuñas that gather in herds like
the chamois upon the snowy pasture lands lures the mighty
birds to this region.

While even the naked eye sees the entire atmosphere to be
inhabited, still greater wonders are revealed to the aided eye.
Rotifers, brachioni, and a host of microscopic creatures are
lifted by the winds from drying waters. Immobile and

submerged in apparent death, they float through the air – until the thaw brings them back to nourishing earth, dissolves the hull that encases their transparent, gyrating bodies, and (probably due to the life-giving material contained by all water) breathes new sensibility into their organs. The yellowish Atlantic 'meteoric dusts' ('dust fogs') that from time to time press far eastward into North Africa, Italy, and Middle Europe from the sea around the Cape Verde islands are, according to Ehrenberg's brilliant discovery, masses of microscopic organisms with siliceous shells. Many of them float, perhaps for years, in the highest layers of the atmosphere, and occasionally drift down, by way of the upper trade winds or by vertical air currents, engaged in organic self-division and capable of life.

Along with the developed creatures, the atmosphere also carries the germinal form of countless future living things: insect eggs and the eggs of plants that are sent, with crowns of hair or feather, upon long autumnal journeys. Even the life-giving dust, the pollen that among species with separate genders is scattered by the male blossom, is carried by winds and by winged insects over land and sea to the lonely female. Wherever the glance of the researcher of Nature is directed, life or the germ of life has been disseminated.

While the moving sea of air, in which we are immersed and above whose surface we have not the capacity to lift ourselves, gives to many organisms their most vital nourishment, these creatures are also in need of the coarser fare offered only at the bottom of this gaseous ocean. This bottom is of two sorts: the lesser portion is formed by dry land in immediate contact with the air, while the greater portion is in the form of water – perhaps having once, millennia ago, coalesced from gaseous materials by means of electrical fire, and now relegated to unceasing activity within the workshop of the clouds, and within the pulsating vessels of animals and plants. Organic forms descend deep into the interior of the Earth – as deep as ever the atmospheric rainwater can penetrate into excavations or natural caverns. Early on, the realm of cryptogamic subterranean flora became a subject of my scientific works. At the highest temperatures, hot springs nourish small hydropores, confervae, and oscillatoriae. Close to the Arctic Circle, at Great Bear Lake in the New Continent, Richardson observed that the ground, which in summer was frozen to a depth of 20 inches, was adorned with blooming vegetation.

It is undecided where there is the greater variety of life: on the land or in the unsounded ocean. Through Ehrenberg's excellent work *Über das Verhalten des kleinsten Lebens*, in the tropical ocean and within the floating and stationary ice of the South Pole, the sphere of organic life, indeed the horizon of life itself, has broadened before our eyes. Siliceous-shelled polygastria, the coscinodiscuses with their green ovaries, have been found 12° from the pole, alive and encased in ice; in the same way, the Podurellae and the little black glacier flea, *Desoria glacialis*, inhabit narrow tubes in the ice of the Swiss glacier investigated by Agassiz. Ehrenberg has shown that upon several microscopic infusoria (*Synedra, Cocconeis*) still other creatures live in the manner of lice and that in the case of Gallionella, with their tremendous capacity for division and mass development, an invisible creature can produce, in four days, two cubic feet of Bilin polishing slate. In the ocean, gelatinlike sea microbes, now alive, now dying out, appear as glimmering stars. Their phosphorescence transforms the greenish surface of the immense ocean to a sea of fire. I will never forget those tropical nights in the South Sea, when the constellations of the high-flying ship Argo and the setting Southern Cross poured out their mild planetary light from the blue gossamer of the heavens while the dolphins drew their glowing wakes in the foaming flood of the sea.

It is not only the ocean, however, but the waters of the swamps as well that hide countless tiny creatures of extraordinary form. Nearly unrecognizable to our eyes are the Cyclidia, the Euglenae, and the host of nymphs, which can be divided into separate branches, like the Lemna whose shade they seek. Surrounded by an air of a different admixture and ignorant of all light, the spotted ascaris breathe within the skin of the earthworm, the silvery leucophras in the body of the riverbank *Naidinae*, and a pentastoma in the wide-celled lungs of the tropical rattlesnake. There are blood-dwelling creatures in frogs and salmon; indeed, according to Nordmann, there are creatures living within the fluids of fisheyes and in the gills of the bream. Thus are the most hidden realms of creation replete with life. But let us remain here a while on the subject of plant species, for upon their existence rests the existence of animal life. Plants ceaselessly organize the raw material of the Earth, preparing to mix together, through the force of life, that which after a thousand transformations is ennobled into animate nerve fibers. The same scrutiny that we devote to the spreading cover of plant life reveals for us the fullness of the animal life that is preserved and nourished by it.

This carpet spread by the blossom-rich flora over the naked body of the Earth is woven in varying ways: thicker where the sun climbs higher in the ever-cloudless sky, sparser toward the slow-moving poles, where the returning frost sometimes kills the grown bud or catches the ripening fruit. Yet everywhere, man joys in the nourishment from plants. If a volcano should part the boiling flood at the bottom of the sea and suddenly (as once occurred between the Greek isles) shove a slag-covered cliff into the air, or (to cite a more peaceful natural phenomenon) should the harmonious lithophytes erect their alveolate dwellings upon the spine of an undersea mountain until, after thousands of years, looming upward over the surface of the water, they die and leave behind a flat coral island: the organic powers are immediately ready to bring the dead rock back to life. Whatever so suddenly brings the seeds, be it wandering birds, or winds, or the waves of the sea, is difficult to discern, given the great distances to the coasts. But as soon as the air first touches the naked stone in the northern countries, webs of silklike fibers form that look like colorful spots to the naked eye. Several of the spots are bordered by exquisite lines, sometimes single and sometimes double; some are cut through with small furrows dividing them into boxes. Their light color darkens with increased age. The vividly bright yellow turns brown, and the bluish-gray of the Lepraria transforms itself gradually to a dusty black. The borders of the aging covering flow into each other and on the dark ground form new, circular lichens of brilliant white. In this way, one organic web rests in layers upon another, and just as the colonizing group of humans must pass through certain stages of moral development, so too is the gradual spread of plants bound by physical laws. Where tall forest trees now lift their tops to lofty heights, there the soilless stone was once covered in such delicate lichens. Mosses, grasses, herbaceous plants, and shrubs fill the gulf of the long but unmeasured era in between. What lichens and moss accomplish in the North is done in the tropics by *Portulaca*, *Gomphrenae*, and other oily shore plants. Thus the history of the covering of plants and their gradual spread over the barren crust of the Earth has its epochs, as does the history of the migrating animal world.

But if the wealth of life is spread everywhere, organic life is also unceasingly occupied with connecting to new forms those elements liberated by death; this richness of life and its renewal differ, however, depending on differences in latitude. In the frigid zone, Nature periodically becomes frozen. However, fluidity being necessary to life, animals and plants (excepting mosses and other cryptogams) will lie sunk in hibernation here for many months. In a great portion of the Earth, then, only such organic beings have been able to develop as can withstand a considerable deprivation of heat and that are capable, without needles or leaves, of a long interruption of life functions. On the other hand, the nearer one comes to the tropics, the greater the variety of shapes, the gracefulness of forms and color combinations, and the perpetual youth and power of organic life.

This increase can easily be doubted by those who have never left our part of the world, or who have neglected the study of basic geography. When one passes out of our thickly leaved forests of oak and descends from the Alps into Welschland or the Pyrenees Range into Spain, indeed, when one merely directs his gaze to the African coast of the Mediterranean, one may easily but wrongly conclude that hot climates are treeless. But one forgets that Southern Europe had a different appearance when agrarian Pelasgic or Carthaginian peoples first gathered there; one forgets that early human civilization pushed back the forests, and that the drive of nations to re-create has gradually robbed the Earth of the sylvan adornment that so pleases those of us in the North and that is more indicative of the youthful period of our moral civilization than of any other part of history. The great catastrophe by which the Mediterranean took on its form when, as a swelling inland sea, it penetrated the strait of the Dardanelles and the Pillars of Hercules – this catastrophe seems to have robbed the bordering countries of much of their topsoil. What is mentioned by the Greek authors of the Samothracian legends points to how recent this destructive natural change was. Also, in all countries that have been flooded by the Mediterranean and that are characterized by tertiary limestone and lower-stage chalk (nummulites and neocomian), a great portion of the ground surface is bare rock. The picturesque quality of regions of Italy rests primarily upon this delightful contrast between uninhabited, desolate stone and the luxuriant vegetation that springs up amidst it like islands. Where this stone is less fissured, keeping the water to the surface, and is covered with earth (as on the charming shores of Lake Albano), even Italy has its oak forests, as shady and green as the inhabitants of the North could wish.

The deserts beyond the Atlas and the immeasurable plains or steppes of South America may also be viewed as merely local phenomena. The latter may be found, at least during the rainy season, to be covered with grass and low, almost herbaceous mimosas; the former are oceans of sand within the Old Continent's interior, great spaces devoid of plants, surrounded by shores of perpetually green forest. Only solitary fan palms serve to remind the traveler that even these wastes are part of a living creation. In the deceptive play of the light brought about by the radiant heat, one might first see the foot of the palm hovering free in the air, and then see its reverse image reflected in the wavelike, quivering layers of air. To the west of the Peruvian Andes, too, on the coast of the Pacific, it took us weeks to traverse such waterless deserts.

The origin of these large expanses of earth devoid of plants in regions otherwise dominated by mighty vegetation is a little-acknowledged geognostic phenomenon that undoubtedly originated in ancient revolutions in Nature, such as floods or volcanic changes to the Earth's crust. If a region has lost all of its plants, if the sand is shifting and lacks all sources of water, then the hot, vertically rising air hinders the precipitation in clouds, and millennia must pass before organic life presses into the interior of the waste from its green shores.

With this in mind, whoever is able to comprehend Nature with a single look and knows to abstract localized phenomena will see how, with the increase in invigorating heat from the poles to the equator, there is also a gradual increase in organic power and abundance of life. But with this increase, certain beautiful aspects are reserved to each different section of the Earth: to the tropics the diversity and immensity of plant forms; to the North the aspect of meadows and the periodic reawakening of Nature upon the first breaths of the spring airs. Besides its particular advantages, each zone has its own character. The old and profound power of organization, despite a certain liberty in the abnormal development of specific cases, binds all animal and vegetable life forms to firm, perpetually returning types. In the same way that one discerns a certain physiognomy in individual organic beings, just as descriptive botany and zoology, in the strict sense of the word, are the analysis of animal and plant forms, so too is there a physiognomy of Nature that applies, without exception, to each section of the Earth.

What the painter indicates with the expression 'Swiss Nature' or 'Italian sky' is the vague feeling of this localized character of Nature. The blue of the sky, illumination, fragrance borne from afar, the forms of the animals, the succulence of the plants, brilliance of the foliage, the outline of the mountains: all of these elements determine the overall impression of a region. Indeed, in all zones of the globe the same types of mountains – trachyte, basalt, porphyry shale, and dolomite – form cliff groups of a single physiognomy. The green-stone crags of South America and Mexico are identical to the German Fichtelgebirge, just as, in the case of animals, the Allco, or the original dog breed of the New Continent, is consistent in form with the breeds of Europe. For the inorganic crust of the Earth is everywhere independent of climatic influences, whether because the difference between climates that one encounters with changes of geographic latitude is a phenomenon newer than the stone, or the hardening, heat-conducting, and heat-discharging mass of the Earth provided its own temperature without having captured it from elsewhere. All geologic formations thus belong to all regions and are manifested in the same way in all. Everywhere, the basalt builds twin peaks and truncated cones; everywhere trap-porphyry appears in grotesque rock masses, granite in gently rounded dome shapes. Similar plant forms too, firs and oaks, enwreathe the mountainsides in Sweden just as they do in the southernmost part of Mexico. Yet amidst all this agreement in form, all this similarity in individual outlines, the groupings of these into a whole takes on the most diverse character.

In the same way that mineralogical knowledge of the types of stone is different from orology, so too is the general physiognomy of Nature different from individual natural descriptions. Georg Forster in his travels and in his shorter writings, Goethe in the natural descriptions found throughout his immortal works, Buffon, Bernardin de St. Pierre, and Chateaubriand have all portrayed with inimitable truth particular places on the planet. But such portrayals are not merely suited to provide enjoyment of the noblest sort; no, the knowledge of the natural character of different parts of the world is connected in the most intimate way to the history of humanity and to that of its culture. For even if the beginning of a culture is not determined by physical influences alone, still a culture's very direction, the character of a people, the bleak or cheerful attitude of humanity depend to a great degree on climatic conditions. How powerfully the sky over Greece affected its inhabitants! Where else but in the happy and beautiful region between the Euphrates, the Halys, and the Aegean Sea did the peoples who came to settle awaken so early to moral dignity and more tender sensibilities? And did not our forebears, when Europe was sinking into new barbarism, when religious zeal had suddenly opened the holy Orient, bring back once more from those gentle valleys gentler customs? The poetic works of the Greeks and the rougher songs of the old Nordic tribes owe much of their individual character to the forms of the plants and animals, to the mountains and valleys that surrounded the poets, and to the airs that swirled around them. Who does not feel a different mood in the dark shade of a beech tree, upon hills crowned with lonely firs, or in the middle of a grassy meadow, where the wind rustles in the trembling leaves of a birch? These native forms of plant life call forth within us images that are melancholy, solemnly uplifting, or merry. The influence of the physical world upon the moral, the mysterious interworking of the sensory and the extrasensory, bestows upon the study of Nature, when lifted to higher considerations, a charm that belongs to it alone, and that remains too little acknowledged.

But even if the character of different regions of the world depends on external phenomena – if the outline of the mountains, the physiognomy of the plants and animals, if the blue of the sky, the shape of the clouds, and the clarity of the atmosphere all exert their influence upon the overall impression – it still cannot be denied that the primary determining factor of this impression is the covering of vegetation. The animal organism lacks the mass: the mobility of individual creatures, and often their small size, keeps them from our view. The plant kingdom, however, impresses our imagination through a constant immensity. Its massive dimensions indicate its age, and in individual plants, age and the impression of a constantly renewing strength are paired with one another. The gigantic dragon tree that I observed on the Canary Islands, which possesses a diameter of 16 feet, continues to bear blossoms and fruit as though in a state of perpetual youth. When French adventurers, the Bétencourts, conquered these happy islands at the beginning of the fifteenth century, the dragon tree of Orotava (sacred to the natives, as was the olive in the Acropolis of Athens or the elm in Ephesus) was of the same colossal size as today. In the tropics, a forest of Hymenaea and Caesalpinia stands as the monument to perhaps more than a millennium.

If one considers at a comprehensive glance all of the phan-erogamic plant varieties that have so far been incorporated into herbaria, the number of which is now estimated to be more than 80,000, one recognizes among this wondrous mul-titude certain primary forms to which many others may be traced back. For the determination of these types, upon whose individual beauty, distribution, and grouping the physi-ognomy of a country's vegetation depends, one need not con-centrate (as happens for other reasons in botanical taxonomy) upon the tiny reproductive organs, the perianths, and the fruits, but rather upon the consideration of that which through its sheer mass individualizes the overall impression of a region. Among the primary forms of vegetation there are of course entire families of so-called natural taxonomies. Banana plants and palms, *Casuarinae* and conifers, are also individually itemized among these. But the botanical taxonomist separates a great number of plant groups that the physiognomist finds himself forced to bind together. Where plants appear in great number, the outlines and divisions of the leaves, the shapes of the trunks and twigs, run one into the other. In the back-ground of a landscape, the painter (and it is exactly to the art-ist's refined feelings toward Nature that this statement applies) differentiates pines or palms from beech trees, but not beech forests from forests of other leafy hardwoods!

The physiognomy of Nature is determined primarily by six-teen plant forms. I am enumerating only those that I observed on my travels through both continents and over the course of years of attention to the vegetation of the various areas between the 60th degree of northern latitude and the 12th degree of southern. Certainly, the numbers of these forms will have noticeably increased once travelers have penetrated more deeply into the interiors of the continents and discovered new genera of plants. In Southeast Asia, in Inner Africa and New Holland (Australia), and in South America from the Amazon to the Chiquitos Province, the vegetation remains completely unknown to us. Imagine if someone were to discover a country where woody sponges, *Cenomyce rangiferina*, or mosses grew into tall trees. *Neckera dendroides*, a German moss, is in fact treelike, and the Bambuseae (treelike grasses), like the tropical treeferns, which are often taller than our lindens and alders, remain for Europeans as astonishing a sight as a forest of tall mosses would be to its first discoverer! The size and degree of development ultimately attained by organisms (plants and animals) belonging to a given family are governed by laws as yet unknown. In each of the great divisions of the animal kingdom – the insects, crustaceans, reptiles, birds, fish, or mammals – bodily dimensions oscillate between certain extreme limits. The measure of variability in size, as determined by observations made up to the present, can be corrected by new discoveries, by seeking out varieties of animals as yet unknown.

Temperature conditions, which are dependent upon latitude, seem above all else to have generated organic development among land animals. The small and slender form of our lizards stretches itself in the South to the colossal, ponderous armored body of the terrible crocodiles. In the immense cats of Africa and America, in the tiger, the lion, and the jaguar, the shape of our little house pet is repeated on a larger scale. If we but penetrate into the Earth's interior, if we stir up the grave sites of plants and animals, not only do the fossils reveal to us a category of forms that contradict the climates of today; they also show us gigantic forms that stand in no less contrast to those that currently surround us than do the dignified, simple, heroic natures of the Hellenic people contrast with that which we, in our time, describe with the term 'greatness of character.' If the temperature of the planet underwent significant, possibly periodically recurring changes, if the proportions of land to sea and even the height of the atmosphere and its pressure have not always been the same, then the size and shape of the organism may likewise have been subject to manifold changes. Powerful pachyderms, elephantlike mastodons, Owen's *Mylodon robustus*, and the Colossochelys, a land tortoise six feet in height – these once inhabited the forests that then consisted of gigantic lepidodendrons, cactuslike stigmaria, and numerous varieties of cycad. As I am incapable of completely depicting this physiognomy of the aging planet according to its current traits, I will venture only to bring up those characteristics that best describe each plant group. Despite all the richness and flexibility of our mother tongue, it is still a difficult undertaking to represent in words that which better befits the painter's imitative art of depiction. Also, one should avoid the impression of tediousness that any enumeration of individual forms must invariably elicit.

We shall begin with the palms, the tallest and noblest of all plants, for the peoples of the world (their earliest civilization having arisen in the Asiatic world of palms and in the area directly adjoining it) have always accorded the palm the prize for beauty. Tall, slender, ringed, and occasionally spiny shafts end in gleaming, outstretched foliage, sometimes fanning out, sometimes feathery. The leaves are often rippled like grass. The smooth trunk attains a height, as I carefully measured it, of 180 feet. The form of the palm diminishes in size and grandeur as one moves away from the equator toward the temperate zone. Among its native plants, Europe possesses but one representative of this form: the dwarf coastal palm, or chamaerops, which in Italy and Spain can be found as far north as the 44th parallel. The actual palm climate of the Earth has an average annual temperature of between $20\frac{1}{2}°$ and $22°$ Réaumur. But the date palm, which is exported to us from Africa and is considerably less attractive than other varieties in this group, will still vegetate in Southern Europe in regions with a mean temperature of $12°$ to $13\frac{1}{2}°$. Palm trunks and elephant ribs lie buried in the ground in Northern Europe; the position in which they lie indicates that they probably did not wash up here in the North from the tropics but that during the great revolutions of our planet, the climate and the physiognomy of Nature that it determines were changed many times.

Together with the palms in all parts of the world occur varieties of the pisang or banana, the botanists' scitaminaea and musaceae, *Heliconia*, *Amomum*, *Strelitzia* – a low but succulent, nearly herbaceous stem, from the tip of which rise thin, loosely interwoven, delicately striped and silkily gleaming leaves. Pisang plants are the jewel of humid regions. The nourishment of nearly all of the inhabitants of the world's torrid zone relies upon their fruit. Like the farinaceous cereals or grains of the North, the pisang stalks have accompanied humanity since the earliest childhood of our culture. Semitic legends place the point of this nourishing plant's origin on the Euphrates, others (with more probability) at the feet of the Himalayas in India. According to Greek legend, the fields of Enna were the fortunate fatherland of the cereal grains. While the Sicilian fruits of Ceres, spread by culture across the northern world, do little in their formation of uniform, widely spreading grasslands to beautify the countenance of Nature, the migrating inhabitant of the tropics, on the other hand, propagates in the cultivation of pisang plants one of the most glorious and noble of plant forms.

The forms of the Malvaceae and Bombaceae are represented by Ceiba, Cavanillesia, and the Mexican hand tree, *Cheirosthemon*: colossally thick trunks with large, velvety, heart-shaped or crenelated leaves and gorgeous crimson blossoms. To this group of plants belongs the monkey bread tree, *Adansonia digitata*, which, while of moderate height, sometimes has a diameter of 30 feet and is probably the most ancient organic monument on our planet. In Italy it is the mallow forms that begin to give the vegetation a particularly southern character.

Our temperate zone in the Old Continent meanwhile is completely without the delicate pinnate foliage of the mimosa forms dominated by *Acacia*, *Desmanthus*, *Gleditsia*, *Porlieria*, and *Tamarindus*. The United States of North America, in which the vegetation is more diverse and luxuriant than in the same latitudes in Europe, is not without this beautiful form. Typical for mimosas is an umbrellalike spreading of the branches, much like the Italian pines. The deep blue of the sky in the tropical climes shimmering through the delicate, feathery leaves creates an extremely picturesque effect.

One plant group whose species are found mostly in Africa comprises the varieties of heath plants. To these belong, in terms of physiognomic character and general appearance, the Epicrideae and the Australian Acacia, the leaves of which are merely leafstalks (phyllodia): a group that has some similarity to the conifers, and which precisely because of this, creates an all the more charming contrast to the conifers thanks to its abundance of bell-shaped blossoms. The arborescent heaths, like some other African plants, reach as far as the northern shore of the Mediterranean. They adorn Welschland and the citrus groves of Southern Spain. I observed them growing at their most luxuriant in Tenerife, on the slopes of Teide Peak. In the Baltic countries and farther north, this plant form is feared as a harbinger of drought and infertility. Our heaths, *Erica (Calluna) vulgaris*, *E. tetralix*, *E. carnea*, and *E. cinerea*, are plants that grow socially, against whose progressive march agrarian peoples have battled for centuries with little success. How strange it is that the main representative of the family can be found on only one side of the planet! Of the 300 currently recognized species of *Erica*, only a single variety exists on the New Continent, from Pennsylvania and Labrador up to Nootka and Alaska.

On the other hand, to the New Continent alone belongs the cactus form: sometimes spherical, sometimes with arms, sometimes in tall and crooked pillars standing upright like organ pipes. This group makes the most conspicuous contrast to the forms of the lily and banana plants. They belong among those plants that Bernardin de St. Pierre calls the 'vegetable springs of the desert.' In the waterless plains of South America, the animals, desperate with thirst, seek out the melon cactus: a ball-shaped plant that grows half-hidden in the sand and whose succulent interior is hidden behind fearsome needles. The columnar cactus stems achieve a height of 30 feet, and, divided like a candelabra and often covered in lichens, they are reminiscent in form of some African Euphorbia.

As these form green oases in deserts otherwise devoid of plants, so do the orchids likewise enliven the tropical tree trunk blackened by the sunlight, or the cracks in the most desolate of rocks. The vanilla form distinguishes itself through light green succulent leaves and by multicolored blooms of remarkable construction. The orchid blooms sometimes resemble winged insects, sometimes the very birds that are attracted by the scent of the nectaries. The life span of a painter would be insufficient, even if concentrating upon only a narrow area, to depict the glorious orchids that adorn the deep-cut valleys of the Peruvian Andes chain.

Like nearly all cactus species, the Casuarineae have a leafless form. They are a plant variety found only in the South Seas and the West Indies – trees with limbs similar to horsetail. But there are traces of this more unusual than attractive variety found in other areas of the world. Plumier's *Equisetum altissimum*, Forskål's *Ephedra aphylla* of North Africa, the Peruvian Colletia, and the Siberian *Calligonum pallasia* are closely related to the Casuarineae.

While the pisang plants accomplish the broadest expansion of the veins in the leaves, it is in the Casuarineae and the conifers that they are most highly contracted. Firs, thujas, and cypresses belong to a northern form that is less common in the tropics and that in some species (*Dammara*, *Salisburia*) features broad, leaflike needles. Their eternally fresh green cheers the barren winter landscape. It also declares to the people of the polar region that when snow and ice cover the ground, the inner life of plants, like promethean fire, is never quenched on our planet.

Besides the orchids, varieties of Pothos, too, spread parasitically over the aging trunks of the forest trees in the tropical world, much as mosses and lichens do in ours. Succulent herbaceous stalks lift up large leaves that, while they are sometimes arrowlike, sometimes palmate or oblong, are always thick-veined. The blossoms of the Aroideae, to increase their warmth, are wrapped in sheaths; without stems, they put forth roots in the air. Related forms are *Pothos*, *Dracontium*, *Caladium*, and *Arum*, the last progressing now as far as the coasts of the Mediterranean, and in Spain and Italy, along with succulent coltsfoot and with tall stands of thistle and *Acanthus*, indicating the luxuriance of southern plant life.

Growing socially with this Arum form are the tropical lianas, displaying in the hot regions of South America the most exquisitely abundant vegetation: *Paullinia*, *Banisteria*, Bignonias, and Passiflora. Our tendrillar hops and grapevines are reminiscent of this plant form of the tropical world. By the Orinoco, the leafless branches of the Bauhinia often reach a length of 40 feet. They sometimes fall vertically from the tops of high Swieteniae, and sometimes they are suspended aslant like a mast line, and the tiger-cat has an admirable agility in climbing up and down them.

Contrasting with the supple and tendrillar lianas, with their fresh, light green, is the free-standing form of the bluish aloe plants: the stems, if there are any, divide hardly at all and are marked by close-set rings winding around like a snake. At the tip are succulent, fleshy, long, and pointed leaves, bunched together and radiating outward. The tall-stemmed aloe plants do not form copses like other, socially growing plants; they stand alone in barren places, thus often lending to the tropical region its own melancholy (one might say 'African') character. The following plants belong to this aloe form, due to the physiognomic similarity in their impressions upon the landscape:

from the Bromeliaceae, the Pitcairnias, which sprout from fissures in the rocks of the Andes chain, the great *Pournetia pyramidata* (Achupalla of the high plains of New Granada), the American aloe (agave), *Bromelia ananas* and *B. Karatas*;

from the Euphorbiaceae, the uncommon varieties with thick, short, candelabralike divided stems;

from the family of the Asphodeleae, the African aloe and the dragon tree *Dracaena draco*;

and finally, from the Liliaceae, the high-blooming yucca.

While the aloe form is characterized by a stolid quiet and firmness, the grass form, especially the physiognomy of the arborescent grasses, is defined by an expression of blithe lightness and mobile slenderness. Bamboo groves form shady archways in both Indies. The smooth, often bowed and swaying stem of the tropical grasses exceeds the height of our alders and oaks. As far north as Italy this form begins to lift itself from the ground in the *Arundo donax*, determining by its height and mass the natural character of the land.

As in the case of the grasses, the form of the ferns in the

hot regions of the Earth is also ennobled. Treelike ferns of up
to 40 feet have an appearance similar to palms, but their trunk
is less slender, shorter, and more roughly scaled than that of
the palms. The foliage is more delicate, loosely intermingled,
and translucent, with neatly serrated edges. These colossal
ferns belong almost exclusively to the tropics, but they prefer
the tropical areas of more moderate climate to the very hot
ones. As the lessening of the heat is a function of increased
altitude, it is accurate to describe mountain regions that rise
two to three thousand feet above sea level as the primary hab-
itat of this form. In South America, tall-stemmed ferns accompany the beneficial tree that provides the bark that is a remedy
for fever. Both of these characterize that happy region of the
Earth in which prevails the eternal mildness of spring.

Yet to be named are the lily plants (*Amaryllis, Ixia, Gladiolus,
Pancratium*), with leaves like those of reed plants and glorious
blooms, a form whose primary place of origin is Southern
Africa; also the willow form, native to all parts of the world,
distinguishing itself on the high plains of Quito in *Schinus molle*
not by the shape of its leaves but by the manner of its branching; the myrtle plants (*Metrosideros, Eucalyptus, Escallonia myrtilloides*); and the Melastoma and Laurel forms.

It would be an undertaking worthy of a great artist to study
the character of all of these plant groups, not in greenhouses
or in the descriptions of botanists but in the vast tropics of
Nature itself. How interesting and instructive to the landscape
painter would be a work that depicts for the eye each of the
sixteen enumerated primary forms, first individually, and then
in contrast to one another. What is more picturesque than a
treelike fern spreading its tenderly woven leaves over the Mexican laurel oak? What is more charming than pisang plants
shaded by tall Guadua and bamboo grasses? To the artist is
left the task of separating the groups, and under his hand the
great, magical image of Nature (if I may venture to use the
expression) reveals itself, much like the written works of men,
in a few simple strokes.

In the glowing sunshine of the tropical sky thrive the most
splendid of plant forms. As the bark of trees in the North is

covered with dry lichens and moss, just so in the tropics do Cymbidium and aromatic vanilla live upon the trunks of the Anacardia and the giant fig trees. The fresh green of the Pothos leaves and the Dracontia contrasts with the multicolored blooms of the orchids. Twining Bauhinia, Passiflora, and yellow-blossomed Banisteria wind about the trunks of the forest trees. Delicate blossoms unfold from the roots of the *Theobroma* and from the dense, rough barks of the Crescentia and *Gustavia*. In this abundance of blossoms and leaves, this luxuriant growth with its confusion of tendrilous plants, it is often difficult for the natural scientist to recognize which blossoms and leaves belong to which stem. A single tree, adorned with Paullinia, Bignonia, and Dendrobium, comprises a group of plants that, if separated from one another, would cover a considerable space of earth.

The plants in the tropics are more extremely succulent, of a fresher green, and arrayed in larger, glossier leaves than are those in northern latitudes. Socially growing plants, which give to European vegetation such uniformity, are virtually absent at the equator. Trees, nearly twice as tall as our oaks, are resplendent with blossoms as grand and gorgeous as our lilies. On the shady banks of the Magdalena River in South America there grows a twining Aristolochia with flowers four feet in circumference, which the Indian boys at play take and pull over their heads. In the southern portion of the Indian Archipelago, the bloom of the *Rafflesia* has a diameter of almost three feet and weighs over fourteen pounds.

Between the tropical lines, the extraordinary elevation to which rise not only single mountains but entire countries, along with the cold that is the result of this elevation, presents to the inhabitant of the tropics a curious perspective. Besides the palms and pisang trees, he is also surrounded by plant forms that would seem indigenous only to northern countries. Cypresses, firs, and oaks, Berberis shrubs and alders (closely related to ours) cover the high plateaus of Southern Mexico as well as the Andes chain below the equator. Nature has thus allowed the inhabitant of the torrid zone to see, without leaving his home, all of the plant forms of the Earth, just as the dome of the heavens from pole to pole hides from him none of its luminous worlds.

The northern peoples are denied these and many other such enjoyments of Nature. Many celestial phenomena and many plant forms – and from these, indeed, the most beautiful (palms, long-stemmed ferns and pisang plants, treelike grasses and feathery mimosas) – remain forever unknown to them. The sickly plants within our greenhouses provide but a weak image of the majesty of tropical vegetation. But in the refinement of our language, in the incandescent imagination of the poet, in the depictive art of the painter there open rich wellsprings of compensation. From this, the power of our imagination creates a living picture of exotic Nature. In the cold of the North, in the starkness of the heath, the lone individual can acquire for himself that which is being explored in the most distant latitudes, and thus create within himself a world that is the work of, and is as free and immortal as, his own spirit.

VI

CONCERNING THE STRUCTURE
AND ACTION OF VOLCANOES
IN VARIOUS REGIONS OF
THE EARTH

IF ONE CONSIDERS the influence that expeditions to different regions and increased knowledge of earth sciences have exerted for centuries on the study of Nature, one soon sees how this influence varies depending on whether the investigations concentrate on the forms of the organic world or on the formations of inanimate earth – the varieties of stone, their relative ages, and their origins. Different forms of plants and animals inhabit the Earth in every zone, be it in the oceanlike plain where the heat of the atmosphere moves according to latitude and the manifold twists and turns of the isothermal lines, or places where the heat moves almost vertically along the steep slopes of mountain chains. Organic Nature gives to each stretch of land a physiognomic character of its own – not so with inorganic Nature, in places where the hard crust of the planet is exposed from under the cover of plants. The same sorts of stone, seeming to attract and repel one another in groups, occur in both hemispheres from the equator to the poles. On a distant isle, surrounded by strange vegetation and under a sky where the old stars no longer shine, the seafarer, joyfully astonished, will recognize the clay slate of home, the comfortably familiar type of rock he knows from his fatherland.

This independence of geognosy from the current

(This treatise was read before the public assembly of the Academy at Berlin on the 24th of January, 1823.)

constitution of the climate does not diminish the beneficial influence that numerous observations made in foreign parts of the world have exerted upon the progress of mineralogy and physical geology; rather, it gives to these sciences their own particular orientation. Each expedition enriches natural history with new plant and animal genera. Sometimes they are organic forms that may be added to long-familiar types, displaying to us the regularly woven, though often seemingly interrupted, network of animated natural creation in its original perfection; sometimes they are forms that appear in isolation, as escaped remnants of extinct genera or, arousing our expectations, as unknown members of groups yet to be discovered. Such diversity is clearly not offered by analysis of the hard crust of the Earth. This reveals rather a consistency in the constituent minerals, the stratification of various masses, and their periodic reappearance, which excites the wonderment of the geognost. In the Andes chain, as in the central range of Europe, one formation seems to some degree to call forth the other. Correspondent masses take the shape of similar forms: basalt and dolerite into twin peaks; dolomite, sandstone, and porphyry as looming cliff walls; trachyte rich in feldspar into bell shapes or high-vaulted domes. In the most distant zones, crystals of the same rock separate themselves as if by inner development from the dense weave of the groundmass, envelop one another, come together in secondary formations, and, as such, announce the proximity of a new and independent formation. Thus every mountainous region of considerable extent reflects, with greater or lesser clarity, the entire inorganic world; yet to recognize completely the important phenomena of the composition, the relative age, and the emergence of the various types of rock, observations from the most disparate regions of the planet must be compared to one another. Problems that have long seemed puzzling to the geognost in his northern homeland find their solution at the equator. If the distant zones, as has often been noted, present to us no new types of rock, i.e., no unknown combinations of basic materials, then they teach us rather how to unmask the great laws that are the same everywhere, the laws by which the layers of the Earth's crust alternately support one another, break apart into channels, or are lifted by elastic forces.

In light of the profit just described that investigation gives to geognostic knowledge, it should not surprise us that one class of phenomena, upon which I will concentrate here, has long been considered all the more one-sidedly as the points of comparison were more difficult, one might even say more painful, to discover. By the close of the previous century, everything that was thought to be known regarding the structure of volcanoes and the action of their subterranean forces was gathered from two mountains of Southern Italy: Vesuvius and Aetna. Since the first is more accessible and (like nearly all short volcanoes) erupts more frequently, it came about that a hill, as it were, came to serve as the generic model by which an entire distant world, the mighty strings of volcanoes of Mexico, South America, and the Asiatic islands, was pictured in the mind. Such a thought process understandably calls to mind Virgil's deluded shepherd who perceived in his narrow hut the model of the regal eternal city of Rome.

Certainly a more painstaking investigation of the entire Mediterranean, especially the eastern islands and coastal lands where humanity first awakened to intellectual civilization and nobler feelings, could have eradicated such a one-sided view of Nature. From the depths of the seafloor here, trachyte cliffs heaved themselves up amidst the Sporades to form islands – similar to what periodically occurred in the Azores, where it happened three times over the course of three centuries and at nearly equal intervals. Between Epidaurus and Troezen, near Methoni, the Peloponnese features a *Monte nuovo*, which was described by Strabo and seen again by Dodwell: taller than the *Monte nuovo* of the Phlegraean Fields of Baiae, perhaps even taller than the new volcano of Jorullo on the Mexican plains, which I found encircled by several thousand small basalt cones that had been pushed out through the surface of the ground and were, at the time, still smoking.

In the Mediterranean basin too, the volcanic fire does not break forth only from permanent craters, isolated mountains with an abiding connection to the interior of the Earth, such as Stromboli, Vesuvius, and Aetna. On Mount Epomeo on the island of Ischia and, according to the reports of the ancients, on the Lelantine Plain near Chalcis, lava has flowed from suddenly opening fissures in the ground. Along with these phenomena (which fall in the realm of historical time, in that narrow region of assured tradition, and which will be collected and elucidated by Carl Ritter in his masterful geographical work), the coasts of the Mediterranean contain manifold remnants of the effects of more ancient fire. Southern France shows us its own enclosed system of volcanoes ordered in rows in the Auvergne region: trachyte domes alternating with volcanic cones from which pour forth ribbonlike streams of lava. The plain of Lombardy, which lies even with the sea and forms the innermost bay of the Adriatic, encloses the trachyte of the Euganean Hills, where domes of granular trachyte, of obsidian, and of perlite rise up: three masses growing out of one another which break through the chalk and nummulite lime below but have never flowed in narrow streams. Similar evidence of ancient revolutions of the Earth can be found in many parts of continental Greece and Western Asia, countries that will offer to the geognost rich material for investigation, once the light returns to the place from which it first shone forth over the West, when tormented humanity is no longer persecuted by the wild barbarism of the Ottomans.

I mention the geographical proximity of these diverse phenomena in order to demonstrate that the basin of the Mediterranean, with its strings of islands, could have provided the attentive observer with everything that has recently been discovered in many various forms and structures in South America, on Tenerife, or in the Aleutians close to the polar region. These objects of observation were certainly all concentrated closely together. But travels to distant climes and the comparison of larger sections of the Earth's surface both within and outside of Europe were necessary in order to recognize the commonality of volcanic phenomena and their dependence upon one another.

Conventional language (which often lends longevity and credibility to the earliest errors, but also often instinctively indicates the truth) describes as 'volcanic' all eruptions of underground fire and molten materials: columns of smoke and vapor that sporadically rise up out of the rocks, as in Colares after the great earthquake of Lisbon; salses, that is, clay cones that spew forth wet mud, bitumen, and hydrogen, like those near Girgenti in Sicily and Turbaco in South America; hot geysers that rise up under the pressure of elastic vapors – in general, all effects of those wild forces of Nature that originate deep in the interior of our planet. In Central America (Guatemala) and in the Philippine Islands, the natives differentiate (and indeed formally) between water and fire volcanoes, *volcanes de agua y de fuego*. With the first of these names, they indicate mountains from which now and then, upon the occasion of sizable seismic shocks, a muffled crack is accompanied by the expulsion of subterranean water.

Without denying the connectedness of the aforementioned phenomena, it still seems advisable to give to the oryctognostic areas of geognosy a more specific language, and not to use the word *volcano* to indicate in one context a mountain that terminates with a permanent mouth of fire and in another any sort of subterranean cause of volcanic phenomena. In the current situation of the Earth, in every region of the planet, the isolated conical mountain (of Vesuvius, Aetna, the peak of Tenerife, of Tungurahua and Cotopaxi) is clearly the usual form of volcanoes; I have seen them in sizes from the lowest hills up to 18,000 feet above sea level. But beside these cone-shaped peaks one also finds permanent chasms of fire, enduring communications with the interior of the Earth upon long-abiding jagged ridges, and not always in the middle but at the lower end of their wall-like tops, near the slope. This is the form of Pichincha, which rises between the Pacific and the city of Quito, and which was first made famous by Bouguer's barometric formulas; so too the volcanoes that rise from the ten-thousand-foot-high steppe of los Pastos. All of these peaks of widely diverse shapes consist of trachyte, once called trap-porphyry: a granular, fissured stone composed of varieties of feldspar (labradorite, oligoclase, albite), augite, hornblende, and occasionally admixed mica or even quartz. Where the evidence of the initial eruption, or I might say where the old structure has remained intact, a high wall of rock, a mantle of accumulated layers surrounds the isolated cone in a circular fashion. Such walls or ring-shaped enclosures are called elevation craters, a large and important phenomenon about which the first geognost, Leopold von Buch, from whose writings I have borrowed many of the views in this essay, presented a truly memorable essay to our academy five years ago.

Volcanoes that communicate with the atmosphere by means of fiery mouths, conical basalt hills, and domed, craterless trachyte mountains (these last being sometimes low, like Sarcouy, sometimes tall, like Chimborazo) form many diverse groups. Sometimes comparative geography shows us small archipelagos, closed mountain systems as it were, with craters and lava flows in the Canary Islands and the Azores, and without craters or actual lava flows in the Euganean Hills and the Siebengebirge near Bonn; other times it describes for us volcanoes lined up in simple or double chains, ranges of several hundred miles, either parallel to the primary direction of the mountains, as in Guatemala, Peru, and Java, or else perpendicularly bisecting the axis of the mountains, as in tropical Mexico. In this land of the Aztecs, fire-spewing trachyte mountains alone attain the height of the snow line, and, probably breaking out along a fault, follow a line of latitude that extends for 105 geographical miles and cuts across the entire continent from the Pacific to the Atlantic.

This concentration of volcanoes, sometimes in separated, somewhat circular groups, and sometimes in double ranges, provides the most convincing evidence that volcanic effects are not dependent upon trivial causes close to the surface but are immense phenomena with deep-rooted causes. The entire metal-poor eastern region of the American continent, in its present condition, is without fiery chasms and trachyte masses, perhaps even without basalt or olivine. All American volcanoes are in the regions that lie across from Asia, in the longitudinally extending 1,800-geographical-mile-long chain of the Andes.

Indeed, the entire plateau of Quito, whose summit is formed by Pichincha, Cotopaxi, and Tungurahua, is a single volcanic hearth. The subterranean fire breaks forth now from one of these openings, now from another, the three of them having been viewed by habit as separate volcanoes. The progressive movement of the fire here has been directed from north to south over the course of the last three centuries. Even the earthquakes that have so devastated this part of the world give peculiar evidence of subterranean connections: not only between countries without volcanoes, which have long been known, but also between mouths of fire that lie at great distances from one another. Thus did the volcano of Pasto, east of the Guaitara River, uninterruptedly pour out a tall column of smoke for three months in 1797, the column then disappearing at the very moment when, 60 miles away, the great earthquake of Riobamba and the mud-eruption, or *Moya*, killed thirty to forty thousand Indians.

The sudden appearance of Sabrina Island in the Azores on 30 January 1811 was the harbinger of the terrible earthquakes far to the west that from May of 1811 to June of 1813 almost unceasingly shook first the Antilles, then the plain of the Ohio and Mississippi, and finally the coastline of Venezuela that lies across from this plain. Thirty days after the total destruction of Caracas, the beautiful capital city of this country, the eruption of the long-dormant volcano of St. Vincent occurred in the nearby Antilles. An odd natural phenomenon accompanied this eruption. In the same moment that this explosion occurred, on 30 April 1812, a terrible subterranean noise was heard in South America throughout an area of 2,200 square geographical miles. The people living on the Apure, near the influx of the Rio Nula, compared the sound to the roar of heavy artillery, as did the most distant inhabitants of the Venezuelan coast. From the confluence of the Rio Nula and the Apure, by way of which I came to the Orinoco, the distance to the volcano of St. Vincent following a straight line measures 157 geographical miles. This noise, which was certainly not propagated through the air, must have had a deep subterranean origin. Its intensity was hardly more extreme on the coasts of the Caribbean, closer to the erupting volcano, than in the country's interior, in the basin of the Apure and Orinoco.

It would serve no purpose to increase the number of such examples as I have collected; but to think of an event that was more historically significant for Europe I need only mention the famous earthquake of Lisbon. Simultaneous to it, on 1 November 1755, not only were the Swiss lakes and the sea on the coast of Sweden violently disturbed, but even in the eastern Antilles around Martinique, Antigua, and Barbados, where the tide never rises above 28 inches, it suddenly rose to twenty feet. All of these phenomena demonstrate that subterranean forces manifest themselves either dynamically, intensely, and convulsively, or else in the productive and chemically altering manner of volcanoes. They also demonstrate that these forces do not exert their influence superficially, coming only from the thin crust of the Earth, but instead deeply, coming from the interior of our planet through clefts and unfilled passages, rising simultaneously to the most distant points on the Earth's surface.

The more complex the structure of volcanoes, that is, the elevated points that contain the channel through which the molten masses of the Earth's interior rise to the surface, the more important it is to fathom this structure by means of exact measurements. The interest in these measurements, which were a particular object of my investigations on another continent, is heightened by the consideration that that which is to be measured is at many points a variable quantity. Natural philosophy is at pains, in this variability of phenomena, to connect the present with the past.

To explore a periodic recurrence or even the laws of progressive alterations in Nature, one needs certain firm points, carefully executed observations that, attached to specific epochs, can be the basis for numerical comparisons. If over the course of millennia the mean temperature of the atmosphere or the average level of the barometer at sea level could have been determined, then we would know to what extent the heat of the climate has risen or decreased, or whether the height of the atmosphere has undergone changes. Just such points of comparison as these are needed for the declination and inclination of the magnetic needle, and for the intensity of the electromagnetic forces, over which two outstanding physicists, Seebeck and Erman, have shed so much light within the halls of this academy. If it is a laudable occupation of learned societies to pursue tenaciously the cosmic changes in heat, air pressure, magnetic direction, and electrical charge, it is on the other hand the duty of the traveling geognost, while determining the irregularities of the Earth's surface, to consider primarily the changeable heights of volcanoes. That which I attempted in the past in the Mexican mountains, on the *volcan de Toluca*, on Popocatepetl, on the *Cofre de Perote* or Naucampatepetl, and on the Jorullo as well as in the Andes of Quito on Pichincha, I have had the opportunity since my return to Europe to repeat at different points in time on Vesuvius. Where complete trigonometric or barometric measurements are not available, carefully taken elevation angles from specifically determined points may be substituted for them. The comparison of such elevation angles measured at different points in time can often be preferable to the complication of complete operations.

Saussure had measured Vesuvius in 1773, at a time when both rims of the crater, the northwest and the southeast, seemed to him to be of equal height. He found their height to be 609 toises or 3,654 Parisian feet. The eruption of 1794 caused a cave-in on the south side, creating the unevenness of the crater rim which the untrained eye can discern even from a great distance. Leopold von Buch, Gay-Lussac, and I measured Vesuvius three times in 1805 and found the north rim, which stands opposite the Somma, *la Rocca del Palo*, to be the same as Saussure had found it, but we found the south rim to be 75 toises lower than it was in 1773. The entire height of the volcano at that time in the direction of Torre del Greco (toward a side on which the fire has been working more or less primarily for 30 years) had decreased by 1/8. The ratio of the cinder cone, relative to the entire height of the mountain, is 1 to 3 on Vesuvius, 1 to 10 on Pichincha, 1 to 22 on the peak of Tenerife. Vesuvius thus has the proportionately tallest cinder cone of these three volcanoes, possibly because it is a low volcano and thus most of its action was from its peak.

A few months ago I was fortunate enough not only to repeat my earlier barometric measurements on Vesuvius but also, in three ascents of the mountain, to undertake a more complete determination of all crater rims. This work is perhaps worthy of attention because it covers the long period of large eruptions between 1805 and 1822, and because it is the only measurement on any volcano yet presented to the public that is comparable in all its parts. It proves that the rims of the craters, not only in cases (such as the peak of Tenerife and all of the volcanoes of the Andes chain) where they are visibly composed of trachyte, but rather in general, are a much more constant phenomenon than was believed after the fleeting observations made before now. According to my latest determinations, the northwestern rim of Vesuvius had since Saussure (i.e., over the last 49 years) seemingly not changed at all, and the southeastern rim, facing Boscotrecase, which became 400 feet lower in 1794, had barely changed by 10 toises (60 feet).

If in the descriptions of great eruptions in published works one finds the completely changed shape of Vesuvius mentioned so often; if one believes these assertions to be substantiated by the picturesque views of the mountain that are sketched in Naples; then the cause of the error lies in the fact that the outline of the crater rim is confused with the outline of the spatter cone, which takes shape in the middle of the crater, resting on the floor around the vent, which has been raised by vapors. Such a spatter cone, made of loosely piled *rapilli* (lapilli) and slag, gradually became visible over the southeastern crater rim in the years 1816 and 1818. The eruption of February 1822 increased its size to the extent that it even grew to be 100 to 110 feet higher than the northwestern crater rim (the *Rocca del Palo*). On the occasion of the last eruption on the night of 22 October, this peculiar cone, which the people of Naples had come to regard as the actual peak of

Vesuvius, caved in with a fearful cracking, such that the floor of the crater, which had been uninterruptedly accessible since 1811, presently lies 750 feet deeper than the north rim of the volcano and 200 feet lower than the south rim. The changeable shape and relative position of the spatter cone, the openings of which must not, as so often occurs, be confused with the crater of the volcano, gives to Vesuvius at different times a particular physiognomy; the historian of the volcano, by means of the outline of the mountaintop, indeed by merely looking at the landscapes by Hackert in the Palace of Portici, would be able to guess the year in which the artist made the sketch study for his painting according to whether the north or south side of the mountain is represented as higher.

One day after the collapse of this 400-foot cone of slag, once the small but numerous lava streams had flowed off, the fiery expulsion of ash and *rapilli* began in the night of the 23rd to the 24th of October. This went on uninterrupted for 12 days, though it was heaviest for the first 4 days. During this time, the detonations inside the volcano were so strong that merely the shocks to the air (there was no trace whatever of earthquake) cracked the ceilings of the Palace of Portici. There appeared in the close-lying villages of Resina, Torre del Greco, Torre dell'Annunziata, and Boscotrecase a curious phenomenon. The atmosphere was so filled with ash that the entire region, in the middle of the day, was wrapped for several hours in the deepest darkness. People on the streets walked with lanterns, as so often happens in Quito at times when Pichincha erupts. Never was there a more universal flight of the inhabitants. They fear lava flows less than eruptions of ash: an event that, to such an extreme, is unknown to us here and that, through the dark legends of the manner in which Herculaneum, Pompeii, and Stabiae were destroyed, fills the human imagination with visions of terror.

The hot steam that rose out of the crater during the eruption and poured into the atmosphere formed in cooling a thick bank of cloud around the 9,000-foot column of ash and fire. Such a sudden condensation of vapors and, as Gay-Lussac demonstrated, the formation of the clouds themselves,

increased the electrical tension. Lightning snaked in all directions from around the pillar of ash, and one could clearly
differentiate the rolling of the thunder from the inner rumbling of the volcano. During no other eruption had the play of
the electrical forces been so apparent.

On the morning of the 26th of October, the uncanny news
spread: a river of boiling water had poured forth from the
crater and come crashing down from the cinder cone. Monticelli, the assiduous and learned observer of the volcano,
soon recognized that an optical illusion had been the cause of
this erroneous rumor. The supposed river was a terrific
amount of dry ash that had shot forth like quicksand from a
cleft in the highest rim of the crater. After a drought that had
rendered the fields desolate had preceded the eruption of
Vesuvius, the volcanic storm just described brought on, near
the end of the eruption, a pouring rain of long duration. In all
zones, such an event is characteristic of the end of an eruption.
Since the cinder cone is usually wrapped in clouds during the
eruption, and since the rainfall is generally heaviest in its vicinity, one will see streams of mud pouring down it on all sides.
The shocked landsman perceives these as water that climbs up
from the interior of the volcano and pours out from the crater;
the deceived geognost believes them to be seawater or mudlike products of the volcano, the so-called *éruptions boueuses*, or,
in the language of old French systematists, products of a
conflagrant-aqueous liquefaction.

When the summits of the volcanoes (and this is usually the
case in the Andes) reach higher than the snow line, or even to
twice the height of Aetna, the inundations described above,
due to the melting and penetrating snow, become extremely
frequent and devastating. These events have a meteorological
connection to the eruption of volcanoes, and they are modified in many ways by the height of the mountains, the girth of
their eternally snow-covered peaks, and the warming of the
walls of the cinder cone, but they cannot be viewed as actual
volcanic phenomena. In broad caves, sometimes on the slope
of the volcano, sometimes at the foot, underground lakes
form that communicate in many directions with the alpine

streams. When earthquakes, which precede all fiery eruptions in the Andes chain, mightily shake the entire mass of the volcano, the subterranean vaults break open and water, fish, and tufflike mud burst forth from them all at once. This is the strange phenomenon that provides the catfish of the Cyclops (*Pimelodes cyclopum*) that the inhabitants of the highlands of Quito call *preñadilla* and that I described shortly after my return. When the peak of the 18,000-foot Carihuairazo north of Chimborazo caved in on the night of 19 to 20 June 1698, all the fields around for some two square miles were covered in mud and fish. Similarly, seven years previous to this, the putrid fever in the city of Ibarra was ascribed to a fish eruption of the volcano Imbaburu.

I call these facts to mind because they shed some light upon the difference between the eruption of dry ash and that of mudlike mixtures of wood, coals, and shells within alluvia of tuff and trass. The amount of ash that Vesuvius recently ejected has been, like all things associated with volcanoes and other terrifying natural phenomena, greatly exaggerated in the published papers; indeed, two Neapolitan chemists, Vicenzo Pepe and Giuseppe di Nobili, even ascribed to the ash, despite contradiction from Monticelli and Covelli, gold and silver content. According to my investigations, the ash layer that fell over 12 days on the slope of the *conus* in the direction of Boscotrecase, where there were also *rapilli* mixed in, reached a thickness of only three feet, and down on the plain, 15 to 18 inches at most. Measurements such as these must not be made in locations where ash, like snow or sand, is blown into heaps by the wind or flooded with water into a sort of slurry. The times are past when, in the way of the ancients, one sought in volcanic phenomena only the wondrous, when someone like Ktesias might describe the ash of Aetna as flying down as far as the Indian Peninsula. Admittedly, a portion of the Mexican lodes of gold and silver are to be found in trachitic porphyry, but in the ash of Vesuvius that I brought with me and that an excellent chemist, Heinrich Rose, examined at my request, there was no trace of gold or silver to be seen.

Though the results that I am developing here (and which

Monticelli's more exact observations substantiate) diverge greatly from those that have been disseminated in the last few months, the ash eruption of Vesuvius from 24 to 28 October remains the most memorable event of its kind (of which there is a reliable report) since the death of Pliny the Elder. The amount of ash is perhaps three times more than has ever been seen to fall since volcanic phenomena have been attentively observed in Italy. A layer of 15 to 18 inches seems at first glance to be insignificant compared to the mass that we find covering Pompeii. But without thinking of the rainfall and alluvia that might certainly have increased this mass over the centuries, without reviving the lively debate which has been carried on with great skepticism on the other side of the Alps regarding the causes of the destruction of the Campanian cities, one may call to mind here that the eruptions of a volcano in epochs widely separated in time may in no way be compared to one another in terms of their intensity. All conclusions based on analogy are insufficient when they are related to quantitative circumstances, to the amounts of lava and ash, to the height of the column of smoke, or to the strength of the detonation.

From the description by Strabo and the judgment of Vitruvius regarding the volcanic origin of pumice stone, one may conclude that until the year of Vespasian's death, that is, until the eruption that covered Pompeii, Vesuvius resembled more a burnt-out volcano than a solfatara. When, after a long quiet period, the forces beneath the ground suddenly opened new passages for themselves, when they again broke through layers of primordial stone and trachyte, powerful events must have been unleashed to which subsequent ones could offer no comparison. From the well-known letters to Tacitus in which Pliny the Younger reports the death of his uncle one can clearly discern that the renewal of eruptions, one could say the reanimation of the slumbering volcano, began with the eruption of ash. This very thing was observed in September 1759 with Jorullo, when the new volcano, penetrating strata of syenite and trachyte, suddenly lifted itself up from the plain. The country people fled, because upon their huts they found ash that had been flung from the many cracks in the ground. In the usual periodic actions of volcanoes, on the other hand, each partial eruption usually ends with the rain of ash. Moreover, the letter of the younger Pliny contains a passage which clearly shows that right at the beginning and without the influence of alluvial deposits, the dry ash that fell from the air reached a height of 4 to 5 feet. 'The court,' the narrative continues, 'through which one came to the room in which Pliny took his afternoon rest was so filled with ash and pumice that, had the sleeper hesitated any longer, he would have found the exit blocked.' In the enclosed space of a court, the effect of winds causing the ash to drift can well have been negligible.

I have interrupted my comparative overview of volcanoes with specific observations made at Vesuvius partly because of the great interest evoked by the last eruption, but also partly because every strong ashfall reminds us almost involuntarily of the classical ground of Pompeii and Herculaneum. In a supplemental text, the reading of which is not really suited to this collection, I have condensed all elements of the barometric measurements that I had the opportunity to make at the end of the past year on Vesuvius and in the Phlegraean Fields.

Thus far we have considered the form and actions of those volcanoes that stand in a state of enduring connection with the interior of the Earth by means of a crater. The peaks of such volcanoes are elevated masses of trachyte and lavas cut through by manifold vents. The permanence of their effects indicates a very complex structure. They have, so to speak, an individual character that remains the same for long periods. Mountains of the same sort situated nearby mostly produce greatly differing materials: leucite and feldspar lavas, obsidian with pumice, basaltlike masses containing olivine. They belong among the newer phenomena of the Earth, they break through most all of the layers of the floetz stone, and their eruptions and lava flows are of later origin than our valleys. Their life, if one may employ this figurative expression, depends upon the type and durability of their connections with the planet's interior. They often rest for centuries, suddenly reignite, and then end up emitting steam and various gases and acids as solfataras; sometimes, however, as was seen in the case of the peak of Tenerife, their top has already become a factory for regenerated sulfur – and yet from the sides of the mountain, powerful streams of lava still pour out, of a type that is like basalt down low, of an obsidian sort with pumice stone above, where the pressure is less.

Independent of these volcanoes with permanent craters, there is another type of volcanic phenomenon that is less frequently observed but that, in a manner especially instructive to the field of geognosy, is reminiscent of the primordial world, that is, of the earliest revolutions of our planet. Trachyte mountains suddenly open, eject lava and ash, and then close themselves up again, possibly forever. So it was with the mighty Antisana in the Andes chain; so too with Epomaeus on Ischia in the year 1302. Such an eruption occasionally occurs even on the plains, as on the plateau of Quito, in Iceland far from the volcano Hekla, and on Euboea in the Lelantine Fields. Many of the elevated islands are the results of these transitory phenomena. The connection with the planet's interior is in these cases not permanent; the effect ceases as soon as the cleft, the communicating canal, is closed again. Channels of basalt, dolerite, and porphyry, which in various parts of the world cut through almost all formations; syenite, augite-porphyry, and amygdaloid masses, which all characterize the newest layers of transition rock and the oldest layer of the floetz strata: all are probably formed in a similar way. In the youthful days of our planet, the materials of the interior that had remained fluid forced their way through the cracks that were everywhere in the Earth's crust; sometimes hardening as granular dike rock, at other times spreading in layers atop one another. What the primordial world has passed down to us as exclusively so-called volcanic rock types did not flow forth ribbonlike, as do the lavas of our isolated cone-shaped mountains. The masses of augite, ilmenite, feldspar, and hornblende may have been the same at different epochs, now more like basalt, now more like trachyte; the chemical materials in mixtures of certain ratios may have aligned themselves in a crystalline fashion (as can be learned from Mitscherlich's

important work and the analogy of artificial products of igni-
tion): time and again we recognize that similarly structured
materials have come to the surface of the ground in greatly
different ways, either lifted up or forced out of temporary fissures, and that, breaking through the older stone strata (that
is to say the parts of the Earth's crust that oxidized earlier),
they finally pour forth as lava flows from conical peaks that
possess a permanent crater. Confusing these actually quite
different phenomena leads the geognosy of volcanoes back
into the darkness from which a great number of comparative
experiences have gradually begun to wrest it away.

The question often arises: what is burning in the volcanoes,
what creates the heat under which melting earth and metals
mingle? Recent chemistry has attempted to answer: 'That
which burns there are the earth, the metals, and the alkalis
themselves; it is the metalloids of these materials. The firm,
already oxidized crust of the Earth separates the surrounding
oxygen-rich atmosphere from the combustible, unoxidized
materials of the interior of our planet. Upon the contact of
these metalloids with the oxygen pressing in, the release of
heat occurs.' The celebrated and ingenious chemist who proposed this explanation of volcanic phenomena would himself
abandon it shortly thereafter. The experiences gathered in
mines and caves in every zone of the Earth, and which Arago
and I collected and presented in a separate treatise, demonstrate that even at shallow depths, the heat of the terrestrial
body is significantly higher than the mean temperature of the
atmosphere at the same location. Such a remarkable and
generally established fact goes along with that which volcanic
phenomena teach us. The depth at which the planetary body
may be considered a molten mass has been calculated. The
primitive cause of this subterranean heat is, as with all planets,
the process of formation itself, the coalescence of a sphere-
forming mass from a vaporous cosmic fluid, the cooling of the
layers of the Earth at different depths through radiation. All
volcanic phenomena are probably the result of a stable or temporary connection between the interior and exterior of our
planet. Elastic vapors push the molten, oxidizing materials

upward through deep fissures. The volcanoes are thus intermediary earth-springs; the liquid mixtures of metals, alkalis,
and earth that settle into lava streams flow softly and quietly
when, lifted up, they find an egress. In a similar way, the
ancients (according to Plato's *Phaeton*) imagined all volcanic
streams of fire as runoffs of the Pyriphlegethon.

I might be permitted, I hope, to add to these considerations
another, more daring, observation. Might not the cause of one
of the most extraordinary phenomena in the study of petrifac-
tion also lie in the interior heat of the planetary body, a heat
that is indicated by the observation of volcanoes and by thermometric experiments on springs that rise from various
depths? Tropical animal forms, arborescent ferns, palms, and
bamboo plants lie buried in the frigid North. Everywhere, the
primeval world shows us a distribution of organic forms that
the current conditions of climate contradict. As a solution to
such an important problem, several hypotheses have been
conceived: the near approach of a comet, a change in the
inclination of the ecliptic, an increased intensity of sunlight.
None of these has been able to satisfy the astronomers, physicists, and geognosts all at once. I am happy to leave unchanged
the axis of the Earth or the light of the sun's disk, from the
spots of which a famed stellar expert explained the fertility
and failure of crops; I believe I can recognize, however, that
in any sort of planet, regardless of its relationship to a central
body or of its astronomical position, there are manifold causes
for the release of heat: through oxidation processes, precipitation, and chemically changed capacity of the planetary body,
through the increase in electromagnetic charge, and through
opened communication between the interior and exterior
parts.

In the places where the deeply fissured crust of the prehistoric world radiated heat from its clefts, there, for perhaps
centuries and over vast stretches of land, palms, arborescent
ferns, and all the animals of the torrid zone could thrive. By
this view of things, which I have already suggested in the
recently released work *Geognostischer Versuch über die Lagerung der
Gebirgsarten in beiden Hemisphären*, the temperature of volcanoes

would be that of the interior of the terrestrial body itself; and the same cause that now brings about such frightful devastation may once, upon the newly oxidized crust of the Earth and on the deeply riven layers of rock, have been able to bring forth in any zone the most luxuriant of vegetation.

Even if one is inclined, by way of explaining the astonishing distribution of tropical forms among their resting places, to accept that the longhaired elephantine creatures now encased in ice floes were originally native to the northern climates, and that similar forms belonging to the same primary type as lions and lynxes could live simultaneously in very different climates, such a means of explaining things would still probably not extend to plant products. For reasons involving plant physiology, palms, pisang trees, and arborescent monocotyledons cannot survive having their appendicular organs stripped away by the northern cold, and in the geognostic problem that we are touching upon here, it seems difficult to me to separate the plant and animal forms from one another. The same line of explanation must apply to both forms.

At the close of this treatise, I have followed the facts that have been collected in the most widely varying regions of the world with uncertain hypothetical assumptions. Natural philosophy transcends a mere description of Nature. It does not consist in a sterile accumulation of facts. It is the privilege of the curious and active mind of humanity to occasionally drift out of the present and into the darkness of prehistory, to gain a sense of what cannot yet be clearly discerned, and thus to take delight in the ancient myths of geognosy in their many recurring forms.

VII

THE PLATEAU OF CAJAMARCA,
THE OLD RESIDENTIAL CITY
OF THE INCA ATAHUALPA;
FIRST SIGHT OF THE PACIFIC
FROM THE RIDGE OF
THE ANDES CHAIN

AFTER SPENDING AN entire year upon the spine of the Anti or Andes chain, within 4° of the equator on the high plains of New Granada, Pastos, and Quito at heights of eight to twelve thousand feet, it is a relief to descend gradually through the cinchona forests of Loja into the plain of the Upper Amazon, an unfamiliar world rich in magnificent forms of vegetation. The small city of Loja has given its name to the most efficacious of all fever barks: *quina*, or *cascarilla fina de Loja*. This bark is the exquisite product of the tree that we botanically described as *Cinchona condaminea*, which had earlier been named *Cinchona officinalis*, under the erroneous assumption that all commercial quinine came from a single species of tree. Fever bark was not brought to Europe until the middle of the seventeenth century, either in 1632 to Alcala de Henares, as Sebastian Badus maintains, or in 1640 to Madrid upon the arrival of the Peruvian viceroy's wife, the Countess of Chinchon, who was accompanied by her personal physician, Juan del Vego, and who had been healed of malaria in Lima. The excellent *quina* of Loja grows two to three miles southeast of the city in the mountains of Uritusinga, Villonaco, and Rumisitana, atop mica schist and gneiss at moderate altitudes between 5,400 and 7,200 feet: about the same elevation as the Grimsel Hospital and the Great St. Bernard pass. The actual limits of the *quina* are the small rivers Zamora and Cachiyacu.

The tree is felled during the first blossoming stage, that is, in the fourth or the seventh year, depending on whether it is the product of a healthy sucker or of a seed. We heard with astonishment that, at the time of my trip, only 110 centners of the fever bark of the *Cinchona condaminea*, by official royal reckoning, were brought in annually from around Loja by the *quina* harvesters (*cascarilleros*, or quinine hunters, *cazadores de quina*). None of this wondrous product was put on the market then; the entire supply was sent via the Pacific harbor of Payta, around Cape Horn, and on to Cadiz for the use of the court. To deliver this modest amount of 11,000 Spanish pounds, eight to nine hundred cinchona trees were felled annually. The older and thicker trunks are becoming ever scarcer, but the abundance of growth is so great that the younger trunks now being used, with a diameter of barely 6 inches, often reach heights of as much as 50 or 60 feet. This appealing tree, adorned with leaves 5 inches long and 2 wide, forever strives when growing in a wild thicket to lift itself above its neighbors. The higher foliage, tossed erratically by the wind, gives off a peculiar reddish shimmer that is recognizable from a great distance. The average temperature in the copses of *Cinchona condaminea* oscillates between 12.5° and 15° Réaumur; this is close to the average annual temperature of Florence and of the island of Madeira, but Loja never reaches the extremes of heat and cold that are observed in these places in the temperate zone. The comparisons of climates at greatly different degrees of latitude to the climate of the high tropical plateaus are by their very nature seldom satisfying.

To travel from the knot of mountains around Loja south-southeast to the hot valley of the Amazon, one must cross the *paramos* of Chulucanas, Guamani, and Yamoca: mountainous wildernesses that we have already considered in other works, and that in the southern reaches of the Andes chain are all encompassed by the term *puna* (a word from the Quechua language). Most of them rise to over 9,500 feet; they are stormy, often wrapped for days in dense fog or afflicted by terrible hailstorms in which the water coalesces not only into multiform hailstones, most of them flattened by rotation, but also into thin, laterally moving individual disks (*papa-cara*) that injure the face and hands. During these meteorological processes I occasionally saw the thermometer sink to 7° or 5° (above freezing) while the electrical tension in the atmosphere, measured by a voltaic electrometer, switched in a few minutes from positive to negative. Below 5°, snow falls in large, widely spaced flakes. It disappears after a few hours. The ragged branching of the small-leaved, myrtlelike shrubbery, the size and abundance of the blossoms, and the eternally fresh leaf organs saturated in the moist air give to the treeless vegetation of the *paramos* a unique physiognomic character. No zone of alpine vegetation in the temperate or frigid regions of the Earth can compare to that of the *paramos* in the tropical Andes.

The solemn impression evoked by the wilderness of the cordilleras is increased in a strange and unexpected way, for still preserved within it are the extraordinary remains of the Inca Road, the enormous construction by which, over a stretch of more than 250 geographical miles, all of the provinces of the empire were connected. Placed here and there along the way, at mostly regular intervals, there are dwellings constructed of well-hewn freestone, caravansaries of a sort called *tambos* or *Inca-pilca* (from *pircca*, 'the wall'?). Some are surrounded like fortresses; others are set up for baths with conduits for warm water, the largest intended for the family of the ruler himself. I had already carefully measured and sketched such well-preserved buildings (called *aposentos de Mulalo* by Pedro de Cieza in the 16th century) at the foot of the Cotopaxi volcano near Callo. On the Andean pass between Alausi and Loja, which is known as the *Paramo del Assuay* (14,568 feet above the sea, a well-used route across the *Ladera de Cadlud* at almost the same elevation as Mont Blanc), we encountered great difficulties on the high plain *del Pullal* leading our heavily laden mules across the swampy ground, while beside us over the course of more than a German mile our eyes were constantly drawn to the magnificent remains of the 20-foot-wide Inca Road. It had a deep base layer and was paved with well-hewn blackish-brown trap-porphyry. What I had seen of Roman roads in Italy, Southern France, and Spain was no more imposing than this work of the ancient Peruvians, and this latter lay, by my barometric measurements, at an elevation of 12,440 feet. This height thus surpasses the summit of the peak of Tenerife by more than a thousand feet. Equally high up on Assuay lie the ruins of the so-called palace of the Inca Tupac Yupanqui, which are known by the name *Paredones del Inca*. From these ruins the road continues southward in the direction of Cuenca to the small but well-preserved fortress of Cañar, probably from the same period as Tupac Yupanqui or his warlike son Huayna Capac.

We saw still grander ruins of the ancient Peruvian road on the trail between Loja and the Amazon River at the Baths of the Inca on the *Paramo de Chulucanas*, not far from Huancabamba, and around Ingatambo near Pomahuaca. Of these ruins, the last-mentioned stand at such a low point that I found the difference in elevation between the Inca Road at Pomahuaca and the Inca Road of the *Paramo del Assuay* to be more than 9,100 feet. The distance in a straight line by astronomical latitude comprises exactly 46 geographical miles, and the road ascends to 3,500 feet higher than the elevation of the pass of Mount Cenis above Lake Como. Of the two paved road systems, cobbled with flat stones or, occasionally, covered with cemented gravel (macadam), one crossed the wide and arid plain between the coast and the Andes chain, while the other went along the slopes of the cordilleras themselves. Milestones declared the distances at regular intervals. Bridges of three sorts – stone, wood, and rope (*puentes de hamaca* or *de maroma*) – crossed over bridges and chasms; water conduits ran to the *tambos* (hostelries) and fortresses. Both systems of maintained roads were directed toward the central point of Cuzco, the royal seat of the great empire (13°31′ south lat.); the elevation of this capital city, according to Pendand's map of Bolivia, is 10,676 feet (Parisian measure) above sea level. Since the Peruvians drove no sorts of vehicles, the roads were intended only for marching troops, porters, and groups of lightly burdened llamas; thus they are found here and there, with the great steepness of the mountains, to be broken by long rows of steps upon which rest areas were installed. Francisco Pizarro and Diego Almagro, who used to such great advantage the military roads of the Incas on the long marches of their own armies, encountered difficulty, especially for the Spanish cavalry, in those places where the road was interrupted by tiers and stairsteps. The hindrance was all the greater because the Spanish at the beginning of the *conquista* employed only the horse, and not the deliberate mule, who appears to consider his every step when he is in the mountains. Only later did the cavalry begin to use the mule.

Sarmiento, who saw the Inca Road when it was still in complete repair, asks himself in a *relacion* that long lay unused, buried in the Biblioteca del Escorial: 'how were a people without the use of iron in high, rocky country able to complete such magnificent works (*caminos tan grandes y tan sovervios*) from Cuzco to Quito and from Cuzco to the coast of Chile?' He adds: 'Emperor Carlos with all his power would not accomplish a fraction of what the well-equipped leadership of the Incas was able to demand of the obedient tribes.' Hernando Pizarro, the most civilized of the three brothers, who atoned for his misdeeds with a 20-year imprisonment at Medina del Campo and, at the age of 100, died in an air of saintliness (*en olor de santidad*), proclaims: 'In the whole of Christendom are no such glorious roads to be seen as the ones we are admiring here.' The two important residential cities of the Incas, Cuzco and Quito, are in direct alignment (SSE to NNW) and (putting aside the many twists and turns of the road) 225 geographical miles apart; including the windings of the road, Garcilaso de la Vega and other conquistadors reckon the distance at about 500 *leguas*. According to the completely credible assertion of the licentiate Polo de Ondegardo, Huayna Capac, whose father had conquered Quito, had certain building materials for the royal buildings (Inca quarters) brought from Cuzco, despite the length of the road. I too found this legend widely circulated among the natives in Quito.

Wherever Nature presents to humankind, through the formation of the land, tremendous hindrances to overcome, there will grow, among the tribes who undertake the enterprise, both the courage and the strength to do so. The despotic centralization of the Inca rulership required both security and speed of communication, especially of troop movements – thus the construction of maintained roads and the perfecting of postal facilities. With peoples who stand at the most differing stages of civilization, one perceives with particular preference national activities moving in specific directions; but the conspicuous development of such isolated activities in no way determines the condition of the entire culture. Egyptians, Greeks, Etruscans, and Romans, Chinese, Japanese, and Indians show us these contrasts. How much time was required to complete the Peruvian Road is difficult to determine. The great works of the northern part of the Inca Empire on the highlands of Quito certainly must have been completed in less than 30 or 35 years – within the short epoch that falls between the conquest of the ruler of Quito and the death of the Inca Huayna Capac; meanwhile, a deep darkness reigns over the age of the southern part of the Peruvian Road that actually lies in Peru.

Generally, the mysterious appearance of Manco Capac is set at 400 years before the landing of Francisco Pizarro upon Puná Island (1532), thus around the middle of the 12th century, almost 200 years before the founding of Mexico City (Tenochtitlan); some Spanish writers give a figure of as much as 500 or even 550 years. But the imperial history of Peru knows only thirteen reigning princes of the Inca dynasty, which, as Prescott correctly notes, could not fill so long a period as 400 or 550 years. Quetzalcoatl, Bochica, and Manco Capac are the three mythical figures to whom are tied the beginnings of the cultures of the Aztecs, Muiscas (actually Chibchas), and Peruvians. Quetzalcoatl, bearded, clothed in black, high priest of Tula, later a penitent on a mountain near Tlaxapuchicalco, comes from the coast of Panuco, that is, the eastern coast of Anahuac on the Mexican plateau. Bochica, or more accurately, the bearded, long-robed Messenger of God, Nemterequeteba (a Buddha of the Muiscas), comes to the plateau of Bogota from the grassy steppes east of the Andes. Civilization already reigned along the picturesque shore of

Lake Titicaca before Manco Capac. The fortress of Cuzco on the hill of Sacsayhuaman was modeled on the older buildings of Tiwanaku. In the same way, the Aztecs imitated the pyramid construction of the Toltecs, and the Toltecs that of the Olmecs (Hulmeks); climbing gradually, one reaches historic ground in Mexico extending back as far as the 6th century of our reckoning. The stepped pyramids of the Toltecs in Cholula are said by Siguenza to repeat the form of the Olmec stepped pyramids of Teotihuacan. So it is that in passing through any layer of civilization, one penetrates into an older one. And while consciousness did not awaken simultaneously in the peoples of the Old and New Continents, the fantastic realm of myth always immediately precedes historical certainty in any people.

Despite the great admiration that the first conquistadors had for the improved roads and water conduits of the Peruvians, these structures were not only neglected but willfully destroyed. This happened more quickly in the littoral (even though it engendered crop failure through lack of water), where the conquistadors used the ready-made stones for new building, than it did on the ridge of the Andes chain or in the deep, gorgelike valleys that cut into this chain. We were compelled during the long day's journey from the syenite rocks of Saulaca to the fossil-rich valley of San Felipe (situated at the foot of the icy *Paramo de Yamoca*) to wade across the Rio Huancabamba 27 times, thanks to its many windings; meanwhile, we were once again continually able to see, on a steep wall of rock nearby, the remains of the straight, high-walled Road of the Incas and its *tambos*. The small torrent, only 120 to 140 feet wide, had a current so fast that our heavily loaded mules were often in danger of being carried away. They were carrying our manuscripts, our dried plants, everything we had collected over the course of a year. At such times, one waits on the far bank in a state of anxiety until the long string of 18 to 20 pack animals is no longer in danger.

The same Rio Huancabamba, in its lower course where it has many waterfalls, is employed in a curious way for correspondence with the Pacific coast. In order to move more quickly the few letters from Trujillo destined for the Province

Jaén de Bracamoros, a swimming postal carrier is employed, *el correo que nada*. In two days, the postman (usually a young Indian) swims from Pomahuaca to Tomependa, first along the Rio Chamaya (the name for this lower end of the Rio Huancabamba), and then along the Amazon. He carefully lays the few letters entrusted to him in a wide cotton towel that he wraps around his head like a turban. At the waterfalls, he leaves the river and walks around the falls through the nearby bushes. So that the long swim does not tire him excessively, he often clings with one arm to a block of lightweight wood (*ceiba*; *palo de balsa*) of the family of the Bombaceae. Sometimes a friend will accompany the swimmer as a partner. The two need not worry about food, for wherever they are, they receive a hospitable welcome in the scattered huts surrounded abundantly by fruit trees in the attractive *Huertas de Pucara* and *Cavico*.

The river is fortunately free of crocodiles; in the upper run of the Amazon too, they are not encountered until one has gone downriver past the cataracts of Mayasi. The ponderous beast prefers the quieter waters. By my measurement, the Rio Chamaya, from the ford (*paso*) of Pucara to its confluence with the Amazon below the village of Choros, a short distance of 13 geographical miles, has a vertical descent of no less than 1,668 feet. The governor of the Province of Jaén de Bracamoros assured me that in using this peculiar water mail system, the letters are rarely soaked or lost. Indeed, shortly after my return from Mexico, I myself received letters in Paris that had come from Tomependa by this very route. Many of the wild Indian tribes that live near the banks of the Upper Amazon make their journeys in a similar fashion, swimming companionably downstream together. I had the opportunity to see some 30 to 40 heads (of men, women, and children) of the Jivaro tribe in the channel arriving at Tomependa. The *correo que nada* makes his way back by land on the arduous paths of the *Paramo del Paredon*.

When one approaches the hot climate of the Amazon basin, one encounters with pleasure a graceful, in some places very luxuriant vegetation. More beautiful citrus trees than those of the *Huertas de Pucara* – mostly sweet oranges (*Citrus aurantium* [Risso]), and in lesser numbers the sour *C. vulgaris* (Risso) – we had never before seen, not even in the Canary Islands or on the hot coastal region of Cumana and Caracas. Laden with many thousands of golden fruits, they reach a height here of 60 feet. Rather than the rounded top, they had branches that strive upward in a manner almost like the laurel. Not far away, near the ford of Cavico, we were surprised by a quite unexpected sight. We saw a copse of small trees, barely 18 feet tall, covered not with green but apparently with completely pink leaves. It was a new species of the genus *Bougainvillaea* that the elder Jussieu had first categorized according to a Brazilian specimen in the Commerson herbarium. The trees had almost no true leaves; what we had thought at a distance were leaves were densely crowded, light pink bracts (blossom-leaves). The sight, in terms of purity and coloration, was quite different from the appearance so gracefully presented by many of our forest trees in autumn. From the Proteaceae family of Southern Africa, a single species, *Rhopala ferruginea*, climbs down from the cold heights of the *Paramo de Yamoca* to the hot plain of Chamaya. We also often found here the delicately pinnate *Porlieria hygrometrica* (of the Zygophylleae), in which the closing of the small leaves, more than by any other member of the Mimosaceae, indicates that a change in the weather is soon to come, especially approaching rain. It seldom misled us.

In Chamaya we found rafts (*balsas*) ready to take us to Tomependa, so that we might determine (it being of some importance to the geography of South America, due to an old observation of La Condamine) the longitudinal difference between Quito and the mouth of the Chinchipe. We slept as usual under the open sky on the sandy bank (*Playa de Huayan-chi*) at the confluence of the Rio Chamaya and the Amazon. The next day, we navigated down the river as far as the cataracts and narrow torrent of Rentema, where cliffs of coarse-grained sandstone (conglomerate) rise like towers, creating a rock dam in the river. I took a baseline measurement on the flat and sandy bank, and found that at Tomependa the Amazon, which to the east becomes so mighty, was only 1,300 feet wide. At the famous narrows of Manseriche between Santiago and San Borja – a mountain gorge that in some places, due to the overhanging cliffs and the roof of foliage, is but poorly lit, and in which all driftwood, including a vast number of tree trunks, is dashed to pieces and disappears – the stream is only 150 feet wide. The cliffs that form all such narrow torrents, or *pongos* (in the Quechua language *puncu*, 'door; gateway') have been subjected to many changes over the course of the centuries. A portion of the Pongo de Rentema mentioned above, for example, was pulverized by the high flood a year before my journey; indeed, among the natives along the Amazon, tradition preserves a lively memory of the collapse of the then very high rock mass of the entire *pongo* at the beginning of the 18th century. The course of the river, due to the collapse and the subsequent damming, was suddenly arrested, and in the village of Puyaya lying below the Pongo de Rentema, the natives looked on with horror as the broad riverbed emptied of water. After a few hours, the river broke through again. It is not believed that earthquakes were the cause of this extraordinary event. On the whole, the mighty stream works without ceasing upon improving its bed; one may well imagine what sort of power it might wield when one sees how it occasionally swells, despite its tremendous width, over 25 feet in 20 to 30 hours.

We stayed in the hot valley of the Upper Marañón or Amazon River for 17 days. In order to leave this valley and come to the coast, one must crest the Andes at the place between Moyobamba and Cajamarca (6°57′ south lat., 80°56′ west long.) where, according to my observations of magnetic inclination, the magnetic equator cuts across the mountain chain. Continuing to climb, one reaches the celebrated silver mines of Chota and there begins to descend (with occasional interruptions) by way of old Cajamarca, where, 316 years ago now, the bloody drama of the Spanish *conquista* was played out, and by way of Aroma and Gangamarca, down into the Peruvian lowlands. Here, as almost everywhere in the Andes and in the mountains of Mexico, the greatest heights are scenically characterized by towering outcroppings of porphyry and trachyte, the ones of porphyry particularly being split into mighty pillars. Such masses give portions of the spine of the mountains the appearance of cliffs in one place, of domes in the next. Here they have broken through a limestone formation that extends enormously on both sides of the equator in the New Continent and that, according to Leopold von Buch's outstanding analyses, belongs to the chalk strata. Between Huambos and Montan, twelve thousand feet above the sea, we found pelagic shell fossils (ammonites with a 14-inch diameter, the large *Pectin alatus*, oyster shells, sea urchins, isocardias, and *Exogyra polygona*). We collected a species of cidaris, which according to Leopold von Buch is no different from one found by Brongniart in the old chalk by the *Perte du Rhône*, both at Tomependa in the Amazon basin and near Moyobamba at an elevation of no less than 9,900 feet. In the Amuich mountain chain in Caucasian Dagestan, the chalk rises in the same fashion from the banks of the Sulak, barely 500 feet above sea level, up to Tschunum, at a full 9,000 feet of elevation, while on the 13,090-foot peak of Mount Shahdagh are found *Ostrea diluviana* (Goldf.) and the same chalk layer. Abich's excellent observations on the Caucasus accordingly corroborate Leopold von Buch's brilliant geognostic views on the alpine distribution of chalk.

From Montan's lonely manor farm surrounded by llama herds, we climbed farther southward on the eastern slope of the cordillera and came to a high plain in which the silver mountain of Hualgayoc, center of the famous mines of Chota, presented to us at nightfall a marvelous vista. The *Cerro de Hualgayoc*, separated by a deep, gorgelike valley (*quebrada*) from the limestone mountain Cormolache, is an isolated cliff of siliceous quartz, shot through with innumerable and often conjoining veins of silver, and deeply, almost vertically shorn off on the northwest face. The highest of the mines lie 1,445 feet above the floor of the gallery, *socabon de espinachi.* The outline of the mountain is interrupted by numerous tower- and pyramidlike points and spires. Its peak also bears the name *Las Puntas.* These deposits most decidedly contrast with the 'gentle exterior' that the miner generally ascribes to metal-rich regions. 'Our mountain,' said a wealthy mine owner whom we encountered, 'stands there like an enchanted castle, *como si fuese un castillo encantado.*' Mount Hualgayoc is somewhat reminiscent of a dolomite cone, but even more of the cloven spine of Montserrat in Catalonia, which I also visited and which was so gracefully described by my brother. The silver mountain Hualgayoc is not only perforated even to its very highest reaches by several hundred mine tunnels bored into it on all sides; the massif of the granular stone itself presents natural fissures through which the vault of the sky, a very deep blue at this mountainous height, may be seen by the onlooker standing at the foot of the mountain. The native people call these openings windows, *las ventanillas de Hualgayoc*; we were shown similar windows in the trachyte walls of the volcano Pichincha, similarly named the *ventanillas de Pichincha.* The strangeness of such a sight is increased still more by the many tunnel portals and workers' cabins that hang like nests on the slopes of the fortresslike mountain, wherever a small clearing allows. The mineworkers carry the ore in baskets down steep and dangerous footpaths to the amalgamation areas.

The value of the silver delivered by the mines in the first 30 years (from 1771 to 1802) probably far exceeds 32 million piasters. Despite the hardness of the stone with its high content of quartz, the Peruvians, even before the coming of the Spanish (as evidenced by old tunnels and shafts), mined for galena rich in silver on the *Cerro de la Lin* and on Chupiquiyacu, and for gold on Curimayo (where there is also natural sulfur in the quartz rock, as in the itacolumite in Brazil). We resided near the mine in the small mountain town of Moyobamba, which sits 11,140 feet above sea level and where, even though it is only 6°43′ away from the equator, the water in every residence freezes nightly throughout a large portion of the year. In this waste, devoid of vegetation, there live three to four thousand people, to whom all provisions are delivered from the warm valleys, as they are able to raise only some varieties of cabbage and very fine lettuce. As in every Peruvian mountain town, boredom drives the wealthier (though not better educated) inhabitants to extremely hazardous games of cards and dice. Quickly won riches are even more quickly lost. It is all reminiscent of the soldier of Pizarro's army who, after plundering the temple of Cuzco, lamented having lost 'a great piece of the sun' (a sheet of gold plate) in a game of chance. The thermometer in Moyobamba at 8 in the morning showed just 1° Réaumur, by noon, 7°. Amidst the slender ichu grass (perhaps our *Stipaerio stachya*) we found a beautiful Calceolaria (*C. sibthorpioides*), which we would not have expected to see at such an elevation.

Close to the mountain town of Moyobamba, on a plateau called *Llanos* or *Pampa de Nevar*, tremendous amounts of red gold ore and wirelike pure silver in 'swirls, spikes, and spreading veins' (*remolinos, clavos, y vetas manteadas*) have been extracted from a piece of ground of more than $\frac{1}{4}$ square geographical mile, only 3 to 4 fathoms under the turf, as if growing together with the roots of the alpine grass. Another plateau, west of Purgatorio and close to the *Quebrada de Chiquera*, is called *Choropampa*, the 'Field of Shells': *churu* is Quechua for 'shell,' especially small, edible varieties like oysters or mussels. The name refers to fossils in the chalk strata, where they are found in such numbers that very early on they drew the attention of the natives. There, from close to the surface, a treasure of pure gold was extracted, richly interwoven with silver. A deposit of this sort shows the dependence of many of the ores that erupt from the interior of the Earth in fissures and channels upon the nature of the surrounding stone and the relative age of the formations penetrated. The stone of the *Cerro de Hualgayoc* and Fuentestiana is very rich in water, but an absolute aridity reigns in Purgatorio. I found there, to my astonishment, and despite the altitude of the land above the sea, that the temperature in the mine was 15.8° Réaumur, while in the *Mina de Guadalupe* nearby, the water in the mine was only about 9°. Since the outside temperature rose to only 4.5°, the naked and hardworking mineworkers call the subterranean heat of the Purgatorio stifling.

The narrow path from Moyobamba to the old Incan city of Cajamarca is difficult, even for the mules. The name of the city was originally *Cassamarca* or *Kazamarca*, i.e., 'City of Frost'; *marca*, when referring to a place, belongs to the northern dialect, Chinchaysuyo or Chinchasuyu, while in the standard Quechua language it means 'stories of a house,' also 'protector' and 'guarantor.' The path led us for five or six hours through a series of *paramos*, on which one is exposed almost without interruption to the wrath of the storms and that sharp-edged hail that is so peculiar to the slopes of the Andes. The elevation of the path keeps itself for the most part to between nine and ten thousand feet. This induced me to make a magnetic observation of general interest: to determine the point at which the northern inclination of the needle changes over to the southern inclination, that is to say, at what point travelers crossed the magnetic equator.

When one has finally reached the last of those mountain wildernesses, the *Paramo de Yanahuanga*, one looks all the more joyfully down into the fertile valley of Cajamarca. It is a charming view, for the valley, with a small river snaking its way across it, forms a tableland of oval shape of 6 to 7 square geographical miles. This tableland is similar to the Savanna of Bogota and, like it, was probably an old lakebed. The only thing missing here is the myth of the miraculous Bochica or Idacanzas, high priest of Iraca, who opened a way for the waters through the cliffs at Tequendama. Cajamarca lies 600 feet higher than Santa Fé de Bogota, thus almost as high as the city of Quito, but due to the protection of the surrounding mountains has a much milder and more pleasant climate. The ground is extremely fertile, filled with crop fields and gardens with avenues of willows and large-blossomed red, white, and yellow *Datura* varieties, interspersed with mimosas and the lovely *quinuar* trees (our *Polylepis villosa*, a Rosacea along with *Alchemilla* and *Sanguisorba*). The wheat in the *Pampa de Cajamarca* produces on the average a 15- or 20-fold yield, but the hopes for rich harvests are occasionally dashed by nighttime frosts not noticeable in the roofed dwellings and caused by the heat being radiated toward the clear sky into the thin, dry mountain air.

Small domes of porphyry (probably once islands in the

ancient lake) rise in the northern part of the plateau and break through widely spread beds of sandstone. On top of one of these porphyry domes, the *Cerro de Santa Polonia*, we enjoyed a captivating view. The old residence of Atahualpa is bordered on this side by fruit orchards and irrigated, pasturelike fields of alfalfa (*Medicago sativa*, *campos de alfalfa*). In the distance rise steam pillars from the hot baths of Pultamarca, which still bear the name *baños del Inca*. I found the temperature of these sulfur springs to be 55.2° Réaumur. Atahualpa spent part of the year at these baths, where some fragile ruins of his palace escaped the *conquistadores'* thirst for destruction. The large, deep water basin (*el tragadero*) in which tradition says one of the golden sedan chairs was sunk (which is forever being sought in vain) seemed to me, considering the regularity of its round form, to have been artificially carved into the sandstone over the mouth of one of the springs.

Likewise, only fragile remnants of the fortress and palace of Atahualpa remain in the city, which is now adorned with beautiful churches. The destruction was accelerated by the fury with which those driven by the lust for gold knocked over walls and weakened the foundations of all of the residential areas, even before the end of the 16th century, in their attempt to dig up the treasures buried deep beneath the ground. The palace of the Inca stood on a hill of porphyry that on the surface (that is, on the outcropping of the stone strata) had originally been carved and hollowed out in such a manner as to surround the primary residence almost like a wall. A city jail and a community meeting house (*la casa del Cabildo*) have been erected on a portion of the ruins. These are the most sizable of the ruins, yet they stand only 13 to 15 feet tall, across from the Cloister of St. Francis; they consist, as one may observe in the apartment of Caciquen, of well-cut ashlar blocks of 2 to 3 feet in length, laid upon one another with no cement, much the same as the *Inca-Pilca* or fortress of Cañar on the plateau of Quito.

Into the porphyry rock a shaft was sunk which once led to underground chambers and a gallery (tunnel entrance), which, it is believed, led to another porphyry dome already

mentioned above, the one at Santa Polonia. These preparations indicate concern about a secure means of escape during
times of war. The burying of treasures was, by the way, a very
widespread custom of the ancient Peruvians. Beneath many
private living quarters in Cajamarca one can still find underground rooms.

We were shown the so-called Footbath of the Inca (*el lavad-
ero de los piés*) and steps that had been carved into the cliff. Such
a washing of the sovereign's feet was accompanied by burden-
some courtly ceremonies. Some of the neighboring buildings
that, according to tradition, were intended for the servants of
the Inca are also constructed with ashlar blocks and built with
gables, while others are made with well-formed tiles alternating with concrete (*muros y obra de tapia*). The latter include vaulted facings (recessed walls), the great age of which I long
doubted, probably erroneously.

In the main building one may still view the room in which
the unfortunate Atahualpa was held prisoner for nine months,
starting in November 1532; travelers are also shown the wall
upon which he made the mark up to which he would fill the
room with gold if he were set free. Xerez, in *Conquista del Peru*
(which Barcia preserved for posterity), Hernando Pizarro in
his letters, and other writers of the time give widely varying
descriptions of the height of this mark. The tormented prince
said that 'the gold bars, sheets, and vessels should be piled as
high as he could reach with his hand.' Xerez describes the
room as 22 feet long and 17 wide. Garcilaso de la Vega, who
had left Peru in 1560, his 20th year, estimates that all that was
gathered together leading up to the fateful day of the 29th of
August, 1533 (the day of the Inca's death), from the treasures
of the Sun Temples of Cuzco, Hualyas, Huamachuco, and
Pachacamac, had a value of 3,838,000 *Ducados de Oro*.

In the chapel of the city jail, which, as I mention above, is
built upon the ruins of the Inca palace, gullible persons are
shown with a shudder the stone upon which there are 'irre-
movable bloodstains.' It is a very thin slab, 12 feet long, that
lies before the altar, and was probably taken from the porphyry or trachyte of the region. An exact analysis involving

taking a chip is not allowed. The three or four supposed stains seem to be hornblende or pyroxene-rich constrictions within the groundmass of the rock type. The licentiate Fernando Montesinos, though he visited Peru barely one hundred years after the conquest of Cajamarca, already begins to spread the tale: Atahualpa was beheaded in the prison, and bloodstains are still visible on the rock upon which the execution took place. It is indisputable, and supported by many eyewitnesses, that the betrayed Inca willingly let himself be baptized under the name Juan de Atahualpa by his fanatical persecutor, the Dominican monk Vicente de Valverde, in order to avoid being burned alive. Strangulation (*el garrote*) finally ended his life, in public under the open sky. Another legend maintains that the chapel was erected upon the stone where the strangling took place, and that Atahualpa's body rests under the stone. The putative bloodstains, then, would clearly remain unexplained. The corpse, however, never lay under this stone; after a mass for the dead and a solemn funeral, which the Pizarro brothers attended in mourning attire (!), it was brought first to the churchyard of the *Convento de San Francisco* and later to Quito, Atahualpa's birthplace. This last relocation was carried out according to the express wishes of the dying Inca. His personal enemy the wily Rumiñaui (called The Eye of Stone due to the loss of one of his eyes to a wart: *rumi*, stone, and *ñaui*, eye in Quechua), with craftiness and political ambition, staged a ceremonious funeral in Quito.

There are still descendants of the monarch living in Cajamarca, in the sad architectural remnants of the glory of days gone by. They are the family of the Indian Cacique (or *Curaca* in the Quechua idiom) Astorpilco. They live in conditions of great need, yet frugally and without complaint, fully resigned to a hard fate that came through no fault of their own. Their descent from Atahualpa by the feminine line is denied nowhere in Cajamarca, but their traces of beard may indicate an infusion of Spanish blood. Those two sons of the great (if, for a Son of the Sun, somewhat free-thinking) Huayna Capac, Huascar and Atahualpa, who both reigned before the Spanish invasion, left behind no acknowledged sons. Huascar became

Atahualpa's prisoner on the plains of Quipaypan and was shortly thereafter murdered on Atahualpa's order. From the other two brothers of Atahualpa, the insignificant young Toparca, whom Pizarro (in the autumn of 1533) had crowned as Inca, and the likewise crowned but subsequently rebellious Manco Capac, there also came no male offspring. Atahualpa left a son with the Christian name don Francisco, who died very young, and a daughter, doña Angelina, with whom Francisco Pizarro produced, in the midst of a wild life of war, a son that he deeply loved, the grandson of the executed ruler. Along with the family of Astorpilco, with whom I spent time in Cajamarca, the Carguaraicos and the Titu-Buscamaytas were also distinguished as relatives of the Inca dynasty, but the Buscamayta line has since died out.

The son of the cacique Astorpilco, a friendly young person of 17 years who accompanied me through the ruins of the old palace in his home city, in his situation of great want had filled his imagination with images of the magnificent subterranean treasures of gold beneath the heaps of rubble upon which we stumped about. He related how one of his forefathers had once bound the eyes of his wife and led her through several deviating pathways carved into the rock, down into the subterranean garden of the Inca. There she saw, artfully replicated in purest gold, trees complete with leaves and fruit, birds sitting on the branches, and the much-sought-after golden sedan chair (*una de las andas*) of Atahualapa. The man commanded his wife to touch nothing, for the long-awaited time (of the reinstatement of the Incas) had not yet come. Anyone who acquired any of this wealth before then must die that very night. Such golden dreams and fantasies as those of this boy are founded upon the memories and traditions of prehistory. The luxury of artificial gardens of gold (*jardines ó huertas de oro*) has been often described by eyewitnesses: by Cieza de Leon, Sarmiento, Garcilaso, and other early historians of the *conquista*. They were found beneath the sun temples in Cuzco, in Cajamarca, and in the graceful valley of Yucay, a favorite seat of the royal family. Where the golden *huertas* were not underground, there stood living plants next to the artful replicas.

The tall stalks and the fruits of maize on cobs (*mazorcas*) are said to have been especially convincing.

The morbid certainty with which the young Astorpilco proclaimed that below me, somewhat to the right of where I stood, a large-blossomed datura tree, a *guanto*, artfully fashioned from sheets and wires of gold, sheltered the couch of the Inca with its branches, made upon me a melancholy impression. Here again, fanciful visions and delusion are comfort for great privation and earthly suffering. 'Do you and your parents not feel,' I asked the boy, 'since you so firmly believe in the existence of this garden, an occasional desire, in light of your want, to dig for the treasures that lie so near?' The boy's answer was so simple, so much the expression of the quiet resignation that characterizes the aboriginal people of this land, that I put it down in my journal in Spanish: 'Such a desire (*tal antojo*) does not come to us; my father says that it would be a sin (*que fuese pecado*). If we had all of the golden branches with all of their golden fruit, then our white neighbors would hate us and harm us. We possess a little field and good wheat (*buen trigo*).' I believe that few of my readers will fault me for remembering here the words of the young Astorpilco and his golden dreams.

The belief, so very widespread among the natives, that to take possession of buried treasures that might have belonged to the Incas is a punishable offense and would bring down misfortune upon an entire people is connected to another belief, especially prevalent in the 16th and 17th centuries, in the eventual reinstatement of an Inca empire. Every oppressed nationality hopes for liberation and a renewal of the old regime. The flight of Manco Inca, brother of Atahualpa, into the forests of Vilcapampa on the slope of the eastern cordillera and the times when Sayri Tupac and Inca Tupac Amaru were forced to abide in those wild reaches left lasting memories. It was believed that descendants of the deposed dynasty might have settled between the rivers Apurimac and Beni, or perhaps even farther east in Guyana. The myth that traveled from the West to the East of El Dorado and the golden city of Manoa increased such dreams. Raleigh's imagination was so inflamed by it 'that he launched an expedition in the hope of conquering the imperial and golden island city, installing a garrison of three to four thousand Englishmen, and levying from the emperor of Guyana, who is descended from Huayna Capac and maintains his court with the same magnificence, an annual tribute of 300,000 pounds sterling as the price of the promised restoration in Cuzco and Cajamarca.' For as far as the Peruvian Quechua language has spread, traces of such expectations of a returning Inca dominion have been preserved in the heads of many natives somewhat versed in the history of their fatherland.

We stayed for five days in the city of the Inca Atahualpa, which at that time had but seven or eight thousand inhabitants. Our departure was delayed by the great number of mules required for the transport of our collections and the careful selection of the drivers who were to lead us over the Andes as far as the entrance to the long but narrow Peruvian sand desert (*Desierto de Sechura*). The transversal of the cordillera was from northeast to southwest. One has hardly left the ancient lake-bed of the lovely plateau of Cajamarca when one is moved to astonishment, while climbing at an elevation of barely 9,600 feet, by the appearance of two grotesque porphyry domes, Aroma and Cunturcaga – a favorite perch of the mighty vulture that we normally call the condor (*cuntur*), *kacca* being, in the Quechua, 'the rock.' The domes consist of 35- to 40-foot pillars with 4 to 7 sides, some bent into curves, some split into vertical sections. The porphyry dome of *Cerro Aroma* is especially picturesque. With its division of overlapping, often converging rows of pillars, it looks like a building with two levels, topped like a cathedral by a thick, rounded rock mass not broken into pillars. Such porphyry and trachyte outcroppings are, as mentioned above, quite characteristic of the high ridge of the cordilleras and give to them a physiognomy very different from that of the Swiss Alps, the Pyrenees, and the Siberian Altai.

From Cunturcaga and Aroma, one zigzags a full 6,000 feet down a steep rock face into the crevasselike Magdalena Valley, the floor of which still sits 4,000 feet above sea level. A few pitiful huts, surrounded by the same cotton trees (*Bombax discolor*) that we first saw by the Amazon, are referred to as an Indian village. The meager vegetation of the valley is similar to that of the Jaén de Bracamoros Province, but we regretfully noted the absence of the red *Bougainvillaea*. The valley is among the deepest I know in the Andes. It is a cleft, a true transversal valley running east–west, hemmed in by the *Altos de Aroma* on one side and *Huangamarca* on the other. Here once more begins the quartz formation that for so long puzzled me, the one we had already observed on the *Paramo de Yanahuanga* between Moyobamba and Cajamarca at an elevation of 11,000 feet, and which attains a mighty size of several thousand feet on the western slope of the cordillera. Since Leopold von Buch demonstrated that the chalk is widespread, even in the highest reaches of the Andes on both the near and far sides of the Isthmus of Panama, that quartz formation, its texture transformed perhaps by volcanic action, belongs to the ashlar sandstone between the upper chalk layer and the gault and greensand. From the mild Magdalena Valley, we now had to climb for three and a half hours, in a westerly direction, the 4,800-foot wall opposite the porphyry groups of the Alto de Aroma. The change in climate was even more palpable there on the rock wall, for we were often wrapped in a cold fog.

After 18 months spent uninterruptedly traversing the restrictive interior of a mountainous country, the longing finally to enjoy once more the unconstrained view of the ocean was heightened by frequent illusions. From the peak of the volcano Pichincha, looking out across the dense forests of the *Provincia de las Esmeraldas*, one cannot clearly discern an ocean horizon due to the height and the great distance to the littoral. One looks out, as if encased in a ball of air, into emptiness; one might have a sense of something but can differentiate nothing. Later, when we reached the *Paramo de Guamani*, where many buildings of the Incas lie in ruins, the mule drivers assured us that beyond the plain, past the depressions of Piura and Lambayeque, we would be able to see the ocean, but a thick fog lay on the plain and on the distant littoral. We saw only rock masses of many shapes, alternately protruding like islands above the billowing sea of fog and then disappearing again, a sight similar to that which we enjoyed on the peak of Tenerife. We encountered nearly the same beguilement of our expectations on the Andean pass of Huangamarca, the traversal of which I will describe here. Each time we had climbed another hour, toiling with suspenseful hope against the slope of the mighty mountain, our guides, not entirely familiar with the track, would promise that our hopes would soon be fulfilled. The layer of mist that enfolded us would seem occasionally to open, but our view would soon be cruelly restricted by heights that yet lay before us.

One's longing to see certain objects is not predicated only on their grandeur, their beauty or importance; it is interwoven in each person with many incidental impressions from their youth, with an early predilection for individual pursuits, with an inclination toward distant places and a life in motion. The improbability of seeing a wish fulfilled is what gives it its peculiar charm. The traveler appreciates in advance the joy of the moment when first he beholds the Southern Cross and the Magellanic Clouds that circle the South Pole, the snow of Chimborazo and the smoke columns of the volcanoes of Quito, a stand of arborescent ferns, or the tranquil Pacific Ocean. The days upon which the fulfillment of such wishes occurs mark the epochs of life with indelible impressions, exciting feelings of such vitality as needs no rational justification. Within the longing for the sight of the Pacific from the spine of the Andes is intermingled the interest with which the small boy listened to the narrative of the bold expedition of Vasco Nuñez de Balboa, the fortunate man who was the first European (followed by Francisco Pizarro) to see, from the Sierra de Querequa on the Isthmus of Panama, the eastern Pacific Ocean. The reed-covered shores of the Caspian Sea, which I first spied from the delta of the Volga, are certainly not what one would call picturesque, and yet that first sight of them was to me all the more joyous for my having been attracted from my earliest youth to the shape of this Asiatic inland sea on maps. That which is awakened within us, whether by childlike impressions or through the element of mere chance in the circumstances of life, will later turn in a more serious direction and will often become a motivation for scientific work, for far-reaching ventures.

When, after many undulations of the ground on the craggy mountainside, we finally reached the highest point of the *Alto de Huangamarca*, the long-veiled vault of the sky suddenly cleared. A sharp southwest wind chased away the mist. The deep blue of the thin mountain air appeared between the highest feathery clouds. The entire western slope of the cordillera near Chorillos and Cascas, covered in monstrous blocks of quartz 12 to 15 feet long, the plains of Chala and Molinos all the way to the seashore at Trujillo lay, as though wondrously close, before our eyes. For the first time, we were seeing the Pacific Ocean; we saw it clearly: next to the littoral, a great body of light, reflecting, ascending to a horizon now more than merely sensed. The joy that my companions, Bonpland and Carlos Montufar, avidly shared caused us to forget to open the barometer on the *Alto de Huangamarca*. By the measurement that we took nearby, somewhat lower than the summit at an isolated farm (the *Hato de Huangamarca*), the point from which we first saw the ocean must lie at only 8,800 or 9,000 feet.

For one who owed part of his education and the nature of many of his wishes to his association with a companion of Captain Cook, there was something solemn about the sight of the Pacific. Georg Forster was familiar with the general outline of my travel plans early on, when I had the privilege of making my first visit to England (now more than a half-century ago) under his guidance. Forster's enchanting descriptions of Tahiti had awakened, especially in Northern Europe, a general and, I might say, yearning interest in the isles of the South Sea. At that time these islands had the good fortune to be seldom visited by Europeans. I too was able to nurture the hope of soon touching some of them, for the purpose of my voyage to Lima was of a dual nature: to observe the transit of Mercury across the disk of the sun, and to fulfill the promise I had made to Captain Baudin upon my departure from Paris, that I would join him in his circumnavigation, as soon as the French republic could deliver the funding it had earlier promised for the purpose.

North American newspapers had spread the report in the Antilles that both corvettes, *le Géographe* and *le Naturaliste*, were to sail around Cape Horn and land in Callao de Lima. In Havana, where I found myself after the completion of the Orinoco journey, upon hearing this news I abandoned my original plan to cross Mexico on my way to the Philippines. I quickly rented a ship that carried me from the Island of Cuba to Cartagena de Indias. But the Baudin expedition took a route quite different from the one that had been announced and expected: it did not sail around Cape Horn, as had been the earlier plan when Bonpland and I had appointed ourselves to meet it; instead, it sailed around the Cape of Good Hope. One goal of my Peruvian journey and the last crossing of the Andes chain thus did not materialize, but I did have the rare good fortune, during an unpropitious time of year, to experience a clear day in the misty country of lowland Peru. I observed the transit of Mercury across the disk of the sun in Callao, an observation that has proved to be of some importance to the accurate determination of the longitude of Lima and the southwestern part of the New Continent. Thus does there often lie, within the entanglement of grave circumstances in life, the germ of a satisfying compensation.

From

VIEWS OF THE CORDILLERAS AND MONUMENTS OF THE INDIGENOUS PEOPLES OF THE AMERICAS

1810–13

Translated by J. Ryan Poynter

HUMBOLDT'S INTRODUCTION

I HAVE BROUGHT together in this work everything that relates to the origin and early technical and artistic advances of the indigenous peoples of the Americas. Two-thirds of the Plates included here depict architectural and sculptural relics, historical scenes, and hieroglyphs relating to the division of time and to the calendar system. Images of monuments relevant to the philosophical study of man are combined here with picturesque views of the most remarkable sites of the new continent. This arrangement was motivated by factors that are stated within the general considerations at the head of this Essay.

Inasmuch as the nature of the subject permits, the description of each Plate constitutes a separate account, and I have given more elaboration to those that might one day cast light on the similarities between the inhabitants of the two hemispheres. It was surprising to discover, toward the end of the fifteenth century, and in a world that we call new, the very kinds of ancient institutions, religious ideas, and shapes of buildings that in Asia seem to date back to the dawn of civilization. It would seem that the characteristics of peoples, not unlike the internal structure of plants, are disseminated across the surface of the earth. The imprint of an original type appears everywhere, despite the differences produced by the nature of the climate, the makeup of the soil, and the combination of several contingent factors.

At the beginning of the conquest of the Americas, the attention of Europe was singularly focused on the gigantic constructions of Cusco [Quechua: Qusqu], the great roads traced through the heart of the Cordilleras, the terraced pyramids, the religion, and the symbolic script of the Mexica. Nowadays, the area surrounding Port Jackson in New Holland and the island of Tahiti are not written about more often than many parts of Mexico and Peru were at that time. One needs to have visited these places to appreciate the naiveté and the authentic local color that characterizes the accounts of the first Spanish travelers. When studying their writings, however, one regrets that the latter were not accompanied by images that might give an exact idea of the many monuments destroyed by fanaticism or fallen into ruin as a result of shameful neglect.

The fervor with which people devoted themselves to studying the Americas began to fade at the start of the seventeenth century. The Spanish colonies, within whose bounds lie the only regions formerly inhabited by civilized peoples, remained closed to foreign nations, and when the Abbot Clavijero recently published his *Storia antica del Messico* in Italy, a number of events to which a crowd of eyewitnesses (including several mutual enemies) attested were viewed with great suspicion. Some famous writers, who were struck more by contrasts than by the harmony of nature, had indulged in portraying the Americas as a swampy land unfavorable for raising animals and newly inhabited by hordes as uncivilized as the inhabitants of the South Seas. In historical studies of the Americans, healthy criticism gave way to absolute skepticism. The declamatory descriptions of Solís and a few other writers who had not left Europe were accorded the same value as the simple and true accounts of the first travelers; it seemed to be the duty of a philosopher to repudiate everything that had been observed by missionaries.

Since the turn of the century, a happy revolution has taken place in our conception of the civilizations of different peoples, and of the factors that either obstruct or encourage progress. We have come to know certain peoples whose customs, institutions, and arts differ as much from those of the Greeks and Romans as the original forms of extinct animals differ from those species that are the focus of descriptive natural history. The Asiatick Society of Calcutta has cast a vivid light on the history of the peoples of Asia. The monuments of Egypt, which are nowadays described with admirable exactitude, have been compared to monuments in the most distant lands, and my study of the indigenous peoples of the Americas appears at a time when we no longer consider as unworthy of our attention anything that diverges from the style that the Greeks bequeathed to us through their inimitable models.

It might have been useful to arrange the materials in this work in geographical order. But the difficulty of both gathering and finishing a large number of Plates in Italy, Germany, and France made it impossible for me to adhere to this principle. To a certain extent, this lack of order is compensated for by the benefit of variety and is, moreover, less objectionable in descriptions contained within a picturesque Atlas than in a formal discourse. I will attempt to remedy this lack through an overview in which the Plates are organized according to the nature of the objects they depict.

[Plates included in this volume are in bold type]

I. Monuments
A. *Mexica*
    Bust of an Aztec Priestess, Plates I and II
    Pyramid of Cholula, Plate VII
    Fortress of Xochicalco, Plate IX
    Bas-Relief Depicting a Warrior's Triumph, Plate XI
    Calendar and Day-Hieroglyphs, Plate XXIII
    Vases, Plate XXXIX
    Bas-Relief around a Cylindrical Stone, Plate XXI
    Ax Covered with Signs, Plate XXVIII
    Funerary Structure of Mitla, Plates XLIX and L
Hieroglyphic Paintings:
    Manuscripts from the Vatican, Plates XIII, XIV, **XXVI**, and LX
    from Velletri, Plates XV, XXVII, and XXXVII
    from Vienna, Plates XLVI, XLVII, and XLVIII
    from Dresden, Plate XLV
    from Berlin, Plates XII, XXXVI, XXXVIII, and LVII
    from Paris, Plates LV and LVI
    from Mendoza, Plates LVIII and LIX
    from Gemelli, Plate XXXII

B. *Peruvian*

House of the Inca at Cañar, Plates XVII, XX,
and LXII

Inga-Chungana, Plate XIX

Ruins of Callo, Plate XXIV

Inti-Guaicu, Plate XVIII

C. *Muisca*

Calendar, Plate XLIV

Sculpted Heads, Plate LXVI

II. Landscapes

A. *Mexican Plateau*

Main Square of Mexico City, Plate III

Basalt Rock of Regla, Plate XXII

Cofre de Perote, Plate XXXIV

Jorullo Volcano, Plate XLIII

Columnar Porphyry of El Jacal, Plate LXV

Los Órganos near Actopan, Plate LXIV

B. *South America's Mountains*

Silla de Caracas, Plate LXVIII

Turbaco Air Volcanoes, Plate XLI

Tequendama Falls, Plate VI

Lake Guatavita, Plate LXVII

Natural Bridge of Icononzo, Plate IV

Quindiu Pass, Plate V

Río Vinagre Falls, Plate XXX

Chimborazo, Plates XVI and **XXV**

Cotopaxi Volcano, Plate X

Top of the Pyramid of Iliniza, Plate XXXV

Nevado of Corazón, Plate LI

Nevado de Cayambe, Plate XLII

Pichincha Volcano, Plate LXI

Rope Bridge at Penipe, Plate XXXIII

Mail Service in Jaén de Bracamoros, Plate XXXI

Raft from the Guayaquil, Plate LXIII

I have attempted to render the objects in these engravings with the greatest possible precision. Those engaged in the practical aspects of the arts know how difficult it is to oversee the large number of Plates that make up a picturesque Atlas. If some of these are less perfect than experts may desire, this imperfection should not be attributed to the artists entrusted with carrying out my work under my supervision but, rather, to the sketches that I made on site in often trying circumstances. Many of the landscapes have been colored, because in this type of engraving snow stands out much better against a sky background, and because the reproduction of Mexica paintings made the use of both colored and black-ink Plates indispensable. We have experienced great difficulty in giving the former the vigor that we so admire in Mr. Daniell's *Oriental Scenerys*.

In my description of the monuments of the Americas, I have proposed to hold to a happy medium between the two paths followed by scholars who have conducted investigations into the monuments, the languages, and the traditions of these peoples. Some scholars have devoted their time to generating theories that, although brilliant, are founded on shaky ground, and they have therefore drawn general conclusions from a small number of isolated facts. They have seen both Chinese and Egyptian colonies in the Americas; they have found both Celtic dialects and the Phoenician alphabet. Although it is still unknown whether the Osci, the Goths, or the Celts were actually transplanted peoples from Asia, some have nonetheless pronounced on the origin of all of the hordes of the new continent. Other scholars have accumulated materials without rising to any general idea, a method as sterile in the history of peoples as it is in the physical sciences. May I have been fortunate enough to avoid the pitfalls that I have just described! A few peoples, very distant from one another – the Etruscans, the Egyptians, the Tibetans, and the Aztecs – exhibit striking parallels in their buildings, their religious institutions, their division of time, their cycles of regeneration, and their mystical ideas. It is the duty of an historian to draw attention to these similarities, which are as difficult to explain as the connections between Sanskrit, Persian, Greek, and the Germanic languages. But in trying to generalize, one must know to stop at the very point where precise data are missing. With these principles in mind, I will bring to light the conclusions to which the knowledge I have hitherto acquired about the indigenous people of the new world appears to lead.

In examining closely the geological makeup of the Americas, in reflecting upon the balance of fluids that are spread across the surface of the earth, one would be hard-pressed to claim that the new continent emerged from the waters at some later point than the old one did. One observes there the same succession of rocky layers as in our hemisphere, and it is likely that the granite, the micaceous schist, or the different gypsum and sandstone formations in the mountains of Peru date from the same periods as their counterparts in the Swiss Alps. The entire globe appears to have undergone the same catastrophes. Fossilized pelagic shells are suspended on the crests of the Andes, at a height exceeding that of Mont Blanc. Fossils of elephant remains are scattered throughout the equinoctial regions; what is particularly remarkable is that they are not found in the steaming plains of the Orinoco but, rather, on the highest and coldest plateaus of the Cordilleras. In the new world, as in the old, generations of now-extinct species preceded those that today populate the earth, the sea, and the air.

There is no proof that the existence of humankind is a much more recent phenomenon in the Americas than in other continents. In the tropics, the vigorous plant life, the size of the rivers, and the partial floods have raised powerful barriers to the migration of peoples. Vast swaths of northern Asia are as thinly populated as the savannahs of New Mexico and Paraguay, and one need not suppose that the lands that have been inhabited the longest are necessarily those with the largest number of inhabitants.

The problem of the original population of the Americas resides no more within the province of history than questions about the origin of plants and animals, and about the distribution of organic germs, lie within the domain of the natural sciences. Venturing back to the earliest times, historical research reveals to us that nearly every part of the earth was once occupied by men who believed themselves to be aboriginal because they were unaware of their filiations. Amidst a multitude of peoples who have succeeded one another and have intermixed, it is impossible to determine what exactly was the initial base of the population, that original layer beyond which begins the domain of cosmogonic tradition.

The peoples of the Americas – with the exception of those bordering the Arctic Circle – form a single race characterized by skull shape, skin color, extremely scarce facial hair, and limp, smooth hair. The American race has unmistakable connections with that of the Mongol people, which includes the descendants of the Xiongnu (formerly known as the Huns), the Khalkha, the Kalmyk, and the Buryats. Recent observations have proved, furthermore, that not only the inhabitants of Unalaska but also many small tribes of South America offer evidence, in the form of certain osteological characteristics of the head, of a transition from the American race to the Mongol race. Once we have more thoroughly studied the brown men of Africa and that swarm of peoples who inhabit the interior and northeast of Asia and to whom traveling categorizers have referred, using the vague terms Tartars and Uralians, then the Caucasian, Mongol, American, Malay, and Negro races will appear less isolated, and we will recognize in this great family of humankind one single organic type, modified by circumstances, which will perhaps remain forever unknown to us.

Although the indigenous peoples of the new continent are united by close ties, they exhibit, in their facial expressions, in their more or less swarthy skin tone, and in their tall stature, differences as striking as those between Arabs, Persians, and Slavs, all of whom belong to the Caucasian race. Nevertheless, the hordes that cross the steaming plains of the equinoctial regions do not have a darker skin tone than the mountain peoples or the inhabitants of the temperate zone, either because, for humankind and for the majority of animals, there is a certain period of organic life after which the influence of climate and diet is more or less nil, or because deviation from the original type becomes noticeable only after a long series of centuries. Moreover, all the evidence suggests that Americans, like the Mongol peoples, have a less mutable physical makeup than other peoples of Asia and of Europe do.

The American race, the least numerous of all, nevertheless occupies the largest territory on earth. That territory stretches across the two hemispheres, from 68 degrees northern latitude to 55 degrees southern latitude. It is the only one of the races that dwells both on the steaming plains bordering the ocean and on the mountainside, where it reaches heights that exceed that of the Peak of Tenerife [Mount Teide] by 200 toises.

The number of distinct languages among the small indigenous tribes in the new continent appears to be much larger than in Africa, where, according to the recent study by Mr. Seetzen and Mr. Vater, more than one hundred and forty languages are spoken. In this respect, the Americas as a whole resemble the Caucasus, Italy prior to the Roman conquest, or Asia Minor, when that small stretch of terrain was home to the Cilicians of the Semitic race, the Phrygians of Thracian origin, the Lydians, and the Celts. The lay of the land, the vigorous plant life, and the fear that mountain peoples in the tropics have of exposing themselves to the heat of the plains obstruct communication and thereby contribute to the astonishing variety of American languages. One also observes that this variety is less evident in the savannahs and in the northern forests that hunters can cross freely, on the banks of the great rivers, along the Ocean coasts, and wherever the Inca had spread their theocracy by force of arms.

When we consider that several hundred languages exist in a continent with a population smaller than that of France, we must acknowledge the differences between languages that have the same relationships between them as do, if not German and Dutch or Italian and Spanish, then at least Danish and German, Chaldean and Arabic, or Greek and Latin. The further one penetrates into the labyrinth of American languages, the more one senses that although several of them can be grouped into families, a large number remain isolated, like Basque among the European languages and Japanese among the Asiatic ones. This isolation is perhaps only superficial, and one has reason to suspect that languages that seem resistant to ethnographic classification are related either to other languages that have been extinct for quite some time or to the languages of peoples whom travelers have not yet encountered.

The majority of American languages, including even those belonging to groups as distinctive as the Germanic, Celtic, and Slavic languages, exhibit a certain degree of conformity in their overall structure, for example in the complexity of their grammatical forms, in the modifications that the verbs undergo according to the nature of the object, and in the multiplicity of additive particles (*affixa* and *suffixa*). The uniform tendency of these languages suggests either a common origin or, at the very least, an extreme uniformity in the intellectual aptitudes of the American peoples from Greenland to the lands of Magellan.

A number of studies conducted with extreme care and following a method that was not formerly employed in the field of etymology have proved that there are a small number of words that are common to all the languages of the two continents. In the eighty-three American languages that Mr. Barton and Mr. Vater analyzed, approximately one hundred and seventy words have been identified that appear to have the same roots; and one is easily persuaded that this similarity is not coincidental, and that its basis lies neither in mimetic harmony nor in the uniform organ shape that makes the first sounds uttered by infants more or less identical. Of the one hundred and seventy words that betray some degree of similarity, three-fifths recall Manchu, Tungus, Mongol, Samoyed, and two-fifths recall the Celtic and Tschud languages, as well as Basque, Coptic, and Congolese. These words were found by comparing all the American languages with all the languages of the old world, for we do not yet know of any language of the Americas that, more than any other, appears to be linked to one of the numerous groups of Asiatic, African, or European languages. What some scholars, relying upon abstract theories, have suggested in regard to the supposed poverty of American languages and the extreme imperfection of their numerical system is as baseless as the claims concerning the weakness and stupidity of humankind in the new continent, the shrinking of the natural realm, and the degeneration of the animals brought from one hemisphere to the other.

Many languages that are the exclusive heritage of barbarian peoples today seem to be the vestiges of rich, supple languages indicative of an advanced culture. We shall not discuss whether the original state of humankind was one of brutish mindlessness or whether the savage hordes descend from peoples whose intellectual faculties were at the same developmental stage as the languages that reflect such faculties. We will merely remark that the little we know of the history of the Americans tends to suggest that the tribes whose migrations led them from north to south already exhibited, in the northernmost countries, the same variety of languages that we find in the Torrid Zone today. From this we can conclude by analogy that the ramification – or, to use an expression not tethered to any system of thought, the multiplicity – of languages is a very old phenomenon. It may be that what we refer to as American languages belong no more to the Americas than Magyar (or Hungarian) and Tschud (or Finnish) belong to Europe.

One cannot deny that the process of comparing the languages of the two continents has not yet led to general conclusions. But we must not lose hope that this investigation might become more fruitful once scholars are able to apply their wisdom to a larger collection of materials. How many languages exist in the Americas and in Central and East Asia whose central mechanism is still as unknown to us as that of Tyrrhenian, Oscan, and Sabine! Among the peoples who disappeared in the old world, there may well be several from which a number of small tribes have been preserved in the vast solitudes of the Americas.

While languages offer only scant proof of prior contact between the two worlds, this contact is undoubtedly evident in the cosmogonies, monuments, hieroglyphs, and institutions of the peoples of both the Americas and Asia. I may flatter myself, perhaps, to think that the following pages will justify this assertion by adding several new pieces of evidence to those that have long been known. An attempt has been made to distinguish carefully between, on the one hand, indices of a common origin and, on the other, the effects experienced by all peoples who find themselves in the situation of beginning to improve their social conditions.

It has hitherto been impossible to determine the period of contact between the inhabitants of the two worlds. It would be rash to suggest a particular group of peoples from the old continent to whom the Toltec, Aztecs, Muisca, or the Peruvians appear most closely connected, for such connections manifest themselves in traditions, monuments, and customs that may actually predate the current division of the Asians into Mongols, Hindus, Tungus, and Chinese.

At the time of the discovery of the new world – or, rather, at the time of the first invasion by the Spanish – the most culturally advanced of the American peoples were the mountain peoples. People born on the temperate plains had followed the ridge of the Cordilleras, which increase in elevation as they approach the Equator. In those lofty regions, they found both a climate and plants resembling those of their native lands.

The faculties develop more easily wherever humans, settled on less fertile land and forced to fight against the obstacles that nature places in their path, do not succumb to this protracted struggle. In the Caucasus and Central Asia, the arid mountains offer a refuge to free barbarian peoples. In the equinoctial regions of the Americas, where verdant savannahs are suspended high above the clouds, we have found only civilized peoples at the heart of the Cordilleras. Their early technical and artistic advances were as old as the bizarre forms of government that did not favor individual liberty.

Like Asia and Africa, the new continent has centers of an original civilization, the mutual connections of which are as unknown to us as those of Meroë, Tibet, and China. Mexico inherited its culture from a country situated to the north; in South America, the great buildings of Tiahuanaco served as models for the monuments that the Inca erected in Cusco. Amid the vast plains of Upper Canada, in Florida, and in the desert bounded by the Orinoco, the Casiquiare, and the

Guainía, embankments of a considerable length, bronze weaponry, and sculpted stone suggest that industrious peoples once inhabited the very lands that hordes of savage hunters cross today.

The unequal distribution of animals across the globe has had a profound impact upon the lot of peoples and their more or less rapid march toward civilization. In the old continent, pastoral life marked the transition from hunting to farming. Ruminants, which are very easy to acclimate to any environment, followed the African Negro as well as the Mongol, the Malay, and the peoples of the Caucasian race. Although several quadrupeds and a larger number of plants are common to the northernmost regions of both worlds, the only bovine creatures native to the Americas are the bison and the musk ox, two animals difficult to domesticate, and whose females produce little milk, despite the richness of the pastures. The tending of herds and the habits of pastoral life did not prepare the American hunter for agriculture. The Andes dweller was never tempted to milk the llama, the alpaca, or the guanaco. Dairy products were formerly unknown among Americans, just as they were among some peoples of East Asia.

Nowhere has the free savage roaming the forests of the temperate zone been seen to abandon voluntarily the life of the hunter to embrace that of the farmer. Only the force of circumstance can bring about this transition, both the most difficult and the most important in the history of human societies. When, during their long migrations, the hordes of hunters, driven by other warlike hordes, reached the plains of the equinoctial region, the dense forests and abundant plant life brought about a change in both their habits and their character. There are lands between the Orinoco, the Ucayali, and the Amazon where the only open space, so to speak, that can be found is in the form of rivers and lakes. Established on the riverbanks, the most savage tribes surrounded their huts with banana plants, jatropha [*Jatropha curcas*], and other food-bearing plants.

Neither historical events nor any legends link the peoples of South America with those who dwell north of the Isthmus of Panama. The annals of the Mexica Empire appear to date back to the sixth century of our time. One finds there the epochs of the migrations, the causes that brought these about, as well as the names of the chiefs issuing from the illustrious Citin family, which led the northern peoples from the unknown regions of Aztlan and Teocolhuacan to the plains of Anahuac. The founding of Tenochtitlan, like that of Rome, falls in heroic times; and it is only since the twelfth century that the Aztec annals, like those of the Chinese and the Tibetans, report without interruption the secular feasts, the genealogy of kings, the tributes imposed upon the conquered, the founding of cities, celestial phenomena, and even the most minute events that had an influence on the state of these nascent societies.

Although their legends do not suggest any direct connection between the peoples of the two Americas, their history nonetheless offers a number of striking links in their respective political and religious upheavals, from which date the civilizations of the Aztecs, Muisca, and Peruvians. Men with beards and lighter skin than that of the natives of Anahuac, Cundinamarca, and the plateau of Cusco appeared, without anyone being able to determine their place of birth. High priests, legislators, lovers of peace and the arts fostered by the latter, these men rapidly changed the condition of the peoples who welcomed them with veneration. Quetzalcoatl, Bochica, and Manco Capac are the sacred names of these mysterious beings. Quetzalcoatl, clothed in black, in priestly habits, came from Panuco, from the shores of the Gulf of Mexico. Bochica, the Buddha of the Muisca, revealed himself in the high plains of Bogotá, where he arrived from the savannahs east of the Cordilleras. The story of these legislators, which I have attempted to develop in this work, is laced with marvels, religious fictions, and features suggestive of allegory. A few scholars have suggested that these strangers are, in fact, shipwrecked Europeans or descendants of those Scandinavians who have visited Greenland, Newfoundland, and perhaps even Nova Scotia since the eleventh century. But one has only to consider the period of the first Toltec migrations, as well as monastic institutions, religious symbols, the calendar, and the form of the monuments of Cholula, Sogamoso, and Cusco, to realize that Quetzalcoatl, Bochica, and Manco Capac did not draw their code of laws from the north of Europe. Everything seems to point toward East Asia, toward those peoples who were in contact with the Tibetans, the Shamanist Tartars, and the bearded Ainu [Aynu or Aino] of the islands of Yezo [Hokkaido] and Sakhalin.

In using the words *monuments of the new world*, *advances in the art of drawing*, and *intellectual culture* throughout the course of this study, I have not intended to suggest a state of affairs that would indicate what is vaguely referred to as a highly advanced civilization. Nothing is more difficult than comparing nations that have taken different paths in their social development. The Mexica and the Peruvians cannot be judged according to principles drawn from the history of peoples whom our own education ceaselessly brings to mind. They are as different from the Greeks and the Romans as they are similar to the Etruscans and the Tibetans. Although the theocratic government of the Peruvians favored the progress of industry, public works, and everything indicative of mass civilization, so to speak, it nevertheless hindered the development of individual faculties. On the contrary, the development of the Greeks, which was so free and so rapid before the time of Pericles, did not correspond to the slow progress of mass civilization. The Inca Empire resembled a great monastic establishment in which some means of contributing to the common good was prescribed to each member of the congregation. By studying on site those Peruvians who have retained their national physiognomy throughout the centuries, one learns to understand the true value of Manco Capac's code of laws and the effects that it produced on customs and public happiness. There was at once general welfare and little private happiness; more resignation to the decrees of the sovereign than love of the fatherland; passive and spineless obedience without courage for daring feats; a sense of order that meticulously regulated even the pettiest actions in one's life; and no reach into the realm of ideas, no elevation in that of character. The most complex political institutions in the history of human society smothered the germ of individual liberty; and the founder of the empire of Cusco, who congratulated himself for his success in forcing people to be happy, reduced the latter to the state of simple machines. Peruvian theocracy was certainly less oppressive than the rule of the Mexica kings. But both contributed to giving to the monuments, worship, and mythology of two mountain peoples the gloomy and somber aspect that so contrasts with the arts and sweet fictions of the peoples of Greece.

Paris, April 1813

PICTURESQUE VIEWS OF THE CORDILLERAS
AND MONUMENTS OF THE INDIGENOUS PEOPLES
OF THE AMERICAS

THERE ARE TWO very different ways in which the monuments of peoples from whom we are separated by centuries can command our attention. If the works of art that have reached us belong to peoples of a highly advanced civilization, then what elicits our admiration is the harmony and beauty of their form and the genius with which they were conceived. Even if no inscription identified the conqueror of Arbela, the bust of Alexander from the gardens of Pison would still be recognized as a precious relic of antiquity. An engraved stone or a coin from the golden age of Greece interests the art lover because of the austerity of its style and finish, even in the absence of any legend or monogram linking such objects to a specific historical period. Such is the privilege of everything produced under the skies of Asia Minor and in the regions of southern Europe.

On the other hand, monuments produced by peoples who did not attain a high level of intellectual culture, or who, for either religious or political reasons or because of the nature of their societal organization, seemed less appreciative of the beauty of forms, can only be considered historical monuments. To this category belong the sculptural relics scattered throughout the vast lands stretching from the banks of the Euphrates to the eastern coasts of Asia. The idols of Tibet and Hindustan and those found on the central plateau of Mongolia attract our attention because they shed light upon the ancient contacts between peoples and the common origin of their mythological traditions.

The crudest works, the most bizarre forms, the masses of sculpted rocks impressive only for their majesty and for the antiquity we attribute to them, and the colossal pyramids that bring to mind teeming throngs of workers – these are all connected to the philosophical study of history.

For this very reason, the scant vestiges of the arts, or, rather, the industry, of the peoples of the new continent merit our attention. Convinced of this truth, I have gathered throughout my travels all that my lively curiosity has led me to discover in countries where, throughout centuries of barbarism, intolerance has led to the destruction of everything related to the customs and religion of the ancient inhabitants; where buildings were dismantled in order to extract stones or seek treasures hidden in them. The connections that I intend to draw between artworks from Mexico and Peru and from the Old World will generate some interest in my own research and in the picturesque Atlas that contains my findings. While I am far removed from any systematic approach, I will nevertheless call attention to naturally occurring parallels, distinguishing the ones that appear to suggest similarities in terms of race from those that most likely result only from strictly internal causes and from the resemblance all peoples exhibit as their intellectual faculties develop. I must limit myself here to a succinct description of the objects depicted in these engravings. The conclusions to which the study of these monuments as a group appears to lead can only be discussed in the narrative of my journey. Since the peoples to whom we attribute these buildings and sculptures still exist, both their physiognomy and an understanding of their customs will serve to illuminate the history of their migrations.

Studies of the monuments erected by peoples still only halfway emerged from barbarism are of interest for yet another reason that we might call psychological: they place before our eyes the spectacle of the uniform and progressive advancement of the human mind. The works of the first inhabitants of Mexico occupy a middle ground between those of the Scythian peoples and the ancient monuments of Hindustan. What an impressive sight the genius of humanity affords us as it covers the space extending from the tombs of Tinian and the statues of Easter Island to the monuments of the Mexica temple of Mitla, and from the crude idols inside this temple to the masterpieces of the chisel of Praxiteles and of Lysippus!

Let us not be surprised by the crudeness of style and the inaccurate contours within the works of the peoples of the Americas. Isolated perhaps at an early stage from the rest of humanity and roaming across a land where humans had to struggle, for a long time, against a wild and forever restless natural realm, these peoples, left to their own devices, were able to develop only slowly. Eastern Asia and western and northern Europe exhibit the same phenomena. In acknowledging these, I shall not undertake to pronounce on the mysterious causes by which the seed of the fine arts has sprouted in only a very small part of the globe. How many peoples of the old continent have lived in a climate similar to that of Greece, surrounded by all that might stir the imagination, without rising to a sense of the beauty of forms, a sense that developed only in those areas where the arts were inspired by the genius of the Greeks? These reflections suffice to establish the objective that I have set for myself in publishing these fragments of American monuments. Their study may become useful like that of the most imperfect languages, the interest of which lies not only in their similarity to known languages but also in the intimate connection that exists between their structure and the degree of ability of humans more or less removed from civilization.

By presenting in a single work the crude monuments of the indigenous peoples of the Americas and the picturesque views of the mountainous lands that these peoples inhabited, I believe to have brought together objects whose connections have not escaped the sagacity of those who are devoted to the philosophical study of the human mind. Although the customs of peoples, the development of their intellectual faculties, and the specific character inscribed in their works all depend at once upon a large number of causes that are not exclusively local, we cannot deny that climate, the lay of the land, the physiognomy of plants, and the prospect of either a cultivated or a wild natural environment have influenced their technical and artistic advances, as well as the style that distinguishes their works. This influence is more appreciable the further removed humans are from civilization. What a contrast between the architecture of a people that dwells inside vast and gloomy caverns and that of the nomadic hordes whose bold monuments recall the slender trunks of desert palms in the shafts of their columns! In order to understand properly the origin of the arts, one must study the nature of the place that witnessed their birth. The only American peoples in whose midst we find remarkable monuments are the mountain peoples. Isolated in the cloud regions on the world's highest plateaus, surrounded by volcanoes whose craters are ringed with eternal ice, they seem to admire, in the solitude of these deserts, only whatever strikes the imagination through the sheer grandeur of its dimensions. The works that they have produced bear the imprint of the wild nature of the Cordilleras.

Part One of this Atlas is intended to be an introduction to the grand scenes that this natural realm presents. I was less interested in depicting those scenes and their picturesque effect than in representing the exact contours of the mountains, the valleys that furrow their sides, and the impressive waterfalls formed by plunging torrents. The Andes are to the High Alps what the Alps are to the Pyrenees. Everything romantic or grand that I have seen on the banks of the Saverne in northern Germany, in the Euganean Hills, in the central mountain range of Europe, or on the steep slopes of the volcano of Tenerife – this is all combined in the Cordilleras of the new world. Several centuries would not be enough time to observe their beauties and to discover the wonders that nature has lavished upon an expanse of two thousand five hundred leagues, from the granite mountains of the Strait of Magellan to the coasts that neighbor eastern Asia. I will consider my goal fulfilled if the humble sketches in this book inspire travelers with a passion for art to visit the regions that I traversed in order to depict faithfully these majestic sites, which cannot be compared to those of the old continent.

PLATE III

View of the Main Square of Mexico City

THE CITY OF Tenochtitlan, capital of Anahuac, founded in 1325 on a small group of islets situated in the western part of the salt lake of Texcoco, was completely destroyed during the siege that the Spanish laid to it in 1521, which lasted seventy-five days. The new city, which counts nearly one hundred and forty thousand inhabitants, was built by Cortés upon the ruins of the former, following the same street pattern; but the canals that crossed these streets were filled in little by little, and Mexico City, radically refurbished by the viceroy, the Count of Revillagigedo, is today comparable to the most beautiful cities of Europe. The main square, depicted on the third Plate, is the site formerly occupied by the great temple of Mexitli, which, like all the *teocalli*, or dwellings of the Mexica gods, was a pyramidal building, similar to the Babylonian monument dedicated to Jupiter Belus. On the right-hand side, we see the palace of the viceroy of New Spain, a building of simple design originally belonging to the Cortés family, which is that of the *Marquis of the Valle de Oaxaca, the Duke of Monteleone*. In the center of the engraving is the cathedral, one part of which (*el sagrario*) is in the ancient Indian or Moorish style commonly called Gothic. Behind the cupola of the *sagrario*, where *Indio triste* runs into Tacuba street, lies King Axayacatl's palace, where Montezuma lodged the Spanish when they arrived in Tenochtitlan. Montezuma's own palace was to the right of the cathedral, across from the present viceroy's palace. I felt it necessary to indicate these locations since they are not without interest to those who study the history of the conquest of Mexico.

Since 1803 the *Plaza mayor*, which must not be confused with the main market of Tlatelolco (which Cortés described in his letters to Emperor Charles V), has been adorned with

PLATE III

the equestrian statue of King Charles IV commissioned by the viceroy Marquis of Branciforte. This bronze statue is of great stylistic purity and beautifully made: it was designed, modeled, cast, and put in place by the same artist, Don Manuel Tolsa, a native of Valencia, Spain, and director of the sculpture class at the fine arts academy of Mexico City. We do not know what we should admire most: this artist's talent or the courage and perseverance that he displayed in a country where everything was yet to be created, and where he had many obstacles to overcome. This beautiful work was a success from the first casting. The statue weighs nearly twenty-three thousand kilograms; it is two decimeters taller than the equestrian statue of Louis XIV in the Place Vendôme in Paris. They had the good taste not to gild the horse and were content to coat it with a brownish olive-colored varnish. As the buildings that border the square are generally low, we see the statue projected against the sky, which, on the ridge of the Cordilleras where the atmosphere is a very deep blue, produces a most picturesque effect. I assisted in the transfer of this enormous piece from the site of its casting to the *Plaza mayor*. It crossed a distance of around sixteen hundred meters in five days. The mechanics that Mr. Tolsa employed to raise it up on a pedestal of exquisite Mexican marble are quite ingenious and merit detailed description.

Today, the main square of Mexico City is of an irregular shape since, contrary to Cortés's plan, they built the square that housed the Parian [set of shops at the southwest corner]. To make the square look less asymmetrical, it was deemed necessary to place the equestrian statue, which the Indians know only by the name of the *great horse*, in a special enclosure. This enclosure is paved in porphyry tile and is more than fifteen decimeters higher than the adjacent streets. The oval, whose major axis is one hundred meters long, is surrounded by four fountains and, to the great dismay of the natives, is closed off by four gates with bronze-decorated grating.

The engraving that I include here is the faithful copy of a drawing made, on a larger scale, by Mr. Ximeno, a distinguished artist who directs the painting class at the academy of

Mexico City. In the figures placed outside the enclosure, this drawing shows the dress of the Guachinangos, the Mexican lower classes.

PLATE V

Quindiu Pass in the Cordillera of the Andes

IN THE KINGDOM of New Granada, from 2°30′ to 5°15′ of northern latitude, the Cordillera of the Andes is divided into three parallel ranges, of which only the two lateral ranges are covered, at extreme heights, with sandstone and other secondary formations. The *eastern range* separates the Magdalena River valley from the plains of the Río Meta. The natural bridges of Icononzo lie on its western slope. Its highest peaks are the Páramo de la *Sumapaz* and that of *Chingaza*. Neither of them reaches the regions of the eternal snows. The middle range divides the waters between the Magdalena River basin and that of the Río Cauca. It often reaches the perpetual snow line, and it surpasses the latter by far in the colossal peaks of *Guanacas*, *Baragan*, and *Quindiu*. At sunrise and sunset, this middle range presents a magnificent spectacle to the inhabitants of Santa Fé; it recalls the view of the Swiss Alps, but on a more impressive scale.

The *western range* of the Andes separates the valley of Cauca from the province of Chocó, as well as from the coasts of the South Sea. Its elevation is barely fifteen hundred meters, and it falls to such a low height between the headwaters of the Río Atrato and those of the Río San Juan that one has difficulty tracing it to the Isthmus of Panama.

These three mountain ranges merge toward the north, at 6° and 7° northern latitude. They form a single group to the south of Popayán in the province of Pastos. We must not, however, mistake them for the division of the Cordilleras that Bouguer and La Condamine observed in the kingdom of Quito, from the equator to 2° of southern latitude.

The city of Santa Fé de Bogotá is located to the west of the Páramo de *Chingasa*, on a plateau at an absolute altitude of two thousand six hundred fifty meters that extends to the ridge of

the *eastern Cordillera*. The result of the Andes' peculiar structure in these parts is that to reach Popayán and the banks of
the Cauca from Santa Fé, one must either descend the *eastern
range* by the *Mesa* and the *Tocaima* or cross the Magdalena River
valley by way of the natural bridges of *Icononzo* and then scale
the middle range. The most heavily traveled pass is that of the
Páramo de Guanacas, which Bouguer described upon his return
from Quito to Cartagena de Indias. Following this path, the
traveler crosses the ridge of the middle Cordillera in a single
day through an inhabited area. We preferred the pass of the
mountain of Quindiu (or *Quindío*), between the cities of Ibagué
and Cartago, to that of Guanacas. The entry to the first pass
is depicted in Plate V. It seemed to me indispensable to provide these geographical details in order to give a better sense
of the position of a place that one would seek in vain on the
best maps of South America, for example, that of La Cruz.

Quindiu Mountain (lat. 4°36′, long. 5°12′) is reported to be
the most difficult passage in the entire Cordillera of the Andes.
It is a dense, completely uninhabited forest that cannot be
crossed in less than ten to twelve days, even in good weather.
There are no huts and no means of livelihood: at all times of
the year, travelers stock up with a month's worth of supplies,
for it often happens that they find themselves cut off by thaw-
ing snow and the sudden swelling of the torrents, unable to
descend from either the Cartago or the Ibagué side. The highest point on this path, the Garito del Páramo, is three thousand
five hundred meters above sea level. As the foot of the mountain is only nine hundred sixty meters high near the banks of
the Cauca, the climate there is appreciably mild and temperate.
The trail by which one ascends the Cordillera is so narrow that
its average width is only four to five decimeters: for the most
part, it resembles a hollowed-out, open-air gallery. In this and
nearly every part of the Andes the rock is coated in a thick
layer of clay. Water trickling down from the mountain has hollowed out ravines six to seven meters deep. One walks in these
mud-filled crevices, whose darkness is exacerbated by thick
vegetation that stretches across their openings. The bodies of
oxen, the beasts of burden commonly used here, pass with

difficulty through these galleries, which can be up to two thousand meters long. If one has the misfortune of encountering one of these animals on the trail, there is no other way of avoiding it than to turn back or to climb onto the earthen wall that runs alongside the gorge and then hold oneself up by hanging on to the roots that reach there from the surface of the soil.

Crossing Quindiu Mountain in October of 1801, on foot and followed by twelve oxen that carried our instruments and collections, we suffered greatly from the continual downpours to which we were exposed throughout the three or four final days of our descent of the western slope of the Cordillera. The path passes through swampy terrain covered with bamboo. The prickles that arm the roots of these gigantic grasses had torn our shoes, forcing us to go barefoot, like all those travelers who do not want to be carried on *man-back*. This peculiar circumstance, plus the constant humidity; the length of the crossing; the muscle strength that one must employ to walk in thick, muddy clay; and the need for wading through deep torrents of icy water, makes this an extremely tiring voyage. But however difficult it may be, one encounters none of the dangers that frighten gullible travelers. Though the path is quite narrow, it skirts precipices only very infrequently. As the oxen have the habit of always stepping in the same tracks, a series of small ditches form in and across the path, separated from one another by very narrow protuberances of earth. During heavy rains these thresholds remain hidden underwater, and the traveler's step is doubly uncertain, for he does not know whether he steps on the dam or in the ditch.

Since few wealthy people in these climes are in the habit of walking on foot and on such difficult paths for fifteen to twenty days in a row, they have themselves carried by men who have chairs tied to their backs; given the current state of the Quindiu pass, it would be impossible to go by mule. In this country one hears the phrase *to go on man-back* (*andar en carguero*), just as one says *to go on horseback*. There is no stigma attached to the job of the *cargueros*. The men who devote their lives to it are not Indians but, rather, Mestizos and sometimes even Whites. One is often surprised to hear naked men,

PLATE V

dedicated to what in our eyes must be a withering profession, arguing in the middle of a forest because one of them refused the other, who claims to have whiter skin, the pompous title of either *Don* or *Su Merced* [Sir or Your Excellency]. The *cargueros* generally carry six to seven *arrobas* (seventy-five to eighty-eight kilograms); the hardiest of them carry up to nine *arrobas*. When one reflects on the enormous fatigue to which these miserable men are exposed as they walk for eight to nine hours a day in mountainous terrain; when one knows that their backs are sometimes bruised like the backs of beasts of burden and that travelers are often so cruel as to abandon them in the forest when they fall ill; when one considers that for a trip from Ibagué to Cartago they earn no more than 12 to 14 piasters (60 to 70 francs) for fifteen, sometimes even twenty-five to thirty, days, one struggles to understand how this profession of *cargueros*, one of the most arduous to which a man might devote himself, is so readily embraced by all the hardy young people who live at the foot of these mountains. The taste for a rootless and vagabond life, as well as the idea of a certain independence in the midst of the forests, causes them to prefer this arduous occupation to sedentary and monotonous employment in the towns and cities.

The Quindiu Mountain pass is not the only part of South America in which one may travel on *man-back*. An entire province, Antioquia, is hemmed in by mountains that are so difficult to cross that those who do not wish to entrust themselves to the nimbleness of a *carguero*, and who are not sufficiently robust to brave the path from Santa Fé de Antioquia to the Boca de Nares or to Río Samana on foot, must simply stay home. I met an inhabitant of this province who was positively enormous: he had only ever encountered two Mestizos capable of carrying him, and it would have been impossible for him to return home had these two *cargueros* died while he was on the banks of the Magdalena, at Mompox or Honda. There are so many young people who perform the job of beasts of burden in Chocó, Ibagué, and Medellín that one sometimes encounters lines fifty or sixty men deep. A few years ago, when the project was conceived of building a mountain path passable for mules from the village of Nares to Antioquia, the *cargueros* formally protested against the improvement of the roads, and the government was weak enough to give in to their demands. It is useful to recall here that in the mines of Mexico there are men whose sole occupation is carrying others on their backs. The sloth of whites in these climes is so great that every mine director has in his employ one or two Indians called his *horses (caballitos)*, because they are saddled every morning and, by leaning on a small cane and thrusting their body forward, they carry their master from one part of the mine to another. The *caballitos* and *cargueros* who have sure footing and a gentle, steady step are singled out and recommended to travelers. It is sad to hear a man's qualities characterized in terms of the gait of horses and mules. Those who have themselves carried in a *carguero*'s chair must sit completely still and lean back for several hours. The least movement would be enough to cause the man carrying them to fall, and such falls are all the more dangerous since the *carguero*, overconfident in his own dexterity, often chooses the steepest slopes or crosses a torrent on a narrow and slippery tree trunk. Accidents are nevertheless very rare, and those that do happen should be attributed to the carelessness of frightened travelers who have jumped from on top of their chairs.

The fifth Plate depicts a quaint site at the entrance to Quindiu Mountain, near Ibagué, at a post called the foot of the Cuesta. The truncated cone of Tolima, covered in perpetual snows, its shape recalling that of Cotopaxi and Cayambe, appears above a mass of granitic rocks. The small river of Combeima, which blends its waters with those of the Río Cuello, winds through a narrow valley and cuts its path across a palm grove. In the background one can make out a part of the city of Ibagué, the great Magdalena River valley, and the eastern range of the Andes. In the foreground a group of *cargueros* is heading to the mountain. One can see here the distinctive way in which the bamboo chair is tied to the shoulders and balanced by a headpiece similar to that worn by horses and oxen. The rolled-up bundle in the third *carguero*'s hand is the roof or, rather, the mobile house that the traveler uses as he crosses the forests of Quindiu.

Upon arrival in Ibagué, and once preparations for the trip are under way, several hundred *vijao* leaves are cut from the neighboring mountains. This plant, which belongs to the same family as the banana tree, forms a new genus related to Thalia and must not be confused with Heliconia bihai. These leaves, membranous and glossy like those of the Musa, have an oval shape with a length of fifty-four centimeters (twenty inches) and a width of thirty-seven centimeters (fourteen inches). They have a silvery white underside covered in a floury substance that flakes off in scales. It is this peculiar *varnish* that makes it resistant to rain for long periods of time. In gathering them, people make an incision at the central vein, which is the extension of the petiole: this incision serves as a hook from which they are hung when it is time to set up the mobile roof; the leaves are then spread out and rolled carefully into a cylindrical bundle. It takes fifty kilograms of leaves to cover a six- to eight-person hut. When one arrives at a place in the middle of the forest where the soil is dry and where one expects to spend the night, the *cargueros* cut a few tree branches that they assemble into a tent shape. In the space of a few minutes this light framework is divided into panes, with lianas or agave threads stretched in parallel lines three or four decimeters apart. During this time the bundle of *vijao* leaves is unrolled, and several people then busy themselves with arranging them on the trellis so that they overlap one another like house tiles. These hastily constructed huts are very cool and comfortable. If, during the night, the traveler feels the rain trickling in, he simply points out the spot with the leak; a single leaf suffices to fix this annoyance. We spent several days in the Boquia valley in one of these leaf tents without getting wet, although the rain was very heavy and almost interminable. Quindiu Mountain is among the richest places in terms of useful and interesting plants. It was there that we found a palm tree (*Ceroxylon andicola*) with a trunk covered in vegetal wax, passion flowers in the trees, and the superb Mutisia grandiflora, whose scarlet flowers are sixteen centimeters (six inches) long.

PLATE VII

Pyramid of Cholula

DESPITE THEIR POLITICAL divisions, five of the peoples who appeared successively on Mexican soil from the seventh to the twelfth century of our time – namely the Toltecs, the Chichimecs, the Acolhua, the Tlaxcalteca, and the Aztecs – spoke the same language, worshiped the same gods, and built pyramidal structures, which they regarded as *teocalli*, that is, as the dwelling places of their gods. Although these structures were of very different dimensions, they all had same shape: terraced pyramids with sides that exactly followed the meridian and the parallel of the site. The *teocalli* [god-dwelling] was raised in the middle of a vast square enclosure surrounded by a wall. This enclosure, comparable to the Greeks περιβολος [*peribolos*, enclosing wall] contained gardens, fountains, the priests' residences, sometimes even armories; like the ancient temple of Baal-berith burned by Abimelech, the dwelling place of every Mexica god was also a fortress. A tall staircase led to the top of the truncated pyramid; on top of this platform were one or two chapels built like towers, which housed colossal idols of the particular deity to which the *teocalli* was dedicated. This part of the structure must be regarded as the most important; it is the ναός [*naos*, temple room] or, rather, the σηκός [*sekos*, sacred area] of Greek temples. This is also the place where the priests kept the sacred flame. The distinctive layout of the structure, which we have just described, made it possible for the sacrificer to be seen by a large crowd of people at the same time. One could see the procession of the *teopixqui* from a distance as they climbed or descended the steps of the pyramid. The structure's interior served as the sepulcher for the kings and the other Mexica dignitaries. It is impossible to read the descriptions of the temple of Jupiter Belus, which Herodotus and Diodorus Siculus bequeathed to us, without being struck by the points of similarity between this Babylonian monument and the *teocalli* of Anahuac.

When the Mexica or Aztecs, one of the seven tribes of the *Anahuatlaca* (*riverine* people), arrived in the equinoctial region of New Spain in the year 1190, they encountered the pyramidal monuments of *Teotihuacan*, *Cholula* (or *Cholollan*), and *Papantla*. They attributed these great constructions to the Toltec, a powerful and civilized people who had lived in Mexico five hundred years earlier, had used hieroglyphic script, and had a calendar year and a chronology that were more exact than those of most of the peoples of the old continent. The Aztecs did not know for certain whether other tribes had inhabited the country of Anahuac before the Toltec. Considering the god-dwellings of Teotihuacan and Cholollan to be the work of the Toltec, they attributed to the latter the most ancient origin they could imagine. It is possible, however, that they were built before the Toltec invasion, that is, before the year 648 of the common era. Let us not be surprised that the history of an American people might begin before the seventh century, and that the history of the Toltec might be as uncertain as that of the Pelasgians and the Ausonians. An insightful scholar, Mr. Schlözer, has provided ample evidence that the history of northern Europe does not go back any further than the tenth century, a period when the Mexican plateau supported a civilization that was much more advanced than that of Denmark, Sweden, or Russia.

The *teocalli* of Mexico City was dedicated to Tezcatlipoca, the most important Aztec deity after Teotl, the supreme and invisible Being, and to Huitzilopochtli, the god of war. It was built by the Aztecs, following the model of the pyramids of Teotihuacan, only six years before the discovery of the Americas by Christopher Columbus. This truncated pyramid, which Cortés called the main Temple, was ninety-seven meters wide at its base and fifty-four meters high. It is not surprising that a structure of such dimensions could be destroyed a few years after the siege of Mexico City. In Egypt, only a few vestiges remain of the enormous pyramids that rose from the waters of Lake Moeris and that, Herodotus claimed, were adorned with colossal statues. In Etruria, the pyramids of Porsena – the description of which seems a bit fanciful, and four of which, according to Varro, were more than eighty meters high – also disappeared.

But whereas the European conquerors toppled the Aztecs' *teocalli*, they did not also succeed in destroying the most ancient monuments, those we attribute to the Toltec people. We shall give a succinct description of these monuments, which are remarkable for both their form and their size.

The pyramid group of *Teotihuacan* is located in the Valley of Mexico at a distance of eight leagues to the northeast of the capital and in a plain that bears the name *Mixcoatl*, or *Pathway of the Dead*. There one can still see two great pyramids dedicated to the sun (*Tonatiuh*) and the moon (*Meztli*) and surrounded by several hundred small pyramids that form roads between them, the direction of which is exactly north–south and east–west. One of the two great *teocalli* has a perpendicular elevation of fifty-five meters, while the other has forty-four meters. Given that the base of the former, the Tonatiuh Yztaqual, is two hundred eight meters long, if we take into consideration the measurements Mr. Oteyza made in 1803, it would appear that this structure is taller than the Mycerinus, the third of the great pyramids of Giza, and that the length of its base is more or less equal to that of Chephren. The small pyramids surrounding the great dwellings of the moon and the sun are barely nine to ten meters high: according to the natives' legends, they served as the tribal chiefs' sepulcher. Similarly, around Cheops and Mycerinus in Egypt, one can make out eight small pyramids arranged in a very symmetrical fashion and parallel to the sides of the large ones. The two *teocalli* of Teotihuacan had four main terraces; each of these was subdivided into small steps, the edges of which can still be made out. Their core is of clay mixed with small rocks and covered with a thick wall of *tezontli*, porous amygdaloids. This construction recalls one of the Egyptian pyramids of Sakkarah, which has six terraces and which, according to Pococke's narrative, is a mass of stones and yellow mortar covered with rough stones on the outside. At the top of the great Mexica *teocalli* were two colossal statues of the sun and the moon. They were made of stone and coated in strips of gold; these strips were removed by Cortés's soldiers. When Bishop Zumárraga, a Franciscan monk, undertook to destroy everything related to the religion, the history, and the antiquities of the indigenous peoples of the Americas, he also had the idols of the Mixcoatl plain burned. One can still see the remains of a staircase built of large cut stones that formerly led to the platform of the *teocalli*.

To the east of the Teotihuacan pyramid group, as one descends from the Cordillera toward the Gulf of Mexico, the Papantla pyramid rises in the midst of a dense forest called *Tajín*. It was only by accident that Spanish hunters discovered it less than thirty years ago, for the Indians prefer to hide from the whites everything that they have long venerated. The shape of this *teocalli*, which had six, perhaps even seven, levels, is slenderer than that of any other monuments of this kind: although it is about eighteen meters high, it is only twenty-five meters long at its base. It is, therefore, almost half as high as the pyramid of Gaius Cestius in Rome, which is thirty-three meters. This small structure is built entirely of extraordinarily large dressed stones with an exquisite, very regular cut. Three staircases lead to its top; the surface of its terraces is adorned with hieroglyphic sculptures and small recesses arranged very symmetrically. The number of these recesses seems to allude to the three hundred eighteen simple and compound signs of the days of the *Cempohualilhuitl*, the Toltec civil calendar.

The greatest, most ancient, and most famous of all the pyramidal monuments of Anahuac is the *teocalli* of Cholula. Today it is called *the handmade mountain* (*monte hecho a mano*). Seeing it from afar, one would indeed be tempted to take it for a natural hill covered in vegetation. It is in its current state of degradation that this pyramid is depicted on the seventh Plate.

A vast plain, that of Puebla, is separated from the Valley of Mexico by the volcanic range that extends from Popocatepetl toward Río Frío and the peak of Telapón. This fertile but treeless plain is rich in relics of Mexica history: it contains the capitals of the three republics of Tlaxcala, Huejotzingo, and

PLATE VII

Cholula, which, despite their continual strife, nonetheless resisted the despotism and the usurpatory spirit of the Aztec kings.

The small city of Cholula, which Cortés compared to the most densely populated cities of Spain in his letters to Emperor Charles V, has barely sixteen thousand inhabitants today. The pyramid is located to the east of the city on the road that leads from Cholula to Puebla. It is very well preserved on its western flank, and it is this side that is depicted in the engraving that we are including here. The Cholula plain exhibits the barren character particular to plateaus with an elevation of two thousand two hundred meters above sea level. In the foreground one can make out a few agave stalks and dragon trees, while in the background one sees the snow-capped top of the Orizaba volcano, a colossal mountain with an absolute elevation of five thousand two hundred ninety-five meters. I have published a sketch of this mountain in my Mexican Atlas, Plate XVII.

The *teocalli* of Cholula has five terraces of equal height. It seems to have been oriented in exact alignment with the four cardinal points; but since the edges of the terraces are not very distinct, it is difficult to discern their original direction. This pyramidal monument has a broader base than any similar structure in the old continent. I have measured it carefully and have confirmed that its perpendicular height is no more than fifty-five meters but that each side of its base is four hundred thirty-nine meters long. Torquemada judged its height to be seventy-seven meters; Betancourt, sixty-five; and Clavijero, sixty-one. Bernal Díaz del Castillo, an ordinary soldier in Cortés's expedition, found a source of distraction in counting the steps in the staircases leading to the platforms of the *teocalli*; he found one hundred fourteen at the great temple of Tenochtitlan, one hundred seventeen at Tetzcoco, and one hundred twenty at Cholula. The base of the Cholula pyramid is twice as large as that of Cheops, but it is only slightly higher than the Mycerinus pyramid. A comparison between the dimensions of the dwelling place of the sun at Teotihuacan and those of the Cholula pyramid suggests that the people who constructed these remarkable monuments intended to build them to the same height, but with bases at a length ratio of one to two. The proportion between the base and the height is also different among the various monuments. The three great pyramids of Giza have a height-to-base ratio of one to one and seven-tenths; for the hieroglyph-covered pyramid of Papantla, this ratio is one to one and four-tenths; for the great pyramid of Teotihuacan, it is one to three and seven-tenths; and for Cholula, it is one to seven and eight-tenths. The last of these monuments is constructed of alternating layers of unfired bricks (*xamilli*) and clay. A number of Cholula Indians assured me that the interior of the pyramid is hollow and that during Cortés's stay in their city, their ancestors had hidden a large number of warriors there in order to swoop down unexpectedly upon the Spanish. Both the material from which this *teocalli* is constructed and the silence of the contemporary historians on this matter seem to cast doubt upon the validity of this claim.

What is indisputable is that in the interior of this pyramid, as in other *teocalli*, there were considerable cavities that served as the natives' sepulcher; a peculiar circumstance occasioned their discovery. Seven or eight years ago, the road from Puebla to Mexico City, which formerly passed by the north side of the pyramid, was redirected; to align this road, they bore straight through the lowest terrace, which left one-eighth of the terrace isolated like a pile of bricks. While boring this hole, they found in the pyramid's interior a square house built of stone and supported by beams of bald cypress (*cupressus disticha*); it contained two corpses, idols in basalt, and a large number of varnished, artistically painted vases. Although they did not bother to preserve these objects, they claim to have verified carefully that this house, covered in bricks and layers of clay, had no exit whatsoever. If one supposes that the pyramid was built not by the Toltec, the first inhabitants of Cholula, but by the prisoners whom the Cholulans took from among the neighboring peoples, it seems plausible that the corpses were those of a few unfortunate slaves deliberately left to die inside the *teocalli*. We have examined the ruins of this subterranean house and have identified a peculiar arrangement of the bricks, which tends to reduce the amount of pressure exerted on the roof. Since the natives did not know how to construct vaulted roofs, they placed especially wide bricks in a horizontal position so that those on top extended past the lower ones. The result was a tiered assembly that functioned somewhat like a Gothic arch; similar vestiges have also been found in several Egyptian structures. It would be interesting to hollow out a gallery through the *teocalli* of Cholula in order to examine its internal construction; remarkably, the desire for finding hidden treasures has not yet prompted such an undertaking. During my trip to Peru, when I visited the vast ruins of the city of Chimu, near Manische, I entered the interior of the famous *Huaca de Toledo*, the tomb of a Peruvian prince, in which García Gutiérrez de Toledo discovered more than five million francs' worth of solid gold while making a gallery in 1576, as is confirmed by the ledgers preserved in the town hall of Trujillo.

At the top of the great *teocalli* of Cholula, also called the mountain of unfired bricks (*Tlalchihualtepec*), was an altar dedicated to Quetzalcoatl, the god of the air. This Quetzalcoatl (whose name means snake dressed in green feathers, from *coatl*, snake, and *quetzalli*, green feather) is probably the most mysterious figure in all of Mexica mythology. He was a white, bearded man, like the Muisca's Bochica, whom we mentioned above in the description of the Tequendama waterfall. He was the high priest at Tula (*Tollan*), a legislator, the head of a religious sect who, like the Sannyasin and the Buddhists of Hindustan, imposed a very cruel penance upon himself: he introduced the custom of piercing the lips and the ears and mortifying the rest of the body with spines from agave leaves and cacti, while inserting reeds into the wounds so that blood streamed out in visible abundance. In a Mexica drawing preserved in the Vatican library, I have seen a figure that represents Quetzalcoatl appeasing the gods' wrath through his penance when, thirteen thousand sixty years after the creation of the world (I am following the extremely vague chronology reported by Father Ríos), there was a great famine in the province of Culan. The saint had retired near Tlaxapuchicalco, on the volcano of Catcitepetl (*the talking mountain*), where he walked barefoot on agave leaves armed with spines. One has the impression of gazing at one of the Rishi [seers or divine scribes], the hermits of the Ganges, whose pious austerity is celebrated in the Puranas.

Quetzalcoatl's reign was the golden age of the peoples of Anahuac. At that time, all animals, even humans, lived in peace; the earth yielded the richest harvests without any need for farming; and the sky was filled with a multitude of birds admired for their song and for the beauty of their plumage. But this reign, like that of Saturn, did not last long, nor did the happiness of the world: the Great Spirit Tezcatlipoca, the Brahma of the peoples of Anahuac, offered Quetzalcoatl a drink that, while rendering him immortal, made him crave travel, giving him in particular an irresistible desire to visit a faraway land that legend calls Tlalpallan. The similarity between this name and that of Huehuetlapallan, the Toltec's homeland, does not appear to be accidental; but how is it plausible that this white man, the priest of Tula, headed, as we will see shortly, for the *southeast*, toward the plains of Cholula, and from there to the eastern coasts of Mexico, only to arrive at this *northerly* land that his ancestors had left in the year 596 of our era?

As Quetzalcoatl crossed the territory of Cholula, he gave in to the pleas of the inhabitants, who offered him the reins of government. He stayed with them for twenty years, taught them how to smelt metal, ordained the great forty-day fasts, and devised the intercalations of the Toltec year. He exhorted men to live in peace and forbade all offerings to the deity other than the first harvests. From Cholula, Quetzalcoatl journeyed to the mouth of the Goatzacoalcos River, where he disappeared after sending word to the Cholulans (*Chololtecatles*) that he would return after a period of time to govern them again and renew their happiness.

It was for the descendants of this saint that the unfortunate Montezuma mistook Cortés's companions. 'We know from our books,' he said in his first interview with the Spanish general, 'that all those who inhabit this country, including myself, are not natives but, rather, foreigners who have come from far away. We also know that the leader who had brought our ancestors returned to his native land for a period of time, and that he came back in search of those who had settled here. He found them married to the women of this land, with numerous offspring, and living in the cities they had built. Our people did not wish to obey their former master, and he went back alone. We have always believed that his descendants would one day come to take possession of this land. Considering that you come from the place where the sun is born, and that, as you claim, you have known us for a long time, I cannot doubt that the king who sends you is our natural master.'

Among the Indians of Cholula a different, quite remarkable legend persists to this day, according to which the great pyramid had not originally been designed for use in the worship of Quetzalcoatl. After my return to Europe I examined the Mexica manuscripts in the Vatican library in Rome and found a record of this very legend in a manuscript by Pedro de los Ríos, a Dominican monk who, in 1566, had copied on site all of the hieroglyphic paintings he could procure. 'Before the great flood (*apachihuiliztli*) that happened four thousand eight years after the creation of the world, the land of Anahuac was inhabited by giants (*Tzocuillixeque*). All those who did not perish were turned into fish, with the exception of seven, who took refuge in caves. When the waters subsided, one of these giants, Xelhua, known as the architect, went to Cholollan where, in memory of Tlaloc Mountain, which had served as a shelter for him and six of his brothers, he built an artificial hill in the shape of a pyramid. He had bricks made in the province of Tlalmanalco at the foot of the Sierra de Cocotl, and in order to transport them to Cholula, he placed a line of men who passed them along by hand. The gods were incensed by the sight of this structure, whose top was meant to reach the clouds; enraged by Xelhua's audacity, they cast fire on the pyramid. Many workers perished, the work was discontinued, and it was afterward consecrated to the god of air, Quetzalcoatl.'

This story recalls the ancient legends of the East, which the Hebrews recorded in their holy books. In Cortés's time, the

Cholulans preserved a stone, shrouded in a globe of fire, that had fallen from the heavens onto the top of the pyramid; this aerolite had the shape of a toad. To prove the ancient origin of the Xelhua fable, Father Ríos noted that it was contained within a canticle that the Cholulans sang at their feasts as they danced around the *teocalli*, and that this canticle began with the words *Tulanian hululaez*, which are not of any current Mexica language. In all corners of the globe, on the ridge of the Cordilleras as on the island of Samothrace in the Aegean Sea, fragments of original languages have been preserved in religious rites.

The platform of the Cholula pyramid, from which I have conducted a great number of astronomical observations, has a surface area of four thousand two hundred square meters. From there one has a magnificent view of Popocatepetl, Iztaccihuatl, Pico de Orizaba, and the Sierra de Tlaxcala, famous for the storms that brew around its summit. It is possible to see in one glance three mountains that are all higher than Mont Blanc, two of them active volcanoes. A small chapel surrounded by cypresses and dedicated to Our Lady de los Remedios has replaced the temple of the god of air, the Mexica Indra; a cleric of the Indian race celebrates mass daily on the top of this ancient monument.

In Cortés's time, Cholula was regarded as a holy city: nowhere could one find a larger number of *teocalli*, more priests and religious orders (*tlamacazque*), more magnificence in worship, and more austerity in fasting and penance. Since the introduction of Christianity among the Indians, the symbols of a new religion have not entirely supplanted the memory of the former; crowds of people come from afar to the top of the pyramid to celebrate the feast of the Virgin. A secret fear and a religious respect seize the natives at the sight of this immense pile of bricks covered in shrubs and perennially green grass.

I have pointed out above the great similarity in construction that can be observed between the Mexica *teocalli* and the temple of Bel (or Belus) in Babylon. This similarity had already struck Mr. Zoëga, although he was only able to obtain very incomplete descriptions of the pyramid group of Teotihuacan. According to Herodotus, who visited Babylon and saw the temple of Belus, this pyramidal monument had eight terraces; it was one stadium high, and the width of the base was equal to its height. The wall that formed the exterior enclosure, the περιβολος [*peribolos*, enclosing wall], was two square stadia (a common Olympic stadium equaled one hundred eighty-three meters: the Egyptian stadium equaled only ninety-eight). The pyramid was built of bricks and asphalt; it had a temple (ναός [*naos*]) at its top and another near its base. According to Herodotus, the former was without statues; there was only a golden table and a bed on which lay a woman chosen by the god Belus. Diodorus Siculus, on the other hand, insisted that this upper temple contained an altar and three statues, to which he gave the names Jupiter, Juno, and Rhea, following concepts taken from Greek religion. But neither these statues nor the monument in its entirety were still in existence at the time of Diodorus and Strabo. In the Mexica *teocalli*, as in the temple of Bel, the lower *naos* was distinguished from the one located on the platform of the pyramid. This very distinction is clearly noted in Cortés's Letters and in the History of the conquest, written by Bernal Díaz, who resided for several months in the palace of King Axayacatl, and thus opposite the *teocalli* of Huitzilopochtli.

None of the ancient authors – neither Herodotus nor Strabo, nor Diodorus, nor Pausanias, nor Arrian, nor Quintus Curtius – mentions that the temple of Belus was oriented in accordance with the four cardinal points, as the Egyptian and Mexica pyramids are. Pliny merely observes that Belus was regarded as the inventor of astronomy: *Inventor hic fait sideralis scientiae* [He was the inventor of the science of the stars]. Diodorus reports that the Babylonian temple served as an observatory for the Chaldeans: 'It is acknowledged,' he says, 'that this construction was extraordinarily tall, and that the Chaldeans used it to conduct observations of the stars, whose rising and setting could be discerned with great exactitude because of the elevation of the building.' The Mexica priests (*teopixqui*) also observed the position of the stars from the top of the *teocalli* and announced the hours of the night to the people by the sound of the horn. These *teocalli* were built in the interval between Muhammad's time and the reign of Ferdinand and Isabella, and it is surprising to learn that American structures, whose form is nearly identical to that of one of the most ancient monuments on the banks of the Euphrates, belong to a relatively recent period.

If one compares the pyramidal monuments of Egypt, Asia, and the new continent, one sees that despite their similarity in form, their purpose was very different. The pyramid groups at Giza and Sakkarah in Egypt; the triangular pyramid of Zarina, queen of the Scythians, which was one stadium high and three stadia wide and adorned with a colossal figure; the fourteen Etruscan pyramids that were said to be contained within King Porsena's labyrinth at Clusium – all of these had been built to serve as sepulchers for illustrious personages. Nothing is more natural to humans than to mark the final resting place of those whose memory they cherish. These were initially simple piles of earth, and afterward *tumuli* of surprising height. Those of the Chinese and the Tibetans are only a few meters high, but the dimensions increase as one moves west: in Lydia, the *tumulus* of Alyattes, the father of Croesus, was six stadia in diameter, while that of Ninus was more than ten stadia. In the north of Europe the sepulchers of the Scandinavian King Gormus and Queen Daneboda are covered in piles of earth three hundred meters wide and thirty meters high. These *tumuli* are found in both hemispheres, in Virginia, in Canada, as well as in Peru, where numerous stone galleries with interlinking shafts fill the insides of the *huacas*, or artificial hills. The Asian sense for extravagance is reflected in the ornamentation, which nevertheless maintains the original form of these rustic monuments; the tombs of Pergamum are earthen cones raised upon an enclosing wall that appears to have formerly been covered in marble.

The *teocalli* or Mexica pyramids were both temples and tombs. We have noted above that the name of the plain where the dwelling places of the sun and the moon of Tenochtitlan rise is the *Pathway of the dead*; but the essential, main section of the *teocalli* was the chapel, the *naos*, at the top of the structure. At the dawn of civilization, peoples chose high places for making sacrifices to the gods. The first altars and temples were erected on mountains. If the mountains were isolated, they preferred to give them regular shapes by cutting terraces into them and making steps in order to climb to the summit more easily. Both continents offer numerous examples of hills that have been terraced and dressed in brick or stone walls. The *teocalli* appear to me nothing more than artificial hills raised in the middle of a plain and designed to serve as a base for altars. Indeed, there is nothing more impressive than a sacrifice that can be seen by an entire people at the same time! The pagodas of Hindustan have nothing in common with the Mexica temples; that of Tanjore [Thanjavur], of which Mr. Daniell made such superb sketches, is a tower with several terraces; but the altar is not found at the top of the monument.

The pyramid of Bel was at once the temple and the tomb of this god. Strabo does not even refer to this monument as a temple; he calls it simply *tomb of Belus*. In Arcadia, the top of the tumulus (χῶμα [*chōma*, funeral mound]) containing the ashes of Callisto bore a temple to Diana; Pausanias described it as a man-made cone covered with ancient vegetation. Here is an example of a remarkable monument in which the temple is more than just an accidental ornament; it serves as a transition, so to speak, between the pyramids of Sakkarah and the Mexica *teocalli*.

PLATE X

Cotopaxi Volcano

IN MY DESCRIPTIONS above of the Iconozo valley, I noted that the huge elevation of the plateaus surrounding the high peaks of the Cordilleras detracts somewhat from the impression that these great rock masses make upon the soul of a traveler accustomed to the majestic scenes of the Alps and the Pyrenees. In all climes what gives a mountainous landscape its particular character is not so much the absolute height of the mountains as their appearance, their shape, and their grouping.

It is the physiognomy of these mountains that I have attempted to depict in a series of drawings, a few of which have already appeared in the *Geographical and Physical Atlas* that accompanies my [*Political*] *Essay on the Kingdom of New Spain*. It seemed to be of great interest to geologists to be able to compare the shapes of mountains in the most remote parts of the globe, just as one compares vegetation from different climates. To date, very few materials have been gathered for this important work. Without the help of geodesic instruments for measuring very small angles, it is practically impossible to determine contours with any great precision. At the same time as I was conducting these measurements in the southern hemisphere on the ridge of the Cordillera of the Andes, Mr. Osterwald (with the assistance of Mr. Tralles, a distinguished geometrician) was following a similar method in drawing the Swiss Alps as seen from the banks of Lake Neufchâtel. This view, which has just been published, is so exact that if the distance to each mountaintop were known, one would be able to find a mountain's relative height merely by factoring into one's calculation the simple measurement of the contours in the drawing. Mr. Tralles used a repeating circle. The angles by which I determined the dimensions of the different parts of a mountain were taken with one of Ramsden's sextants, the limb of which reliably indicated six to eight seconds. If this work were repeated century after century, we would eventually come to understand the random changes that the surface of the globe undergoes. In a country susceptible to earthquakes and thrown into upheaval by volcanoes, it is extremely difficult to resolve the question of whether ejections of ashes and scoria lead to imperceptible decreases or increases in the size of the mountains. This question will be resolved more effectively by taking simple height angles in select stations than by conducting complete trigonometric measurements, the results of which are affected by the errors that one might make in measuring not only the base but also the oblique angles.

A comparison of the mountains of both continents reveals a similarity in shape that would be unimaginable if one reflected upon the combination of forces that, in the primal world, had a tumultuous effect on the soft surface of our planet. The volcanoes' fire spews cones of ash and pumice stone out through its craters; bubbles that resemble extraordinarily tall domes appear to have been produced by the expansive force of elastic fumes alone; earthquakes either raised or straightened seashell-filled layers; ocean currents furrowed the bottoms of basins that today form circular valleys or plateaus surrounded by mountains. Each region of the globe has its specific physiognomy; but even when one is surrounded by characteristic features that give the natural realm such a rich and varied appearance, one is struck by a resemblance in shape that is based on both similar causes and local circumstances. As one navigates among the Canary Islands and observes the basalt cones of Lanzarote, Alegranza, and Graciosa, one has the impression of seeing the Euganean Hills [in Italy] or the trappean hills in Bohemia. The granite, micaceous schist, ancient sandstone, and limestone formations to which mineralogists have given the formation names *Jura*, *High Alps*, or *transition limestone* lend a peculiar character to the contour of these tall masses and to the rifts in the ridge of the Andes, the Pyrenees, and the Urals. The nature of the rocks has shaped the outward appearance of mountains everywhere.

Cotopaxi, whose top is shown on the tenth Plate, is the

PLATE X

highest of the volcanoes in the Andes to have erupted in recent memory. Its absolute elevation is five thousand seven hundred fifty-four meters (two thousand nine hundred fifty-two toises), or double the height of Mount Canigou [in the Pyrenees]. It is therefore eight hundred meters higher than Vesuvius would be if it were stacked on top of the Peak of Tenerife [Teide]. Cotopaxi is also the most feared of all the volcanoes in the kingdom of Quito, the one with the most frequent and most devastating explosions. Considering the amount of scoria and rock pieces ejected from this volcano and strewn across the surrounding valleys over an area of several square leagues, one imagines that their combined mass would form a colossal mountain. In 1738 the flames of Cotopaxi rose to a height of nine hundred meters above the edge of the crater. In 1744 the roaring of the volcano could be heard as far away as Honda, a city located two hundred common leagues away on the banks of the Magdalena River. On April 4, 1768, the quantity of ash spewed from the mouth of Cotopaxi was so great that in the cities of Ambato and Latacunga it was still nighttime at three o'clock in the afternoon, forcing the inhabitants to carry lanterns with them in the streets. The explosion that took place in January of 1803 was preceded by a terrifying phenomenon: the sudden melting of the snows that cap the mountain. For more than twenty years, no smoke, no visible vapor, had been emitted from the crater, but in a single night, the subterranean fire became so intense that by sunrise the outer walls of the cone had been raised to such a high temperature that they appeared bare and of the blackish color that is peculiar to vitrified scoria. In the port of Guayaquil, fifty-two leagues, as the crow flies, from the edge of the crater, we heard the volcano roaring night and day, like the repeated discharge of a battery; we could make out the dreadful noise even in the South Sea to the southwest of Puná Island.

Cotopaxi is located twelve leagues to the south-southeast of the city of Quito, between Rumiñahui Mountain, whose crest, spiked with small, isolated boulders, stretches forth like an enormously high wall, and the Quilindaña volcano [in Ecuador], which soars to the region of eternal snows. In this part of the Andes, a valley running lengthwise divides the Cordilleras into two parallel ranges. Since the bottom of this valley is still three thousand meters above ocean level, when viewed from the Licán and Mulaló plateaus, Chimborazo and Cotopaxi appear only as high as Col du Géant [in the Mont Blanc Massif] and Cramont [in the Swiss Alps], as measured by Saussure. As there is reason to suppose that the proximity of the Ocean helps to stoke volcanic fire, the geologist is surprised to note that the most active volcanoes in the kingdom of Quito – Cotopaxi, Tungurahua, and Sangay – belong to the eastern range of the Andes, thus to the range farther from the coast. With the exception of Rucu-Pichincha, the peaks that crown the western Cordilleras all appear to be volcanoes that have been extinguished for several centuries. The mountain depicted in our drawing, which is 2°2′ away from the nearest coasts – those of La Esmeralda and San Mateo Bay – neverthe-less shoots out sprays of fire periodically, desolating the surrounding plains.

The shape of Cotopaxi is the most beautiful and the most regular of all the colossal peaks in the upper Andes. It is a perfect cone that, cloaked in an enormous layer of snow, shines dazzlingly at sunset and stands out delightfully against the azure sky. This snow cover hides the smallest irregularities in the ground from the observer: neither boulder tips nor rocky masses pierce through these eternal ice fields to disturb the regularity of the conical shape. The summit of Cotopaxi resembles the sugarloaf (*pan de azúcar*) at the top of the Teide, but its cone is six times higher than that of the great volcano of the island of Tenerife.

It is only near the edge of the crater that one notices the rock banks that are never covered in snow and that from a distance seem like deep black lines. What causes this phenom-enon is probably the steep slope of this part of the cone and the crevices through which currents of hot air escape. This crater, similar to that of the Peak of Tenerife, is surrounded by a short enclosing wall that, when examined with good bin-oculars, looks like a parapet; one can make it out particularly well from the southern slope, when one is positioned either on the *Mountain of Lions* (Puma Urcu) or on the banks of the tiny lake of Yuracoche. To acquaint my readers with the volcano's peculiar structure, I have added to the bottom of the Plate the view of the crater's southern edge, exactly as I sketched it near the perpetual snow line (at an absolute elevation of four thousand four hundred eleven meters) at Suniguaicu, on the porphyric mountain ridge that joins Cotopaxi to the Nevado de Quilindaña.

The conical part of the Peak of Tenerife is very accessible; it rises in the midst of a pumice-covered plain, where a few clusters of Spartium supranubium grow. When scaling the volcano of Cotopaxi, however, it is extremely difficult to reach the lower edge of the perpetual snow line. We experienced this difficulty ourselves during an excursion we undertook in May of 1802. The cone is surrounded by deep crevices that during eruptions carry scoria, pumice, water, and blocks of ice toward the Río Napo and the Río de los Alaques. When one has examined the summit of Cotopaxi firsthand, one can say with some degree of certainty that it would be impossible to reach the edge of the crater.

Given the regularity of the cone's shape, it is all the more striking to find a small rock mass on the southwest side, half-hidden under the snow and spiked with points, which the natives call the *Head of the Inca*. The origin of this bizarre moniker is uncertain. According to a folk belief that exists in the country, this isolated boulder was once part of Cotopaxi's summit. The Indians claim that when the volcano first erupted, it hurled forth a rocky mass that had covered the enormous cavity containing the underground fire like the calotte of a dome. Some insist that this extraordinary catastrophe took place a short time after the Inca Tupac Yupanqui had invaded the kingdom of Quito and that the rock piece that one can make out on the tenth Plate to the left of the volcano is called the Head of the Inca because its fall was the sinister omen of the conqueror's death. Others, even more gullible, insist that this mass of *pechstein*-based porphyry was dislodged in an explosion that happened at the very moment that the Inca Atahualpa was strangled by the Spanish at Cajamarca. It seems, in fact, quite certain that there was an eruption at Cotopaxi when Pedro Alvarado's army corps left Puerto Viejo for the Quito plateau, although Piedro de Cieza [de León] and Garcilaso de la Vega refer only vaguely to a mountain that spewed out ashes, whose sudden fall startled the Spanish. But to believe that the boulder called *Cabeza del Inca* took its current position at that time, one must assume that Cotopaxi had not undergone any prior eruptions. This assumption is all the more flawed in that the walls of the Inca's palace at Callo, built by Huayna Capac, contain rocks of volcanic origin hurled from the mouth of Cotopaxi. We shall discuss elsewhere the important question of whether this volcano had likely already reached its current height at the moment when the underground fire broke through its top, or whether several geological facts do not jointly prove that its cone, like the Vesuvius's *Somma*, is composed of a large number of lava layers stacked on top of one another.

I sketched Cotopaxi and the *Head of the Inca*, to the west of the volcano, from the tenanted farm of *La Ciénaga*, on the terrace of a lovely country house belonging to our friend the young marquis of Maenza, who has just inherited his grandeeship and the title of Puñonrostro. In these views of the Andes summits, to distinguish the mountains that are still active volcanoes from those that no longer erupt, I took the liberty of including a thin plume of smoke above the crater of Cotopaxi, although I did not see any smoke emitted when I made this sketch. Built by a close acquaintance of Mr. La Condamine, the house at La Ciénaga is located in the vast plain that stretches between the two branches of the Cordilleras, from the hills of Chisinche and Tiopullo all the way to Ambato. There one can observe all at once, and in frightening proximity, the colossal volcano of Cotopaxi, the slender peaks of Iliniza, and the Nevado de Quilindaña. It is one of the most majestic and impressive sites that I have seen in either hemisphere.

PLATE XVII

The Peruvian Monument of Cañar

THE HIGH PLAINS that extend across the ridge of the Cordilleras from the equator to near 3° of southern latitude end at a mass of mountains four thousand eight hundred meters high, which link the eastern and western crests of the Andes of Quito like an enormous embankment. This group of mountains, in which micaceous schist and other rocks of original formation are covered in porphyry, is known as the *Páramo del Azuay.* We were forced to cross it in order to travel from Riobamba to Cuenca and to the beautiful forests of Loja, which are renowned for their abundance in cinchona. The pass of Azuay is especially formidable in the months of June, July, and August, when an immense quantity of snow falls, and when the icy winds from the South blow in these lands. Since the main road, according to the measurements that I took in 1802, nearly reaches the elevation of Mont Blanc, travelers there are exposed to extreme cold, and not a year passes when a few do not perish. Midway through this pass, at an absolute elevation of four thousand meters, one crosses a plain that stretches over more than six square leagues. This plain – and this remarkable fact sheds some light on the formation of high plateaus – is almost at the height of the savannahs surrounding the part of the Antisana volcano that is covered in eternal snows. The plateaus of Azuay and Antisana, the geological compositions of which are so strikingly similar, are nevertheless separated by a distance of over fifty leagues. They contain freshwater lakes of great depth that are lined with dense patches of alpine grass. But there are no fish and hardly any aquatic insects to enliven their solitude.

The soil of the *Llano del Pullal* (the name of the high plains of Azuay) is extremely marshy. We were surprised to find there, at elevations far exceeding the top of the Peak of Tenerife, the

PLATE XVII

magnificent ruins of a trail built by the Inca of Peru. Lined with large cut stones, this roadway can be compared with the most beautiful Roman roads that I have seen in Italy, France, and Spain. It is perfectly straight and maintains the same direction over a distance of six to eight thousand meters. As we saw firsthand, it extends to the vicinity of Cajamarca, one hundred twenty leagues south of Azuay, and people there believe that it once led all the way to the city of Cusco. Near the Azuay road, at an absolute elevation of four thousand forty-two meters (two thousand seventy-four toises), are the ruins of the Inca Tupac Yupanqui's palace, the shell of which, commonly called *los paredones*, is of relatively low height.

Descending from the Páramo of Azuay toward the south, between the farms of Turche and Burgay, one comes upon another masterpiece of ancient Peruvian architecture, which is known as *Ingapirca*, or the fortress of Cañar. This fortress, if one can use this term for a hill topped with a platform, is much less remarkable for its size than for its perfectly preserved condition. A wall built of thick-cut stones, five to six meters high, forms an extremely regular oval, with a major axis that is thirty-eight meters long. Inside this oval is a talus covered with gorgeous vegetation that adds to the charming impression of the landscape. At the center of the enclosure rises a house that has only two chambers and is nearly seven meters high. Both this house and the enclosure, shown on the seventeenth Plate, belong to a system of walls and fortifications over one hundred fifty meters long; we shall speak of them below. The cut of the stones, the layout of the gates and the recesses, and the perfect similarity between this structure and those of Cusco leave no doubt as to the origin of this *military monument*, which served as lodging for the Inca during those princes' occasional journeys from Peru to the kingdom of Quito. The foundations of a large number of buildings surrounding the enclosure offer evidence that there was once enough space at Cañar to lodge the small army corps that usually accompanied the Inca on their travels. In these foundations I found a very artfully carved stone, which is depicted in the left foreground of the painting; I was unable to ascertain the use of this particular cut.

What is most striking about this small monument, surrounded by a few trunks of *schinus molle* trees, is the shape of its roof, which makes it perfectly resemble European houses. One of the first historians of the Americas, Pedro de Cieza de León, who began writing about his travels in 1541, speaks in detail of several of the Inca's houses in the province of *Los Cañares*. He states plainly that 'the structures of Tomabamba have a covering of rushes, which is so well-made that, unless destroyed by fire, it can be preserved for centuries with no deterioration whatsoever.' This observation necessarily leads one to suspect that the gable on the house at Cañar was added after the conquest. What appears most to confirm this theory is the existence of window openings in this part of the building, for it is certain that in the structures built by the ancient Peruvians, windows are found as frequently as in the ruins of houses in Pompeii and Herculaneum – that is, never.

In a very interesting paper on a number of ancient monuments of Peru, Mr. La Condamine also tends toward the opinion that the gable on the small monument of Cañar is not from the time of the Inca. He says that 'it is perhaps of modern construction, and that it is not built of cut stones like the rest of the walls but, rather, of a kind of air-dried brick permeated by straw.' Elsewhere, this same scholar adds that the use of these bricks, which the Indians call *tica*, was known to the Peruvians long before the arrival of the Spanish, and that for this reason the top of the gable, although it is made of bricks, might well be of ancient construction.

I deeply regret not having been acquainted with Mr. La Condamine's paper before my journey to the Americas. By no means do I intend to cast doubt upon the observations of that famous traveler, whose work necessitated a lengthy stay in the area around Cañar and who had much more time than I did to examine this monument. I am, however, surprised that while debating on site the question of whether this structure's roof was added at the time of the Spanish, Mr. Bonpland and I were not struck by the difference in construction that allegedly exists between the wall and the top of the gable. I did not see any bricks (*ticas* or *adobes*); I noticed only some cut stones coated with a kind of yellowish stucco that was easily removable and embedded with *ichu*, cut straw. The proprietor of a nearby farm who accompanied us on our excursion to the Cañar ruins boasted that his ancestors had contributed greatly to the destruction of these buildings. He told us that the sloped roof had been covered not with tiles, in the European fashion, but with very thin, well-polished slabs of stone. It was this circumstance in particular that made me, at that time, lean toward the probably baseless theory that with the exception of the four windows, the rest of the structure was the same as it had been at the moment of its construction by the Inca. Be that as it may, one must agree that acute-angle roofs would have been quite useful in a mountainous country with plentiful rain. These sloped roofs are known to the natives in the northwest coast of the Americas; in the earliest times, they were even known in southern Europe, as several Greek and Roman monuments suggest, especially the reliefs of the Trajan column and the landscape paintings found in Pompeii and formerly preserved in the magnificent collection of Portici. Among the Greeks, the rooftop angle was oblique; it became a right angle among the Romans, who lived under less beautiful skies than those of Greece. The roofs become more sloped the farther one moves to the north.

The drawing whose engraving is shown on the seventeenth Plate is based on my own sketch; it was made in Rome by Mr. Gmelin, an artist who is rightly celebrated both for his talent and for the breadth of his knowledge. During my most recent stay in Italy, he honored me by extending his friendship, and I am largely indebted to his care for anything in my work that might not be utterly unworthy of the public's attention.

PLATE XVIII

Boulder of Inti-Guaicu

IN DESCENDING THE hill whose summit is crowned by the Cañar fortress, one encounters, in a valley hollowed out by the Gulán River, a number of small tracks carved into the rock. These tracks lead to a crevice that, in the Quechua language, is called *Inti-Guaicu*, the *ravine of the sun*. In this lonely place fringed with lovely, vigorous plant life rises an isolated sandstone mass no more than four to five meters high. One of the faces of this small boulder is remarkably white. It drops off sharply, as though it had been cut by human hands. On this smooth, white background one can make out a number of concentric circles that represent the image of the sun as it was depicted by all the peoples of the earth at the dawn of civilization. The circles are of a blackish-brown color; in their interiors one can identify some half-faded lines that suggest two eyes and a mouth. The base of the boulder is carved into steps that lead to a seat cut into the same stone and positioned in such a way that one can contemplate the image of the sun from the bottom of a hollow.

The natives say that when the Inca Tupac Yupanqui advanced with his army to seize the kingdom of Quito, then ruled by the Conchocando of Licán, the priests discovered on the stone the image of the deity whose worship was soon to be introduced among the conquered peoples. The inhabitants of Cusco were convinced that they saw the image of the sun everywhere, just as Christians everywhere saw either crosses or the footprint of the apostle St. Thomas painted on rocks. The prince and the Peruvian soldiers regarded the discovery of the stone of Inti-Guaicu as an excellent omen: it very likely prompted the Inca to build a residence at Cañar, for it is known that the descendants of Manco-Capac saw themselves as the children of the sun, a belief that makes for a remarkable point of comparison between the first legislator of Peru and that of India, who was also called *Vaivasvata*, son of the sun.

A close examination of the Inti-Guaicu boulder reveals that the concentric circles are thin filaments of brown iron ore, very common in all sandstone formations. The lines indicating the eyes and the mouth are obviously cut with a metal tool; one must assume that they were added by the Peruvian priests to deceive the people more easily. Upon the arrival of the Spanish, the missionaries found it in their interest to hide from the eyes of the natives everything that the latter had venerated for centuries; one can indeed still make out the traces of the chisel used to deface the image of the sun.

According to Mr. Vater's interesting research, the word *inti*, sun, bears no resemblance to any other language known to the old continent. All in all, of the eighty-three American languages examined by this estimable scholar and by Mr. Barton of Philadelphia, only one hundred thirty-seven roots have thus far been identified that are also found in the languages of Asia and Europe – that is, in those of the Manchu Tartars, the Mongols, the Celts, the Basques, and the Estonians. This curious finding appears to confirm what we suggested above in our discussion of Mexica mythology. It is undeniable that the majority of the natives of the Americas belong to a race of men separated from the rest of humanity since the beginning of the world, and who exhibit, in the nature and the diversity of their languages, as in their features and the shape of their skulls, incontrovertible proof of their long and complete isolation.

PLATE XVIII

PLATE XIX

Inga-Chungana near Cañar

TO THE NORTH of the Cañar ruins rises a hillside that slopes
gently down toward the Inca's house, although it drops steeply
on the Gulán valley side. According to native legend, this hill
was part of the gardens that surrounded the ancient Peruvian
fortress. As near the *ravine of the sun*, we identified here a large
number of small tracks hollowed out by human hands on the
slope of a rock that is only lightly covered with topsoil.

In the gardens of Chapultepec near Mexico City, the European traveler contemplates with interest cypresses whose
trunks have a circumference of more than sixteen meters and
which, it is believed, were likely planted by the kings of the
Aztec dynasty. In the Inca's gardens near Cañar, we searched
in vain for a tree at least a half-century old; nothing in those
lands suggests that the Inca once resided there, with the possible exception of a small stone monument positioned on the
edge of a precipice, the purpose of which is a subject of dis-
agreement among the inhabitants of the country.

This small monument, which they call the *Inca's game*, consists of a small mass of stones. The Peruvians used the same
trick to build it that the Egyptians used to sculpt the Sphinx
at Giza, of which Pliny plainly states: '*e saxo naturali elaborate* [it
is made of natural stone].' The boulder of quartziferous sandstone that serves as its base was eroded, so that after the layers
that formed its summit were removed, all that remained was
a seat surrounded by a wall, which is depicted on this Plate. It
is surprising that a people who had stacked such a prodigious
number of cut stones on the beautiful Azuay roadway resorted
to such a bizarre method to erect a wall only one meter high.
Every Peruvian work exhibits the character of a hardworking
people who liked digging into the rock, who sought out chal-
lenges in order to show off their skill by overcoming them, and

PLATE XIX

who gave all their buildings, even the most humble ones, a character of permanence, which might lead one to believe that at a different time they might have erected more significant monuments.

Seen from afar, *Inga-Chungana* resembles a settee with a back adorned by a chain-shaped arabesque. Entering into the oval-shaped enclosure, one sees that there is room on the seat for only one person, but that this person is very comfortably positioned and enjoys the most delightful view of the Gulán valley. A small river winds through this valley, forming several waterfalls whose froth is visible through clusters of gunnera and melastoma. This rustic seat would not be out of place in the gardens of Ermenonville or Richmond, and the prince who chose this site was not insensitive to the beauties of nature; he belonged to a people whom we do not have the right to call barbarians.

In this construction I saw only a backed chair located in a pleasant spot on the edge of a precipice, on the steep slope of a hillside overlooking a valley. Some of the older Indians, who are the local antiquarians, find this explanation too simple; they maintain that the incised chain on the edge of the wall was used to hold small balls that were raced for the prince's amusement. One cannot deny that the edge with the arabesque is somewhat sloped, and that the ball, if cast forcibly, could have rolled up from the point where the wall is visibly lower, just as easily as it had rolled down there. But if this theory were accurate, would one not find some hole that would have held the balls at the end of their race? The lowest part of the surrounding wall, the point opposite the seat, corresponds to an opening in the rock at the edge of the precipice. A narrow track cut into the sandstone leads to this grotto in which, according to native legend, there are treasures hidden by Ata-hualpa. People maintain that a trickle of water once flowed down this track. Is it there that one should search for the *Inca's game*, and was the wall positioned such that the prince could see comfortably whatever was happening on the steep slope of the boulder? We shall reserve our discussion of this grotto for the narrative of our journey to Peru.

PLATE XX

Interior of the Inca's House at Cañar

THIS PLATE SHOWS the plan and the interior of the small building that occupies the center of the esplanade in the Cañar citadel and that Mr. La Condamine believed to have been built as a guardroom. I took all the more care to render this drawing as precisely as possible, since the relics of Peruvian architecture, scattered across the ridge of the Cordilleras from Cusco to Cayambe or from 13° southern latitude to the equator, all display the same character in the cut of the stones, the shape of the doors, the symmetrical distribution of the recesses, and the total absence of external decoration. This uniformity of construction is so complete that all of the inns (*tambos*) located along the major roads, which the locals call the houses or palaces of the Inca, seem to be perfectly identical. Peruvian architecture did not rise above the needs of a mountain people; it had neither pilasters nor columns nor round arches. Born in a land spiked with boulders, on virtually treeless plateaus, it did not imitate the structure of a wooden framework, as did the architecture of the Greeks and the Romans. Simplicity, symmetry, and solidity are the three favorable characteristics that all Peruvian buildings shared.

The Cañar citadel and the square buildings that surround it are not made of the same quartziferous sandstone that covers the clayey schist and the porphyry of Azuay, and that is visible on the surface of the Inca's garden as one descends toward the Gulán valley. Nor are the stones used in the structures at Cañar granite, as Mr. La Condamine believed, but, rather, an extremely hard trappean porphyry within which are embedded both vitreous feldspar and amphibole. Perhaps this porphyry was extracted from the large quarries found at an elevation of four thousand meters near the lake of Culebrilla, more than three leagues from Cañar. It is at least certain that those quarries furnished the gorgeous stone used in the Inca's house in the plain of Pullal at an elevation nearly equal to what Puy-de-Dôme would reach were it placed on top of Canigou.

One does not find the enormous stones of the Peruvian structures in Cusco and the adjacent lands in the ruins of Cañar. Acosta measured some at Traquanaco that were twelve meters (thirty-eight feet) long, 5.8 meters (eighteen feet) wide, and 1.9 meters (six feet) thick. Pedro Cieza de León saw the same dimensions in the ruins of Tiahuanaco [Tiwanaku]. I did not notice any stones in the Cañar citadel that were over twenty-six decimeters (eight feet) long. They are, in general, much less remarkable for their massive size than for their exquisite cut: the majority of them are joined together with absolutely no appearance of cement, although the latter is visible in some of the buildings that surround the citadel, as well as in the Inca's three houses in Pullal, each one of which is more than fifty-eight meters long. The citadel is made from a mixture of small stones and clayey marl that effervesces upon contact with acid; it is true mortar, and I was able to remove considerable amounts of it using a knife to dig in the cracks between the parallel courses of stones. This fact is worthy of some attention, since all the travelers who had preceded me insisted that the Peruvians were not at all accustomed to using cement; but it was just as wrong to impute an ignorance of cement to them as it was to the ancient Egyptians. The Peruvians did not only use marly mortar: in the great structures of Pacaritambo, they used asphalt (*betún*) cement, a mode of construction that, on the banks of the Euphrates and the Tigris, dates back to the earliest times.

The porphyry used in the structures at Cañar is cut into parallelepipeds, with such precision that the joints of the stones would be imperceptible, as Mr. La Condamine justly notes, if their external surface were flat; but the outward-facing side of each stone is slightly convex and beveled on the edges, so that the joints form small flutes that serve as decorations, like the gaps between stones in rustic works. This cut of stone, which Italian architects call *bugnato*, is also found in the ruins of Callo, near Mulaló [Vallecaucano], where I drew it in detail. It lends

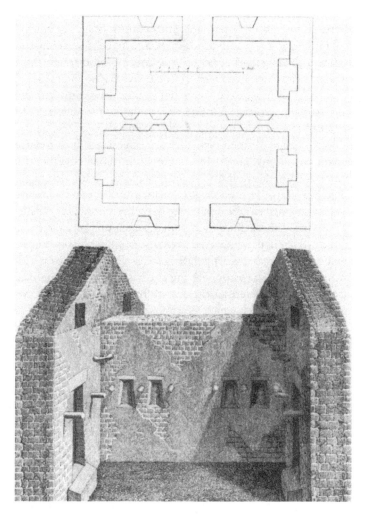

PLATE XX

the walls of Peruvian structures a strong resemblance to certain Roman constructions, for example, the *muro di Nerva* in Rome.

What is especially characteristic of the monuments of Peruvian architecture is the shape of the doors, which were typically nineteen to twenty decimeters (six to eight feet) high, so that the Inca and other high lords could pass through them even when carried in a litter, on the shoulders of their vassals. The jambs of these doors were not parallel but slanted, probably so that stone lintels of a lesser width could be used. The recesses (*hoco*) built into the walls, which served as cabinets, echo the shape of these *porte rastremate*: the slant of their jambs makes the Peruvian structures resemble those of Egypt, in which the lintels are always shorter than the lower door openings. Between the *hocos* are smooth-surfaced, five-decimeter-long cylindrical stones that jut forth from the wall; the natives claimed that these were used to hang weapons or clothes. In addition, strangely shaped struts made of porphyry are visible in the corners of the walls. Mr. La Condamine believes that these were meant to connect the two walls; but I am inclined to think that the ropes of the *hamacs* [hammocks] were looped around these struts, which serve this very purpose at least in all the Indians' huts in the Orinoco, where they are made of wood.

The Peruvians display an incredible ability for cutting the hardest stones. At Cañar there are curved tracks carved into the porphyry to replace the door hinges. In ancient structures built in the time of the Inca, La Condamine and Bouguer saw porphyry decorations that represent animal muzzles, with pierced nostrils bearing mobile rings of the same stone. When, traversing the Cordillera by the Páramo of Azuay, I saw the enormous piles of cut stones extracted from the porphyry quarries of Pullal for the Inca's great roads, I was already skeptical of the claim that the Peruvians had no other tools besides stone axes; I suspected that friction was not the only method they had employed to level stones or give them a regular, uniform convexity. I consequently embraced a theory that was at odds with received wisdom: I hypothesized that the Peruvians had possessed copper tools that obtained great hardness when mixed with tin in a certain proportion. This hypothesis was substantiated by the discovery of an ancient Peruvian chisel found in Vilcabamba [Quechua: Willkapampa, sacred plain] near Cusco, in a silver mine worked during the time of the Inca. This precious instrument, which I owe to the kindness of Father Narciso Girbal and which I was fortunate to bring back with me to Europe, is twelve centimeters long and two centimeters wide. Its material composition was analyzed by Mr. Vauquelin, who detected 0.94 copper and 0.06 tin. The Peruvians' *sharp copper* is almost identical to that of the Gallic axes, which chop wood just as well as steel does. At the dawn of the civilization of peoples, the use of copper mixed with tin (*aes*, χαλκός [*chalkos*, bronze]) prevailed over that of iron everywhere in the old continent, even in areas where iron had long been in use.

PLATE XXV

Chimborazo Viewed from the Tapia Plateau

THE MOUNTAIN HAS been drawn exactly as it is seen from the arid plain of Tapia, near the village of Licán, the former residence of the sovereigns of Quito before the conquest of the Inca Tupac Yupanqui. Licán is five leagues away from the summit of Chimborazo, as the crow flies. Plate XVI shows this colossal mountain with a belt of permanent snow, which near the equator occurs only at a height of four thousand eight hundred meters above sea level. Plate XXV shows Chimborazo as we saw it after one of the heaviest snowfalls in memory, on June 24, 1802, only one day after our excursion to the top. I thought that it might be interesting to give an exact idea of the imposing appearance of the Cordilleras at the time of both *maximum* and *minimum* snow levels.

Only those travelers who have seen the summits of Mont Blanc and Mont Rose are able to grasp the character of this imposing, calm, and majestic scene. Chimborazo is of such enormous size that the visible area near permanent snow line is seven thousand meters wide. The extreme thinness of the air layers through which one sees the tops of the Andes greatly enhances the sparkle of the snow and the magical effect of its reflections. In the tropics, at a height of five thousand meters, the azure vault of the heavens takes on a shade of indigo. The contours of the mountain stand out against the background of this pure, limpid atmosphere, while the lower air layers, which rest upon a grassless plateau and reflect its radiant heat, are misty and seem to veil the distant countryside.

The Tapia plateau, which stretches to the east all the way to the foot of El Altar and Condorasto, is at an elevation of three thousand meters. Its height is more or less equal to that of Canigou, one of the highest peaks of the Pyrenees. In the arid plain grow a few stalks of Schinus molle, Cactus, Agave, and

PLATE XXV

Molina. In the foreground, one sees llamas (*Camelus lacma*), drawn from life, and a few groups of Indians heading to the Licán market. The mountainside presents the very gradation of plant life that I have attempted to outline in my *Tableau de la Géographie des Plantes*, and which one can follow on the western slope of the Andes from the impenetrable palm groves to the permanent snow, lined by a thin layer of lichen.

At an absolute elevation of three thousand five hundred meters, the woody plants with their glossy, tough leaves gradually disappear. The region of shrubs is separated from that of grasses by alpine herbs, tufts of Nertera, Valerians, Saxifrages, and Lobelia, and small crucifer plants. The grasses constitute a very large belt occasionally covered in snow that lasts only for a few days. This zone, which the locals call the *pajonal*, appears from afar like a golden carpet. Its color contrasts delightfully with that of the scattered snow masses; it is the result of the stems and leaves of the grasses being burnt by the rays of the sun during great drought periods. Above the *pajonal* one finds oneself in the region of the cryptogamic plants, which here and there cover the porphyritic rocks, devoid of humus. A little farther on the line of permanent ice marks the end of organic life.

However surprising the height of Chimborazo, its summit is still four hundred fifty meters below the point at which Mr. Gay-Lussac, during his memorable air [balloon] voyage, conducted experiments that were as important for meteorology as they were for understanding the laws of magnetism. The natives of Quito province have preserved a legend according to which one peak from the eastern crest of the Andes, which today is called the Altar (*el Altar*) and which partially collapsed in the fifteenth century, was once taller than Chimborazo. In Bhutan, Soomoonang, the highest mountain for which the English travelers have given us the measurements, is only 4419 meters (2,268 toises) high: but, according to Colonel Crawford, the tallest peak in the Cordilleras of Tibet is over twenty-five thousand English feet, or 7617 meters (3,909 toises) high. If this estimate is based on an exact measurement, then there is a mountain in central Asia that is one thousand ninety meters higher than Chimborazo. The absolute elevation of mountains is an unimportant phenomenon to the true geologist, who, being engaged in the study of rock *formations*, is accustomed to viewing nature on a large scale. He will hardly be surprised if at some point in the future and in some other part of the globe, someone discovers a peak that surpasses Chimborazo by as much as the highest mountain in the Alps soars above the highest point in the Pyrenees.

A distinguished architect, Mr. Thibault, who combines a knowledge of the monuments of antiquity with a deep appreciation of the beauties of nature, was gracious enough to execute the colored drawing [reproduced in black and white in this Everyman edition] whose engraving forms the main decorative illustration in this work. The sketch that I had made on site served no other purpose than to give an exact indication of the contours of Chimborazo. The faithfulness of the work as a whole and its details has been scrupulously maintained. To make it easier for the naked eye to perceive the gradation of the different levels and to grasp the expanse of the plateau, Mr. Thibault has enlivened the scene with figures that are grouped very intelligently. It is always a joy to acknowledge favors granted by the most selfless of friends.

PLATE XXVI

Epochs of Nature According to Aztec Mythology

THE MOST ASTONISHING of all the observable similarities among the monuments, customs, and traditions of the peoples of Asia and the Americas is revealed in Mexica mythology in the cosmogonic myth of the periodic destructions and regenerations of the Universe. This mythic fiction, which links the return of the great cycles to the notion of the renewal of matter presumed to be indestructible and which attributes to space characteristics that seem to belong only to time, dates back to the earliest period of antiquity. The sacred books of the Hindus, especially the *Bhagavata Purana*, already speak of the four ages and the *pralayas* or cataclysms that have led to the destruction of the human species in various epochs. A tradition of *five ages*, similar to that of the Mexica, can also be found on the high plateau of Tibet. If it is true that this astrological fiction, which became the foundation of a particular cosmogonic system, was conceived in Hindustan, then it is also plausible that it spread from there, via Iran and Chaldea, to the peoples in the west. One cannot disregard a certain resemblance between the Indian tradition of the *yuga* and the *kalpa*, the cycles of the ancient inhabitants of Etruria, and the series of annihilated generations that Hesiod characterized through the emblem of the four metals.

'The peoples of Culhua or Mexico,' wrote Gómara, who wrote in the mid-sixteenth century, 'believe, according to their hieroglyphic paintings, that before the sun that now shines upon them, four suns had already existed and had been extinguished, one after the other. These five suns constitute the ages in which humankind was wiped out by floods, earthquakes, an all-consuming blaze, and the effect of fierce storms. After the destruction of the fourth sun, the world was plunged into shadows for a period of twenty-five years. It was in the midst of this deep night, ten years before the fifth sun reappeared, that humanity was regenerated. At that time, the gods created one man and one woman for the fifth time. The day on which the last sun appeared bore the sign *tochtli* (rabbit), and the Mexica counted eight hundred fifty years from that time to 1552. Their annals date back all the way to the fifth sun. They used historical paintings (*escritura pintada*) in the four preceding ages as well; but these paintings were destroyed, they claim, because everything must be renewed with each new age.' According to Torquemada, this fable about the revolution of time and the regeneration of nature is of Toltec origin; it is a national tradition that belongs to the group of peoples whom we know as the Toltec, Chimichec, Acolhua, Nahua, Tlaxcalteca, and Aztecs and who, speaking the same language, had migrated from north to south beginning in the middle of the sixth century of our era.

While examining in Rome the *Cod[ex] Vaticanus*, number 3738, copied in 1566 by the Dominican friar Pedro de los Ríos, I came across the Mexica drawing shown on Plate XXVI. Since it indicates the duration of each epoch using signs whose value is known to us, this historical monument is all the more intriguing. In Father Ríos's commentary, the order in which the catastrophes occurred is completely wrong: he places the final one, the flood, first. This same error is found in the works of Gómara, Clavijero, and the majority of Spanish writers, who, forgetting that the Mexica arranged their hieroglyphs from right to left, starting from the bottom of the page, necessarily reversed the order of the four destructions of the world. I will adhere to the order shown in the Mexica painting from the Vatican library and described in a very curious story written in the Aztec language, a few fragments of which have been preserved for us by the Indian Fernando de Alva Ixtlilxochitl. The testimony of a native author and the copy of a Mexica painting made on site shortly after the conquest are probably more trustworthy than the accounts of the Spanish historians. Besides, this discrepancy, the reasons for which we have just indicated, applies only to the order of the destructions, for Gómara, Pedro de los Ríos, Ixtlilxochitl, Clavijero, and Gama all report the circumstances that accompanied each of them in the most consistent manner possible.

First cycle. Its duration is 13 × 400 + 6 = 5,206 years: this number is indicated on the right in the lower painting through nineteen circles, thirteen of which have a *feather* placed above them. We observed above, in our discussion of the calendar, that the hieroglyph for twenty squared is a feather, and that the Mexica used simple dots to represent the number of years, in the same way that Etruscans and the Romans used nails. This first age, which corresponds to the Hindus' age of justice (*Satya Yuga*), was called *Tlaltonatiuh*, epoch of the earth; it is also the age of the giants (*Qzocuilliexeque* or *Tuinametin*), for the historical legends of all peoples begin with brawls among giants. The Olmec (or Hulmec) and the Xicalanc, two peoples who preceded the Toltecs and who prided themselves on their ancient origins, claimed to have come across giants when they arrived in the Tlaxcala plains. According to the sacred *Puranas*, Bacchus (or the young Rama) won his first victory over Ravana, the king of the giants of the island of Ceylon.

The year presided over by the sign *ce acatl* was a year of lack, and the first generation of humans perished in the famine. This catastrophe began on the day 4 *tiger* [jaguar] (*nahui ocelotl*), and it is probably because of the hieroglyph for this day that other traditions maintain that the giants who did not die of starvation were devoured by the very tigers [jaguars] (*tequanes*) whose appearance the Mexica dreaded at the end of each cycle. The hieroglyphic painting depicts an evil spirit who descends to earth to rip out grass and flowers. Three human figures – among whom one can easily identify a woman by a hairstyle composed of two small plaits that resemble horns – are each holding a sharp instrument in their right hand and fruits or cut sheaves of grain in the left. The spirit who announces the famine is wearing one of those prayer-bead chains that have been used in Tibet, China, Canada, and Mexico since time immemorial and that spread from the east to the Christians in the west. Despite the fact that among all the peoples of the world, the fictional stories of the giants, the Titans, and the Cyclops appear to refer to the conflict of the elements or the state of the globe upon its emergence from chaos, it is undeniable that in both Americas the enormous fossilized skeletons of animals scattered across the surface of the earth have had a great impact on mythological history. At Punta Santa Elena to the north of Guayaquil, there are giant remains of unknown cetaceans: some Peruvian legends thus maintain that a colony of giants who slaughtered one another had once disembarked in this very spot. Both the kingdom of New Granada and the ridge of the Mexican Cordilleras are teeming with fossilized remains of mastodons and elephants belonging to species that have disappeared from the surface of the globe. It is for this very reason that the plain that stretches from Sua-cha toward Santa Fé de Bogotá at an elevation of two thousand seven hundred meters bears the name *Field of Giants*. It is likely that the Hulmecs' claim that their ancestors had fought against the giants on the fertile plateau of Tlaxcala derives from find-ings of mastodon and elephant molars, which people across the country take for the teeth of colossally sized men.

Second cycle. Its duration is 12 × 400 + 4 = 4,804 years; it was the age of fire, *Tletonatiuh*, or the red age, *Tzonchichilteque*. The god of fire, Xiuhteuctli, descends to earth in the year pres-ided over by the sign *ce tecpatl*, on the day *nahui quiahuitl*. Since only birds could escape the all-consuming blaze, legend has it that all humans were transformed into birds, except for one man and one woman who found safety inside a cave.

Third cycle, the age of the wind or the air, *Ehecatonatiuh*. Its duration is 10 × 400 + 10 = 4,010 years. The catastrophe occurred on the day 4 wind (*nahui ehecatl*) of the year *ce tecpatl*. The drawing shows the hieroglyph for the air or the wind, *ehecatl*, repeated four times. Humans perished in the storms, and some of them were transformed into monkeys; these animals did not appear in Mexico until this third epoch. I do not know which deity it is that descends to earth, armed with a sickle – might it be Quetzalcoatl, the god of the air, and might the sickle imply that the storm uproots the trees as though they had been felled? In any case, I doubt that the yellow streaks allude to the shape of the clouds battered by the storm, as one Spanish commentator suggests. Monkeys are generally less numerous in the hot regions of Mexico than in South America. These animals undertake distant migrations whenever they are driven by hunger or inclement weather to abandon their original abode. I know lands in the mountainous parts of Peru where the people recall the time when new monkey colonies settled in one valley or another. Might the tradition of the five epochs bear some relation to the history of animals? Might it refer to a particular year in which great storms and upheavals caused by the volcanoes incited the monkeys to make forays into the mountains of Anahuac? In this *cycle of tempests*, only two humans survived the catastrophe by taking refuge inside a cave, just as at the end of the preceding age.

Fourth cycle, the age of water, *Atonatiuh*, the duration of which was $10 \times 400 + 8 = 4,008$ years. A great flood, which began in the year *ce calli* on the day 4 water (*nahui atl*), destroyed the human species; this was the last of the great revolutions that the world suffered. Humans were transformed into fish, with the exception of one man and one woman who escaped into the trunk of an *ahahuete*, a bald cypress. The drawing shows the goddess of water, called *Matlalcueje* or *Chalchiuhcueje*, and regarded as the companion of Tlaloc, diving toward the earth. Coxcox, the Noah of the Mexica, and his wife *Xochiquetzal* are seated in a tree trunk covered in leaves and are floating in the midst of the floodwaters.

These four epochs, which are also known as *suns*, together contain eighteen thousand twenty-four years; that is, six thousand years more than the four Persian ages described in the Zend-Avesta. I do not see any indication anywhere of the number of years that elapsed from the flood of Coxcox to the sacrifice of Tlalixco, or until the reform of the Aztec calendar; but however short an interval one assumes between these two epochs, one always finds that the Mexica viewed the world as having been in existence for more than twenty thousand years. This duration certainly conflicts with the Hindus' great period, which is four million three hundred twenty thousand years long, and especially with the cosmogonic fiction of the Tibetans, according to which humankind has already passed through eighteen revolutions, each of which contains several

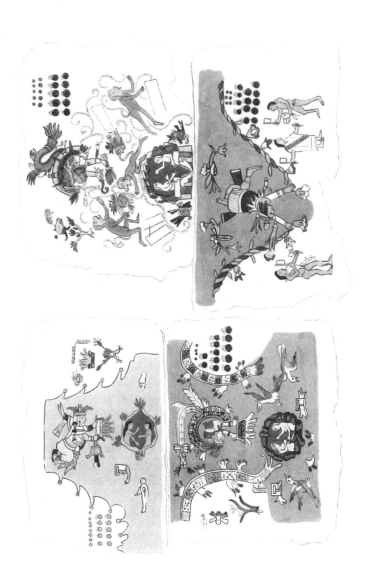

PLATE XXVI

padu represented by sixty-two-digit numbers. It is, nevertheless, remarkable to find an American people who, using the
same calendar system that they employed when Cortés
arrived, mark the days and the years of twenty centuries ago,
when the world suffered great catastrophes.

Le Gentil, Bailly, and Dupuis have offered clever explanations for duration of the great cycles of Asia. I was unable to
determine any special property in the number 18,028 years: it
is not a multiple of 13, 19, 52, 60, 72, 360, or 1440, which are
the numbers that one finds in the cycles of the Asian peoples.
If the duration of the *four Mexica suns* was three years, and if
one replaced the numbers 5,206, 4,804, 4,010, and 4,008 years
with the numbers 5,206, 4,807, 4,009, and 4,009, one might
believe that these cycles were derived from the knowledge of
the nineteen-year lunar period. Whatever their true origin, it
seems clear that they are fictions of astronomical mythology,
modified either by a vague recollection of some great revolution that our planet underwent or in accordance with theories
about natural history and geology that the physical appearance
of marine petrifactions and fossilized remains inspires, even
among those peoples furthest removed from civilization.

Examining the paintings shown on Plate XXVI, one finds
in the four destructions the emblem of four elements: *earth*,
fire, *air*, and *water*. These same elements were also represented
by the four year-hieroglyphs: *rabbit, dwelling, flint,* and *reed. Calli,*
or *dwelling,* seen as the symbol of fire, recalls the customs of a
northern people whom the inclement weather forced to heat
their huts, as well as the idea of Vesta ('Εστια [Hestia]), which,
in the most ancient system of Greek mythology, represents
not only the *house* but also the *hearth* and the *fire* in the hearth.
The sign *tecpatl, flint,* was dedicated to the god of the air, *Quetzalcohuatl,* a mysterious figure who belongs to the heroic
period of Mexica history, and of whom we have had occasion
to speak at many points in this work. According to the Mexica
calendar, *tecpatl* is the *night-sign* that accompanies the hieroglyph for the day called *ehecatl, wind,* at the beginning of the
cycle. Perhaps the story of an aerolite that fell from the
heavens onto the top of the Cholula pyramid, dedicated to

Quetzalcohuatl, inspired the Mexica to conceive this bizarre relationship between fire-starting flint (*tecpatl*) and the god of the winds.

We have seen that the Mexica astrologers gave a historical character to the tradition of the destructions and the regenerations of the world by citing the days and years of the great catastrophes in accordance with the calendar they used in the sixteenth century. Only a very simple calculation was needed for them to find the hieroglyph for a year that came 5,206 or 4,804 years before a given epoch. It was in this manner that, according to Macrobius and Nonnus, the Chaldean and Egyptian astrologers determined even the position of the planets both at the time of the creation of the world and at that of the great flood. Using the system of the periodic series, I recalculated the signs that presided over the years several centuries before the sacrifice at Tlalixco (in the year *ome acatl*, 2 *reed*, which corresponds to the year 1091 of the Christian era) and found that the dates and signs did not correspond exactly to the duration of each Mexica epoch. These dates are also not indicated in the Vatican paintings; I took them from a fragment of Mexica history preserved by Alva Ixtlilxochitl, who sets the length of the four ages not at 18,028 but only at 1,417 years. This discrepancy in astrological calculations should not surprise us, for the first number contains almost as many indictions as the second does years. Likewise, in the Hindus' mystical chronology, substituting days for *divine years* reduces the four ages from 4,320,000 years to 12,000.

SYSTEM OF THE CODEX VATICANUS, No. 3738	SYSTEM OF THE TRADITION PRESERVED BY IXTILXOCHITL
Duration of the *first age*............ 100 × 52 + 6 = 5,206 years	13 × 52 + 676 years
Period of the first destruction.....................................	.... 1 *Acat.*
Duration of the catastrophe	.... 13 years
Duration of the *second age*.......... 92 × 52 + 20 = 4,804 years	7 × 52 = 364 years
Period of the second destruction	.... 1 *Tecpa*
Duration of the *third age*............ 77 × 52 + 6 = 4,010 years	6 × 52 = 312 years
Period of the third destruction.....................................	.... 1 *Tecpa*
Duration of the *fourth age*........... 76 × 52 + 4 = 4,008 years	1 × 52 = 52 years
Period of the fourth destruction	.... 1 *Cal*
346 cycles of 52 years + 36 = 18,028 years	109 indictions of 13 years or 1,417 years

Examining the numbers in this table in accordance with the Mexica calendar system, one sees that two ages separated by an interval cannot have different signs if the number of years in the interval is a multiple of 52. It is impossible for the fourth destruction to have taken place in the year *calli* if the third occurred in the year *tecpatl*. I cannot imagine what might have caused this error; it may be, however, that it merely appears to be an error, and that in the historical monuments that have been handed down to us, no mention was made of the small number of years that nature required for each regeneration. The Hindus make a distinction between the interval separating two cataclysms and the amount of time that each of them actually lasted. Similarly, in the fragment from Alva Ixtlilxochitl, we read that the first catastrophe is separated from the second by seven hundred seventy-six years but that the famine that killed the people lasted for thirteen years, or one-quarter of a cycle. In the two chronological systems that we have just described, the epoch of the creation of the world, or better, the starting point for the great periods, is the year presided over by *tochtli*; this sign was for the Mexica what the catasterism *aries* [the ram] was for the Persians. The astrological traditions of all peoples note the position of the sun at the moment when the stars begin their course; and in our discussion above of the observable connections between the fiction of the epochs and the meaning of the hieroglyph *ollin*, we have suggested the likelihood that *tochtli* corresponds to one of the solsticial points.

In the Mexica system, the four great revolutions of nature are caused by the four elements: the first catastrophe is the devastation of the productive force of the earth, while the other three are due to the effect of fire, air, and water. The human species regenerates after each destruction, and any members of the previous race who did not perish are transformed into birds, monkeys, or fish. These transformations also recall the legends of the East; yet in the Hindus' system the ages, *yugas*, all end in floods, while in that of the Egyptians the cataclysms alternate with conflagrations, and men find refuge either on the mountains or, at other times, in the valleys. We would digress from our topic were we to explain here the small local revolutions that occurred on several occasions in the mountainous part of Greece and discuss the famous passage from the second book of Herodotus, which has so challenged commentators' wisdom. It seems quite clear that it is not a question of *apocatastases* in this passage but, rather, of four (visible) changes that affected the moments of sunset and sunrise and that were brought about by the precession of the equinoxes.

Since one might be surprised to find five ages, *suns*, among the peoples of Mexico, while the Hindus and the Greeks recognize only four, it is useful to observe here that Mexica cosmogony aligns closely with that of the Tibetans, who also regard the present age as the fifth one. By examining closely the lovely passage of Hesiod in which he explains the Eastern system of the renewal of nature, one sees that this poet actually counts five generations within four epochs. He divides the Bronze Age into two parts that cover the fourth and fifth generations, and one may be surprised that such a clear passage has occasionally been misinterpreted. We do not know the number of ages mentioned in the books of the Sibyl, but we believe that the similarities we just highlighted are not accidental, and that it is not unimportant for the philosophical history of humanity to note that the same fictional stories are widespread, from Etruria to Latium to Tibet and from there all the way to the ridge of the Cordilleras of Mexico.

In addition to the tradition of the four suns and the costumes that we described above, the *Cod[ex] Vatican[us] Anon[ymous]* Number 3738 contains several other peculiar images, among which we cite the following: Folio 4, the *chichiuhalquehuitl*, *milk tree* or *celestial tree*, which secretes milk from the tips of its branches and around which are seated the children who died a few days after their birth; Folio 5, a three-pound molar, perhaps from a mastodon, which Father Ríos gave to the viceroy Don Luis de Velasco in 1564; Folio 8, the volcano *Catcitepetl*, the *speaking mountain*, famous for the penance exercises of Quetzalcohuatl and designated by a mouth and a tongue, which are the hieroglyphs for speech; Folio 10, the pyramid of Cholula; and Folio 67, the seven chiefs of the seven Mexica tribes, dressed in rabbit skins and emerging from the seven caves of Chicomortoc. From folio 68 to 93, this manuscript contains copies of hieroglyphic paintings made after the conquest: here one sees natives hung from trees, holding crosses in their hands; a number of Cortés's soldiers on horseback setting fire to a village; friars who are baptizing unfortunate Indians at the very moment when the latter are put to death by being cast into the water. In these images, one recognizes the arrival of the Europeans in the new world.

PLATE XXIX

Aztec Idol Made of Basaltic Porphyry,
Found under the Cobblestones of the
Main Square of Mexico City

WITH THE SOLE exception of the group of figures shown on Plate XI, all the remnants of Mexica painting and sculpture that we have examined thus far demonstrate a complete ignorance of the proportions of the human body, a great deal of coarseness and inaccuracy in the drawing, but also an effort toward meticulous fidelity in rendering the details of the accessories. One may be surprised to find the arts of imitation present in such an unrefined state among a people whose political existence had for centuries suggested a certain degree of civilization, yet among whom idolatry, astrological superstitions, and the desire to preserve the memory of events magnified the number of idols, sculpted stones, and historical paintings. One must not forget, however, that several peoples who played a role on the world stage (particularly the peoples of central and eastern Asia, whom the inhabitants of Mexico seem to resemble through quite close ties) exhibit this very contrast between social perfection and artistic infancy. One might be tempted to apply to both the inhabitants of Tartary and the mountain peoples of Mexico what a great historian of antiquity said about the Arcadians. 'The somber, cold climate of Arcadia lends a hard, austere character to its inhabitants, since it is natural for men, in their customs, their figure, their color, and their institutions, to resemble the climate in which they live.' But the more one examines the state of our species in various regions and becomes accustomed to comparing the physiognomy of countries with that of the peoples who settled there, the less faith one has in the specious theory that attributes exclusively to the climate the effects of a combination of numerous moral and physical circumstances.

Among the Mexica, the cruelty of their customs, sanctioned by a bloodthirsty religion, the tyranny exercised by nobles and priests, the fanciful concepts of astrology, and the frequent use of symbolic script all appear to have greatly contributed to perpetuating a lack of artistic refinement and a predilection for inaccurate, hideous forms. These idols, before which the blood of human victims flowed daily, 'these original deities spawned by fear,' had features that combined the strangest aspects of nature. The character of the human figure disappeared under the weight of the garments, the helmets shaped like the heads of carnivorous animals, and the serpents wound around bodies. A religious respect for signs resulted in each idol's having its individual type, from which it was forbidden to diverge. It was in this manner that the religion perpetuated the inaccuracy of forms, and the people became accustomed to these assemblages of monstrous parts, which were nevertheless arranged in accordance with systematic ideas. Both astrology and the complicated manner of graphically representing temporal divisions were largely responsible for these lapses in imagination. Each event appeared to be influenced not only by the hieroglyph that presided over that day but also by those that ruled the half-decade and the year; hence the idea of pairing signs and creating those purely fantastical creatures we find repeated so many times in the astrological paintings that have been transmitted to us. The genius of the American languages, which, like Sanskrit, Greek, and the languages of Germanic origin, enables one to convey a large number of ideas in a single word, probably facilitated these wondrous creations of mythology and the mimetic arts.

Faithful to their original habits, all peoples – regardless of their intellectual culture – pursue for centuries the course that they once set for themselves. In regard to the imposing simplicity of the Egyptian hieroglyphs, one shrewd writer remarked that 'these hieroglyphs show a lack of imitation rather than an excess of it.' It is, on the contrary, precisely this excess of imitation, this predilection for the minutest details, and the repetition of the most common forms that characterizes Mexica historical paintings. We have already cautioned above that

Fig. 3.

Fig. 2.

Fig. 1.

Fig. 6.

Fig. 5.

PLATE XXIX

one must not confuse images in which almost everything is individualized with simple hieroglyphs capable of representing abstract ideas. Whereas the Greeks drew from the latter a sense of the ideal style, the Mexica peoples encountered insurmountable obstacles to the progress of the mimetic arts in their frequent use of historical and astrological paintings and their respect for forms that were frequently bizarre and always inaccurate. It was in Greece that religion became the wellspring of those arts to which it gave birth. The imagination of the Greeks was able to endow even the gloomiest of subjects with sweetness and charm. But among a people who bear the yoke of a bloodthirsty religion, death manifests itself everywhere in the most terrifying emblems: it is engraved onto each stone; one finds it inscribed on each page of their books; the religious monuments have no other purpose than to incite terror and dread.

I thought it necessary to recall these ideas before focusing the reader's attention on the monstrous idol on Plate XXIX. This rock, sculpted on all sides, is over three meters high and two meters wide. It was found under the cobblestones of the *Plaza Mayor* in Mexico City, within the walls of the great temple, in August of 1790, and thus only a few months before people discovered the enormous stone that shows both the celebrations and the day-hieroglyphs of the Aztec calendar. Workers carrying out excavations for the construction of an underground aqueduct discovered it in a horizontal position, thirty-seven meters to the west of the viceroy's palace and five meters to the north of the *Acequia de San José*. Since it is hardly likely that while burying the idols to remove them from the natives' sight, Cortés's soldiers had ordered masses of considerable weight to be transported quite far from the *sacellum* [chapel] where they had been originally placed, it is important to give an exact indication of those places where each remnant of Mexica sculpture was found. These ideas will be of particular interest should some government, eager to cast light upon the ancient civilization of the Americans, decide to dig around the cathedral in the main square of the former Tenochtitlan and in the market of Tlatelolco, where, in the final days of the siege, the Mexica had retreated with their household gods (*Tep-itotan*), their sacred books (*Teoamoxtli*), and all of their most precious possessions.

Looking at the idol represented in Plate XXIX as it appears when seen from the front (*Figure* 1), from behind (*Figure* 3), from the side (*Figure* 2), from above (*Figure* 4), and from below (*Figure* 5), one might at first be tempted to believe that this monument is a *teotetl*, a *divine stone*, a kind of betyl [omphalos] adorned with sculptures, a rock on which hieroglyphic signs have been engraved. Yet when one examines this shapeless mass more closely, one can make out in the upper part the heads of two monsters positioned side by side, and one finds on each face (*Figures* 1 *and* 3) two eyes and a wide mouth armed with four teeth. Perhaps these monstrous figures represent only masks, for it was a custom among the Mexica to mask the idols whenever the king was ill and during any other public calamity. The arms and feet are hidden under a drapery ringed by enormous serpents that the Mexica called *cohuatlicuye*, *garment of serpents*. All of these accessories, especially the feather-shaped fringes, are sculpted with great care. Mr. Gama suggested in a separate paper that this idol (*Figure* 3) very likely represents the god of war, *Huitzilopochtli*, or *Tlacahuepancuexcot-zin*, and his wife (*Figure* 1), called *Teoyamiqui* (from *miqui*, to die, and *teoyao*, divine war), because she led the souls of the warriors who died defending the gods to the *house of the Sun*, the paradise of the Mexica, where she transformed them into humming-birds. The skulls and the severed hands, four of which sur-round the goddess's breast, recall the horrific sacrifices (*teoquauhquetzoliztli*) celebrated in the fifteenth thirteen-day period after the summer solstice in honor of the god of war and his companion *Teoyamiqui*. The severed hands alternate with the images of particular vessels in which incense was burned. These vessels were called *top-xicalli*, *calabash-shaped bags* (from *toptli*, purse woven from century plant fiber, and *xicalli*, calabash).

Since all of the faces of this idol were sculpted, even the underside (*Figure* 5) where one finds an image of *Mictlanteuhtli*, *lord of the realm of the dead*, it was undoubtedly held up in the air by means of two columns that supported parts A and B, in figures 1 and 3. This odd positioning meant that the head of the idol was actually raised five to six meters above the floor of the temple, such that when the priests (*Teopixqui*) dragged the unfortunate victims to the altar, they made them pass under the figure of *Mictlanteuhtli*.

The viceroy, the count of Revillagigedo, had this monument brought to the building of the University of Mexico, which he regarded as 'the most appropriate place in which to preserve one of the most peculiar remnants of American antiquity.' But the professors of that University, friars of the Dominican order, did not want the Mexica youth to gaze upon this idol; they buried it anew, half a meter deep in the corridors of the college. I would not have been so fortunate as to examine it if the bishop of Monterrey, Don Feliciano Marín, who passed through Mexico City on his way to his diocese, had not, at my request, petitioned the rector of the University to have it disinterred. I found Mr. Gama's drawing, which I have had copied on Plate XXIX, to be very accurate. The stone used in this monument is bluish-gray basaltic *wacke*, cracked and filled with vitreous feldspar.

In January of 1791, the same excavations to which we owe the sculptures shown on Plates XXI, XXIII, and XXIX also led to the discovery of a tomb two meters long and one meter wide, filled with very fine sand and containing the well-preserved skeleton of a carnivorous quadruped. The tomb was square and formed of slabs of a porous amygdaloid called *tezontli*. The animal appeared to be a *coyote* or Mexica wolf. Clay vessels and small, well-molten bronze bells had been placed next to the remains. This tomb was probably that of some sacred animal; for sixteenth-century writers inform us that the Mexica erected small chapels dedicated to the wolf (*chantico*), the tiger ([jaguar] *tlatocaocelotl*), the eagle (*quetzalhuexoloquauhtli*), and the grass snake. The *cu*, or *sacellum* [chapel], of the *chantico* was called *tetlanman*; and what is more, the priests of the sacred wolf formed a special congregation, whose monastery bore the name *Tetlacmancalmecac*.

One can easily imagine how the zodiac divisions and the

names of the signs that preside over the days, the semilunar months, and the years might lead men to the worship of animals. The nomadic peoples count by lunar months; they distinguish the moon of the rabbits from that of the tigers and of the goats, et cetera, depending on the different periods of the year in which wild or domestic animals bring them joy or inspire fear among them. As the temporal divisions gradually become spatial divisions and peoples form the dodecatemoria of the *full-moon zodiac*, the names of the wild and domestic animals pass over to the constellations themselves. It is thus that the Tartar zodiac, which contains only true ζώδια [*zōdia*], can be considered to be the *zodiac of the hunting and herding peoples*; the tiger, unknown in Africa, lends it an exclusively Asian character. This animal is no longer found within the Chaldean, Egyptian, and Greek zodiacs, in which the tiger, the hare, the horse, and the dog were replaced by the lion of Africa, Thrace, and western Asia; the scales; the twins; and, what is quite remarkable, agricultural symbols. The Egyptian zodiac is a *farming people's zodiac*. As peoples became civilized and the mass of their ideas grew, the names of the zodiac constellations lost their original uniformity and the number of *celestial animals* decreased; this number has nevertheless remained considerable enough to exert a noticeable influence on religions. The imaginative excesses of astrology led men to attach a great importance to the signs that preside over the various divisions of time. In Mexico City, each day-sign had its own altar. In the main *teocalli* (θεῦ καλια) [*theoũ kalia*, dwelling of the god), near the column that supported the image of the planet Venus (*Ilhuicatitlan*), one could see small chapels for the catasterisms *macuilcalli* (5 dwelling), *ome tochtli* (2 rabbit), *chicome atl* (7 water), and *nahui ocelotl* (4 jaguar). Since the majority of the day-hieroglyphs were composed of animals, the worship of the latter was closely tied to the calendar system.

PLATE XXXII

Hieroglyphic History of the Aztecs,
from the Great Flood to the
Founding of Mexico City

THIS HISTORICAL PAINTING was already published at the end of the seventeenth century in Gemelli Careri's travel narrative. Although the *Giro del Mondo* by that author is a widely known work, we found it necessary to reproduce this piece, whose authenticity has been the subject of some rather baseless conjectures that warrant scrupulous examination. It is only by bringing together a large number of monuments that one can hope to shed some light on the history, the customs, and the civilization of those peoples of the Americas who were not acquainted with the admirable art of breaking down sounds and representing them either as isolated or as grouped signs. Comparing monuments to one another not only makes it easier to explain them; it also provides reliable information about the degree of trustworthiness of the Aztec traditions recorded in the writings of the first Spanish missionaries. I think that these powerful motives will provide ample justification for our having chosen a few monuments scattered in printed works to supplement the numerous previously unpublished ones in this collection.

The hieroglyphic drawing shown in Plate XXXII has been all the more neglected until now because of its inclusion in a book that, due to the most extraordinary skepticism, has been considered a mass of frauds and lies. 'I did not dare speak of Gemelli Careri,' writes the illustrious author of the *History of America,* 'because it appears to be a generally accepted opinion now that this traveler never left Italy, and that his *Tour of the World* [*Giro del mondo*] is the account of a fictitious voyage.' It is true that even though he voices this opinion, Robertson appears not to share it, for he adds prudently that the grounds for this accusation of deceit do not appear very plausible to him. I shall not judge whether or not Gemelli ever went to China or Persia; but having traveled a large part of the itinerary in Mexico that the Italian traveler so meticulously described, I can say that it is just as undeniable that Gemelli was in Mexico City, Acapulco, and the small villages of Mazatlán and San Augustin de las Cuevas as it is certain that Pallas was on the Crimea and Mr. Salt in Abyssinia. Gemelli's descriptions have that local color that constitutes the main charm of travel narratives, even when they are written by the least enlightened of men, and that only those who have had the advantage of seeing with their own eyes can provide. A respectable cleric, the Abbot Clavijero, who had traveled across Mexico nearly half a century before me, already raised his voice in defense of the author of the *Giro del Mondo*. He very rightly observed that had Gemelli never left Italy, he would not be able to speak with such great precision, characteristic of the people of his time, about the monasteries of Mexico City and the churches of several villages whose names were unknown in Europe. The same truthfulness – and we must insist on this point – is not, however, evident in the ideas that the author claims to have drawn from his friends' accounts. Gemelli Careri's work, like that of a famous traveler who has been subjected to such harsh treatment in our own day, seems to show an inextricable mixture of errors and precisely reported facts.

This drawing of the Aztecs' migration was once part of the famous collection of Dr. Sigüenza, who had inherited the hieroglyphic paintings from a noble Indian, Juan de Alva Ixtlilxochitl. As the Abbot Clavijero assures us, this collection was preserved intact in the Jesuits' college in Mexico City until 1759. It is not known what became of it after the destruction of the order; I have looked in vain through the Aztec paintings preserved in the library of the university without being able to find the original of the drawing that is shown in Plate XXXII. But there exist in Mexico City several old copies that were certainly not made from Gemelli Careri's engraving. If one compares all the symbolic and chronological content in the painting of the migrations to the hieroglyphs contained in the manuscripts at Rome and Velletri and in the collections of Mendoza and Gama, one will certainly not be inclined to give any credence to the theory that Gemelli's drawing is the fictitious creation of some Spanish monk who attempted to prove, through apocryphal testimony, that the legends of the Hebrews are also found among the indigenous peoples of the Americas. Everything we know about the history, the religion, the astrology, and the cosmogonic fables of the Mexica forms a system with tightly interconnected components. The paintings, the bas-reliefs, the decorations of the idols, and the *divine stones* (*teotetl* among the Aztecs, θεοῦ πέτρα [*theoū petra*], stone of god, among the Greeks) – everything has the same character, the same physiognomy. The cataclysm with which the history of the Aztecs begins, and from which Coxcox escapes in a boat, is shown with the very same circumstances in the drawing that depicts the destructions and the regenerations of the world. The four indictions (*tlatpilli*) that are related to these catastrophes or the subdivisions of the *long year* are sculpted on a stone discovered in 1790 in the foundations of the *teocalli* of Mexico City.

In the most recent edition of his work, Robertson, whose pursuit of facts demonstrates a most exacting critical perspective, has also acknowledged the authenticity of the paintings in Sigüenza's museum. It is undeniable, this great historian writes, that these paintings were produced by the natives of Mexico, and the accuracy of the drawing seems to prove only that this copy was either made or retouched by some European artist. This latter observation does not, however, appear to be entirely corroborated by the large number of hieroglyphic paintings preserved in the archives of the viceroyalty in Mexico City. One detects in these paintings a noticeable improvement in the standard of drawing since the conquest, and especially since the year 1540. In Boturini's collection I have seen only cotton canvases or rolls of agave paper that show, with quite faithful contours, bishops mounted on mules, Spanish lancers on horseback, oxen pulling a plow, ships landing at Veracruz, and several other objects unknown to the Mexica prior to Cortés's arrival. These paintings were made not by

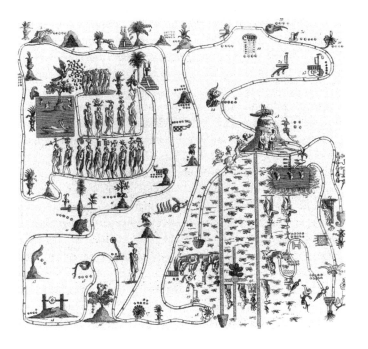

PLATE XXXII

Europeans but by Indians and Mestizos. Leafing through hieroglyphic manuscripts from different periods, one follows with interest the progressive advance of the arts toward a higher level of perfection. The once stocky figures become slimmer; the limbs become more distinct from the torso; when the heads are seen in profile, the eyes do not gaze directly at the viewer; the horses that in Aztec paintings resembled Mexican stags gradually assume their true form. The figures are no longer grouped in *procession style*; their interactions become more frequent; one sees them in action; and symbolic painting, which involves alluding to or recalling events more than expressing them, is thereby subtly transformed into an animated style that uses only a few phonetic hieroglyphs for the names of persons and places. I am inclined to believe that this painting, which Sigüenza passed on to Gemelli, is a copy made after the conquest by either a native or a Mexican Mestizo. The painter probably did not want to reproduce the inaccurate forms of the original; he imitated the hieroglyphs of the names and the cycles with scrupulous precision, but he changed the proportions of the human figures, which he clothed in a manner similar to that which we have acknowledged in other Mexica paintings.

Here, then, are the principal events depicted on Plate XXXII, according to Sigüenza's explanation, to which we shall add some concepts taken from the Mexica's historical annals.

History begins with the great flood of Coxcox, or the fourth destruction of the world, which in Aztec cosmogony concludes the fourth great cycle, *atonatiuh*, the *age of water*. According to the two accepted chronological systems, this cataclysm occurred either one thousand four hundred seventeen or eighteen thousand twenty-eight years after the beginning of the *age of the earth*, *tlatonatiuh*. The huge difference between these numbers should surprise us, especially if we recall the theories on the duration of the Hindus' four *yugas* that Bailly, William Jones, and Bentley have recently advanced. Among the various peoples who lived in Mexico, the Aztecs, the Mixteca, the Zapoteca, the Tlaxcalteca, and the Michoacans were all found to have paintings that represented Coxcox's flood.

The Noah, Xisuthros, or Manu of these peoples is called Coxcox, Teo-Cipactli, or Tezpi. Together with his wife, Xochiquetzal, he saved himself in either a small boat or, according to other legends, a raft made of Ahuahete (*Cupressus distichia*). The painting shows Coxcox adrift on the water, stretched out in a boat.

The mountain whose tree-crowned summit soars above the waters is the Ararat of the Mexica, the Peak of Culhuacan. The horn on the left is the phonetic hieroglyph for Culhuacan. At the base of the mountain, one sees the heads of Coxcox and his wife; the latter is identifiable by the two horn-shaped plaits that specify the female gender, as we have already mentioned several times. The humans born after the flood were mute; a dove perched on top of a tree distributes to them tongues imaged as small commas. One must not confuse this dove with the bird that brought to Coxcox the news that the waters had receded. According to a legend preserved among the peoples of Michoacan, Coxcox, whom they call Tezpi, boarded a spacious *acalli* with his wife, children, several animals, and seeds whose conservation was of the utmost importance to the human species. When the great Tezcatlipoca commanded the waters to retreat, Tezpi ordered a vulture, zopilote (*Vultur aura*), to leave the boat. This bird, which feeds on dead flesh, did not return because of the large number of corpses strewn across the recently dried land. Tezpi sent out other birds, among which only the hummingbird returned, holding in its beak a leaf-covered branch. Then, seeing that the ground was being covered anew with greenery, Tezpi left his boat near Culhuacan Mountain.

These legends, we repeat here, recall others of a high and venerable antiquity. Among peoples who had no contacts with each other, finding the fossils of sea creatures on the highest mountain tops might well have inspired the idea of great floods that had temporarily extinguished organic life on earth. But is it not imperative to acknowledge the traces of a common origin wherever the cosmogonic ideas and the earliest legends of peoples exhibit striking analogies, even in very minor details? Does not Tezpi's hummingbird recall Noah's dove, that of Deucalion, as well as the birds that, according to Berosus, Xisutrus ordered to leave his ark to determine whether the waters had ebbed, and whether he could begin building altars to the patron gods of Chaldea?

Since the tongues that the dove had distributed to the peoples of the Americas (Number 1) varied infinitely from one another, these peoples scattered, and only fifteen heads of family, who spoke the same language and from whom the Toltecs, the Aztecs, and the Acolhua descended, banded together and arrived in Aztlan (land of herons or flamingos). The bird in the hieroglyph for water, *atl,* refers to Aztlan. The terraced pyramidal monument is a *teocalli.* I am surprised to find a palm tree near this *teocalli*: this plant surely does not suggest a northerly region, yet it is almost certain that the original homeland of the Mexica peoples – *Aztlan, Huehuetlapallan,* and *Amaquemecan* – must have been north of at least the 42nd degree of latitude. Perhaps the Mexica painter, an inhabitant of the Torrid Zone, placed a palm tree next to the temple of Aztlan merely because he was unaware that this tree does not grow in the lands of the North. The simple hieroglyphs for the names of the fifteen chiefs are placed above their heads.

The images placed along the road from the Aztlan *teocalli* to Chapultepec mark the places where the Aztecs stayed for some time and the cities they built: *Tocolco* and *Oztotlan* (numbers 3 and 4), *humiliation* and *place of caves*; *Mizquiahuala* (number 5), identified by a fruit-bearing mimosa next to a *teocalli*; *Teotzapotlan* (number 11), *place of the divine fruits*; *Ilhuicatepec* (number 12); *Papantla* (number 13), *wide-leaved herb*; *Tzompango* (number 14), *place of human remains*; *Apazco* (number 15), *clay pot*; *Atlicalaguian* (slightly above the preceding hieroglyph), crevice into which a stream plunges; *Quauhtitlan* (number 16), the grove where the eagle dwells; *Atzcapozalco* (number 17), *anthill*; *Chalco* (number 18), *place of precious stones*; *Pantitlan* (number 19), *the place of spinning*; *Tolpetlac* (number 20), *mats made of rushes*; *Quauhtepec* (number 9), *the Eagle's mountain*, from Quauhtli, eagle, and tepee (in Turkish, tepe), mountain; *Tetepanco* (number 8), *wall composed of many small stones*; *Chicomortoc* (number 7), *the seven caves*; *Huitzquilocan* (number 6), *place of thistles*;

Xaltepozauhcan (number 22), *the place where sand originates*; *Cozca-quauhco* (number 33), name of a vulture; *Techcatitlan* (number 31), place of obsidian mirrors; *Azcaxochitl* (number 21), *ant flower*; *Tepetlapan* (number 23), the spot where one finds *tepetate*, a clayey breccia that contains amphibole, vitreous feldspar, and pumice stone; *Apan* (number 32), *place of water*; *Teozomaco* (number 24), place of the divine monkey; *Chapultepec* (number 25), *mountain of the grasshoppers*, a site shaded by ancient cypresses and famous for the magnificent view that one enjoys from the top of the hill; *Coxcox*, king of Culhuacan (number 30), identified by the same phonetic hieroglyphs found in the square that depicts both Coxcox's flood and Culhuacan mountain; *Mixiuhcan* (number 29), *birthing place*; the city of *Temazcatitlan* (number 26); the city of *Tenochtitlan* (number 34), identified both by the causeways that cross its swampy terrain and by the Indian fig (*cactus*) on which the eagle reposes, which the oracle had designated as the spot where the Aztecs were to build their city and end their migrations; the founders of *Tenochtitlan* (number 35); those of *Tlatelulco* (number 27); the city of *Tlatelulco* (number 28), which today is but a suburb of Mexico City.

We shall not enter into historical detail about the events to which the simple and composed hieroglyphs of Sigüenza's painting refer. These events are reported in Torquemada and the ancient history of Mexico published by the Abbot Clavijero. This painting is less interesting as a historical monument than for the method that the artist employed to link these events together. Suffice it to mention here that the ribbon-tied bunches of rushes (number 2) do not represent four-hundred-year periods, as Gemelli claimed, but rather cycles or bindings of years, Xiuhmolpilli, of fifty-two years. The painting as a whole shows only eight of these bindings, or four hundred sixteen years. If one recalls that the city of Tenochtitlan was founded in the twenty-seventh year of a Xiumolpilli, one finds that according to the chronology of the painting (Plate XXXII), the departure of the Mexica peoples from Aztlan took place five cycles before the year 1298, or in the year 1038 of the Christian era. Gama's estimate for this departure, based on other information, is 1064. The dots accompanying the hieroglyph of a binding of years had been tied since the famous sacrifice of Tlalixco. Yet in the painting that we are examining, the hieroglyph of the cycle is followed by four nails, or units, placed near the hieroglyph of the city of Culhuacan (number 30). It was therefore in the year 208 of their era that the Aztecs emerged from their enslavement under the kings of Culhuacan, and this timing conforms to Chimalpahin's annals. The dots placed next to the hieroglyphs for the cities (numbers 14 and 17) mark the number of years that the Aztec people remained in each place before resuming their migrations. I think that binding number 2 represents the cycle that ended at Tlalixco; for according to Chimalpahin, the festival of the second cycle was celebrated in Cohuatepetl, and that of the third cycle in Apuzco, while the fourth- and fifth-cycle festivals took place in Culhuacan and in Tenochtitlan, respectively.

The odd idea of recording on such a small sheet what in other Mexica paintings often fills canvases or skins ten to twelve feet long made this historical summary quite incomplete. It deals only with the Aztecs' migration, not with that of the Toltec, who preceded the Aztecs in the land of Anahuac by more than five centuries, and who differed from the latter by the same love for the arts and the same religious and peace-loving character that distinguish the Etruscans from the original inhabitants of Rome. The heroic period of Aztec history extended to the eleventh century of the Christian era. Up to then, the deities had been involved in the actions of men; at that time appeared, on the coasts of Panuco, Quetzalcoatl, the Buddha of the Mexica, a white, bearded man, both priest and legislator, devoted to strict penance, and the founder of monasteries and congregations similar to those of Tibet and western Asia. Everything prior to the departure from Aztlan is mixed with childish fables. Among the barbarous peoples, who lack the means to preserve the memory of their deeds, self-awareness is a relatively recent phenomenon; there is a point in their existence beyond which they no longer measure the intervals between events. Distant objects approach one another both in time and in space and become confused. The very cataclysm that the Hindus, the Chinese, and all the peoples of the Semitic race place thousands of years before the perfecting of their social state is believed by the Americans, a people no less ancient perhaps, but whose awakening occurred later, to have taken place only two cycles before their departure from Aztlan.

From

POLITICAL ESSAY ON THE
ISLAND OF CUBA

1826

Translated by J. Bradford Anderson, Vera M. Kutzinski
and Anja Becker

HERE, I END the *Political Essay on the Island of Cuba*, in which I have recounted the state of this important Spanish possession as it is today. As a historian of America, I wanted to clarify facts and specify ideas by means of comparisons and statistical data. An investigation of such minute detail seems necessary at a point in time when the enthusiasm that inspires benign gullibility on the one hand and, on the other, spiteful passions that threaten the new republics' safety has given rise the vaguest and most erroneous observations. It was my plan from the start to abstain from all reasonable speculations about future developments or probable changes that a shift in foreign policy might bring about in the Antilles. I have examined only what pertained to the organization of human societies: the unequal distribution of rights and of life's enjoyment and the threats and dangers that legislators' wisdom and voluntary moderation can avert – whatever the form of government. It befits the traveler, who witnessed up close the torment and degradation of humanity, to bring the laments of the wretched to the ears of those who have the power to assuage them. I have observed the conditions and circumstances of blacks in countries where laws, religion, and national customs tend to soften their lot. Nevertheless, when leaving America, I still harbored the same hatred for slavery with which I had left Europe. It is in vain that wily writers have invented phrases such as *black peasants of the Antilles*, *black vassalage*, and *patriarchal protection* in order to veil institutionalized barbarity in ingenious linguistic fictions. It is a profanation of the noble arts of the spirit and the imagination to use illusory compromises and misleading sophistries to excuse the excesses that afflict humanity and bring about violent upheavals. Do people really consider themselves exempt from compassion when they compare[1] the status of black people with that of medieval serfs or with the yoke under which certain classes of humans in northern and Eastern Europe still groan? In the times in which we live, the comparisons, the rhetoric, and the disdainful impatience with which some shrug off as chimerical even the hope for slavery's gradual abolition are useless weapons. The great revolutions that the American continent and the Antillean archipelago have seen since the beginning of the nineteenth century have affected ideas and public reason even in countries where slavery exists and is now beginning to change. Many reasonable men with a vested interest in the political stability of the *sugar and slave islands* sense that a free accord among owners, along with measures initiated by those familiar with the localities, can overcome a state of crisis and malaise, whose dangers are exacerbated by indolence and obstinacy. I will conclude this section by forecasting the prospects of such measures, and I will prove, through citations taken directly from official documents, that the local authorities in Havana which are most closely connected to the metropole have, on occasion, been favorably

---

1. These comparisons calm only those secret partisans of the slave trade who seek to numb themselves to the afflictions of the black race and thus resist, in a manner of speaking, all emotions that might surprise them. Often one confuses a caste's permanent condition, founded upon legal and institutional barbarity, with an excess of power temporarily wielded over a few individuals. This is why Mr. Bolingbroke, who lived in Demerary and visited the Antilles, does not hesitate to repeat 'that on board a British warship, the whip is used more often than on the plantations of the British colonies.' He adds 'that, normally, one seldom whips blacks but has thought up other, more reasonable correctional methods, such as forcing them to eat boiling, heavily spiced soup or to drink a solution of Glauber salt with a small spoon.' The slave trade strikes him as a *universal benefit*, and he is convinced that if one were to let the blacks, who enjoyed 'all the comforts of a slave's life' in Demerary for twenty years, return to the African coast, they would serve as wonderful recruiters, bringing entire nations under British domination (*Voyage to Demerary*, 1807, pp. 107, 108, 116, 136). Here, we have a clear example of the very stubborn, naïve *colonist's faith*. Nevertheless, as many other passages in his book prove, Mr. Bolingbroke is a moderate man full of kind intentions toward slaves.

disposed toward improving the conditions of black people, long before foreign affairs could have had any influence on their opinions.

Slavery is possibly the greatest evil ever to have afflicted humanity, no matter if one focuses on the individual slave ripped from his family in the country of his birth and thrown into the hold of a slave ship[1] or considers him as part of the herd of black men penned up in the Antilles. Still, there are degrees of suffering and deprivation. What a difference there is between a slave who works in a rich man's house in Havana or Kingston, or who works for himself and gives his master only a daily amount, and a slave who labors in a sugar factory! The threats with which masters attempt to discipline an unruly black show the degrees of human depravity. The *calesero* [coachman] is threatened with the *coffee plantation*, the *cafetal*, while the slave who works on a *cafetal* is threatened with the *sugar plantation*. On the sugar plantation, the black man – affectionate like most Africans are – who has a wife and lives in his own cabin finds comfort after work in the midst of an impoverished family. His lot cannot be compared to that of a slave who is isolated and lost in the crowd. This difference is lost on those who have never set foot on the Antilles. Gradual improvements even among the enslaved caste explain how the masters' luxuries and the possibility of gain through work could have drawn more than 80,000 slaves to Cuba's cities, and how manumission, which sensible laws favor, could have become so effective that, in our day, it has produced more than 130,000 free people of color. The colonial administration will find ways of improving the conditions of the blacks by considering each class' relative position, by rewarding

---

1. 'If one whips the slaves,' said one of the witnesses in a *parliamentary inquiry* in 1789, 'to make them dance on the slave ship's deck, or one forces them to sing in choir: *messe, messe, mackerida* (that one should live happily among whites), this only proves the care we show for their health.' Such delicate care reminds me of a description I have of an auto-da-fé wherein one boasts of the generosity with which refreshments are distributed to the condemned and of 'these steps erected by the inquisition's friends in the midst of the pyre for the comfort of the *relajados* [recidivists].'

intelligence, love of work, and domestic virtues according to a descending scale of dispossession. Philanthropy does not mean 'a little more cod and fewer lashes of the whip.' Genuine improvement for the enslaved class must consider the human condition as a whole, both moral and physical.

The European governments that value human dignity and know that injustice carries within it the seeds of destruction can take the lead. Yet, their leadership (regretfully) will have no effect if landowners, colonial assemblies, or *legislatures*, do not adopt the same views and do not act according to well-orchestrated plans, whose final end is slavery's cessation in the Antilles. Until then, one can count the lashes of the whip, decrease the number of lashes that a person can receive at any one time, require the presence of witnesses, and name slave protectors. But all these regulations, created with the best of intentions, are easy to evade. The plantations' isolation renders their enforcement impossible. Such regulations presuppose a system of domestic control that is incompatible with what one refers to, in the colonies, as 'acquired rights.' The conditions of slavery in their entirety cannot be improved peaceably without the combined efforts of the free men in the Antilles (whites and men of color); of colonial assemblies and *legislatures*; of those who enjoy high moral standing and positions of influence among their fellow-citizens and who, because they understand the locales, know how to calibrate the means of improvement to each island's mores, customs, and circumstances. Preparing this work for a large part of the Antillean Archipelago would benefit from looking back and weighing the circumstances under which many humans were freed in medieval Europe. When one wishes to improve a situation without causing upheavals, it is necessary to let new institutions grow from institutions that have evolved during centuries of barbarism. One day, people will hardly believe that, before 1826, no law existed in any of the Greater Antilles against selling young children and separating them from their parents, or prohibiting the degrading practice of branding blacks with a hot iron simply to be able to identify the human chattel more easily. To remove even the possibility of such

barbaric practices, I offer the following as the most urgent
subjects for colonial legislators: enact laws that fix the numbers of female blacks, and of blacks in relation to each other,
for each sugar plantation; grant freedom to every slave who
has served 15 years and every black woman who has raised 4
or 5 children; emancipate both under the condition that they
work a certain number of days for the plantation's profit; give
slaves some of the net profits to incentivize their interest in
the growth of agricultural wealth;[1] and set aside a certain
amount of public funds in the *budget* for buying slaves' freedom and improving their lives.

The Spanish *conquest* of the American continent and the
slave trade in the Antilles, in Brazil, and in the southern United
States have thrown together in the same place the most heterogeneous of populations. Yet, this strange combination of Indians, whites, blacks, people of different racial admixtures [métis
and mulâtres], and *zambos* seems to be part of the dangers that
strong and unrestrained passions produce during these hazardous times, when a society, shaken to its foundations, is on
the brink of a new era. The *colonial system*'s hateful logic of
safety founded upon enmity between castes, which has been
propagated for centuries, is now exploding with violence. Fortunately the number of black people is so insignificant in the
new continental states that, except for the cruelties in Venezuela, where the royal faction had armed the slaves, vengeful
acts on the part of the enslaved population have not sullied

---

1. Already in 1785, General Lafayette, whose name is connected to everything
that promises to contribute to human freedom and the improvement of the human
condition through institutions, propagated a plan to buy a settlement in Cayenne to
be shared among the blacks who farm it, and whose owner would renounce all gain
for himself or his decendents. He had interested preachers from the Holy Spirit Mission, who owned land in French Guiana, in his noble enterprise. A letter to the Mar-
shal of Castries dated June 6, 1785 proves that the unfortunate King Louis XVI,
dispensing his compassionate intentions even to blacks and free people of color, had
ordered similar experiments to be undertaken at the government's expense. Mr. de
Richeprey, charged with dividing the land among the blacks by Mr. de Lafayette, died
as a result of Cayenne's climate.

the fight between the independents and the loyalist soldiers. Free men of color (blacks, mixed-race, and *mestizos*) have embraced the national cause warmly. The copper-colored indigenous race, however, in its timid suspicion and its mysterious indifference, has remained aloof from these movements, even though it will benefit from them in spite of itself. Long before the revolution, Indians were free, poor farmers. Isolated by language and customs, they lived separately from whites. If, in disregard of Spanish laws, the greed of the *chief magistrates*, *corregidores*, and the *missionaries'* meddlesome practices often hampered Indians' freedom, there was still a big difference between this oppressive state, black chattel slavery, and the serfdom that peasants experience in Europe's Slavic regions. The small number of blacks and the freedom of the aboriginal races, of whose representatives America preserves eight and a half million without any admixture of foreign blood, characterizes the former Spanish continental possessions and renders their moral and political predicament entirely different from that of the Antilles, where the *logic of the colonial system* could develop with greater energy because of the disproportion between free men and slaves. In this archipelago, as in Brazil – two parts of America that have more than three million two hundred thousand slaves – the fear of a reaction among blacks and of the perils that surround whites have been, to this day, the most powerful force behind the metropoles' safety and the survival of the Portuguese dynasty. Can this safety, by its very nature, last very long? Does it justify the inaction of governments that neglect to remedy the evil while there is still time? I doubt it. When fears will have weakened under the influence of extraordinary circumstances, and when countries in which the accumulation of slaves has created an explosive mix of heterogeneous elements are dragged into an external conflict, perhaps despite themselves, civil strife will erupt in all its violence, and European families, who are not responsible for a social order not of their own making, will face the most imminent of dangers.

One cannot praise enough the intelligent legislation of Spanish America's new republics, which, since their inception, have been seriously concerned with slavery's total cessation. In this respect, this vast part of the earth has an immense advantage over the South of the United States, where, during the fight against Britain, whites established their freedom for their own profit and where the slave population, already at a million and six hundred thousand, grows still more rapidly than the white population. If civilization moved ahead rather than just spread; if, following great and appalling upheavals in Europe, the part of America between Cape Hatteras and the Missouri River became the foremost home of Christianity's beacon, what a spectacle this center of civilization would offer when, in freedom's sanctuary, one were able to attend a *slave sale after the death of the master*, hearing parents wail as they are torn away from their children! We hope that the generous principles that have animated *legislatures* in the northern United States for quite some time now[1] will gradually extend toward the south and toward the western regions beyond the Alleghenies and the banks of the Mississippi, where slavery and its iniquities have spread in the wake of the adoption of an imprudent and harmful law.[2] We hope that the force of public opinion, the progress of enlightenment, the improvement of mores, the legislation of the new continental republics, and the momentous and felicitous recognition of Haiti by the French government will have – either through fear and foresight or through more decent and disinterested sentiments – a beneficent influence on the condition of black men and

1. Already in 1769 (forty-six years before the declaration of the Congress of Vienna, and thirty-eight years before the slave trade's cessation was decreed in Washington and London), the Massachusetts house of representatives had inveighed against 'the unnatural and unwarrantable custom of enslaving mankind' (see Walsh, *Appeal to the United States*, 1819, p. 312). The Spanish writer Avendaño is perhaps the first to speak forcefully not only against the commerce in slaves, abhorred even by the Afghanies (Elphinstone, *An Account of the Kingdom of Caubul*, p. 245), but also against slavery in general and against 'all the iniquitous sources of colonial wealth.' [Avendaño,] *Thesaurus indicus*, Vol. I, book 9, chap. 2.

2. Rufus King, *Speeches on the Missouri Bill* (New York, 1819). *North-American Review*, no. 26, pp. 137–68.

women in the rest of the Antilles, the Carolinas, the Guianas, and Brazil.

To succeed at undoing slavery's ties gradually, one needs the strictest enforcement of laws against the slave trade, humiliating punishments against those who infringe upon them, the formation of mixed tribunals, and the right of mutual inspections carried out with equitable reciprocity. It is sad to learn that the slave trade, having become crueler for being more hidden, still wrests almost the same number of black people from Africa as it did before 1807, all because of the disdainful and guilty negligence of certain European governments. Yet, one cannot posit, as do the secret partisans of slavery, the practical impossibility of the beneficent measures enacted first in Denmark, the United States, Great Britain, and then in the rest of Europe. What happened between 1807 and the time when France regained possession of some of its former colonies and what is happening today in the nations that sincerely desire the abolition of the slave trade and its abominable practices proves the fallacy of this conclusion. Also, is it reasonable to compare numerically slave imports from 1825 to slave imports in 1806? Considering the activity at the core of all industrial enterprises, what kind of increase would we have seen in the importation of blacks to the British Antilles and the southern United States, had the slave trade, entirely without constraints, continued to deposit new slaves, thus rendering unnecessary any care for the conservation and growth of the former slave population? Is it believable that British trade would have limited itself to the sale of 53,000 slaves, as it did in 1806? That the United States would have restricted itself to the sale of 15,000? We know with enough certainty that the British Antilles alone received more than 2,130,000 slaves ripped from Africa's coasts during the 106 years before 1786. At the time of the French Revolution, the slave trade (according to Mr. Norris) brought in 74,000 slaves per year, of which the British colonies absorbed 38,000 and the French colonies 20,000. It would be easy to prove that the entire Antillean Archipelago, which has barely 2.4 million blacks and persons of mixed race (frees and slaves) today, received five million Africans (*negros bozales*) between 1670 and 1825. These dreadful calculations about the consumption of human beings do not even account for the number of unfortunate slaves, who either died during the Middle Passage or were thrown overboard like damaged goods. By how many thousands would losses have to be increased, if the two peoples who show the most passion and aptitude for commercial and industrial development – the British and the inhabitants of the United States – had continued to take as liberal a part in the slave trade after 1807 as the other peoples of Europe did? Sad experience proved how catastrophic for humanity were the treaties from July 15, 1814 and January 22, 1815, in which Spain and Portugal still reserved[1] 'the privilege of trading black people' for a certain number of years.

Local authorities – or, to be more precise, the rich land-owners who comprise Havana's *Ayuntamiento* [city council], the *Consulado* [merchant guild], and the *Patriotic Society* – have been favorably disposed toward the improvement of the slaves' lot on several occasions.[2] If the metropole's government had known to take advantage of these happy circumstances and of the rise of men of talent among their compatriots instead of fearing even the appearance of innovation, the state of society would have changed progressively and the inhabitants of the island of Cuba would have already enjoyed some of the improvements that had been discussed thirty years ago. The disturbances in Saint-Domingue in 1790 and in Jamaica in 1794 caused so much alarm among Cuba's *hacendados* that means to preserve the country's tranquility were debated

---

1. 'Dicen nuestros Indios del Río Caura cuando se confiesan que ya entienden que es pecado comer carne humana; pero piden que se les permita desacostumbrarse poco a poco: quieren comer la carne humana una vez al mes, despues cada tres meses, hasta que sin sentirlo pierdan la costumbre' [During confession, our Indians on the Río Caura admit that they understand that eating human flesh is a sin; but they ask that they be permitted to wean themselves of it gradually: they want to eat human flesh once a month, then once every three months, until they lose the habit without realizing it]. *Cartas de los Reverentes Padres Observantes*, no. 7 (unpublished).

2. [Abad y Queipo,] *Representación al Rey de 10 de Julio de 1799* (manuscript).

passionately at a *Junta económica* [economic summit]. They regulated the pursuit of fugitives,[1] an activity that had, up to then, led to the most shameful of excesses. They proposed to increase the number of female blacks on sugar plantations; to take better care of the raising of children; to curtail slave imports from Africa; to invite white colonists from the Canary Islands and Indian colonists from Mexico; to establish schools in the countryside to improve the mores of the lower classes and to thus mitigate the effects of slavery in an indirect way. These proposals did not have the desired effect. The court opposed all immigration policies, and most owners, given over to old fantasies of safety, did not want to restrict the slave trade at a time when high crop prices fed hopes for extraordinary profits. It would be unfair, however, not to point to the hopes and principles that some of Cuba's inhabitants articulated during this fight between private interests and prudent policies – either in their own name or in the name of rich and powerful corporations. 'Our legislation's humanity,' Mr. Arango y Parreño[2] gallantly stated in an account from 1796,

---

1. [Zamora y Coronado,] *Reglamento sobre los negros cimarrones de 20 Dec. de 1796.* Before 1788, there were many fugitive slaves (*cimarrones*) in the Jaruco Mountains, where they were sometimes *apalancados*, that is, many of these unfortunates built little trenches with tree trunks for their common defense. The maroons, *bozales* born in Africa, are easy to capture, for the majority walk day and night to the east in the vain hope of finding their homeland. They are so exhausted from fatigue and hunger when they are taken that they cannot be saved unless they are fed small amounts of broth over many days. Creole maroons hide in the forest during the day and steal provisions at night. Until 1790, the right to capture fugitive slaves belonged only to the *Alcalde mayor provincial* [provincial mayor], a hereditary position in Count Barreto's family. Today, every inhabitant may seize a maroon, and the slave owner pays 4 piasters per head plus food expenses. If the master's name is unknown, the *Consulado* uses the maroon for public works. These manhunts, which have brought a deplorable renown to Cuba's (as well as Haiti and Jamaica's) dogs, were conducted in the cruelest possible manner prior to the regulation that I cited above.

2. *Informe sobre negros fugitivos* (*de 9 de Junio* 1796), by Don Francisco de Aranngo y Parreño, Oidor honorario y síndico del Consulado [honorary magistrate and trustee of the council].

'bestows four rights (*cuatro consuelos*) upon the slave, which go some way toward alleviating his suffering and which have been constantly denied him in other countries. These rights are: the choice of a less severe master;[1] the right to marry whom he pleases; the possibility of working to purchase his freedom[2] or of receiving it as reward for his good services; the right to own property and to pay for his wife and children's freedom with acquired property.[3] Despite the wisdom and leniency of Spanish legislation, to how many excesses does the slave remain

1. It is the right to *buscar amo*, to find a new master. As soon as a slave has found a new master who wishes to buy him, he may leave the first about whom he feels he has something to complain: such is the letter and spirit of a compassionate law that is nevertheless often evaded like all laws that protect slaves. It is in hope of exercising the privilege to *buscar amo* that blacks often ask travelers whom they meet a question that is never posed out loud in civilized Europe, though one sometimes sells one's vote or one's opinion: 'quiere Vm. [Vuestra Merced] Comprarme' [Would Your Highness like to buy me]?

2. According to the law, the slave in the Spanish colonies should be put at the lowest price: during my trip, this estimate was 200 to 380 piasters, depending on the locale. We saw above that the price of an adult slave on the island of Cuba was 450 piasters in 1825. In 1788, the French market offered slaves for 280 to 300 piasters (Page, *Traité d'économie politique des colonies*, Vol. VI, pp. 42 and 43). Among the Greeks, a slave cost 300 to 600 drachmas (54 to 108 piasters), while a worker cost one-tenth of a piaster a day. While Spanish laws and institutions favor every kind of *manumission*, the master in the non-Spanish Antilles pays the treasury five to seven hundred piasters for every freed slave!

3. What a contrast between the humanity of the oldest Spanish laws concerning slavery and the traces of barbarity that one finds on every page of the *Code noir*, and in certain provincial laws in the British Antilles! Barbados's laws, from 1688, and Bermuda's, from 1730, command that the master who kills his slave while punishing him cannot be prosecuted, while the master who kills his slave out of malice will pay 10 pound sterling to the royal treasury. A law in St. Christophe [St. Kitts] from March 11, 1784 begins with these words: 'Whereas some persons have *of late* been guilty of cutting off and depriving slaves of their ears, we decree that whosoever will have plucked out an eye, torn out a slave's tongue, or cut off his nose, will pay 500 pounds sterling and shall be condemned to six months in prison.' I need not add that these British laws, in effect 30 or 40 years ago, have been abolished and replaced by more

exposed in the solitude of a farm or plantation where a brutal *capataz* [overseer] armed with a *machete* and a whip exercises absolute authority with impunity! The law limits neither the slave's punishment nor his work's duration. Nor does it dictate the quality or the quantity of his provisions.[1] It is true that the law grants the slave recourse to a magistrate, who can enjoin the master to be more equitable; but this recourse is nearly entirely illusory, because there is another law according to which one must arrest and return to his master every slave discovered more than a league and a half from his plantation without a pass. How can an abused slave, exhausted by hunger and excessive work, appear before a magistrate? If he does, how is he to defend himself against a powerful master, who calls his salaried accomplices as witnesses?'

I will end by quoting another most remarkable extract from the *Representación [...] del Ayuntamiento, Consulado y Sociedad Patriótica* from July 20, 1811. 'Everything about proposed changes in the conditions of the *enslaved class* has less to do with our fears about declines in agricultural wealth than with the safety of white people, something so easily compromised by imprudent measures. Besides, those who accuse the council and the Havana municipality of stubborn resistance forget that, after 1799, these same authorities unsuccessfully proposed that one should concern oneself with the condition of black people on the island of Cuba (*del arreglo de este delicado asunto* [the mending of this sensitive matter]). What is more: we are far from adopting principles that European nations, which brag about their level of *civilization*,[2] saw as indisputable. For instance, that

---

humane legislation. I wish I could say as much of the legislation in the French Antilles, where six young slaves suspected of wanting to escape had *the tendons in the backs of their knees severed* after being arrested in 1815!

1. A *cédula* from May 31, 1789 had attempted to regulate food and clothing, but this *cédula* was never implemented.

2. 'Hasta abandono hemos [hecho] de [e]species muy favorable[s] que pasan por inconc[l]usas en esas *naciones cultas*. Tal es la de que sin negros esclavos no pudiera haber colonias. Nosotros contra este dictamen decimos que sin esclavitud, y aún sin negros, pudo haber lo que [por] colonia[s] se entiende, y que la diferencia habría

without slaves, there could not be any colonies. On the contrary, we declare that colonies could have existed without slaves, and even without blacks, and that the only difference would lie in greater or lesser profit and in more or less rapid growth in productivity. But if this is our firm conviction, we should recall to Your Majesty that a social organization cannot be changed in unreflecting haste once slavery has been introduced as a factor. We are far from denying that dragging slaves from one continent to another was an evil contrary to moral principles, and that it was a political mistake not to listen to the complaints of Hispaniola's governor, Ovando, against the importation and accumulation of so many slaves alongside such a small number of free men. But once these moral crimes and abuses are already deeply rooted, we must avoid worsening our position and that of our slaves by violent means. What we ask, Sire, is consistent with a wish articulated by one of the most ardent protectors of human rights, the most relentless enemy of slavery. Like he, we wish that civil law deliver us from both abuse and danger at the same time.'

Here is the solution to the problem upon which depends the safety of 875,000 free people (whites and people of color[1]) in the Antilles alone, excluding Haiti, and the adjudication of the fates of 1,150,000 slaves. We have demonstrated that this cannot be achieved by peaceful means without the participation of local authorities, whether *colonial assemblies* or landowner meetings known by names less threatening to the old metropoles. Direct influence from the authorities is indispensable, and it is a grave mistake to believe 'one can let time take

---

estado en las mayores ganancias o en los mayores progresos' [We have even abandoned favorable ideas that pass for undisputed in those cultured nations. For example, that without black slaves, there could be no colonies. We say against this dictum that, without slavery and even without blacks, there might be recognizable colonies; the difference would be in higher profits or greater progress] ([Arango,] *Documentos [. . .] sobre el tráfico y esclavitud de negros*, 1814, pp. 78–80).

1. Specifically: 452,000 whites, of whom 342,000 were in the only two Spanish Antilles (Cuba and Puerto Rico), and 423,000 free people of color, persons of mixed race, and blacks.

its course.' Time will work simultaneously on slaves, on the relations between the islands' and the mainland's inhabitants, and on events that one cannot control any longer, because one will have waited for them in a state of apathetic inaction. Wherever slavery is long established, civilization's advance influences the treatment of slaves far less than one would care to admit. A nation's civilization rarely extends to a large number of individuals. It does not reach those in workplaces who are in direct contact with black people. Owners – I have known some who are very humane – recoil before the difficulties on large plantations. They hesitate to trouble the established order, to adopt innovations that fall short of their ends – where they are not simultaneously supported by legislation, or, what would be more effective, by the general will – and perhaps worsen the lot of those whom they would like to help. Such timid considerations inhibit the good in those men whose intentions are the most benevolent and who suffer under the barbaric institutions that are their sad legacy. Familiar with local conditions, they know that, to produce a basic change in the status of slaves and gradually to lead them to the enjoyment of freedom, the local authorities must have a strong will, support from rich and enlightened citizens, and a comprehensive plan that considers all possibilities for disorder and repressive means. Without this community of action and effort, slavery will sustain itself with its pains and excesses, as it did in ancient Rome,[1] side by side with elegant manners, with enlightenment's much trumpeted progress, with all the glories of a civilization that its presence condemns and that it threatens to devour when the time for revenge will have come. Both civilization, on the one hand, and a slow brutalization of

1. The argument in favor of slavery derived from Roman and Greek civilizations is very popular in the Antilles, where occasionally one indulges in adorning it with all of the trappings of philological erudition. Because of this, in a 1795 speech before Jamaica's *legislative assembly*, it was argued that the example of elephants used in Pyrrhus's and Hannibal's wars justified importing a hundred dogs and forty hunters to track down maroons. Bryan Edwards, [*The History, Civil and Commercial, of the British Colonies in the West Indies,*] Vol. I, p. 570.

peoples on the other only prepare minds for future events. But to bring about large changes in the social order, the coincidence of certain events, whose moment cannot be determined in advance, is necessary. Such is the complexity of human destiny that the very cruelties that covered the conquest of both Americas in blood are returning before our eyes during a time we believed to be characterized by enlightenment's prodigious progress and by a general softening of mores. The course of one man's life sufficed to see the French Reign of Terror, the Saint-Domingue expedition,[1] and Spain and Naples's political reaction. I could add the Chio, Ipsara, and Missolonghi massacres, the work of barbarians from Eastern Europe that the civilized peoples of the west and north did not believe themselves able to prevent. In slave countries, where long-standing habits tend to legitimize institutions that are the most opposed to justice, one can count on the influence of enlightenment, intellectual culture, or the softening of mores only insofar as they all accelerate government initiative and facilitate the implementation of measures once they are adopted. Without the governments' and *legislatures'* guiding action, peaceful change is not to be hoped for. The danger becomes particularly imminent when a general restlessness seizes the spirit and when the faults and responsibilities of governments are revealed in the midst of political upheavals that agitate neighboring peoples. Then, calm can only be restored by a power that knows how to control events by itself initiating improvements out of a noble sense of its strength and its right.

1. [Review of Vastey in] *North American Review*, 1821, no. 30, p. 116. Battles against slaves fighting for their freedom are deplorable not only because of the atrocities they unleashed on both sides, but also because such wars contribute to the confusion of all feelings of justice and injustice once emancipation is achieved. 'Certain colonists condemned to death the entire male population above the age of six. They hold that an example before the eyes of those who did not bear arms could become contagious. This lack of moderation is the result of the colonists' long misfortunes.' Charault, *Réflexions sur Saint-Domingue*, 1814, p. 16.

From

COSMOS

SKETCH OF A PHYSICAL DESCRIPTION
OF THE UNIVERSE
1845−61

Nature as vero rerum vis atque majestas in omnibus momentis fide caret, si quis modo partes ajus as non totam complectatur animo. − PLIN. H. N. lib. vii. c. 1.

Translated by Elizabeth Juliana Sabine

AUTHOR'S PREFACE

IN THE LATE evening of a varied and active life, I offer to the German public a work of which the undefined type has been present to my mind for almost half a century. Often the scheme has been relinquished as one which I could not hope to realize, but ever after being thus abandoned, it has been again, perhaps imprudently, resumed. In now presenting its fulfilment to my contemporaries, with that hesitation which a just diffidence of my own powers could not fail to inspire, I would willingly forget that writings long expected are usually least favourably received.

While the outward circumstances of my life, and an irresistible impulse to the acquisition of different kinds of knowledge, led me to occupy myself for many years, apparently exclusively, with separate branches of science, – descriptive botany, geology, chemistry, geographical determinations, and terrestrial magnetism, tending to render useful the extensive journeys in which I engaged, – I had still throughout a higher aim in view; I ever desired to discern physical phænomena in their widest mutual connection, and to comprehend Nature as a whole, animated and moved by inward forces. Intercourse with highly-gifted men had early led me to the conviction, that without earnest devotion to particular studies such attempts could be but vain and illusory. The separate branches of natural knowledge have a real and intimate connection, which renders these special studies capable of mutual assistance and fructification: descriptive botany, no longer restricted to the narrow circle of the determination of genera and of species, leads the observer, who traverses distant countries and lofty mountains, to the study of the geographical distribution of plants according to distance from the equator and elevation above the level of the sea. Again, in order to elucidate the complicated causes which determine this distribution, we must investigate the laws which regulate the diversities of climate and the meteorological processes of the atmosphere; and thus the observer, earnest in the pursuit of knowledge, is led onwards from one class of phænomena to another, by their mutual connection.

I have enjoyed one advantage which few scientific travellers have shared to an equal degree, in having seen not merely coasts, and districts little removed from the margin of the ocean, as in voyages of circumnavigation, – but in having, moreover, traversed, both in the new and the old world, extensive continental districts presenting the most striking contrasts; on the one hand the tropical and alpine landscapes of Mexico and South America, and on the other the dreary uniformity of the steppes of Northern Asia. Such opportunities could not fail to encourage the tendencies of a mind predisposed to generalization, and were well fitted to animate me to the attempt of treating in a special work our present knowledge of the sidereal and terrestrial phænomena of the universe in their empirical connection. 'Physical Geography', the limits of which have been hitherto somewhat vaguely defined, has been thus expanded, by perhaps too bold a plan, into a scheme comprehending the whole material creation, or into that of a 'Physical Cosmography'.

Such a work, if it would aspire to combine with scientific accuracy any measure of success as a literary composition, has to surmount great difficulties, arising from the very abundance of the materials which the presiding mind must reduce to order and clearness, while yet the descriptions of the varied forms and phænomena of nature must not be deprived of the characteristic traits which give them life and animation. A series of general results would be no less wearisome than a mere accumulation of detached facts. I cannot venture to flatter myself that I have adequately satisfied these various conditions, or avoided the dangers which I have not failed to perceive; the faint hope which I cherish of success rests on the particular favour which my countrymen have long bestowed on a small work which I published, soon after my return from

Mexico, under the title of *Ansichten der Natur,** and which treated some portions of physical geography, such as the physiognomy of plants, savannahs, deserts, and cataracts, under general points of view. Doubtless the effect which this small volume produced was far more attributable to its indirect action, in awakening the faculties of young and susceptible minds endowed with imaginative power, than to any thing which it could itself impart. In my present work, as in the one to which I have just alluded, I have endeavoured to shew practically, that a certain degree of scientific accuracy in the treatment of natural facts is not incompatible with animated and picturesque representation.

Public discourses or lectures have always appeared to me well adapted to test the success or failure of an endeavour to unite detached branches of a general subject in a systematic whole; with this view a series of lectures on the Physical Description of the Universe, as I had conceived it, was delivered both in Berlin and in Paris, in German and in French. These discourses were not committed to writing; and even the notes preserved by the diligence of some attentive auditors have remained unknown to me; nor have I chosen to have recourse to them in the execution of the present work, the whole of which, with the exception of a portion of the Introduction, was written for the first time in the years 1843 and 1844; the discourses in Berlin having been delivered from November 1827 to April 1828, previous to my departure for Northern Asia. A representation of the actual state of our knowledge, in which year by year the acquisitions of new observations imperatively demand the modification of previous opinions, must, as it appears to me, gain in unity, freshness, and spirit, by being definitely connected with some one determinate epoch.

The first volume contains a general view of nature, from the remotest nebulæ and revolving double stars to the terrestrial phænomena of the geographical distribution of plants, of animals, and of races of men; preceded by some preliminary

[* *Views of Nature.* – Ed.]

considerations on the different degrees of enjoyment offered by the study of nature and the knowledge of her laws; and on the limits and method of a scientific exposition of the physical description of the Universe. I regard this as the most important and essential portion of my undertaking, as manifesting the intimate connection of the general with the special, and as exemplifying in form and style of composition, and in the selection of the results taken from the mass of our experimental knowledge, the spirit of the method in which I have proposed to myself to conduct the whole work. In the two succeeding volumes I design to consider some of the particular incitements to the study of Nature, – to treat of the history of the contemplation of the physical universe, or the gradual development of the idea of the concurrent action of natural forces co-operating in all that presents itself to our observation, – and lastly, to notice the specialities of the several branches of science, of which the mutual connection is indicated in the general view of nature in the present volume. References to authorities, together with details of observation, have been placed at the close of each volume, in the form of Notes. In the few instances in which I have introduced extracts from the works of my friends, they are indicated by marks of quotation; and I have preferred the practice of giving the identical words, to any paraphrase or abridgment. The delicate and often contested questions of discovery and priority, so dangerous to introduce in an uncontroversial work, are rarely touched upon: the occasional references to classical antiquity, and to that highly favoured transition period marked by the great geographical discoveries of the fifteenth and sixteenth centuries, have had for their principal motive, the wish, which is occasionally felt when dwelling on general views of nature, to escape from the more severe and dogmatical restraint of modern opinions, into the free and imaginative domain of earlier presentiments.

It has sometimes been regarded as a discouraging consideration, that whilst works of literature, being fast rooted in the depths of human feeling, imagination, and reason, suffer little from the lapse of time, it is otherwise with works which treat of subjects dependent on the progress of experimental knowledge. The improvement of instruments, and the continued enlargement of the field of observation, render investigations into natural phænomena and physical laws liable to become antiquated, to lose their interest, and to cease to be read. Such reflections are not entirely destitute of foundation; yet none who are deeply penetrated with a true and genuine love of nature, and with a lively appreciation of the true charm and dignity of the study of her laws, can ever view with discouragement or regret that which is connected with the enlargement of the boundaries of our knowledge. Many and important portions of this knowledge, both as regards the phænomena of the celestial spaces and those belonging to our own planet, are already based on foundations too firm to be lightly shaken; although in other portions, general laws will doubtless take the place of those which are more limited in their application, new forces will be discovered, and substances considered as simple will be decomposed, whilst others will become known. I venture, then, to indulge the hope, that the present attempt to trace in animated characters such a general view of the grandeur of nature, and of the permanent relations and laws discernible through apparent fluctuation, as the knowledge of our own age permits us to form, will not be wholly disregarded even at a future period.

POTSDAM, NOV. 1844.

COSMOS

A PHYSICAL DESCRIPTION OF THE UNIVERSE
VOL. I

ON THE DIFFERENT DEGREES OF ENJOYMENT
OFFERED BY THE ASPECT OF NATURE AND
THE STUDY OF HER LAWS.

IN ATTEMPTING, AFTER a long absence from my country, to unfold a general view of the physical phænomena of the globe which we inhabit, and of the combined action of the forces which pervade the regions of space, I feel a double anxiety. The matter of which I would treat is so vast, and so varied, that I fear, on the one hand, to approach it in an encyclopaedic and superficial manner, and on the other, to weary the mind by aphorisms presenting only dry and dogmatic generalities. Conciseness may produce aridity, whilst too great a multiplicity of objects kept in view at the same time leads to a want of clearness and precision in the sequence of ideas.

But nature is the domain of liberty; and to give a lively picture of those ideas and those delights which a true and profound feeling in her contemplation inspires, it is needful that thought should clothe itself freely and without constraint in such forms and with such elevation of language, as may be least unworthy of the grandeur and majesty of creation.

If the study of physical phænomena be regarded in its bearings, not on the material wants of man, but on his general intellectual progress, its highest result is found in the knowledge of those mutual relations which link together the various powers of nature. It is the intuitive and intimate persuasion of the existence of these relations which at once enlarges and elevates our views, and enhances our enjoyment. Such extended views are the growth of observation, of meditation, and of the spirit of the age, which is ever reflected in the

operations of the human mind whatever may be their direction. Those who by the light of history should trace back
through past ages the progress of physical knowledge to its
early and remote sources, would learn how for thousands of
years the human mind has laboured to lay hold of the sure
thread of the invariability of natural laws, amid the perplexities
of ceaseless change; and in so doing has gradually conquered,
so to speak, great part of the physical universe. In following
back this mysterious track, still the same image of the *Cosmos*
reappears, which, in its earlier revelation, shewed itself as a
presentiment of the true harmony and order of the universe,
and which, in our days, presents itself as the fruit of long-
continued and laborious observation. Each of these two
epochs of the contemplation of the external world has its own
proper enjoyment: that belonging to the first awakening of
such reflections is well suited to the simplicity of the earlier
ages of the world; to them the undisturbed succession of the
planetary movements, and the progressive development of
animal and vegetable life, were pledges of an order yet undis-
covered in other relations, but of which they instinctively
divined the existence. To us in an advanced civilization
belongs the enjoyment of the precise knowledge of phænomena. From the time when man in interrogating nature began
to experiment, or to produce phænomena under definite conditions, and to collect and record the fruits of experience, so
that investigation might no longer be restricted by the short
limits of a single life, the *philosophy of nature* laid aside the vague
and poetic forms with which she had at first been clothed, and
has adopted a more severe character: – she now weighs the
value of observations, and no longer divines, but combines
and reasons. Exploded errors may survive partially among the
uneducated, aided in some instances by an obscure and mystic
phraseology: they have also left behind them many expressions by which our nomenclature is more or less disfigured;
while a few of happier, though figurative origin, have gradually
received more accurate definition, and have been found
worthy of preservation in our scientific language.

The aspect of external nature, as it presents itself in its

generality to thoughtful contemplation, is that of unity in diversity, and of connection, resemblance and order, among created things most dissimilar in their form; – one fair harmonious whole. To seize this unity and this harmony, amid such an immense assemblage of objects and forces, – to embrace alike the discoveries of the earliest ages and those of our own time, – and to analyse the details of phænomena without sinking under their mass, are efforts of human reason in the path wherein it is given to man to press towards the full comprehension of nature, to unveil a portion of her secrets, and, by the force of thought, to subject, so to speak, to his intellectual dominion, the rough materials which he collects by observation.

If we attempt to analyse the different gradations of enjoyment derived from the contemplation of nature, we find, first, an impression which is altogether independent of any knowledge of the mode of action of physical powers, and which does not even depend on the particular character of the objects contemplated. When we behold a plain bounded by the horizon, and clothed by a uniform covering of any of the social plants (heaths, grasses, or cistusses), – when we gaze on the sea, where its waves, gently washing the shore, leave behind them long undulating lines of weeds, – then, while the heart expands at the free aspect of nature, there is at the same time revealed to the mind an impression of the existence of comprehensive and permanent laws governing the phænomena of the universe. The mere contact with nature, the issuing forth into the open air, – that which by an expression of deep meaning my native language terms *in das Freie*, – exercises a soothing and a calming influence on the sorrows and on the passions of men, whatever may be the region they inhabit, or the degree of intellectual culture which they enjoy. That which is grave and solemn in these impressions is derived from the presentiment of order and of law, unconsciously awakened by the simple contact with external nature; it is derived from the contrast of the narrow limits of our being with that image of infinity, which everywhere reveals itself in the starry heavens, in the boundless plain, or in the indistinct horizon of the ocean.

Other impressions, better defined, affording more vivid enjoyment and more congenial to some states of the mind, depend more on the peculiar character and physiognomy of the scene contemplated, and of the particular region of the earth to which it belongs. They may be excited by views the most varied; either by the strife of nature, or by the barren monotony of the steppes of Northern Asia, or by the happier aspect of the wild fertility of nature reclaimed to the use of man, fields waving with golden harvests, and peaceful dwellings rising by the side of the foaming torrent; for I regard here less the force of the emotion excited, than the relation of the sensations and ideas awakened to that peculiar character of the scene which gives them form and permanence. If I might yield here to the charm of memory, I would dwell on scenes deeply imprinted on my own recollection – on the calm of the tropic nights, when the stars, not sparkling, as in our climates, but shining with a steady beam, shed on the gently heaving ocean a mild and planetary radiance; – or I would recall those deep wooded valleys of the Cordilleras, where the palms shoot through the leafy roof formed by the thick foliage of other trees, above which their lofty and slender stems appear in lengthened colonnades, 'a forest above a forest'; – or the Peak of Teneriffe, when a horizontal layer of clouds has separated the cone of cinders from the world beneath, and suddenly the ascending current of the heated air pierces the veil, so that the traveller, standing on the very edge of the crater, sees through the opening the vine-covered slopes of Orotava, and the orange gardens and bananas of the coast. In such scenes it is no longer alone the peaceful charm, of which the face of nature is never wholly destitute, which speaks to our minds, but the peculiar character of the landscape, the new and beautiful forms of vegetable life, the grouping of the clouds, and the vague uncertainty with which they mingle with the neighbouring islands, and the distant horizon half visible through the morning mist. All that the senses but partially comprehend, and whatever is most grand and awful in such romantic scenes, open fresh sources of delight. That which sense grasps but imperfectly offers a free field to creative fancy; the outward impressions change with the changing phases of the mind; and this without destroying the illusion, by which we imagine ourselves to receive from external nature that with which we have ourselves unconsciously invested her.

When far from our native country, after a long sea voyage, we tread for the first time the lands of the tropics, we experience an impression of agreeable surprise in recognizing, in the cliffs and rocks around, the same forms and substances, similar inclined strata of schistose rocks, the same columnar basalts, which we had left in Europe: this identity, in latitudes so different, reminds us that the solidification of the crust of the earth has been independent of differences of climate. But these schists and these basalts are covered with vegetable forms of new and strange aspect. Amid the luxuriance of this exotic flora, surrounded by colossal forms of unfamiliar grandeur and beauty, we experience (thanks to the marvellous flexibility of our nature) how easily the mind opens to the combination of impressions connected with each other by unperceived links of secret analogy. The imagination recognizes in these strange forms nobler developments of those which surrounded our childhood; the colonist loves to give to the plants of his new home names borrowed from his native land, and these strong untaught impressions lead, however vaguely, to the same end as that laborious and extended comparison of facts, by which the philosopher arrives at an intimate persuasion of one indissoluble chain of affinity binding together all nature.

It may seem a rash attempt to endeavour to analyse into its separate elements the enchantment which the great scenes of nature exert over our minds, for this effect depends especially on the combination and unity of the various emotions and ideas excited; and yet if we would trace back this power to the objective diversity of the phænomena, we must take a nearer and more discriminating view of individual forms and variously acting forces. The richest and most diversified materials for such an analysis present themselves to the traveller in the landscapes of Southern Asia, in the great Indian Archipelago, and, above all, in those parts of the new continent where the highest summits of the Cordilleras approach the upper surface of the aerial ocean by which our globe is enveloped, and where the subterranean forces which elevated those lofty chains still shake their foundations.

Graphic descriptions of nature, arranged under the guidance of leading ideas, are calculated not merely to please the imagination, but also to indicate to us the gradation of those impressions to which I have already alluded, from the uniformity of the sea beach or of the steppes of Siberia, to the rich luxuriance of the torrid zone. If we represent to ourselves Mount Pilatus placed on the Shreckhorn, or the Schneekoppe of Silesia on the summit of Mont Blanc, we shall not yet have attained to the height of one of the colossi of the Andes, the Chimborazo, whose height is twice that of Etna; and we must pile the Rigi or Mount Athos on the Chimborazo, to have an image of the highest summit of the Himalaya, the Dhavalagiri. But although the mountains of India far surpass in their astonishing elevation (long disputed, but now confirmed by authentic measurements) the Cordilleras of South America, they cannot, from their geographical position, offer that inexhaustible variety of phænomena by which the latter are characterized. The impression produced by the grandest scenes of nature does not depend exclusively on height. The chain of the Himalaya is situated far without the torrid zone. Scarcely is a single palm tree found so far north as the beautiful valleys of Kumaoon and Nepaul. In 28° and 34° of latitude, on the southern slope of the ancient Paropamisus, nature no longer displays that abundance of tree ferns, or arborescent grasses, of Heliconias, and of Orchideous plants, which, within the tropics, ascend towards the higher plateaux of the mountains. On the slopes of the Himalaya, under the shade of the Deodar and the large-leaved oak peculiar to these Indian Alps, the rocks of granite and of mica schist are clothed with forms closely resembling those which characterize Europe and Northern Asia; the species indeed are not identical, but they are similar in their aspect and physiognomy, comprising junipers, alpine birches, gentians, parnassias, and prickly species of Ribes. The chain of the Himalaya is also wanting in those imposing volcanic phænomena, which, in the Andes and in the Indian Archipelago, often reveal to the inhabitants, in characters of terror, the existence of forces residing in the interior of our planet. Moreover, on the southern declivity of the Himalaya, where the vapour-loaded atmosphere of Hindostan deposits its moisture, the region of perpetual snow descends to a zone of not more than 11,000 or 12,000 (11,700 or 12,800 Eng.) feet of elevation: thus the region of organic life ceases at a limit nearly three thousand feet below that which it reaches in the equinoctial portion of the Cordilleras.

But the mountainous regions which are situated near the equator possess another advantage, to which attention has not been hitherto sufficiently directed. They are that part of our planet in which the contemplation of nature offers in the least space the greatest possible variety of impressions. In the Andes of Cundinamarca, of Quito, and of Peru, furrowed by deep barrancas, it is permitted to man to contemplate all the families of plants and all the stars of the firmament. There, at a single glance, the beholder sees lofty feathered palms, humid forests of bamboos, and all the beautiful family of Musaceæ; and, above these tropic forms, oaks, medlars, wild roses, and umbelliferous plants, as in our European homes; there, too, both the celestial hemispheres are open to his view, and, when night arrives, he sees displayed together the constellation of the Southern Cross, the Magellanic clouds, and the guiding stars of the Bear which circle round the Arctic pole. There, the different climates of the earth, and the vegetable forms of which they determine the succession, are placed one over another, stage above stage; and the laws of the decrement of heat are indelibly written on the rocky walls and the rapid slopes of the Cordilleras, in characters easily legible to the intelligent observer. Not to weary the reader with details of phænomena which I long since attempted to represent graphically, I will here retrace only a few of the more comprehensive features which, in their combination, form those pictures of the torrid zone. That which, in impressions received solely by our senses, partakes of an uncertainty, similar to the effect of the misty atmosphere, which, in mountain scenery, renders at times every outline dim and indistinct, – when scrutinized by reasoning on the cause of the phænomena, may be clearly viewed and correctly resolved into separate elements, to each of which its own individual character is assigned; and thus, in the study of nature, as well as in its more poetic description, the picture gains in vividness and in objective truth by the well and sharply-marked lines which define individual features.

Not only is the torrid zone, through the abundance and luxuriance of its organic forms, most rich in powerful impressions, – it has also another advantage, even greater in reference to the chain of ideas here pursued, in the uniform regularity which characterizes the succession both of meteorological and of organic changes. The well-marked lines of elevation which separate the different forms of vegetable life, seem there to offer to our view the invariability of the laws which govern the celestial movements, reflected as it were in terrestrial phænomena. Let us dwell for a few moments on the evidences of this regularity, which is such, that it can even be measured by scale and number.

In the burning plains which rise but little above the level of the sea, reign the families of Bananas, of Cycadeæ, and of Palms, of which the number of species included in our floras of the tropical regions has been so wonderfully augmented in our own days by the labours of botanic travellers. To these succeed, on the slopes of the Cordilleras, in mountain valleys, and in humid and shaded clefts of the rocks, tree ferns raising their thick cylindrical stems, and expanding their delicate foliage, whose lace-like indentations are seen against the deep azure of the sky. There, too, flourishes the Cinchona, whose fever-healing bark is deemed the more salutary the more often the trees are bathed and refreshed by the light mists which form the upper surface of the lowest stratum of clouds. Immediately above the region of forests the ground is covered with white bands of flowering social plants, small Aralias, Thibandias, and myrtle-leaved Andromedas. The Alp rose of the Andes, the magnificent Befaria, forms a purple girdle round the spiry peaks. On reaching the cold and stormy regions of the Paramos, shrubs and herbaceous plants, bearing large and richly-coloured blossoms, gradually disappear, and are succeeded by a uniform mantle of monocotyledonous plants. This is the grassy zone, where vast savannahs (on which graze lamas, and cattle descended from those brought from the old world) clothe the high table lands and the wide slopes of the Cordilleras, whence they reflect afar a yellow hue. Trachytic rocks, which pierce the turf, and rise high into those strata of the atmosphere which are supposed to contain a smaller quantity of carbonic acid, support only plants of inferior organization – Lichens, Lecideas, and the many-coloured dust of the Lepraria, forming small round patches on the surface of the stone. Scattered islets of fresh-fallen snow arrest the last feeble traces of vegetation, and are succeeded by the region of perpetual snow, of which the lower limit is distinctly marked, and undergoes extremely little change. The elastic subterranean forces strive, for the most part in vain, to break through the snow-clad domes which crown the ridges of the Cordilleras; – but even where these forces have actually opened a permanent channel of communication with the outer air, either through crevices or circular craters, they rarely send forth currents of lava, more often erupting ignited scoriæ, jets of carbonic acid gas and sulphuretted hydrogen, and hot steam. The contemplation of this grand and imposing spectacle appears to have produced on the minds of the earlier inhabitants of those countries only vague feelings of astonishment and awe. It might have been imagined, that, as we have before said, the well-marked periodic return of the same phænomena, and the uniform manner in which they group themselves in ascending zones, would have rendered easier a knowledge of the laws of nature; but so far as history and tradition enable us to trace, we do not find that the advantages possessed by those favoured regions have been so improved. Recent researches have rendered it very doubtful whether the primitive seat of Hindoo civilization, one of the most wonderful phases of the rapid progress of mankind, were really within the tropics. Airyana Vaedjo, the ancient cradle of the Zend, was to the north-west of the Upper Indus; and after the separation of the Iraunians from the Brahminical institution, it was in a country bounded by the Himalaya and the small Vindhya chain, that the language which had previously been common to the Iraunians and Hindoos, assumed among the latter (together with manners, customs, and the social state), an individual form in the Magadha, or Madhya Desa. The extension of the Sanscrit language and civilization to its south-easternmost limit, far within the torrid zone, has been described by my brother, Wilhelm von Humboldt, in his great work on the Kawi, and other languages of kindred structure.

Notwithstanding the greater difficulties with which in more northern climates, the discovery of general laws was surrounded, by the excessive complication of phænomena, and the perpetual local variations, both in the movements of the atmosphere and in the distribution of organic forms, it was to the inhabitants of the temperate zone that a rational knowledge of physical forces first revealed itself. It is from this northern zone, which has shown itself favourable to the progress of reason, to the softening of manners, and to public liberty, that the germs of civilization have been imported into the torrid zone, either by the great movements of the migration of races, or by the establishment of colonies, very different in their institution in modern times from those of the Greeks and Phœnicians.

In considering the influences which the order and succession of phænomena may have exercised on the greater or less facility of recognizing their producing causes, I have indicated that important point in the contact of the human mind with the external world, at which there is added to the charm attendant on the simple contemplation of nature, the enjoyment springing from a knowledge of the laws which govern the order and mutual relations of phænomena. Thenceforth the persuasion of the existence of an harmonious system of fixed laws, which was long the object of a vague intuition, gradually acquires the certainty of a rational truth, and man, as our immortal Schiller has said – 'Amid ceaseless change, seeks the unchanging pole.'

In order to reascend to the first germ of this more thoughtful enjoyment, we need only cast a rapid glance on the earliest glimpses of the *Philosophy of Nature*, or of the ancient doctrine of the *Cosmos*. We find amongst the most savage nations (and my own travels have confirmed the truth of this assertion), a secret and terror-mingled presentiment of the unity of natural forces, blending with the dim perception of an invisible and spiritual essence manifesting itself through these forces, whether in unfolding the flower and perfecting the fruit of the food-bearing tree, or in the subterranean movements which shake the ground, and the tempests which agitate the atmosphere. A bond connecting the outward world of sense with the inward world of thought may be here perceived; the two become unconsciously confounded, and the first germ of a philosophy of nature is developed in the mind of man without the firm support of observation. Amongst nations least advanced in civilization, the imagination delights itself in strange and fantastic creations. A predilection for the figurative influences both ideas and language. Instead of examining, men content themselves with conjecturing, dogmatizing, and interpreting supposed facts which have never been observed. The world of ideas and of sentiments does not reflect back the image of the external world in its primitive purity. That which in some regions of the earth, and among a small number of individuals gifted with superior intelligence, manifests itself as the rudiment of natural philosophy, appears in other regions and among other races of mankind as the result of mystic tendencies and instinctive intuitions. It is in the intimate communion with external nature, and the deep emotions which it inspires, that we may also trace, in part, the first impulses to the deification and worship of the destroying and preserving powers of nature. At a later period of human civilization, when man, having passed through different stages of intellectual development, has arrived at the free enjoyment of the regulating power of reflection, and has learned, as it were by a progressive enfranchisement, to separate the world of ideas from that of the perceptions of sense, a vague presentiment of the unity of natural forces no longer suffices him. The exercise of thought then begins to accomplish its noble task, and, by observation and reasoning combined, the students of nature strive with ardour to ascend to the causes of phænomena.

The history of science teaches us how difficult it has been for this active curiosity always to produce sound fruits. Inexact and incomplete observations have led, through false inductions, to that great number of erroneous physical views which have been perpetuated as popular prejudices among all classes of society. Thus, by the side of a solid and scientific knowledge of phænomena, there has been preserved a system of pretended results of observation, the more difficult to shake because it takes no account of any of the facts by which it is overturned. This empiricism – melancholy inheritance of earlier times – invariably maintains whatever axioms it has laid down; it is arrogant, as is everything that is narrow-minded; whilst true physical philosophy, founded on science, doubts because it seeks to investigate thoroughly, – distinguishes between that which is certain and that which is simply probable, – and labours incessantly to bring its theories nearer to perfection by extending the circle of observation. This assemblage of incomplete dogmas bequeathed from one century to another, – this system of physics made up of popular prejudices, – is not only injurious because it perpetuates error with all the obstinacy of the supposed evidence of ill-observed facts, but also because it hinders the understanding from rising to the level of the great views of nature. Instead of seeking to discover the *mean* state, around which, in the midst of apparent independence and irregularity, the phænomena really and invariably oscillate, this false science delights in multiplying apparent exceptions to the dominion of fixed laws; and seeks, in organic forms and in the phænomena of nature, other marvels than those presented by internal progressive development, and by regular order and succession. Ever disinclined to recognize in the present the analogy of the past, it is always disposed to believe the order of nature suspended by perturbations, of which it places the seat, as if by chance, sometimes in the interior of the earth, sometimes in the remote regions of space.

It is the special object of this work to combat these errors, which, originating in vicious empiricism and defective induction, have survived even amongst the higher classes of society (often by the side of much literary cultivation), and thus to augment and ennoble the enjoyments which nature affords, by imparting a deeper view into her inner being. Such enjoyment (as our Carl Ritter has well shewn) is highest, when the whole mass of facts collected from different regions of the earth is comprehended in one glance, and placed under the dominion of intellectual combination. Increased mental cultivation, in all classes of society, has been accompanied by an increased desire for the embellishment of life through the augmentation of the mass of ideas, and of the means of generalizing those already received. Nor is such a desire unworthy of notice in reference to vague accusations, which represent the minds of men, in this our age, as occupied almost exclusively by the material interests of life.

I touch, almost with regret, on a fear which seems to me to arise either from a too limited view, or from a certain feeble sentimentality of character; I mean the fear that nature may lose part of her charms, and part of the magic of her power over our minds, when we begin to penetrate her secrets, – to comprehend the mechanism of the movements of the heavenly bodies, – and to estimate numerically the intensity of forces. It is true that, properly speaking, the forces of nature can only exert over us a magical power, by their action being to our minds enveloped in obscurity, and beyond the conditions of our experience. Even supposing that they would thus be the better fitted to excite our imagination, that assuredly is not the faculty which we should prefer to evoke, whilst engaged in those laborious subsidiary observations, which have for their ultimate object the knowledge of the grandest and most admirable laws of the universe. The astronomer occupied in determining, by the aid of the heliometer, or of the doubly refracting prism, the diameter of planetary bodies; or patiently engaged for years in measuring the meridian altitudes of certain stars and their distances apart, – or, searching for a telescopic comet among a crowded group of nebulæ, does not feel his imagination more excited, (and this is the very warrant of the accuracy of his work,) than the botanist who is intent on counting the divisions of the calix, the number of stamens, or the sometimes connected, and sometimes independent, teeth of the capsule of a moss. And yet it is these precise angular measurements, and minute organic relations, which prepare and open the way to the higher knowledge of nature and of the laws of the universe. The physical philosopher (as Thomas Young, Arago, and Fresnel,) measures with admirable sagacity the waves of light of unequal length, which by their interferences reinforce or destroy each other, even in respect to their chemical action; the astronomer armed with powerful telescopes, penetrates space, and contemplates the satellites of Uranus at the extreme confines of our solar system*, or (like Herschel, South, and Struve) decomposes faintly sparkling points into double stars, differing in colour and revolving round a common centre of gravity; the botanist discovers the constancy of the gyratory motion of the chara in the greater number of vegetable cells, and recognizes the intimate relations of organic forms in genera, and in natural families. Surely the vault of heaven studded with stars and nebulæ, and the rich vegetable covering which mantles the earth in the climate of palms, can scarcely fail to produce on these laborious observers impressions more imposing, and more worthy of the majesty of creation, than on minds unaccustomed to lay hold of the great mutual relations of phænomena. I cannot therefore agree with Burke when he says, that our ignorance of natural things is the principal source of our admiration, and of the feeling of the sublime. The illusion of the senses, for example, would have nailed the stars to the crystalline dome of the sky; but astronomy has assigned to space an indefinite extent; and if she has set limits to the great nebula to which our solar system belongs, it has been to shew us further and further beyond its bounds, (as our optic powers are increased,) island after island of scattered nebulæ. The feeling of the sublime, so far as it arises from the contemplation of physical extent, reflects itself in the feeling of the infinite which belongs

[* Written, the reader will remember, before the discovery of the planet Le Verrier. – Ed.]

to another sphere of ideas. That which it offers of solemn and imposing it owes to the connexion just indicated; and hence the analogy of the emotions and of the pleasure excited in us in the midst of the wide sea; or on some lonely mountain summit, surrounded by semi-transparent vaporous clouds; or, when placed before one of those powerful telescopes which resolve the remoter nebulæ into stars, the imagination soars into the boundless regions of universal space.

The mere accumulation of unconnected observations of details, without generalization of ideas, may no doubt have conduced to the deeply-rooted prejudice, that the study of the exact sciences must necessarily tend to chill the feelings, and to diminish the nobler enjoyment attendant on the contemplation of nature. Those who in the present day cherish such an error in the midst of rapid progress and new vistas of knowledge, fail in appreciating the value of every enlargement of the sphere of intellect, and of the tendency to rise from separate facts to results of a higher and more general character. To this fear of sacrificing, under the influence of scientific reasoning, something of the free enjoyment of nature, is often added another fear, namely, that the extent of the field of natural knowledge forbids to the greater part of mankind access to its enjoyments. It is true that in the midst of the universal fluctuation of forces, and of the seemingly inextricable network of organic life, alternately developed and destroyed, every step in the more intimate knowledge of nature leads to the entrance of new labyrinths; but to those engaged in the pursuit the very multiplicity of paths presenting themselves, the exciting effort of divining the true one, the presentiment of fresh mysteries to be unveiled, are all full of enjoyment. The discovery of each separate law indicates, even if it does not reveal, to the intelligent observer the existence of some other higher and more general law. Nature, according to the definition of a celebrated physiologist, and as the word itself indicated with the Greeks and Romans, is 'that which is in perpetual growth and progress, and which subsists in continual change of form and internal development'. The series of organic types presented to our view gradually gains enlargement and completeness, as previously unknown regions are penetrated and surveyed, – as living organic forms are compared with those which have disappeared in the great revolutions which our planet has undergone, – as microscopes have been rendered more perfect, and have been more extensively employed. Amid this immense variety of animal and vegetable forms and their transformations, we see, as it were, incessantly renewed the primordial mystery of all organic and vital development, the problem of metamorphosis, so happily treated by Goethe, – a solution corresponding to our intuitive desire to arrange all the varied forms of life under a small number of fundamental types. As observation, continually increasing, reveals yet more and more of the treasures of nature, man becomes imbued with the intimate conviction that, whether we regard the surface or the interior of the earth, the depths of the ocean, or the celestial spaces, the scientific conqueror will never complain with the Macedonian, that there are no fresh worlds to subject to his dominion. General considerations, whether relating to matter agglomerated in the celestial bodies, or to the distribution of organic life on the surface of the earth, are not only in themselves more attractive than special studies, but they also offer peculiar advantages to the greater number of men who can devote but little time to such occupations. The different branches of the study of natural history are only accessible in certain positions of social life; nor do they present the same charm in all seasons and in all climates. If our interest is fixed exclusively upon one class of objects, the most animated accounts of travellers from distant regions will have no attraction for us, unless they happen to touch on the chosen subjects of our studies.

As the history of nations, if it were possible that it could always successfully trace back events to their true causes, would no doubt solve to us the ever-recurring enigma of the alternately impeded and accelerated progress of human society; so, likewise, the physical description of the universe, the science of the Cosmos, if grasped by a powerful intellect, and based on the knowledge of all that has been discovered up to a given epoch, would remove many of those apparent contradictions, which the complication of phænomena, caused by a multitude of simultaneous perturbations, presents at the first glance.

The knowledge of laws, whether revealing themselves in the ebb and flow of the ocean, in the paths of comets, or in the mutual attractions of multiple stars, renders us more conscious of the 'calm of nature': and we might say that 'the discord of the elements', – that long-cherished phantasm of the human mind in its earlier and more intuitive contemplations – is gradually dispelled as science extends its empire. General views lead us habitually to regard each organic form as a definite part of the entire creation, and to recognize, in the particular plant or animal, not an isolated species, but a form linked in the chain of being to other forms living or extinct. They assist us in comprehending the relations which exist between the most recent discoveries, and those which have prepared the way for them. They enlarge the bounds of our intellectual existence, and while we ourselves may be living in retirement they place us in communication with the whole globe. Under their guidance we follow with eager interest the investigations of travellers and observers in every variety of climate. We accompany, in thought, the bold navigators of the polar seas; and, amidst the realm of perpetual ice, view with them that volcano of the antarctic pole, whose fires are seen from afar, even at the season when no night favours their brightness. The intellectual objects, both of these adventurous voyages, and of those stations of observations recently established in almost every latitude, are not strange to us; for we can comprehend some of the wonders of terrestrial magnetism, and general views lend an irresistible attraction to the consideration of those *magnetic storms*, which embrace the whole circumference of the earth at the same instant of time.

Let me be permitted to elucidate the preceding considerations, by touching on a few of those discoveries whose importance cannot be justly appreciated without some general knowledge of physical science. For this purpose I will select instances which have recently attracted much attention. Who, without some general knowledge of the ordinary paths of comets, could perceive how fruitful in consequences was Encke's discovery, by which a comet, that in its elliptic orbit never passes out of our planetary system, reveals the existence of an ethereal fluid obstructing its tangential force? A rapidly-spreading half-knowledge brings scientific results ill understood into the conversation of the day, and the supposed danger of collision between two heavenly bodies, or of a deterioration of climate from cosmical causes, are again brought forward in a new and more deceptive form. Clear views of nature, even if merely historical, are sufficient preservatives against these dogmatizing fancies. The history of the atmosphere, and of the annual variations of its temperature, extends already sufficiently far back to shew that these consist in repeated small oscillations around the mean temperature of a station, thereby dispelling the exaggerated fear of a general and progressive deterioration of the climates of Europe. Encke's comet, which is one of the three interior comets, completing its course in 1,200 days, must, from its position and the form of its path, be as harmless to the inhabitants of our globe as Halley's great comet of 1759 and 1835, which has a period of seventy-six years. The path of another comet of short period, Biela's, which completes its course in six years, does, indeed, intersect the earth's path, but it can only approach us when its perihelion coincides with our winter solstice.

The quantity of heat received by a planetary body (the unequal distribution of which determines the great meteorological processes of our atmosphere) depends conjointly on the light-evolving power of the sun (*i. e.* the nature of its surface, or the state of its gaseous covering), and on the relative positions of the sun and planet. There are, indeed, periodical variations, which the form of the earth's orbit and the obliquity of the ecliptic undergo in obedience to the universal law of gravitation; but these changes are so slow, and restricted within such small limits, that their thermic effects would hardly be appreciable by our present thermometric instruments in many thousands of years. Supposed cosmical causes of diminished temperature or moisture, or of epidemic diseases, – of which the idea has been entertained in modern times, as well as in the middle ages, – are, therefore, wholly beyond the range of our actual experimental knowledge.

I may also borrow from physical astronomy other examples, of which the grandeur and the interest cannot be felt without some general knowledge of the forces which animate the universe, and may adduce the elliptic revolutions of many thousands of double stars, or suns, around each other, or rather around their common centre of gravity, revealing the existence of the Newtonian attraction in those distant worlds; – the periodical abundance or paucity of spots on the sun (openings in the opaque but luminous envelope of the solid nucleus); – and the periodic appearance, observed for some years past about the 12th or 13th of November and the 10th or 11th of August, of countless multitudes of shooting stars, moving with planetary swiftness, which probably form a belt of asteroids intersecting the orbit of the earth.

Descending from the skies to the earth, we may notice how the oscillations of a pendulum in air (the theory of which has been perfected by Bessel's acuteness) have thrown light on the internal density, I might say on the degree of solidification, of our planet; they have also served, in a certain sense, to sound terrestrial depths, conveying information respecting the geological nature of strata otherwise inaccessible. In this manner, as well as in others, we are enabled to trace a striking analogy between the production of granular rocks in lava currents which have flowed down the slopes of active volcanoes, and those granites, porphyries, and serpentines, which, issuing from the interior of the earth, have broken, as eruptive rocks, through the secondary strata, modifying them by contact, hardening them by the introduction of silex, or changing them into dolomite, or causing in them the formation of crystals of various kinds. The elevation of sporadic islets, of domes of trachyte, and of cones of basalt, by the elastic forces which emanate from the fluid interior of our planet, conducted the first geologist of our age, Leopold von Buch, to the theory of the elevation of continents and of mountain chains generally. This action of subterranean forces, in breaking through and elevating sedimentary rocks, of which the coast of Chili has offered a recent example, shows us how the oceanic shells which M. Bonpland and myself found on the ridge of the Andes, at an elevation of more than 4,600 metres (about 15,100 English feet), may have been conveyed there, not by a rise of the ocean, but by volcanic agencies elevating into ridges the heat-softened crust of the globe.

I use the term volcanic agency in its most general sense, applying it, whether on the earth or on her satellite the moon, to that reaction of the interior of a planet on its crust, which on our globe at least has been very different at different epochs. Those who are unacquainted with the experiments which show the increase of internal heat at increasing depths in the earth to be so rapid, that granite is supposed to be in a state of fusion about twenty geographical miles below the surface, cannot have a clear comprehension of the causes of the simultaneity of volcanic eruptions occurring at great distances apart, – of the extent and intersection of circles of commotion in earthquakes, – of the constancy of temperature and of chemical composition in thermal springs during many years of observation, – or of the difference of temperature of Artesian wells of unequal depth. And yet the knowledge of the internal terrestrial heat throws a faint light on the early history of our planet, by showing the possibility of a generally prevalent tropical climate, arising from the heat issuing from crevices in the recently oxydized crust of the globe; a state of things in which the temperature of the atmosphere would depend far more on the reaction of the interior of the planet upon its crust, than on its relative position in respect to the central body or sun.

The cold zones of the earth present to the researches of the geologist many buried products of a tropical climate: – in the coal formations, upright stems of palms, coniferæ, and tree ferns, goniatites, and fishes with rhomboidal enamelled scales; – in the Jura limestone, colossal skeletons of crocodiles and long-necked Plesiosauri, Planulites, and stems of Cycadeæ; – in the chalk, small Polythalamia and Bryozoa, in part identical with some of our living marine animals; – in tripoli or polishing slate, in semi-opal, and in the substance called mountain meal, agglomerated masses of fossil infusoria, such as Ehrenberg's all-animating microscope has disclosed to us; – and lastly, in transported soils and in caves, bones of hyenas, lions, and elephantine Pachydermata. An enlarged knowledge of other natural phænomena renders these objects no longer an occasion for mere barren curiosity and wonder, but for intelligent study and profound meditation.

The multiplicity of diverse objects, which I have here purposely crowded together, leads directly to the question, whether general views of nature can possess a sufficient degree of clearness, without a deep and earnest application to separate studies, whether of descriptive natural history, of geology, of physics, or of mathematical astronomy? In attempting a reply, we must discriminate carefully between the teacher who undertakes the selection, combination, and presentation of the results, and the person who receives them, when thus presented, as something not sought out by himself, but communicated to him by another. To the first, some exact knowledge of the special is indispensably necessary; before proceeding to the generalization of ideas, he should have wandered long in the domains of the separate sciences, and have himself observed, experimented, and measured. I cannot deny that where positive knowledge is wanting in the reader, general results, which in their mutual connection lend so great a charm to the contemplation of nature, are not susceptible of being always developed with equal clearness; but, nevertheless, I permit myself the pleasure of thinking, that in the work which I am preparing, the greater number of the truths presented will admit of being exhibited without the necessity of always reascending to fundamental principles and ideas. The picture of nature thus drawn, even though some part of its outline may be less sharply defined, will still possess truth and beauty, and will still be suited to enrich the intellect, to enlarge the sphere of ideas, and to nourish and vivify the imagination.

Our scientific literature has been reproached, and perhaps not without justice, with not sufficiently separating the general from the special – the view of that already gained, from the

ALEXANDER VON HUMBOLDT

long recital of the means which have led to it. This reproach
even led the greatest poet of our age to exclaim with impatience, that 'the Germans have the gift of rendering the
sciences inaccessible'. Whilst the scaffolding stands, it
obscures the effect of the finished building. Who can doubt
that the uniformity of figure observed in the distribution of
our continental masses, by which they taper towards the south,
and spread out in breadth towards the north (a fact or law on
which the distribution of climates, the prevailing direction of
atmospheric and oceanic currents, and the great extension of
tropical forms into the southern temperate zone so materially
depend), may be fully apprehended, together with its consequences, without any acquaintance with those geodesical
and astronomical determinations, by means of which the precise forms and dimensions of the continents have been delineated in our maps? Thus, too, the physical description of the
earth teaches us that the length of the equatorial axis of our
planet exceeds that of its polar axis by a certain number of
miles, and informs us of the mean equality of the compression
of the northern and southern hemispheres, without the necessity of relating in detail the measurements of degrees and the
pendulum experiments, by means of which we have arrived at
the knowledge that the true figure of the earth is that of an
irregular ellipsoid of revolution, and is reflected in the irregularity of the movements of the earth's satellite, the moon.

Enlarged views of physical geography have been essentially
advanced by the appearance of the admirable work ('Erdkunde
im Verhältniss zur Natur and zur Geschichte des Menschen,
oder allgemeine vergleichende Geographie') in which Carl
Ritter has characterized so powerfully the physiognomy of our
globe, and has shewn the influence of its external configuration, both on the physical phenomena which take place on its
surface, and on the migration of nations, their laws, their
manners, and their history.

France possesses an immortal work, Laplace's 'Exposition
du Système du Monde', in which the results of the highest
mathematical and astronomical labours of all preceding ages
are presented, detached from all details of demonstration. In

this work the structure of the heavens is reduced to the simple solution of a great problem in mechanics; and yet, assuredly, it has never been accused of incompleteness, or want of profoundness. The separation of the general from the special not only renders it possible to embrace at one view, with greater clearness, a wider field of knowledge, but it also lends to the treatment of natural science a character of greater elevation and grandeur. By the suppression of details the masses are better seen, and the reasoning faculty is enabled to grasp that which might otherwise escape our limited powers of comprehension.

The high degree of improvement which the last half century has witnessed in the study of all the separate branches of natural science, but especially in those of chemistry, general physics, geology, and descriptive natural history, is eminently favourable to the presentation of general results. When first looked at singly and superficially all phænomena appear unconnected; as observations multiply and are combined by reflection, and as a deeper insight into natural powers is obtained, more and more points of contact and links of mutual relation are discovered, and it becomes more and more possible to develop general truths with conciseness, without superficiality. In an age of such rapid and brilliant progress as the present, it is a sure criterion of the number and value of the discoveries to be hoped for in any particular science, if, though studied with great assiduity and sagacity, its facts still appear for the most part unconnected, with little mutual relation, or even in some instances in seeming contradiction with each other. Such is the kind of expectation at present excited by meteorology, by many parts of optics, and, since the admirable labours of Melloni and Faraday, by the study of radiant heat and of electro-magnetism. The circle of brilliant discoveries has here still to be run through; although the Voltaic pile already reveals the wondrous connection of electrical, magnetical, and chemical phænomena. Who will venture to affirm, that we yet know with precision that part of the atmosphere which is not oxygen, or that thousands of gaseous substances affecting our organs may not be mixed with the nitrogen? or who will say that we already know even the whole number of the forces which pervade the universe?

It is not the purpose of this work to attempt to reduce all sensible phænomena to a small number of abstract principles, having their foundation in pure reason only. The physical cosmography of which I attempt the exposition does not aspire to the perilous elevation of a pure rational science of nature. Leaving to others, who may perhaps adventure on them with more success, these depths of a purely speculative philosophy, my essay on the Cosmos consists of *physical geography*, joined with the *description of the heavenly bodies in space*: its aim is to present a view of the material universe, which may rest on the experimental foundation of the facts registered by science, compared and combined by the operations of the intellect. It is within these limits alone that the undertaking can harmonize with the wholly objective tendency of my mental disposition, and with the labours which have occupied my long scientific career. The unity which I seek to attain in the development of the great phænomena of nature, is similar in kind to that which historical compositions may offer. All that belongs to the specialities of the actual, – to its individualities, variabilities, and accidents, whether in the form and connection of natural objects and phænomena, or in the struggle of man with the elements, or of nations with each other, – does not admit of being *rationally constructed*, that is to say, of being deduced from ideas alone. I venture to think that a like degree of empiricism attaches to the description of the material universe, and to civil history; but in reflecting on physical phænomena and historical events, and in reasoning backward to their causes, we recognize more and more the grounds of that ancient belief, that the forces inherent in matter, and those which regulate the moral world, exert their action under the government of a primordial necessity, and in recurring courses of greater or less period. It is this necessity, this occult but permanent connection, this periodical recurrence in the progressive development of forms, of phænomena and of events, which constitute nature obedient to the first-imparted impulse of the Creator. Physical science, as the name imports, limits itself to the explanation of the phænomena of the material world by the properties of matter. All beyond this belongs not to the domain of the physics of the universe, but to a higher class of ideas. The discovery of laws, and their progressive generalization, are the objects of the experimental sciences. Kant, who has never been deemed an irreligious philosopher, has traced with rare sagacity the limits of physical explanations, in his celebrated 'Essay on the Theory and Structure of the Heavens', published at Königsberg, in 1755.

The study of a science which promises to lead us over the wide range of creation, may be likened to a journey in a distant country. Before undertaking it, we are inclined to measure, perhaps not without mistrust, both our own strength and that of the guide who offers to conduct us. But our fears may be lessened by remembering how in our days, an increasing knowledge of the mutual relation of phænomena, leading to the attainment of general results, has more than kept pace with the vast increase of separate observations. The chasms which divide facts from each other are rapidly filling up; and it has often happened that facts observed at a distance have thrown a new and unexpected light on others nearer home, which had long seemed to resist all efforts at explanation. Plants and animals which had long appeared insulated, become connected with others by the discovery of intermediate forms before unknown; and the geography of beings endowed with organic life receives completeness, as we behold species, genera, and whole families, peculiar to one continent, reflected, so to speak, in analogous forms, or, as it were, in *equivalents*, in the opposite continent. These transitions may be traced, in the sometimes fuller, sometimes more rudimentary, development of particular parts, or in their different relative importance in the balance of forces, or in the junction of distinct organs, or sometimes in resemblances to intermediate forms, not permanent, but only characteristic of particular phases of a normal development. Passing to the consideration of inorganic bodies, and to examples which characterize strongly the advances of modern geology, we see how, according to the grand views of Elie de Beaumont, chains of mountains, dividing different climates, floras, and nations, reveal to us their *relative* age, by the nature of the sedimentary rocks uplifted by them, and by the directions which they follow over the long crevices produced by the action of the forces which have elevated in ridges portions of the crust of the globe. Relations of superposition of trachyte and of syenitic porphyry, of diorite and of serpentine, which remain doubtful if studied in the auriferous soils of Hungary, in the platinum district of the Oural, or on the South Western slope of the Siberian Altai, are clearly made out by the aid of observations on the high table-lands of Mexico and Antioquia, and in the unhealthy ravines of the Choco. The most important of the materials which in modern times have afforded a solid basis for physical geography have not been accumulated by chance. In conformity with its characteristic tendencies, our age has recognized, that facts obtained by observations in different regions of the earth, can only be expected to prove fruitful in results, when the traveller is previously acquainted with the state and wants of the science which he seeks to advance, and when his researches are conducted under the guidance of sound ideas, and some insight into the character and connection of natural phænomena.

By means of the happy, though often too easily satisfied tendency towards general conceptions, a tendency dangerous only in its abuse, a considerable portion of the results of natural knowledge may become the common property of all educated persons, producing a sound information very different both in substance and in form from those superficial compilations, which contained the sum of what, up to the close of the last century, was complacently designated by the unsuitable term of *popular scientific knowledge*. I take pleasure in persuading myself that it is possible for scientific subjects to be presented in language, grave, dignified, and yet animated; and that those who are able to escape occasionally from the restricted circle of the ordinary duties of civil life, and regret to find that they have so long remained strangers to nature, may thus have opened to them access to one of the noblest enjoyments which the activity of the rational faculties can afford to man. The study of general natural knowledge awakens in us as it were new perceptions which had long lain dormant; we enter into a more intimate communion with the external world, and no longer remain without interest or sympathy for that which at once promotes the industrial progress and intellectual ennoblement of man.

The clearer our insight into the connection of phænomena, the more easily shall we emancipate ourselves from the error of those, who do not perceive that for the intellectual cultivation and for the prosperity of nations, all branches of natural knowledge are alike important; whether the measuring and describing portion, or the examination of chemical constituents, or the investigation of the physical forces by which all matter is pervaded. It has not been uncommon presumptuously to depreciate investigations arbitrarily characterized as 'purely theoretic', forgetting that in the observation of a phænomenon which shall at first sight appear isolated, may lie concealed the germ of a great discovery. When Galvani first stimulated the nervous fibre by the contact of two dissimilar metals, his immediate contemporaries could not have foreseen that the voltaic pile would discover to us in the alkalis, metals of a silvery lustre, easily inflammable, and so light as to float in water; that it would become the most important instrument of chemical analysis, and at the same time a thermoscope and a magnet. When Huygens first applied himself, in 1678, to the enigma of the phænomena of polarization of light exhibited in doubly-refracting spar, and observed the difference between the two portions into which a beam of light divides itself in passing through such a crystal, it was not foreseen that through the admirable sagacity of a physical philosopher of the present day, the phænomena of *chromatic polarization* would lead us to discern, by means of a minute fragment of Iceland spar, whether the light of the sun proceeds from a solid nucleus, or from a gaseous covering; whether comets are self-luminous, or reflect borrowed light.

An equal appreciation of all parts of natural knowledge is an especial requirement of the present epoch, in which the material wealth and increasing prosperity of nations are in great measure based on a more enlightened employment of natural products and forces. The most superficial glance at the present condition of European states shews, that those which linger in the race cannot hope to escape the partial diminution, and perhaps the final annihilation, of their resources. It is with nations as with nature, which, according to a happy expression of Goethe, knows no pause in unceasing movement, development, and production, and has attached a curse to standing still. The danger to which I have alluded must be averted by the earnest cultivation of natural knowledge. Man can only act upon nature, and appropriate her forces to his use, by comprehending her laws, and knowing those forces in relative value and measure. Bacon has said that, in human societies, knowledge is power, – both must rise or sink together. Knowledge and thought are at once the delight and the prerogative of man; and they are also a part of the wealth of nations, and often afford to them an abundant indemnification for the more sparing bestowal of natural riches. Those states which remain behind in general industrial activity, in the selection and preparation of natural substances, in the application of mechanics and chemistry, – and where a due appreciation of such activity fails to pervade all classes, – must see their prosperity diminish; and that the more rapidly as neighbouring states are meanwhile advancing, both in science and in the industrial arts, with, as it were, renewed and youthful vigour.

The improvement of agriculture in the hands of freemen, and on properties of moderate extent, – the flourishing state of the mechanical arts freed from the trammels of the spirit of corporation, – commerce augmented and animated by the multiplied contact of nations with each other, – are brilliant results of the general progress of intelligence, and of the amelioration of political and civil institutions in which that progress is reflected. The picture presented by modern history ought to convince those who seem tardy in apprehending the instruction which it is fitted to convey. Nor let it be feared that the predilection for industrial progress and for those branches of natural science most immediately connected with it, which characterizes the age in which we live, has any necessary tendency to check intellectual exertion in the fair fields of classical antiquity, history, and philosophy; or to deprive of the life-giving breath of imagination, the arts and the literature which embellish life. Where all the blossoms of civilization unfold themselves with vigour under the shelter of wise laws and free institutions, there is no danger of the development of the human mind in any one direction proving prejudicial to it in others. Each offers to the nation precious fruits, – those which furnish necessary subsistence and comfort, and are the foundation of material wealth, – and those fruits of creative fancy which, far more enduring than that wealth, transmit the glory of the nation to the remotest posterity. The Spartans, in spite of the Doric severity of their mode of thought, 'prayed the Gods to grant them the beautiful with the good'.

As in that higher sphere of thought and feeling to which I have just alluded, in philosophy, poetry, and the fine arts, the primary aim of every study ought to be an inward one, that of enlarging and fertilizing the intellect; so the direct aim of science should ever be the discovery of laws, and of the principles of unity, order, and connection, which everywhere reveal themselves in the universal life of nature. But by that happy connection, whereby the useful is ever linked with the true, the exalted, and the beautiful, science thus followed for her own sake will pour forth abundant, overflowing streams, to enrich and fertilize that industrial prosperity, which is a conquest of the intelligence of man over matter.

The influence of mathematical and physical knowledge on national prosperity, and on the present condition of Europe, requires here only a passing allusion: the well-nigh boundless course which we have to travel over, warns me that it would ill become me to digress more widely from the leading object of our undertaking, – the contemplation of nature as a whole. Accustomed to distant excursions, I have perhaps fallen into the error of describing the path before us as more smooth and pleasant than it will be really found, as those are wont to do who love to guide others to the summit of lofty mountains: they praise the view, even when great part of the distant prospect is hidden by the clouds; knowing, indeed, that this half transparent misty veil is itself not altogether without a secret charm for the imagination. I too ought to fear, that from the height to which this physical description of the universe aspires, many parts of the wide horizon may appear dimly lighted and imperfectly defined, – that much of the prospect may remain vague and obscure, and this not only by reason of the want of connection arising from the imperfect state of some branches of science, but also still more, (and how, in so comprehensive a work, should I not willingly own it?) because of the deficiencies of the guide who has imprudently ventured to attempt to scale these lofty summits.

The object of this introductory discourse has been less to represent the importance of natural knowledge, which is admitted by all, and may well dispense with any eulogium, than to shew how, without prejudice to the thorough and fundamental study of separate branches, a higher point of view may be indicated, from whence all the forms and the forces of nature may be contemplated in intimate and living connection.

The idea of physical geography, extended so as to embrace all that we know of the material creation in space as well as on our own globe, passes into that of physical cosmography; the one term is moulded upon the other. But the science of the Cosmos, as I understand it, is not the mere encyclopædic aggregation of the most general and important results, extracted from separate works on natural history, physics, and astronomy. Such results are only to be used as materials, and in so far as they illustrate the concurrent action of the various forces in the universe, and the manner in which they reciprocally call forth or limit each other. The distribution of organic types in different regions and climates (*i. e.* the geography of plants and animals,) differs as widely from descriptive botany and zoology, as does a geological knowledge of the globe from mineralogy properly so called. The physical description of the universe is not therefore to be confounded with *encyclopædias of the natural sciences*. In the work before us it is proposed to consider partial facts only in their relation to the whole. The higher the point of view here indicated, the more the study requires a peculiar mode of treatment, and to be presented in animated and picturesque language.

But thought and language are of old intimately allied: if the language employed lends to the presentation grace and clearness, if by its organic structure, its richness, and happy flexibility, it favours the attempt to delineate the phænomena of nature, it at the same time reacts almost insensibly on thought itself, and breathes over it an animating influence. *Words*, therefore, are more than signs and forms; and their mysterious and beneficent influence is there most powerfully manifested, where the language has sprung spontaneously from the minds of the people, and is on its own native soil. Proud of my country, whose intellectual unity is the firm foundation of every manifestation of her power, I look with joy to these privileges of my native land. Highly favoured indeed is he, who, in attempting an animated representation of the phænomena of the universe, is permitted to draw from the depths of a language, which through the elevation and free exercise of powerful thought, in the domain of creative fancy no less than in that of searching reason, has for centuries exerted so powerful an influence over the minds and the destinies of men.

IN THE PRECEDING discourse, I have sought to make manifest, and to illustrate by examples, how greatly the enjoyment
of nature, varying as it does in the inward sources from which
it springs, may be heightened by a clear insight into the connection of phænomena, and of the laws by which they are
regulated. I have now to examine more particularly the spirit
of the method of exposition, and to indicate the limits of the
science of physical cosmography, such as I have conceived it,
and have now endeavoured to display it, after many years of
preparatory studies in many regions of the earth. Would, that
in so doing, I might flatter myself with the hope of thereby
justifying the bold title of my work, and freeing it from the
reproach of presumption!

Before entering on the view of nature, which forms the
larger portion of the present volume, I would touch on some
general considerations intimately connected with each other,
with the nature of our knowledge of the external world,
and with the relations which this knowledge presents, at
different epochs of history, to the different phases of the intellectual cultivation of nations. These considerations will have
for their objects: –

1. The idea and the limits of physical cosmography as a distinct and separate science.

2. A rapid review of the known phænomena of the universe,
under the form of a general view of nature.

3. The influence of the external world on the imagination
and feelings. This, in modern times, has acted as a powerful
incitement to the study of the natural sciences, through the
instrumentality of animated descriptions of distant regions,
descriptive poetry (a branch of modern literature), of landscape painting when it seizes the characteristic physiognomy

of vegetable or of geological forms, and by the cultivation and arrangement of exotic plants, in well-contrasted groups.

4. The history of the contemplation of nature, or the progressive development of the idea of the Cosmos, with the exposition of the historical and geographical facts which have led to the systematic connection of the phænomena as they are thus presented.

The higher the point of view from which all the phænomena are to be regarded in this study, the more necessary it is to circumscribe it within its just limits, and to distinguish it from all analogous and auxiliary ones. The physical description of the universe is founded on the contemplation of all the material creation (whether substances or forces) co-existing in space. For man, as an inhabitant of the earth, it may be ranged under two leading divisions; the telluric and the celestial. I will pause a few moments on the first of these, (or on that portion of the science of the Cosmos which concerns the Earth,) in order to illustrate the independence of the study, and the nature of its relation to general physics, descriptive natural history, geology, and comparative geography. An encyclopædic aggregation of these would no more constitute the telluric portion of the Cosmos, than a mere dry enumeration of the philosophical opinions prevailing in different ages, would deserve to be called the history of philosophy.

The confusion between the boundaries of closely allied branches of study has been the greater, because for centuries different portions of our empirical knowledge have been designated by terms which are either too comprehensive, or too restricted, for the notions they were intended to convey: and which have besides the disadvantage of having borne a very different sense in the languages of classical antiquity from which they have been borrowed. The terms of physics, physiology, natural history, geology, and geography, arose and grew into general use long before clear ideas were entertained of the diversity of the objects which those sciences ought to embrace, and consequently of their respective limits. Such is the influence of long habit upon language, that in one of the nations of Europe most advanced in civilization, the word 'physic' is applied to medicine; and in a Society of justly deserved and universal renown, writings on technical chemistry, geology, and astronomy experipirically treated, (all branches of purely experimental science), are classed under the general title of 'Philosophical Transactions'. The attempt has often been made, and almost always in vain, to substitute new and more appropriate names for those ancient terms, – vague, it is true, but which, however, are now generally understood. These changes have been proposed, for the most part, by those who have occupied themselves with the general classification of all branches of human knowledge; from the great Encyclopædia (Margarita Philosophica) of Gregory Reisch, Prior of the Chartreuse of Freiburg towards the end of the fifteenth century, to Lord Bacon; from Bacon to D'Alembert; and still more recently to a sagacious physicist of our own time, André-Marie Ampère. The selection of an inappropriate Greek nomenclature has, perhaps, been even more prejudicial to the last of these attempts, than the abuse of the binary division and the excessive multiplication of groups.

The physical description of the universe as an object of external sense, does indeed require the aid of general physics and of descriptive natural history; but the consideration of the material creation, all the parts of which are linked together by mutual connection, under the figure of a natural whole animated and moved by inward forces, gives to the science which now occupies us a peculiar character. Physical science dwells on the general properties of matter; it is an abstract representation of the manifestations of physical forces, and in the work in which its earliest foundations were laid, in the eight books of Physics of Aristotle, all the phænomena of nature are depicted as the moving vital activity of a universal force or power.

The telluric portion of the physical description of the universe, to which I preserve the old and expressive title of *physical geography*, treats of the distribution of magnetism on our planet in its relations of intensity and direction, but does not teach the laws of magnetic attraction and repulsion, or the means of eliciting powerful electro-magnetic effects, whether transitorily or permanently. Physical geography describes in bold and general outlines the compact or indented configuration of continents, and the distribution of their masses in both hemispheres, – a distribution which powerfully influences the differences of climates and the most important meteorological processes of the atmosphere; it seizes the predominant character of mountain chains, whether parallel, or transverse and intersecting, and whether belonging to the same or to different epochs and systems of elevation; it examines the *mean* height of continents above the present surface of the sea, or the position of the centre of gravity of their volume; the relation of the highest summits of the great chains to the general line of their crests, to the vicinity of the sea, and to the mineral character of the rocks of which they consist. It depicts to us the eruptive rocks as active principles of movement, traversing, uplifting, and inclining at various angles, the passive sedimentary rocks. It considers volcanoes either as isolated, or ranged in single or in double series, and extending their sphere of action to various distances, either by means of long narrow bands of erupted rocks, or by earthquakes operating in circles which widen or contract in the course of centuries. It describes the strife of the liquid element with the firm land; it shews the features which are common to all great rivers in the upper and in the lower portion of their course, and how they become subject to bifurcation. It characterizes rivers either as breaking their way through great mountain chains, or following, for a time, a course parallel to them, either close to their foot or at a considerable distance, according to the influence which the elevation of the mountain system may have exercised on the neighbouring plains. It is only the general results of comparative orography and hydrography which belong to the science whose proper limits I am endeavouring to trace, and not the enumeration of our loftiest mountains, active volcanoes, or rivers with the extent of their watershed and the number of their tributaries. All these details belong to geography properly so called, in its most restricted sense. We here consider phænomena only in their mutual connection, and in their relations to the different zones of our planet, and to its general

physical constitution. The specialities either of inanimate substances or of organic beings, classed according to analogy of
form and composition, do indeed form a highly interesting
subject of study, but quite foreign to the present work.

Particular descriptions of countries are, it is true, the most
available materials for a general physical geography; but the
most careful successive accumulation of such descriptions
would be as far from affording a true picture of the general
conformation of the irregular surface of our planet, as a series
of all the floras of different regions would be from forming
what I should designate by the term of a 'Geography of
Plants'. It is the work of the intellect, by comparing and
combining isolated observations, to extract from the specialities of organic formation (morphology and the descriptive
natural history of plants and animals,) that which is common
to them in regard to their climatic distribution; – to investigate
the numerical laws, or the proportion of certain forms or particular families to the whole number of species; – to assign
the latitude or geographical position of the zone where (in the
plains) each of these forms reaches its maximum number of
species, and its highest organic development. These considerations will lead us to perceive the manner in which the picturesque character of the landscape in different latitudes, and
the impression which it produces on the mind, depend principally on the laws of the geography of plants, or the relative
number and more vigorous growth of those which predominate in the general mass. The systematically-arranged cata-
logues, to which the too pompous name of 'Systems of
Nature' was formerly given, present to us an admirable connection and arrangement by analogies of structure, whether
completely developed, or (according to views of an evolution
in spirals) in the different phases passed through in vegetables,
by the leaves, bracteas, calix, blossom, and fruit, and in animals
by their cellular and fibrous tissues, and their articulations or
less perfectly developed parts. But these ingeniously classified
so called 'systems of nature', do not shew us organic beings as
they are grouped over the surface of our planet, in districts,
zones of latitude, or of elevation, and according to other

climatic influences arising from general and often very distant causes. But, as we have already said, the final aim of physical geography is to recognize unity in the vast variety of phænomena, and by the exercise of thought and the combination of observations, to discern that which is constant through apparent change. In the exposition of the terrestrial portion of the Cosmos, we may sometimes find occasion to descend to very special facts, but it will only be for the purpose of recalling the connection existing between the laws of the actual distribution of organic beings over the surface of the globe, and the laws of the ideal classification by natural families, analogy of internal organization, and progressive evolution.

It follows from these discussions on the limits of different sciences, and particularly from the distinction which it is necessary to draw between descriptive botany (morphology) and the geography of plants, that, in the physical description of the globe, the innumerable multitude of organized bodies, which form so large a portion of the beauties of creation, ought to be considered rather with reference to *zones of habitation*, and to the differently inflected *isothermal curves*, than according to principles of gradation in the development of their internal organization. But botany and zoology, which are the two branches of the descriptive natural history of organized bodies, are the fruitful sources from whence we draw the materials, without which the study of the relations and connection of phænomena would want a solid foundation.

We will here add an important observation. The first general glance over the vegetation of an extensive portion of a continent, shews us an assemblage of dissimilar forms, – gramineæ, orchideæ, coniferæ, and oaks: we perceive these families and genera, instead of being locally associated, scattered apparently as it were by chance: but this irregular dispersion is only apparent; and it is the province of physical geography to shew that vegetation everywhere presents constant numerical relations in the development of its forms and types; that, in the same climates, species which are wanting in one country, are replaced in a neighbouring one by other species of the same families, according to a law of substitution, which seems to belong to the yet unknown relations of organized beings; and by which the numerical proportion of particular great families to the whole mass of the phænogamous floras in adjoining countries is maintained. There is thus revealed in the multitude of organic forms by which these regions are peopled a principle of unity, a primitive plan of distribution. There is also discovered in each zone, diversified according to the families of plants, a slow but continuous action on the aerial ocean, an action which depends on the influence of light – that primary and essential condition of all organic vitality on the solid or liquid surface of our planet. It might be said, according to a fine expression of Lavoisier, that the marvel of the ancient mythus of Prometheus is incessantly renewed before our eyes.

When we apply the course which it is proposed to follow in the exposition of the physical description of the earth, to the sidereal part of the science of the Cosmos, or to the description of what is known to us of the regions of space, and of the heavenly bodies which they contain, we shall find our task remarkably simplified. If, according to ancient but inexact forms of nomenclature, we distinguish between *physics*, or the general consideration of matter, its forces, and its movements, – and *chemistry*, or the consideration of the different nature of substances, their elementary composition, and their attractions not depending on relations of mass or the laws of gravitation, – we must of course recognize that the telluric portion of our study embraces both *physical* and *chemical* processes. By the side of the fundamental force of gravitation, we discover around us on the earth the action of other forces, taking effect either when the particles of matter are in contact, or at exceedingly small distances apart; to which forces we give the name of *chemical affinity*. Under various modifications, by electricity, by heat, by condensation in porous bodies, or by the contact of an intermediate substance, these forces are incessantly in action in inorganic matter, and in the tissues of animals and plants. But, in the regions of space, we are only cognizant by direct observation of physical phænomena, and among these (excepting in the case of the small asteroids, which appear to us under the form of aerolites or shooting stars,) we know with certainty only those effects which depend on the quantitative relations of matter or the distribution of masses; and which may therefore be contemplated as governed by simple dynamic laws. Effects due to specific differences, or to heterogeneous qualities of matter, do not as yet enter into our calculations of the celestial mechanics.

It is only through the phænomena of light (the propagation of luminous waves) and the effects of gravitation, that the inhabitants of our earth enter into relation with matter in space, whether existing in spheroids, or in a dispersed form. The existence of a periodical influence of the sun or moon on the variations of terrestrial magnetism is still highly problematical. The only direct experimental knowledge which we possess of any of the specific properties or qualities of matter not belonging to our planet, is derived from the fall of the aerolites or meteoric stones, already alluded to. Their direction and enormous velocity of projection (a velocity wholly planetary) render it more than probable, that these masses, enveloped in vapours and reaching the earth in a state of high temperature, are small heavenly bodies, which the attraction of our planet has caused to deviate from their previous path. The aspect so familiar to us of these asteroids, and the analogy which their composition presents to the minerals of which the crust of our globe is formed, are indeed very striking. The inference to which they point appears to me to be, that the planetary and other masses were agglomerated in rings of vapour, and afterwards in spheroids, under the influence of a central body; and that being originally integral parts of the same system, they consist of substances chemically identical. Pendulum experiments, and especially those made by Bessel with so high a degree of precision, confirm the Newtonian axiom, that the acceleration occasioned by the attraction of the earth is identical in bodies the most heterogeneous in composition, – viz., water, gold, quartz, granular limestone, and portions of different aerolites. Purely astronomical observations add their testimony to the proofs afforded by the pendulum. The almost identical results found for the mass of

Jupiter, from its influence on his own satellites, on Encke's comet of short period, and on the small planets, Vesta, Juno, Ceres, and Pallas, equally teach that, as far as our observations reach, the attraction of gravitation is determined solely by the quantity of matter.

This absence of all perception (derived either from observation or from theoretical considerations) of any heterogeneous qualities of matter, gives to celestial mechanics a high degree of simplicity. The study of the immense regions of space being directed by the laws of motion only, the sidereal portion of the Cosmos draws from the pure and abundant sources of mathematical astronomy, as the terrestrial portion does from those of physics, chemistry, and organic morphology. But the domain of the three last-named sciences embraces phænomena so complex, and, to the present time, so little susceptible of the application of rigorously exact methods, that the physical knowledge of the globe cannot boast of the certainty and simplicity in the exposition of facts and of their mutual connection, which characterize the celestial portion of the Cosmos. This difference may be the true reason why, in the early times of the intellectual cultivation of the Greeks, the natural philosophy of the Pythagoreans was directed to the heavenly bodies in space, rather than to the earth and her productions; and became through Philolaus, and subsequently through the analogous views of Aristarchus of Samos, and Seleucus of Erythrea, of far greater avail towards the knowledge of the true system of the universe, than the natural philosophy of the Ionic school could ever become to the physical knowledge of the earth. Giving less heed to the properties and specific differences of the various kinds of matter, the great *statical* school, in its Doric gravity, preferred to turn its regards towards all that relates to measure, form, and number; while the Ionic school dwelt on the qualities of matter, its real or supposed transformations, and its relations of origin. It was reserved to the powerful genius, and to the at once profoundly philosophical and practical mind of Aristotle, to enter equally deeply and successfully into the world of abstract ideas, and into that of the rich diversity of material substances, of organized beings, and animated existence.

Several highly esteemed treatises on physical geography have prefixed to them an introductory astronomical section, in which the earth is first considered in its planetary dependence, and in its relation to the solar system. This order of proceeding is opposite to that which I propose to follow. The dignity of the physical description of the universe requires that the sidereal portion, which Kant has called the natural history of the heavens, should not be made subordinate to the terrestrial portion. In the science of the Cosmos, according to the expression of Aristarchus of Samos – that ancient herald of the Copernican doctrine – the sun (together with all his satellites) is viewed but as one of the countless host of stars. It is then with these celestial bodies with which space is peopled, that the physical description of the universe ought to begin. It should commence with such a graphic sketch of the universe (such a true *map of the world*) as was traced by the bold hand of the elder Herschel. If, notwithstanding the smallness of our planet, the telluric portion of the present work occupies the largest space, and is treated with the greatest fulness, this arises only from the unequal amount of our knowledge of that which is within and that which is beyond our reach. The subordination of the celestial to the terrestrial portion is met with, however, in the great geographical work of Bernard Varenius, written in the middle of the seventeenth century, who distinguishes, with great acuteness, between general and special geography; subdividing the first into an absolute, or properly *terrestrial* portion (when treating of the surface of the earth in its different zones), and a relative or planetary one, when considering the solar and lunar relations of our planet. It is a permanent glory to Varenius, that his 'General and Comparative Geography' was found capable of fixing, in a high degree, the attention of Newton. In the imperfect state, in the time of Varenius, of the auxiliary branches of knowledge from which his resources had to be drawn, it was not possible that the execution of the work should correspond to the greatness of the undertaking. It was reserved to our own time to see comparative geography, in its most extended sense, and even embracing its influence on the history of man, treated in a masterly manner by my own countryman, Carl Ritter.

The enumeration of the more important results of the astronomical and physical sciences, which in the Cosmos radiate towards a common centre, may justify, in some degree, the title which I have ventured to affix to this work, written in the late evening of my life. I might add, that the title is perhaps more adventurous than the enterprise itself, circumscribed within the limits which I have proposed. In all my previous investigations, I have hitherto avoided, as much as possible, the introduction of new names to express general ideas. When I have attempted to enlarge our nomenclature, it has been solely in the specialities of descriptive botany and zoology, when objects observed for the first time rendered new names necessary. The expression of physical cosmography, or a physical description of the universe, is formed on that of physical geography, or a physical description of the earth, which has long been used. The powerful genius of Descartes has left us some fragments of a great work, which he intended should appear under the title of 'Monde', and for which he had begun to study special subjects, and even human anatomy. The little used, but precise expression of the *science of the Cosmos*, recalls to the inhabitant of our globe that we are treating of a wider horizon, of the assemblage of all the material things with which space is filled, from the remotest nebulæ, to the climatic distribution of the thin vegetable tissues of variously coloured lichens, which clothe the surface of rocks.

In every language, views entertained in the infancy of nations have led to a confusion of the ideas of *earth* and *world*: the common expressions of 'voyages round the world', 'map of the world', 'new world', are instances of this confusion. The more accurate and more noble expressions* of 'system of the world', 'creation of the world', and others of a similar nature,

---

* Our language does not possess all the expressions referred to by M. de Humboldt. We have no direct English equivalents for the expressive German terms 'Weltgebäude', 'Weltraum', and 'Weltkörper'.   Translator

relate either to the whole of the bodies with which celestial space is filled, or to the origin of the entire universe.

It was natural that, amidst the extreme variability of the phænomena presented by the surface of the earth and the surrounding aerial ocean, men should have been impressed by the aspect of the vault of heaven and the regular and uniform movements of the sun and planets. The word *Cosmos*, which, in its primitive signification in the Homeric times, expressed the ideas of *ornament* and *order*, was subsequently applied to the order and harmony observed in the movements of the heavenly bodies; then to those bodies generally; and finally, to the universe itself. It is asserted by Philolaus, – the genuine fragments of whose writings have been commented on with so much sagacity by M. Böekh, – that, according to the general testimony of antiquity, 'Pythagoras was the first who used the word Cosmos to express the order which reigns in the universe, or the world or universe itself.' From the Italic school of philosophy, the term used in this sense passed into the language of the poets of nature, Parmenides and Empedocles, and thence into that of prose writers. We need not enter here into the distinction, which, following the Pythagorean views, Philolaus draws between Olympus, Uranus, and Cosmos, or how the latter word, used in the plural, has been applied individually to celestial bodies (the planets) circling round the central 'hearth', or focus of the world, or to 'world-islands', or groups of stars. In my work, the word Cosmos is employed as signifying the heavens and the earth, or the whole world of sense, or the material universe; agreeably to general Hellenic usage subsequently to the time of Pythagoras, and in conformity with its definition by the unknown author of the treatise, entitled 'De Mundo', which was long erroneously attributed to Aristotle. If scientific names had not long varied from their true linguistic meaning, the present work might properly have been entitled '*Cosmography*', divided into *Uranography* and *Geography*. The desire of imitating the Greeks led the later Romans, in their feebler philosophical essays, to give the signification of universe to the word *mundus*, the primary meaning of which was merely that of *ornament*, without including order or regularity in the arrangement of parts. The introduction of this technical term, in the same double signification as the Greek word Cosmos, was probably due to Ennius, who was a follower of the Italic school, and translated the writings of Epicharmus, or one of his imitators, on the Pythagorean Philosophy. A physical *history* of the universe, in the extended sense of the word, ought, if materials for writing it existed, to trace the variations to which the Cosmos has been subjected in the course of ages, from those new stars which have suddenly become visible or have disappeared in the firmament, from nebulæ dissolving or condensing towards their centres, – to the first cryptogamic vegetation on the surface of the recently cooled crust of the globe, or that which now clothes the coral reef newly risen above the ocean. On the other hand, the object of a physical *description* of the universe is to present a view of all that co-exists in space, and of the simultaneous action of natural forces, with the resulting phænomena. But if we wish to comprehend existing nature well, we cannot separate entirely and absolutely the consideration of the present state of things, from that of the successive phases through which they have previously passed. The mode of formation, or of production, is often an important element of their character. Nor is it in the organic world only that matter is constantly undergoing change, and dissolving to be formed into new combinations: the globe on which we live also reveals the knowledge of an earlier state: the strata of sedimentary rocks, – which compose a large portion of its crust, present to us earlier forms of organic life, which have now almost entirely disappeared; and these forms are associated in groups, successively replacing each other. The different superimposed strata thus present to us the buried faunas and floras of different epochs. In this sense the description of nature cannot be separated from its history; for, in studying the present, the geologist, in tracing the mutual relations of the facts which come before him, is conducted back to ages long past: this intermixture of past and present is in some respects analogous to that which may be observed in the study of languages, where the etymologist finds traces of successive grammatical developments, leading him back to the primitive state of the idiom reflected as it were in forms of speech now in use. In the material world, this reflex of the past is the clearer, from our now seeing similar eruptive and sedimentary rocks in process of formation. The particular forms of domes of trachyte, basaltic cones, bands of amygdaloid with long parallel pores, and white deposits of pumice with black scoriæ intermixed, give in the eye of the geologist a peculiar kind of animation to the landscape, acting on his imagination as traditional monuments of an earlier world. Their form is their history.

The sense in which the Greeks and Romans employed the word *history* shows that they too had the intimate persuasion, that, to form a complete idea of the actual condition of things, it was necessary to consider them in their succession. It is not, however, in the definition given by Verrius Flaccus, but in the zoological writings of Aristotle, that the word *history* presents itself as signifying an exposition of the results of experience and observation. The elder Pliny's physical description of the world bears the title of 'Natural History'; and in his nephew's letters, the nobler appellation of 'History of Nature'. The earlier Greek historic writers scarcely separated the description of countries from the relation of events of which they had been the theatre. In their writings, physical geography and history were long gracefully and pleasingly interwoven, until the increasing complexity of political interests, and the agitations of civil life, expelled the geographical element from the history of nations, and obliged it to become the subject of a separate study.

It remains to examine, whether we can hope, by the operation of thought, to reduce the immense diversity of phænomena comprehended by the Cosmos, to a unity of principle, similar to that presented by the evidence of what are specially called 'rational truths'. In the present state of our empirical knowledge at least, we dare not entertain such a hope. Experimental sciences, founded on observation of the external world, cannot aspire to completeness; the nature of things and the imperfections of our organs are alike opposed to it. We shall never succeed in exhausting the inexhaustible riches of nature, and no generation of men will ever be able to boast of having comprehended all phænomena. It is only by distributing them into groups, that we have been able to discover in some the empire of laws, grand and simple as Nature herself. Doubtless, the bounds of this empire will be enlarged as the physical sciences gradually enlarge their domain, and become more perfect. Brilliant examples of such progress have appeared in our own times, in the phænomena of electro-magnetism, and in those of the propagation of luminous waves and of radiant heat. The doctrine of evolution shows us how, in organic development, all that is formed is sketched out as it were beforehand, and how the tissues of both vegetable and animal matter are uniformly produced by the multiplication and transformation of cells.

The generalization of laws which were first applied to smaller groups of phænomena advances by successive gradations, and their empire is extended, and their evidence strengthened, so long as the reasoning process is directed to really analogous phænomena. But as soon as dynamic views no longer suffice, and the specific properties of heterogeneous matter come into play, fear may be entertained lest, in the too obstinate pursuit of laws, we may arrive at impassable chasms: the principle of unity fails, and the guiding clue breaks, when, in tracing the effects of natural forces, we come to specific kinds of action. The law of equivalents, and of definite numerical proportions in compound substances, so happily recognized by modern chemists and proclaimed under the antique form of atomic symbols, remains hitherto isolated, and unsubjected to the mathematical laws of motion and gravitation.

Natural productions, which are objects of direct observation, may be logically distributed in classes, orders, and families. Such distribution does no doubt give greater clearness to descriptive natural history; but the study of organized bodies, arranged in linear connection, though it gives greater unity and simplicity to the distribution of groups, cannot rise to the height of a classification founded on a sole principle of composition and internal organization. As different gradations are presented by natural laws, according as they embrace narrower or wider circles of phænomena, so there are successive steps in empirical investigation. It begins by single perceptions, which are afterwards classed according to their analogy or dissimilarity. Observation is succeeded, at a much later epoch, by experiment, in which phænomena are made to arise under conditions previously determined on by the experimentalist, guided by preliminary hypotheses, or a more or less just intuition of the true connection of natural objects and forces. The results obtained by observation and experiment lead by the path of induction and analogy to the discovery of empirical laws; and these successive phases in the application of the human intellect have marked different epochs in the life of nations. It has been by adhering closely to this inductive path, that the great mass of facts has been accumulated which now forms the solid foundation of the natural sciences.

Two forms of abstraction govern the whole of this class of knowledge; viz. relations of *quantity*, comprehending the ideas of number and magnitude; and relations of *quality*, embracing the specific properties of heterogeneous matter. The first of these forms, more accessible to the exercise of thought, belongs to the domain of mathematics; the other, more difficult to seize, and apparently more mysterious, to that of chemistry. In order to submit phænomena to calculation, recourse is had to a hypothetical construction of matter by a combination of molecules and atoms whose number, form, position, and polarity, determine, modify, and vary the phæno-mena. The suppositions of imponderable matter, and vital forces peculiar to each mode of organization, have compli-cated and perplexed the view. Meanwhile, the prodigious mass of empirical knowledge is enlarging with increasing rapidity; and investigating reason tries at times, with varying success, to break through ancient forms and symbols invented to effect the subjection of rebellious matter to mechanical constructions.

We are yet very far from the time, even supposing it possible that it should ever arrive, when a reasonable hope could be entertained of reducing all that is perceived by the senses to the unity of a single principle. The complication of the problem, and the immeasurable extent of the Cosmos, seem to forbid the expectation of such success in the field of natural philosophy being ever achieved by man; but the partial solution of the problem – the tendency towards a general comprehension of the phænomena of the universe – does not the less continue to be the high and enduring aim of all natural investigation. For my own part, faithful to the character of my earlier writings, and to that of the labours which have occupied my scientific career, in measurements, experiments, and in investigation of facts, I limit myself in the present work to the sphere of empirical conceptions. It is the only ground on which I feel myself able to move without a sense of insecurity. This mode of treating an aggregation of observed facts does not exclude their combination by reasoning, their arrangement under the guidance of leading ideas, their generalization wherever it can be justly effected, and the constant tendency to the discovery of laws. A purely rational conception of the universe, founded on principles of speculative philosophy, would no doubt assign to the science of the Cosmos a still more elevated aim. I am far from blaming efforts which I have not myself attempted, solely because their success hitherto has been extremely doubtful. Contrary to the wishes and counsels of those profound and powerful thinkers who have given new life to speculations belonging to antiquity, systems of a philosophy of nature have in our country (Germany) turned men's minds for a time from the graver studies of the mathematical and physical sciences. The intoxication of supposed conquests already achieved, – a novel and extravagantly symbolical language, – a predilection for formulas of scholastic reasoning more contracted than were ever known to the middle ages, – have, through the youthful abuse of noble powers, characterized the short saturnalia of a purely ideal science of nature. I say abuse of powers, for superior minds, which have embraced both speculative studies and the experimental sciences, took no part in these saturnalia. The results obtained by serious investigations in the path of induction, cannot be at variance with a true philosophy of nature. If there is contradiction, the fault must be either in the unsoundness of the speculation, or in the exaggerated pretensions of empiricism, which thinks that it has proved by its experiments more than is really deducible from them.

The natural world may be opposed to the intellectual, or nature to art, taking the latter term in its higher sense as embracing the manifestations of the intellectual power of man; but these distinctions (which are indicated in the most polished languages) must not be suffered to lead to such a separation of the domain of physics from that of the intellect, as would reduce the physics of the universe to a mere assemblage of empirical specialities. Science only begins for man from the moment his mind lays hold of matter, – when he strives to subject the mass accumulated by experience to rational combinations: science is mind applied to nature. The external world only exists for us so far as we receive it within ourselves, and as it shapes itself within us into the form of a contemplation of nature. As intelligence and language, thought and the signs of thought, are united by secret and indissoluble links, so in like manner, and almost without our being conscious of it, the external world and our ideas and feelings melt into each other. 'External phænomena are translated,' as Hegel expresses it, in his Philosophy of History, 'in our internal representation of them.' The objective world, received into our thoughts and reflected, is subjected to the unchanging, necessary, and all-conditioning forms of our intellectual being. The activity of the mind exerts itself on the elements furnished to it by the perceptions of the senses. Thus, in the youth of nations, there manifests itself in the simplest intuition of natural facts, in the first efforts made to comprehend them, the germ of the philosophy of nature. These tendencies vary, and are more or less powerful, according to national individualities of character, turn of mind, and stage of mental culture, and whether attained amidst scenery fitted to excite and charm, or to repress and chill the imagination.

History has preserved the record of the varied and hazardous attempts which have been made to comprehend all phænomena in a theoretical conception, and to discover in them a single natural force pervading, setting in motion, and transforming all matter. In classical antiquity the earliest of these attempts are found in the treatises of the Ionic school on the principles of things; treatises in which the whole of nature was subjected to rash speculation, with only an extremely scanty basis of observation. This ardour for deductively determining the essence of things and their mutual connection from an ideal construction and purely rational principles, has gradually subsided, with the increasingly brilliant development of the natural sciences resting on the firm support of observation. Nearer to our own time, the mathematical portion of natural philosophy has received the grandest and most admirable enlargement. The method, and the instrument (analysis), have both been perfected together. We are of opinion, that what has been conquered by means so diverse, – by the ingenious application of atomic suppositions, – by the more general and more intimate study of phænomena, – and by new and improved apparatus, – is the common property of mankind; and cannot now, any more than in the times of the ancients, be withdrawn from the free exercise of speculative thought. It cannot be denied that the results of experience may have been sometimes undervalued in the course of such processes; nor ought we to be too much surprised if in the perpetual fluctuations of speculative views, as the author of Giordano Bruno has ingeniously remarked, 'most men see in philosophy only a succession of passing meteors; and even the grander forms under which she has revealed herself partake in the popular estimation of the fate of comets, which they regard as belonging not to the class of permanent celestial bodies, but to that of mere passing igneous vapours'. But the abuse of speculative thought, and the false paths into which it has sometimes strayed, ought not to lead to a view, dishonouring to intellect, which would regard the world of ideas as essentially a region of phantom-like illusions, and philosophy as a hostile power, by which the accumulated treasures of experimental knowledge are threatened. It is unsuitable to the spirit of the age to reject with distrust any attempted generalization of views, or investigation in the path of reasoning and induction. Nor is it consonant with a due estimation

of the dignity of the human intellect, and the relative importance of the faculties with which we are endowed, to condemn,
at one time, severe reason applied to the investigation of
causes and their connection, and at another, that exercise of
the imagination which is often precursive to discoveries, – for
the achievement of which the imaginative power is indeed an
essential auxiliary.

COSMOS

A PHYSICAL DESCRIPTION OF THE UNIVERSE
VOL. II

INCITEMENTS TO THE STUDY OF NATURE.

Action of the external world on the imaginative faculty, and the reflected image produced – Poetic descriptions of nature – Landscape painting – Cultivation of those exotic plants which determine the characteristic aspect of the vegetation in the countries to which they belong.

WE NOW PASS from the domain of objects to that of sensations. The principal results of observation, in the form in which, stripped of all additions derived from the imagination, they belong to a pure scientific description of nature, have been presented in the preceding volume. We have now to consider the impression which the image received by the external senses produces on the feelings, and on the poetic and imaginative faculties of mankind. An inward world here opens to the view, into which we desire to penetrate, not, however, for the purpose of investigating – as would be required if the philosophy of art were our aim – what in æsthetic performances belongs essentially to the powers and dispositions of the mind, and what to the particular direction of the intellectual activity, – but that we may trace the sources of that animated contemplation which enhances a genuine enjoyment of nature, and discover the particular causes which, in modern times especially, have so powerfully promoted, through the medium of the imagination, a predilection for the study of nature, and for the undertaking of distant voyages.

I have alluded, in the preceding volume, to three kinds of incitement more frequent in modern than in ancient times; 1st, the æsthetic treatment of natural scenery by vivid and graphical descriptions of the vegetable and animal world, which is a very modern branch of literature; 2d, landscape painting, so far as it portrays the characteristic aspect of vegetation; and, 3d, the more extended cultivation of tropical plants, and the assemblage of contrasted exotic forms. Each of these subjects might be historically treated and investigated at some length; but it appears to me better suited to the spirit and object of my work, to unfold only a few leading ideas relating to them, – to recall how differently the contemplation of nature has acted on the intellect and the feelings of different races of men, and at different periods of time, – and to notice how, at epochs when there has been a general cultivation of the mental faculties, the severe pursuit of exact knowledge, and the more delicate workings of the imagination, have tended to interpenetrate and blend with each other. If we would describe the full majesty of nature, we must not dwell solely on her external phænomena, but we must also regard her in her reflected image – at one time filling the visionary land of physical myths with graceful phantoms, and at another developing the noble germs of imitative art.

I here limit myself to the consideration of incitements to a scientific study of nature; and, in so doing, I would recall the lessons of experience, which tell us how often impressions received by the senses from circumstances seemingly accidental, have so acted on the youthful mind as to determine the whole direction of the man's course through life. Childish pleasure in the form of countries and of seas, as delineated in maps; the desire to behold those southern constellations which have never risen in our horizon; the sight of palms and of the cedars of Lebanon, figured in a pictorial bible, may have implanted in the spirit the first impulse to travels in distant lands. If I might have recourse to my own experience, and say what awakened in me the first beginnings of an inextinguishable longing to visit the tropics, I should name George Forster's descriptions of the islands of the Pacific – paintings, by Hodge, in the house of Warren Hastings, in London, representing the banks of the Ganges – and a colossal dragon tree in an old tower of the Botanic Garden at Berlin. These objects, which I here cite as exemplifications taken from fact, belong respectively to the three classes above noticed, viz. to descriptions of nature flowing from a mind inspired by her contemplation, to imitative art in landscape painting, and to the immediate view of characteristic natural objects. Such incitements are, however, only influential where general intellectual cultivation prevails, and when they address themselves to dispositions suited to their reception, and in which a particular course of mental development has heightened the susceptibility to natural impressions.

IT HAS OFTEN been said, that if delight in nature were not
altogether unknown to the ancients, yet that its expression was
more rare and less animated among them than in modern
times. Schiller, in his considerations on naïve and sentimental
poetry, remarks, that 'when we think of the glorious scenery
which surrounded the ancient Greeks, and remember the free
and constant intercourse with nature in which their happier
skies enabled them to live, as well as how much more accord-
ant their manners, their habits of feeling, and their modes of
representation, were with the simplicity of nature, of which
their poetic works convey so true an impress, we cannot but
remark with surprise how few traces we find amongst them of
the sentimental interest with which we moderns attach ourselves to natural scenes and objects. In the description of
these, the Greek is indeed in the highest degree exact, faithful,
and circumstantial, but without exhibiting more warmth of
sympathy than in treating of a garment, a shield, or of a suit
of armour. Nature appears to interest his understanding rather
than his feelings; he does not cling to her with intimate
affection and sweet melancholy, as do the moderns.' Much as
there is that is true and excellent in these remarks, they are
far from being applicable to all antiquity, even in the sense
ordinarily attached to the term; I cannot, moreover, but regard
as far too limited, the restriction of antiquity (as opposed to
modern times), exclusively to the Greeks and Romans: a profound feeling of nature speaks forth in the earliest poetry of
the Hebrews and of the Indians; – in nations, therefore, of
very different descent, Semitic, and Indo-Germanic.

We can only infer the feeling with which the ancients
regarded nature from the portions of its expression which

have reached us in the remains of their literature; we must therefore seek for such passages the more diligently, and pronounce upon them the more circumspectly, as they present themselves but sparingly in the two great forms of epical and lyrical poetry. In Hellenic poetry, at that flowery season of the life of mankind, we find, indeed, the tenderest expression of the love and admiration of nature mingling with the poetic representation of human passion, in actions taken from legendary history; but specific descriptions of natural scenes or objects appear only as subordinate; for in Grecian art all is made to concentre within the sphere of human life and feeling.

The description of nature in her manifold diversity, as a distinct branch of poetic literature, was altogether foreign to the ideas of the Greeks. With them the landscape is always the mere background of a picture, in the foreground of which human figures are moving. Passion breaking forth in action riveted their attention almost exclusively; the agitation of politics, and a life passed chiefly in public, withdrew men's minds from enthusiastic absorption in the tranquil pursuit of nature. Physical phænomena were always referred to man by supposed relations or resemblances either of external form or of inward spirit. It was almost exclusively by such applications that the consideration of nature was thought worthy of a place in poetry in the form of comparisons or similitudes, which often present small detached pictures, full of objective vividness and truth.

At Delphi, pæans to spring were sung – probably to express men's joy that the privations and discomforts of winter were past. A natural description of winter has been interwoven (may it not be by a later Ionian rhapsodist?) with the 'Works and Days' of Hesiod. This poem, full of a noble simplicity, but purely didactic in its form, gives advice respecting agriculture, and directions for different kinds of work and profitable employment, together with ethical exhortations to a blameless life. Its tone rises to a more lyrical character when the poet clothes the miseries of mankind, or the fine allegorical mythus of Epimetheus and Pandora, with an anthropomorphic garb. In Hesiod's Theogony, which is composed of various ancient and dissimilar elements, we find repeatedly (as, for example, in the enumeration of the Nereides), natural descriptions veiled under the significant names of mythic personages. In the Bœotian bardic school, and generally in all ancient Greek poetry, the phænomena of the external world are introduced only by personification under human forms.

But if it be true, as we have remarked, that natural descriptions, whether of the richness and luxuriance of southern vegetation, or the portraiture in fresh and vivid colours of the habits of animals, have only become a distinct branch of literature in very modern times, it was not that sensibility to the beauty of nature was absent, where the perception of beauty was so intense, – or the animated expression of a contemplative poetic spirit wanting, where the creative power of the Hellenic mind produced inimitable master works in poetry and in the plastic arts. The deficiency which appears to our modern ideas in this department of antiquity, betokens not so much a want of sensibility, as the absence of a prevailing impulse to disclose in words the feeling of natural beauty. Directed less to the inanimate world of phænomena than to that of human action, and of the internal spontaneous emotions, the earliest and the noblest developments of the poetic spirit were epical and lyrical. These were forms in which natural descriptions could only hold a subordinate, and, as it were, an accidental place, and could not appear as distinct productions of the imagination. As the influence of antiquity gradually declined, and as its blossoms faded, the rhetorical spirit shewed itself in descriptive as well as in didactic poetry; and the latter, which, in its earlier philosophical and semi-priestly character, had been severe, grand, and unadorned, as in Empedocles' 'Poem of Nature', gradually lost its early simple dignity.

I may be permitted to illustrate these general observations by a few particular instances. Conformably to the character of the Epos, natural scenes and images, however charming, appear in the Homeric songs always as mere incidental adjuncts. 'The shepherd rejoices in the calm of night, when the winds are still; in the pure ether, and in the bright stars shining in the vault of heaven; he hears from afar the rushing of the suddenly-swollen forest torrent, bearing down earth and trunks of uprooted oaks.' The fine description of the sylvan loneliness of Parnassus, and of its dark, thickly-wooded rocky valleys, contrasts with the smiling pictures of the many-fountained poplar groves of the Phæacian Islands, and especially with the land of the Cyclops, 'where swelling meads of rich waving grass surround the hills of undressed vines'. Pindar, in a vernal dithyrambus recited at Athens, sings 'the earth covered with new flowers, what time in Argive Nemea the first opening shoot of the palm announces the approach of balmy spring'; he sings of Etna, 'the pillar of heaven, the nurse of enduring snows'; but he quickly hastens to turn from the awful form of inanimate nature, to celebrate Hiero of Syracuse, and the Greeks' victorious combats with the powerful Persian nation.

Let us not forget that Grecian scenery possesses the peculiar charm of blended and intermingled land and sea; the breaking waves and changing brightness of the resounding ocean, amidst shores adorned with vegetation, or picturesque cliffs richly tinged with aerial hues. Whilst to other nations the different features and the different pursuits belonging to the sea and to the land appeared separate and distinct, the Greeks, not only of the islands, but also of almost all the southern portion of the mainland, enjoyed the continual presence of the greater variety and richness, as well as of the higher character of beauty, given by the contact and mutual influence of the two elements. How can we imagine that a race so happily organized by nature, and whose perception of beauty was so intense, should have been unmoved by the aspect of the wood-crowned cliffs of the deeply-indented shores of the Mediterranean, the varied distribution of vegetable forms, and, spread over all, the added charms dependent on atmospheric influences, varying by a silent interchange with the varying surfaces of land and sea, of mountain and of plain, as well as with the varying hours and seasons? Or how, in the age when the poetic tendency was highest, can emotions of the mind thus awakened through the senses have failed to resolve themselves into ideal contemplation? The Greeks, we know, imagined the vegetable world connected by a thousand mythical relations with the heroes and the gods: avenging chastisement followed injury to the sacred trees or plants. But while trees and flowers were animated and personified, the prevailing forms of poetry in which the peculiar mental development of the Greeks unfolded itself, allowed but a limited space to descriptions of nature.

Yet, a deep sense of the beauty of nature breaks forth sometimes even in their tragic poets, in the midst of deep sadness, or of the most tumultuous agitation of the passions. When Œdipus is approaching the grove of the Furies, the chorus sings, 'the noble resting-place of glorious Colonos, where the melodious nightingale loves to dwell, and mourns in clear and plaintive strains': it sings 'the verdant darkness of the thick embowering ivy, the narcissus bathed in the dews of heaven, the golden beaming crocus, and the ineradicable, ever fresh-springing olive tree'. Sophocles, in striving to glorify his native Colonos, places the lofty form of the fate-pursued, wandering king, by the side of the sleepless waters of the Cephisus, surrounded by soft and bright imagery. The repose of nature heightens the impression of pain called forth by the desolate aspect of the blind exile, the victim of a dreadful and mysterious destiny. Euripides also takes pleasure in the picturesque description of 'the pastures of Messenia and Laconia, refreshed by a thousand fountains, under an ever mild sky, and through which the beautiful Pamisus rolls his stream'.

Bucolic poetry, born in the Sicilian fields, and popularly inclined to the dramatic, has been called, with reason, a transitional form. These pastoral epics on a small scale depict human beings rather than scenery: they do so in Theocritus, in whose hands this form of poetry reached its greatest perfection. A soft elegiac element is indeed everywhere proper to the idyll, as if it had arisen from 'the longing for a lost ideal'; or as if in the human breast a degree of melancholy were ever blended with the deeper feelings which the view of nature inspires.

When the true poetry of Greece expired with Grecian liberty, that which remained became descriptive, didactic, instructive; – astronomy, geography, and the arts of the hunter and the fisherman, appeared in the age of Alexander and his successors as objects of poetry, and were indeed often adorned with much metrical skill. The forms and habits of animals are described with grace, and often with such exactness that our modern classifying natural historians can recognize genera and even species. But in none of these writings can we discover the presence of that inner life – that inspired contemplation – whereby to the poet, almost unconsciously to himself, the external world becomes a subject of the imagination. The undue preponderance of the descriptive element shews itself in the forty-eight cantos of the Dionysiaca of the Egyptian Nonnus, which are distinguished by a very artfully constructed verse. This poet takes pleasure in describing great revolutions of nature; he makes a fire kindled by lightning on the wooded banks of the Hydaspes burn even the fish in the bed of the river; he tells how ascending vapours produce the meteorological processes of storm and electric rain. Nonnus of Panopolis is inclined to romantic poetry, and is remarkably unequal; at times spirited and interesting, at others verbose and tedious.

A more delicate sensibility to natural beauty shews itself occasionally in the Greek Anthology, which has been handed down to us in such various ways, and from such different periods. In the pleasing translation by Jacobs, all that relates to plants and animals is collected in one section: these passages form small pictures, most commonly, of only single objects. The plane tree, which 'nourishes among its boughs the grape swelling with rich juice', and which, in the time of Dionysius the Elder, reached the banks of the Sicilian Anapus from Asia Minor, through the Island of Diomedes, occurs perhaps but too often; still, on the whole, the antique mind shews itself in these songs and epigrams as more inclined to dwell on animal than on vegetable forms.

The vernal idyll of Meleager of Gadara in Cœlo-Syria is a noble and more important composition. I am unwilling, were it only for the ancient renown of the locality, to omit all notice of the description of the wooded Vale of Tempe given by

Ælian, probably from an earlier notice by Dicearchus. It is the most detailed description of natural scenery by a Greek prose writer which we possess; and, although topographic, is at the same time picturesque. The shady valley is enlivened by the Pythian procession (theoria), 'which gathers from the sacred laurel the reconciling bough'.

In the latest Byzantine epoch, towards the end of the fourth century, we find descriptions of scenery frequently introduced in the romances of the Greek prose writers; as in the pastoral romance of Longus, in which, however, the author is much more successful in the tender scenes taken from life, than in the expression of sensibility to the beauties of nature.

It is not the object of these pages to introduce more than such few references to particular forms of poetic art, as may tend to illustrate general considerations respecting the poetic conception of the external world; and I should here quit the flowery circle of Hellenic antiquity, if, in a work to which I have ventured to give the name of 'Cosmos', I could pass over in silence the description of nature, with which the pseudo Aristotelian book of the Cosmos (or 'Order of the Universe') commences. This description shews us 'the terrestrial globe adorned with luxuriant vegetation, abundantly watered, and, which is most worthy of praise, inhabited by thinking beings'. The rhetorical colouring of this rich picture of nature, so unlike the concise and purely scientific manner of the Stagirite, is one of the many indications by which it has been judged not to have been his composition. Conceding this point, and ascribing it to Appuleius, or to Chrysippus, or to any other author, its place is fully supplied by a brief but genuine fragment which Cicero has preserved to us from a lost work of Aristotle. 'If there were beings living in the depths of the earth, in habitations adorned with statues and paintings, and every thing which is possessed in abundance by those whom we call fortunate, and if these beings should receive tidings of the dominion and power of the gods, and should then be brought from their hidden dwelling places to the surface which we inhabit, and should suddenly behold the earth, and the sea, and the vault of heaven; should perceive the broad expanse of the clouds and the strength of the winds; should admire the sun in his majesty, beauty, and effulgence; and, lastly, when night veiled the earth in darkness, should gaze on the starry firmament, the waxing and waning moon, and the stars rising and setting in their unchanging course, ordained from eternity, they would, of a truth, exclaim, "there are gods, and such great things are their work".' It has been justly said, that these words would alone be sufficient to confirm Cicero's opinion of 'the golden flow of the Aristotelian eloquence', and that there breathes in them somewhat of the inspired genius of Plato. Such a testimony as this to the existence of heavenly powers, from the beauty and infinite grandeur of the works of creation, is indeed rare in classical antiquity.

That which we miss with regard to the Greeks, I will not say in their appreciation of natural phænomena, but in the direction which their literature assumed, we find still more sparingly among the Romans. A nation which, in conformity with the old Siculian manners, manifested a marked predilection for agriculture and rural life, might have justified other hopes; but with all their capacity for practical activity, the Romans, in their cold gravity, and measured sobriety of understanding, were, as a people, far inferior to the Greeks in the perception of beauty, and far less sensitive to its influence; and were much more devoted to the realities of everyday life, than to an idealizing poetic contemplation of nature.

These inherent differences between the Greek and Roman mind are faithfully reflected, as is always the case with national character, in their respective literatures; and I must add to this consideration, that of the acknowledged difference in the organic structure of the two languages, notwithstanding the affinity between the races. The language of ancient Latium is regarded as possessing less flexibility, a more limited adaptation of words, and 'more of realistic tendency' than of 'ideal mobility'. The predilection for the imitation of foreign Greek models in the Augustan age, might, moreover, have been unfavourable to the free outpourings of the native mind and feelings in reference to nature; but yet, powerful minds, animated by love of country, have effectually surmounted these varied obstacles, by creative individuality, by elevation of ideas, and by tender grace in their presentation. The great poem which is the fruit of the rich genius of Lucretius, embraces the whole Cosmos: it has much affinity with the works of Empedocles and Parmenides; and the grave tone in which the subject is presented is enhanced by its archaic diction. Poetry and philosophy are closely interwoven in it; without, however, falling into that coldness of composition, which, as contrasted with Plato's views of nature so rich in imagination, is severely blamed by the rhetor Menander, in the sentence passed by him on the 'hymns to nature'. My brother has pointed out, with great ingenuity, the striking analogies and diversities produced by the interweaving of metaphysical abstraction with poetry in the ancient Greek didactic poems, in that of Lucretius, and in the Bhagavad-Gita episode of the Indian epic Mahabharata. In the great physical picture of the universe traced by the Roman poet, we find contrasted with his chilling atomic doctrine, and his often extravagantly wild geological fancies, the fresh and animated description of mankind exchanging the thickets of the forest for the pursuits of agriculture, the subjugation of natural forces, the cultivation of the intellect and of language, and the formation of civil society.

When, in the midst of the busy and agitated life of a statesman, and in a mind excited by political passions, an animated love of nature and of rural solitude still subsists, its source must be sought in the depths of a great and noble character. Cicero's writings shew the truth of this assertion. Although it is generally recognized that in the book De Legibus, and in that of the Orator, many things are imitated from the Phædrus of Plato, yet the picture of Italian nature does not lose its individuality and truth. Plato, in more general characters, praises the dark shade of the lofty plane tree, the luxuriant abundance of fragrant herbs and flowers, the sweet summer breezes, and the chorus of grasshoppers. In Cicero's smaller pictures, we find, as has been recently well remarked, all those features which we still recognize in the actual landscape: we see the Liris shaded by lofty poplars; and in descending the steep mountain side to the east, behind the old castle of Arpinum, we look on the grove of oaks near the Fibrenus, as well as on the island now called Isola di Carnello, which is formed by the division of the stream, and into which Cicero retired, as he says, to 'give himself up to his meditations, to read, or to write'. Arpinum, on the Volscian Mountains, was the birthplace of the great statesman; and his mind and character were doubtless influenced in his boyhood by the grand scenery of the vicinity. In the mind of man, the reflex action of the external aspect of surrounding nature is early and unconsciously blended with that which belongs to the original tendencies, capacities, and powers of his own inner being.

In the midst of the stormy and eventful period of the year 708 (from the foundation of Rome), Cicero found consolation in his villas, alternately at Tusculum, Arpinum, Cumæ, and Antium. 'Nothing,' he writes to Atticus, 'can be more delightful than this solitude; more pleasing than this country dwelling, the neighbouring shore, and the prospect over the sea. In the lonely island of Astura, at the mouth of the river of the same name, and on the shore of the Tyrrhenian sea, no human being disturbs me; and when, early in the morning, I hide myself in a thick wild forest, I do not leave it until the evening. Next to my Atticus, nothing is so dear to me as solitude, in which I cultivate intercourse with philosophy; but this intercourse is often interrupted with tears. I strive against these as much as I can, but I have not yet prevailed.' It has been repeatedly remarked, that in these letters, and in those of the younger Pliny, expressions resembling those so common amongst the sentimental writers of modern times may be unequivocally recognized; I find in them only the accents of a mind deeply moved, such as in every age, and every nation or race, escape from the heavily-oppressed bosom.

From the general diffusion of Roman literature, the master works of Virgil, Horace, and Tibullus, are so widely and intimately known, that it would be superfluous to dwell on individual instances of the delicate and ever wakeful sensibility to nature, by which many of them are animated. In the Æneid, the epic character forbids the appearance of descriptions of natural scenes and objects otherwise than as subordinate and

accidental features, limited to a very small space; individual
localities are not portrayed, but an intimate understanding and
love of nature manifest themselves occasionally with peculiar
beauty. Where have the soft play of the waves, and the repose
of night, ever been more happily described? and how finely
do these mild and tender images contrast with the powerful
representations of the gathering and bursting tempest in the
first book of the Georgics, and with the descriptions in the
Æneid of the navigation and landing at the Strophades, the
crashing fall of the rock, and of Ætna with its flames. We might
have expected from Ovid, as the fruit of his long sojourn in
the plains of Tomi in Lower Mæsia, a poetic description of the
aspect of nature in the steppes; but none such has come down
to us from antiquity, either from him or from any other writer.
The Roman exile did not indeed see that kind of steppe which
in summer is thickly covered by rich herbage and flowering
plants from four to six feet high, which, as each breeze passes
over them, present the pleasing picture of an undulating many-
coloured sea of flowers and verdure. The place of his banishment was a desolate marshy district. The broken spirit of the
exile, which yielded to unmanly lamentations, was filled with
recollections of the social pleasures and the political occurrences of Rome, and had no place for the contemplation of
the Scythian desert by which he was surrounded. On the other
hand, this richly-gifted poet, so powerful in vivid representation, has given us, besides general descriptions of grottos,
fountains, and silent moonlight nights, which are but too frequently repeated, an eminently-characteristic, and even geo-
logically-important description of the volcanic eruption at
Methone between Epidaurus and Trœzene, which has been
referred to in the 'General View of Nature' contained in the
preceding volume.

It is especially to be regretted that Tibullus should not have
left us any great composition descriptive of natural scenery,
general or individual. He belongs to the few among the poets
of the Augustan age who, being happily strangers to the Alex-
andrian learning, and devoted to retirement and a rural life,
full of feeling and therefore simple, drew from their own

resources. Elegies are indeed portraits of mind and manners of which the landscape forms only the background; but the Lustration of the Fields and the 6th Elegy of the first book shew what might have been expected from the friend of Horace and Messala.

Lucan, the grandson of the rhetor Marcus Annæus Seneca, is indeed only too nearly related to his progenitor in the rhetorical ornateness of his style; yet we find among his writings a fine description of the destruction of a Druidic forest on the now treeless shore of Marseilles, which is thoroughly true to nature: the severed oaks, leaning against each other, support themselves for a time before they fall; and, denuded of their leaves, admit the first ray of light to penetrate the awful gloom of the sacred shade. Those who have lived long in the forests of the New Continent, feel how vividly the poet has depicted, with a few traits, the luxuriant growth of trees whose giant remains are still found buried in turf bogs in France.

In a didactic poem entitled Ætna, written by Lucilius the Younger, a friend of L. Annæus Seneca, the phænomena of a volcanic eruption are described, not inaccurately, but yet in a far less animated and characteristic manner than in the 'Ætna Dialogus' of the youthful Bembo, mentioned with praise in the preceding volume.

When, after the close of the fourth century, poetry in its grander and nobler forms faded away, as if exhausted, poetic attempts, deprived of the magic of creative imagination, were occupied only with the drier realities of knowledge and description: and a certain rhetorical polish of style could ill replace the simple feeling for nature, and the idealizing inspiration, of an earlier age. We may name as a production of this barren period, in which the poetic element appears only as an accidental and merely external ornament, a poem on the Moselle, by Ausonius, a native of Aquitanian Gaul, who had accompanied Valentinian in his campaign against the Allemanni. The 'Mosella', which was composed at ancient Trèves, describes sometimes not unpleasingly the already vine-covered hills of one of the loveliest rivers of Germany; but the mere topography of the country, the enumeration of the streams which flow into the Moselle, and the characters, in form, colour, and habits, of some of the different kinds of fish which are found in the river, are the principal objects of this purely didactic composition.

In the works of Roman prose writers, among which we have already referred to some remarkable passages by Cicero, descriptions of natural scenery are as rare as in those of Greek writers of the same class; but the great historians – Julius Cæsar, Livy, and Tacitus – in relating the conflicts of men with natural obstacles and with hostile forces, are sometimes led to give descriptions of fields of battle, and of the passage of rivers, or of difficult mountain passes. In the Annals of Tacitus, I am delighted with the description of Germanicus's unsuccessful navigation of the Amisia, and with the grand geographical sketch of the mountain chains of Syria and of Palestine. Curtius has left us a fine natural picture of a forest wilderness to the west of Hekatompylos, through which the Macedonian army had to pass in entering the humid province of Mazanderan; to which I would refer more in detail, if, in a writer whose period is so uncertain, we could distinguish with any security between what he has drawn from his own lively imagination, and what he has derived from historic sources.

The great encyclopædic work of the elder Pliny, which, as his nephew, the younger Pliny, has finely said, is 'varied as nature herself', and which, in the abundance of its contents, is unequalled by any other ancient work, will be referred to in the sequel, when treating of the 'History of the Contemplation of the Universe'. This work, which exerted a powerful influence on the whole of the middle ages, is a most remarkable result of the disposition to comprehensive, but often indiscriminate collection. Unequal in style – sometimes simple and narrative, sometimes thoughtful, animated, and rhetorically ornate – it has, as, indeed, might be expected from its form, few individual descriptions of nature; but wherever the grand concurrent action of the forces in the universe, the well-ordered Cosmos (naturæ majestas), is the object of contemplation, we cannot mistake the evidences of true inward poetic inspiration.

We would gladly adduce the pleasantly-situated villas of the Romans, on the Pincian Mount, at Tusculum, and Tibur, on the promontory of Misenum, and near Puteoli and Baiæ, as evidences of a love of nature, if these spots had not, like those in which were the villas of Scaurus and Mæcenas, Lucullus and Adrian, been crowded with sumptuous buildings – temples, theatres, and race-courses alternating with aviaries and houses for rearing snails and dormice. The elder Scipio had surrounded his more simple country seat at Liturnum with towers like a fortress. The name of Matius, a friend of Augustus, has been handed down to us as that of the individual whose predilection for unnatural constraint first introduced the custom of cutting and training trees into artificial imitations of architectural and plastic models. The letters of the younger Pliny furnish us with pleasing descriptions of two of his numerous villas, Laurentinum and Tuscum. Although buildings, surrounded by box cut into artificial forms, are more numerous and crowded than our taste for nature would lead us to desire, yet these descriptions, as well as the imitation of the Vale of Tempe in the Tiburtine villa of Adrian, shew us that among the inhabitants of the imperial city, the love of art, and the solicitous care for comfort and convenience manifested in the choice of the positions of their country houses with reference to the sun and to the prevailing winds, might be associated with love for the free enjoyment of nature. It is cheering to be able to add, that on the estates of Pliny this enjoyment was less disturbed than elsewhere by the painful features of slavery. The wealthy proprietor was not only one of the most learned men of his period, but he had also those compassionate and truly humane feelings for the lower classes of the people who were not in the enjoyment of freedom, of which the expression at least is most rare in antiquity. At his villas fetters were unused; and he provided that the slave, as a cultivator of the soil, should freely bequeath that which he had acquired.

No description of the eternal snows of the Alps, when tinged in the morning or evening with a rosy hue, of the beauty of the blue glacier ice, or of any part of the grandeur of the scenery of Switzerland, have reached us from the ancients, although statesmen and generals, with men of letters in their train, were constantly passing through Helvetia into Gaul. All these travellers think only of complaining of the difficulties of the way; the romantic character of the scenery never seems to have engaged their attention. It is even known that Julius Cæsar, when returning to his legions in Gaul, employed his time, while passing over the Alps, in preparing a grammatical treatise 'De Analogia'. Silius Italicus, who died under Trajan, when Switzerland was already in great measure cultivated, describes the district of the Alps merely as an awful and barren wilderness; although he elsewhere loves to dwell in verse on the rocky ravines of Italy, and the wood-fringed banks of the Liris (Garigliano). It is deserving of notice that the remarkable appearance of groups of jointed basaltic columns, such as are seen in several parts of the interior of France, on the banks of the Rhine, and in Lombardy, never engaged the attention of the Romans sufficiently to lead their writers to describe or even to mention them.

At the period when the feelings which had animated classical antiquity, and had directed the minds of men to the active manifestation of human power, almost to the exclusion of the passive contemplation of the natural world, were expiring, a new influence, and new modes of thought, were gaining sway. Christianity gradually diffused itself; and, as where it was received as the religion of the state, its beneficent action on the lower classes of the people favoured the general cause of civil freedom, so also did it render man's contemplation of nature more enlarged and free. The forms of the Olympic gods no longer fixed the eyes of men: the fathers of the church proclaimed, in their æsthetically correct, and often poetically imaginative language, that the Creator shews himself great no less in inanimate than in living nature; in the wild strife of the elements as well as in the silent progress of organic development. But during the gradual dissolution of the Roman Empire, vigour of imagination, and simplicity and purity of diction, declined more and more, first in the Latin countries, and afterwards in the Greek or eastern portion of the empire.

A predilection for solitude, for saddened meditation, and for an internal absorption of mind, seems to have influenced simultaneously both the language itself and the colouring of the style.

Where a new element appears to develop itself suddenly and generally in the feelings of men, we may almost always trace earlier indications of a deep-seated germ existing previously in detached and solitary instances. The softness of Mimnermus has often been called a sentimental direction of the mind. The ancient world is not abruptly separated from the modern; but changes in the religious sentiments and apprehensions of men, in their tenderest moral feelings, and in the particular mode of life of those who influence the ideas of the masses, gave a sudden predominance to that which previously escaped notice.

The tendency of the Christian mind was to shew the greatness and goodness of the Creator from the order of the universe and the beauty of nature; and this desire to glorify the Deity through his works, favoured a disposition for natural descriptions. We find the earliest and most detailed instances of this kind in the writings of Minucius Felix, a rhetorician and advocate living in Rome in the beginning of the third century, and a contemporary of Tertullian and Philostratus. We follow him with pleasure in the evening twilight to the sea shore near Ostia, which, indeed, he describes as more picturesque, and more favourable to health, than we now find it. The religious discourse entitled 'Octavius' is a spirited defence of the new faith against the attacks of a heathen friend.

This is the place for introducing from the Greek fathers of the church extracts descriptive of natural scenes, which are probably less known to my readers than are the evidences of the ancient Italian love for a rural life contained in Roman literature. I will begin with a letter of the great Basil, which has long been an especial favourite with me. Basil, who was a native of Cesarea in Cappadocia, left the pleasures of Athens when little more than thirty years of age, and, having already visited the Christian hermitages of Cœlo-Syria and Upper Egypt, withdrew, like the Essenes and Therapeuti before

Christianity, into a wilderness adjacent to the Armenian river
Iris. His second brother, Naucratius, had been drowned there
while engaged in fishing, after leading for five years the life of
a rigid anchorite. Basil writes to his friend Gregory of Nazianzum, 'I believe I have at last found the end of my wanderings:
my hopes of uniting myself with thee – my pleasing dreams, I
should rather say, for the hopes of men have been justly called
waking dreams, – have remained unfulfilled. God has caused
me to find a place such as has often hovered before the fancy
of us both; and that which imagination shewed us afar off, I
now see present before me. A high mountain, clothed with
thick forest, is watered towards the north by fresh and ever
flowing streams; and at the foot of the mountain extends a
wide plain, which these streams render fruitful. The surrounding forest, in which grow many kinds of trees, shuts me in as
in a strong fortress. This wilderness is bounded by two deep
ravines; on one side the river, precipitating itself foaming from
the mountain, forms an obstacle difficult to overcome; and the
other side is enclosed by a broad range of hills. My hut is so
placed on the summit of the mountain, that I overlook the
extensive plain, and the whole course of the Iris, which is both
more beautiful, and more abundant in its waters, than the Stry-
mon near Amphipolis. The river of my wilderness, which is
more rapid than any which I have ever seen, breaks against the
jutting precipice, and throws itself foaming into the deep pool
below – to the mountain traveller an object on which he gazes
with delight and admiration, and valuable to the native for the
many fish which it affords. Shall I describe to thee the fertilizing vapours rising from the moist earth, and the cool breezes
from the broken water? shall I speak of the lovely song of the
birds, and of the profusion of flowers? What charms me most
of all is the undisturbed tranquillity of the district: it is only
visited occasionally by hunters; for my wilderness feeds deer
and herds of wild goats, not your bears and your wolves. How
should I exchange any other place for this! Alcmæon, when he
had found the Echinades, would not wander farther.' In this
simple description of the landscape and of the life of the forest, there speak feelings more intimately allied to those of

modern times than anything that Greek and Roman antiquity have bequeathed to us. From the lonely mountain hut to which Basilius had retired, the eye looks down on the humid roof of foliage of the forest beneath; the resting-place for which he and his friend Gregory of Nazianzum have so long panted is at last found. The sportive allusion at the close to the poetic mythus of Alcmæon sounds like a distant lingering echo, repeating in the Christian world accents belonging to that which had preceded it.

Basil's Homilies on the Hexaemeron also bear witness to his love of nature. He describes the mildness of the constantly serene nights of Asia Minor, where, according to his expression, the stars, 'those eternal flowers of heaven', raise the spirit of man from the visible to the Invisible. When, in speaking of the creation of the world, he desires to praise the beauty of the sea, he describes the aspect of the boundless plain of waters in its different and varying conditions – 'how, when gently agitated by mildly-breathing airs, it gives back the varied hues of heaven, now in white, now in blue, and now in roseate light; and caresses the shore in peaceful play!'

We find in Gregory of Nyssa, the brother of Basil, the same delight in nature, the same sentimental and partly melancholy vein. 'When,' he exclaims, 'I behold each craggy hill, each valley, and each plain clothed with fresh-springing grass; the varied foliage with which the trees are adorned; at my feet the lilies to which nature has given a double dower, of sweet fragrance, and of beauty of colour; and in the distance the sea, towards which the wandering cloud is sailing, – my mind is possessed with a sadness which is not devoid of enjoyment. When, in autumn, the fruits disappear, the leaves fall, and the branches of the trees, stripped of their ornaments, hang lifeless, in viewing this perpetual and regularly recurring alternation the mind becomes absorbed in the contemplation, and rapt as it were in unison with the many-voiced chorus of the wondrous forces of nature. Whoso gazes through these with the inward eye of the soul feels the littleness of man in the greatness of the universe.'

While the early Christian Greeks were thus led, by

glorifying God in a loving contemplation of nature, to poetic descriptions of her various beauty, they were at the same time full of contempt for all works of human art. We find in Chrysostom many such passages as these: 'when thou lookest on the glittering buildings, if the ranges of columns would seduce thy heart, turn quickly to contemplate the vault of heaven and the open fields, with the flocks grazing by the water's side. Who but despises all that art can shew whilst he gazes at early morn, and, in the silence of the heart, on the rising sun pouring his golden light upon the earth; or when seated by the side of a fountain in the cool grass, or in the dark shade of thick foliage, his eye feeds the while on the wide-extended prospect far vanishing in the distance.' Antioch was at this period surrounded by hermitages, in one of which Chrysostom dwelt: it might have seemed that eloquence had found again her element, freedom, on returning to the bosom of nature in the then forest-covered mountain districts of Syria and Asia Minor.

But when, during the subsequent period, so hostile to all intellectual cultivation, Christianity spread among the Germanic and Celtic races, who had previously been devoted to the worship of nature, and who honoured under rude symbols its preserving and destroying powers, the close and affectionate intercourse with the external world of phænomena which we have remarked among the early Christians of Greece and Italy, as well as all endeavours to trace the action of natural forces, fell gradually under suspicion, as tending towards sorcery. They were therefore regarded as not less dangerous than the art of the sculptor had appeared to Tertullian, Clemens of Alexandria, and almost all the most ancient fathers of the church. In the twelfth and thirteenth centuries, the Councils of Tours (1163) and of Paris (1209) forbade to monks the sinful reading of writings on physical science. These intellectual fetters were first broken by the courage of Albertus Magnus and Roger Bacon; when nature was pronounced pure, and reinstated in her ancient rights.

Hitherto we have sought to depict differences which have

shewn themselves in different periods of time; and in two literatures so nearly allied as were those of the Greeks and the Romans. But not only are great differences in modes of feeling produced by time, – by the changes which it brings with it, in forms of government, in manners, and in religious views, – but diversities still more striking are produced by differences of race and of mental disposition. How different in animation and in poetic colouring are the manifestations of the love of nature and the descriptions of natural scenery among the Greeks, the Germans of the north, the Semitic races, the Persians, and the Indians! An opinion has been repeatedly expressed, that the delight in nature felt by northern nations, and the longing desire for the pleasant fields of Italy and Greece, and for the wonderful luxuriance of tropical vegetation, are principally to be ascribed to the long winter's privation of all such enjoyments. We do not mean to deny that the longing for the climate of palms seems to diminish as we approach the South of France and the Iberian Peninsula; but the now generally employed, and ethnologically correct name of Indo-Germanic races, might alone be sufficient to remind us that we must be cautious lest we generalize too much respecting the influence thus ascribed to northern winters. The richness of the poetic literature of the Indians teaches us, that within and near the tropics south of the great chain of the Himalaya, the sight of ever verdant and ever flowering forests has at all times acted as a powerful stimulus to the poetic and imaginative faculties of the East-Arianic nations, and that these nations have been more strongly inclined to picturesque descriptions of nature than the true Germanic races, who, in the far inhospitable north, had extended even into Iceland. A deprivation, or, at least, a certain interruption of the enjoyment of nature, is not, however, unknown even to the happier climates of Southern Asia. The seasons are there abruptly divided from each other by alternate periods of fertilizing rain and of dusty desolating aridity. In the Persian plateau of West Aria, the desert often extends in deep bays far into the interior of the most smiling and fruitful lands. In Middle and in Western Asia, a margin of forest often forms as it were the shore of a widely extended inland sea of steppe; and thus the inhabitants of these hot countries have presented to them the strongest contrasts of desert barrenness and luxuriant vegetation, in the same horizontal plane, as well as in the vertical elevation of the snow-capped mountain chains of India and of Afghanistan. Wherever a lively tendency to the contemplation of nature is interwoven with the whole intellectual cultivation, and with the religious feelings of a nation, great and striking contrasts of season, of vegetation, or of elevation, are unfailing stimulants to the poetic imagination.

Delight in nature, inseparable from the tendency to objective contemplation which belongs to the Germanic nations, shews itself in a high degree in the earliest poetry of the middle ages. Of this the chivalric poems of the Minnesingers during the Hohenstauffen period afford us numerous examples. Many and varied as are its points of contact with the romanesque poetry of the Provençals, yet its true Germanic principle can never be mistaken. A deep felt and all pervading love of nature may be discerned in all Germanic manners, habits, and modes of life; and even in the love of freedom characteristic of the race. The wandering Minnesingers, or minstrels, though living much in courtly circles (from which, indeed, they often sprang), still maintained frequent and intimate intercourse with nature, and preserved, in all its freshness, an idyllic, and often an elegiac, turn of thought. I avail myself on these subjects of the researches of those most profoundly versed in the history and literature of our German middle ages, my noble-minded friends Jacob and Wilhelm Grimm. 'The poets of our country of that period,' says the last named writer, 'never gave separate descriptions of natural scenery designed solely to represent, in brilliant colours, the impression of the landscape on the mind. Assuredly the eye and the feeling for nature were not wanting in these old German masters; but the only expressions thereof which they have left us are such as flowed forth in lyrical strains, in connection with the occurrences or the feelings belonging to the narrative. To begin with the best and oldest monuments of the popular epos, we do not find any description of scenery either in the Niebelungen or in

Gudrun, even where the occasion might lead us to look for it. In the otherwise circumstantial description of the chase during which Siegfried is murdered, the only natural features mentioned are the blooming heather and the cool fountain under the linden tree. In Gudrun, which shews something of a higher polish, a finer eye for nature seems also discernible. When the king's daughter, with her companions, reduced to slavery, and compelled to perform menial offices, carry the garments of their cruel lord to the sea-shore, the time is indicated as being the season "when winter is just dissolving, and the birds begin to be heard, vying with each other in their songs; snow and rain still fall, and the hair of the captive maidens is blown by the rude winds of March. When Gudrun, hoping for the approach of her deliverer, leaves her couch, the morning star rises over the sea, which begins to glisten in the early dawn and she distinguishes the dark helmets and the shields of her friends." The words are few, but they convey to the fancy a visible picture, suited to heighten the feeling of expectation and suspense previous to the occurrence of an important event in the narrative. In like manner, when Homer paints the island of the Cyclops and the gardens of Alcinous, his purpose is to bring before our eyes the luxuriant fertility and abundance of the wild dwelling-place of the giant monsters, and the magnificent residence of a powerful king. In neither poet is the description of nature a primary or independent object.'

'Opposed to these simple popular epics, are the more varied and artificial narrations of the chivalrous poets of the thirteenth century; among whom, Hartmann von Aue, Wolfram von Eschenbach, and Gottfried von Strasburg, in the early part of the century, are so much distinguished above the rest, that they may be called great and classical. It would be easy to bring together from their extensive writings sufficient proof of their deep feeling for nature, as it breaks forth in similitudes; but distinct and independent descriptions of natural scenes are never found in their pages; they never arrest the progress of the action to contemplate the tranquil life of nature. How different is this from the writers of modern poetic compositions! Bernardin de St-Pierre uses the occurrences of his narratives only as frames for his pictures. The lyric poets of the 13th century, especially when singing of love, (which is not, however, their constant theme), speak, indeed, often of "gentle May", of the "song of the nightingale", and "the dew glistening on the bells of heather", but always in connection with sentiments springing from other sources, which these outward images serve to reflect. Thus, when feelings of sadness are to be indicated, mention is made of fading leaves, birds whose songs are mute, and the fruits of the field buried in snow. The same thoughts recur incessantly, not indeed without considerable variety as well as beauty in the manner in which they are expressed. Walther von der Vogelweide, and Wolfram von Eschenbach, the former characterized by tenderness and the latter by deep thought, have left us some lyric pieces; unfortunately only few in number, which are deserving of honourable mention.'

'If it be asked whether contact with Southern Italy, and, by means of the crusades, with Asia Minor, Syria, and Palestine, did not enrich poetic art in Germany with new imagery drawn from the aspect of nature in more sunny climes, the question must, on the whole, be answered in the negative. We do not find that acquaintance with the East changed the direction of the minstrel poetry of the period: the crusaders had little familiar communication with the Saracens, and there was much of repulsion even between the warriors of different nations associated for a common cause. Friedrich von Hausen, who perished in Barbarossa's army, was one of the earliest German lyrical poets. His songs often relate to the crusades, but only to express religious feelings, or the pains of absence from a beloved object. Neither he nor any of the writers who had taken part in the expeditions to Palestine, as Reinmar the Elder, Rubin, Neidhart, and Ulrich of Lichtenstein, ever take occasion to speak of the country in which they were sojourning. Reinmar came to Syria as a pilgrim, it would appear, in the train of Duke Leopold VI. of Austria: he complains that the thoughts of home leave him no peace, and draw him away from God. The date-tree is occasionally mentioned, in speaking of the palms which pious pilgrims should

bear on their shoulders. Neither do I remember any indication
of the loveliness of Italian nature having stimulated the imagination of those minstrels who crossed the Alps. Walther von
der Vogelweide, though he had wandered far, had in Italy seen
only the Po; but Freidank was in Rome, and he merely remarks
that "grass now grows in the palaces of those who once ruled
there".'

The German Thier-epos, which must not be confounded
with the oriental 'fable', originated in habitual association and
familiarity with the animal world; to paint which was not, however, its purpose. This peculiar class of poem, which Jacob
Grimm has treated in so masterly a manner, in the introduction to his edition of Reinhart Fuchs, shews a cordial delight
in nature. The animals, not attached to the ground, excited by
passion, and gifted by the poet with speech, contrast with the
still life of the silent plants, and form a constantly active element enlivening the landscape. 'The early poetry loves to look
on the life of nature with human eyes, and lends to animals,
and even to plants, human thoughts and feelings; giving a fanciful and childlike interpretation to all that has been observed
of their forms and habits. Plants and flowers, gathered and
used by gods and heroes, are afterwards named from them. In
reading the old German epic, in which brutes are the actors,
we breathe an air redolent as it were with the sylvan odours of
some ancient forest.'

Formerly we might have been tempted to number among
the memorials of Germanic poetry having reference to external nature, the supposed remains of the Celto-Irish poems,
which, for half a century, passed as shapes of mist from nation
to nation, under the name of Ossian; but the spell has been
broken since the complete discovery of the literary fraud of
the talented Macpherson, by his publication of the supposed
Gaelic original text, now known to have been a retranslation
from the English work. There are, indeed, ancient Irish Fingal-
ian songs belonging to the times of Christianity, and perhaps
not even reaching as far back as the eighth century; but these
popular songs contain little of the sentimental description of
nature which gives a particular charm to Macpherson's poems.

We have already remarked, that if sentimental and romantic turns of thought and feeling in reference to nature belong in a high degree to the Indo-Germanic races of Northern Europe, it should not be regarded only as a consequence of climate; that is, as arising from a longing desire enhanced by protracted privation. I have noticed, that the literatures of India and of Persia, which have unfolded under the glowing brightness of southern skies, offer descriptions full of charm, not only of organic, but also of inorganic nature; of the transition from parching drought to tropical rain; of the appearance of the first cloud on the deep azure of the pure sky, and the first rustling sound of the long desired etesian winds in the feathered foliage of the summits of the palms.

It is now time to enter somewhat more deeply into the subject of the Indian descriptions of nature. 'Let us imagine,' says Lassen, in his excellent work on Indian antiquity, 'a portion of the Arianic race migrating from their primitive seats, in the north-west, to India: they would there find themselves surrounded by scenery altogether new, and by vegetation of a striking and luxuriant character. The mildness of the climate, the fertility of the soil, the profusion of rich gifts which it lavishes almost spontaneously, would all tend to impart to the new life of the immigrants a bright and cheerful colouring. The originally fine organization of this race, and their high endowments of intellect and disposition, the germ of all that the nations of India have achieved of great or noble, early rendered the spectacle of the external world productive of a profound meditation on the forces of nature, which is the groundwork of that contemplative tendency which we find intimately interwoven with the earliest Indian poetry. This prevailing impression on the mental disposition of the people, has embodied itself most distinctly in their fundamental religious tenets, in the recognition of the divine in nature. The careless ease of outward life likewise favoured the indulgence of the contemplative tendency. Who could have less to disturb their meditations on earthly life, the condition of man after death, and on the divine essence, than the Indian anchorites, the Brahmins dwelling in the forest, whose ancient schools constituted one of the most peculiar phænomena of Indian life, and materially influenced the mental development of the whole race?'

In referring now, as I did in my public lectures under the guidance of my brother and of others conversant with Sanscrit literature, to particular instances of the vivid sense of natural beauty which frequently breaks forth in the descriptive portions of Indian poetry, I begin with the Vedas, or sacred writings, which are the earliest monuments of the civilization of the East Arianic nations, and are principally occupied with the adoring veneration of nature. The hymns of the Rig-Veda contain beautiful descriptions of the blush of early dawn, and the appearance of the 'golden-handed' sun. The great heroic poems of Ramayana and Mahabharata are later than the Vedas, and earlier than the Puranas; and in them the praises of nature are connected with a narrative, agreeably to the essential character of epic poetry. In the Vedas, it is seldom possible to assign the particular locality whence the sacred sages derive their inspiration; in the heroic poems, on the contrary, the descriptions are mostly individual, and attached to particular localities, and are animated by that fresher life which is found where the writer has drawn from impressions of which he was himself the recipient. Rama's journey from Ayodhya to the capital of Dschanaka, his sojourn in the primeval forest, and the picture of the hermit life of the Panduides, are all richly coloured.

The name of the great poet Kalidasa, who flourished at the highly polished court of Vikramaditya, contemporaneously with Virgil and Horace, has obtained an early and extensive celebrity among the nations of the west: nearer our own times, the English and German translations of Sacontala have further contributed, in a high degree, to the admiration so largely felt for an author, whose tenderness of feeling, and rich creative imagination, claim for him a distinguished place among the poets of all countries. The charm of his descriptions of nature is seen also in the lovely drama of 'Vikrama and Urvasi', in which the king wanders through the thickets of the forest in search of the nymph Urvasi; in the poem of 'The

Seasons'; and in 'The Meghaduta', or 'Cloud Messenger'. The last named poem paints, with admirable truth to nature, the joyful welcome which, after a long continuance of tropical drought, hails the first appearance of the rising cloud, which shews that the looked-for season of rains is at hand. The expression, 'truth to nature', which I have just employed, can alone justify me in venturing to recall, in connection with the Indian poem, a sketch of the commencement of the rainy season traced by myself, in South America, at a time when I was wholly unacquainted with Kalidasa's Meghaduta, even in Chézy's translation. The obscure meteorological processes which take place in the atmosphere, in the formation of vapour, in the shape of the clouds, and in the luminous electric phænomena, are the same in the tropical regions of both continents; and idealizing art, whose province it is to form the actual into the ideal image, will surely lose none of its magic power by the discovery that the analysing spirit of observation of a later age confirms the truth to nature of the older, purely graphical and poetical representation.

We pass from the East Arians, or the Brahminic Indians, and their strongly marked sense of picturesque beauty in nature, to the West Arians, or Persians, who had migrated into the northern country of the Zend, and were originally disposed to combine with the dualistic belief in Ormuzd and Ahrimanes a spiritualized veneration of nature. What we term Persian literature does not reach farther back than the period of the Sassanides; the older poetic memorials have perished; and it was not until the country had been subjugated by the Arabs, and the characteristics of its earlier inhabitants in great measure obliterated, that it regained a national literature, under the Samanides, Gaznevides, and Seldschuki. The flourishing period of its poetry, from Firdusi to Hafiz and Dschami, can hardly be said to have lasted four or five centuries, and extends but little beyond the epoch of Vasco de Gama. The literatures of Persia and of India are separated by time as well as by space; the Persian belonging to the middle ages, while the great literature of India belongs strictly to antiquity. In the Iraunian highlands, nature does not present the luxuriance of arborescent vegetation, or the admirable variety of form and colour, which adorn the soil of Hindostan. The Vindhya chain, which was long the boundary of the East Arianic nations, is still within the torrid zone, while the whole of Persia is situated beyond the tropics, and its poetic literature even belongs in part to the northern soil of Balkh and Fergana. The four paradises celebrated by the Persian poets, were the pleasant valley of Soghd near Samarcand, Maschanrud near Hamadan, Tcha'abi Bowan near Kal'eh Sofid in Fars, and Ghute the plain of Damascus. Both Iran and Turan are wanting in the sylvan scenery and the hermit life of the forest which influenced so powerfully the imaginations of the Indian poets. Gardens refreshed by springing fountains, and filled with rose bushes and fruit trees, could ill replace the wild and grand scenery of Hindostan. No wonder, therefore, that the descriptive poetry of Persia has less life and freshness, and is even often tame, and full of artificial ornament. Since, in the judgment of the Persians, the highest meed of praise is given to that which we term sprightliness and wit, our admiration must be limited to the productiveness of their poets, and to the infinite variety of forms which the same materials assume under their hands: we miss in them depth and earnestness of feeling.

In the national epic of Persia, Firdusi's Shahnameh, the course of the narrative is but rarely interrupted by descriptions of landscape. The praises of the coast land of Mazanderan, put into the mouth of a wandering bard, and describing the mildness of its climate, and the vigour of its vegetation, appear to me to have much grace and charm, and a high degree of local truth. In the story, the king (Kei Kawus) is induced by the description to undertake an expedition to the Caspian, and to attempt a new conquest. Enweri, Dschelaleddin Rumi (who is considered the greatest mystic poet of the East), Adhad, and the half Indian Feisi, have written poems on spring, parts of which breathe poetic life and freshness, although in other parts our enjoyment is often unpleasingly disturbed by petty efforts in plays on words and artificial comparisons. Joseph von Hammer, in his great work on the history of Persian poetry, remarks of Sadi, in the Bostan and Gulistan (Fruit and Rose Gardens), and of Hafiz, whose joyous philosophy of life has been compared with that of Horace, that we find in the first an ethical teacher, and in the love songs of the second, lyrical flights of no mean beauty; but that in both the descriptions of nature are too often marred and disfigured by turgidity and false ornament. The favourite subject of Persian poetry, the loves of the nightingale and the rose, is wearisome, from its perpetual recurrence; and the genuine love of nature is stifled in the East under the conventional prettinesses of the language of flowers.

When we proceed northwards from the Iraunian highlands through Turan (in the Zend Tuirja), into the chain of the Ural which forms the boundary between Europe and Asia, we find ourselves in the early seat of the Finnish races; for the Ural is as deserving of the title of the ancient land of the Fins as the Altai is of that of the Turks. Among the Fins who have settled far to the west in European lowlands, Elias Lönnrot has collected, from the lips of the Karelians and the country people of Olonetz, a great number of Finnish songs, in which Jacob Grimm finds, in regard to nature, a tone of emotion and of reverie rarely met with except in Indian poetry. An old epic of nearly three thousand lines, which is occupied with the wars between the Fins and the Lapps, and the fortunes and fate of a godlike hero named Vaino, contains a pleasing description of the rural life of the Fins; especially where the wife of the ironworker, Ilmarine, sends her flocks into the forest, with prayers for their safeguard. Few races present more remarkable gradations in the character of their minds and the direction of their feelings, as determined by servitude, by wild and warlike habits, or by persevering efforts for political freedom, than the race of Fins, with its subdivisions speaking kindred languages. I allude to the now peaceful rural population among whom the epic just mentioned was discovered, – to the Huns, (long confounded with the Monguls,) who overrun the Roman world, – and to a great and noble people, the Magyars.

We have seen that the vividness of the feeling with which nature is regarded, and the form in which that feeling manifests itself, are influenced by differences of race, by the particular character of the country, by the constitution of the state, and by the tone of religious feeling; and we have traced this influence in the nations of Europe, and in those of kindred descent in Asia (the Indians and Persians) of Arianic or Indo-Germanic origin. Passing from thence to the Semitic or Aramean race, we discover in the oldest and most venerable memorials in which the tone and tendency of their poetry and imagination are displayed, unquestionable evidences of a profound sensibility to nature.

This feeling manifests itself with grandeur and animation in pastoral narratives, in hymns and choral songs, in the splendour of lyric poetry in the Psalms, and in the schools of the prophets and seers, whose high inspiration, almost estranged from the past, is wrapped in futurity.

Besides its own inherent greatness and sublimity, Hebrew poetry presents to Jews, to Christians, and even to Mahometans, local reminiscences more or less closely entwined with religious feelings. Through missions, favoured by the spirit of commerce, and the territorial acquisitions of maritime nations, names and descriptions belonging to oriental localities, preserved to us in the writings of the Old Testament, have penetrated far into the recesses of the forests of the new continent, and into the islands of the Pacific.

It is characteristic of Hebrew poetry in reference to nature, that, as a reflex of monotheism, it always embraces the whole world in its unity, comprehending the life of the terrestrial globe as well as the shining regions of space. It dwells less on details of phænomena, and loves to contemplate great masses. Nature is portrayed, not as self-subsisting, or glorious in her own beauty, but ever in relation to a higher, an over-ruling, a spiritual power. The Hebrew bard ever sees in her the living expression of the omnipresence of God in the works of the visible creation. Thus, the lyrical poetry of the Hebrews in its descriptions of nature is essentially, in its very subject, grand and solemn, and, when touching on the earthly condition of man, full of a yearning pensiveness. It is deserving of notice, that notwithstanding its grand character, and even in its highest lyrical flights elevated by the charm of music, the Hebrew poetry, unlike that of the Hindoos, scarcely ever appears unrestrained by law and measure. Devoted to the pure contemplation of the Divinity, figurative in language, but clear and simple in thought, it delights in comparisons, which recur continually and almost rhythmically.

As descriptions of natural scenery, the writings of the Old Testament shew as in a mirror the nature of the country in which the people of Israel moved and dwelt, with its alternations of desert, fruitful land, forest, and mountain. They portray the variations of the climate of Palestine, the succession of the seasons, the pastoral manners of the people, and their innate disinclination to agriculture. The epic, or historical and narrative, portions are of the utmost simplicity, almost more unadorned even than Herodotus; and from the small alteration which has taken place in the manners, and in the usages and circumstances of a nomade life, modern travellers have been enabled to testify unanimously to their truth to nature. The Hebrew lyrical poetry is more adorned, and unfolds rich and animated views of the life of nature. A single psalm, the 104th, may be said to present a picture of the entire Cosmos: – 'The Lord covereth himself with light as with a garment, He hath stretched out the heavens like a canopy. He laid the foundations of the round earth that it should not be removed for ever. The waters springing in the mountains descend to the valleys, unto the places which the Lord hath appointed for them, that they may never pass the bounds which He has set them, but may give drink to every beast of the field. Beside them the birds of the air sing among the branches. The trees of the Lord are full of sap, the cedars of Lebanon which He hath planted, wherein the birds make their nests, and the fir trees wherein the stork builds her house.' The great and wide sea is also described, 'wherein are living things innumerable; there move the ships, and there is that leviathan whom Thou hast made to sport therein'. The fruits of the field, the objects of the labour of man, are also introduced; the corn, the cheerful vine, and the olive garden. The heavenly bodies complete this picture of nature. 'The Lord appointed the moon for seasons, and the sun knoweth the term of his course. He bringeth darkness, and it is night, wherein the wild beasts roam. The young lions roar after their prey, and seek their meat from God. The sun ariseth and they get them away together, and lay them down in their dens': and then 'man goeth forth unto his work and to his labour until the evening'. We are astonished to see, within the compass of a poem of such small dimension, the universe, the heavens and the earth, thus drawn with a few grand strokes. The moving life of the elements is here placed in opposition to the quiet laborious life of man, from the rising of the sun, to the evening when his daily work is done. This contrast, the generality in the conception of the mutual influence of phænomena, the glance reverting to the omnipresent invisible Power, which can renew the face of the earth, or, cause the creature to return again to the dust, give to the whole a character of solemnity and sublimity rather than of warmth and softness.

Similar views of the Cosmos present themselves to us repeatedly in the Psalms, (as in the 65th, v. 7–14, and in the 74th, 15–17), and with perhaps most fulness in the ancient, though not premosaic, book of Job. The meteorological processes taking place in the canopy of the clouds, the formation and dissolution of vapour as the wind changes its direction, the play of colours, the production of hail, and the rolling thunder, are described with the most graphic individuality; many questions are also proposed, which our modern physical science enables us indeed to propound more formally, and to clothe in more scientific language, but not to solve satisfactorily. The book of Job is generally regarded as the most perfect example of Hebrew poetry; it is no less picturesque in the presentation of single phænomena than skilful in the didactic arrangement of the whole. In all the various modern languages into which this book has been translated, its imagery, drawn from eastern nature, leaves on the mind a deep impression. 'The Lord walks on the heights of the sea, on the ridges of the towering waves heaped up by the storm' (chap. xxxviii. v. 16.) 'The morning dawn illumines the border of the earth, and moulds variously the canopy of clouds, as the hand of man moulds the ductile clay' (chap. xxxviii. v. 13–14.) The habits of animals are depicted, of the wild ass and the horse, the buffalo, the river horse of the Nile, the crocodile, the eagle, and the ostrich. We see (chap. xxxvii. v. 18) during the sultry heat of the south wind, 'the pure ether spread over the thirsty desert like a molten mirror'. Where the gifts of nature are sparingly bestowed, man's perceptions are rendered more acute, so that he watches every variation in the atmosphere around him and in the clouds above him; and in the desert, as on the billows of the ocean, traces back every change to the signs which foretold it. The climate of the arid and rocky portions of Palestine is particularly suited to give birth to such observations.

Neither is variety of form wanting in the poetic literature of the Hebrews: while from Joshua to Samuel it breathes a warlike tone, the little book of Ruth presents a natural picture of the most naïve simplicity, and of an inexpressible charm. Goethe, at the period of his enthusiasm for the East, said of it, that we have nothing so lovely in the whole range of epic and idyllic poetry.

Even in later times, in the earliest memorials of the literature of the Arabians, we discover a faint reflex of that grandeur of view in the contemplation of nature, which so early distinguished the Semitic race: I allude to the picturesque description of the Bedouin life of the deserts, which the grammarian Asmai has connected with the great name of Antar, and has woven (together with other pre-mohamedan legends of knightly deeds), into a considerable work. The hero of this romantic tale is the same Antar of the tribe of Abs, son of the princely chief Sheddad and of a black slave, whose verses are preserved among the prize poems, (moallakät), which are hung up in the Kaaba. The learned English translator, Terrick Hamilton, has called attention to the biblical tones in the style of Antar. Asmai makes the son of the desert travel to Constantinople, and thus introduces a picturesque contrast of Greek culture with nomadic simplicity. We should be less surprised at finding that natural descriptions of the surface of the Earth occupy only a very small space in the earliest Arabian poetry, since, according to the remark of an accomplished Arabic scholar, my friend Freytag of Bonn, narratives of deeds of arms, and praises of hospitality and of fidelity in love, are its principal themes, and since scarcely any, if any, of its writers were natives of Arabia Felix. The dreary uniformity of sandy deserts or grassy plains is ill fitted to awaken the love of nature, excepting in rare instances and in minds of a peculiar cast.

Where the earth is unadorned by forests, the imagination, as we have already remarked, is the more occupied by the atmospheric phenomena of storm, tempest, and long desired rain. Among faithful natural pictures of this class, I would instance particularly Antar's Moallakat, which describes the pasture fertilized by rain, and visited by swarms of humming insects; the fine descriptions of storms, both by Amru'l Kais, and in the 7th book of the celebrated Hamasa, which are also distinguished by a high degree of local truth; and lastly, the description in the Nabegha Dhobyani of the swelling of the Euphrates, when its waters roll down masses of reeds and trunks of trees. The eighth book of the Hamasa, which is entitled 'Travel and Sleepiness', naturally attracted my attention: I soon found that the 'sleepiness' belongs only to the first fragment of the book, and even there is more excusable, as it is ascribed to a night journey on a camel.

I have endeavoured in this section to unfold in a fragmentary manner the different influence which the external world, that is, the aspect of animate and inanimate nature, has exercised at different epochs, and among different races and nations, on the inward world of thought and feeling. I have tried to accomplish this object by tracing throughout the history of literature, the particular characteristics of the vivid manifestation of the feelings of men in regard to nature. In this, as throughout the whole of the work, my aim has been to give not so much a complete, as a general, view, by the selection of such examples as should best display the peculiarities of the various periods and races. I have followed the Greeks and Romans to the gradual extinction of those feelings which have given to classical antiquity in the West an imperishable lustre; I have traced in the writings of the Christian fathers of the Church, the fine expression of a love of nature nursed in the seclusion of the hermitage. In considering the Indo-Germanic nations, (the denomination being here taken in its most restricted sense), I have passed from the poetic works of the Germans in the middle ages, to those of the highly cultivated ancient East Arianic nations (the Indians); and of the less gifted West Arians, (the inhabitants of ancient Iran). After a rapid glance at the Celtic or Gaelic songs, and at a newly discovered Finnish epic, I have described the rich perception of the life of nature which, in races of Aramean or Semitic origin, breathes in the sublime poetry of the Hebrews, and in the writings of the Arabians. Thus I have traced the reflected image of the world of phænomena, as mirrored in the imagination of the nations of the north and the south-east of Europe, of the west of Asia, of the Persian plateaus, and of tropical India. In order to conceive Nature in all her grandeur, it seemed to me necessary to present her under a two-fold aspect; first objectively, as an actual phænomenon; and next as reflected in the feelings of mankind.

After the fading of Aramaic, Greek, and Roman glory – I might say after the destruction of the ancient world – we find in the great and inspired founder of a new world, Dante Alighieri, scattered passages which manifest the most profound sensibility to the aspect of external nature. The period at which he lived followed immediately that of the decline of the minstrelsy of the Suabian Minnesingers, on the north side of the Alps, of whom I have already spoken. Dante, when treating of natural objects, withdraws himself for a time from the passionate, the subjective, and the mystic elements of his wide range of ideas. Inimitably does he paint, for instance, at the close of the first canto of the Purgatorio, the sweet breath of morning, and the trembling light on the gently agitated distant mirror of the sea, (il tremolar de la marina); in the fifth canto, the bursting of the clouds and the swelling of the rivers, which, after the battle of Campaldino, caused the body of Buonconte da Montefeltro to be lost in the Arno. The entrance into the thick grove of the terrestrial paradise reminds the poet of the pine forest near Ravenna: 'la pineta in sul lito di Chiassi', where the early song of birds is heard in the tall trees. The local truth of this natural picture contrasts with the description of the river of light in the heavenly paradise, from which 'sparks burst forth, sink amidst the flowers on the banks, and then, as if intoxicated by their perfumes, plunge again into the stream'. It seems not impossible that this fiction may have had for its groundwork the poet's recollection of that peculiar state of the ocean, in which, during the beating of the waves, luminous points dash above the surface, and the whole liquid plain forms a moving sea of sparkling light. The extraordinary conciseness of the style of the Divina Commedia augments the depth and earnestness of the impression produced.

Lingering on Italian ground, but avoiding those frigid compositions, the pastoral romances, I would next name the sonnet in which Petrarch describes the impression which the lovely valley of Vaucluse made on him when Laura was no more; then, the smaller poems of Boiardo, the friend of Hercules of Este; and at a later period some noble stanzas by Vittoria Colonna.

When the sudden intercourse which took place with Greece in her low state of political depression caused a more general revival of classical literature, we find, as the first example among prose writers, a charming description of nature from the pen of the lover of the arts, the counsellor and friend of Raphael, Cardinal Bembo. His juvenile work, entitled Ætna Dialogus, gives us an animated picture of the geographical distribution of plants on the declivity of the mountain, from the rich corn fields of Sicily to the snow-covered margin of the crater. The finished work of his maturer years, the Historiæ Venetæ, characterizes in a still more picturesque manner the climate and the vegetation of the new continent.

At that period every thing concurred to fill the mind at once with views of the suddenly enlarged boundaries both of the earth, and of the powers of man. In antiquity, the march of the Macedonian army to the Paropamisus, and to the forest-covered river-valleys of Western Asia, left impressions derived from the aspect of a richly adorned exotic nature, of which the vividness manifested itself whole centuries afterwards in the works of highly gifted writers; and now, in like manner, the western nations were acted upon a second time, and in a higher degree than by the crusades, by the discovery of America. The tropical world, with all the richness and luxuriance of its vegetation in the plain, with all the gradations of organic life on the declivities of the Cordilleras, with all the reminiscences of northern climates in the inhabited plateaus of Mexico, New Grenada, and Quito, was now first disclosed to the view of Europeans. Imagination, without which no truly great work of man can be accomplished, gave a peculiar charm to the descriptions of nature traced by Columbus and Vespucci. The description of the coast of Brazil, by the latter, is characterized by an accurate acquaintance with the poets of ancient and modern times; that given by Columbus of the mild sky of Paria, and of the abundant waters of the Orinoco, flowing as he imagines from the east of Paradise, is marked by an earnestly religious tone of mind, which afterwards, by the influence of increasing years, and of the unjust persecutions which he encountered, became touched with melancholy, and with a vein of morbid enthusiasm.

In the heroic times of the Portuguese and Castilian races, it was not the thirst of gold alone (as has been asserted, in ignorance of the national character of the period), but rather a general excitement which led so many to dare the hazards of distant voyages. In the beginning of the sixteenth century, the names of Hayti, Cubagua, and Darien, acted on the imagination of men as in more recent times, since Anson and Cook, those of Tinian and Tahiti have done. If the tidings of far distant lands then drew the youth of the Iberian peninsula, of Flanders, Milan, and Southern Germany, under the victorious banners of the great Emperor, to the ridges of the Andes and to the burning plains of Uraba and Coro; – in more modern times, under the milder influence of a later cultivation, and as the earth's surface became more generally accessible in all its parts, the restless longing for distant regions acquired fresh motives and a new direction. The passionate love for the study of nature which proceeded chiefly from the north, inflamed the minds of men; intellectual grandeur of view became associated with the enlargement of material knowledge; and the particular poetic sentimental turn belonging to the period, has embodied itself, since the close of the last century, in literary works under forms which were before unknown. If we once more cast our eyes on the period of those great discoveries which prepared the way for the modern tendency of which we have been speaking, we must in so doing refer preeminently to those descriptions of nature which have been left us by Columbus himself. It is only recently that we have obtained the knowledge of his own ship's journal, of his letters to the treasurer Sanchez, to Donna Juana de la Torre governess of the Infant Don Juan, and to Queen Isabella. In my critical examination of the history of the geography of the 15th and 16th centuries, I have sought to show with how deep a feeling and perception of the forms and the beauty of nature the great discoverer was endowed, and how he described the face of the earth, and the 'new heaven' which opened to his view, ('viage nuevo al nuevo cielo i mundo que fasta entonces estaba en occulto'), with a beauty and simplicity of expression which can only be fully appreciated by those who are familiar with the ancient force of the language as it existed at the period.

The aspect and physiognomy of the vegetation; the impenetrable thickets of the forests, 'in which one can hardly distinguish which are the flowers and leaves belonging to each stem'; the wild luxuriance which clothed the humid shores; the rose-coloured flamingoes fishing at the mouth of the rivers in the early morning, and giving animation to the landscape; – attract the attention of the old navigator while sailing along the coast of Cuba, between the small Lucayan islands and the Jardinillos, which I also have visited. Each newly discovered land appears to him still more beautiful than those he had before described; he complains that he cannot find words in which to record the sweet impressions which he has received. Wholly unacquainted with botany, (although through the influence of Jewish and Arabian physicians some superficial knowledge of plants had at that time extended into Spain), the simple love of nature leads him to discriminate truly between the many strange forms presented to his view. He already distinguished in Cuba seven or eight different kinds of palms 'more beautiful and loftier than date-trees', (variedades de palmas superiores a las nuestras en su belleza y altura); he writes to his friend Anghiera, that he has seen on the same plain palms and pines, (palmeta and pineta), wonderfully grouped together; he regards the vegetation presented to his view with a glance so acute, that he was the first to observe that, on the mountains of Cibao, there are pines whose fruits are not fir cones, but berries like the olives of the Axarafe de Sevilla; and, to cite one more and very remarkable example, Columbus, as I have already noticed, separated the genus Podocarpus from the family of Abietineæ.

'The loveliness of this new land,' says the discoverer, 'far surpasses that of the campiña de Cordoba. The trees are all bright with ever-verdant foliage, and perpetually laden with fruits. The plants on the ground are tall and full of blossoms. The breezes are mild like those of April in Castille; the nightingales sing more sweetly than I can describe. At night other small birds sing sweetly, and I also hear our grasshoppers and frogs. Once I came into a deeply enclosed harbour, and saw high mountains which no human eye had seen before, from which the lovely waters (lindas aguas) streamed down. The mountain was covered with firs, pines, and other trees of very various form, and adorned with beautiful flowers. Ascending the river which poured itself into the bay, I was astonished at the cool shade, the crystal clear water, and the number of singing birds. It seemed to me as if I could never quit a spot so delightful, – as if a thousand tongues would fail to describe it, – as if the spell-bound hand would refuse to write. (Para hacer relacion a los Reyes de las cosas que vian, no bastaran mil lenguas a referillo, ni la mano para lo escribir, que le parecia questaba encantado.)'

We here learn from the journal of an unlettered seaman, the power which the beauty of nature, manifested in her individual forms, may exert on a susceptible mind. Feelings ennoble language; for the prose of the Admiral, especially when, on his fourth voyage, at the age of 67, he relates his wonderful dream on the coast of Veragua, is, if not more eloquent, yet far more moving than the allegorical pastoral romance of Boccaccio and the two Arcadias of Sannazaro and of Sydney; than Garcilasso's Salicio y Nemoroso; or than the Diana of Jorge de Montemayor. The elegiac idyllic element was unhappily too long predominant in Italian and Spanish literature; it required the fresh and living picture which Cervantes has drawn of the adventures of the Knight of La Mancha, to efface the Galatea of the same author. The pastoral romance, however ennobled in the works of these great writers by beauty of language and tenderness of feeling, is from its nature, like the allegorical artifices of the intellect of the middle ages, cold and wearisome. Individuality of observation alone leads to truth to nature; in the finest descriptive stanzas of the 'Jerusalem Delivered', impressions derived from the poet's recollection of the picturesque landscape of Sorrento have been supposed to be recognized.

That truth to nature which springs from actual contemplation, shines most richly in the great national epic of Portuguese literature; it is as if a perfumed air from Indian flowers breathed throughout the whole poem, written under the sky of the tropics, in the rocky grotto near Macao and in the Moluccas. It is not for me to confirm a bold sentence of Friedrich Schlegel's, according to which the Lusiad of Camoens excels Ariosto in colouring and richness of fancy; but as an observer of Nature, I may well add that in the descriptive portion of the Lusiad, the poet's inspiration, the ornaments of language, and the sweet tones of melancholy, never impair the accuracy of the representation of physical phænomena. Rather, as is always the case when art draws from pure sources, they heighten the living impressions of grandeur and of truth in the pictures of nature. Inimitable are the descriptions in Camoens of the never ceasing mutual relations between the air and sea, between the varying form of the clouds above, their meteorological changes, and the different states of the surface of the ocean. He shews us this surface at one time, as, when curled by gentle breezes the short waves glance sparklingly in the play of the reflected sunbeams; and at another, when the ships of

Coelho' and Paul de Gama, overtaken by a dreadful tempest, sustain the conflict of the deeply agitated elements. Camoens is in the most proper sense of the term, a great sea painter. He had fought at the foot of Atlas in the empire of Morocco, in the Red Sea, and in the Persian Gulf; twice he had sailed round the Cape, and for sixteen years watched the phænomena of the ocean on the Chinese and Indian shores. He describes the electric fires of St Elmo, (the Castor and Pollux of the ancient Greek navigators) 'the living light, sacred to the mariner'. He paints the danger-threatening water-spout in its gradual development; 'how the cloud, woven of thin vapour, whirls round in a circle, and sending down a slender tube sucks up the flood as if athirst; and how, when the black cloud has drunk its fill, the foot of the cone recedes, and flying back to the sky, restores to the waves, as fresh water, the salt stream which it had drawn from them with a surging noise'. 'Let the book-learned,' says the poet – and his taunt might almost as well apply to the present time – 'try to explain the wonderful things hidden from the world; they who, guided by (so-called) science and their own conceptions only, are so willing to pronounce as false, what is heard from the mouth of the sailor whose only guide is experience.'

Camoens shines, however, not only in the description of single phænomena, but also where large masses are comprehended in one view. The third canto paints with a few traits the whole of Europe, from the coldest north, 'to the Lusitanian kingdom, and the strait where Hercules accomplished his last labour'. The manners and state of civilization of the different nations are alluded to. From the Prussians, the Muscovites, and the tribes 'que o Rheno frio lava', he hastens to the glorious fields of Hellas, 'que creastes os peitos eloquentes, e os juizos de alta phantasia'. In the tenth canto the view becomes still more extended; Thetys conducts Gama to the summit of a lofty mountain to shew him the secrets of the structure of the universe ('machina do mundo'), and to disclose to him the courses of the planets, (according to the views of Ptolemy). It is a vision in the style of Dante, and as the Earth is the centre of motion, we have in the description of the globe, a review of all the countries then known, and of their productions. Even the 'land of the Holy Cross', (Brazil), is named, and the coasts which Magellan discovered 'by the act, but not by the loyalty of a son of Lusitania'.

When I before extolled Camoens as especially a marine painter, it was to indicate that the aspect of nature on the land seems to have attracted him less vividly. Sismondi has remarked with justice, that the whole poem contains absolutely no trace of graphical description of the vegetation of the tropics, and its peculiar physiognomy and forms. He only notices the spices and other productions which have commercial value. The episode of the magic island does, indeed, present a charming landscape picture, but, as befits an 'Ilha de Venus', the vegetation consists of 'fragrant myrtles, citrons, lemon trees, and pomegranates'; all belonging to the climates of South Europe. In the writings of the great discoverer of the new world, we find far greater delight in the forests of the coasts seen by him, and far more attention to the forms of the vegetable kingdom; but it should be remarked, that Columbus, writing the journal of his voyage, records in it the living impressions of each day. The epic of Camoens, on the other hand, is written to celebrate the great achievements of the Portuguese. To have borrowed from native languages uncouth names of plants, and to have interwoven them in the descriptions of landscapes forming the background to the actors in his narrative, might have appeared but little attractive to the poet accustomed to harmonious sounds.

By the side of the knightly form of Camoens has often been placed the equally romantic one of a Spanish warrior who served under the banners of the great Emperor in Peru and Chili, and sung in those distant regions the deeds of arms in which he had borne a distinguished part. But in the whole Epic of the Araucana of Don Alonso de Ercilla, the immediate presence of volcanoes clad with eternal snows, of valleys covered with tropical forests, and of arms of the sea penetrating far into the land, have scarcely called forth any description which can be termed graphical. The excessive praise which Cervantes bestows on Ercilla, on the occasion of the ingenious satirical review of Don Quixote's books, is probably to be attributed only to the vehement rivalry subsisting at that time between Spanish and Italian poetry, though it would appear to have misled Voltaire and several modern critics. The Araucana is, indeed, a work imbued with a noble national feeling; and the description which it contains of the manners of a wild race who perish in fighting for the freedom of their native land, is not without animation; but Ercilla's style is heavy, loaded to excess with proper names, and without any trace of true poetic inspiration.

We recognize this essential element, however, in several strophes of the Romancero Caballeresco; we perceive its presence, mixed with a vein of religious melancholy, in the writings of Fray Luis de Leon, – as, for example, where he celebrates the 'eternal luminaries (resplandores eternales) of the starry heaven'; – and we find it in the great creations of Calderon. The most profound critic of the dramatic literature of different countries, my friend Ludwig Tieck, has remarked the frequent occurrence in Calderon and his contemporaries of lyrical strains in varied metres, often containing dazzlingly beautiful pictures of the ocean, of mountains, of wooded valleys, and of gardens; but these pictures are always introduced in allegorical applications, and are characterized by a species of artificial brilliancy. In reading them we feel that we have before us ingenious descriptions, recurring with only slight variations, and clothed in well-sounding and harmonious verse; but we do not feel that we breathe the free air of nature; the reality of the mountain scene, and the shady valley, are not made present to our imagination. In Calderon's play of 'Life is a Dream', (la vida es sueno), he makes Prince Sigismund lament his captivity in a series of gracefully drawn contrasts with the freedom of all living nature. He paints the birds, 'which fly across the wide sky with rapid wing', the fish, which, but just escaped from the sand and shallows where they were brought to life, seek the wide sea, whose boundless expanse seems still too small for their bold range. Even the stream meandering among flowers, finds a free path through the meadow: 'and I', exclaims Sigismund despairingly, 'who have more life than they, and a spirit more free, must endure an existence in which I enjoy less freedom'. In a similar manner, too often disfigured by antitheses, witty comparisons, and artificial turns from the school of Gongora, Don Fernando speaks to the king of Fez in the 'Steadfast Prince'.

I have referred to particular instances, because they show how in dramatic poetry, which is chiefly concerned with action, passion, and character, 'descriptions of natural objects become as it were only mirrors in which the mental emotions of the actors in the scene are reflected. Shakspeare, who amidst the pressure of his animated action has scarcely ever time and opportunity to introduce deliberate descriptions of natural scenes, does yet so paint them by occurrences, by allusions, and by the emotions of the acting personages, that we seem to see them before our eyes, and to live in them. We thus live in the midsummer-night in the wood; and in the latter scenes of the Merchant of Venice we see the moonshine brightening the warm summer night, without direct descriptions. An actual and elaborate description of a natural scene occurs, however, in King Lear, where Edgar, who feigns himself mad, represents to his blind father, Gloucester, while on the plain, that they are mounting to the summit of Dover Cliff. The picture drawn of the downward view into the depths below actually turns one giddy.'

If in Shakspeare the inward life of feeling, and the grand simplicity of the language, animate thus wonderfully the individual expression of nature, and render her actually present to our imagination; in Milton's sublime poem of Paradise Lost, on the other hand, such descriptions are, from the very nature of the subject, magnificent rather than graphic. All the riches of imagination and of language are poured forth in painting the loveliness of Paradise; but the description of vegetation could not be otherwise than general and undefined. This is also the case in Thomson's pleasing didactic poem of The Seasons. Kalidasa's poem on the same subject, the Ritusanhara, which is more ancient by above seventeen centuries, is said by critics deeply versed in Indian literature to individualize more vividly the vigorous nature of the vegetation of the tropics;

but it wants the charm which, in Thomson, arises from the more varied division of the seasons which is proper to the higher latitudes; the transition from fruit-bringing autumn to winter, and from winter to reanimating spring; and the pictures afforded by the varied laborious or pleasurable pursuits of men belonging to the different portions of the year.

Arriving at the period nearest to our own time, we find that, since the middle of the last century, descriptive prose has more particularly developed itself, and with peculiar vigour. Although the study of nature, enlarging on every side, has increased beyond measure the mass of things known to us, yet amongst the few who are susceptible of the higher inspiration which this knowledge is capable of affording, the intellectual contemplation of nature has not sunk oppressed under the load, but has rather gained a wider comprehensiveness and a loftier elevation, since a deeper insight has been obtained into the structure of mountain masses (those storied cemeteries of perished organic forms), and into the geographical distribution of plants and animals, and the relationship of different races of men. The first modern prose writers who have powerfully contributed to awaken, through the influence of the imagination, the keen perception of natural beauty, the delight in contact with nature, and the desire for distant travel which is their almost inseparable companion, were in France, Jean Jacques Rousseau, Buffon, Bernardin de St-Pierre, and (to name exceptionally one living writer), my friend Auguste de Chateaubriand; in the British islands the ingenious Playfair; and in Germany, George Forster, who was the companion of Cook on his second voyage of circumnavigation, and who was gifted both with eloquence and with a mind peculiarly favourable to every generalization in the view of nature.

I must not attempt in these pages to examine the characteristics of these different writers; or what it is that, in works so extensively known, sometimes lends to their descriptions of scenery such grace and charm, or at others disturbs the impressions which the authors desire to awaken; but it may be permitted to a traveller who has derived his knowledge principally from the immediate contemplation of nature, to introduce here a few detached considerations respecting a recent, and on the whole little cultivated, branch of literature.

Buffon, with much of grandeur and of gravity, – embracing simultaneously the structure of the planetary system, the world of organic life, light, and magnetism – and far more profound in his physical investigations than his contemporaries were aware of – when he passes from the description of the habits of animals to that of the landscape, shews in his artificially-constructed periods, more rhetorical pomp than individual truth to nature; rather disposing the mind generally to the reception of exalted impressions, than taking hold of it by such visible paintings of the actual life of nature, as should render her actually present to the imagination. In perusing even his most justly celebrated efforts in this department, we are made to feel that he has never quitted middle Europe, and never actually beheld the tropical world which he engages to describe. What, however, we particularly miss in the works of this great writer, is the harmonious connection of the representation of nature with the expression of awakened emotion; we miss in him almost all that flows from the mysterious analogy between the movements of the mind and the phænomena perceived by the senses.

Greater depth of feeling, and a fresher spirit of life, breathe in Jean Jacques Rousseau, in Bernardin de St-Pierre, and in Chateaubriand. If in the first-named writer (whose principal works were twenty years earlier than Buffon's fanciful Epoques de la Nature) I allude to his fascinating eloquence, and to the picturesque descriptions of Clarens and La Meillerie on Lake Leman, it is because, in the most celebrated works of this ardent but little informed plant-collector, poetical inspiration shews itself principally in the inmost peculiarities of the language, breaking forth no less overflowingly in his prose, than in Klopstock's, Schiller's, Goethe's, and Byron's imperishable verse. Even where an author has no purpose in view immediately connected with the study of nature, our love for that study may still be enhanced by the magic charm of a poetic representation of the life of nature, although in regions of the earth already familiar to us.

In referring to modern prose writers, I dwell with peculiar complacency on that small production of the creative imagination to which Bernardin de St-Pierre owes the fairest portion of his literary fame – I mean Paul and Virginia: a work such as scarcely any other literature can shew. It is the simple but living picture of an island in the midst of the tropic seas, in which, sometimes smiled on by serene and favouring skies, sometimes threatened by the violent conflict of the elements, two young and graceful forms stand out picturesquely from the wild luxuriance of the vegetation of the forest, as from a flowery tapestry. Here, and in the Chaumière Indienne, and even in the Etudes de la Nature, (which are unhappily disfigured by extravagant theories and erroneous physical views), the aspect of the sea, the grouping of the clouds, the rustling of the breeze in the bushes of the bamboo, and the waving of the lofty palms, are painted with inimitable truth. Bernardin de St-Pierre's master-work, Paul and Virginia, accompanied me into the zone to which it owes its origin. It was read there for many years by my dear companion and friend Bonpland and myself, and there – (let this appeal to personal feelings be forgiven) – under the silent brightness of the tropical sky, or when, in the rainy season on the shores of the Orinoco, the thunder crashed and the flashing lightning illuminated the forest, we were deeply impressed and penetrated with the wonderful truth with which this little work paints the power of nature in the tropical zone in all its peculiarity of character. A similar firm grasp of special features, without impairing the general impression or depriving the external materials of the free and animating breath of poetic imagination, characterizes in an even higher degree the ingenious and tender author of Atala, René, the Martyrs, and the Journey to Greece and Palestine. The contrasted landscapes of the most varied portions of the earth's surface are brought together and made to pass before the mind's eye with wonderful distinctness of vision: the serious grandeur of historic remembrances could alone have given so much of depth and repose to the impressions of a rapid journey.

In our German fatherland, the love of external nature

showed itself but too long, as in Italian and Spanish literature, under the forms of the idyl, the pastoral romance, and didactic poems: this was the course followed by the Persian traveller Paul Flemming, Brockes, Ewald von Kleist, in whom we recognize a mind full of feeling, Hagedorn, Solomon Gessner, and by one of the greatest naturalists of all times, Haller, whose local descriptions present, however, better defined outlines and more objective truth of colour. At that time the elegiac idyllic element predominated in a heavy style of landscape poetry, in which, even in Voss, the noble and profound classical student of antiquity, the poverty of the materials could not be veiled by happy and elevated, as well as highly finished diction. It was not until the study of the earth's surface gained depth and variety, and natural science, no longer limited to tabular enumerations of extraordinary occurrences and productions, rose to the great views of comparative geography, that this finish of language could become available in aiding to impart life and freshness to the pictures of distant zones.

The older travellers of the middle ages, such as John Mandeville (1353), Hans Schiltberger of Munich (1425), and Bernhard von Breytenbach (1486), still delight us by an amiable naïveté, by the freedom with which they write, and the apparent feeling of security with which they come before a public who, being wholly unprepared, listen with the greater curiosity and readiness of belief, because they have not yet learnt to feel ashamed of being amused or even astonished. The interest of books of travels was at that period almost wholly dramatic; and the indispensable mixture of the marvellous which they so easily and naturally acquired, gave them also somewhat of an epic colouring. The manners of the inhabitants of the different countries are not so much described, as shewn incidentally in the contact between the travellers and the natives. The vegetation is unnamed and unheeded, excepting where a fruit of particularly pleasant flavour or curious form, or a stem or leaves of extraordinary dimensions, induce a special notice. Amongst animals, the kinds which they are most fond of remarking are, first, those which show some resemblance to the human form, and next those which are most wild and most formidable to man. The contemporaries of these travellers gave the fullest credence to dangers which few among them had shared; the slowness of navigation, and the absence of means of communication, caused the Indies, as all tropical countries were then called, to appear at an immeasurable distance. Columbus was as yet scarcely justified in saying, as he did in his letter to Queen Isabella, 'the earth is not very large: it is much less than people imagine'.

In respect to composition, these almost-forgotten books of travels of the middle ages had, notwithstanding the poverty of their materials, great advantages over most of our modern voyages. They had the unity which every work of art requires: everything was connected with an action, *i. e.* subordinated to the journey itself. The interest arose from the simple, animated, and usually implicitly believed narrative of difficulties overcome. Christian travellers, unacquainted with the previous travels of Arabs, Spanish Jews, and proselytizing Buddhists, always supposed themselves to be the first to see and describe everything. The remoteness and even the dimensions of objects were magnified by the obscurity which seemed to veil the East and the interior of Asia. This attractive unity of composition is necessarily wanting in the greater part of modern travels, and especially in those undertaken for scientific purposes; in these, what is done yields precedence to what is observed; the action almost disappears under the multitude of observations. A true dramatic interest can now only be looked for, in arduous, though perhaps little instructive ascents of mountains, and above all adventurous navigation of untraversed seas in voyages of discovery properly so called, and in the awful solitudes of the Polar regions, where the surrounding desolation and the lonely situation of the mariners, cut off from all human aid, isolate the picture, and cause it to act more stirringly on the imagination of the reader. If the above considerations render it undeniably evident that in modern books of travels the active element necessarily falls into the background, affording for the most part merely a connecting thread whereby the successive observations of nature or of manners are linked together, yet ample compensation may be derived from the treasures of observation, from grand views of the universe, and from the laudable endeavour in each writer to avail himself of the peculiar advantages which his native language may possess for clear and animated description. The benefits for which we are indebted to modern cultivation are the constantly advancing enlargement of our field of view, the increasing wealth in ideas and feelings, and their active mutual influence. Without leaving our native soil, we may now not only be informed what is the character and form of the earth's crust in the most distant zones, and what are the plants and animals which enliven its surface, but we may also expect to be presented with such pictures as may produce in ourselves a vivid participation in a portion at least of those impressions which in each zone man receives from external nature. To satisfy these demands, – this requirement of a species of intellectual delight unknown to the ancient world, – is one of the efforts of modern times; the effort prospers, and the work advances, both because it is the common work of all cultivated nations, and because the increasing improvement of the means of transport, both by sea and land, renders the whole earth more accessible, and brings into comparison its remotest portions.

I have here attempted to indicate, however vaguely, the manner in which the traveller's power of presenting the result of his opportunities of observation, the infusion of a fresh life into the descriptive element of literature, and the variety of the views which are continually opening before us on the vast theatre of the producing and destroying forces, may all tend to enlarge the scientific study of nature and to incite to its pursuit. The writer who, in our German literature, has, according to my feelings, opened the path in this direction with the greatest degree of vigour and success, was my distinguished teacher and friend George Forster. Through him has been commenced a new era of scientific travelling, having for its object the comparative knowledge of nations and of nature in different parts of the earth's surface. Gifted with refined æsthetic feeling, and retaining the fresh and living pictures with which Tahiti and the other fortunate islands of the Pacific had filled his imagination (as in later years that of Charles Darwin), George Forster was the first gracefully and pleasingly to depict the different gradations of vegetation, the relations of climate, and the various articles of food, in their bearing on the habits and manners of different tribes according to their differences of race and of previous habitation. All that can give truth, individuality, and graphic distinctness to the representation of an exotic nature, is united in his writings: not only his excellent account of the second voyage of Captain Cook, but still more his smaller works, contain the germ of much which, at a later period, has been brought to maturity. But, for this noble, sensitive, and ever-hopeful spirit, a fortunate and happy life was not reserved.

If a disparaging sense has sometimes been attached to the terms 'descriptive and landscape poetry', as applied to the numerous descriptions of natural scenes and objects which in the most modern times have more especially enriched German, French, English, and North American literatures, yet such censure is only properly applicable to the abuse of the supposed enlargement of the field of art. Versified descriptions of natural objects, such as at the close of a long and distinguished literary career were given by Delille, cannot be regarded, notwithstanding the refinements of language and of metre expended on them, as the poetry of external nature in the higher sense of the term: they lack poetic inspiration, and are therefore strangers on true poetic ground; they are cold and meagre, as is all that glitters with mere outward ornament. But if what has been called (as a distinct and independent form) 'descriptive poetry', be justly blamed, such disapprobation cannot assuredly apply to an earnest endeavour, by the force of language, – by the power of significant words, – to bring the richer contents of our modern knowledge of nature before the contemplation of the imagination as well as of the intellect. Should means be left unemployed whereby we may have brought home to us not only the vivid picture of distant zones over which others have wandered, but also a portion even of the enjoyment afforded by the immediate contact with nature? The Arabs say figuratively but truly that the best description is that in which the ear is transformed into an eye. It is one of the evils of the present time that an unfortunate predilection for an empty species of poetic prose, and a tendency to indulge in sentimental effusions, has seized simultaneously in different countries on authors otherwise possessed of merit as travellers, and as writers on subjects of natural history. This mixture is still more unpleasing, when the style, from the absence of literary cultivation, and especially of all true inward spring of emotion, degenerates into rhetorical inflation and spurious sentimentality. Descriptions of nature, I would here repeat, may be sharply defined and scientifically correct, without being deprived thereby of the vivifying breath of imagination. The poetic element must be derived from a recognition of the links which unite the sensuous with the intellectual; from a feeling of the universal extension, the reciprocal limitation, and the unity of the forces which constitute the life of Nature. The more sublime the objects, the more carefully must all outward adornment of language be avoided. The true and proper effect of a picture of nature depends upon its composition, and the impression produced by it can only be disturbed and marred by the intrusions of elaborate appeals on the part of its presenter. He who, familiar with the great works of antiquity, and in secure possession of the riches of his native tongue, knows how to render with simplicity and characteristic truth that which he has received by his own contemplation, will not fail, in the impression which he desires to convey; and the risk of failure will be less, as in depicting external nature, and not his own frame of mind, he leaves unfettered the freedom of feeling in others.

But it is not alone the animated description of those richly adorned lands of the equinoctial zone, in which intensity of light and of humid warmth accelerates and heightens the development of all organic germs, which has furnished in our days a powerful incentive to the general study of nature: the secret charm excited by a deep insight into organic life is not limited to the tropical world; every region of the earth offers the wonders of progressive formation and development, and the varied connection of recurring or slightly deviating types. Everywhere diffused is the awful domain of those powerful forces, which in the dark storm clouds that veil the sky, as well as in the delicate tissues of organic substances, resolve the ancient discord of the elements into harmonious union. Therefore, wherever spring unfolds a bud, from the equator to the frigid zone, our minds may receive and may rejoice in the inspiration of nature pervading every part of the wide range of creation. Well may our German fatherland cherish such belief; where is the more southern nation who would not envy us the great master of our poetry, through all whose works there breathes a profound feeling of external nature, seen alike in the Sorrows of Werter, in the Reminiscences of Italy, in the Metamorphoses of Plants, and in his Miscellaneous Poems. Who has more eloquently excited his contemporaries to 'solve the sacred enigma of the universe' ('des Weltalls heilige Räthsel zu lösen'); and to renew the ancient alliance which in the youth of human kind united philosophy, physical science, and poetry in a common bond? Who has pointed with more powerful charm to that land, his intellectual home, where

Ein sanfter Wind vom blauem Himmel weht,
Die Myrte still, und hoch der Lorbeer steht?

II.—LANDSCAPE PAINTING—GRAPHICAL REPRESENTATION OF THE PHYSIOGNOMY OF PLANTS—CHARACTERISTIC FORM AND ASPECT OF VEGETATION IN DIFFERENT ZONES.

AS FRESH AND vivid descriptions of natural scenes and objects are suited to enhance a love for the study of nature, so also is landscape painting. Both shew to us the external world in all its rich variety of forms, and both are capable, in various degrees, according as they are more or less happily conceived, of linking together the outward and the inward world. It is the tendency to form such links which marks the last and highest aim of representative art; but the scientific object to which these pages are devoted, restricts them to a different point of view; and landscape painting can be here considered only as it brings before us the characteristic physiognomy of different positions of the earth's surface, as it increases the longing desire for distant voyages, and as, in a manner equally instructive and agreeable, it incites to fuller intercourse with nature in her freedom.

In classical antiquity, from the peculiar direction of the Greek and Roman mind, landscape painting, like the poetic description of scenery, could scarcely become an independent object of art: both were used only as accessories. Employed in complete subordination to other objects, landscape painting long served merely as a background to historical composition, or as an accidental ornament in the decoration of painted walls. The epic poet, in a similar manner, sometimes marked the locality of particular events by a picturesque description of the landscape, or, as I might again term it, of the background, in front of which the acting personages were moving. The history of art teaches how the subordinate auxiliary gradually became itself a principal object, until landscape painting, separated from true historical painting, took its place as a distinct form. Whilst this separation was being gradually effected, the human figures were sometimes inserted as merely secondary features in a mountainous or woodland scene, a marine or a garden view. It has been justly remarked, in reference to the ancients, that not only did painting remain subordinate to sculpture, but more especially, that the feeling for picturesque beauty of landscape reproduced by the pencil was not entertained by them at all, but is wholly of modern growth.

Graphical indications of the peculiar features of a district must, however, have existed in the earliest Greek paintings, if (to cite particular instances) Mandrocles of Samos, as Herodotus tells us, had a painting made for the great Persian king of the passage of the army across the Bosphorus; or if Polygnotus painted the destruction of Troy in the Lesche at Delphi. Among the pictures described by the elder Philostratus mention is even made of a landscape, in which smoke was seen to issue from the summit of a volcano, and the stream of lava to pour itself into the sea. In the very complicated composition of a view of seven islands, the most recent commentators think that they recognize the representation of a real district; viz, the small volcanic group of the Æolian or Lipari islands, north of Sicily.

Perspective scene painting, which was made to contribute to the theatrical representation of the master-works of Æschylus and Sophocles, gradually extended this department of art, by increasing a demand for the illusive imitation of inanimate objects, such as buildings, trees, and rocks. In consequence of the improvement which followed this extension, landscape painting passed with the Greeks and Romans from the theatre into halls adorned with columns, where long surfaces of wall were covered, at first with more restricted scenes, but afterwards with extensive views of cities, sea-shores, and wide pastures with grazing herds of cattle. These pleasing decorations were not, indeed, invented by the Roman painter, Ludius, in the Augustan age, but were rendered generally popular by him, and enlivened by the introduction of small figures. Almost at the same period, and even half a century earlier, amongst the Indians, in the brilliant epoch of

Vikramaditya, we find landscape painting referred to as a much practised art. In the charming drama of 'Sacontala', the king, Dushmanta, has the picture of his beloved shewn him; but not satisfied with her portrait only, he desires that 'the paintress should draw the places which Sacontala most loved: – the Mal-ini river, with a sandbank on which the red flamingoes are standing; a chain of hills, which rest against the Himalaya, and gazelles reposing on the hills'. These are no small requisitions: they indicate a belief, at least, in the possibility of executing complicated representations.

In Rome, from the time of the Cæsars, landscape painting became a separate branch of art, but so far as we can judge by what the excavations at Herculaneum, Pompeii, and Stabia, have shewn us, the pictures were often mere bird's-eye views, resembling maps, and aimed rather at the representation of seaport towns, villas, and artificial gardens, than of nature in her freedom. That which the Greeks and the Romans regarded as attractive in a landscape, seems to have been almost exclu-sively the agreeably habitable, and not what we call the wild and romantic. In their pictures, the imitation might possess as great a degree of exactness as could consist with frequent inaccuracy in regard to perspective, and with a disposition to conventional arrangement; their compositions of the nature of arabesques, to the use of which the severe Vitruvius was averse, contained rhythmically recurring and tastefully arranged forms of plants and animals; but, to avail myself of an expression of Otfried Müller's, 'the dreamy twilight of mind which speaks to us in landscape appeared to the ancients, according to their mode of feeling, incapable of artistic representation'.

The specimens of ancient landscape painting in the manner of Ludius, which have been brought to light by the excavations at Pompeii (lately so successful), belong most probably to a single and very limited epoch, namely, from Nero to Titus; for the town had been entirely destroyed by earthquake sixteen years before the catastrophe caused by the celebrated eruption of Vesuvius.

From Constantine the Great to the beginning of the middle

ages, painting, though connected with Christian subjects, preserved a close affinity to its earlier character. An entire treasury of old memorials is found both in the miniatures adorning superb manuscripts still in good condition, and in the scarcer mosaics of the same period. Rumohr mentions a manuscript Psalter, in the Barberina at Rome, containing a miniature in which 'David is seen playing on the harp, seated in a pleasant grove from amongst the branches of which nymphs look forth and listen: this personification marks the antique character of the whole picture'. From the middle of the sixth century, when Italy was impoverished and in a state of utter political confusion, it was Byzantine art in the eastern empire which did most to preserve the lingering echoes and types of a more flourishing period. Memorials, such as we have spoken of, form a kind of transition to the more beautiful creations of the later middle ages: the fondness for ornamented manuscripts spread from Greece in the east to the countries of the west and the north, – into the Frankish monarchy, among the Anglo-Saxons, and into the Netherlands. It is therefore a fact of no little importance in respect to the history of modern art, 'that the celebrated brothers, Hubert and John van Eyck, belonged essentially to a school of miniature painters, which, since the second half of the fourteenth century, had reached a high degree of perfection in Flanders'.

It is in the historical paintings of the brothers Van Eyck that we first meet with a careful elaboration of the landscape portion of the picture. Italy was never seen by either of them; but the younger brother, John, had enjoyed an opportunity of beholding a south European vegetation, having, in 1428, accompanied the embassy which Philip the Good, Duke of Burgundy, sent to Lisbon, to prefer his suit to the daughter of King John I. of Portugal. We possess, in the Berlin Museum, the volets of the magnificent painting which these artists, the true founders of the great Netherlands school of painting, executed for the cathedral at Ghent. On the sides which present the holy hermits and pilgrims, John van Eyck has adorned the landscape with orange trees, date palms, and cypresses, which are marked by an extreme fidelity to nature, and impart to the other dark masses a grave and solemn character. In viewing this picture, we feel that the painter had himself received the impression of a vegetation fanned by soft and warm breezes.

The master-works of the brothers Van Eyck belong to the first half of the fifteenth century, when oil painting, though it had only just begun to supersede fresco, had already attained high technical perfection. The desire to produce an animated representation of natural forms was now awakened; and if we would trace the gradual extension and heightening of the feelings connected therewith, we should recall how Antonello of Messina, a scholar of the brothers Van Eyck, transplanted to Venice a fondness for landscape; and how, even in Florence, the pictures of the Van Eyck school exerted a similar influence over Domenico Ghirlandaio, and other masters. At this period, the efforts of the painters were, for the most part, directed to a careful, but almost painfully solicitous and minute imitation of natural forms. The representation of nature first appears conceived with freedom and with grandeur in the masterworks of Titian, to whom, in this respect also, Giorgione had served as an example. I had the opportunity, during many years, of admiring, at Paris, Titian's painting of the death of Peter Martyr, attacked in a forest by an Albigense in the presence of another Dominican monk. The form of the forest trees, their foliage, the blue mountainous distance, the management of the light and the subdued tone of colouring, produce an impression of grandeur, solemnity, and depth of feeling, pervading the whole composition of the landscape, which is of exceeding simplicity. Titian's feeling of nature was so lively, that not only in paintings of beautiful women, as in the background of the Venus in the Dresden Gallery, but also in those of a severer class, as in the portrait of the poet Pietro Aretino, he gives to the landscape or to the sky a character corresponding to that of the subject of the picture. In the Bolognese school, Annibal Caracci and Domenichino remained faithful to this elevation of style and character. If, however, the sixteenth century was the greatest epoch of historic painting, the seventeenth is that of landscape. As the riches of nature became better known and more carefully studied, art-istic feeling could extend itself over a wider and more varied range of subjects; and, at the same time, the technical means of representation had also attained a higher degree of perfection. Meanwhile, the landscape painter's art becoming more often and more intimately connected and associated with inward tone and feeling, the tender and mild expression of the beauti-ful in nature was enhanced thereby, as well as the belief in the power of the emotions which the external world can awaken within us. When, conformably to the elevated aim of all art, this awakening power transforms the actual into the ideal, the enjoyment produced is accompanied by emotion; the heart is touched whenever we look into the depths either of nature or of humanity.

We find assembled, in the same century, Claude Lorraine, the idyllic painter of light and of aerial distance; Ruysdael's dark forest masses and threatening clouds; Gaspar and Nich-olas Poussin's heroic forms of trees; and the faithful and simply natural representations of Everdingen, Hobbema, and Cuyp. This flourishing period in the development of art com-prised happy imitations of the vegetation of the north of Europe, of southern Italy, and of the Iberian peninsula: the painters adorned their landscapes with oranges and laurels, with pines and date trees. The date (the only member of the magnificent family of Palms which the artists had themselves seen, except the small native European species, the Chamæ-rops maritima) was usually represented conventionally, with scaly and serpentlike trunks, and long served as the representative of tropical vegetation generally, – much as Pinus pinea (the stone pine) is, by a still widely prevailing idea, regarded as exclusively characteristic of Italian vegetation. The outlines of lofty mountains were yet but little studied: and naturalists and landscape painters still regarded the snowy summits, which rise above the green pastures of the lower Alps, as inaccessible. The particular characters of masses of rock were rarely made objects of careful imitation, except where associated with the foaming waterfall. We may here remark another instance of the comprehensiveness with which the varied forms of nature are seized by a free and artistic spirit. Rubens, who in his great hunting pieces has depicted with inimitable truth and animation the wild movements of the beasts of the forest, has also apprehended, with peculiar felicity, the characteristics of the inanimate surface of the earth, in the arid desert and rocky plateau on which the Escurial is built.

The department of art to which we are now referring might be expected to advance in variety and exactness as the geographical horizon became enlarged, and as voyages to distant climates facilitated the perception of the relative beauty of different vegetable forms, and their connection in groups of natural families. The discoveries of Columbus, Vasco de Gama, and Alvarez Cabral in Central America, Southern Asia, and Brazil, the extensive commerce in spices and drugs carried on by the Spaniards, Portuguese, Italians, Dutch, and Flemings, and the establishment, between 1544 and 1568, of botanic gardens (not yet however furnished with regular hothouses), at Pisa, Padua, and Bologna, did indeed afford to painters the opportunity of becoming acquainted with many remarkable exotic productions even of the tropical world; and single fruits, flowers, and branches, were represented with the utmost fidelity and grace by John Breughel, whose celebrity had commenced before the close of the sixteenth century; but until near the middle of the seventeenth century there were no landscapes which reproduced the peculiar aspect of the torrid zone from actual impressions received by the artist himself on the spot. The first merit of such representation probably belongs (as I learn from Waagen), to a painter of the Netherlands, Franz Post of Haarlem, who accompanied Prince Maurice of Nassau to Brazil, where that prince, who took great interest in tropical productions, was the Statholder for Holland in the conquered Portuguese possessions from 1637 to 1644. Post made many studies from nature near Cape St Augustine, in the bay of All Saints, on the shores of the Río San Francisco, and on those of the lower part of the river of the Amazons. Some of these were afterwards executed by himself as pictures, and others were etched with much spirit. There are preserved in Denmark, (in a gallery of the fine castle at Frederiksborg), some large oil paintings of great merit belonging to the same epoch by the painter Eckhout, who, in 1641, was also in Brazil with Prince Maurice. In these pictures, palms, papaws (Carica papaya), bananas, and heliconias, are most characteristically portrayed, as are likewise the native inhabitants, birds of many-coloured plumage, and small quadrupeds.

These examples were followed by few artists of merit until Cook's second voyage of circumnavigation: what Hodges did for the western islands of the Pacific, and our distinguished countryman, Ferdinand Bauer, for New Holland and Van Diemen Island, has been since done in very recent times in a much grander style, and with a more masterly hand, for tropical America, by Moritz Rugendas, Count Clarac, Ferdinand Bellermann, and Edward Hildebrandt; and for many other parts of the earth by Heinrich von Kittlitz, who accompanied the Russian admiral, Lutke, on his voyage of circumnavigation.

He who with feelings alive to the beauties of nature in mountain, river, or forest scenery, has himself wandered in the torrid zone, and beheld the variety and luxuriance of the vegetation, not merely on the well-cultivated coasts, but also on the declivities of the snow-crowned Andes the Himalaya or the Neilgherries of Mysore, or in the virgin forests watered by the network of rivers between the Orinoco and the Amazons, can feel, – and he alone can feel, – how almost infinite is the field which still remains to be opened to landscape painting in the tropical portions of either continent, and in the islands of Sumatra, Borneo, and the Philippines; and how all that this department of art has yet produced, is not to be compared to the magnitude of the treasures, of which at some future day it may become possessed. Why may we not be justified in hoping that landscape painting may hereafter bloom with new and yet unknown beauty, when highly-gifted artists shall oftener pass the narrow bounds of the Mediterranean, and shall seize, with the first freshness of a pure youthful mind, the living image of the manifold beauty and grandeur of nature in the humid mountain valleys of the tropical world?

Those glorious regions have been hitherto visited chiefly by travellers to whom the want of previous artistic training, and a variety of scientific occupations, allowed but little opportunity of attaining perfection in landscape painting. But few among them were able, in addition to the botanical interest excited by individual forms of flowers and leaves, to seize the general characteristic impression of the tropical zone. The artists who accompanied great expeditions supported at the expense of the states which sent them forth, were too often chosen as it were by accident, and were thus found to be less prepared than the occasion demanded; and perhaps the end of the voyage was approaching, when even the most talented among them, after a long enjoyment of the spectacle of the great scenes of nature, and many attempts at imitation, were just beginning to master a certain degree of technical skill. Moreover, in voyages of circumnavigation, artists are seldom conducted into the true forest regions, to the upper portions of the course of great rivers, or to the summits of the mountain chains of the interior. It is only by coloured sketches taken on the spot, that the artist, inspired by the contemplation of these distant scenes, can hope to reproduce their character in paintings executed after his return. He will be able to do so the more perfectly, if he has also accumulated a large number of separate studies of tops of trees, of branches clothed with leaves, adorned with blossoms, or laden with fruit, of fallen trunks of trees overgrown with pothos and orchideæ, of portions of rocks and river banks, as well as of the surface of the ground in the forest, all drawn or painted directly from nature. An abundance of studies of this kind, in which the outlines are well and sharply marked, will furnish him with materials enabling him, on his return, to dispense with the misleading assistance afforded by plants grown in the confinement of hot-houses, or by what are called botanical drawings.

Great events in the world's history, the independence of the Spanish and Portuguese Americas, and the spread and increase of intellectual cultivation in India, New Holland, the Sandwich Islands, and the southern colonies of Africa, cannot

fail to procure, not only for meteorology and other branches
of natural knowledge, but also for landscape painting, a new
and grander development which might not have been attain-
able without these local circumstances. In South America
populous cities are situated 13,000 feet above the level of the
sea. In descending from them to the plains, all climatic gradations of the forms of plants are offered to the eye. What may
we not expect from the picturesque study of nature in such
scenes, if after the termination of civil discord and the establishment of free institutions, artistic feeling shall at length
awaken in those elevated highlands!

All that belongs to the expression of human emotion and to
the beauty of the human form, has attained perhaps its highest
perfection in the northern temperate zone, under the skies of
Greece and Italy. By the combined exercise of imitative art
and of creative imagination, the artist has derived the types of
historical painting, at once from the depths of his own mind,
and from the contemplation of other beings of his own race.
Landscape painting, though no merely imitative art, has, it may
be said, a more material substratum and a more terrestrial
domain: it requires a greater mass and variety of direct impressions, which the mind must receive within itself, fertilize by
its own powers, and reproduce visibly as a free work of art.
Heroic landscape painting must be a result at once of a deep
and comprehensive reception of the visible spectacle of external nature, and of this inward process of the mind.

Nature, in every region of the earth, is indeed a reflex of the
whole; the forms of organized being are repeated everywhere
in fresh combinations; even in the icy north, herbs covering
the earth, large alpine blossoms, and a serene azure sky, cheer
a portion of the year. Hitherto, landscape painting has pursued
amongst us her pleasing task, familiar only with the simpler
forms of our native floras, but not therefore without depth of
feeling or without the treasures of creative imagination. Even
in this narrower field, highly-gifted painters, the Caracci, Gas-
pard Poussin, Claude Lorraine, and Ruysdael, have, with magic
power, by the selection of forms of trees and by effects of light,
found scope wherein to call forth some of the most varied

and beautiful productions of creative art. The fame of these master works can never be impaired by those which I venture to hope for hereafter, and to which I could not but point, in order to recall the ancient and deeply-seated bond which unites natural knowledge with poetry and with artistic feeling, for we must ever distinguish, in landscape painting as in every other branch of art, between productions derived from direct observation, and those which spring from the depths of inward feeling and from the power of the idealizing mind. The great and beautiful works which owe their origin to this creative power of the mind applied to landscape painting, belong to the poetry of nature, and like man himself and the imagination with which he is gifted, are not riveted to the soil or confined to any single region. I allude here more particularly to the gradation in the forms of trees from Ruysdael and Everdingen, through Claude Lorraine to Poussin and Annibal Caracci. In the great masters of the art we perceive no trace of local limitation; but an enlargement of the visible horizon, and an increased acquaintance with the nobler and grander forms of nature, and with the luxuriant fulness of life in the tropical world, offer the advantage not only of enriching the material substratum of landscape painting, but also of affording a more lively stimulus to less gifted artists, and of thus heightening their power of production.

I would here be permitted to recall some considerations which I communicated to the public nearly half a century ago, and which have an intimate connection with the subject which is at present under notice; they were contained in a memoir which has been but little read, entitled 'Ideen asseiner Physiognomik der Gewächse' (Ideas towards a physiognomy of plants). When rising from local phenomena we embrace all nature in one view, we perceive the increase of warmth from the poles to the equator accompanied by the gradual advance of organic vigour and luxuriance. From Northern Europe to the beautiful coasts of the Mediterranean this advance is even less than from the Iberian Peninsula, Southern Italy and Greece, to the tropic zone. The carpet of flowers and of verdure spread over our bare and naked earth is unequally woven;

thicker where the sun rises high in a sky either of a deep azure purity or veiled with light semi-transparent clouds; and thinner towards the gloomy north, where returning frosts are often fatal to the opening buds of spring, or destroy the ripening fruits of autumn. If in the frigid zone the bark of trees is covered with lichens or with mosses, in the zone of palms and finely-feathered arborescent ferns, the trunks of Anacardias and of gigantic species of Ficus are enlivened by Cymbidium and the fragrant vanilla. The fresh green of the Dracontias, and the deep-cut leaves of the Pothos, contrast with the many-coloured flowers of the Orchideæ. Climbing Bauhinias, Passifloras, and yellow flowering Banisterias, entwining the stems of the forest trees, spread far and wide, and rise high in air; delicate flowers unfold themselves from the roots of the Theobromas, and from the thick and rough bark of the Crescentias and the Gustavia. In the midst of this abundance of leaves and blossoms, this luxuriant growth and profusion of climbing plants, the naturalist often finds it difficult to discover to which stem different flowers and leaves belong; nay, a single tree adorned with Paullinias, Bignonias, and Dendrobium, presents a mass of vegetation and a variety of plants which, if detached from each other, would cover a considerable space of ground.

But to each zone of the earth are allotted peculiar beauties; to the tropics, variety and grandeur in the forms of vegetation; to the north, the aspect of its meadows and green pastures, and the periodic long-desired reawakening of nature at the first breath of the mild air of spring. As in the Musaceæ we have the greatest expansion, so in the Casuarinæ and needle trees we have the greatest contraction of the leafy vessels. Firs, Thuias, and Cypresses, constitute a northern form which is extremely rare in the low grounds of the tropics. Their ever-fresh verdure cheers the winter landscape; and tells to the inhabitants of the north, that when snow and ice cover the earth, the inward life of plants, like the Promethean fire, is never extinct upon our planet.

Each zone of vegetation, besides its peculiar beauties, has also a distinct character, calling forth in us a different order of impressions. To recall here only forms of our native climates, who does not feel himself differently affected in the dark shade of the beech or on hills crowned with scattered firs, and on the open pasture where the wind rustles in the trembling foliage of the birch? As in different organic beings we recognize a distinct physiognomy, and as descriptive botany and zoology, in the more restricted sense of the terms, imply an analysis of peculiarities in the forms of plants and animals, so is there also a certain natural physiognomy belonging exclusively to each region of the earth. The idea which the artist indicates by the expressions 'Swiss nature', 'Italian sky', &c. rests on a partial perception of local character. The azure of the sky, the form of the clouds, the haze resting on the distance, the succulency of the herbage, the brightness of the foliage, the outline of the mountains, are elements which determine the general impression. It is the province of landscape painting to apprehend these, and to reproduce them visibly. The artist is permitted to analyse the groups, and the enchantment of nature is resolved under his hands, like the written works of men (if I may venture on the figurative expression), into a few simple characters.

Even in the present imperfect state of our pictorial representations of landscape, the engravings which accompany, and too often only disfigure, our books of travels, have yet contributed not a little to our knowledge of the aspect of distant zones, to the predilection for extensive voyages, and to the more active study of nature. The improvement in landscape painting on a scale of large dimensions (as in decorative or scene painting, in panoramas, dioramas, and neoramas), has of late years increased both the generality and the strength of these impressions. The class of representations which Vitruvius and the Egyptian Julius Pollux satirically described as 'rural satyric decorations', which, in the middle of the sixteenth century, were, by Serlio's plan of sliding scenes, made to increase theatrical illusion, may now, in Barker's panoramas, by the aid of Prevost and Daguerre, be converted into a kind of substitute for wanderings in various climates. More may be effected in this way than by any kind of scene painting; and this partly because in a panorama, the spectator, enclosed as in a magic circle and withdrawn from all disturbing realities, may the more readily imagine himself surrounded on all sides by nature in another clime. Impressions are thus produced which in some cases mingle years afterwards by a wonderful illusion with the remembrances of natural scenes actually beheld. Hitherto, panoramas, which are only effective when they are of large diameter, have been applied chiefly to views of cities and of inhabited districts, rather than to scenes in which nature appears decked with her own wild luxuriance and beauty. Enchanting effects might be obtained by means of characteristic studies sketched on the rugged mountain declivities of the Himalaya and the Cordilleras, or in the recesses of the river country of India and South America; and still more so if these sketches were aided by photographs, which cannot indeed render the leafy canopy, but would give the most perfect representation possible of the form of the giant trunks, and of the mode of ramification characteristic of the different kinds of trees. All the methods to which I have here alluded are fitted to enhance the love of the study of nature; it appears, indeed, to me, that if large panoramic buildings, containing a succession of such landscapes, belonging to different geographical latitudes and different zones of elevation, were erected in our cities, and, like our museums and galleries of paintings, thrown freely open to the people, it would be a powerful means of rendering the sublime grandeur of the creation more widely known and felt. The comprehension of a natural whole, the feeling of the unity and harmony of the Cosmos, will become at once more vivid and more generally diffused, with the multiplication of all modes of bringing the phænomena of nature generally before the contemplation of the eye and of the mind.

III.—CULTIVATION OF TROPICAL PLANTS—
ASSEMBLAGE OF CONTRASTED FORMS—IMPRESSION
OF THE GENERAL CHARACTERISTIC PHYSIOGNOMY OF
THE VEGETATION PRODUCED BY SUCH MEANS.

THE EFFECT OF landscape painting, notwithstanding the multiplication of its productions by engravings and by the modern improvements of lithography, is still both more limited and less vivid, than the stimulus which results from the impression produced on minds alive to natural beauty by the direct view of groups of exotic plants in hot-houses or in the open air. I have already appealed on this subject to my own youthful experience, when the sight of a colossal dragon tree and of a fan palm in an old tower of the botanic garden at Berlin, implanted in my breast the first germ of an irrepressible longing for distant travel. Those who are able to reascend in memory to that which may have given the first impulse to their entire course of life, will recognize this powerful influence of impressions received through the senses.

I would here distinguish between those plantations which are best suited to afford us the picturesque impression of the forms of plants, and those in which they are arranged as auxiliaries to botanical studies; between groups distinguished for their grandeur and mass, as clumps of Bananas and Heliconias alternating with Corypha Palms, Araucarias and Mimosas, and moss-covered trunks from which shoot Dracontias, Ferns with their delicate foliage, and Orchideæ rich in varied and beautiful flowers, on the one hand; and on the other, a number of separate low-growing plants classed and arranged in rows for the purpose of conveying instruction in descriptive and systematic botany. In the first case, our consideration is drawn rather to the luxuriant development of vegetation in Cecropias, Carolinias, and light-feathered Bamboos; to the picturesque apposition of grand and noble forms, such as adorn the banks of the upper Orinoco and the forest shores of the Amazons, and of the Huallaga described with such truth to nature by Martius and Edward Poppig; to impressions which fill the mind with longing for those lands where the current of life flows in a richer stream, and of whose glorious beauty a faint but still pleasing image is now presented to us in our hot-houses, which formerly were mere hospitals for languishing unhealthy plants.

Landscape painting is, indeed, able to present a richer and more complete picture of nature than can be obtained by the most skilful grouping of cultivated plants. Almost unlimited in regard to space, it can pursue the margin of the forest until it becomes indistinct from the effect of aerial perspective; it can pour the mountain torrent from crag to crag, and spread the deep azure of the tropic sky above the light tops of the palms, or the undulating savannah which bounds the horizon. The illumination and colouring, which between the tropics are shed over all terrestrial objects by the light of the thinly veiled or perfectly pure heaven, give to landscape painting, when the pencil succeeds in imitating this mild effect of light, a peculiar and mysterious power. A deep perception of the essence of the Greek tragedy led my brother to compare the charm of the *chorus* in its effect with the *sky in the landscape*.

The multiplied means which painting can command for stimulating the fancy, and concentrating in a small space the grandest phænomena of sea and land, are indeed denied to our plantations in gardens or in hot-houses; but the inferiority in general impression is compensated by the mastery which the reality everywhere exerts over the senses. When in the palm house of Loddiges, or in that of the Pfauen-insel near Potsdam (a monument of the simple feeling for nature of our noble departed monarch), we look down from the high gallery, during a bright noonday sunshine, upon the abundance of reed-like and arborescent palms, a complete illusion in respect to the locality in which we are placed is momentarily produced; we seem to be actually in the climate of the tropics, looking down from the summit of a hill upon a small thicket of palms. The aspect of the deep blue sky, and the impression of a greater intensity of light, are indeed wanting, but still the illusion is greater, and the imagination more vividly active, than from the most perfect painting: we associate with each vegetable form the wonders of a distant land; we hear the rustling of the fan-like leaves, and see the changing play of light, as, gently moved by slight currents of air, the waving tops of the palms come into contact with each other. So great is the charm which reality can give. The recollection of the needful degree of artificial care bestowed no doubt returns to disturb the impression; for a perfectly flourishing condition, and a state of freedom, are inseparable in the realm of nature as elsewhere; and in the eyes of the earnest and travelled botanist, the dried specimen in an herbarium, if actually gathered on the Cordilleras of South America, or the plains of India, often has a greater value than the living plant in an European hot-house: cultivation effaces somewhat of the original natural character; the constraint which it produces disturbs the free organic development of the separate parts.

The physiognomic character of plants, and their assemblage in happily contrasted groups, is not only an incitement to the study of nature, and itself one of the objects of that study, but attention to the physiognomy of plants is also of great importance in landscape gardening – in the art of composing a garden landscape. I will resist the temptation to expatiate in this closely adjoining field of disquisition, and content myself with bringing to the recollection of my readers that, as in the earlier portion of the present volume, I found occasion to notice the more frequent manifestation of a deep feeling for nature among the Semitic, Indian, and Iraunian nations, so also the earliest ornamental parks mentioned in history belonged to middle and southern Asia. The gardens of Semiramis, at the foot of the Bagistanos mountain, are described by Diodorus, and the fame of them induced Alexander to turn aside from the direct road, in order to visit them during his march from Chelone to the Nysäic horse pastures. The parks of the Persian kings were adorned with cypresses, of which the form, resembling obelisks, recalled the shape of flames of fire, and which, after the appearance of Zerdusht

(Zoroaster), were first planted by Gushtasp around the sanctuary of the fire temple. It was, perhaps, thus that the form of the tree led to the fiction of the Paradisaical origin of cypresses. The Asiatic terrestrial paradises (παραδεισοι), were early celebrated in more western countries; and the worship of trees even goes back among the Iraunians to the rules of Hom, called, in the Zend-Avesta, the promulgator of the old law. We know from Herodotus the delight which Xerxes took in the great plane tree in Lydia, on which he bestowed golden ornaments, and appointed for it a sentinel in the person of one of the 'immortal ten thousand'. The early veneration of trees was associated, by the moist and refreshing canopy of foliage, with that of sacred fountains. In similar connection with the early worship of nature, were, amongst the Hellenic nations, the fame of the great palm tree of Delos, and of an aged plane tree in Arcadia. The Buddhists of Ceylon venerate the colossal Indian fig tree (the Banyan) of Anurahdepura, supposed to have sprung from the branches of the original tree under which Buddha, while inhabiting the ancient Magadha, was absorbed in beatification, or 'self-extinction' (nirwana). As single trees thus became objects of veneration from the beauty of their form, so did also groups of trees, under the name of 'groves of the gods'. Pausanias is full of the praise of a grove belonging to the temple of Apollo, at Grynion, in Æolis; and the grove of Colonè is celebrated in the renowned chorus of Sophocles.

The love of nature which showed itself in the selection and care of these venerated objects of the vegetable kingdom, manifested itself with yet greater vivacity, and in a more varied manner, in the horticultural arrangements of the early civilized nations of Eastern Asia. In the most distant part of the old continent, the Chinese gardens appear to have approached most nearly to what we now call English parks. Under the victorious dynasty of Han, gardens of this class were extended over circuits of so many miles that agriculture was affected, and the people were excited to revolt. 'What is it,' says an ancient Chinese writer, Lieu-tscheu, 'that we seek in the pleasures of a garden? It has always been agreed that these plantations should make men amends for living at a distance from what would be their more congenial and agreeable dwelling-place, in the midst of nature, free, and unconstrained. The art of laying out gardens consists, therefore, in combining cheerfulness of prospect, luxuriance of growth, shade, retirement, and repose, so that the rural aspect may produce an illusion. Variety, which is a chief merit in the natural landscape, must be sought by the choice of ground with alternation of hill and dale, flowing streams, and lakes covered with aquatic plants. Symmetry is wearisome; and a garden where every thing betrays constraint and art becomes tedious and distasteful.' A description which Sir George Staunton has given us of the great imperial garden of Zhe-hol, north of the Chinese wall, corresponds with these precepts of Lieu-tscheu – precepts to which our ingenious contemporary, who formed the beautiful park of Moscow, would not refuse his approbation.

The great descriptive poem, composed in the middle of the last century by the Emperor Kien-long to celebrate the former Mantchou imperial residence, Moukden, and the graves of his ancestors, is also expressive of the most thorough love of nature sparingly embellished by art. The royal poet knows how to blend the cheerful images of fresh and rich meadows, wood-crowned hills, and peaceful dwellings of men, all described in a very graphic manner, with the graver image of the tombs of his forefathers. The offerings which he brings to his deceased ancestors, according to the rites prescribed by Confucius, and the pious remembrance of departed monarchs and warriors, are the more special objects of this remarkable poem. A long enumeration of the wild plants, and of the animals which enliven the district, is tedious, as didactic poetry always is; but the weaving together the impression received from the visible landscape (which appears only as the background of the picture,) with the more elevated objects taken from the world of ideas, with the fulfilment of religious rites, and with allusions to great historical events, gives a peculiar character to the whole composition. The consecration of mountains, so deeply rooted among the Chinese, leads the author to introduce careful descriptions of the aspect of inanimate nature, to which the Greeks and the Romans shewed themselves so little alive. The forms of the several trees, their mode of growth, the direction of the branches, and the shape of the leaves, are dwelt on with marked predilection.

As I do not participate in that distaste to Chinese literature which is too slowly disappearing amongst us, and as I have dwelt, perhaps, at too much length on the work of a contemporary of Frederic the Great, it is the more incumbent on me to go back to a period seven centuries and a half earlier, for the purpose of recalling the poem of 'The Garden', by See-ma-kuang, a celebrated statesman. It is true that the pleasure grounds described in this poem are, in part, overcrowded with numerous buildings, as was the case in the ancient villas of Italy; but the minister also describes a hermitage, situated between rocks, and surrounded by lofty fir trees. He praises the extensive prospect over the wide river Kiang, with its many vessels: 'here he can receive his friends, listen to their verses, and recite to them his own'. See-ma-kuang wrote in the year 1086, when, in Germany, poetry, in the hands of a rude clergy, did not even speak the language of the country. At that period, and, perhaps, five centuries earlier, the inhabitants of China, Transgangetic India, and Japan, were already acquainted with a great variety of forms of plants. The intimate connection maintained between the Buddhistic monasteries was not without influence in this respect. Temples, cloisters, and burying-places were surrounded with gardens, adorned with exotic trees, and with a carpet of flowers of many forms and colours. The plants of India were early conveyed to China, Corea, and Nipon. Siebold, whose writings afford a comprehensive view of all that relates to Japan, was the first to call attention to the cause of the intermixture of the floras of widely-separated Buddhistic countries.

The rich and increasing variety of characteristic vegetable forms which, in the present age, are offered both to scientific observation and to landscape painting, cannot but afford a lively incentive to trace out the sources which have prepared for us this more extended knowledge and this increased enjoyment. The enumeration of these sources is reserved for the succeeding section of my work, *i. e.* the history of the contemplation of the universe. In the section which I am now closing, I have sought to depict those incentives, due to the influence exerted on the intellectual activity and the feelings of men by the reflected image of the external world, which, in the progress of modern civilization, have tended so materially to encourage and vivify the study of nature. Notwithstanding a certain degree of arbitrary freedom in the development of the several parts, primary and deep-seated laws of organic life bind all animal and vegetable forms to firmly established and ever recurring types, and determine in each zone the particular character impressed on it, or *the physiognomy of nature*. I regard it as one of the fairest fruits of general European civilization, that it is now almost everywhere possible for men to obtain, – by the cultivation of exotic plants, by the charm of landscape painting, and by the power of the inspiration of language, – some part, at least, of that enjoyment of nature, which, when pursued by long and dangerous journeys through the interior of continents, is afforded by her immediate contemplation.

INDEX

This book is set in GARAMOND, the first typeface in
the ambitious programme of matrix production
undertaken by the Monotype Corporation
under the guidance of Stanley Morrison
in 1922. Although named after the
great French royal typographer,
Claude Garamond (1499–
1561), it owes much to
Jean Jannon of Sedan
(1580–1658).